Cultural Atlas of
JAPAN

Editor Graham Speake
Art Editor Andrew Lawson
Map Editor Olive Pearson
Picture Editor Linda Proud
Index Ann Barrett
Design Adrian Hodgkins
Production Clive Sparling

AN EQUINOX BOOK

Published by Phaidon Press Ltd,
Littlegate House, St Ebbe's
Street, Oxford OX1 1SQ, England

Planned and produced by
Equinox (Oxford) Ltd, Littlegate
House, St Ebbe's Street, Oxford
England, OX1 1SQ

British Library Cataloguing in
Publication Data
Collcutt, Martin, *1939–*
    Cultural atlas of Japan.
    1. Japanese civilization, to 1987
    I. Title   II. Jansen, Marius B.
    III. Kumakura, Isao 952

    ISBN 0-7148-2526-3

Origination by Scantrans,
Singapore

Maps drawn and originated by
Lovell Johns Ltd, Oxford, and
Alan Mais, Hornchurch, Essex

Filmset by Hourds Typographica,
Stafford, England

Printed in Spain by Heraclio
Fournier SA, Vitoria

Frontispiece Illustrations of
proper dress for a samurai family
of the Edo period.

Cultural Atlas of
JAPAN

by Martin Collcutt,
Marius Jansen
and Isao Kumakura

Phaidon·Oxford

CONTENTS

List of Maps

CHRONOLOGICAL TABLE

	50 000 BC	11 000 BC	300 BC	300 AD	552	710	794
PERIOD	PALEOLITHIC	JŌMON	YAYOI	KOFUN	LATE YAMATO	NARA	HEIAN
POLITICAL MOVEMENTS	clan heads the only rulers	little political differentiation; clan or village heads as rulers	57 AD King Nu of Wa receives gold seal from Chinese emperor 239 AD Queen Himiko sends embassy to China	*uji* chieftains as local rulers late 5th century five kings of Wa mentioned in Chinese chronicles Yamato chieftains (*ōkimi*)	593–628 Empress Suiko reigns; Prince Shōtoku regent 593–622 beginnings of political centralization along Chinese lines; transition from clan to imperial system 645 Taika reform 672–86 Emperor Temmu reigns 694 Empress Jitō establishes new capital at Fujiwara	710 Empress Gemmyō designates Heijō (Nara) the new capital 724–49 Emperor Shōmu reigns 752 Emperor Shōmu consecrates Great Buddha at Tōdaiji 784 Emperor Kammu (reigns 781–806) moves capital to Nagaoka and later (794) to Heian	early Heian phase of strong imperial authority 858 Fujiwara Yorifusa becomes regent for nine-year-old Emperor Seiwa: marks beginning of Fujiwara domination of court government 995–1027 Fujiwara no Michinaga dominant 1086–1156 *insei,* cloistered rule by cloistered emperors to offset power of the Fujiwara 1156 Hōgen insurrection 1159 Heiji insurrection 1180–85 Gempei War

A cord-marked lamp of the Middle Jōmon period, c. 3000 BC.

A *haniwa-koto* player from the Kofun period, 6th century AD.

The Hōryūji at Nara, founded by Prince Shōtoku in 607.

The Great Buddha Hall of the Tōdaiji at Nara, founded in 745.

	50 000 BC	11 000 BC	300 BC	300 AD	552	710	794
CULTURE AND RELIGION	stone tools and microliths	Jōmon pottery, shell mounds, figurines	Yayoi pottery	great and lesser tombs	552 introduction of Buddhism 607 foundation of the original Hōryūji monastery	712 *Kojiki* 720 *Nihon shoki* 777 *Manyoshū* six schools of Nara Buddhism Buddhism as court religion reconciliation of Shinto and Buddhism 741 provinces ordered to build monasteries and nunneries	805 Saichō establishes the Tendai school of Buddhism 806 Kūkai founds Shingon school of Buddhism Although direct contact with China is broken off (894), Japanese art, architecture and literature continue to be influenced by China, while showing Japanese innovations 905 *Kokinshū* anthology of verse 985 Genshin teaches Pure Land Buddhism 1010 *Tale of Genji* by Lady Murasaki Shikibu 1175 Hōnen founds Pure Land school
SOCIETY AND ECONOMICS	preceramic Stone Age hunting-and-gathering economy	Stone Age hunting-and-gathering ceramic culture	wet rice cultivation, agricultural implements, bronze bells, mirrors and weapons, weaving	builders of the great tombs; heads of a powerful confederation of *uji*; evidence of military and horseriding culture	645 all land brought under imperial control 702 Taihō codes promulgated 708 copper and silver coins officially minted		935 Taira Masakado's insurrection in the eastern provinces 1010 private estates (*shōen*) developing within the public land system; warrior bands (*bushidan*) proliferating in the provinces
INTERNATIONAL RELATIONS			petty rulers of Wa in contact with China		607 embassy of monks and scholars sent to Sui China 630–894 15 official embassies journey to Tang China 663 Japanese fleet destroyed off Korean coast by Silla	754 Ganjin arrives from China	805 Saichō returns from China 806 Kūkai returns from China 894 suspension of official embassies to China

1185	1333	1392	1568	1600	1868	1912	1926–
KAMAKURA	**NORTHERN AND SOUTHERN COURTS**	**MUROMACHI**	**MOMOYAMA**	**EDO**	**MEIJI**	**TAISHŌ**	**SHŌWA**

KAMAKURA

1185 destruction of Taira by Minamoto; Yoritomo establishes Bakufu at Kamakura
1192 beginning of warrior government and shogunal rule
1219 Minamoto Sanetomo assassinated; Hōjō regents dominate Kamakura Bakufu
1221 Jōkyū War
1333 overthrow of Kamakura Bakufu

NORTHERN AND SOUTHERN COURTS

1336 Go-Daigo flees Kyoto and establishes southern court in Yoshino; Takauji establishes Muromachi Bakufu in Kyoto
1338 Takauji takes title of Seiitaishogun; followed by 14 generations of Ashikaga shoguns

MUROMACHI

1368–94 Ashikaga Yoshimitsu rules, a strong shogun
1392 Yoshimitsu unifies the two courts
1467–77 Ōnin War
1449–73 Yoshimasa rules, 8th shogun, a weak ruler; imperial court impoverished

MOMOYAMA

1568 Oda Nobunaga marches into Kyoto, ends Ashikaga shogunate (1573) and conquers much of central Japan
1582 Nobunaga assassinated; Toyotomi Hideyoshi succeeds, unifies Japan and rules as Kampaku

EDO

1600 Tokugawa Ieyasu establishes his supremacy at Sekigahara
1603 Ieyasu takes title of Seiitaishogun; establishes Bakufu in Edo; succeeded by 14 generations of Tokugawa shoguns who rule Japan through the *Baku-han* system
1615 siege of Osaka castle

MEIJI

1868 Bakufu overthrown by samurai alliance; imperial restoration; Emperor Mutsuhito moves court to Edo (renamed Tokyo)
1890 Meiji constitution; political parties formed; first general election for House of Representatives

TAISHŌ

1912 death of Meiji emperor; Taishō emperor succeeds; two-party civilian government until 1932

SHŌWA

1926 accession of Shōwa emperor, Hirohito
1945 atomic bombs on Hiroshima and Nagasaki lead to Japanese surrender
1945–52 allied occupation under General Douglas MacArthur
1946 emperor renounces claims to divinity promulgation of postwar constitution of Japan
1952 Japan regains full independence
1972 Okinawa reverted to Japan

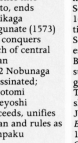

The Great Buddha at Kamakura, height 11·5 meters, c. 1252.

Oda Nobunaga (1534–82), first of the unifiers.

A jar in the Imari style, late 19th century.

Hiroshima, August 1945.

---

development of fine swords, armor and military equipment
1207 Shinran exiled to Echigo: origin of True Pure Land school
1225 *Tales of the Heike* and other war tales
1253 Nichiren asserts exclusive efficacy of *Lotus Sūtra:* origin of Nichiren school
1289 death of Ippen, founder of "Timely" school of Pure Land Buddhism

spread of Zen culture revival of Kyoto as a commercial and cultural center
Noh theater develops
1394 Yoshimitsu builds Golden Pavilion in Kyoto
1420–1506 Sesshū the painter
1421–1508 Sōgi the poet
Tea Ceremony developing outside Zen monastic circles
1549–1639 the Christian century

1576 Nobunaga completes Azuchi castle on Lake Biwa
1587 proscription of Catholic missionary activity

1609 prohibition of Catholicism
1637 promotion of Neo-Confucianism
1688–1703 Genroku era: flowering of Kabuki and puppet theater, prints of the floating world, poetry and narrative fiction
1730–1801 Shinto revival; National Learning Movement
1760–1849 Katsushika Hokusai
1767–1858 Andō Hiroshige

1896 movies imported; start of domestic film production

1916 death of Natsume Sōseki, novelist
1922 death of Mori Ōgai, surgeon-general and novelist
1925 start of radio broadcasting

1953 start of televised broadcasting

1232 compilation of *Jōei shikimoku*, first legal code for warrior society

1467–77 the age of wars: Japan breaks up into many semi-independent feudal domains ruled by *daimyō*
1500 Japanese pirates roam seas of east and southeast Asia
1543 introduction of firearms

1582–98 land surveys
1588 sword hunt edict; separation of samurai from peasants

1637 suppression of Shimabara uprising
1688–1703 rapid growth of Edo, Osaka and castle towns
1701–02 affair of the 47 *Rōnin*
1781–88 Temmei famine; great hardship in many villages, large-scale peasant uprisings and urban riots

1871 return of *daimyō* domains to emperor
1872 Tokyo – Osaka telegraph opened; Yokohama – Tokyo railroad opened; development of light industry
1894 strike at a cotton mill in Osaka
1904 development of heavy industry

1923 great Kantō earthquake

1945–52 democratization of economic activity and free labor movement proposed by SCAP
1946 land reform policy
1947 SCAP bans planned general strike
1960 Prime Minister Ikeda announces Income Doubling plan: economic miracle under way
1964 first Bullet Train from Tokyo to Osaka
1973 oil crisis
1988 Seikan Tunnel links Hokkaido and Honshu; Seto Bridge links Honshu and Shikoku

---

1200 Eisai and Dōgen introduce Rinzai and Sōtō traditions of Zen from China
1274–81 Mongol invasions

1543 Portuguese arrive at Tanegashima
1549 Francis Xavier comes to Japan

1592 Hideyoshi launches unsuccessful invasions of Korea and (1597) China

1604 Red Seal licenses issued to Japanese vessels trading with Luzon, Siam etc
1609 Dutch trading post established at Hirado
1635 ban on Japanese travel abroad
1853 arrival of Captain Matthew Perry at Uraga precipitates crisis

1894 Sino-Japanese War
1904 Russo-Japanese War
1910 annexation of Korea

1912 first participation in Olympic Games
1914 Japan declares war on Germany
1920 Japan admitted to League of Nations

1933 withdrawal from League of Nations
1937 Japan declares war on China
1941 Japan attacks Pearl Harbor
1950 outbreak of Korean War
1951 San Francisco Peace Treaty and US-Japan Security Pact signed
1956 admitted to UN
1964 Tokyo Olympic Games
1970 World Expo in Osaka
1979 5th Summit Conference held in Tokyo
1986 12th Summit Conference held in Tokyo

PREFACE

Rapid air transportation and telecommunications have brought modern Japan within easy reach of the rest of the world. Japanese cars, cameras and electronic products are everywhere. Japanese businesspeople, students and tourists are flocking abroad: more than 7 million in 1988, for instance. Japanese factories are springing up in many countries. Japanese dance troupes, traditional and avant-garde theatrical groups, musicians, fashion designers, movies, food and art exhibits spread knowledge of the country and of its traditional and contemporary culture. In spite of the soaring yen, foreign businesspeople, travelers and students are visiting Japan in growing numbers. As tariff barriers have come down and the yen has risen, the Japanese domestic market has opened up to foreign goods. The country is constantly in the news. Known as the economic super-achiever of the late 20th century, Japan is increasingly visible on the international scene and the Japanese themselves talk constantly of the "internationalization" of their society.

Japan has not yet, however, transcended geography. Nor has the country severed its ties with its history, or broken the thread of cultural continuity with its past. Older Japanese today sometimes talk disparagingly about a "new race" (*shin-jinrui*) of Japanese. They have in mind those born since World War II who seem to have very different interests and values. The younger generation seems less disciplined, frugal and work-oriented, more assertive, individualistic, Westernized and consumer-oriented. But the *shin-jinrui* clearly share most of the cultural values of their parents. They still emphasize values that have contributed to Japan's recent economic success: education, hard work, discipline, family and group harmony, consensus and the primacy of national over personal goals. More comfortable with Western culture than their parents, they still maintain a clear sense of their cultural identity as Japanese.

History and geography have shaped the country's present and will continue to contribute to its future. For most of its history Japan's location at the eastern fringe of Asia and the westernmost edge of the Pacific Ocean has left the country relatively remote. It was never entirely isolated, however. Cultural influences from the continent constantly affected the country, and at times the Japanese themselves made gargantuan efforts to seek advanced civilization from China or the West.

Geography and climate have influenced Japan's development in other ways too. Japan's seasonal climate and its landscape, flora and fauna have all been reflected in the rich literature, art and mythology of the country. Most of Japan proved suitable for wet rice cultivation when that technology was introduced in the Yayoi period (300 BC–300 AD). The manifold aspects of social organization, economy, religious ideas and political structure, centering on paddyfield rice cultivation, helped shape Japan until the 19th century and have remained a major economic and political determinant in the age of industrialization and high technology of the 20th century.

Although nature has been kind to the Japanese, it has not been munificent. The volcanic land has always been subject to severe earthquakes. It is crowded and overbuilt, and minerals and other resources are in short supply. For centuries the Japanese have thought of themselves as poor, especially in natural resources. In modern times this perception of inadequate domestic resources contributed to a drive for expansion in Korea and Manchuria, to a willingness to fight for oil supplies rather than give ground in China in 1945, and to postwar economic development that has hinged on the import of raw materials and technology and the export of high-quality finished goods. It has also contributed to a psychological attitude that one hears even today, when the Japanese are believed by many in the West to be enjoying great affluence and security. Proud of their achievements, and at times dismissive of the West, the perception of relative poverty, of vulnerability, of separateness from, but of dependence on, the outside world frequently surfaces. Old habits of thought die hard. Many Japanese do indeed find it difficult to believe in the durability of their new-found affluence. They look at their society less optimistically and more critically than most outsiders.

This *Cultural Atlas of Japan* is written for general readers and travelers who would like to relate the rich cultural history of Japan to the physical environment in which it has developed. It does not presuppose any familiarity with Japanese history, geography or culture. But it is hoped that it will also be of interest to readers who know Japan well. The coverage is broad, from the stone tools of Paleolithic man to the computer terminals of contemporary kindergarten children, and the selection of maps correspondingly diverse.

The book is a collaborative effort. Chapters on geography, ancient history and the medieval age were written by Martin Collcutt. The chapter on Edo culture was provided by Isao Kumakura and translated by Akiko Collcutt. The chapters on Meiji and modern Japan were written by Marius B. Jansen. Maps, illustrations and artwork were produced by Olive Pearson, Linda Proud and Andrew Lawson, whose concern for quality is evident on every page of the book. Graham Speake was a dedicated and demanding editor, coordinating the efforts of the whole team, without whose enthusiasm and hard work the book might never have been completed. Thanks are also due to the many publishers, museums, private collectors and libraries who have generously given permission for the illustrations.

PART ONE
ORIGINS

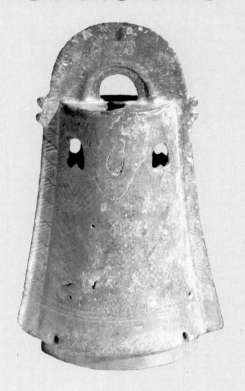

THE GEOGRAPHY OF JAPAN

Like all peoples the Japanese and their culture have been shaped by the land and climate in which they live. The location of Japan, its natural features and seasonal climate have provided both limits and opportunities for cultural development. Had the islands of Japan been further north, or less blessed with snow-capped mountains, rivers and fertile plains, the cultivation of paddy-field rice, which has left a deep imprint on ancient and modern Japanese culture, might never have taken hold. Had Japan been located further from the Asian continent, it might not have been the beneficiary of such powerful Chinese and Korean cultural impulses. Had it been closer to China, it might well have developed a much less distinctive culture. Over the centuries the Japanese took the country's resources, its climate and location to shape a distinctive civilization. In general the Japanese have believed that they have been favored by geography; that in spite of occasional volcanic eruptions, earthquakes and typhoons the islands and the climate have always been generous to them. In ancient times this belief in the beneficence of their land was expressed in a land-creation myth in which the islands were created by the coupling of the gods Izanagi and Izanami: "Izanagi and Izanami stood on the floating bridge of Heaven and held counsel together, saying: 'Is there not a country beneath?' Thereupon they thrust down the jewel-spear of Heaven, and groping about therewith found the ocean. The brine which dripped from the point of the spear coagulated and became an island which received the name Onogoro-jima. The two Deities thereupon descended and dwelt in the islands. Accordingly they wished to become husband and wife together, and to produce countries."

Topography and structure of the archipelago

The Japanese archipelago is part of the circum-Pacific arc of mountains lying along the eastern edge of the Asian continent. The archipelago consists of four larger and more than 1000 smaller islands covering some 370 000 square kilometers (145 000 square miles). This corresponds roughly in size to the countries of Finland or Italy, or to the states of Montana or California in the United States. The four largest islands are Hokkaido, a little smaller than Ireland, approximately 83 000 square kilometers (30 000 square miles), Honshu, a little larger than Great Britain, 231 000 square kilometers (89 000 square miles), Kyushu, a little larger than Taiwan, 42 000 square kilometers (16 000 square miles), and Shikoku, about the size of Sardinia, 19 000 square kilometers (7000 square miles). Among the many lesser islands the largest are Okinawa, in the Ryukyuan chain, and Sado, off the coast of northern Honshu. At the end of the Pacific War in 1945 Japan lost control of many territories that had been claimed as part of the prewar Japanese empire. These included the Kuril Islands (Chishima Rettō), southern Sakhalin (Karafuto), the Ryukyu Islands and other Pacific islands, Taiwan and Korea. The Bonin (Ogasawara) Islands were returned by the United States in 1968 and Okinawa in 1972. Japan's claim to the four northern Kuril Islands, occupied by the Soviet Union since 1945, remains a major source of friction between the two countries.

The topography of the archipelago, as we now know it, dates from the end of the ice ages, some 12 000 years ago. From fossils and archaeological remains it is clear that Japan was part of the Asiatic mainland during the ice ages. As temperatures fell, polar ice built up, oceans receded and land bridges to the continent were created. Animals of all kinds from the Asian mainland roamed through Japan, including mammoths, wolves, deer and brown bears from the north and the Naumann elephants and antelopes from the south. The animals were followed by hunters who came and settled in what is now Japan. Toward the end of the ice age temperatures began to rise, the polar ice caps receded and sea levels rose again. Some 12 000 years ago the rising seas severed the land bridges and separated the archipelago from the Asian mainland.

Although we now think of it as the industrial giant of Asia—a hive of crowded cities, bustling ports, ultramodern factories, clogged highways and bullet trains—Japan remains a land of soaring mountains, fiery volcanoes, deeply etched valleys, silent forests, fast-flowing rivers and shimmering seas. Mountains dominate the landscape. The archipelago is formed from mountains, many of them volcanic, rising from the floor of the western Pacific. Volcanoes, thermal hot springs and earthquakes are features of the country. More than 180 volcanoes are known to have been active since the Quaternary geological period and over 40 are active today. Mount Fuji is now dormant, but volcanoes like Sakurajima, Aso, Asama, Bandai and Mihara spew plumes of smoke from active craters.

Earth tremors are frequent. The Japanese may experience as many as 1000 a year. Earthquakes of magnitude 4 to 6 on the Richter scale are not uncommon. A quake measuring 6·6 on the Richter scale, for instance, struck the Chiba-Tokyo area at noon on 17 December 1987. Two people were killed, and more than 50 injured, by falling buildings or concrete block walls. All train services were halted temporarily. The destructive Tokyo earthquake of 1923 had a magnitude of 8·2. With very large quakes seeming to run on a 60-year cycle, many Japanese expect another devastating quake in the Tokyo area before very long. Today, however, buildings are more resistant. The 40-story skyscrapers of central Tokyo are built on flexible foundations designed to absorb the worst shocks of severe earthquakes. Quakes under the sea can give rise to destructive tidal waves known as *tsunami* that ravage coastlines hundreds or thousands of miles from their source.

meters
3000
2000
1000
200
0 sea level
500

—·— international boundary
■ capital city
□ other important city
▲ mountain summit
(height in meters)

CHINA

USSR

SEA OF OKHOTSK

Sakhalin

La Pérouse Str
(Sōya Str)
C Sōya

Rebun
Rishiri

C Shiretoko

Kunl Is

Vladivostok

DAISETSU MTS
Mt Asahi
▲2290

L Kussharo

Ishikari Bay

Ishikari
Plain

Kushiro

N KOREA

Sapporo

L Shikotsu

Tokachi

HIDAKA MTS

HOKKAIDO

Ch'ongjin

Okushiri

Uchiura
Bay

C Erimo

Hakodate

Tsugaru Str

Mutsu
Bay

▲ Mt Iwaki
1625

SEA OF JAPAN

Akita

Omono

▲ Mt Chokai
2230

Kitakami

Mogami

ECHIGO MTS

Sendai

Matsushima
Bay

Sado

Ullung

Niigata
Agano
Niigata
Plain

JAPAN

Noto Pen

Toyama
Bay

Shinano

MIKUNI MTS

PACIFIC OCEAN

Kanazawa

JAPAN ALPS

Mt Yarigo
3180

Utsunomiya

HONSHU

Nishi

Oki

Mt Haku
2702▲

Tone
Kanto Plain

REA

Wakasa Bay

L Biwa

Kiso

Nobi
Plain

AKAISHI MTS

Tokyo

C Inubo

Pusan

CHUGOKU MTS

Kyoto

Nagoya

Yokohama

Boso
Pen

Mt Fuji
3776

Sagami
Bay

Korea Strait
(Tsushima Str)

Okayama

Kobe

Osaka
Plain

Ise
Bay

Izu
Pen

Oshima

Tushima

Hiroshima

Osaka

Awaji

KII
MTS

Nii

Kozu

Tanegashima
Ōsumi Is

Yaku

Yakujima Str

Higashi Str

Iki

Takamatsu

Yoshino

Kii Channel

Miyake

Mikura

Izu Is

Hirado

Fukuoka

INLAND SEA

SHIKOKU MTS

C Muroto

Ō Is

Chikugo
Tsukushi
Plain

Kitakyushu

Mt Kuju ▲
1788

SHIKOKU

C Shio

Hachijo

Amami

Kikai

Fukue

Nagasaki

Shimo

Burgo Channel

C Ashizuri

Tokuno

Okino erabu

Kagoshima

KYUSHU MTS

KYUSHU

Okinawa Islands

Ōsumi Str

Ōsumi Is

Tanegashima

Kerama

Naha

Okinawa

Yakujima Str

Yaku

scale 1:6 500 000

0   300 km

0   200 mi

EAST CHINA SEA

PACIFIC OCEAN

TAIWAN

Sakashima Islands

Miyako

Iriomote

Ishigaki

continuation southwest at same scale

Natural vegetation of Japan
Due to its mountainous structure Japan still has a very rich vegetation for a highly industrialized country. Some 70 percent of the country is either mountain forest or scrubland. Centuries ago broad-leaved evergreens and deciduous species predominated at lower altitudes over the southwest of the country, with conifers at higher altitudes. In central and eastern Japan deciduous woodlands were extensive, with needle-leaved evergreens common in the north. Today much of the forest has been replanted, chiefly with broad-leaved evergreens or conifers. Alpine vegetation is found at higher altitudes in the mountains.

Most of Japan is mountainous. Some 75 percent of the land is in slopes of over 15 degrees. In many parts of the country the mountains run down almost to the heavily indented coastline, leaving only river valleys and fan-shaped coastal plains for settlement, agriculture and industrial development. This accounts for the heavy concentration of cities and industrial development along the narrow Pacific coastal strip from Tokyo to Osaka and along the coasts of the Inland Sea. The largest alluvial plains in Japan include the Ishikari Plain of Hokkaido, the Niigata Plain of northern Honshu, the Kantō Plain at the head of Tokyo Bay, the Nobi Plain around Nagoya in central Honshu, the Osaka Plain and the Tsukushi Plain of northern Kyushu. Of these the Kantō Plain, covering an area of 32 375 square kilometers, is the largest.

Several rugged mountain arcs meet to form the horned spine of the Japanese archipelago. Hokkaido is dominated by the mountain ranges of Dai-

NATURAL VEGETATION

- alpine
- coniferous forest
- broadleaf deciduous forest
- broadleaf evergreen forest
- coastal dunes

scale 1:10 000 000

| 0 | 300 km |
| 0 | 200 mi |

and have contributed to the sense of awe and grandeur reflected in a long tradition of mountain worship and mountain asceticism.

Mountains have also helped shape Japan's basic irrigation and river patterns. Japan has many rivers. Most are short, less than 300 kilometers long, and flow rapidly from the mountains to the sea. Only a few, like the Ishikari in Hokkaido, the Tone in the Kantō (east of the barrier) and the Yodo in the Kansai (west of the barrier), wind their way across substantial plains. Very few rivers are navigable, except in their lower reaches. Most streams swell into torrents during the spring snow melt or after typhoon rains, then subside again into rocky channels. Before the development of modern bridging and road-building techniques rivers provided serious obstacles to transportation and communication. Woodblock prints from the Edo period frequently show travelers on the major highway to Edo (modern Tokyo), the Tōkaidō, being ferried, or carried, across the rivers that cut the road.

The combination of heavy precipitation and many river channels has meant that historically Japan has been blessed with plentiful supplies of water for irrigation. Through much of Japan's history there was an ongoing struggle to tame unruly rivers and harness them for irrigation or, more recently, for hydroelectric power. Although abundant, river water alone has been insufficient to sustain industrial, agricultural and residential needs for water and energy. Surface water has been supplemented with ground water and hydroelectric power with oil and nuclear energy. Japan is heavily dependent upon imported oil for some 60 percent of its total energy consumption.

setsu and Hidaka. The Northern and Southern Alps comprise several ranges running down the spine of Honshu with more than 20 peaks rising to over 3000 meters, and Mount Fuji soaring to 3776 meters. Most of the Kii peninsula is mountainous, and the Chūgoku range splits western Honshu into San'in and Sanyō districts. The islands of Kyushu and Shikoku and smaller islands to the south are all mountainous and volcanic.

In earlier times the mountain chains made transportation, especially across Honshu, rather difficult and encouraged the development of settlement and culture in the narrow valleys and larger coastal basins. They thus contributed to regional differences and local character, and in the premodern period to local control by entrenched families or feudal lords. But mountains and volcanoes have also given Japan hydroelectric power, thermal hot springs, summer and winter resorts and many spectacular national parks. They have been celebrated in mythology, art and literature

Ocean currents around Japan
The two major ocean-current systems washing Japan's shores have a profound impact on climate. The warm Kuroshio (Japan) Current contributes to the warmth of Japan's southern coastlines, resulting in muggy summers and heavy snowfalls on coastlines facing the Sea of Japan. The cold Oyashio (Okhotsk) Current tempers the summers and contributes to a shorter growing season in Hokkaido and northeastern Japan. Where the Kuroshio and the Oyashio meet off the coast of northeastern Honshu are some of the world's richest fishing grounds.

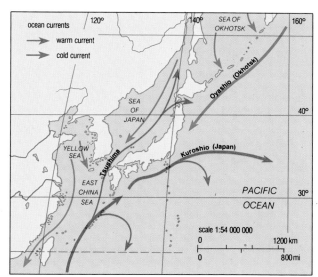

Japan is surprisingly heavily forested. Some 70 percent of the country, including large sections of the upland area, is forest. This compares closely with Scandinavian countries and is much higher than the world average of 30 percent. Corresponding to the subarctic, cold temperate, temperate and subtropical climatic zones of Japan, there are four main forest zones. In the north, in Hokkaido, the forests are mainly needle-leaved evergreens, in northern Honshu broad-leaved evergreens, in southern Honshu broad-leaved deciduous trees, and in the Ryukyu Islands tropical forests of broad-leaved evergreens. Bamboo groves are still to be found in Honshu and southern parts of the country. These woodlands are almost entirely in upland areas. Few towns and cities in Japan have extensive wooded areas within their boundaries.

Under human pressure, the pattern of afforestation has changed with time. Originally the whole of Japan was heavily forested. The Jōmon people, a non-agricultural hunting-and-gathering people who inhabited the islands between 10 000 and 300 BC, exploited the deciduous forests of central and eastern Japan. After the introduction of the cultivation of rice and other cereal crops in the Yayoi period (300 BC–300 AD) fields were burned out of woodland. Over time, rice paddies took the place of woodland in the major plains, and then climbed hillsides as intricately layered terraces, cutting into the lower edges of the forests. Until modern times, and the opening of Hokkaido, forests were generally not sacrificed for pasture. Shortage of suitable grassland and Buddhist prohibitions on the taking of animal life were among the factors contributing to a lack of emphasis on animal husbandry and livestock farming prior to the 19th century. Moreover, in the native Shinto cults various mountains and forests were regarded as sacred and remained intact and inviolable for centuries.

The growth of towns, the use of iron tools and the need for charcoal for smelting or firewood for pottery kilns put forests under greater pressure. The building of the capitals of Nara and Heian in the 8th and 9th centuries and the surge of castle building and urbanization in the 16th and 17th centuries made particularly heavy inroads into premodern timber resources. Shoguns (military rulers) and feudal lords, however, saw the value of forest not only as hunting range but as a means of limiting soil erosion and flooding. They adopted deliberate policies of nurturing and protecting forests, they limited lumbering and enforced replanting.

Modern industrialization, urbanization and population growth, with their concomitant demands for construction materials and fuel, have again put pressure on woodlands. Natural deciduous forest has dwindled and been replaced by planted forest, most of it conifer—Japanese cedar, cypress, black pine and red pine—which now accounts for more than 25 percent of Japan's woodland. In spite of its extensive forest resources, Japan imports great quantities of lumber from the United States and other parts of the world. Much of the forest is suitable for fuel but not for commercial construction use. Access is difficult on steep mountain slopes and many forest areas are of very mixed character. Lumber for building, furniture, woodchips and pulp is imported from America, Canada, the Soviet Union, Indonesia and other countries.

The significance of the sea

Few places in Japan are far from the sea, and the seas, like the mountains, have shaped Japan's character. The Pacific Ocean, the Sea of Japan and the Inland Sea have a profound effect on Japan's climate. The Pacific Ocean tends to keep the air masses moving in from the east warm and moist. It contributes to the generally mild, sunny climate of the Pacific coast and spawns the typhoons that bring rain, and sometimes destruction, to the islands. The deep waters of the Sea of Japan add warmth and moisture to the cold, dry Siberian winds that strike northern Japan in winter. This contributes to the heavy snows that fall on the

Below: Japan in the Far East.

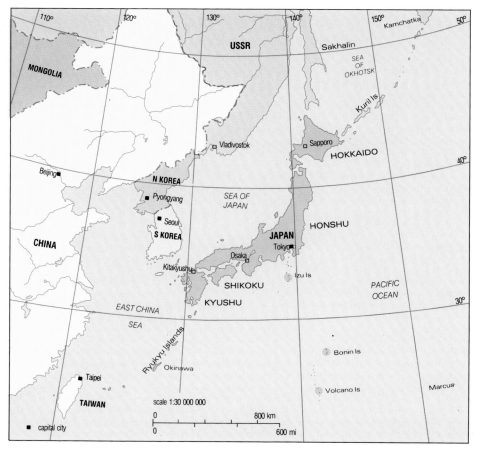

15

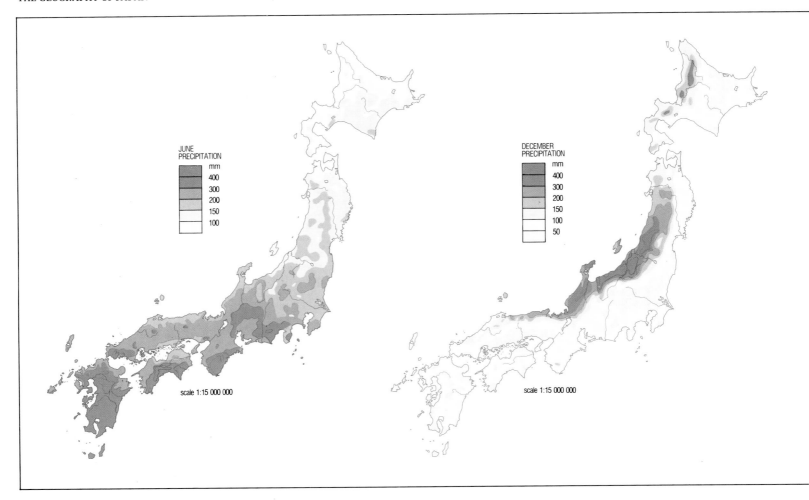

JUNE
PRECIPITATION

mm
400
300
200
150
100

scale 1:15 000 000

DECEMBER
PRECIPITATION

mm
400
300
200
150
100
50

scale 1:15 000 000

mountains. Two ocean current systems also have profound effects upon climate. The waters of the Kuroshio, flowing from the western Pacific, warm the southern coastal areas and contribute to the long growing seasons there. Hokkaido and the coasts of northern Honshu are washed by colder currents coming from the Sea of Okhotsk. Where these warm and cool currents mingle, at around latitude 36 degrees north, marine life is particularly rich. The Inland Sea is a protected warm-water channel, rich in marine life, though subject recently to heavy industrial development and severe pollution.

The seas around Japan have always been vital sources of food. From the very beginnings of their history the Japanese have depended heavily on seaweed, fish and shellfish for food and fertilizer. They have farmed the seas almost as intensively as they have farmed the land. Industrial pollution, dwindling fish stocks, concern for whales and other endangered sea creatures, and the efforts of other countries to extend control over their territorial waters now threaten to restrict Japan's ability to farm the seas as heavily as in the past. Still, small vessels from fishing villages around the coasts of Japan continue to fish the rich inshore waters as they have done for centuries while larger ships scour the oceans of the world to supply the insatiable Tokyo and Osaka markets.

Japan's insular location has had a profound impact on its history and culture. The seas have been a major regulator of contact with the outside world. The distance between Japan and Korea is 200 kilometers (125 miles). The distance to China across the Sea of Japan at its widest point is more

than 800 kilometers (500 miles). In these days of rapid air travel these do not seem great distances. From Tokyo one can be in Seoul or Beijing, Hong Kong or Honolulu, or even Moscow, New York or London in a matter of hours. In earlier times, however, with the only transportation an open boat and navigation techniques uncertain, the seas around Japan were daunting barriers to travel and communication. These seas can be rough and are subject to typhoons at certain times of the year. This maritime barrier has protected Japan. There have been few invasion attempts and it was generally easy to regulate maritime contacts. Restricted communication fostered a distinct and homogeneous culture within the archipelago. Attempted invasions by Mongol fleets in the 13th century were foiled by typhoons and waves. Japan's insularity made it possible for a regime like the Tokugawa shogunate to restrict contact with the outside world in the interests of domestic order and stability. Far from being sterile periods, these were times of distinctive cultural creativity. Yet, even in periods of so-called "seclusion," some degree of communication with the outside world was maintained. The maritime obstacle was not insurmountable. Japan has never been totally isolated.

From the very beginnings of Japanese history the seas have also been the principal channel of communication, cultural infusion and trade. During the early centuries Chinese and Korean influences constantly trickled into Japan, while the Japanese themselves in the 7th and 8th centuries sent many large embassies to China to acquire advanced knowledge of continental civilization. In the 16th century Iberian missionaries and traders

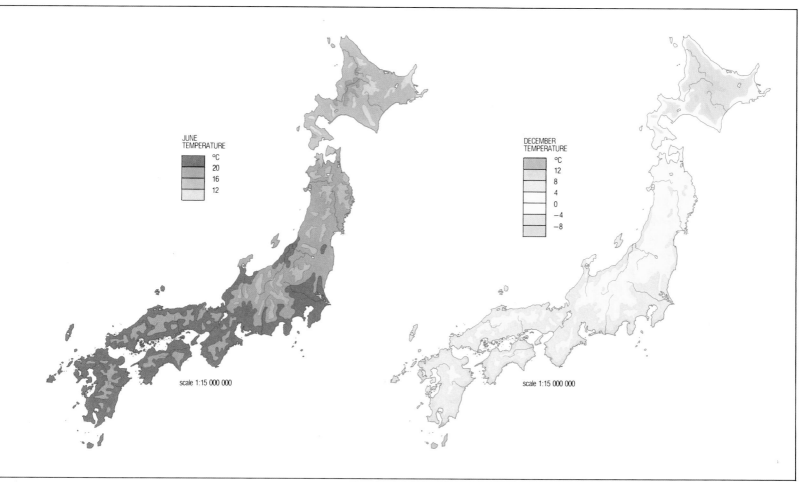

JUNE TEMPERATURE
°C
20
16
12

scale 1:15 000 000

DECEMBER TEMPERATURE
°C
12
8
4
0
−4
−8

scale 1:15 000 000

Climate of Japan
With the exception of semitropical Okinawa and the Ryukyu Islands, the archipelago of Japan enjoys a well-defined seasonal climate. The months of July, August and early September are hot and humid over most of the country except Hokkaido with temperatures ranging well into the 90s (Fahrenheit). Summer is preceded in June and early July by a rainy season, which spreads eastward over Kyushu and most of Honshu, and is often followed by typhoons in September and October. Spring (March, April and May) and fall (October through November) bring warm days and cool nights, with stable moderate temperatures. December, January and February bring frigid temperatures to northern Japan with heavy snowfalls on the Sea of Japan coast and the central mountain ranges. The Pacific and Inland Sea coasts, east of the mountains, tend to be cold but clear and dry in winter.

brought Christianity, guns and Western culture to Japan. On their way they encountered Japanese merchants and seamen who sailed the seas of Asia and traded as far south as Malacca. Even during the Tokugawa period there was always some coming and going by sea. The Dutch maintained a trading post in Nagasaki, while Chinese traders and Korean and Ryukyuan envoys came and went. In the 19th century the threat to the Tokugawa seclusion policy, and the catalyst that brought an end to the feudal regime, came by sea: Russian ships probed from the north, English vessels from the south, and Americans, culminating in Commodore Perry's squadron, from the east. Having recognized the potent influence of naval power and maritime commerce, the leaders of the Meiji government gave great attention to building up a Japanese navy and merchant marine as vital components of a rich and powerful modern nation-state.

Even in these days of rapid air travel, Japan still relies on the sea for its highly successful trade. The country is heavily dependent on imports of foodstuff and raw materials and on exports of manufactured products. Most of those imports and exports are carried by sea. Foreign pressure is now forcing the Japanese government and consumers to become less export-oriented and to absorb more imports. This, however, has barely reduced the flow of freighters carrying automobiles, machine tools or electronic products to world markets. Almost 100 percent of Japan's oil is imported by sea, as is 95 percent of its aluminum, nickel, iron ore, tin and copper. Two-thirds of the grain consumed by the Japanese and most of the soybeans

are also imported by sea. This heavy dependence on exports and imports moving via extended sealanes contributes to a sense of vulnerability on the part of many Japanese, while it is at the same time undeniably a source of recent prosperity.

Today the seas are much less of a barrier to communication. Modern sea and air transportation, especially discounted charter flights, are bringing Japan closer to the rest of the world and the world closer to Japan. Ease of travel, combined with the international reach of the Japanese economy, the growing wealth of the Japanese and strength of the Japanese yen, has encouraged millions of Japanese to travel abroad on business, study and leisure. Japan, even with the yen at all-time highs against many other currencies, remains a fascinating country for foreign visitors and students. The opening of Japanese financial markets to foreign securities houses and the lure of the rich but difficult Japanese market to foreign corporations have brought many more foreign residents to Tokyo, Osaka and some other cities. The Japanese talk of the "internationalization" of their country. That is an attitude of mind that many would say still has to be achieved, but it is true that the Japanese have become much more cosmopolitan in the past decade.

Climate
The long narrow Japanese archipelago covers nearly 22 degrees of latitude from the northern tip of Hokkaido to the southern Ryukyu Islands. This range in latitude corresponds to that between northern Italy and southern Egypt or between Montreal in Canada and southern Florida in the

United States. Climatically Japan has much in common with the eastern seaboard of the United States, but with greater contrasts between summer and winter precipitation, and complicated by the fact that it is a mountainous archipelago located in proximity to a vast continental land mass. Among the most notable features of the climate are considerable yearly temperature fluctuations, distinct seasonal change and heavy rainfall. Because of the length of the archipelago and the complexity of the land formation, however, there is much seasonal regional variation. Northern Japan has warm summers and long hard winters with heavy snowfalls. Central Japan has hot, humid summers and cold, but short, winters. The average January temperature in Tokyo, for instance, is lower than that of Reykjavik in Iceland, which is considerably further north. Southwestern Japan has long, hot and humid summers and mild winters. Okinawa and the Ryukyu Islands enjoy a subtropical climate.

Japan's climate is regulated by a complex interaction of Pacific and continental air masses and frontal movements. This produces frequent variations of weather, depending on the season. During the winter months from December to February most of Japan's climate is dominated by the high-pressure areas of the Siberian continental air mass, at the center of which is the mass of cold dry polar air stretching from Lake Baikal to the Mongolian border. Cold waves from this frigid continental air mass and seasonal northwest winds from Siberia flow over the Sea of Japan where they encounter warmer northerly air currents. They absorb large quantities of moisture which is deposited as snow on the mountainous areas of the Sea of Japan side of the country. With their heavy winter snowfalls and well-developed resorts Honshu and Hokkaido are a skiers' paradise, at least for those who do not mind crowded slopes.

The mountain chains and surrounding ocean currents also affect climate significantly. The northwest coast of Honshu, facing the continent, gets heavy snowfalls from Siberian air depositing precipitation before crossing the mountains. Precipitation is intensified by the fact that the Sea of Japan is a deep-water sea and therefore warmer in winter than surrounding land masses. It warms, moistens and destabilizes the lower masses of Siberian air. Elsewhere in Japan precipitation in winter is much lighter and 70 to 80 percent of the annual precipitation falls in summer rather than winter. The warm-water Kuroshio Current, the Pacific equivalent of the Atlantic's Gulf Stream, warms the coasts of southern Japan and the Pacific coastal areas. In a contrary movement, cold currents from the Sea of Okhotsk move southward along the eastern coast of Hokkaido and the western and eastern coasts of northern Honshu.

During the summer months of June, July and August Japan is affected by high-pressure areas moving in from the Pacific. Hot, moist air streams flow from west to east and from south to north to fill low-pressure areas over Siberia. The Japanese use a summer discomfort index, calculated on the basis of temperature and humidity. Most summer days in Tokyo and Osaka register a disagreeable level of discomfort. To escape the heat many Japanese head for summer mountain resorts or,

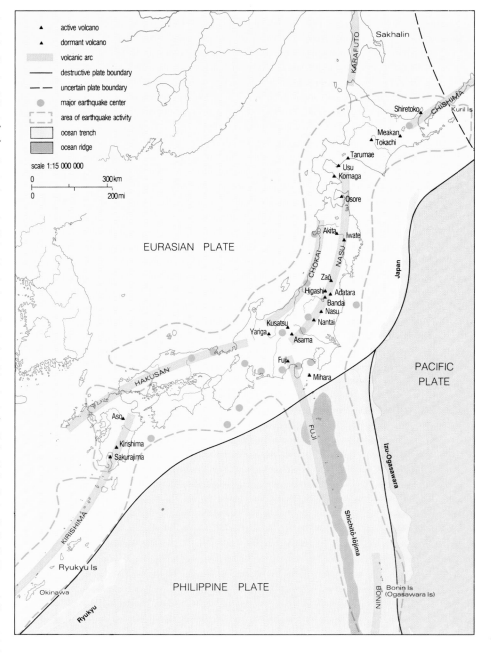

increasingly, go abroad for their vacations.

At the start of the summer, in June and early July, there is a rainy season (*baiu*) which opens in the south and gradually moves northward. This is the product of cold high-pressure air currents from the Sea of Okhotsk encountering warm, moist air currents from the south Pacific. These air masses linger to produce several weeks of heavy rainfall over western and central Japan. The rains are important for rice cultivation and the replenishment of water supplies but severe downpours can be a cause of flooding and landslides.

With the end of summer, in September and October, comes the major typhoon season. Typhoons are powerful tropical storms produced in low-pressure areas of southern oceans near the Equator. They generally have wind speeds at the center of more than 17 meters per second. They sometimes move in toward Japan in early spring, but more commonly in the fall. Like Atlantic hurricanes or the cyclones of the Indian Ocean they bring torrential rains over wide areas and can cause severe damage. The typhoons that wrecked Mongol vessels in the late 13th century in response

Geology of Japan

Geologically, the archipelago of Japan comprises several volcanic arcs. Those through the Kuril Islands, northeastern Honshu and down to the Bonin Islands form one continuous island arc making up northeastern Japan. The arcs of southwestern Honshu and the Ryukyu Islands make up the geologically older southwestern Japan.

Located on the edge of the continental crust of the Eurasian plate, the islands of Japan lie at the intersection of the Eurasian, Pacific and Philippine plate systems. Geological crustal movements of these plates over millions of years have contributed to the intensity and pattern of Japan's continuing seismic and volcanic activity.

The Pacific plate, for instance, which occupies most of the bed of the Pacific Ocean, is moving westward at a speed of several centimeters a year. Where it submerges at the edge of the Eurasian plate, it has created the Japan Trench and intensified the pattern of volcanic activity.

to the prayers of priests and people were named divine winds (*kamikaze*). The weather stabilizes in mid-October and winter seasonal wind patterns begin to develop.

In spring (March to May) and fall (October to November) continental and oceanic high-pressure areas tend to balance over Japan giving fine, steady weather patterns. These are delightful seasons, celebrated in poetry since ancient times. While nights may remain cool, the climate is mild during these months. In February people wait eagerly for the first warm spring wind and follow the zone of plum and cherry blossom moving northward. In fall the skies are sometimes brilliantly clear and maple viewing, best in a light rain, draws millions to parks, temple gardens and mountain trails.

Geology and soil structure

Located on the edge of the Eurasian continental plate and in contact with the Pacific and Philippine plates, the archipelago is subject to severe tectonic movements—both long-term movements and spasmodic seismic activity. It was probably formed as a result of a series of orogenic movements that thrust mountains upward rather than as the product of a single crustal eruption. Its geological origin dates from at least the Silurian phase of the Paleozoic era, about 400 million years ago, and the crustal movement is still continuing. Offshore in the Pacific are several deep trenches and troughs where the crust is considerably thinner. The Kuril-Kamchatka Trench, the Japan Trench and the Izu-Ogasawara Trench may be thought of as one long channel some 9000 meters (30 000 feet) deep following the arc of northeastern Japan. The Nankai Trough and the Ryukyu Trench are separate deep-water channels to the south. The depth of the crust varies from 7 kilometers (23 000 feet) on the floor of the Japan Trench to 36 kilometers (118 000 feet) in the central mountain ranges.

Geologically Japan is divided into northeastern and southwestern zones. The northeastern zone is formed largely by rock strata from the Neocene period of the Cenozoic era. Volcanoes have been active since the Quaternary period. Volcanic activity is much greater in the northeastern zone, occurring in the Chishima, Chōkai and Nasu volcanic arcs. Earthquake activity is also more vigorous in the northeastern zone. Hypocenters of earthquakes in the northeastern zone frequently occur inside the arc made by the Japan Trench.

The southwestern zone was formed in a comparatively early period. Most of the rock strata in southwestern Japan were formed during the Paleozoic or Mesozoic eras. Southwestern Japan is divided into an inner belt facing the Sea of Japan and an outer belt facing the Pacific by the great fault known as the Median Tectonic Line running longitudinally through Wakayama Prefecture, Shikoku and north-central Kyushu. There are fewer volcanoes in southwestern Japan and volcanic activity there tends to be concentrated in the area facing the Sea of Japan and in Kyushu. Earthquake activity is also less vigorous.

Japan's soils naturally reflect its geological structure and surface configuration. More than two-thirds of the soils are thin mountain soils containing varying quantities of beach sand and volcanic ash. Of the remainder, about 20 percent

are zonal soils including podzolic soils at higher altitudes and in the north, with brown, and red and yellow podzolics at lower altitudes. About 15 percent, mostly in the lowlands, are alluvial soils, created by river deposits. It is this 15 percent which both supports the intense practice of Japanese agriculture and serves as the site of residential settlement and industrial use.

Energy resources and minerals

Japan is endowed with coal and water for energy but must import petroleum and natural gas. Like France and the Soviet Union, the country has also committed itself to the use of nuclear power to provide a substantial proportion of its future energy needs and reduce its dependence on imported supplies. Coal supplies are plentiful in northern Kyushu and Hokkaido. However, the coal is of poor quality, it lies in deep and scattered seams, and is difficult and expensive to mine. Coal still supplies about one-fifth of the country's total energy needs but its relative share continues to shrink as Japan relies more heavily on petroleum, hydroelectric power and nuclear energy.

The fast-flowing rivers of the country still provide a useful source of energy. To tap this resource several large storage dams and many smaller dams have been built. The largest such hydroelectric scheme is the Kurobe Dam, 186 meters high, blocking the Kurobe River in Toyama Prefecture. Water from the dam is fed through tunnels carved through the Japan Alps to more than 14 generating plants. Japan has a potential of 20 million kilowatts of water power of which it uses some 12 million. Although the amount of hydroelectric energy used has been rising over the past 40 years, the relative proportion of hydroelectric power used has declined as the use of more efficient petroleum, natural gas and nuclear energy has risen rapidly. Today hydroelectric power accounts for only about 5 percent of Japan's total energy use, compared with about 20 percent from coal.

Japan does have some deposits of oil and natural gas. These, however, are minuscule and account for less than 1 percent of total consumption. The economic miracle of the 1970s and 1980s has been fueled with imported energy, mostly petroleum. The Japanese are intensely conscious that a political or international crisis that cut off oil supplies from the Persian Gulf, or sent oil prices skyrocketing again, or closed the Straits of Hormuz, Malacca or Lombok could have the most drastic repercusions for the Japanese economy. Since the oil crisis of 1973 the government has pursued a number of policies to reduce this vulnerability. These have included stockpiling, the shrinking or exporting of energy-intensive industries, acceleration of research on alternative energy sources, diversifying sources of oil supply and greater reliance on nuclear power. Because of its perceived vulnerability Japan has striven to develop a vigorous merchant marine, to maintain good diplomatic relations with other countries, to remain neutral in the Iran-Iraq war and to promote strategic development projects with ASEAN and other countries.

Japanese government planners see nuclear power as a possible solution to energy vulnerability and limited domestic energy resources.

Nuclear power already produces some 20 percent of Japan's electricity. This amount is projected to increase to more than 50 percent in coming decades. The Japanese people are sensitive to the risks of nuclear accidents but see little alternative if the country is to reduce its heavy dependence on imported fossil fuel for power generation.

Japan is also heavily dependent on foreign sources for its mineral needs. Japanese swords, ironware, bronze gilt statues, filigree gold and other metal objects are famous. Japan has domestic supplies of ferrous and non-ferrous minerals but the quantities are limited. Copper is mined in Akita Prefecture and the Kantō Plain. Iron ore is found in Iwate Prefecture and other parts of the northeast. Chromite, zinc and lead are also fairly abundant. None of these, however, is sufficient to meet more than 5 percent of the enormous industrial demand. Again Japan's heavy dependence on foreign supplies of critical resources influences its international diplomacy. Maintaining good commercial relations with large suppliers of minerals like South Africa becomes a policy imperative.

Population and settlement patterns

The image of Japan held by most outsiders is that of a small, isolated, overcrowded island country in which every square centimeter of usable land is either farmed intensively, settled as teeming cities or used for ultramodern factories. This image is in some ways quite misleading. In comparison with countries like the United States, Canada, China, India, Brazil or the Soviet Union Japan does seem very small. However, although Japan is only about the size of the state of Montana in area, it is about half as large again as West Germany or the United Kingdom and larger than Poland and Italy.

Nor is its population—about 121 million—particularly large by the standards of the most populous countries of the world. Japan ranks seventh after China, India, the Soviet Union, the United States, Indonesia and Brazil. The sense of overcrowding comes not so much from sheer population size, as from population distribution. Japan's overall population density, 322 per square kilometer, is less than that of Belgium or the Netherlands; but with only about one-quarter of the land area usable, the actual population density is considerably higher. More than 75 percent of the

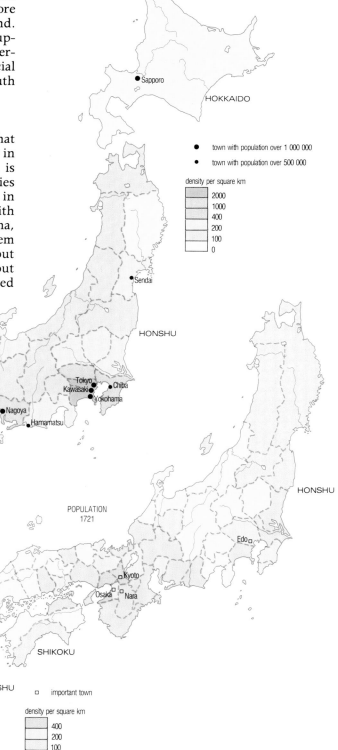

Population of Japan in 1721 and 1980

In 1986 Japan's population stood at 121·5 million, the seventh largest in the world. Whereas average population density per square kilometer for the world is 36 people, in Japan it is 322. Among countries of any size only Bangladesh, South Korea and the Netherlands are more densely populated.

Because much of Japan is mountainous, its highly urbanized population is concentrated on the coastal plains. Nearly 50 percent of the population lives in three great conurbations of greater Tokyo (including Kawasaki, Yokohama and Chiba), greater Nagoya (including Aichi and Mie Prefectures) and greater Osaka (including Hyōgo and Kyoto Prefectures).

Estimates of population in the early 17th century range from 7 to 18 million. There is general agreement that the population grew rapidly until about 1720 when the first shogunate census counted 26 million. (If allowance is made for samurai, court nobles and outcasts, this would have totaled about 30 million.) Thereafter, overall population growth was slower with considerable regional variation. With thriving cities and garrison towns like Osaka, Kyoto, Edo (Tokyo) and Nagoya, Japan was highly urbanized for a preindustrial society.

population is concentrated in urban centers; and those urban and industrial centers all cluster on the lowland alluvial quarter of the land area. The Tokyo-Kawasaki-Yokohama conurbation has a population of over 25 million, the largest in the world, while the Osaka-Kobe-Kyoto conurbation has more than 13 million people living in an area of less than 1300 square kilometers, a density of more than 10 000 per square kilometer.

The Japanese think of themselves as a homogeneous population. In general this perception is valid. But there are several significant minority groups whose position in the society is not always an easy one. The Korean minority makes up 0·5 percent of the population. Since the Japanese government employs the principle of lineage in determining citizenship, members of the Korean community, even those born in Japan and speaking fluent Japanese, are aliens. They face discrimination in education, job opportunities and marriage prospects. Another group still facing considerable prejudice is the *burakumin,* the descendants of outcast communities of the premodern period. Although legally protected against overt discrimination, *burakumin* still face severe prejudice. They are often refused employment in any but menial jobs. Those who want to avoid discrimination are sometimes forced to try to hide their origin when seeking employment, marriage or residence.

Since World War II there has been an accelerating movement of population away from the countryside and into urban centers. However, these urban centers are generally located close to what were always agrarian areas of Japan. This has created certain problems. Urbanization has meant a concomitant loss of agricultural land. Although Japanese farming is highly intensive and efficient, Japanese farmers cannot produce rice and other crops as economically as the large farmlands of the United States and other countries. From a purely economic view the mass of the population would benefit from unrestricted and internationally competitive imports of grains, citrus fruit and meat.

Below: ancient provinces
The basic administrative structure of Japan was defined in the Chinese-style centralized reforms of the 7th and 8th centuries. The country, or as much of it as was then under the control of the imperial court, was divided into some 60 provinces, or *kuni*. Each province was originally governed by a provincial governor and his staff who were sent out periodically from the court in Heian. This centralized administrative structure was gradually eroded, first by the creation of private estates (*shōen*) within the provinces during the Heian and Kamakura periods, then by warrior aggrandizement during the feudal age. But the provincial system persisted in name until the 19th century.

Left: modern prefectures
In 1871 the Meiji government announced the abolition of all feudal domains. Japan was redivided into three urban prefectures (*fu*) and 72 other prefectures (*ken*) under governors appointed by the central government. These divisions, with considerable adjustments, have since remained the basis for local government. In 1889 the number was reduced to three urban and 42 other prefectures excluding Hokkaido and the Ryukyu Islands. Today Japan's administrative structure is described as "*to-dō-fu-ken.*" The only *to* (metropolis) is Tokyo; the single *dō* (district) is Hokkaido; *fu* (urban prefectures) include Osaka and Kyoto; and there are 47 *ken* (prefectures).

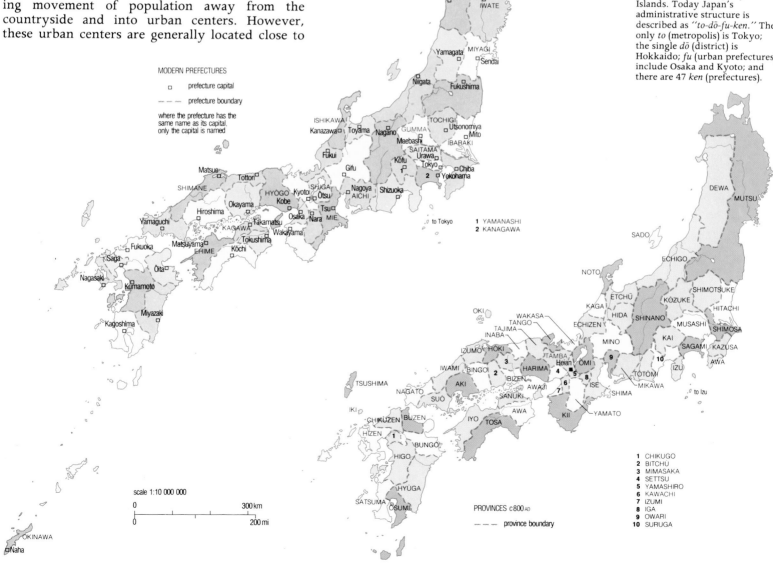

MODERN PREFECTURES
□ prefecture capital
- - - prefecture boundary

where the prefecture has the same name as its capital, only the capital is named

1 YAMANASHI
2 KANAGAWA

scale 1:10 000 000
0 — 300 km
0 — 200 mi

PROVINCES c 800 AD
- - - province boundary

1 CHIKUGO
2 BITCHU
3 MIMASAKA
4 SETTSU
5 YAMASHIRO
6 KAWACHI
7 IZUMI
8 IGA
9 OWARI
10 SURUGA

The Japanese government, however, views the maintenance of a domestic farm industry as a strategic necessity. Moreover, the ruling Liberal Democratic Party relies heavily on the farm vote and farmers are a powerful political lobby. To protect agriculture, and hold rural votes, the government has offered subsidies to farmers to keep fields in production or has maintained artificially high prices for rice and other commodities. To some extent this has robbed the city dweller to pay the farmer. It has also kept off the market farmland that might otherwise have been used for housing, contributing to the astronomical land values in Tokyo and other urban centers. Urbanization and population increase have merely reinforced the traditional patterns of population distribution. By far the greatest bulk of the population increase in modern Japan has been in the urban industrial centers. In gross terms Japan's rural population has declined quite slowly. In 1900 rural population was over 30 million. In 1965 it was about 33 million. By 1970 it was under 30 million, and it has continued to fall. The percentage shift from rural to urban, however, has been much more dramatic: 75 percent of the population now lives in urban areas.

In 1867, at the time of the Meiji restoration, Japan's population was about 33 million. By 1900 it had reached 44 million, and in 1920 was over 55 million. By 1940 it was over 70 million and it continued to rise during the war to 83 million in 1950 and over 93 million in 1960. It moved above 100 million in 1967 and is now estimated to be over 121 million. Thus it has almost quadrupled in the century since the Meiji restoration. The rate of growth, however, is less dramatic than it seems. Annual rates of increase have, on the whole, not been above 1·5 percent in the modern era and have fallen well below 1 percent since the 1960s, much lower than the United States, France and many other countries. Birth rates have declined even faster than mortality rates. In 1985 the birth rate was 12·0 per 1000. Deaths per 1000 were 6·0 and the natural rate of population increase 0·06 per-

cent. Having gone through a baby boom in the immediate postwar period, Japan now has an aging population as life expectancy has risen to one of the highest in the world for both men and women. Life expectancy at birth is 75·2 years for males and 80·9 for females. Among the serious social problems of the late 20th and early 21st centuries will be those of social welfare, care for the elderly and labor supply. At the same time, the acceptance of regular employment for married as well as single women, the rapid growth of a service-oriented economy and the surge in robotics are all contributing to changing patterns of labor supply and demand that the Japanese are already coming to grips with.

The major regions of Japan
Although the population is largely homogeneous and the land area of the Japanese archipelago is relatively small, the latitudinal range from subarctic to subtropical, combined with the mountainous character of the islands, makes for considerable regional diversity. This diversity is reflected in life-styles, dialects and speech patterns, local products, flora and fauna, and in differing patterns of historical and economic development. At the same time, regional diversity is modulated by easy access between city and countryside, by rapid communications and by the universal diffusion of highly sophisticated mass media. Japan is now a land of urbanized villages and cosmopolitan cities. Only some of the smaller islands can now be described as remote.

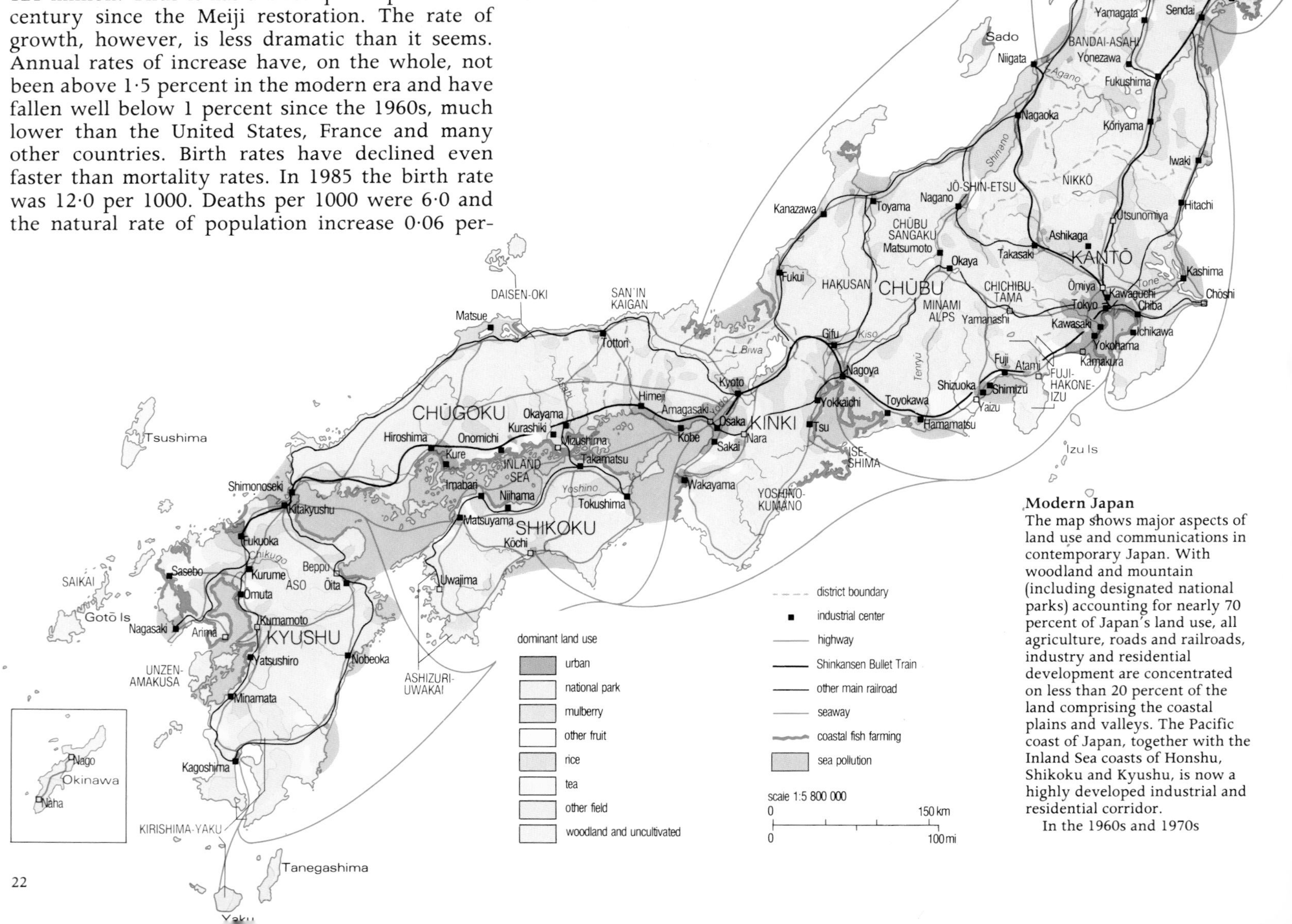

Modern Japan
The map shows major aspects of land use and communications in contemporary Japan. With woodland and mountain (including designated national parks) accounting for nearly 70 percent of Japan's land use, all agriculture, roads and railroads, industry and residential development are concentrated on less than 20 percent of the land comprising the coastal plains and valleys. The Pacific coast of Japan, together with the Inland Sea coasts of Honshu, Shikoku and Kyushu, is now a highly developed industrial and residential corridor.

In the 1960s and 1970s

dominant land use
- urban
- national park
- mulberry
- other fruit
- rice
- tea
- other field
- woodland and uncultivated

- - - - district boundary
■ industrial center
——— highway
——— Shinkansen Bullet Train
——— other main railroad
——— seaway
~~~~ coastal fish farming
sea pollution

scale 1:5 800 000
0   150 km
0   100 mi

Hokkaido

Hokkaido is Japan's northern frontier. Dominated by the Daisetsu mountain range and national park, Hokkaido is an island of forests, rivers, sheer cliffs and rolling pastures. Located at roughly the same latitude as New England or southern France, Hokkaido is bounded by the Sea of Okhotsk to the north and east, the Sea of Japan to the west, and the Pacific Ocean to the south. It is 83 517 square kilometers in area, a little smaller than Ireland. Its population density, at 71 persons per square kilometer, is less than one-fifth that of Honshu. Because of its northern location and the fact that its coasts are washed by cold ocean currents from the Sea of Okhotsk, its climate is quite different from that of Honshu, with colder temperatures, lower rainfall, no rainy season, few typhoons, and a much shorter growing season of only 120 to 140 days a year. Hokkaido was outside the rice-growing area in premodern Japan, but modern cold-resistant strains will grow there and it now produces large quantities of rice as well as livestock, dairy produce, fish, potatoes and other crops. The principal city and center of develop-

ment of modern Hokkaido is Sapporo (1·5 million).

Before the Meiji restoration of 1868 Hokkaido was known as Ezochi, Land of the Ezo, and was populated mainly by the Ainu, a Caucasoid people racially distinct from the inhabitants of the rest of Japan. In premodern times the Ainu are thought to have inhabited not only Hokkaido but also northern Honshu, southern Sakhalin and the Kuril Islands. They lived by hunting deer, salmon and seal. Now numbering fewer than 20 000, they are being rapidly assimilated into the main Japanese population. Some Ainu customs, festivals and crafts are preserved, but largely for tourist interest.

After the Meiji restoration the new government established the Hokkaido Development Agency to settle the area and preempt southern expansion by Russia. Hokkaido was developed by Japanese pioneers from Honshu under strong Western influence. Hokkaido University, originally the Sapporo Agricultural College, was established by the American scientist, missionary and educator William S. Clark (1826–86), president of the Massachusetts Agricultural College. Other foreign experts invited by the Hokkaido Development Board included the agronomist Horace Capron (1804–85). Western crops and dairy-farming methods were introduced early on, and wheat, beans, potatoes, oats and sugar beet are cultivated.

Japan's air, seas and rivers suffered heavy pollution as a byproduct of the single-minded pursuit of industrial growth. The horror of mercury poisoning at Minamata and Niigata and the heavy incidence of respiratory disorders at places like Yokkaichi, Kawasaki and Amagasaki convinced citizens and their government of the need for basic laws to protect the environment and make corporations accept responsibility for industrial pollution.

Right Sapporo, the site of the Hokkaido prefectural government and location of the 1980 Winter Olympic Games, is now a thriving city with a population of 1 500 000. In the 19th century it was little more than a cluster of huts belonging to Ainu and a few immigrants from Honshu. The city grew rapidly, however, as the center of the government-sponsored development of Hokkaido. Laid out on a grid-shaped pattern like Kyoto, Sapporo has until recently been principally an administrative and commercial center with little industry other than the Sapporo Brewery. It was at the Sapporo Agricultural College, established by William S. Clark in 1876, that Clark and Horace Capron introduced to Hokkaido many of the farming practices of New England as well as their Christian faith. Sapporo is now a center of winter sports and the site of an annual snow festival held in the first week of February in which teams compete in the building of elaborate and fanciful snow sculptures with themes from Japanese history, legend, sports or cartoons.

Rice is also grown on a large scale. About 90 percent of Japan's pastureland is found in Hokkaido and nearly as much of its dairy produce comes from there. With its wooded terrain, pasturelands, herds of cattle, large farms and silos Hokkaido has something of the look of New England to it. Individual farms are larger than those further south and the population is less dense. The coal-mining, forestry and fishing industries are important and industrial development is taking place around Sapporo.

The question of Japan's northern frontiers was first raised in the days of the Edo shogunate. A Russo-Japanese Amity treaty in 1855 stipulated that the Kuril Islands north of and including Urup Island would be Russian territory and those to the south, including Etorofu (Iturup), would belong to Japan. People of both nationalities were allowed to settle in Sakhalin (Karafuto), but after the Meiji restoration of 1868 Japan chose to move out of that island and concentrate on developing Hokkaido instead. A treaty of 1875 settled the issue formally, giving Sakhalin to Russia and all the Kuril Islands to Japan, along with fishing rights in northern waters. After World War II, however, Russia occupied Etorofu, Kunashiri, Shikotan and the Habomai island group and still holds them today despite repeated Japanese protests that the islands, and offshore fishing rights, are Japanese. This dispute is the single major issue remaining unsettled from World War II and still impedes the conclusion of a complete peace treaty with the Soviet Union.

Above and left Since its opening up in the late 19th century, Hokkaido has been a center of agriculture, forestry, fishing, mining and to a lesser extent manufacturing industry. With hard winters and a short growing season, farming has tended to be more extensive and mechanized than elsewhere in Japan. Dairy farms predominate. Rice is grown, but potatoes, beans, wheat, oats and sugar beets are equally important. Although Hokkaido is still Japan's northern frontier with thousands of hectares of mountain, forest and wild shoreline, its environment has been subject to heavy pressure from agricultural, industrial and residential development. In the process the rich wildlife of the island has been reduced and in some cases threatened with extinction. Environmental deterioration in the 1960s and 1970s led to sharp decreases in the numbers of such species as the red-crested crane or Japanese crested ibis. Efforts are now being made to protect the fragile habitat of such rare creatures as the white owl. The completion of the Seikan rail tunnel linking Hokkaido directly with Honshu, however, has added to the pressure for development and the erosion of Hokkaido's natural environment.

HONSHU

Honshu

The island of Honshu, at 231 000 square kilometers, is larger than Great Britain and is very much more densely populated, 404 persons per square kilometer. It is broken by a spine of mountain arcs into a number of regions with overlapping, but recognizably distinct, characteristics depending on their latitude and which sea they face. The coastal plains of Honshu were for centuries the heartland of Japanese rice agriculture. They have also been the site of dense urban settlement and heavy industrial development.

The northeastern part of Honshu, comprising the prefectures of Aomori, Iwate, Akita, Yamagata, Miyagi and Fukushima, is known as the Tōhoku, or northeastern, region. Traditionally labeled the granary of Japan, it is still predominantly a farming area, supplying Sendai and the huge Tokyo-Yokohama market with rice and other commodities. Farms in northern Tōhoku, while smaller than some dairy farms in Hokkaido, are larger than the national average. From the windows of the Shinkansen Bullet Train, which now runs to Morioka and will soon link Aomori with Tokyo, travelers see acres of rice fields spread in regular grids over the broad valleys. Today rice farming is highly mechanized, but one still sees women stooping in the fields, transplanting seedlings or weeding.

The long cold winters make double cropping difficult and farmers are in general less prosperous than those in the southeast. Rice prices, however, have been supported by the government. Lumber and fishing are important and there are growing pockets of high-technology industrial development. Tourism is also a major industry: the islands of Matsushima Bay, Lake Towada, the Rikuchū Coastline National Park and the Bandai-Asahi National Park all attract visitors. Mount Bandai (1819 meters) is still active, and more than 400 people were killed in an eruption there in 1888. The building of dams and the extension of the Shinkansen into the northeast have brought greater prosperity to the region. The major city in the Tōhoku region is Sendai which grew up around the castle town of the feudal lord Date Masamune (1567–1636). It lies on the Sendai alluvial plain, traversed by the Hirose River. It is now a thriving industrial and university city, with electronics, special steel plants, synthetics, machine tools and the Tōhoku National University.

The Kantō, literally "east of the barrier," comprises the seven prefectures around Tokyo on the broad Kantō Plain. They are Kanagawa Prefecture, Tokyo Metropolitan Prefecture, Saitama, Gumma, Tochigi, Ibaraki and Chiba. The Izu and Bonin Islands are administratively part of metropolitan Tokyo. The alluvial plain, watered by several rivers rising in the mountains of central Honshu, is surrounded by mountains to the west and north, and hills to the east. Once the heartland of feudal

The magnificent, perfectly conical profile of Mount Fuji soars 3776 meters into the sky above the Fuji-Hakone-Izu National Park. Although a thin whisp of smoke can sometimes be seen above its snow-capped summit, Fuji has not been active for several centuries. Eighteen eruptions are on record. The worst occurred in 800, 864 and 1707, blanketing the city of Edo in 15 centimeters of ash. The volcano has been celebrated in art and literature for centuries and regarded as a sacred mountain since antiquity. Until the Meiji restoration women were forbidden to climb it. Today more than 300000 people climb the six trails each year.

power, the Kantō has been at the core of modern Japanese development. The Tokyo-Kawasaki-Yokohama conurbation, with a population in 1985 of over 25 million in an area of 2500 square kilometers, is Japan's greatest population center and industrial zone, its seat of government, and the hub of its largest cluster of universities and cultural amenities. Industry is located in the Keihin (Tokyo-Yokohama) belt and in Saitama Prefecture. The range includes petrochemicals, automobiles, robotics, electronics, precision instruments and textiles.

Much of the Kantō Plain has been eaten up by residential and commercial or industrial construction, but the remainder of the plain is still intensively farmed and produces rice, tea, beans, vegetables and other crops for the Tokyo metropolitan market. It still produces mulberries, the basis of a small silkworm industry. The growing season averages about 215 days.

The Chūbu, or central, region spans the country from the Sea of Japan to the Pacific coast across the Japan Alps, where some of the country's highest peaks are to be found. It includes the nine prefectures of Niigata, Toyama, Ishikawa, Fukui, Nagano, Yamanashi, Gifu, Shizuoka and Aichi. The first four are also known as the Hokuriku area. Climate is varied. The Japan Alps divide the country into two—the sunnier Pacific side, also known as the front of Japan, *omote*-Nihon, and the colder Sea of Japan side, known as *ura*-Nihon, or the back of Japan. Historically the Sea of Japan coast has been less prosperous than the Pacific side, but the extension of the Shinkansen to Niigata is opening up the region and bringing it greater prosperity. Like the Tōhoku region, Hokuriku is a major wet-rice-producing area, with Niigata Prefecture the largest producer. The growing season is shorter than on the Pacific coast with single cropping the norm. Most of its precipitation of between 200 and 250 millimeters falls as snow in winter. The Pacific side is generally sunnier and drier, receiving its 150 to 200 millimeters of rainfall in the rainy or typhoon seasons. The region is famous for its oranges and tea, and Yamanashi produces grapes and peaches. The mountain prefecture of Nagano, the "Switzerland of Japan," was famous for sericulture before World War II but now is known mainly for tourism and fruit growing. The Pacific coastal prefectures of Shizuoka and Aichi are known as Tōkai, eastern seaboard. Shizuoka and Aichi used to produce a great deal of seafood from coastal areas but industrialization and accompanying pollution have cut into this. Shizuoka, however, still draws large fish catches from its deep-water port of Yaizu.

The largest city and center of the industrial core of the Pacific side of the Chūbu region is Nagoya with a population of over 2 million. Located on the old Tōkaidō route, Nagoya developed from the 17th century as the castle town of Owari domain. By 1692 it had a population of 40 000. In the late 19th century Nagoya was an important railroad junction between Tokyo and Osaka. Destroyed by bombing during World War II, Nagoya has been completely rebuilt and has flourished as one of the major centers of Japanese automobile production, the home of Toyota. Among the important cities in the Hokuriku area are Niigata and Kanazawa. Kanazawa, capital of Ishikawa Prefecture, flourished

Below With city streets clogged by traffic and parking in short supply, commuters rely heavily on trains and buses to get them to and from schools and offices. Bicycles carry people to the local station but create their own parking problems and test the patience and orderly instincts of their owners. In 1986 Japanese factories produced 7 810 000 automobiles, of which 4 573 000 were exported. In the same year Japan produced 6 583 000 bicycles, of which only 682 000 were exported.

Left The Japanese have always harvested the sea. Today, small vessels like these at Jōdogahama in Iwate Prefecture fish inshore waters while modern Japanese fishing fleets scour the oceans of the world to supply the Japanese market.

Below left Volcanic Japan is blessed with abundant thermal springs. There are hundreds of natural hot-spring resorts in the mountains and around the coasts. Some famous spas such as Atami, Arima and Beppu are large commercialized entertainment centers. Others, like the one shown here deep in the Nikkō National Park, are simple, open-air hot springs. For centuries Japanese have used these hot springs for relaxation and medicinal purposes.

Below The bustling modern port city of Kobe developed out of the small premodern port of Hyōgo. Hyōgo was among the ports opened under Western pressure in the 1860s. Since that time it has been among the most international cities in Japan. Backed by steep mountains, the modern port could only be extended by reclamation from the sea.

Left Reduced to rubble by firebombing in early 1945, Tokyo has since been rebuilt several times. Central Tokyo is now a metropolis of concrete and glass, elevated highways and underground shopping arcades. Once a staging point on the Kōshū Kaidō route from Edo to Suwa, Shinjuku is now one of the busiest rail terminals and business centers in Tokyo. Skyscrapers of 48 stories tower over fashionable shops and department stores and one of the liveliest entertainment districts in Tokyo. Shinjuku is now experiencing a further surge of development and land prices with the building of the new Tokyo Metropolitan Government building, the tallest in the city.

from the late 16th century as the castle town of the wealthy Maeda family. Spared bombing in World War II, it is a center of crafts, especially Kutani pottery and painted silks, known as Kaga Yuzen. With its old samurai residences, the city offers a reminder of Japan's feudal past.

The cities of Osaka, Kyoto, Kobe and Nara form the core of the Kansai region, "west of the barrier." Speech patterns, foods and customs differ from those of the Kantō centering on Tokyo. Kyoto combines a courtly past—it was the capital of Japan from 794 to 1868—with a thriving present as a university city, center of craft production and hub of new high-technology industry. Kyoto today is a bustling city of 1·5 million people. It is a city of quiet temples and palaces, crowded business streets, handmade crafts and, increasingly, research centers and high-technology development in ceramics and other materials.

Within the Kansai, the prefectures of Shiga, Mie, Kyoto, Nara, Osaka, Wakayama and Hyōgo make up the Kinki district. The industrial center of the region is the Hanshin industrial belt running through Osaka and Kobe cities. Osaka is built on a delta formed by the Yamato and Yodo rivers. Once named the "city of 808 bridges" or the "Venice of Japan," it has lost most of its old canal network to urban development. Osaka was a center of trade from the 17th century, the principal rice market and "kitchen" of Japan, and a city of vibrant urban culture. In the modern period with a population of 2·6 million it has become a commercial port and industrial city second only to Tokyo. In industrial production Osaka Prefecture ranks after

Tokyo, and Hyōgo Prefecture is sixth. Kobe is the most important international port in western Japan. It handles over 10 000 vessels annually. Known as a natural deep-water harbor since the 3rd century, it has played a major role in foreign trade throughout Japanese history. One of several ports opened to foreign vessels in the mid-19th century, it still has many Western-style buildings, giving the city a strong cosmopolitan flavor. Coastal areas around Osaka have been extensively reclaimed. The planned new Osaka international airport will be built entirely on reclaimed land in Osaka Bay. The Kansai area is home to many of Japan's largest corporations, including such industries as electronics, computers, synthetics, chemicals, metals and robotics. Farms in the region are small, intensively cultivated and mostly double cropped. They produce fruit, vegetables and livestock, including Kobe beef, for the Kansai market.

The western part of Honshu is known as the Chūgoku, or central provinces, region. It comprises the five prefectures of Tottori, Shimane, Okayama, Hiroshima and Yamaguchi. The region is divided by the Chūgoku mountain range into two distinct parts: San'in, "in the shade of the mountains," to the north, facing the Sea of Japan, and Sanyō, "the sunny side of the mountains," fronting the Inland Sea. The whole Inland Sea region, including Sanyō, has undergone rapid development. Hiroshima, for instance, devastated by the atomic bomb in 1945, is now an industrial city of more than 900 000 people. San'in, by contrast, is less industrially developed and relies more heavily on lumber, livestock and fishing.

Shikoku

Kyushu

The island of Shikoku takes its name from the "four provinces" of Sanuki (modern Kagawa Prefecture), Awa (Tokushima), Tosa (Kōchi) and Iyo (Ehime). A mountainous island, except for plains around the Inland Sea and Pacific coasts, Shikoku supports a population of 4 million people and is about the size of Sardinia. The northern part of the island around Tokushima and in Ehime and Kagawa Prefectures is part of the Seto Inland Sea industrial belt. The southern part of the island concentrates on citrus production, lumber and fishing. The growing season is very long, 260 days. Shikoku is the location of an ancient pilgrimage, in honor of Kūkai, still carried on today.

Much of the Seto Inland Sea is designated a national park. It has areas of striking beauty with white-sand beaches, pine-clad islands, steep cliffs and shrines like Itsukushima that seem to float on the waves. But it is also a busy fishing area, shipping channel and a major industrial center. Eleven prefectures border the Inland Sea and annually produce millions of metric tons of steel, chemicals, petrochemicals, pulp, paper and oil. The industrial activity and massive reclamation projects have ravaged the coastline in places and brought pollution to the waters and problems for the fishing grounds.

Kyushu, meaning "nine provinces" from its ancient administrative structure, is a mountainous island a little larger than Taiwan, divided into an increasingly wealthy, urbanized, industrialized north and a poorer, still mainly agricultural south. Although the warm climate and long growing season make double cropping easy, arable land is quite scarce. Kyushu is connected to Honshu by the Kammon Bridge (1500 meters) over the fast-flowing Kammon Straits and by three tunnels, including one for the Shinkansen.

Throughout the modern period northern Kyushu has been an industrial center, first for silk and cotton production and then, from around 1900, for steel production at the Yawata Iron and Steel Works (now the Yawata Works, Japan Steel Corporation), using coal from Kyushu mines and ore imported from China. In 1963 the five cities of Moji, Kokura, Yahata, Tobata and Wakamatsu merged to form the city of Kitakyushu (North Kyushu). Kitakyushu and Fukuoka each have populations of over a million.

To the southeast of Fukuoka is the sulfurous barren landscape of the Aso National Park, at the center of which is the active volcano, Mount Aso, with its huge caldera. Nakadake, the active crater, is 600 by 1200 meters across and 160 meters deep.

Below Japan's economy depends on the import of raw materials and the export of manufactured goods. With suitable land in short supply, many of Japan's industrial complexes have been built on land reclaimed from the sea. This large industrial complex at Mizushima near Kurashiki, built on reclaimed land on both sides of the Takahashi River, includes oil refineries, petrochemical plants, steelworks and other heavy industry. Industrial development and the consequent pollution have had a severe impact on the fishing industry in this part of the Inland Sea.

Left and below Mount Aso, an active volcano with the largest caldera in the world, lies at the center of the Aso National Park in Kumamoto Prefecture, Kyushu. Mount Aso is the general name for five volcanic peaks, of which Nakadake (altitude 1323 meters) is the most active, constantly sending up plumes of black smoke and spewing volcanic ash. The sulfurous landscape has a desolate, somber beauty. To the north and south of the five peaks lie two extensive plains making up the old crater of the volcano. They contain several towns and villages with a total population of 56 000 people and cover an area of 400 square kilometers. Like other national parks Mount Aso attracts crowds of visitors, many of whom take advantage of Sundays and holidays to drive to the summit and look down into the broiling crater of Nakadake.

Smoke and gas pour menacingly from crevices in its sides.

Nagasaki lies at the head of the deeply indented and beautiful Nagasaki Bay which opens outward to the continent and the south. Nagasaki was a port for Iberian, English, Dutch, Korean and Chinese trade from the 16th century. After other Western countries were expelled from Japan in the early 17th century, the Dutch were permitted to maintain a trading post on the small fan-shaped island of Dejima in Nagasaki harbor throughout the so-called period of seclusion. In modern times Nagasaki has maintained its commercial character. Through the Meiji and Taishō periods the city traded widely with China and Southeast Asia. With its fine natural harbor the city was also a center of shipbuilding. On 9 August 1945 it was destroyed by the second atomic bomb. More than 73 000 people were killed and many more have since died from radiation sickness. Rebuilt, Nagasaki is again a busy commercial and industrial city. The Mitsubishi Corporation has shipbuilding, steelmaking and machine industries there. Although shipping and steel have been depressed in recent years, the Mitsubishi works are still big local employers. Nagasaki has also sought to develop trade with Taiwan and the Chinese mainland.

Kagoshima, with a population of about 514 000, is the most important city in southern Kyushu. It has a magnificent location, looking across the bay at the active volcano Sakurajima. For centuries the area was ruled by the Shimazu family of Satsuma domain. Young Kagoshima samurai played a major role in the Meiji restoration. The area is famous for rice spirits (*shōchū*) and ceramics. Sakurajima is part of Kirishima-Yaku National Park which contains more than 20 volcanic craters and includes Yaku Island with its virgin cedar forests and Mount Miyanoura which rises to more than 1930 meters.

Below The Japanese archipelago curves from the semitropical Okinawa (seen here) and the Ryukyu Islands in the south to the Siberian climate of Hokkaido and the Kuril Islands in the north. From ancient times the Ryukyu Islands, under the influence of China, served as cultural stepping stones between Japan and the continent. Left largely to themselves, the Ryukyuan people developed their own distinctive culture. Wrested from China in the early 17th century, the Ryukyus were controlled by Satsuma domain and exploited as a source of sugar.

Okinawa

Okinawa

The island of Okinawa, largest in the Ryukyuan chain, is 140 kilometers long and between 3 and 19 wide. Its subtropical climate differs from that of the larger islands in having no frost and a year-round growing season. There is little industry and few mineral resources. Livestock, fish, sugar, pineapples and tobacco provide some income but the production of rice, sweet potatoes and silk is declining or stagnant. Some crafts have been revived, especially the vividly patterned fabric known as *bingata* and ceramics. But the economy of Okinawa relies heavily on the service industries and tourism.

The Okinawa Islands, located between Japan and China, have traditionally maintained relations with both their powerful neighbors. From 1609 the Shimazu family of Satsuma controlled Okinawa and exploited it for sugar, which they sold into the Osaka market at a good profit. After 1868 the new Meiji government took over the Ryukyu kingdom. Chinese claims to the Ryukyus were ended with the Sino-Japanese war (1894–95). Japan controlled Okinawa until the end of World War II after which it was governed by the United States until its reversion to Japan in 1972. The cliffs and caves of Okinawa saw some of the most bitter fighting between the Allies and Japanese troops between April and June 1945. Thousands of Okinawan non-combatants were killed and most of the older buildings on the island were demolished.

Modern communications and the Bullet Train
Modern air, road and rail communications have linked the islands of the archipelago much more closely in recent decades. New highways, bridges and tunnels, reliable rail services, the Shinkansen and frequent air services have all played their role in breaking down regional differences and restructuring the archipelago. The Shinkansen has had a perceptible effect. First linking Kyoto, Osaka, Hiroshima and Fukuoka with Tokyo, the Bullet Train was then extended to Niigata and Morioka. Future extensions will take it to Aomori at the tip of Honshu and along the coast of Hokuriku. Wherever the Shinkansen has gone, it has spurred new commercial and residential development and extended the metropolitan corridor dominated by Tokyo and Osaka. The newly opened Seikan Tunnel between Aomori and Hakodate links Hokkaido directly to Honshu and will contribute to further rapid development of Hokkaido. A new bridge, the Seto Ōhashi, opened in April 1988, links Shikoku with Honshu. The traveler who looks now for a more leisurely, less streamlined Japan has to move beyond that corridor. There is still a more "local" feel to cities like Kanazawa, Kumamoto, Nagasaki and Kagoshima which have so far not been tied in to the metropolitan corridor of high-speed rail transport. They too will be incorporated into the Shinkansen network in time. Meanwhile the Japanese are actively developing the next generation of high-speed rail transport for the 21st century—a linear motor-driven train.

THE ARCHAEOLOGICAL ORIGINS OF JAPANESE CULTURE AND SOCIETY

Who were the ancestors of the Japanese? What were their origins, and when did they begin to inhabit the fiery arc of volcanic islands that we call Japan? Written records, whether Japanese or Chinese, are not very helpful. The earliest Japanese chronicles, the *Kojiki* (Records of Ancient Matters) and *Nihon shoki* (Chronicles of Japan), date from the early 8th century AD. In its later sections the *Nihon shoki* becomes a more detailed chronicle, useful to historians. The *Kojiki* and the early sections of the *Nihon shoki,* however, present only the mythological origins of the country and its ruling dynasty in an age of the gods on the plain of high heaven. Japan, under the name "Land of the people of Wa," appears in Chinese chronicles from the 1st century AD, but the early Chinese accounts, though fascinating to read, were based on hearsay rather than first-hand observation or direct contact.

To probe the origins of Japanese culture we have to rely on the findings of archaeologists. Fortunately, the study of archaeology has blossomed in Japan since World War II and with it our understanding of the earliest phases of Japanese society. The scientific study of Japanese archaeology began in the late 19th century under the influence of the American E. S. Morse (1838–1925) who, while Professor of Zoology at Tokyo University, excavated the Ōmori shell mound near Tokyo and published the first scientific monograph on the subject, *The Shell Mounds of Ōmori,* in 1879. By the early 20th century Japanese archaeologists were excavating ancient sites stratigraphically and classifying the early culture known as Jōmon, which Yamanouchi Sugao (1902–70) dated to 3000 BC.

These promising prewar developments were hampered by a changing political climate as Japan became embroiled in imperialism and militarism. In the oppressive thought-controlled atmosphere of the 1930s and early 1940s the national myth tracing the Japanese emperor and state back to a legendary ancestor, Jimmu, descendant of the Sun Goddess, who was believed to have come to the throne in 660 BC, nullified active critical speculation about the origins of Japanese society. Archaeologists could dig, but they risked imprisonment if they broadcast theories that would in any way qualify the national myth.

Archaeologists, like historians, have been liberated in the postwar period as intellectual taboos have been lifted. They have also benefited from Japan's economic and industrial recovery and from its rapidly burgeoning technological expertise. Since the war more than 15 000 sites have been excavated by means of the latest techniques of meticulous stratification, radiocarbon dating and laboratory analysis of botanical and zoological remains. The economic boom has brought spectacular finds to light. At the same time much has also been covered in newly laid concrete. In many cases researchers have been forced to carry out rapid salvage archaeology, keeping just ahead of the blades of bulldozers for new factories, housing developments, subways, airports and highways. Archaeological enthusiasm has been encouraged by the tremendous fascination the Japanese of all ages show in the origins of their society and culture. Every bookstore in Japan seems to have a section devoted to archaeology and minor finds, and important discoveries like the Takamatsuzuka painted tomb, opened in 1972, are reported in the pages of the daily newpapers and the evening television news broadcasts.

These archaeological excavations have pushed the boundaries of Japanese prehistory steadily backward. Whereas a few decades ago the origins of human activity in Japan would have been set at the Jōmon ceramic period (10 000 BC–300 BC), it is now clear that a rich Paleolithic culture existed prior to Jōmon and that the islands of the Japanese archipelago have been inhabited for perhaps as long as 50 000 years.

Japan's prehistory is normally discussed in four phases. Each phase has its own distinct characteristics, yet there are strong continuities running through them. We can detect cumulative, if not always steady, cultural development. Over many thousands of years there was a gradual movement from Stone Age culture through a pottery-making and hunting-and-gathering phase to a metal-using agricultural society, and then to one characterized by huge burial mounds whose local chieftains had the power to draft tens of thousands of laborers to build enormous mounded tombs. The transitions from one phase to the next may have involved the influx of peoples from the continent and occasional local conquest. They seem, however, to have been characterized less by conquest from outside than by the accretion of new techniques overlaying older cultural patterns. Most of these techniques

Above The American zoologist E.S. Morse, who served as the first Professor of Zoology in the new Tokyo University from 1877 to 1879, made important contributions to the study of Japanese culture as well as the study of Western science in Japan. Morse led the first scientific excavation at the Ōmori shell mounds, opening a window on Japan's Jōmon culture.

Right: Paleolithic Japan
Since the first excavation of the Iwajuku site in 1946 the existence of Paleolithic cultures in Japan has been confirmed and their antiquity has been steadily pushed backward in time by radiocarbon dating and other modern techniques to at least 30000 years ago. Stone tools recently excavated from the Zasaragi site may date from 50000 years ago. More than 2000 Paleolithic sites have now been identified throughout Japan. They have yielded stone choppers, knives, scrapers and fine flake and blade tools. Later Paleolithic sites (13500–10000 years ago) have yielded many fine microliths made of obsidian.

Inset: the continental land bridges
Geological evidence, surviving plants of continental origin and animal fossil remains all indicate that during the ice ages of the later Pleistocene epoch Japan was linked to the Asian land mass. Paleolithic hunters following mammoths, Naumann elephants, great deer and smaller animals crossed what is now the Korea (Tsushima) Strait from Korea to Japan or the La Pérouse (Sōya) Strait from Siberia to Hokkaido. Deeper straits in the northern Ryukyu Islands and between Hokkaido and Honshu were usable as land bridges for shorter periods. Japan's geographical isolation began some 20000 years ago as the great glaciers melted and sea levels rose, creating the major straits now separating the islands from each other and the whole archipelago from the continent.

Paleolithic Period	
Early	c.50 000-30 000 years ago
Late	c.30 000-12 000 years ago
Jōmon Period	
Incipient	11 000 BC-7500 BC
Earliest	7500 BC-5500 BC
Early	5500 BC-3500 BC
Middle	3500 BC-2500 BC
Late	2500 BC-1500 BC
Latest	1500 BC-300 BC
Yayoi Period	
Early	300 BC-100 BC
Middle	100 BC-100 AD
Late	100 AD-300 AD
Kofun Period	
Early	300 AD-400 AD
Middle	400 AD-500 AD
Late	500 AD-650 AD

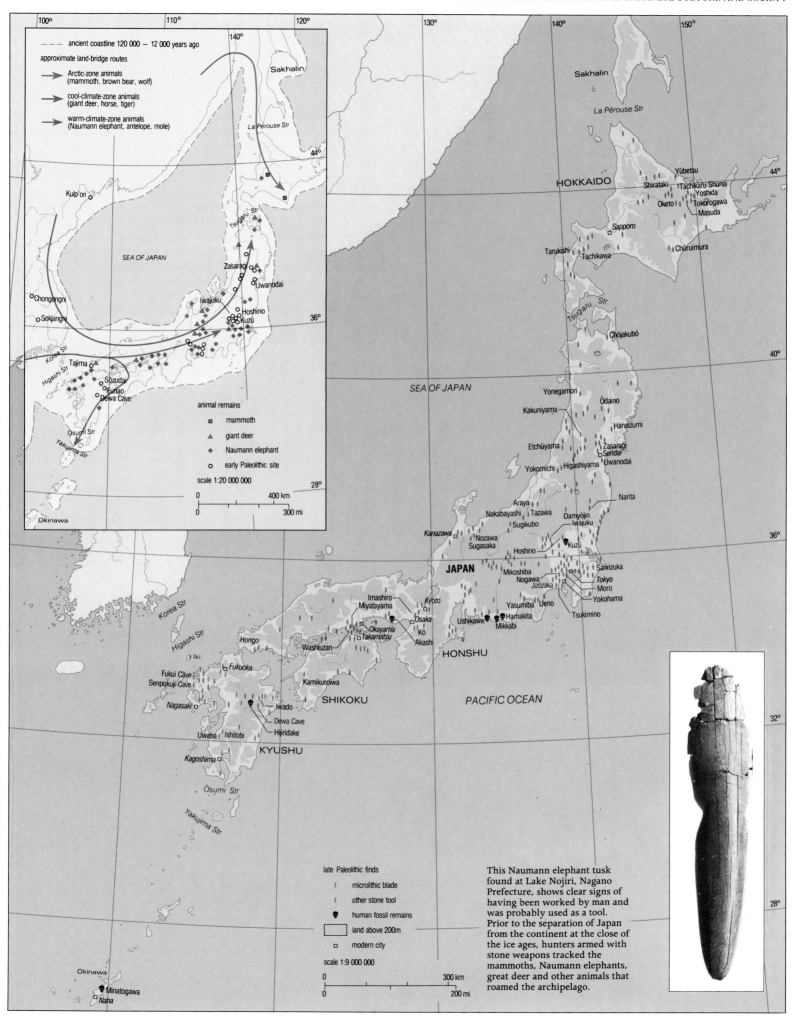

ancient coastline 120 000 – 12 000 years ago

approximate land-bridge routes

→ Arctic-zone animals
(mammoth, brown bear, wolf)

→ cool-climate-zone animals
(giant deer, horse, tiger)

→ warm-climate-zone animals
(Naumann elephant, antelope, mole)

animal remains

▫ mammoth

▲ giant deer

◆ Naumann elephant

○ early Paleolithic site

scale 1:20 000 000

0 ____ 400 km

0 ____ 300 mi

Sakhalin

La Pérouse Str

Kulp'ori

SEA OF JAPAN

Tsugaru Str

Zasaragi
Uwanodai

Chongonghi

Iwajuku
Hoshino
Kuzū

Sokjanghi

Korea Str
Tajima
Higashi Str
Sōzudai
Funao
Dewa Cave

Osumi Str

Yakujima Str

Okinawa

Sakhalin

La Pérouse Str

HOKKAIDO

Yūbetsu
Shirataki   Tachikaru Shunai
Yoshida
Oketo   Tokorogawa
Masuda

Sapporo

Chūruimura

Tarukishi
Tachikawa

Tsugaru Str

Chōjakubō

SEA OF JAPAN

Yonegamori

Kakuniyama   Ōdaino

Hanaizumi

Etchūyama   Zasaragi
Seridai
Yokomichi   Higashiyama   Uwanodai

Araya   Narita
Nakabayashi   Tazawa
Sugikubo   Damyōjin
Kanazawa   Iwajuku
Nozawa   Hoshino   Kuzū
Sugasaka

JAPAN
Sanrizuka
Mikoshiba   Tokyo
Imashiro   Nogawa   Moro
Miyatayama   Kyōto   Jizōzaka   Yokohama
Osaka   Yasumiba   Ueno   Tsukimino
Okayama   Kō   Ushikawa   Hamakita
Takamatsu   Akashi   Mikkabi

Imashiro
Miyatayama

HONSHU

Hongo

Washiuzan   PACIFIC OCEAN

Iki

Kamikuroiwa

SHIKOKU

Fukuoka

Fukui Cave
Senpukuji Cave

Nagasaki

Iwado
Dewa Cave
Hijiridake
Uwaba   Ishitobi

KYUSHU

Kagoshima

Ōsumi Str

Yakujima Str

late Paleolithic finds

┃ microlithic blade

┃ other stone tool

☠ human fossil remains

▢ land above 200m

▫ modern city

scale 1:9 000 000

0 ____ 300 km

0 ____ 200 mi

Okinawa

Minatogawa
Naha

This Naumann elephant tusk
found at Lake Nojiri, Nagano
Prefecture, shows clear signs of
having been worked by man and
was probably used as a tool.
Prior to the separation of Japan
from the continent at the close of
the ice ages, hunters armed with
stone weapons tracked the
mammoths, Naumann elephants,
great deer and other animals that
roamed the archipelago.

were continental in origin, but much of their diffusion and development seems to have gone on in Japan. Thus stone tools and Jōmon-influenced ceramic modes persisted long after the introduction of metal and agricultural technologies.

The earliest phase of Japanese prehistory was Paleolithic—a hunting-and-gathering culture that had mastery of stone tools and weapons but did not know ceramic techniques. It was followed from about 10 000 BC by a ceramic Mesolithic phase known as Jōmon, or "cord-marked," after its very distinctive pottery. Around 300 BC Jōmon culture was being overlaid by the Yayoi culture of people who worked metals, wove cloth and engaged in agriculture. From around 300 AD the physical and cultural landscape was transformed by the appearance of great tombs centering on the Yamato region at the eastern end of the Inland Sea. This tomb phase saw the emergence of Japan's first clearly defined political entity, the Yamato dynasty.

Because of the different names of these phases, it is easy to think that there were cultural breaks between them, perhaps invasions, and that each successive phase was carried on by very different people. Some historians and archaeologists have suggested the possibility of invasions, either in the Yayoi period or in the tomb period, and it is true that there were changes in physique produced by diet and life-style. But it seems that these phases were basically internally driven, with some groups in the society learning and benefiting from new technologies introduced by small groups of immigrants arriving from the Korean peninsula or China or from northern Asia via the Kuriles.

The first tool makers: Paleolithic culture

From radiocarbon-dated finds at sites like Iwajuku we know that people who made and used stone tools and weapons inhabited the islands at least 30 000 years ago, and perhaps very much earlier. During the ice ages of the Pleistocene epoch, when the seas receded, Japan was periodically linked by land to continental Asia. Hokkaido was joined to Siberia by what is now the Sōya Strait. Western Japan was linked to the Korean peninsula via the Tsushima Strait. There were also land connections between Hokkaido and Honshu and between the northern Ryukyus and Kyushu. Small bands of hunters using stone-tipped weapons would have followed herds of wild animals including mammoths, Naumann elephants and great deer over these land routes. The late Pleistocene was also a period of considerable volcanic activity. Layers of volcanic ash built up the Kantō loam of eastern Japan, in the topmost layers of which most of the Paleolithic finds have been made.

Japan's acidic volcanic soils have not preserved many human fossil remains. The only sites for which human fossil remains from this period have been claimed are those at Akashi, Ushikawa, Mikkabi, Hamakita and Kuzū. But hundreds of Paleolithic sites have provided a rich store of animal fossils and flake and pebble-stone choppers, blades, handaxes, scrapers and points. From around 13 000 years ago there is evidence of the existence of extensive microlith production, very fine flake tools, made from the plentiful supplies of obsidian.

The Jōmon potters

From about 10 000 BC there was a worldwide warming trend which peaked around 3000 BC. Sea levels rose while volcanic activity lessened. Honshu and Hokkaido were again separated, and Japan was once more divided from the Asian continent and set in greater geographical isolation. Some of the large animal species died out when their links to the continent were severed, but there was a compensating enrichment in plant and animal life brought by a warmer climate.

At about this time the inhabitants of the islands mastered the technique of coiling and firing pottery. It is possible that the technique was imported, but few clear continental models have yet been found. The closest may be cord-marked vessels found in the Amur River in eastern Siberia and in Korean sites. These finds, however, postdate the earliest Jōmon pottery. The technique of firing clay shaped into vessels meant enhancement of life through the cooking of food, better storage and greater freedom of movement away from immediate sources of water. Pots, shaped by coiling clay, were fired in open pits at fairly low temperatures, perhaps 500–600 degrees centigrade.

The Jōmon period, about 10 000 BC–300 BC, takes its name from this very distinctive earthenware pottery produced throughout the period. Jō-mon means "cord-marked," and many of the pieces were patterned by impressing cords or branches into the soft clay or by marking with bamboo. Thousands of sites have been found, and tens of thousands of pots and shards carefully classified. Imposing some order on the almost bewildering variety of Jōmon pottery, archaeologists usually classify it by age, with certain regional types being predominant in different phases. Incipient (Subearliest) and Earliest Jōmon pots, from 11 000 to 5000 BC, look unstable, typically having rounded or pointed bottoms, perhaps because they were mainly used for cooking outdoors and could be stood among the stones of a hearth or steadied in soft ash or sand. Pottery from the Fukui Cave in Nagasaki Prefecture, the Kamikuroiwa site in Ehime Prefecture and several other sites has been dated to 10 750 (± 500) by radiocarbon dating. This makes Incipient Jōmon the earliest clearly dated pottery so far found anywhere in the world. By the Early Jōmon, 5500–3500 BC, flat bottoms had become customary, perhaps indicating that pots were now being used more indoors where they had to be set on baked earthen floors. Northeastern Honshu and southern Hokkaido produced fine cord-marked cylindrical vessels, while a herringbone decoration was common in Kyushu. Middle Jōmon pottery is particularly striking with luxuriant forms and powerful surface decoration. The rims of Umataka pots from Niigata, for instance, clearly suggest leaping flames, while some pottery from Nagano Prefecture shows a snake's head design. The fanciful decoration of these pots suggests ritual as well as purely functional purposes. Late Jōmon, 2500–1500 BC, saw the production of thinner-walled, functional vessels of many different kinds in many areas. There is greater variety of function and aesthetic effect. The Kamegaoka style in northeastern Japan, for instance, included smallish pots, with polished surfaces and zoned markings.

The Jōmon hunting-and-gathering culture (c. 11000 BC–300 BC) takes its name from its rich and distinctive "cord-marked" (jōmon) pottery. Initial Jōmon pots (far right) from sites such as Natsushima in Tokyo Bay were simple in shape and surface design, and generally pointed at the foot. By Middle Jōmon (below right) the shapes and surface designs, created with cords, vines or bamboo, were complex and powerful. Some of the most vigorous forms, like the pot shown here, show leaping flames, twining shapes or human faces. Flattened bases suggest that these pots were made to be set on flat interior floors. Late Jōmon pottery became more subdued and functionally diverse.

Middle and Late Jōmon sites also yield many ritual earthenware figurines of animals or human figures known as dogū (right). First crafted as two-dimensional images, they grew in volume by Late Jōmon. Most of the figures are female, some with distinctive snow-goggle faces. Since many seem to have been deliberately broken, they are thought to have been used as sympathetic talismans to draw away the pain of childbirth or sickness.

Middle Jōmon culture
Evidence for the life-style of the Stone Age hunting-and-gathering Jōmon culture (c. 11000–300 BC) has been unearthed from thousands of sites scattered throughout Japan. The map shows some of the major Middle Jōmon (c. 3500–2500 BC) sites. Shell mounds, like that at Ōmori between Tokyo and Yokohama, in which the Jōmon people left not only seashells and bones but also stone tools, ornaments, pottery and ritual figurines (dogū), have been very revealing. Jōmon has been intricately classified on the basis of regional variations and pottery styles. Some sites have provided evidence of semipermanent Jōmon villages, consisting of clusters of part-submerged house sites with interior fireplaces. A few sites, such as the stone circles of Ōyu, provide evidence of Jōmon ritual practices. During the warm Middle Jōmon there seems to have been a tendency for Jōmon people to move away from the coast and make greater use of upland sites in central Japan.

The Kantō Plain (inset), around modern Tokyo, is dotted with Jōmon sites. The analysis of such sites as Ōmori, Ubayama and Kasori helped to establish the contours of Jōmon society and pottery types. Two styles of pottery found plentifully in the Kantō region and the central mountains in the Middle Jōmon period were vigorous, full-bodied designs named for finds from the Katsusaka and Otamadai sites.

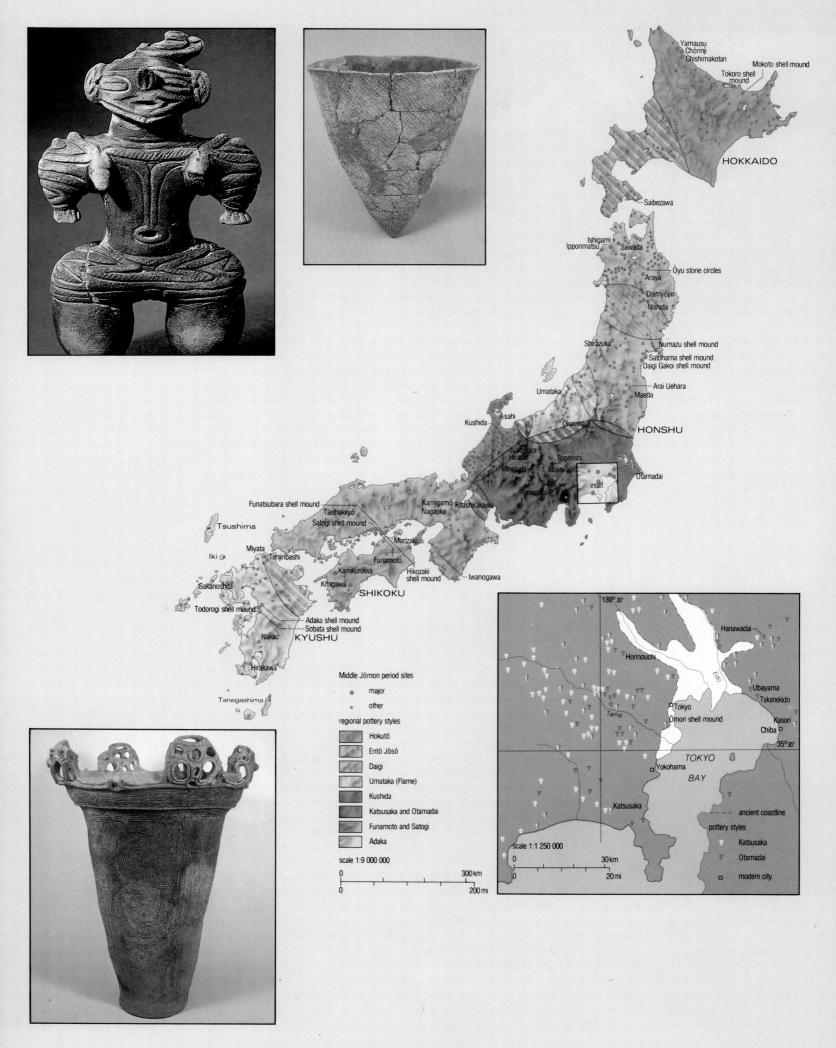

Middle Jōmon period sites
● major
· other

regional pottery styles

Hokutô
Entô Jōsō
Daigi
Umataka (Flame)
Kushida
Katsusaka and Otamadai
Funamoto and Satogi
Adaka

scale 1:9 000 000

0 ——— 300 km
0 ——— 200 mi

HOKKAIDO

Yamausu
Chôrinji
Chishimakotan
Mokoto shell mound
Tokoro shell mound

Saibezawa

Ishigami
Ipponmatsu   Sawada
Ôyu stone circles
Araya
Daimyôjin
Nishida
Shirazuka
Numazu shell mound
Satohama shell mound
Daigi Gakoi shell mound
Arai Uehara
Maeda

Umataka
Kushida   Asahi
Okinahara   **HONSHU**
Nakahara
Hiraide   Toganishi
Minehata   Idojin
Sakai   inset   Otamadai
Yanagida

Funatsubara shell mound
Taishakkyô
Satogi shell mound
Kamigamô Kitashirakawa
Nagaoka
Morizaki
Tsushima
Miyata   Funamoto
Iki   Kamikuroiwa   Hikozaki shell mound
Tenjinbashi   Iwanogawa
Sakanoshita   Kitagawa
Todorogi shell mound   **SHIKOKU**
Adaka shell mound
Sobata shell mound
Nakao   **KYUSHU**
Hirakawa

Tanegashima

Inset map:

139°30′
Hanawadai
Horinouchi
Ubayama
Takanekido
Tokyo
Kasori
Ômori shell mound   Chiba
35°30′
Tama   *Edo*
TOKYO BAY
Yokohama
Katsusaka

ancient coastline

pottery styles
⚲ Katsusaka
⚲ Otamadai
□ modern city

scale 1:1 250 000
0 ——— 30 km
0 ——— 20 mi

Much of what we know about Jōmon society, including its pottery, comes from the excavation of its garbage sites, the shell mounds or middens, and storage pits found near Jōmon settlements which preserved many remains of the diet, daily life and burial practices. The Jōmon people were hunters and gatherers who lived on nuts, fruit, roots, animal flesh, fish and shellfish. The warming trend between about 8000 and 3000 BC, encouraged breeding by shellfish along the coasts and river estuaries. These were a rich resource for Early Jōmon people who made their settlements nearby and left behind great piles of shells and other refuse. From these piles have come deer, boar and bear bones, the bones and shells of dozens of kinds of fish and shellfish, stone and wooden tools, bows and arrowheads, fishhooks, sinkers, harpoon heads, oars, bone needles, ornaments and net fragments.

In the warm climate of the Middle Jōmon period deciduous trees flourished and many large Jōmon sites were built in upland areas in central Japan, modern Nagano Prefecture. Animals were hunted, acorns, chestnuts, walnuts and other nuts, yams and wild grapes were gathered. Around 2500 BC, with deteriorating climate, colder winters and heavier rainfall, upland settlements faced harsher conditions and Jōmon people drifted back to the coasts, accounting for the many large coastal shell mounds like those of Ōmori, Kasori or Ubayama that are characteristic of Late Jōmon.

Many Jōmon settlements were at least semi-permanent, consisting of a small cluster of thatch-roofed semisunken house sites, each house containing five or six people. Interior central fireplaces were lined with stone slabs, and surrounded by five or six postholes. In some Late Jōmon communities there were house pits considerably larger than their fellows. These may have been ritual sites or perhaps the homes of village chiefs. Most communities probably tried to be self-sufficient, but there is some indication of local or regional exchange, with salt from the coastal regions finding its way to mountain settlements and obsidian and stone for tools moving from mountain sources to coastal regions. There has been considerable debate as to whether Late Jōmon people engaged in agriculture. Some scholars have pointed to the cultivation of a kind of millet (*hie*) or the herb *Perilla*. Most would suggest that, while the Jōmon people knew where to find particular plants, how to leach tannins from plants and how to store food and preserve it in salt, they had not mastered the systematic cultivation of crops.

From Jōmon pottery and other objects we can get some insight into the artistic and ritual imaginations of these people. The vigorous pottery had not yet become standardized and each piece was a work of creative art in itself. Some large jars were used for infant burial in Middle and Late Jōmon. Jars were also used for the burial of religious offerings. Stone phalli have been found in house sites and on hillsides. Among the most striking artifacts from the Jōmon period are carved stones and clay figurines known as *dogū*. Found from Kyushu to Aomori in the north, they became increasingly elaborate in the northeastern part of the country in Middle and Late Jōmon. Many of these were clearly anthropomorphic, resembling pregnant females with masklike faces and protuberant eyes.

They may have been intended to facilitate child-birth, alleviate disease or simulate burial. In many sites they are found broken in such a way as to suggest that they may have been used in rituals in which disease was transferred from the suffering human to the clay figure. In northern Japan a number of stone-circle sites have been identified. At Ōyu in Akita two circles have been unearthed, one surrounding a single standing stone that may have had phallic significance. At Kinsei in Yamagata Prefecture a central stone is surrounded by a wide ring of stones 1·5 meters high. These and similar sites were too large for single village rituals and must have been used by several villages, perhaps for rituals relating to hunting or salmon fishing. Jōmon grave sites and shell mounds have yielded lacquered combs, bone hairpins, shell earrings and other ornaments. Some Jōmon shell-mound burials were flexed and by Late Jōmon several inhumations took place in the same grave site. Ritual teethpulling was practiced, especially for males at the age of puberty.

While some linguists have detected southeast Asian traces in the Japanese language, the prevailing opinion traces the roots of Japanese to Korean and other Altaic languages. It seems likely that what eventually developed as Japanese entered Japan during the Jōmon period.

Jōmon sites have been found in Hokkaido, the home of the Ainu people. The Ainu are a north Asian Caucasoid people who entered the islands at a very early period. They spread over Hokkaido and into northeastern Japan where there are still many Ainu names. Some Ainu words bear a strong resemblance to the Japanese. *Kamui* in Ainu sounds very like the Japanese word for the gods, *kami*. Some archaeologists have argued that Latest Jōmon in northeastern Japan was an Ainu culture period, but the role of Ainu culture within Late and Latest Jōmon is far from clear. In succeeding centuries the Ainu, or Ezo or Emishi, as they were known, were driven further northward by the expansive and racially different tribes in Honshu. Their culture has survived into the 20th century, but they have been under great pressure from the flood of migrants from Honshu in the past century and are now being rapidly assimilated. Although Ainu bear and salmon festivals are still performed in Hokkaido, few purebred Ainu now survive.

Yayoi: rice farmers and metal workers

In the 600 years or so between 300 BC and 300 AD the daily life of the inhabitants of the islands was greatly enriched by the introduction and diffusion of new pottery techniques, wet rice cultivation, metal technologies and weaving techniques. Although it was a pottery find at Yayoichō in Tokyo that gave its name to this cultural phase, it was probably the advent of wet rice cultivation that had the most far-reaching social implications. It set a stamp on the pattern of much of Japanese village life and culture up until the present day.

Rice was being grown in the Yangzi basin of China from at least 5000 BC. It was being grown in the Korean peninsula from about 1500 BC. It is likely that small groups from the continent carried the technology to western Japan and that it was there eventually adopted by some Jōmon groups. The earliest sites were probably natural wet lands

Below This photograph shows an Ainu village around the year 1900. Ainu dwellings were rectangular and built of poles, with walls and roofs step-thatched with miscanthus or bamboo. The eastern ends of houses normally had a single window known as a spirit window. Interiors contained a centrally located hearth, ceremonial altar and treasure platform.

The Ainu of Hokkaido

The Ainu people of Hokkaido, a vanishing culture, have attracted considerable scholarly attention, but still remain something of an enigma. They are an indigenous minority people with many non-Japanese physical characteristics. It is estimated that between 17000 and 24000 Ainu of pure or mixed blood survive in Hokkaido and a few hundred in southern Sakhalin in the USSR. Because of facial features, body hair and fullness of beard Ainu are commonly said to be of Caucasoid origin. Recent serological and skeletal studies, however, indicate closer ties with the Uralic populations of Siberia. In any case, they lived in northeastern Honshu long enough to have left Ainu place names.

Left Early Ainu life was based on a hunting-and-gathering economy. Bear, salmon and other animals had spiritual as well as economic significance and festivals were held in their honor. During special three-day bear festivals shamans called on the spirit of a sacrificed bear to carry messages to ancestral spirits.

Below Men and women wore decorated headbands and long coats made of cotton or *attush,* a textile woven from elm bark fibers, decorated with curvilinear cotton appliqué designs. Formerly women wore tattoos around their mouths.

Left Since the beginning of the Meiji period (1868) there has been a steady process of assimilation in the direction of Japanese housing, clothing, food and other aspects of life and economy, with traditional dress and religious objects now used only for ceremonial occasions. There has also been a shift from hunting, fishing and gathering of wild plants to agricultural and commercial marine fishing and, with the initiation of compulsory education, an emphasis on the use of Japanese by the younger generations.

Far Left There are now very few surviving speakers of Ainu. Although three major dialects have been isolated (Hokkaido, Sakhalin and Kuril), the relationship of Ainu to other languages has not been clearly established. Its phonemic structure has much in common with languages of northern Asia but other aspects of grammar resemble those of Southeast Asia and Oceania.

with little in the way of man-made irrigation. At first rice was a sporadic supplement to the prevailing Jōmon diet. Gradually, however, the farming of rice became more systematic as flooded fields, irrigation channels and storage facilities were prepared and new tools introduced. Rice and grains began to assume a more important role in the diet. Paddyfield rice cultivation is intensive, calling as it does for cooperative efforts to prepare fields, organize irrigation and carry through the harvest. But rice is also capable of supporting greater population levels than other foodstuffs, and the Yayoi period may have experienced some population increase.

A number of Yayoi period rice-producing sites have been carefully excavated. Early Yayoi sites were mostly in marshy lowland areas where people could take advantage of flooding and natural water tables. In succeeding centuries, as control over irrigation techniques improved, rice fields were constructed at higher elevations. One of the earliest agricultural sites is at Itazuke, Fukuoka. About 30 houses seem to have been occupied at any one time. Wooden palings were used to mark off rice fields, some of which were 400 square meters in area. Judging from implements found at the site, cultivating was done with stone reapers, wooden rakes and hoes.

Perhaps the most revealing mid-Yayoi period site is at Toro, Shizuoka. There is a museum on the site and a number of house sites and granaries have been restored. Toro gives us a good idea of a Yayoi period rice-farming village of a kind that was to become rapidly more common in succeeding centuries. The site is on low ground near the mouth of the Abe River. It comprised a village with several dwellings and storehouses to the north and rice fields running downward to the south. There is evidence of fairly elaborate irrigation and drainage systems. Wooden slats were carefully cut, probably with iron-tipped tools, to hold in place the paths between the rice paddies. The houses were oval in shape, about eight meters by six. Thatched roofs were supported by crossbeams on four heavy posts set in postholes and resting on boards to prevent them sinking. The houses had semisunken floors surrounded by earthen banks to keep out groundwater and with shallow hearths toward the center of the space. Some food was stored in jars, but by mid-Yayoi in sites like Toro quite well-designed raised wooden storehouses were in use. The storehouses were raised on piles about a meter off the ground, and the rice was protected from rodents by wooden collars set on the supporting posts. The storehouse, a vital building for the community and the individual family, was represented in scratched designs on early bronze bells and on *haniwa* (see below, p.43). The raised style later influenced shrine and palace architecture.

Aomori Prefecture was the northern limit of Yayoi period rice farming. It was not until modern cold-resistant strains of rice were developed that Hokkaido saw significant rice production. In the less hospitable environment of northern Japan fields were smaller. The Tareyanagi site, Aomori Prefecture, excavated in 1981, has yielded rice paddy remains from mid-Yayoi, with small paddies of 12–15 square meters in area.

Yayoi period rice farmers used a mixture of stone, wooden and iron tools. Stone axes and a stone reaping knife newly introduced from the continent were still basic tools. So were wooden rakes, shovels and hoes, rice paddy clogs, and pestles and mortars for pounding rice. Some iron-tipped axes, adzes and digging tools were also in use. Iron does not survive for long when buried and finds of iron-tipped tools are therefore scanty but the regularity of paddyfield palings and wooden storehouse planks indicates considerable use of iron in cutting blades.

Like the Jōmon period, Yayoi is named from its distinctive pottery. Archaeologists have distinguished five major types. In general Yayoi pottery was less organic than Jōmon. It was charac-

Above Bronze was the aristocrat's symbol of power in Yayoi society. Among the finest bronze finds from the period are bronze bells, *dōtaku*, like this one (475 mm high) from Sumiyoshi-chō, Higashi Nada, Kōbe, dating from the 2nd or 3rd century AD. Early *dōtaku* were small, poorly cast copies of Korean bells. By the 2nd century AD, however, the Japanese had mastered the technology of making sandstone molds and casting the bells. The latest of the bells are large, thin-walled and elegant. Some are decorated in relief with flowing-water designs or (as *top right*) in panels showing stick-figure scenes of animals, hunting and farming.

Below left: the spread of rice agriculture
Although rice has been a staple of the Japanese diet for centuries and has had a profound effect on the shaping of Japanese society and culture, the crop was not originally native to Japan and the technology had to be learned. The cultivation of rice in flooded fields had its origins in tropical Asia several thousand years ago. The technology spread via southeastern China and the Korean peninsula to Japan by about 300 BC. The Late Jōmon people may have known slash-and-burn agriculture, but the diffusion of rice growing is generally associated with the Yayoi period.

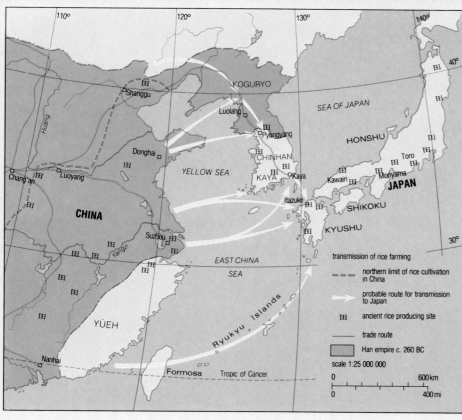

transmission of rice farming

- - - - northern limit of rice cultivation in China

⟶ probable route for transmission to Japan

⊞ ancient rice producing site

—— trade route

▨ Han empire c. 260 BC

scale 1:25 000 000

0 ———————— 600 km
0 ———————— 400 mi

Right: Yayoi society
The colors on the map suggest the stages in the diffusion of paddyfield rice growing through the Yayoi period. Although rice-field sites have been excavated in these areas, they are few in number, suggesting that the techniques were known in pockets and not widely pervasive. Red symbols indicate important sites from which bronze objects have been recovered. It is noticeable that bronze bells tend to cluster in the Kinki region, spearheads and halberds in Kyushu and Shikoku, and swords along the Inland Sea region. Also shown is the site in north Kyushu where a gold seal was found, thought to have been sent by a Chinese emperor to a local petty chieftain. The map does not attempt to show the location of the many sites from which bronze mirrors have been unearthed.

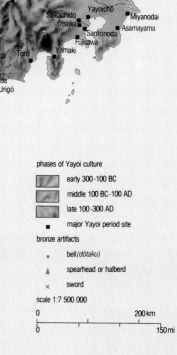

phases of Yayoi culture

▨ early 300–100 BC

▨ middle 100 BC–100 AD

▨ late 100–300 AD

■ major Yayoi period site

bronze artifacts

• bell (dōtaku)

▲ spearhead or halberd

✕ sword

scale 1:7 500 000

0 ———————— 200 km
0 ———————— 150 mi

terized by smooth lines and surfaces, burnished or sometimes painted, with geometric designs. It was probably fired in open charcoal kilns at higher temperatures than Jōmon, 800–900 degrees centigrade. The pieces are often elegant and carefully finished. Yayoi pots show some tendency toward specialization. But they are more interesting aesthetically than the following Haji ware which seems to have been made in large quantities by professional potters with little regard for aesthetic appeal. Jōmon cord-marking influence was still felt in northeastern Japan well into the Yayoi period. The pottery demonstrates functional and ritual uses. There were plenty of cooking utensils and storage jars. Certain kinds of vermilion-painted pottery were used for ritual ware and offerings in some sites. Pottery was also used in some burial rituals. Large jars, set mouth to mouth, were used for burials in some mid-Yayoi sites. More than 50 jar burials have been found at Itazuke, for instance. Such large jars could only have been made by expert and specialized potters.

Jar burials were not the only kind of interment. Dolmens, like those found in the Korean peninsula, covering jar burials or stone cists were common. So too were cemeteries with individual wooden or stone coffins, jars or chambers. In late Yayoi some chieftains and their families were buried in rectangular mounds with shaft graves in them. These have been seen by some specialists as precursors of the great mound tombs of the 4th and 5th centuries. In contrast to most Jōmon grave sites where little social distinction was evident in the burial, grave goods and evidence of consciousness of social rank become more obvious in Yayoi. Grave goods included bronze mirrors, semi-precious beads in cylinder or comma shape, bronze and stone weapons, iron, wooden bird figurines, flat wooden dolls and personal ornaments.

Mastery of metal technology acquired during these centuries added immeasurably to Japanese social and aesthetic development. Japan entered its

Toro

Below Located on lowlying land beside the Abe River, the Toro site slopes from north to south. House sites and reconstructed houses cluster to the north, while more than a dozen rice paddies, divided by slatted pathways and fed by irrigation channels and sluice gates, slope away to the south.

The city of Shizuoka contains a number of interesting sites, among them the Kunōzan Mausoleum to Tokugawa Ieyasu, the Rinzaiji Zen monastery, the Serizawa Textile Museum and the Toro archaeological site. Of the many Yayoi period sites that have now been excavated, that at Toro, with its paddy fields held in place by carefully cut wooden slats, complex irrigation trenches, sluices, reconstructed houses and granaries and nearby archaeological museum containing farming tools and pottery, gives one of the fullest impressions of agricultural and domestic life in the late Yayoi and Kofun periods.

Below Yayoi period houses are fairly uniform. Oval in shape and semisunken, a house floor measures about 8 × 6 meters. The superstructure consisted of a thatched roof with a central ventilator, supported by four heavy posts and cross beams. Posts were sunk with boards set under their bases.

Bottom Unreconstructed sites of pit dwellings are oval, with four postholes and in most cases a shallow sunken hearth toward the center. Most Yayoi period communities kept their rice in storage pots or pits. The Toro community built collective storehouses very like those seen scratched on bronze *dōtaku*.

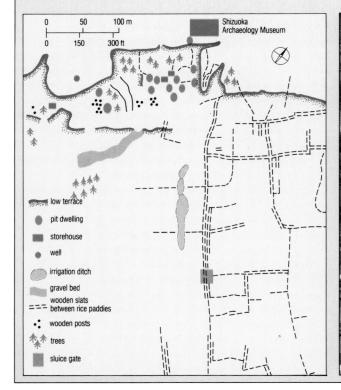

0 50 100 m
0 150 300 ft

Shizuoka Archaeology Museum

low terrace

● pit dwelling

■ storehouse

• well

⬭ irrigation ditch

▬ gravel bed

--- wooden slats between rice paddies

•.• wooden posts

🌲🌲 trees

▬ sluice gate

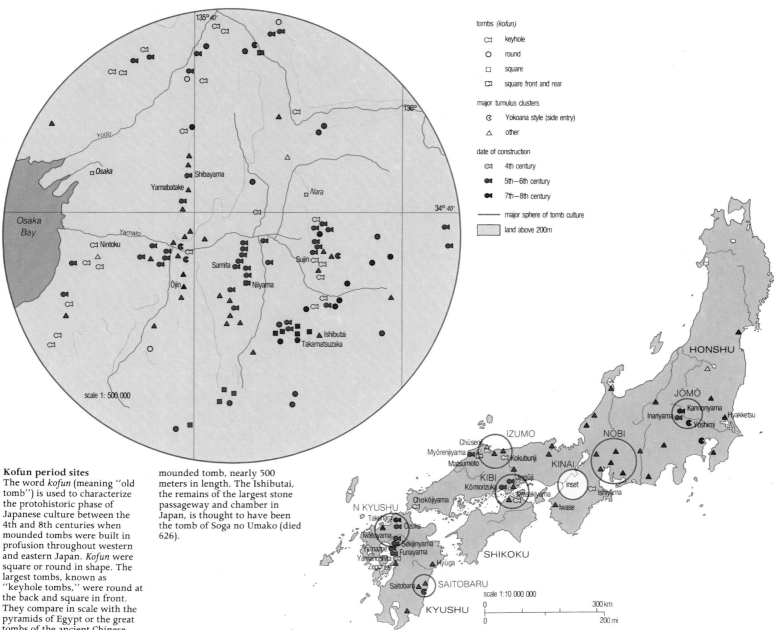

tombs (kofun)

⊏⊐ keyhole
○ round
□ square
⊏⊐ square front and rear

major tumulus clusters

Ϭ Yokoana style (side entry)
△ other

date of construction

⊏⊐ 4th century
◖⊐ 5th—6th century
◖⊐ 7th—8th century

—— major sphere of tomb culture
▨ land above 200m

scale 1: 500,000

Kofun period sites

The word *kofun* (meaning "old tomb") is used to characterize the protohistoric phase of Japanese culture between the 4th and 8th centuries when mounded tombs were built in profusion throughout western and eastern Japan. *Kofun* were square or round in shape. The largest tombs, known as "keyhole tombs," were round at the back and square in front. They compare in scale with the pyramids of Egypt or the great tombs of the ancient Chinese emperors and were clearly built for chieftains who could command the labor of many thousands of men and women.

The greatest concentration of large tombs is in the Kinai region near modern Osaka-Nara. They are associated with the Yamato rulers, ancestors of the present imperial line. The small round Takamatsuzuka tomb, excavated in 1972, was found to contain brightly colored wall and ceiling paintings. Tombs of the 5th century show clear evidence of horse-riding culture and have given rise to the controversial hypothesis of an invasion by horseriders.

Among the many great tombs in the Kinai region (*inset*) are the huge moated *kofun* said to be the burial places of the emperors Sujin, Nintoku and Ōjin. According to the ancient chronicles, Sujin was the tenth emperor. His tomb is thought to be the oldest of the keyhole-shaped imperial tombs. Nintoku, the sixteenth emperor, ruled from the early to mid-5th century AD. He is said to have started to build his tomb in the 67th year of his reign and died 20 years later. His is the largest

mounded tomb, nearly 500 meters in length. The Ishibutai, the remains of the largest stone passageway and chamber in Japan, is thought to have been the tomb of Soga no Umako (died 626).

bronze and iron ages simultaneously. Iron was the more utilitarian metal, bronze the metal of ritual and power. Both had long been in use in China and Korea. They were being worked in Japan by the 1st century AD. Bronze weapons included halberds, swords and throwing spears. When first introduced, the weapons were probably functional. The Japanese copied them and in some cases enlarged them to give them ritual uses. Bronze bells (*dōtaku*) were also copied from continental, probably Korean, models. They grew in size and artistic quality as the Japanese improved the techniques of casting. Later bells have panel decorations and thin walls, too thin to be really functional as bells, and it has been conjectured that they may have been ritual symbols of power, used as dispensations of political authority. This possibility is strengthened by the fact that they were often buried in clusters on hillsides some way from village sites and that several widely scattered bells were obviously made from a single mold.

It is in the Yayoi period that we can begin to discern village organization and local political power taking recognizable form. Control over agriculture and metals, added to control over irrigation and rice production, gave some chieftains the chance to extend their power over their neighbors. Caches of mirrors, metal swords and spears, and bronze bells from different parts of Japan suggest locally centralized petty political entities. These differences in wealth and status were also reflected in Yayoi period grave sites, which typically yield many more objects than Jōmon sites. By late Yayoi, chiefs and their families were sometimes being buried in special ritual areas, mounds demarcated from ordinary cemeteries. Ritual objects also included deer bones that had obviously been heated and cracked for divination. We do not know what auguries were sought or given, but it is not unlikely that some appeals concerned the expediency of making war or peace, as well as those concerning sickness and childbirth.

The age of the great tombs

Many of the features discernible in the Yayoi period—such as irrigated rice fields and sedentary agricultural life, the increasing use of iron and bronze, weaving, specialization in the production of metals, pottery and salt, tomb burials of chieftains with numerous grave goods, social differentiation and the consolidation of warring petty states—continued to develop and intensify in succeeding centuries. Rice paddies were constructed at higher elevations, irrigation systems became more elaborate, pottery became more commonplace, and iron tools and weapons were used more extensively.

One of these phenomena, the building of tombs or tumuli known in Japanese as *kofun,* has seemed so striking to archaeologists and historians that it has given its name to the age. The period between the 3rd and 7th centuries AD is commonly known as the Kofun period. The largest of these tombs, built in the Yamato region, are seen as expressions of the sheer power of an extensive political regime, one from which the subsequent Japanese imperial line traced descent.

The burial mounds of petty chieftains and powerful rulers of these centuries may have had their origins in the ditched stone-chambered tombs and raised mounds of the late Yayoi period, but they were often on a considerably larger scale or in larger clusters. Thousands of individual tombs and tomb clusters have been found from southern Kyushu to northern Honshu. The largest clusters were built in the modern Nara-Kyoto-Osaka region, in modern Okayama Prefecture, in northern Kyushu and in northern and northeastern Honshu. These are considered the main centers of political and cultural activity in these centuries. The greatest of the tombs are found in the Nara basin and the Kawachi Plain at the eastern end of the Inland Sea. Shapes varied from round, the most common, to square and combinations of both. The largest and most characteristically Japanese of the tombs were "keyhole-shaped" or "square-front round-back" tombs. The earliest tombs were frequently built into the side of an existing hill or had a trench for several burials cut into the top of the mound. Later large tombs comprised more extensive mounds over stone burial chambers built vertically or laterally. The coffins were either lowered from above into a stone-walled chamber or carried in through a stone-lined passageway.

From the 4th century great moated keyhole tombs several hundred meters in length were built. The tombs reached their greatest scale in the 5th century. The so-called Nintoku tomb, for instance, is among the great monuments of the world. It rivals the pyramids and is only dwarfed by the tomb of the first emperor of the Qin dynasty of China with its vast spectral army of life-size clay soldiers and horses. Nintoku was a legendary emperor whose reign, according to the *Nihon shoki,* lasted nearly 90 years. During it he is said to have conceived and built the enormous tomb. Surrounded by three moats and covering 80 acres (32 hectares), it is nearly 500 meters long and 35 meters high. These later tombs were entered from the side by stone-lined passageways. Finely laid stone burial chambers, sometimes with vividly painted walls, held stone sarcophagi and grave objects.

Tombs with an imperial connection are now under the control of the Imperial Household Agency. Access to them is restricted and many remain unexcavated. Some tombs were pillaged over the centuries. Those that have been excavated have provided rich material finds and insights into the culture and burial practices of the period. Early tombs have yielded many small stone replicas of personal effects, bracelets, knives, mirrors, weapons, tools, clogs, and batons thought to be shamanistic symbols. Later tombs contained iron swords, armor, pottery, beads, domestic and farm tools, crowns and bronze mirrors.

The largest keyhole-shaped tomb (*kofun*) on the Osaka Plain is said to belong to the semilegendary Emperor Nintoku. According to the *Nihon shoki* Nintoku reigned from 313 to 399. Modern scholarship rejects this dating, but allows that he may have been one of the Five Kings of Wa (Japan) mentioned in Chinese sources of the 5th century. The great tomb, nearly 500 meters long and surrounded by three moats with intervening green belts, is thought to date from the early 5th century.

Art of the Great Tombs

Literally meaning "rings of clay," *haniwa* were clay cylinders, inanimate objects, animals and human figures set on the slopes of the mounded tombs (*kofun*) built between the 4th and 7th centuries. According to an entry for the reign of Emperor Suinin in the *Nihon shoki*, they were substitutes for live burials. They may well have developed from simple cylinders or jars placed systematically to keep soil in place on the outer slopes of the tombs or simply for decorative effect. First made in western Japan in the 4th century, they became the major art form of the tomb period and reflect many aspects of life in prehistoric Japan. A single tomb might have had thousands of *haniwa* surrounding it, frequently culminating in a *haniwa* "procession" to welcome the deceased.

Below left This *haniwa* warrior from Ōta, 125·7 cm high, is fully armored in a visored helmet with cheek plates, shoulder and neck protector, long pleated hauberk and pleated trousers. It is characteristic of the detailed *haniwa* warriors found on tombs in the Kantō region. The large number of warrior figures, helmets, suits of armor and quivers gives a strong impression of the martial and aristocratic character of Kofun society.

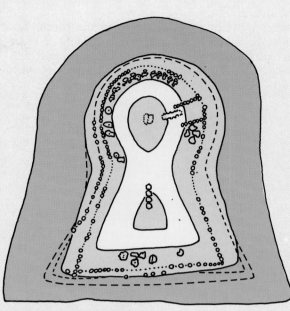

Above The plan of the Futatsuyama tomb in Gumma Prefecture shows how *haniwa* were arranged on a late keyhole-style tomb with stone burial chamber. The front slope of the forward mound was decorated with a mixture of houses, fans and human figures. *Haniwa* in the shape of hats, archer's wristlets, horses and human figures were found on the rear mound.

Left Boats for crossing between Japan and Korea or China must have been much like this 6th-century *haniwa* model found on one of the Saitobaru tombs in southern Kyushu. It displays quite complex construction methods.

Above This finely shaped head, recovered from the Nintoku tumulus, is one of the oldest anthropomorphic *haniwa* figures. It may well have represented a young shaman. Realistically conceived, the head shows a slight fullness at the edges of the mouth and eyes, and the cheeks are rounded.

Left Many *haniwa* of horses have been recovered from scattered 5th-century tombs, contributing to the hypothesis of an invasion by mounted riders. This fully caparisoned horse is ornamented with bells and the high saddle is set on a saddlecloth.

Many tombs dated to the 5th and 6th centuries have provided evidence of a horse-riding culture. Grave goods began to include bridle bits, stirrups, saddle decorations, body plates, and strap ornaments. Horse bones also appear from some late 5th- and 6th-century tombs. The appearance of these horse trappings and the obvious existence of a horse-riding aristocracy forcibly marshaling the human and material reserves of the society to build great tombs for its chieftains has given rise to the theory advocated most vigorously by Professor Egami Namio that during the 4th century there was an invasion of Japan by a horse-riding people from the Korean peninsula. Many archaeologists question the timing and logistics of such an "invasion" as a single epic event. It is clear, however, that the skill of horse riding had found its way to Japan, perhaps brought by repeated influxes of small groups from Silla or Paekche, and that it had been adopted as a military technique by tribal chieftains who used it to extend their power regionally. That there were close, though not always friendly, contacts between the tribal groups in Japan and the Korean kingdoms is evident from the tombs themselves and from the bronze, iron and other grave goods found in them.

One distinctive art form of this period, known as *haniwa*, was found mostly on the outside of tombs. *Haniwa* began as earthenware cylinders to keep the earthen mounds in place. They gradually evolved into a rich art form expressing many of the aspects of daily life of the age. There are figures of warriors, priestesses, mothers with children, horses and other animals, boats, houses and storehouses. With some tombs the *haniwa* seem to have been laid out in ritual order as if to welcome the deceased and surround them with familiar objects. The thousands of *haniwa* needed for a mound like that over the Nintoku tomb were probably made by specialized craftspeople at nearby kilns.

Yamato society

The number and size of the tombs and the other rich archaeological evidence have led to much speculation about the political and social system of Japan at this time. What was the political organization that could mobilize human resources on such a scale? By the 5th and 6th centuries it is possible to speculate about the contours of the society from entries in later Japanese historical records or Chinese and Korean sources. The evidence from these various sources meshes and clearly points to the existence of a confederation of tribal states, some very powerful, many of which had contacts with the continent, dominated by an increasingly powerful, centralizing dynasty located in the Yamato region. The rulers of Yamato, which itself may have been a shifting confederation of intermarried tribal chieftains, claimed descent from the Sun Goddess, extended their power westward and eastward, and were able to build for themselves the most imposing burial mounds. Mirrors cast from the same molds seem to have been distributed widely as symbols of Yamato authority over other tribes well beyond the Kyoto-Nara-Osaka region. Local families in alliance with Yamato constructed tumuli with large caches of grave goods, many of which seem to have been gifts from the central Yamato regime. Many objects found at Okino-

shima, an island in the Japan Sea and a shrine for safe passage, are similar to those found in Yamato tombs, suggesting that Yamato chieftains may have sponsored rituals on the island. The similarity between an inscription on an iron sword found at Inariyama in Saitama Prefecture in eastern Japan, stressing the duties of loyal service by vassals, and a sword inscription from the Etafunayama tumulus near Kumamoto in Kyushu suggests centralization of power, and many scholars see the political reach of the Yamato chieftains spreading from the Kantō region to northern Kyushu. Land-ceding myths in the account of the Izumo people in the *Kojiki* have been read as implying a defeat of Izumo by Yamato, coupled with a recognition by Yamato of the right of the Izumo people to maintain their own gods and ritual forms.

Archaeologists and historians do not fully agree on the origins or dynamics of Yamato power. But it is fairly clear that society in the tomb period was quite sharply stratified, with Yamato seeking to exert its control and influence over a confederation of rival clans, or *uji,* organized along similarly stratified lines. By the 5th or 6th century a single kingly line seems to have been asserting its pre-eminence within Yamato. According to inscriptions on mirrors Yamato chieftains were known as Daiō (Great King), also read as Ōkimi. The term that has historically been used to describe the sovereigns of Japan, *tennō,* did not come into use until the 7th century. Yamato kingship had many elements to it. One element was kinship. Blood ties remained a powerful factor in the imperial family throughout Japanese history. Another element was military supremacy. Yet another was the ability to manipulate and monopolize the symbolism of the sun myth to enhance their authority. The rituals of access to the Sun Goddess were blended with an ideology of heavenly origin for the Yamato lineage. Other elements included the balancing of rival tribal interests by the awarding of titles, selective intermarriage, tying the interests of the more powerful clans into those of the central dynasty, and the acquisition of dynastic lands (*miyake*).

Beneath the Yamato court, clan society was organized as *uji, be* and slave groups. The heads of the great *uji* were also known as Ōkimi. Among the powerful *uji* closely associated with the Yamato dynasty were the Soga, Mononobe, Nakatomi, Kasuga, Ki, Ōtomo and Haji. Their chieftains were given titles, on the basis of kinship or service, that ranked them in relative proximity to the court. Among these titles were Omi and Muraji, Tomo no miyatsuko (Attendant Families) and Kuni no miyatsuko (Leaders of Provinces). Many of these *uji* had continental origins and connections and were purveyors of special skills and services. The *uji* chieftains performed tribal rituals, propitiated the local deities (*kami*) and led ancestral worship.

Beneath the *uji,* and serving them, were semi-servile groups known as *be.* These were occupational groups that produced special products such as paper, cloth, arms or agricultural products or performed hereditary services as grooms or scribes for the court or local *uji.* They were somewhat above the level of slaves (*yatsuko*) taken in war or born into slavery. Immigrant groups, including the Aya and Hata families, with advanced skills in writing, diplomacy, agriculture, ironworking,

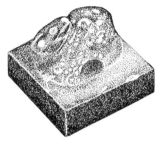

Well before Japan had anything like a centralized ruling dynasty, local chieftains in western Honshu and Kyushu were in contact with Korean and Chinese rulers seeking legitimation and gifts. The *Chronicles of the Later Han Dynasty* record the presentation of tribute by a "King Nu of Wa" in 57 AD, and the grant of a golden seal by the Chinese emperor. In 1784 a gold seal was found in a field on Shikanoshima, northern Kyushu, bearing the inscription: "King Nu of Wa [vassal] of Han." The seal is 2·4 cm square at the base and 2·4 cm high. The handle is carved in the shape of an animal with a serpent's head. Believed to be a forgery at first, the seal is now generally accepted as the one mentioned in the Chinese records.

weaving and pottery played important roles in the society both among the *uji* and the *be*.

Relations with the continent: Yamatai and Yamato

Throughout these early centuries of the Yayoi and Kofun periods there were intermittent but close connections between clans in Japan and peoples on the continent, in China but especially in the Korean peninsula. The eastern barbarians of the countries of Wa were of interest to Chinese chroniclers. The *Chronicles of the Later Han Dynasty* refer to the bestowal by the Chinese emperor on one of these chieftains in 57 AD of a golden seal bearing the inscription ''King Nu of Wa of Han.'' The inscription implies that King Nu of Wa was a vassal of Han. By strange chance a seal bearing this same inscription and dating from the period was found in a field in Shikanoshima, northern Kyushu, in 1784. A Chinese record of 107 AD states that 160 slaves were received from a Wa ruler, with a request for an imperial audience. Chinese chronicles of the 2nd century AD talk of 100 countries of Wa. These fragments of evidence have been interpreted to suggest that many rival petty states existed by the 2nd century in Wa, that some of these had contact with China, and that a process of unification of these village states seems to have been taking place.

During the late 2nd century the Han empire weakened and was replaced by the three kingdoms of Wei in the north, Wu in the east and south, and Shu in the Sichuan basin. In 265 AD the Wei was succeeded by the Western Jin. This was an unstable period with each of the three kingdoms trying to spread its influence and unite the country. Wei was active in Manchuria and northern Korea and, contending with Koguryŏ in the north, strengthened control over Chinese colonies in Lolang and Daifang. The Wei court also developed an interest in Wa and sent at least one embassy. Wa peoples from Kyushu for their part were active in the southern part of the peninsula and in contact with Wei.

In Wa, according to the *Wei Chronicle* (*Wei Zhi*) account of the Wa people among the ''accounts of the eastern barbarians,'' 30 countries had been unified under the leadership of a shaman-queen Himiko of Yamatai by the mid-3rd century. The account gives a detailed description of social customs in Yamatai and even purports to provide actual traveling distances for getting there from China. Yamatai was also mentioned in Korean records. But there is no mention of Yamatai or Himiko in the *Kojiki* or *Nihon shoki*. The account of Yamatai in the *Wei Zhi* set off one of the longest debates in ancient Japanese history: where exactly was Yamatai? and how, if at all, did it relate to

Many Yayoi and Kofun period sites have yielded bronze mirrors, brightly polished on the face and embossed and decorated on the reverse. The earliest mirrors were probably imported from China, but craftsmen in the islands quickly mastered the technology and began to produce small mirrors modeled on the Chinese imports. The mirror illustrated here shows a common Chinese decorative theme of gods and mythical beasts. Around the raised boss, at the four compass points, are a seated immortal, a tiger, another seated immortal and a dragon. Around them is a band with raised congratulatory calligraphic inscription and outer bands of abstract geometric designs. The whole thing is 21 cm in diameter. Bronze mirrors seem to have been regarded more as treasures or ritual implements than as functional objects. The fact that many mirrors made from the same mold have been found in widely distributed tombs suggests that they were granted as symbols of political legitimation. A mirror was included among the ancient imperial regalia.

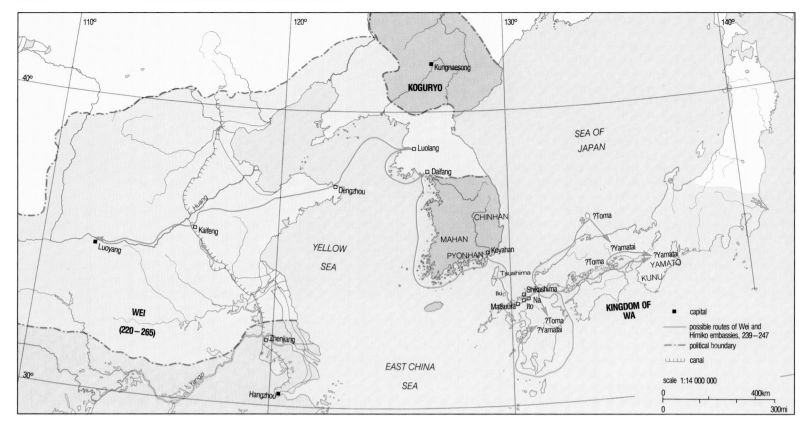

Yamato? The debate started in the 11th century when scholars assumed that Yamatai was in the Yamato area. Since then it has been located almost everywhere. Some proponents argue that the figures, when adjusted as they have to be, place Yamatai in Kyushu, others that it was in the Yamato region at the eastern end of the Inland Sea. If Yamatai was in Kyushu, then it was an extensive local polity by the date of the *Wei Chronicle* account. If it was indeed in Yamato, then what we think of as the Yamato dynasty had been established by the 3rd century. Moreover the range of Yamatai influence was very much more extensive than a locally based Yamatai in Kyushu.

As Chinese influence over the Korean peninsula waned in the 4th century, the kingdoms of Silla and Paekche gained ground in the south, while Koguryō tried to extend its power from the north. Japanese historians believe that the Yamato dynasty (Wa) established diplomatic relations with Paekche in 366 and established a foothold in the south, the colony of Mimana (Kaya), which it governed until ousted by Silla in 562. Korean historians tend to play down the extent of Japanese control over Kaya. After 562 Yamato tried to recover some influence in the peninsula by aiding Paekche in its struggles with Silla and its allies. In 663 Tang Chinese armies and Silla forces routed Paekche, supported by Yamato, at the battle of Hakusukinoe. In one of the major battles of the ancient period Japan was driven from the peninsula in a major reverse. From this point, unable to secure their influence by military means, Japanese rulers turned to cultural and diplomatic contacts with China in what can be described as a great effort at domestic self-strengthening along Chinese lines.

According to a Chinese record, the *Song shu*, between 413 and 478 five chieftains, or kings, of Wa sent a total of nine embassies with tribute to China. Some scholars have suggested that their motive in engaging in diplomacy was to seek support for Yamato's position in the Korean peninsula. These kings were known in the Japanese readings of their names as San, Mi, Sei, Kō and Bu. Attempts have been made to link them with early *tennō* mentioned in the *Nihon shoki* but with little certainty. What is certain is that in these centuries Yamato was drawing heavily on Paekche, Silla and Chinese kingdoms for cultural and technological skills and that it was in active contact with China, perhaps trying to protect its interests in the peninsula. These contacts naturally enriched the cultural level of Yamato. There is plenty of evidence for the presence of many immigrant families, *uji* and *be*, providing high-level cultural skills to the Yamato clans in every area of political and social activity. It is during these centuries, for instance, that the Japanese were introduced to the Chinese writing system. Mirrors and swords with inscriptions have been found. The bearers of these skills were originally immigrant groups who served the Yamato court or great *uji* as scribes and chroniclers. At this stage in its cultural development Japan can hardly be thought of apart from its continental neighbors.

Tombs were still being built in the 7th century. But by then Japanese society was being transformed by new cultural elements from the continent. The transformation first affected the spiritual life of the leading families and then the political and administrative organization of the country. By the mid-6th century, Buddhism, which had taken deep hold in China and Korea, was finding its way to Japan via immigrant communities. Gradually Buddhist temples replaced the great tombs as the places of ritual burial for ruling groups in Japan. But Buddhism was only the first impulse in a great surge of reform and emulation of China that was to reshape the country between 600 and 800 AD.

Routes to Yamatai
The most extensive and colorful description of prehistoric Japanese society is that provided in the late 3rd-century account of the country called Yamatai in the *Wei-Zhi* "accounts of the eastern barbarians." The *Wei-Zhi* account describes in considerable detail the customs of the people of Yamatai, ruled by their shaman-queen Himiko. It also describes how to get to Yamatai: 7000 *li* from Daifang to Koyahan, 1000 *li* to Tsushima, 100 *li* to Iki, 1000 *li* to Matsuura (Matsuro), 500 *li* east to Itō, 100 *li* to Na and thence by Toma to Yamatai. Unfortunately, distances and directions are all uncertain. When adjusted, they place Yamatai in different parts of Kyushu, western Honshu or at the head of the Inland Sea (later Yamato). Although the true location of Yamatai may never be known, the debate is not entirely frivolous. It goes to the heart of questions of political power and state formation in ancient Japan.

PART TWO
THE HISTORICAL PERIOD

THE ANCIENT WORLD

The origins of Shinto and Japanese mythology
Shinto, Buddhism, Confucianism, and to a lesser extent Taoism and Christianity, have all in their different ways exerted a profound influence on Japanese culture and the spiritual lives of individual Japanese. Of these, what later came to be known as Shinto, or the Way of the Gods, is the oldest and deepest spiritual influence. Originating in the dawn of Japanese history, Shinto has touched every aspect of Japanese emotional experience and shaped Japanese responses to nature, life and death, community life, social organization, political ideology, festivals and aesthetics. In the 18th and early 19th centuries Shinto formed the core of a movement of national revival, the National Learning movement, that sought to define the features of Japanese culture that made it distinct from China and the West in terms of the Japanese classics and Shinto virtues of simplicity and purity of heart. Politicized in the late 19th and early 20th centuries and turned into a nationalist state cult supporting the ideological edifice of veneration for the imperial house, Shinto was purged of political connections in the postwar occupation reforms. Since 1945 shrines have returned to their earlier roles as centers of community festivals and family rituals.

When Buddhism was first introduced to Japan in the 6th century, the Japanese already had their own system of spiritual beliefs and ritual practices. Without knowledge of writing, these beliefs and practices had existed uncodified and inchoate for centuries. Although they were very ancient, it is unlikely that these notions had first originated within the islands of Japan. Some of these practices, such as rituals for hunting and fishing, animistic devotion to natural deities and powerful forces, prayers for fertility or the exorcising of sickness and evil, were brought by early migrants from continental Asia and date from the Jōmon period or earlier. Community rituals relating to the cycle of agricultural life must have developed during the Yayoi period. Others, expressing respect for clan ancestors and divinities, and the Yamato court mythology of divine dynastic ancestry were further refined during the Kofun period. From tombs of the period have come *haniwa* figures of priestesses with bead necklaces and mirrors at their waists. The strong cultic association of the curved jewel (*magatama*), mirror and sword is also evident by the tomb period. These family and local cult practices, however, lacked a clear descriptive definition. Under the influence of Buddhism, which was also known as the Way of the Buddha, they came to be known as Shinto, the Way of the Kami. Like Buddhism, the indigenous cult began to order its divinities into a well-defined hierarchy, and to compile a written mythology in the *Kojiki* and *Nihon shoki*.

The word Shinto expresses the centrality of the concept of *kami* within the developing tradition.

The *kami* are numberless and numinous powers or spirits inherent in nature and associated with the forces of growth and renewal. The relationship between the *kami* and nature is stressed from the introduction of the creation myth in the *Nihongi*: "Before Heaven and Earth were produced, there was something which might be compared to a cloud floating over the sea. It had no place of attachment for its root. In the midst of this a thing was generated which resembled a reed-shoot when it was first produced in the mud. This became straightway transformed into [a god]."

The *kami* were neither personalized forces nor heavenly figures sitting in judgment on the affairs of men. However, they could be called upon to aid men and women or, if angered, be mollified by ritual purification and entertainment. Said to number eight million, the *kami* were actually numberless because any person, living or dead, and any place or object with numinous or transcendent qualities could be venerated as a *kami*. Including emperors, courtiers and warriors as well as fearsome spirits, they customarily resided in the sky, in rocks, trees, waterfalls or islands. Their messengers included deer, foxes and other animals. Their wills could be interpreted by priests and shamans.

At first there was little need for any special building. *Kami* were probably first worshiped by individuals and communities in an open, natural setting. An imposing natural setting would have been sufficient, or perhaps a sacred open space among trees or rocks. Later they were worshiped by clan chieftains in their palaces or in specially dedicated shrines. By the late 6th century priestly families of hereditary ritual specialists such as the Nakatomi were emerging. When shrines did come to be built, the natural setting was always important. Today shrines are found in the back streets of busy cities as well as in the countryside and mountains. Some, like Miyajima in the Inland Sea, are spectacularly located. But even those that do not enjoy a fine natural setting usually incorporate some trees and rocks. *Kami* are not always present in the shrine. They come as visitors when called upon by prayers and offerings. The inner sanctum of the shrine included a *shintai*, a receptacle, or form of the *kami,* often a mirror into which the *kami* worshiped in the shrine could enter. From antiquity shrines were marked by entrance gates or *torii*. Tall trees or rocks were regarded as useful conductors (*yorishiro*) in drawing the *kami* down to the sacred precinct. In some cases an island or a waterfall rather than any building is the *shintai*.

The early history of Shinto is heavily colored by political ideology in the form of the assertion in the *Kojiki* and *Nihon shoki* of the divine lineage of the Yamato clan as the sole legitimate ruling house of Japan. The *Kojiki* may be read as a ranking of the various *kami* setting the Sun Goddess and her pro-

At the heart of Shinto is worship of the *kami*, the numinous forces of nature and ancestral spirits. Long before shrines were built, devotion was offered to waterfalls, islands, rocks, tall trees and sacred animals as *kami* or their receptacles (*shintai*). These "wedded rocks" (*meoto-iwa*) are located just off the coast of Ise, site of the most sacred shrines in Japan. They are traditionally associated with Izanagi and Izanami, the primal pair of *kami* who, in myth, gave birth to the islands of Japan, the Sun Goddess and other gods. A *torii*, or sacred gateway, stands on one rock and the pair are joined by a straw rope which is renewed each new year.

Ise

The plan shows the sanctuary of the Inner Shrine, surrounded by four wooden fences, with the vacant alternate site alongside. For centuries, with some interruptions, the buildings at Ise have been rebuilt every 20 (more recently 21) years on alternating sites.

When the first Japanese chronicles were written in the early 8th century, Ise was already an ancient sacred site associated with the imperial lineage and the Sun Goddess, Amaterasu Ōmikami, from whom it claimed direct descent. Historically, the shrines probably date from the 4th or 5th century AD. Ise comprises an Inner Shrine (*naikū*) dedicated to the Sun Goddess and an Outer Shrine (*gegū*) to Toyouke-no-ōkimi, divinity of rice and harvests.

Until the impoverishment of the imperial house in the 15th century the Ise shrines were visited only by members of the imperial family. When Ise priests began to seek popular patronage in the 15th and 16th centuries, Ise became the focus of popular pilgrimage. In the Edo period thousands of pilgrims took the roads to Ise every year. Buddhist temples and entertainment quarters were built on the outskirts of Ise.

In the prewar period Ise became the focus of militant nationalism. Today it is once more a place of tranquil spirituality and popular veneration of the *kami*.

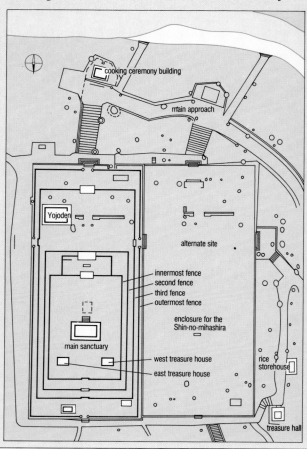

This view looks down on both sites of the sanctuary of the Inner Shrine. The alternate site is in the foreground. In the center is the main sanctuary, flanked by the treasure houses and surrounded by a fourfold wooden fence delineating the sacred precinct. Visitors worship outside the southern gate. Entry to the inner precinct is reserved for priests and members of the imperial family.

genitors, Izanagi and Izanami, in a paramount cosmological position and tracing the imperial lineage from them. According to the creation myth the divine brother and sister, Izanagi and Izanami, gave birth to the islands of Japan and a number of deities. Izanami died in giving birth to the god of fire, and Izanagi, Orpheus-like, followed her to the world of the dead but was driven away by the stench of putrefaction. Purifying himself in a stream, he gave birth to more deities of whom the most important were Amaterasu and her brother, the Storm God, Susa-no-ō. From their union more gods were born. Susa-no-ō was unruly and offended his sister by damaging her rice fields and defecating in her palace. She plunged the world into darkness by retreating into a cave. The other deities performed a lewd dance to lure her out again, but Susa-no-ō was banished to Izumo where

he became the progenitor of a line of rulers who warred with the descendants of the Sun Goddess, until their eventual defeat by Yamato.

Just as the myths ranked the various *kami*, in the same way the Yamato chieftains ranked the local rulers over whom they extended their power and brought their *kami* into subordinate positions. According to Shinto mythology, the sovereigns of Japan are descended from Amaterasu Ōmikami, the Sun Goddess and supreme deity of the Shinto pantheon. The earliest texts were at pains to make this linkage explicit: "Then she commanded her August Grandchild, saying: 'This Reed-plain-1500-autumns-fair-rice-ear Land is the region which my descendants shall be lords of. Do thou, my August Grandchild, proceed thither and govern it. Go! and may prosperity attend thy dynasty, and may it, like Heaven and Earth, endure forever' "

Top The main sanctuary at Ise is built in the *shimmei-zukuri* style of Shinto architecture. It is raised approximately 2 meters off the ground in the style of ancient granaries. Its pillars and walls are of natural untreated cypress.

Above The major rituals conducted at Ise are daily services of purification (as here) and annual observances to pray for good harvests and imperial wellbeing.

Right The Great Shrine of Izumo in Shimane Prefecture ranks with the Ise shrines in antiquity and importance. Built in the imposing *taisha-zukuri* style, Izumo has been rebuilt many times. The present shrine building dates from the mid-18th century. It is approximately 24 meters high and approached by 15 large steps. The main shrine is built around nine pillars, including the great central pillar (*shin-no-mihashira*) which is itself made of nine smaller pillars locked together. The main festivals are in May, when all the *kami* from throughout Japan assemble, and October, in thanks for the harvest. Prayers to the *kami* of Izumo are thought to be particularly efficacious for marital and agricultural blessings.

(*Nihongi*). Ninigi, the grandson of the Sun Goddess, descended to earth in southern Kyushu bringing with him the three sacred regalia: the mirror (an obvious symbol of the sun), a sacred sword, which the Storm God Susa-no-ō had found in the belly of an eight-headed serpent, and a curved jewel (*magatama*). Ninigi's grandson fought his way eastward, to Yamato, where he ascended the throne as the first emperor Jimmu in 660 BC and founded the imperial line. Jimmu's descendants finally defeated the rulers of Izumo and other areas and brought the Izumo people and their gods under Yamato control, although allowing worship of Susa-no-ō at the great shrine of Izumo.

Naturally the *kami* of the Sun was the subject of particular devotion within the Yamato court. The Grand Shrine of Ise, devoted to Amaterasu, is said to have been established in the late 5th century AD (478, reign of Yūryaku). From ancient times the tradition was established that it should be constantly renewed by faithful reconstruction every 20 years. The Izumo people worshiped Ōkuninushi and Susa-no-ō at a shrine that survives as the Great Shrine of Izumo in Shimane Prefecture. Other *uji* had their own deities. Like Yamato, the powerful clans claimed divine ancestry. The Nakatomi family, for instance, who later became the Fujiwara, traced their ancestry to the age of the gods. Major court ceremonies were the Kinensai, a spring planting festival in the second month, and Niinamesai, offering thanks for harvest. Ritual control over these festivals for the realm as well as for the dynasty strengthened the sacred and ritual aspects of early imperial power. Within the court political and sacerdotal hegemony merged. The early term

for government or rule was *matsurigoto*, which also carries the connotation of ritual. At the same time we need not assume that Shinto, or access to the *kami*, had been completely coopted by the Yamato court or powerful *uji*. The *kami* were ubiquitous and could be found, and venerated, in the simplest of natural settings: a grove of tall trees, or a weathered rock, or a welling spring of clear water.

Clearly, early Shinto did not have an elaborate philosophy or metaphysical system. Until spurred by Buddhism, it lacked texts, ethical concerns and an established artistic tradition. Its world view was positive and optimistic, concerned with here and now rather than a remote salvation or distant afterlife. Affinities between man, nature and the *kami* were stressed. There was a strong reverence for nature and respect for simple "natural" materials, forms and processes. The natural universe was viewed as good and ethical. Human nature was dependent on harmony with the forces of nature. Good was identified with natural purity and harmony, evil with impurity. *Makoto*, sincerity or purity of heart and action, quickly emerged as a central virtue. Shrines were not only places of ritual and prayer but also centers of dancing, merrymaking, sumo wrestling, horse racing and archery to please the gods. Impurity or interference with the normal rhythms of nature was considered destructive and sinful. The myth of Izanami and Izanagi in the land of darkness, *yomi no kuni*, speaks of horror of pollution, blood and death. The most heinous crime in the ancient myths was that of the unruly deity Susa-no-ō who desecrated a purification hall and broke down the barriers between rice paddies.

A Shinto Pantheon

Shinto means "Way of the *kami*." Veneration of *kami*, which can be translated as deities or powerful spirits, is central to Shinto. Before the advent of Buddhism in the 6th century Shinto lacked literary and artistic representation of its varied myths and beliefs, so it had no clearly defined pantheon. The *kami* were numberless and ubiquitous, since any person – living or dead – or any object or place possessing a numinous or transcendent quality might be regarded as a *kami*. A Shinto pantheon gradually developed under several influences. Mahayana Buddhism offered the example of rich literary and artistic representation of a cosmic Buddhist order. The political ideology enshrined in the myths of the *Kojiki* and *Nihon shoki* involved an ordering of Shinto *kami* to establish a lineage running from the Sun Goddess to the Yamato rulers. The establishment of shrines by the imperial house and nobility also contributed to the elaboration of the growing pantheon.

Right Nakatsu-hime. In Shinto art the *kami* were frequently depicted as noblewomen and children. Princess Nakatsu was the consort of Emperor Ōjin. She figures in the Hachiman cult as an incarnation of the compassionate Bodhisattva Kannon and as an attendant image for Hachiman. She usually appears with the long tresses of a Heian beauty, wearing the Tang-style robes popular at the Heian court.

Left Zenmyō Nyoshin. Japanese Buddhist monks who went to China or Korea in search of Buddhist teachings brought back many guardian deities of Buddhist or Taoist origin. Zenmyō was a beautiful Chinese girl who fell in love with a Korean monk Ui-sang who was studying Kegon Buddhism in China. Broken-hearted when he had to return to Korea, she was transformed into a dragon who guided and protected his vessel. She was treated as a protective deity of Kegon Buddhism and enshrined as one of the Shinto guardians of the Kegon monastery of Kōzanji in Kyoto in 1225.

Below Izu-san Gongen. This plump jovial figure is a local *kami* of the Izu mountain range in modern Shizuoka Prefecture. His origins are obscure, but like many of the images of the *kami* he developed under strong Buddhist influence. Here he is shown wearing a courtier's cap and a Buddhist priest's stole over one shoulder. An incarnation of the 1000-armed Kannon, he was an object of devotion to Minamoto and Hōjō warriors during the Kamakura period.

Left Zaō Gongen. One powerful current in Japanese religious life was the assimilation of Buddhism and Shinto. In this syncretic belief Shinto *kami* were regarded as protective deities and manifestations of Buddhas and Bodhisattvas. Zaō Gongen is associated with Mount Kinpu in the Yoshino mountains south of Nara and was probably initially a minor local *kami*. He became a special guardian of the Shugendō cult of mountain asceticism tracing its origins to the legendary En no Gyōja and was regarded as the Shinto manifestation of several Buddhas. His ferocious expression aims not to terrify devotees but to ward off evil.

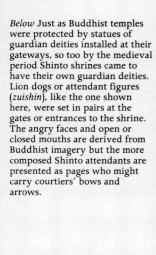

Below Just as Buddhist temples were protected by statues of guardian deities installed at their gateways, so too by the medieval period Shinto shrines came to have their own guardian deities. Lion dogs or attendant figures (*zuishin*), like the one shown here, were set in pairs at the gates or entrances to the shrine. The angry faces and open or closed mouths are derived from Buddhist imagery but the more composed Shinto attendants are presented as pages who might carry courtiers' bows and arrows.

Right Wakamiya Hachiman. Hachiman is a *kami* identified with the legendary Emperor Ōjin and later considered a war god and tutelary deity of the Minamoto warrior clan. By the Heian period he had become the center of an extensive devotional cult represented in many shrines. Hachiman appears in painting and sculpture in a variety of guises, most commonly that of a monk. He is associated closely with the Shinto goddess Hime-gami (Nakatsu-hime, *facing page top right*) and is commonly an incarnation of the Buddha Amida.

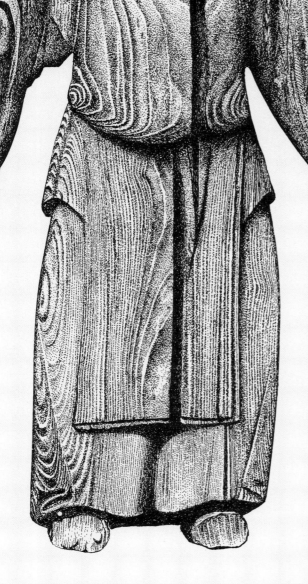

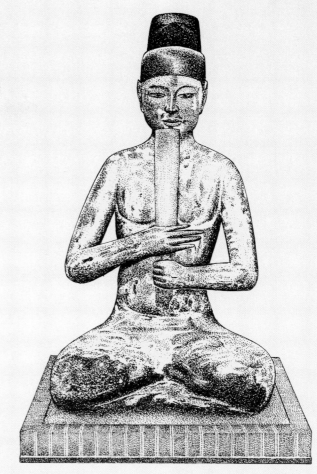

Below If one current in the artistic representation of Shinto *kami* was to present them as incarnations of Buddhas, another current was to present them as noble courtly figures. This figure, like many of the most powerful and expressive works of Shinto sculpture, was carved from a single block of cypress wood and then polychromed. The flowing robes, distinctive cap and staff of office indicate that this was a courtier. The posture radiates meditative energy.

The introduction of Buddhism

Buddhism has been integral to Japanese culture since at least the 6th century AD. In the early centuries it served both to broaden spiritual possibilities for the Japanese and to give them greater access to Chinese civilization. Patronized at first by powerful families and the ancient state, Buddhist teachings of universal salvation spread widely among the common people from the 12th century when Japan can be said to have fully entered its Buddhist age. The influence of Buddhism continued strong until well into the early modern period, but it came under criticism by nativist thinkers in the 18th and 19th centuries as a superstitious and alien teaching inimical to the rationalism of Confucianism, to Japanese native Shinto traditions and to the interests of Japanese rulers. In the 1870s Buddhism was forcibly separated from Shinto by the new Meiji government which was bent on promoting Shinto as a national creed (see below, p. 169). It also had to face competition from Christian missionaries whose activities were again permitted. Although Buddhism suffered something of an eclipse, it was not eradicated and by the late 19th century was making a recovery. Today, through its different schools, it continues to exert a pervasive influence on the minds of millions of Japanese.

During the first five or six centuries of our era the teachings attributed to the Buddha Sākyamuni (c. 563–483 BC) were spreading rapidly through east Asia. Brought by camel caravans from India and western Asia to China in the 1st century AD, they put down deep roots in China during the Han dynasty before being carried to Korea in the 4th century. To distinguish it from the Theravada Buddhist tradition, the "teaching of the elders" of Sri Lanka and southeast Asia, east Asian Buddhism is generally described as Mahayana Buddhism, the Buddhism of the "great vehicle" that will carry all living beings to enlightenment. This division within Buddhism occurred around the 1st century BC. Advocates of the great vehicle argued that their more powerful and all-embracing teachings offered a better chance of salvation than those Theravada doctrines they denigrated as "small vehicle" teachings.

Although there were some important differences of emphasis between early Mahayana and Theravada, there was also much common ground. Both held out as their ideal the life and spiritual quest of the Buddha. Accounts of the Buddha's life and teaching were not written down until several centuries after his death. Then they were compiled by faithful believers whose aim was to extol the virtues of the Buddha. They contain many miraculous features, but through these we can see the Buddha, not as a god, but as a humane troubled man seeking spiritual insight in the face of change, suffering and death.

According to tradition Gautama Siddhārtha was born into a princely family in northern India and brought up in luxury. Shocked when, at the age of 29, he encountered the realities of sickness, old age and death, he abandoned his palace to seek deeper spiritual understanding. After subjecting himself to severe austerities for six years he renounced the ascetic path as too harsh and embarked instead on a more moderate path, the middle way, of medi-

tation. One night, while meditating under a tree, he attained enlightenment, or nirvana, a perfect understanding of the insubstantiality of being. Recognized as the Buddha, the "enlightened one," he spent the remainder of a long life wandering and teaching a growing following of lay patrons and mendicant disciples who formed the earliest Buddhist communities of monks and nuns. After the Buddha's death his followers and later commentators continued to spread his message and work out the philosophical implications of the teachings, the *dharma*, in a huge scriptural canon known as the Tripitaka or "three baskets," including sermons attributed to the Buddha himself (*sūtras*), later commentaries (*abhidharma*) and monastic rules (*vinaya*).

At the core of the Buddha's *dharma* is the conviction that all living beings are subject to suffering and impermanence and bound by ignorance and craving to a cycle of birth, death and rebirth (*samsāra*). Actions, or *karma*, springing from attachment that is rooted in ignorance, perpetuate the cycle of birth and rebirth in sentient form. The only way to break the cycle of *samsāra*, to attain nirvana, is to follow the example of the Buddha, abandon all attachment, seek transcendent wisdom and recognize the intrinsic emptiness of reality. This teaching is enshrined in the Four Noble Truths and the Noble Eightfold Path: that life is suffering, that the source of this suffering is craving or desire, that to stop suffering desire must be stopped, and that to stop desire the seeker must live a moral life according to the Noble Eightfold Path.

The Noble Eightfold Path, as described in the Fourth Noble Truth, consisted of right views, right intentions, right speed, right action, right livelihood, right effort, right mindfulness and right concentration. Here was outlined an ethical program

Transmission of Buddhism Between the death of the Buddha in the 5th century BC and the 6th century AD, his teachings spread throughout Asia in two great streams. One stream, known as Theravada Buddhism, "the teaching of the elders," was carried southward to Sri Lanka and Southeast Asia. The other current, Mahayana Buddhism, "the teaching of the great vehicle" on which all beings can ride to salvation, was carried across mountains and deserts to Gandhara (Afghanistan), Tibet and China. From China Buddhism was introduced to Korea by the 4th century AD and from thence to Japan in the mid-6th century. To Japan Buddhism offered not only a sophisticated philosophical and moral system. It also brought rich art and music, Chinese, Korean and Indian culture, and the economic and social organization of the monastery.

Above right This *sūtra* dating from the Nara period illustrates the recital by Sakyamuni of his own life history. The central teaching of Buddhism is that life is impermanent and that men and women are blinded by flames of passion and bound by attachments to the cycle of birth, death and rebirth. But the Buddha taught, and showed in his own life, that men and women can control the flames of passion through meditation and moral behavior and thus break the cycle of rebirth.

Right This scene from a 17th-century handscroll shows the death of the Buddha, or rather his passing into nirvana (*nehan* in Japanese).

that involved respect for all living beings, honesty, compassion and the avoidance of lust, theft and immorality. Enfolding this ethical life within a meditative religious life involving celibacy, vegetarianism and abstinence from alcoholic beverages allowed the sincere seeker to accumulate good *karma* and eventually attain the insight that offers release from the painful cycle of birth and rebirth.

While Theravadan teachers held to a traditional emphasis on the austere meditative life of the mendicant seeker after Buddhahood, the ideal of the Arhant, Mahayanists broadened the *dharma* to draw in people who did not have the time, training, education or means to follow the rigorous practices of the mendicant seeker. There developed a powerful current of devotionalism and salvationism in which the Buddha came to be venerated by priests as well as by laypeople and set at the head of an expanding pantheon of Buddhas, Bodhisattvas and attendants, all of whom were working for the realization of the *dharma* and the common goal of bringing all sentient beings to enlightenment. Among the Buddhas, Vairocana became a representation of cosmic universalism, Amitābha (Amida) who inhabited the Western Paradise had vowed to save the faithful, while Maitreya would come in the future to purify the world.

The ideal of the Bodhisattva was a particularly powerful one in Mahayana Buddhism. These were

enlightened beings of transcendent wisdom and compassion on the brink of Buddhahood who postponed their own Buddhahood in order to work in the world to save other beings. Like the Virgin Mary and the Christian saints, the Bodhisattvas themselves became objects of veneration. Among the many Bodhisattvas, Avalokiteśvara (Guanyin in Chinese, Kannon in Japanese), for example, emerged as a popular cult figure of supreme compassion. Transformed from male to female, Kannon was frequently depicted with a thousand arms to draw sentient beings to salvation.

The teachings of Buddhism probably began to filter into Yamato via Korean immigrants there in the late 5th or early 6th century AD. They were not, however, taken up seriously in court circles until the mid-6th century. In 552, according to the *Nihon shoki* (538 by some accounts), the king of Paekche, hoping to secure Yamato's support in his struggles against Silla, sent Buddhist texts and a gilt statue to the Yamato ruler, Kimmei, and commended the religion to the Yamato court as a new and higher form of wisdom and magical power.

This action aroused tension within the court. Some of the tension may have been caused by a division of opinion over the wisdom of supporting Paekche's political aims in the peninsula, but some of it seems to have swirled about the new teaching and the wisdom of adopting a new and alien religion that might be inimical to existing practices. Several powerful and conservative *uji*, led by the Nakatomi clan, who were ritualists, and the Mononobe, a family of military specialists, opposed the acceptance of this foreign *kami*. Other *uji*, led by the powerful Soga family, threw their weight behind acceptance. Kimmei permitted Soga no Iname to worship the Buddha statue as a family *kami*. Buddhism suffered a setback, however, when the traditionalists blamed an epidemic on Buddhism and had the statue thrown into a canal. Soga no Umako's victory over the Mononobe in 587 assured fuller acceptance of Buddhism. By then, monks, nuns, scribes, architects and makers of Buddhist statues were arriving from Korea. Proponents of Buddhism argued that angry Buddhas were causing plague and epidemic. They too should be placated and venerated. Gradually Buddhism gained a foothold within the Yamato court and its associated families. At first very little of its intellectual or devotional potential was realized, however. It was viewed more as a powerful miracle-working and healing force.

Soga no Umako, who died in 626, is a shadowy figure. Clearly in his day he was a powerful political force and an active patron of Buddhism. Between 588 and 609 in gratitude for his victory over the Mononobe he established the Hōkoji (Asukadera) using Korean craftsmen. He controlled the Yamato court by placing his relatives on the throne and removing them when it suited him. In order to set his niece Suikō on the throne he is said to have had his nephew Sushun assassinated. Suikō entrusted government to her nephew and regent, Prince Shōtoku (Shōtoku Taishi).

Prince Shōtoku (572–622) is one of Japan's most revered cultural heroes. An enthusiastic promulgator of Buddhism and patron saint of Japanese Buddhists, he was regarded by many as a reincarnation of the Buddha himself and became the

The Hōryūji at Nara

The western precinct of Hōryūji, with its main hall, pagoda, cloisters and great lecture hall, dates from the late 7th century. The eastern precinct, added in the 8th century, centers on an octagonal hall, the Yumedono or Hall of Dreams, dedicated to Prince Shōtoku.

Built originally by Prince Shōtoku between 601 and 607, destroyed by fire in 670 and immediately rebuilt, the Hōryūji is the oldest surviving monastic compound in Japan and a great repository of architecture and art of the pre-Nara era. Originally a modest temple, the Ikarugadera, built close to Shōtoku's Ikaruga Palace, the Hōryūji became a center for Yogic practice and the Hossō school of Buddhism which taught that existence is merely a manifestation of the human mind. As devotion to Prince Shōtoku spread, the Hōryūji became the focus of the popular cult.

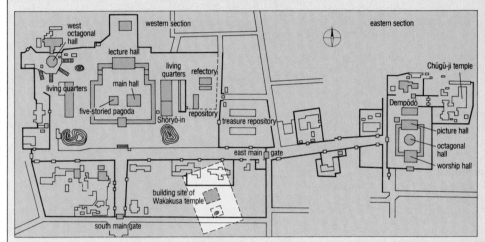

Left The first pagoda is said to have been built in Japan in 585. The graceful five-story pagoda from Hōryūji built in the late 7th century is the oldest surviving pagoda in Japan. Standing to a height of 32 meters, it tapers slightly at each story to create an impression of lightness and stability. Like other pagodas, the one at Hōryūji was believed to enshrine a relic of the Buddha. Its location and scale attest to its importance in early Buddhist religious life.

object of cultic veneration as early as the 8th century. The account of his activities in the *Nihon shoki* was written a century after his death and it is difficult to be sure he was responsible for all the innovations attributed to him, but he seems to have been a remarkable statesman and a devout Buddhist. As a builder of temples he is thought to have established the Shitennōji (Temple of the Four Heavenly Kings) in Naniwa after the Soga victory over the Mononobe. He later founded the Hōryūji and traditionally 300 other temples. This last number is certainly an exaggeration. The *Nihon shoki* states that there were 46 temples, 816 monks and 569 nuns in Japan in 622, the year after his death. It was many decades after his death before 300 temples were built. He studied the *sutras* with the aid of a Korean monk and is said to have written commentaries on at least three: the *Lotus Sūtra* (Hoke-kyō), the *Vimalakīrti Sūtra* (Yuima-kyō) and the *Sūtra of Queen Srīmālā* (Shōman-gyō). Shōtoku wrote the protection of Buddhism into his "Seventeen-Article Constitution." Its second article begins "Revere the Three Treasures [the Buddha's teaching, the monastic community, and the monastic rule]." He is credited with the statement: "All is illusion, the Buddha alone is real." If there is any truth in the attribution, then he was among the first Japanese to realize the spiritual depth of Buddhism.

Buddhism, although not fully understood at first, made massive contributions to Japanese culture. In the spiritual sphere it offered the model of the historical Buddha who found enlightenment by the middle path of meditation. It brought the teachings of the Buddha as these had been developed in the *sutras* and the Mahayana tradition of the great vehicle on which all might ride to salvation. It brought notions of moral behavior, *karma* and personal salvation through recognition of the Four Noble Truths and practice of the Noble Eight-fold Path. It brought both the Theravada teaching of the Arhant, or seeker after Buddhahood, and the Mahayana ideal of the compassionate Bodhisattva. It addressed itself to human suffering with a depth and directness unmatched in the native beliefs. It also provided a well-developed body of doctrine, art, magic and medicine, music and ritual, even notions of heavens and hells for those who found the abstract concept of nirvana hard to grasp.

Intellectually, Buddhism offered a literate and highly sophisticated philosophical and cultural tradition developed in India, China and Korea to a society in which literacy and philosophical discussion were still very new. The Three Baskets of teachings (*sutras*), commentaries and rules for monks and nuns comprised a vast canonical corpus. It provided a rich textual tradition in which hundreds of *sutras* were made available to Japanese monks and their lay patrons. The *Lotus Sūtra*, the *Vimalakīrti Sūtra*, the *Sūtra of the Golden Light* and the *Sūtra of Queen Srīmālā* could be read, or heard, as imaginative literature as well as spiritual teaching.

Moreover, Buddhism was not simply a spiritual or intellectual force. It also brought new physical and artistic models to Japan. Buddhist monasteries, with their distinctive layouts and great buildings—pagodas, gates, cloisters, golden halls and lecture halls—were completely new architectural

Evolution of the pagoda. A pagoda is simply a multistoried tower used to enshrine relics of the Buddha. Pagodas derived in design and function from Indian stupas, which originated from burial mounds. After Sakyamuni's death eight stupas were erected to hold his relics. The Mahayana movement within Buddhism may have begun with a group of disciples who practiced stupa worship. As Buddhism spread, the stupa retained its reliquary function but was transformed into an increasingly elaborate towered structure, the pagoda. The Yakushiji pagoda (7), c. 698, is a three-story pagoda, with intervening subsidiary sections to add to the height (35 meters).

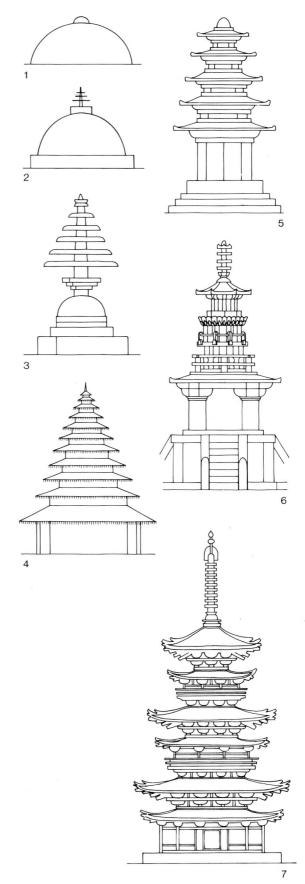

Below This gilt bronze triad, showing the Buddha Sakyamuni with two attendants, is now the central image in the main hall of the Hōryūji. Made in the contemporary Chinese (Northern Wei) style—like images in the Longmen caves in Henan—it is thought to date from 623 and to be the work of Kuratsukuri no Tori, the most renowned sculptor of his day. The triad was commissioned to commemorate the death of Prince Shōtoku.

Above This aerial view shows the oldest buildings in the western quarter: the middle gate, cloisters, five-storied pagoda and main hall (Kondō) set side by side, and the great lecture hall behind. The original monastery (Ikarugadera) was built in the Shitennōji style, transmitted from Korea, with its pagoda and main hall on a single vertical axis. When Hōryūji was rebuilt the architects broke with continental styles in setting pagoda and hall side by side, using the height of the pagoda to balance the breadth of the hall.

forms in Japan. The regulated life of monks and nuns was new. So too were the statues built by professional sculptors with their identifying marks of the Buddha and complex hand positions, and the paintings and ritual implements associated with Buddhist ritual.

Buddhism quickly came to assume certain functions in society which had not been fully provided for by early Shinto. These functions related very directly to daily life. One was to provide for the repose of the dead and for the pacification and relief of troubled spirits or violent ghosts. At first these funereal and memorial obsequies were performed for members of the court or noble families. Gradually they came to be a major element in the relationship between Buddhist temples and the local community. A second function was to provide prayers for immediate mundane benefits such as relief from sickness and famine, a bountiful harvest, ease of childbirth, a male heir or rain in time of drought. This function of offering prayers for immediate benefits also became an enduring, and profitable, feature of most Japanese Buddhist schools. A third function in early Japanese Buddhism was that of protection of the nation, *chingo kokka*. Like the *kami*, the Buddhas were seen as protective deities, while monks and nuns were expected to pray and work as fervently for the spiritual needs of the state as they did for their own salvation or that of their fellow men. This ensured the prosperity and state support of Buddhism in ancient Japan, but it also tended to subordinate Buddhist spiritual ideals to secular needs.

Finally, Buddhism enriched the range of political discourse. Texts recounting the story of Emperor Asoka, the great patron of Buddhism in India, made the point that the Buddhist ruler who patronized the Three Treasures would surely prosper and that his state would enjoy the protection of the Buddhas. This message was certainly recognized by Yamato rulers in their patronage of Buddhism. On an even more universal level a ruler could set himself up as a human counterpart of a Buddha radiating light at the apex of a cosmic order. This conceit was used by more than one later emperor, but especially by Shōmu who built the great Buddha of Tōdaiji. In a more tangible way great monasteries in the capital, patronized by the ruler or the state, could serve as the hub of a provincial network of monasteries whose local patrons were thus linked to the center of political power. On the other hand, monks and monasteries, if allowed to go unchecked, could present a threat to the state. For this reason the secular authorities sought to impose discipline on the developing Buddhist institution.

Buddhism and Shinto

After the initial tension over its reception Buddhism settled into an easy complementary relationship with the indigenous cults. Early Shinto was no match for Buddhism in philosophical depth, textual sophistication or artistic imagination, but devotion to the *kami* was pervasive and too deeply rooted to be easily abandoned. The fact that the native cult did not present challenging intellectual or doctrinal positions gave it staying power and allowed for a melding of Buddhist and Shinto practices and an easy association between the *kami* and

Mandalas are symmetrically organized symbolic diagrams used in Hinduism, Buddhism and Shinto to express fundamental, and frequently esoteric, religious doctrines. The earliest Japanese mandalas were Buddhist. From the late Heian period, however, mandalas expressing indigenous Shinto and Shinto-Buddhist beliefs were produced. These included *suijaku* mandalas, in which Shinto deities were presented as reincarnations of corresponding Buddhas or Bodhisattvas, and shrine mandalas illustrating the features of famous shrines. Many mandalas were produced as part of the cult of the Kasuga shrine. Founded in 709 by Fujiwara no Fuhito to protect the new capital at Heijō, Kasuga was dedicated to the divinities (*kami*) of the Fujiwara family. It was closely associated with nearby Kōfukuji, the family temple of the Fujiwara. This mandala, dating from the 14th century, depicts Buddhas associated with Kōfukuji in the lower ground, the Kasuga shrine and Mount Mikasa above them, and the five deities of Kasuga in the upper section.

Below Prince Shōtoku was so revered as statesman, sage and patron of Buddhism that a devotional cult in his honor sprang up shortly after his death. The veneration permeated most branches of Japanese Buddhism and reached a peak in the Kamakura period when the prince was adopted in popular belief as a patron of arts and crafts. This wooden image depicts the prince as an infant when, according to legend, he faced eastward and intoned the mantra "Namu Butsu," "Praise to the Buddha."

the Buddhas. To promote Buddhism, Buddhist priests portrayed the Buddhas as simply superior *kami*. In order to legitimize Buddhism, they also called upon the *kami* for protection. Early temples were built close to or within shrine precincts and the *kami* were viewed as protectors of Buddhist temples. Buddhist statues were often carved on behalf of the *kami*. *Kami* of a region were asked for "permission" before a temple was built. Later temples had small shrines built within their precincts. Many temples had close relations with nearby shrines—for instance, Kōfukuji and the Kasuga shrine in Nara or Enryakuji and the Hie shrine near Kyoto.

Buddhist temples, Shinto shrines and Nara administration
During the 7th and 8th centuries Japan was transformed from a clan society headed by a great chieftain to an imperial state on the Tang model ruled by a heavenly sovereign. The transformation was based on the importation, first of Buddhism, then of a whole series of Chinese administrative and legal institutions, known as the *ritsuryō* codes. After the Taika reform (646) and the building of the new capitals at Fujiwara and Heijō, Japan was divided up into provinces and circuits with provincial capitals where governors supervised tax collection and local order. Roads were improved, new land and tax systems introduced.

At the time of Prince Shōtoku's death in 622 Japan had 46 Buddhist temples and 1345 ordained clergy, mostly clustered in the Asuka region. With the establishment of the new capital of Heijō and a new centralized imperial government, Buddhist monasteries were incorporated into the fabric of the state and Buddhist clergy acquired considerable political power. Of the great monasteries, Tōdaiji was made the apex of a system of provincial monasteries and nunneries (*kokubunji*). At the same time, Shinto shrines were reorganized and a system of major provincial shrines introduced.

Thus developed the close association between Buddhism and Shinto that characterized Japanese religious life until their separation by imperial decree after 1868. Through this association individual Buddhas were paired off with particular *kami* in what has been called a uniting of gods and Buddhas, *shinbutsu shūgo*. Under the influence of later Tendai and Shingon esoteric Buddhist thought (see below, pp. 85 and 87), an increasingly systematic syncretism of Buddhist and Shinto beliefs was worked out during the 10th and 11th centuries in which the *kami* were viewed as native Japanese manifestations (*suijaku*) of the universal Buddhist deities who were their original forms (*honji*). This *honji-suijaku* synthesis found frequent expression in art and literature and became deeply embedded in Japanese religious thought. While the Shinto *kami* were placed on a lower plane than the Buddhas, they were, in the process, given new status and cultural identity. In time some pro-Shinto advocates would argue that the native *kami* were in fact the original forms and the Buddhas their traces.

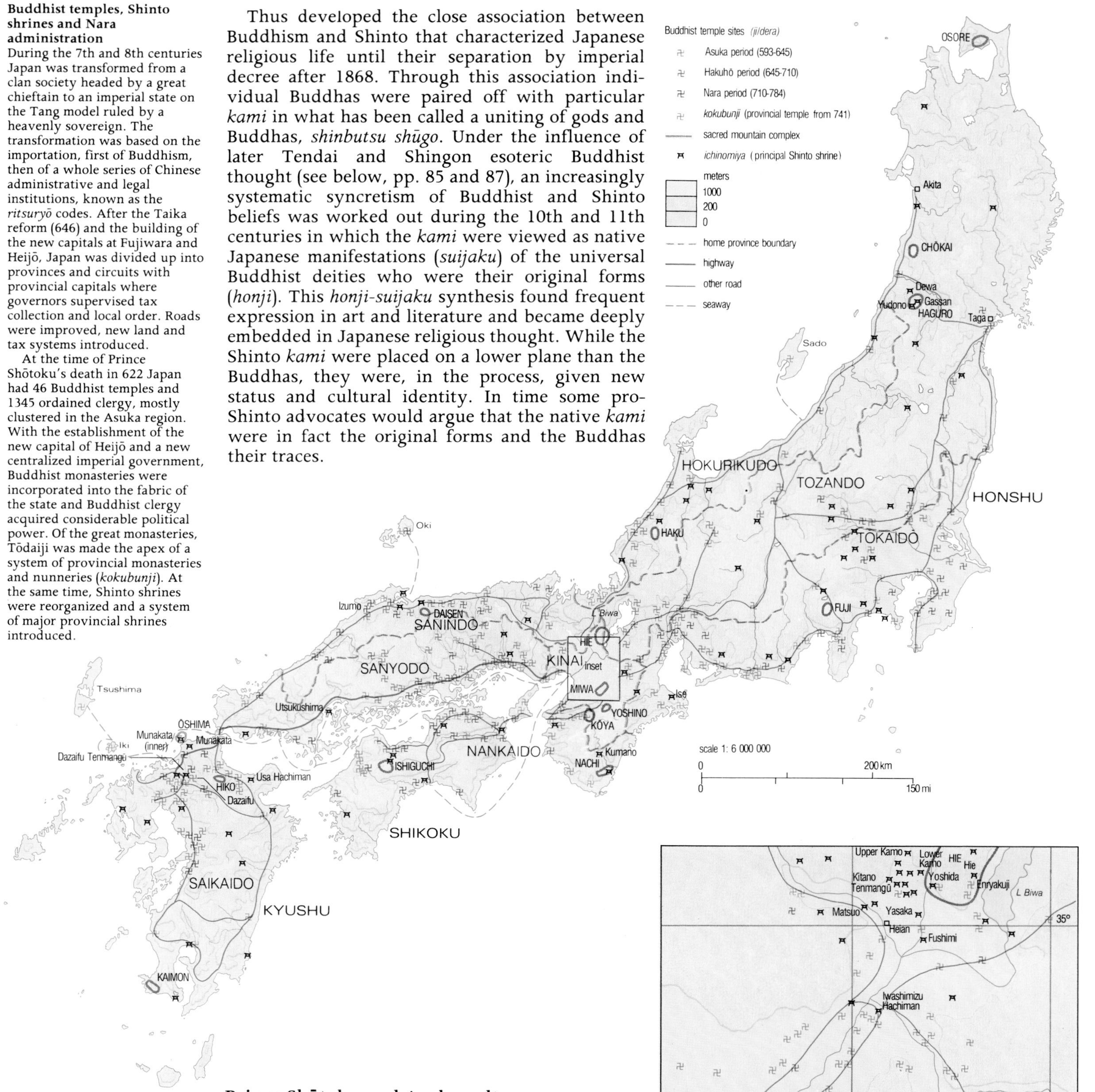

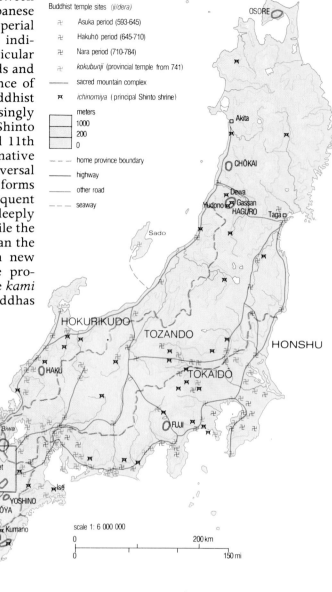

Buddhist temple sites (*ji/dera*)
卍 Asuka period (593–645)
卍 Hakuhō period (645–710)
卍 Nara period (710–784)
卍 *kokubunji* (provincial temple from 741)
⸺ sacred mountain complex
�֍ *ichinomiya* (principal Shinto shrine)

meters
1000
200
0

‒ ‒ home province boundary
⸺ highway
⸺ other road
‒ ‒ seaway

scale 1: 6 000 000
0   200 km
0   150 mi

Prince Shōtoku and Asuka culture
During the late Kofun period of the late 6th and early 7th centuries in which Prince Shōtoku was active, the center of political and cultural activity within Yamato was in the Asuka region. This period is therefore commonly referred to as the Asuka period. Styles of Buddhist architecture and sculpture patronized by Shōtoku and the court are known as Asuka culture. According to the account of the reign of Empress Suiko in the *Nihon shoki*, Prince Shōtoku was not merely an active patron of Buddhism. Politically he used the Chinese imperial model to provide the blueprint for a stronger state and to elevate the position of the Yamato rulers above the ruck of clan politics. New court ranks,

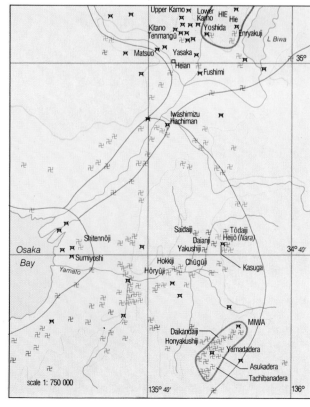

scale 1: 750 000

the 12 cap ranks introduced in 603, were based on Chinese practice and intended to facilitate a reordering of political power around the court by weakening the hereditary power of old clan chieftains and promoting men of talent from among the lesser clan leaders.

He is also credited with writing a "constitution" or directive for ministers in 17 articles. This document assumed the existence of an official bureaucracy and stressed Chinese Confucian and legalist principles of loyalty, harmony, dedication and ability in government as ideals to be realized in Japanese political life. The opening article stresses harmony and decries factionalism of the kind that beset Yamato clan society: "Harmony is to be valued and an avoidance of wanton opposition to be honored." Article 3 enjoins obedience to the throne: "When you receive the imperial commands fail not scrupulously to obey them. The lord is Heaven. The vassal is Earth. Heaven overspreads. The Earth upbears." Other articles urged officials to be impartial, diligent, trustworthy and fair to the people whom they would govern. The document has come down to us as a set of moral precepts aimed at inculcating an ideal of social harmony, strengthening an ethic of bureaucratic service to the throne and elevating the ruler above clan rivalries.

Shōtoku has been particularly revered for his elevation of the imperial office. According to an entry in the Chinese chronicle of the Sui dynasty, Shōtoku angered the Chinese emperor by addressing greetings "from the Son of Heaven in the land where the sun rises to the Son of Heaven in the land where the sun sets." We do not know whether Shōtoku actually intended to assert Japan's equality with China. Conceivably he could have been unaware of the niceties of diplomatic language in dealing with China. But the statement has been remembered as a first clear assertion of Japan's separate national identity and cultural parity with her great continental neighbor. It is also viewed as a major step in elevating the imperial dignity from that of "Great Chieftain" (ōkimi) to "Heavenly Sovereign" (tenshi or tennō or, in the honorific Japanese pronunciation, sumera-mikoto).

Shōtoku also laid the basis for a further surge of Chinese reforms. When it became clear that Japan could not maintain a position in Korea, he turned to diplomacy, sending several official embassies to the Sui court. Scholars and priests who went with the embassies returned years later to participate in a further wave of reforms. These large-scale organized contacts with China increased Japan's receptivity to a broad range of Chinese influences including Buddhism, Confucianism, the Chinese calendar, concepts of government and administrative codes for a centralized state.

Shōtoku did not have a free hand politically. He had to compromise with powerful uji like the Soga. It is doubtful if many of Shōtoku's reforms were actually implemented in his day. Cap ranks and the "constitution" were probably stronger in aspiration than in realization. Even so, he set a model as an enlightened Buddhist and Confucian statesman, loyal proponent of imperial sovereignty, patron of religion and the arts, and a model for later court officials and holders of political power in Japan. Within a few centuries of his death he was apotheosized as an incarnation of the Buddha and became the focus of a popular cult.

The Taika reforms

Prince Shōtoku died of sickness in 622. After his death the impulse for centralization and political and cultural reform flagged. No one was appointed to succeed him as regent and the Soga family, led by Emishi and his son Iruka, reasserted their

This splendid Buddha head in the Tang style is 42 cm high. It is thought to have been the head of the central image in a large triad made for the Yamadadera in Asuka. During the 12th century the triad was removed to Kōfukuji in Nara where most of it was later destroyed.

Right The fields of Asuka have yielded mounded tombs, temple and palace foundations and enigmatic stones. Whimsically carved stone figures, like the one shown here, were used as field and roadside guardians, field markers and fertility symbols.

The tomb of Prince Shōtoku. Shōtoku is believed to be buried with his mother and one of his consorts at a place now called Taishi-chō on the Osaka side of Mount Nijō. Nearby are tombs of the rulers Bidatsu, Yōmei, Suiko and Kotoku. Empress Suiko, whom Shōtoku served as regent, is buried close by. She ordered the erection of a temple beside his tomb, but nothing of that now survives.

Asuka

Below The cradle of Japanese history, Asuka lies in a level valley studded with gentle hills and steeper mountains on its periphery. The remains of more than 50 temples, palaces and burial mounds have been found. Its most impressive building is the restored Asukadera, originally built in 596.

The gentle valley of Asuka, bounded by the Three Mountains of Yamato and crossed by the Asuka River, was the heartland of political authority and Buddhist culture in the late 6th and 7th centuries. Rich in palaces, tombs and temples, it was here that Empress Suiko and her regent Shōtoku held court. Asuka sprang into the limelight again in 1972 with the discovery of the painted Takamatsuzuka tomb.

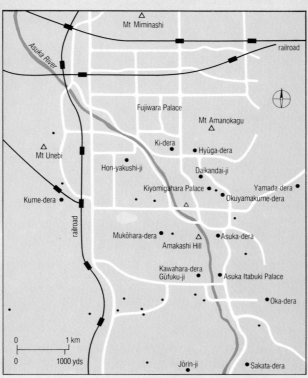

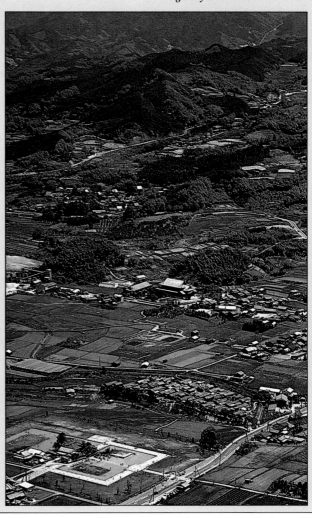

Below The cradle of Japanese history, Asuka lies in a level valley studded with gentle hills and steeper mountains on its periphery. The remains of more than 50 temples, palaces and burial mounds have been found. Its most impressive building is the restored Asukadera, originally built in 596.

control over the throne. With no clear leadership pressing for centralization, clan rivalries reasserted themselves and the court was again mired in intrigue and bloodshed. In 643 Iruka had Prince Yamashiro, Shōtoku's son and a rival to the Soga for power, assassinated. This and other oppressive Soga actions caused revulsion among those courtiers who were hostile to the Soga and eager to continue the process of centralization and reform. In 645 an imperial prince, Naka no Ōe, and the head of one of the powerful clans, Nakatomi no Kamatari, led a coup in which they first slashed Iruka to death at a banquet for a visiting Korean envoy and then executed Emishi.

To mark this as a renewed start on the path to reform a new emperor, Kōtoku, was installed. Prince Naka later became Emperor Tenji. Kamatari was given the new name Fujiwara, thus becoming the ancestor of one of the most influential families in Japanese history, one that was to support, intermarry with and dominate the imperial line for centuries. The capital was moved briefly to Naniwa. The era was renamed Taika, or "Great Change," and edicts outlining the direction of the reform were issued in 646.

The declared aims of the coup leaders were to recover power for the rulers (*tennō*), to shake off the baneful influences of clan domination of the court and to create a system of centralized and effective government along the lines outlined earlier by Shōtoku, using Chinese administrative codes and the model of Sui and Tang imperial government to create a just and effective administration. The Taika reform edicts presaged sweeping political and social changes. Private landholding was to be abolished. All land was to be put under control of the emperor and, following the model of the Chinese "equal field system," rice fields were to revert to the state for reallocation each generation. *Be* were abolished and removed from their role of supporting the *uji*. To provide income for a new capital, a central bureaucracy, new roads, post stations and military establishment, a new tax system had to be imposed. Taxes in kind or in labor or military service were to be levied on those who worked the land. This in turn called for regular census taking. The provincial *uji* chieftains were to be coopted into acceptance of the new system by being granted titles and offices in the local administration of the new districts created within their provinces and by being guaranteed peace and stability through the backing of the central government. To add impulse to the reforms, Prince Naka set an example by giving his lands to the state.

The renewed drive for centralization and self-strengthening may well have been hastened by a disastrous naval defeat suffered by Japanese forces at the hands of Chinese and Silla forces at the battle of Hakusukinoe (Paek-kang) in Korea in 663 in which Japan is said to have lost 170 ships and 27 000 men. This defeat forced a complete Japanese withdrawal from the Korean peninsula. Japan even expected an invasion from Tang and built up its defenses in north Kyushu, including the city of Dazaifu. Dazaifu was a military and administrative center of great importance in the administration of the western provinces and the trade and diplomacy with China and Korea. As the fear of invasion receded, the Japanese began to send a series of missions to Tang China to establish solid diplomatic relations and import Tang institutions and culture.

The "Great Change" was far too ambitious and far-reaching to be imposed overnight. The first census, for example, was not taken until 670. But the reform edicts had set a course and the transformation of Japan along Chinese lines proceeded steadily in the late 7th and 8th centuries by means of a series of compilations based on Chinese penal and administrative codes (*ritsu* and *ryō*). Of these the most extensive was the Taihō *ritsuryō* code, promulgated in 702. The importance of these Chinese administrative codes in the reshaping of Japan in these centuries is reflected in the term "*ritsuryō* system," used by modern historians to describe Japanese politics and society in the Nara and Heian periods.

Politics and culture in the Nara period

Until the late 7th century the Japanese rulers had not felt the need for a permanent capital. The capital was simply the ruler's palace. At the ruler's death it was generally abandoned, probably to avoid the pollution associated with death, and a new one built. Changes of ruler and palace also reflected the twists and turns of clan rivalries within the court. As the Japanese began to build an imperial regime and adopt Chinese administration, the central bureaucracy grew rapidly and the need was felt for less peripatetic and more spacious capitals with a great palace surrounded by government buildings. The first of these, Fujiwara-kyō (*kyō* means "capital"), was a substantial capital on the grid-shaped model of Chang'an which served three emperors between 694 and 710 when it was abandoned.

In 708 Empress Gemmyō decided to move her capital from the city of Fujiwara to a new site known as Heijō-kyō (to the west of the modern city of Nara). Heijō was much larger than Fujiwara, measuring some 4·5 kilometers east–west by 4 kilometers north–south. Occupied in 710, Heijō was built as a smaller version of Chang'an with the imperial palace to the north and administrative offices, residences of the new nobility, temples and markets to the south. At its peak in the mid-8th century it is thought by some scholars to have had a population of 200 000. Heijō remained the capital until 784 when the site was again abandoned. This stable 70-year period is known as the Nara period.

During the 8th century the extension and

Below The imperial palace compound was to the north of the city. The residences of nobles and commoners, temples, shrines and markets were further south. The city was cut by two main thoroughfares, one running north–south to the palace, the other east–west just in front of the palace.

Heijō

The building of a new capital at Heijō commenced in 710. Within a decade an elegant grid-shaped Chinese-style city was taking shape. The city measured 4·5 by 4 kilometers. It was planned on a scale of 36 by 32 *chō*, each *chō* measuring 120 meters. Internally the city was divided into nine blocks, known as *jō*, running north–south and eight blocks, known as *bō*, running east–west. Each block was further subdivided to provide space for the homes of nobles and commoners.

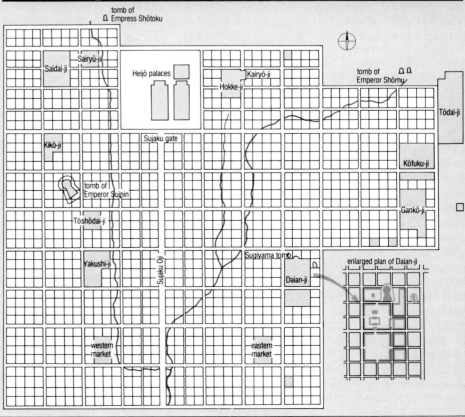

Right To help enforce the new
land, tax and conscription
systems introduced under the
Ritsuryō codes from the late 7th
century, provincial officials were
ordered to compile detailed
household census and tax
registers at six-yearly intervals.
The seals on this one read:
"Buzen Province Seal."

consolidation of the *ritsuryō* system on the basis of
the Taihō code and its emendations continued. The
administration and organization of the country
were modeled more closely on those of Tang
China. The whole country was divided administratively into provinces, districts and villages. The
landscape in many of the central provinces was
transformed as rice fields were reshaped into the
characteristic grid patterns that lent themselves to
easy subdivision and reallocation. The former cultivators now worked public lands as commoners
who bore the burden of taxation to the state. They
were organized into village units, mutually responsible for each other's behavior. Taxes were to be
collected in kind, in the form of rice, textiles and
other local products, and labor service. The state
also enforced compulsory military service on the
male population. Although the threat of foreign
invasion had receded, these centuries witnessed
the expansion of central government authority into
southern Kyushu and northern Japan (see map
p. 73) and there was a demand for conscript
soldiers.

The old clan aristocracy remained on the land in
their localities but derived their authority and
income as district officials of the central government. Court nobles were sent out to the provinces
as governors to oversee local administration and
the enforcement of census and annual taxes. The
members of the swelling court nobility who staffed
the central bureaucracy with its departments,
ministries and council of state were drawn from the
more influential clans in the Yamato region and
awarded extensive rights to income from the state
treasury and the public domain. This court aristocracy quickly became hereditary. Unlike China,
Japan did not resort to an examination system to
choose its bureaucratic leaders. Birth and personal
recommendation rather than merit or performance
in office remained the criteria for appointment and
promotion. Buddhist temples were established in
the new capital and enjoyed the protection and
patronage of the state. They, like the nobility, were
granted extensive public lands and tax
concessions.

At the apex of the new Chinese-style bureaucracy was the imperial office (*tennō*) that drew
heavily on the Chinese imperial model while
retaining very distinctive Japanese characteristics.
Chinese concepts were borrowed to strengthen the
throne, not to circumscribe it. As a "son of
heaven" or heavenly sovereign (*tennō*) the
Japanese ruler, like the Chinese emperor, enjoyed a
divine mandate. Unlike his Chinese counterpart's,
however, the Japanese emperor's mandate was
inviolable and irrevocable. There was no acceptance of the Chinese notion of a transferable mandate. It was recognized by all contenders for power
in Japan that the mandate had been entrusted for
all time to the imperial house by virtue not of the
military prowess or political sagacity of the *tennō*,
but by its divine descent from the Sun Goddess.

The emperors Tenji and Temmu in the 7th
century and Shōmu and Kammu in the 8th can be
described as active rulers who made and carried
through political decisions. But power and leadership were not essential for the imperial office.
Weak emperors, child emperors and empresses, if
accepted as belonging to the sacred lineage, could

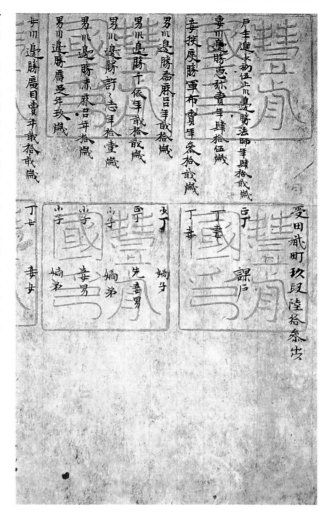

perform the priestly rituals that were the root of
Japanese imperial power. While the Japanese
imperial office was heightened with Chinese
notions of imperial rule and Buddhist notions of
the cosmic ruler who brings prosperity to his state
by protecting the three treasures of Buddhism, at
bottom it continued to rely heavily on sanctions
derived from the native cult of the *kami*. Moreover, at the heart of the new Chinese-style bureaucratic system a place was found for a Department of
Rituals responsible for the ceremonial functions
performed for the native *kami*. Throughout
history, Japanese emperors have performed rituals,
including the important rites of spring planting
and autumn harvest, as part of their office.

Although the Japanese made a determined effort
to impose Chinese-style reforms on the country in
the 7th and 8th centuries, many areas of life either
remained untouched, being regarded as sacrosanct,
or quickly reverted to earlier patterns. Although a
land allotment system was established and worked
for some decades, it did not undercut the wealth or
status of aristocratic families or religious institutions. It tended rather to enhance them. Just as
the imperial line could not lose its claim on the
throne, aristocratic birth was protected by the
Japanese preference for a hereditary principle.
Government office at both central and local levels
was never fully bureaucratized or based on merit.
It continued to be monopolized by the well connected and well born.

Although life for the nobility in the capital was
luxurious and the worst of internecine clan rivalry
had been brought under control, Japanese society

The economy of Japan in the
Nara period was basically a
commodity economy in which
taxes in the form of rice, cloth or
other commodities were levied
on the peasants who worked the
public lands. Recently
discovered wooden tallies
(*mokkan*) record these
commodity flows in considerable
detail. To facilitate the payment
of taxes the government sought
to follow Chinese example and
use coins. Chinese coins of the
kind shown here were imported
between the 7th and 12th
centuries. From 708 the
government began to issue its
own coins, but they were soon
debased and fell out of use.

The Tōdaiji at Nara

The Tōdaiji, or Great Eastern Temple, was built between 745 and 752, at the direction of Emperor Shōmu (701–56, reigned 724–49), to house a giant bronze statue of the Buddha Vairocana. Shōmu was an ardent Buddhist who in 741 had ordered the building of state-sponsored monasteries and nunneries in every province. The Tōdaiji was to serve as the hub of this provincial system. Its great Buddha was intended to bring relief from plague and political strife and to symbolize the union of Buddhism with the state.

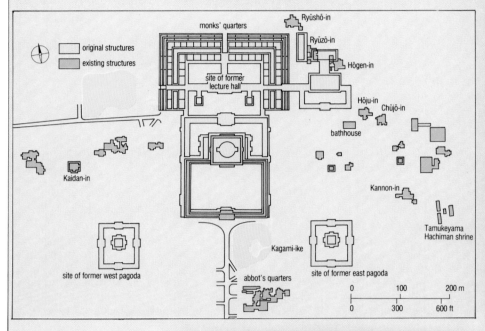

When originally built, Tōdaiji was an immense complex covering seven blocks of the capital. Pillaged and ravaged by fire over the centuries, little now survives of the early buildings.

Right This wooden statue of the aged and emaciated Pure Land monk Shunjōbō Chōgen (1121–1206), intoning the sacred title of Amida, is one of the finest examples of what has been called the "realistic" sculpture of the Kamakura period. In 1180 Tōdaiji was razed by the Taira general Shigehira for supporting the Minamoto cause. The court, with the backing of Minamoto Yoritomo, ordered Chōgen to supervise the fund raising and rebuilding. Under his devoted direction the great Buddha, main hall, central and southern gates and cloisters were all restored, largely in a new style derived from Song Chinese and Indian inspiration.

in the Nara period was not always at ease. Conscription and heavy taxation put pressure on the peasantry and forced many to abscond. As Wayne Farris has shown in a recent study, plagues, including smallpox, were common and periodically decimated the population in the 8th and 9th centuries. Within the capital the new nobility struggled for influence within the government and over the throne. The Fujiwara were already beginning to set aside other noble contenders for power, but they had not yet achieved anything like a complete hegemony by the end of the Nara period. Prelates from the Nara temples were also active in court politics and came to exert what many nobles regarded as a dangerous influence over impressionable sovereigns. The threat of clerical domination of the court was brought out most starkly in the Dōkyō affair. Dōkyō was a monk of the Hossō school of Buddhism who sought to advance his political fortunes through the infatuation of Empress Shōtoku. She housed him in the palace, awarded him offices of state, and the title of *hōō*, King of the Buddhist Law, which was reserved for abdicated emperors entering the priesthood. When it was hinted that Dōkyō had designs on the imperial throne itself, he was banished and died in exile. The removal of Dōkyō represented a political victory for aristocratic factions, especially the Fujiwara. The struggles among aristocrats and Buddhist clergy, however, eventually convinced Kammu and his closest advisers that it was time to think seriously about relocating the capital.

Literary arts

The surge of sinification also brought growing familiarity with Chinese legal and historical writing, poetry, and Confucian and Buddhist texts. The Nara period saw a flowering of literary culture by Japanese who had mastered the Chinese writing system. Although spoken Chinese and Japanese are linguistically poles apart, the Japanese found that they could either express the meaning of their thoughts in Chinese characters or use the characters, not for their meanings, but as a complex syllabary to express the various sounds of Japanese. Of the two earliest Japanese texts, the *Nihon shoki*, which purported to be a historical work, was written in Chinese. The myths recorded in the *Kojiki*, however, were presented in a mixed style that sometimes used Chinese characters for their meanings and sometimes only for their sounds.

This difference of usage is also evident in the earliest poetry collections. The *Kaifūsō*, an anthology from the mid-8th century, was written in Chinese. The *Manyōshū* (Collection of Ten Thousand Leaves) anthology used Chinese characters to represent the sounds of Japanese, giving poets more direct and spontaneous expression than they had in Chinese. The *Manyōshū* is regarded as the first powerful expression of the poetic sensibilities of the Japanese and the greatest anthology in the language. Although many longer poems (*chōka*) were included, it established the 31-syllable short-verse form, in lines of 5-7-5-7-7 syllables (*tanka*), as the prevailing form for Japanese poetry. Poems included in the anthology were written by people of many different stations in life including emperors and empresses, nobles, garrison soldiers, priests and young women. They speak of love and long-

ing, joy and desolation, an abiding love of the land of Yamato and veneration for local spirits (*kami*). Among the poets represented, the most powerful was Kakinomoto Hitomaro. This simple *tanka* expresses his sorrow at the prospect of his own death in the province of Iwami:

> Not knowing I am pillowed
> Among the crags of Kamo Mountain,
> My wife must still be waiting
>   for my return.

It is followed by two poems by his wife expressing her sorrow at the news of his death:

> Today, today!
> Each day I have waited for you,
> and now do they not say
> you are strewn with the shells
>   Of Ishi River?

> Never again to meet him
>   in the flesh—
> Rise, o clouds, and spread
> over Ishi River,
> That, gazing on you,
> I may remember him.

Buddhism in the Nara period

Buddhism took deeper root in the capital and the provinces during the Nara period as many new monasteries and nunneries were established under the patronage of the imperial family and the central and local nobility. The Hōryūji, originally established by Prince Shōtoku and later destroyed by fire, was rebuilt in 670. Several monasteries, including the Yakushiji, Daianji and Gankōji, that had existed at Fujiwara, were rebuilt on a grand scale in Heijō. Other great temples were added to make up the "seven great monasteries of Nara." The Kōfukuji, for instance, became the family temple of the Fujiwara and exercised control over the Fujiwara family shrine of Kasuga. In 745, with the country beset by natural disasters, Emperor Shōmu set in motion the building of an enormous universal Buddha and a massive building to house it. This monastery was known as Tōdaiji, the Great Eastern Temple. The Tōdaiji later became the hub of a network of provincial monasteries and nunneries offering prayers for the nation. Known as *kokubunji*, these were built in each province with contributions from the local nobility. When Shōmu was sick in 747, his daughter ordered the building of a western counterpart to the Tōdaiji, the Saidaiji, or Great Western Temple.

Although growing numbers of Japanese were committing themselves to the religious life, many of the great monasteries in the capital were still headed by Korean or Chinese monks. Among the Chinese monks who brought new Buddhist teachings to Japan was Ganjin (Jianzhen), a specialist in the precepts of monastic life (*vinaya*), who reached Japan in 753 after six frustrated attempts and the loss of his sight. Ganjin established the elegant Tōshōdaiji monastery which reminds us of the powerful influence of Tang dynasty Buddhism in Nara Japan while providing an impression of the Tang architectural style that must have been common in public buildings in Nara. The Tōshōdaiji venerates a sculpted portrait of Ganjin, one of the finest expressions of Japanese portrait sculpture.

Left This recent aerial view shows the central gate, cloisters and great Buddha Hall of Tōdaiji, the largest wooden building in the world. Rebuilt several times, the present hall dates mostly from 1709. It was reroofed in 1980.

Left The great Buddha Vairocana, filling the huge Buddha Hall of Tōdaiji, is the most famous of several giant Buddha images in Japan. It was twice badly damaged (in 1180 and 1567) and extensively repaired. The only original parts of the existing statue are fragments of the lotus-petal throne. Even so, the towering statue still conveys a sense of the devotion that inspired the building and rebuilding of Tōdaiji.

Above Tōdaiji contains other examples of sculpture that date from the 8th century. This fearsome visage with its flaming hair belongs to a clay guardian figure.

Japanese Buddhism took on new philosophical depth as more *sūtras* became available to the Japanese. Especially influential in the Nara period were the *Kegon-kyō*, or *Flower Garland Sūtra* (Sanskrit *Avatamsaka Sūtra*), and the *Sūtra of the Golden Light*. The *Flower Garland* was believed to expound the fullest undiluted teaching of the Buddha. It set the Buddha Vairocana, source of light, at the center of the Buddhist cosmos and emphasized the doctrine of Buddha nature that permeates all things in both the spiritual and physical realms in a fundamental all-pervasive harmony of interdependent causation. The *Sūtra of the Golden Light* taught the omnipresence of the Buddha, the all-embracing reach of his compassion, and the accessibility of Buddhahood to all sentient beings through the operation of the inner light of transcendent wisdom (*prajnā*). The *sūtra* ends with the wonderful parable of the compassionate Buddha giving himself to feed a hungry lion. In several chapters the *sūtra* dealt with the political relationship between Buddhism and the state, stressing the harmony of the Buddhist law and the imperial law and promising the protection of Buddhism to rulers who promoted the teachings of the Buddha and sponsored the development of the order (*samgha*). It also advocated a theory of kingship based upon karmic merit attained through the performance of good works and sponsorship of Buddhism in previous existences. This Buddhist notion of "divine" authority was used by Japanese rulers like Shōmu to enhance and reinforce the notion of a divine and unchallengeable mandate from the Sun Goddess.

A variety of teachings or schools were represented within Nara monasteries. The six major schools of Nara Buddhism—Hossō, Jōjitsu, Kegon, Kusha, Sanron and Ritsu—had all originated in India or China and were brought to Japan in the 7th and 8th centuries by returning Japanese monks or by Chinese masters. They should not be thought of as clearly defined sects but rather as currents of philosophical thought focusing on one or other of the *sūtras*. They were not necessarily exclusive. Several schools might be represented within a single monastery as monks espoused different teachers or texts. Although these teachings were important in laying the doctrinal basis for subsequent monastic Buddhism in Japan, they were too abstruse to be well understood by any but the most learned clerics in the major monastic centers. The Sanron ("Three Treatises") school, for instance, taught the Mahayana Mādhyamika philosophy of the middle path of dialectical eightfold negation leading to the recognition of truth as emptiness or void. The Hossō ("Dharma character" or Yogācāra) school taught the doctrine of *vijnāpitimātra*, that existence beyond thought is illusory and that enlightenment can be attained only through mind. The Kegon school was based on the *Avatamsaka (Flower Garland) Sūtra* which taught the sublime doctrine of the universe as an interdependent whole. Of the six, the Ritsu (or Vinaya) school, introduced by Ganjin in 753, was the most concrete with its emphasis on the detailed observance of the precepts for monastic life and the proper performance of the rituals of clerical ordination. The schools were extremely important in training Japanese monks in the intricacies of Budd-

hist textual tradition and philosophical thinking and in inculcating standards of clerical behavior and performance, but they made little direct impression on the lives of ordinary Japanese.

For elite patrons and ordinary people the main attractions of Buddhism remained its impressive art and architecture, its elaborate rituals, its promised exorcism of ghosts and evil spirits, its burial and memorial services, and its magical spells for temporal benefits (*gense riyaku*) in this world, which remained a powerful feature of Japanese Buddhism through the centuries. Many among the elite patronized Buddhism for its ritual and healing power. In return for their good works laypeople hoped for recovery from sickness, transfer of merit to some deceased person, or "protection of the nation." The *sūtras* were used less as guides to personal enlightenment than as formulas or spells for rain, for an emperor's recovery from sickness, for the birth of a male heir, or the alleviation of sickness and epidemic. The *Sūtra of the Golden Light*, for instance, contains a chapter devoted to the Buddha's healing powers. The Buddha of healing, Yakushi, was at the center of a popular cult and a splendid bronze image depicting the healing Buddha was the principal icon of the great monastery of Yakushiji in Heijō.

In Indian pre-Buddhist thought Ashuras were regarded as demonic evil forces, enemies of the heavenly gods. In Buddhism they were incorporated as powerful protectors of the Buddhist law. In the six realms of karmic transition the realm of the Ashuras was between the heavenly and human realms on the one hand and the realms of hells, hungry ghosts and beasts on the other. The four faces and many arms of this Ashura contribute to its protective functions. The statue, 1·5 meters high in dry lacquer, is a fine example of Tempyō period (729–48) art.

The building of Tōdaiji

The most obvious example of this kind of imperial patronage of Buddhism for the protection of the nation was the casting by Emperor Shōmu of the great Buddha of Tōdaiji. The enormous bronze statue 16 meters high represented Vairocana, cosmic Buddha of the sun and fitting counterpart of the imperial eminence in the earthly realm. Shōmu is said to have exhausted the country's supply of bronze and precious metals to build the statue and the lofty hall enclosing it. In an edict he urged the whole population to contribute "even a twig or a handful of dirt" if they had nothing else. Fund raisers were sent out to the provinces to harness the spiritual energies of the people. Thousands of monks came from all corners of Japan and Asia to join courtiers, foreign ambassadors and military officials at the eye-opening ceremony in 752. With his consort at his side Shōmu held cords attached to a giant brush with which an Indian monk, Bodhisena (704–60), standing high on a scaffold, painted in the irises of the statue, thus imbuing it with life. Entertainment was provided by court dancers and musicians performing the Chinese and Central Asian masked dances known as *gagaku*. During the ceremonies Shōmu declared himself to be a "servant of the three treasures," thus taking Japan as far as it was ever to go in the recognition of a Buddhist sanction for imperial authority.

The great Buddha and the Buddha Hall of Tōdaiji have been razed and rebuilt several times. Little now survives of the originals, but the monastery is still a vast repository of Buddhist art and ritual objects, having at least 140 designated national treasures and hundreds of important cultural properties. Of the many seasonal rituals that were performed there, some have been carried on for centuries. Among the best-known is the new-year water-drawing ritual (*omizutori*), held in the Nigatsu-dō at the beginning of the new year by the old lunar calendar. The festival, in which freshly drawn water from a well is offered before an image of an 11-headed Kannon, is conducted in bitter cold at 1.30 in the morning by the light of blazing cypress brands. Combining Shinto with Buddhist features, it is the culmination of a rigorous month-long purification ritual performed by monks for their own spiritual salvation, the welfare of the nation, the imperial family and all sentient beings.

The Tōdaiji, in keeping with Vairocana's central role in the Buddhist cosmos, became the chief temple in the land and the center of a provincial network of monasteries and nunneries (*kokubunji*). In 741 Shōmu ordered that a Buddhist monastery and nunnery incorporating a seven-storied pagoda should be built in every province. Each province was also to have ten copies of the *Lotus Sūtra* (*Hoke-kyō*) and the *Sūtra of the Golden Radiant Victorious Kings* (*Konkōmyō-saishō-ō-kyō*). Monks and nuns were to chant these and other *sūtras* continuously for the intentions of the emperor and the welfare of the state. Tōdaiji was designated the apex of this system and the monastery in which the monks of the *kokubunji* were trained. The head nunnery was the Hokkeji.

As the dedication ceremony at the completion of the great Buddha indicates, 8th-century Japan was a participant in the cosmopolitan culture of Asia and the easternmost terminus of the silk road. Precious objects, including musical instruments, glass vessels, gold ritual objects, fabrics, mirrors, screens and objects in mother-of-pearl from all over Asia were presented to Shōmu's court. At his death they were installed by his widow in a specially built repository, the Shōsōin. Built of roughly hewn cypress logs in a simple, pre-Buddhist style, the Shōsōin was designed to be airtight in the humid summer months and to allow adequate ventilation in the dry months. It housed a priceless collection of treasures from the silk road.

The Nara government did not actively encourage the diffusion of Buddhism among the common people. Copies of invocations from the *Sūtra of the Golden Light* were dispensed to the provinces, but probably only to the homes of powerful local families. Shōmu also proclaimed that each household should have a Buddhist altar. Again it is likely that only the provincial elite were in a position to comply. There was some concern that popular preachers would contribute to political instability by using magical spells to attract a mass following. The government, not always successfully, sought to restrict private ordinations and to regulate closely the lives of monks and nuns. One such itinerant holy man was the priest Gyōki (668–749). Gyōki was instrumental in raising funds for the building of Tōdaiji and rose to become senior prelate (*daisōjō*), but he devoted much of his life to charitable works among the people such as the building of irrigation systems, ponds and simple medical facilities. For his efforts he was venerated as a living Bodhisattva. If the common people were beginning to grasp the teachings of Buddhism, it was through contact with mendicants like Gyōki, or through their sense of involvement on however small a scale with a great project like the building of Tōdaiji, or through the gradual diffusion of such simple notions of karmic retribution as that good actions quickly contribute to benefits and that evil actions bring unfortunate consequences. These popular notions of *karma* were reflected in the *Nihon ryōiki*, a selection of Buddhist cautionary tales compiled by the monk Kyōkai in the early 9th century. In this work we see again a Japanese tendency to telescope Indian notions of limitless kalpic time into a system of immediate rewards and punishments.

In 784 the court, under the rule of Emperor Kammu, again moved the capital, this time from Heijō north to Nagaoka, and then, when that proved inauspicious, to a site known as Heian. Taboos associated with pollution may have been among the reasons for the move. But it has also been suggested that it was an attempt by the emperor and court nobles to sidestep the growing influence of Buddhist clerics over court life. That influence had reached crisis proportions in the infatuation of Empress Shōtoku and her lover, the priest Dōkyō (see above, p. 65). Dōkyō was banished, but the fear of undue clerical influence lingered. The court's move to a new capital effectively reduced the influence of the great Nara temples which were forbidden to follow or set up branches in the new capital. At the same time, the Dōkyō affair made it very difficult for empresses to take the imperial throne and only two reigned in their own right in subsequent centuries.

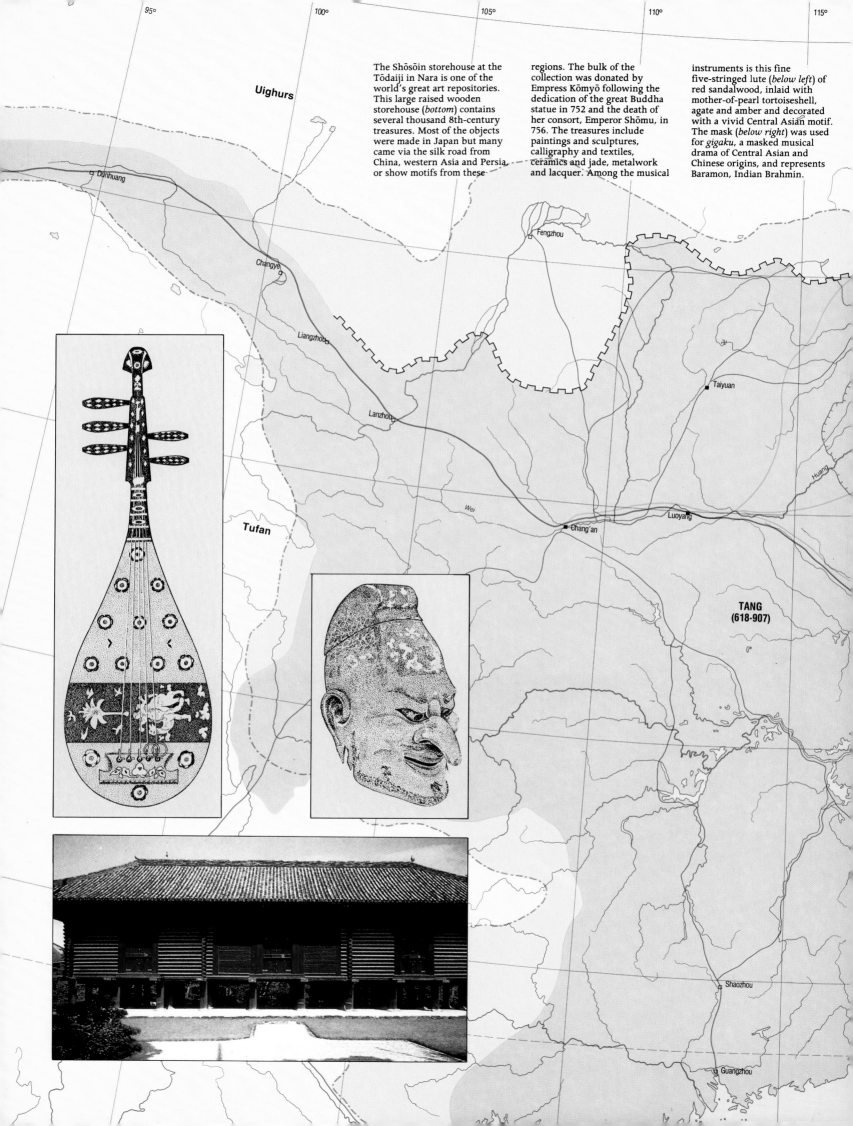

The Shōsōin storehouse at the Tōdaiji in Nara is one of the world's great art repositories. This large raised wooden storehouse (*bottom*) contains several thousand 8th-century treasures. Most of the objects were made in Japan but many came via the silk road from China, western Asia and Persia, or show motifs from these regions. The bulk of the collection was donated by Empress Kōmyō following the dedication of the great Buddha statue in 752 and the death of her consort, Emperor Shōmu, in 756. The treasures include paintings and sculptures, calligraphy and textiles, ceramics and jade, metalwork and lacquer. Among the musical instruments is this fine five-stringed lute (*below left*) of red sandalwood, inlaid with mother-of-pearl tortoiseshell, agate and amber and decorated with a vivid Central Asian motif. The mask (*below right*) was used for *gigaku*, a masked musical drama of Central Asian and Chinese origins, and represents Baramon, Indian Brahmin.

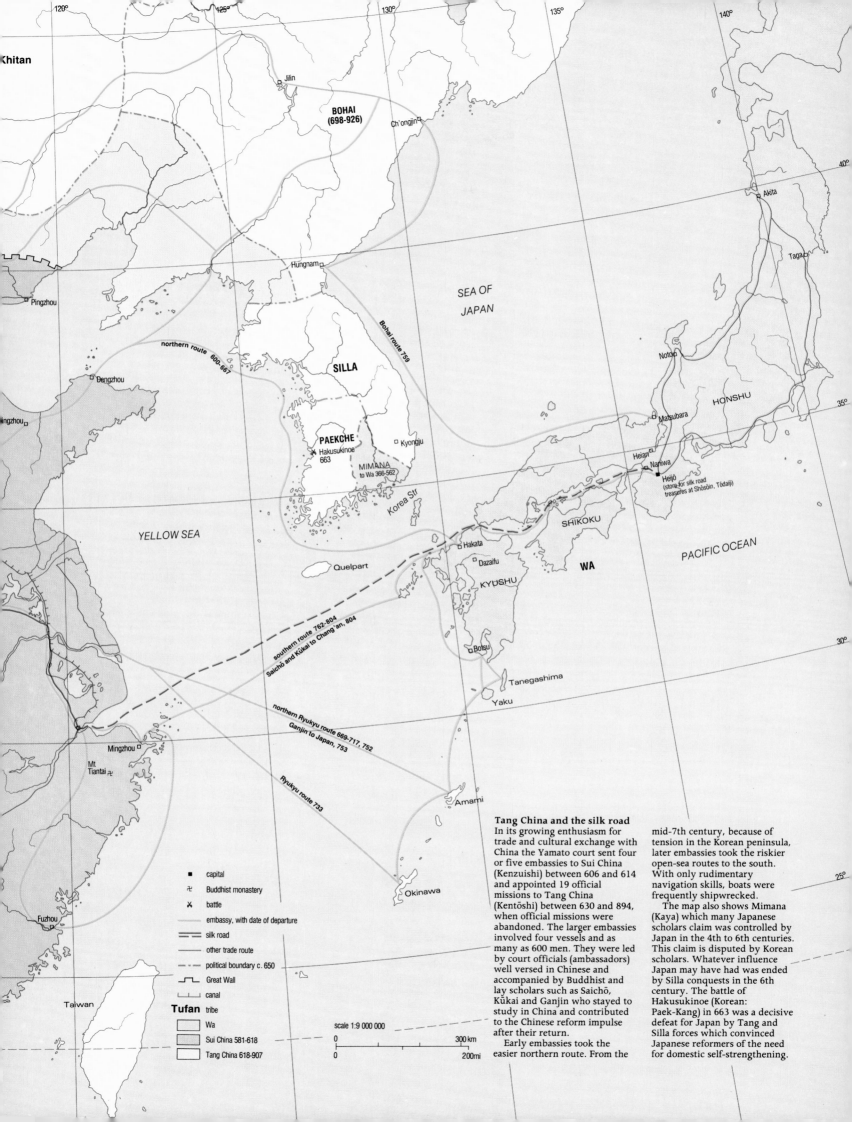

Khitan

Jilin

BOHAI
(698-926)

Ch'ongjin

SEA OF
JAPAN

Akita

Taga

Pingzhou

Hungnam

Bohai route 759

Notoo

HONSHU

northern route 600-667

Dengzhou

SILLA

Matsubara

Mingzhou

PAEKCHE

Heian

× Hakusukinoe
663

Kyongju

Naniwa

Heijō
(store for silk road
treasures at Shōsōin, Tōdaiji)

MIMANA
to Wa 366-562

Korea Str

YELLOW SEA

Quelpart

SHIKOKU

PACIFIC OCEAN

Hakata

Dazaifu

WA

KYUSHU

southern route 762-804
Saichō and Kūkai to Chang'an, 804

Botsu

Tanegashima

northern Ryukyu route 669-717, 752
Ganjin to Japan, 753

Yaku

Mingzhou

Ryukyu route 733

Amami

Mt
Tiantai 卍

Fuzhou

Okinawa

Tang China and the silk road

In its growing enthusiasm for trade and cultural exchange with China the Yamato court sent four or five embassies to Sui China (Kenzuishi) between 606 and 614 and appointed 19 official missions to Tang China (Kentōshi) between 630 and 894, when official missions were abandoned. The larger embassies involved four vessels and as many as 600 men. They were led by court officials (ambassadors) well versed in Chinese and accompanied by Buddhist and lay scholars such as Saichō, Kūkai and Ganjin who stayed to study in China and contributed to the Chinese reform impulse after their return.

Early embassies took the easier northern route. From the mid-7th century, because of tension in the Korean peninsula, later embassies took the riskier open-sea routes to the south. With only rudimentary navigation skills, boats were frequently shipwrecked.

The map also shows Mimana (Kaya) which many Japanese scholars claim was controlled by Japan in the 4th to 6th centuries. This claim is disputed by Korean scholars. Whatever influence Japan may have had was ended by Silla conquests in the 6th century. The battle of Hakusukinoe (Korean: Paek-Kang) in 663 was a decisive defeat for Japan by Tang and Silla forces which convinced Japanese reformers of the need for domestic self-strengthening.

- ■ capital
- 卍 Buddhist monastery
- × battle
- —— embassy, with date of departure
- ▬▬ silk road
- —— other trade route
- —·—·— political boundary c. 650
- ⊏⊐⊔ Great Wall
- ⊔⊔ canal

Tufan tribe

Wa

Sui China 581-618

Tang China 618-907

scale 1:9 000 000

0   300 km

0   200 mi

Taiwan

THE COURTLY AGE OF HEIAN

The Heian period

In 784 Emperor Kammu (737–806) decided to move the imperial capital from Heijō. He instructed Fujiwara no Tanetsugu, his supervisor of construction, to locate a suitable site. Tanetsugu chose Nagaoka to the north of Heijō and work began. From the start the project was bedeviled by political intrigue and factional rivalries. Tanetsugu was assassinated by rival courtiers and the site beset by natural disasters. Taking these events as omens, Kammu abandoned the half-completed project and ordered that a new site be found. A site to the north between the Katsura and Kamo rivers was selected and planning and construction began anew. The new capital was called Heian-kyō, "capital of peace and tranquility." Heian-kyō, later known as Kyoto, was to remain the capital of Japan until the Meiji restoration of 1868 when the young Meiji emperor moved his court eastward to Tokyo to head a new government.

The four centuries between the transfer to the new capital at Heian-kyō in 794 and the consolidation of warrior rule in Kamakura in 1185 by Minamoto no Yoritomo are known as the Heian period. This long period, which seems stable and tranquil when viewed from the point of view of the imperial court, saw considerable domestic change. The early Heian period witnessed the active assimilation of the Chinese administrative and cultural model and the refurbishing of the centralized Chinese-style institutions introduced under the Nara period *ritsuryō* codes. From the 10th century, however, political and economic changes in the court and the provinces undermined the original bureaucratic intent of the *ritsuryō* system and contributed to privatization and a resurgence of clan influence both within the court and throughout the provinces. At the same time, the court stopped sending official embassies to China. During the 11th and 12th centuries violence became more frequent in the provinces and even in the capital itself. Leisured aristocratic life continued in the capital, but the nobility were dependent on warrior chieftains to enforce the edicts of the court and maintain order in the provinces. It was not long before some of these warrior chieftains entertained designs on political power themselves.

The mid-Heian period, around the year 1000, saw the flowering of a distinctively Japanese aristocratic culture centering on the court. Heian was the apogee of aristocratic court culture in Japan and an age of great creativity in literature, religion and the arts. The *Tale of Genji* (*Genji monogatari*) and the *Kokinshū* anthology of Japanese poetry are only two of the superb literary creations of the age. The Heian age also set styles in aristocratic residential architecture and garden design, in scroll painting and Buddhist sculpture. Tendai, Shingon and Pure Land Buddhism flourished. Chinese literary arts and Confucianism remained

influential, but the Japanese language also found easier vernacular expression in prose and verse through the development of *kana* syllabaries (see below, p. 79).

The new capital: Heian-kyō

Emperor Kammu's decision to establish a new capital did not imply an abandonment of the ideals of a centralized system of administration that had been established in the Nara period. He no doubt hoped for a fresh political start in a new environment through liberation from the succession disputes, clan rivalries and clerical interference that had beset the court at Heijō.

Like the Fujiwara and Heijō capitals, the new Heian capital was modeled on Chang'an (modern Xi'an/Sian). Unlike Chang'an and other Chinese cities, however, ancient Japanese capitals were not protected by walls. Heian-kyō was set on a broad plain surrounded to north, east and west by low mountains. The northeast and northwest corners of the capital were protected by the two peaks of Hieizan and Atogayama. Heian enjoyed a better water supply than Heijō. The Kamo, Katsura and Shirakawa rivers flowed down from the hills around the city and into the Yodo River which linked the capital with the port of Naniwa and the sea. The new capital was grander in conception than Heijō, measuring 4·5 kilometers east–west by 5·2 kilometers north–south. At first only part of the planned site was occupied. It gradually expanded eastward across the Kamo River.

As in Chang'an and Heijō, the great palace enclosure and seat of government (*daidairi*) was constructed to the north of the city. The grand official buildings were resplendent with red pillars and green roof tiles in the Chinese style. In contrast, the imperial residence within the residential compound (*dairi*) was a simple structure built of unpainted wood and roofed with cedar bark. The city was constructed on a grid pattern of avenues and streets making up some 1200 uniform residential blocks. A central avenue, the Suzakuōji, divided it into left and right sectors, *ukyō* and *sakyō*. The residences of the aristocracy were situated close to the *daidairi* to the northeast of the city around the first three cross streets. The only Buddhist monasteries originally allowed within the city were the state-sponsored eastern and western temples, Tōji and Saiji. State-sponsored markets were also established in the eastern and western sectors.

Like Heijō, Heian was primarily an administrative capital, the political, social and cultural center of the country. Apart from the court nobles its inhabitants included petty officials, artisans, storekeepers, military guards and a few monks. The total population of the capital in the 9th century was perhaps 100 000, of whom 10 000 or so were nobles and lesser officials. The commoner population gradually swelled to satisfy the consumer

Although Kyoto has been ravaged by warfare, earthquakes, fire and floods over the centuries and little now remains from the earliest days of its existence, it has always been rebuilt in the characteristic grid-shaped pattern. The present palace was rebuilt after a fire in 1855 on a more easterly site. It was modeled on buildings erected in 1790 after earlier styles. This aerial view of the palace area (*below*), seen from the north, gives an impression of the early form of the city in which a great central avenue, the Suzakuōji, led directly to the walled administrative enclosure (*daidairi*) with its palaces, ministries and offices. The inner imperial residence (*dairi*) was a walled compound to the northeast of the administrative enclosure. Two major restored buildings in this compound are the sovereign's private residence (*seiryōden*) and the Great Ceremonial Hall (*shishinden*), shown here (*right*).

Heian

In an effort to revitalize the centralized *ritsuryō* administrative system and escape the influence of the great Nara monasteries, Emperor Kammu moved the seat of government from Heijō-kyō to Nagaoka-kyō in 784 and then in 794 to Heian-kyō, literally the capital of peace and tranquillity. Heian, or Kyoto as it was increasingly called from the 11th century, remained the capital of Japan until the emperor moved his court to Tokyo in 1868. The only break in this long span was a period of six months in 1180 when Taira no Kiyomori moved the capital to Fukuhara-kyō in Settsu Province. Heian became a center of courtly culture, the site of Buddhist temples and Shinto shrines, and a vigorous merchant and artisan community.

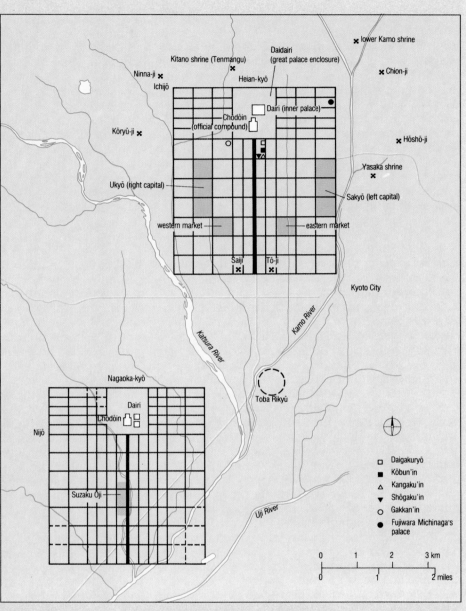

Above The plan shows the layout of Heian as originally envisaged. Around the great palace enclosure and inner palace to the north, the city was divided into regular blocks (*bō*), each further subdivided into 16 *chō* (1450 square meters each), cut by avenues running north–south and streets running east–west. Heian-kyō was bisected by the broad avenue Suzakuōji (85 meters wide) into eastern (Sakyō) and western (Ukyō) districts. Kammu restricted the number of temples in the capital to eastern and western temples, of which the eastern temple, Tōji, developed as a major center of Shingon Buddhism.

Left The emperor's private chambers in the inner palace contained a raised dais surrounded by decorated screens. Lacquer washing and toilet utensils are part of the furnishings.

needs of the aristocracy. Horses were used to carry taxes and other goods to government storehouses and the residences of the nobility. Stalls and stores began to appear in competition with the government-sponsored markets. As shrines, temples and palaces were built and rebuilt, artists and craftsmen set up studios and workshops. Commoners built shacks along the banks of the Kamo River below the fourth cross street as the city straggled eastward. With the breakdown of civil order after the 10th century the city suffered crime, arson and pillage. Unruly soldier-monks (sōhei) from Enryakuji or the Nara monasteries frequently threatened the court unless their demands were met. Footloose warriors and thugs roamed the streets. Robberies were committed in broad daylight. The walled residences of the aristocracy were not immune and they were often pillaged or burned. There were frequent fires in the emperor's quarters in the dairi and the palace buildings. The Great Audience Hall, symbol of imperial prestige, was not rebuilt after a third major fire in 1156.

Although the old temples had been forbidden to relocate, Buddhism was not entirely excluded from Heian. Kammu was not hostile to Buddhism. He merely wished to assert unchallenged imperial control over the capital and the Buddhist clerics living there. In fact he was an active sponsor of Buddhism. He patronized a number of monks, including Saichō (767–822) and Kūkai (774–835), both of whom he sent to China to bring back new teachings and texts. They brought back the teachings that were to develop as Tendai and Shingon Buddhism. Saichō established his monastery of Enryakuji on Mount Hiei to the northeast of the city. It was to become one of the most influential monastic centers in Japan and the womb of much of subsequent Japanese Buddhism. Kūkai established a mountain monastery, Kōyasan, far to the south of the capital but was also granted the headship of Tōji in the south of the city itself. Kammu was thus able to shake off the worst of the influence of the old Nara temples and promote a newer Buddhist institution more in accord with his notions of the proper place of Buddhism in society. It is hardly surprising that both Saichō and Kūkai should have stressed the renewal of monastic discipline and the training of monks who would be of service to the nation as spiritual leaders. In time other Buddhist temples sponsored by members of the imperial family and the nobility were built in the hills around the city.

Kammu was an active emperor. He introduced changes to recover the flagging ideals of the Taika reforms. He enforced closer inspection of government officials, set up new agencies, outside the ritsuryō codes, to advise the throne, and established an imperial police force. He used a new militia system to press forward the subjugation of the Ezo tribes in the northeast. Kammu's attempt at reinvigoration of the ritsuryō system was carried on, but less energetically, by his successor Saga. These were, however, among the last active tennō. The remainder of the Heian period is characterized less by imperial assertion than by the spreading domination of the court by the nobility, especially members of the northern branch of the Fujiwara family. Emperors continued to function as the titular heads of government, symbols of legitima-

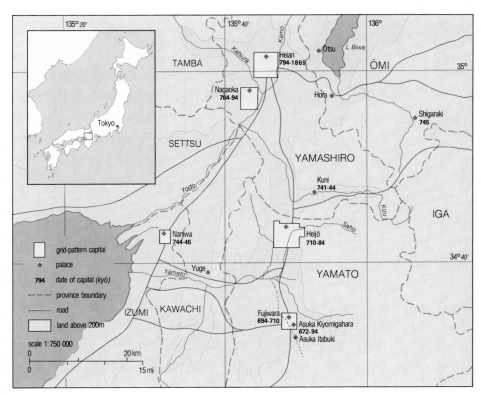

tion and objects of veneration by virtue of their divine descent. But actual power was increasingly exercised by Fujiwara leaders in their roles as regents or maternal grandfathers, uncles or fathers-in-law. This represented the privatization of political power and a reversion to clan or lineage politics within an ostensibly official and bureaucratic system of rule. In this process of privatization, the formal machinery of government, although maintained in its entirety, was increasingly bypassed by clan chieftains, even by members of the imperial family, and by the great temples and shrines.

Fujiwara domination of the imperial court was so pervasive that the period from 858 to 1185 is commonly described as the Fujiwara age. Like the reigning emperor himself, the central bureaucracy established by the reforms became more and more ceremonial. It remained only as a convenient source of honors and an organ to legitimize the emerging centers of power. Emperors continued to reign but it was the Fujiwara who ruled. Indirect rule of this kind became one of the ongoing characteristics of Japanese political behavior. As the Heian period progressed, there was increasing privatization in court politics, in provincial landholding and in local military organization.

The Fujiwara

The Fujiwara were influential from the beginning of imperial rule. The house was founded by Nakatomi no Kamatari, head of the Nakatomi clan of Shinto ritualists, who had helped Prince Naka no Ōe in the coup of 645 (see above, p. 61). Kamatari was given the name Fujiwara ("Wisteria Field") by Emperor Tenji in 669 in memory, it is said, of the spot where the plot to overthrow the Soga was hatched. Kamatari's son Fuhito (659–720) was active in the compilation of the Taihō code. He became Great Councillor and minister of the right. He was the father-in-law of two emperors, Mommu and Shōmu, and the grandfather of another. His

Above: movement of capitals from Asuka to Heian
Among the earliest centers of government were the palaces of ruling chieftains in the Asuka region. The small scale of government, frequent succession disputes and prevailing belief that a site was polluted by death or sickness led to frequent abandonment of palace sites. By the 7th century the idea of a more sedentary capital was taking root. These capitals became steadily more extensive cities built on the grid-shaped model of Chinese imperial cities, and tended to move northward toward Lake Biwa. The first Chinese-style capital city was Fujiwara-kyō used by Mommu between 694 and 710. Heijō (Nara), a larger city, served as capital between 710 and 784. During that period Emperor Shōmu moved the court briefly to palaces at Kuni, Naniwa and Shigaraki between 741 and 745. Heijō was abandoned by Emperor Kammu in 784. After an ill-omened attempt to build at Nagaoka, the site known as Heian was chosen. Construction began in 794 on the great city that was to remain the capital of Japan until 1868.

Right: conquest of the north
The imperial court in Heijō (710–84) and Heian (from 794) took several centuries to assert its control over the periphery of the country. In the north it met armed resistance from tribes known as the Ezo. Between the 7th and 10th centuries, the frontier was gradually pressed northeastward.

Above right Kasuga is the family shrine of the Fujiwara where their four principal tutelary kami are venerated. Originally built at the foot of Mount Mikasa, Kasuga was moved closer to the capital in 769. Though famous, its iron lanterns are not particularly old.

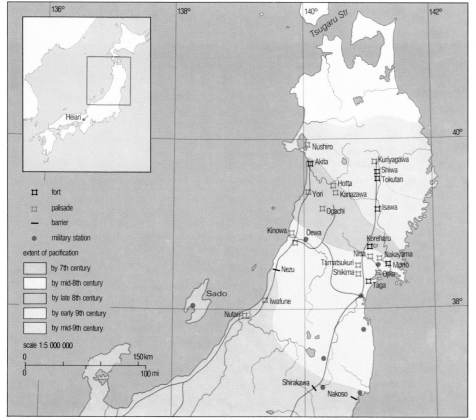

four sons headed the four branches of the Fujiwara house. The Fujiwara suffered a temporary setback in the mid-Nara period when four of Fuhito's sons died in an epidemic in 737, but the family fortunes quickly recovered. In the late Nara period the Fujiwara pushed the Tachibana and other noble families aside and led the resistance to the priestly pretender Dōkyō. It was the northern branch of the family, descended from Fuhito's son Fusaaki (681–737), that came to the forefront of politics in the Heian period.

The Fujiwara excercised and extended their power in a variety of ways. In the process they proved themselves masters of all aspects of the game of courtly politics. Isolating and excluding rivals, they were not above plotting incidents which they blamed on others. They were adept and patient in marriage politics, intertwining themselves inexorably with the imperial line through the birth of imperial princes and heirs apparent. They added to their private wealth and power by accumulating holdings in private estates (*shōen*), and then used this wealth to bestow largesse on lesser families.

But the key to long-term Fujiwara success was the maximization of the powers of regency to institutionalize their power. They monopolized advisory offices to the throne, offices that had not been provided for by the *ritsuryō* system. The two key offices were *sesshō*, regent for a minor, and *kampaku*, regent for an adult emperor. By persuading emperors to retire early and then installing themselves as regents for their child successors, the Fujiwara found a way of controlling the throne without actually taking it. They were able to build up a semipermanent regency that ruled in the name of the *tennō*.

Control over the regency was consolidated from 858 when Fujiwara no Yoshifusa (804–72), the Great Mininster of State, placed his own nine-year-old grandson on the throne as Emperor Seiwa (850–80) and took the office of *sesshō*. This was the first time that someone not of the imperial blood had held the office of regent. Mototsune (836–91) was the first Fujiwara to continue as regent after the maturity of an emperor, taking the title of *kampaku*. This practice allowed the same Fujiwara nobleman to continue as effective spokesman and director of policy throughout the lifetime of a reigning emperor. Fujiwara no Tadahiro (880–949) was *sesshō* for Emperor Suzaku from 939 to 941 and *kampaku* from 941 to 949.

Some emperors who did not have Fujiwara mothers or who for some reason did not have a regent looking over their shoulders tried to reassert imperial leadership. Emperors Uda (867–931), Daigo (885–930) and Murakami (926–67) all sought to rule without Fujiwara regents. They turned to other rival noble families, and branches of the Fujiwara, to resist or counter Fujiwara influence. One course was to try to promote talented non-Fujiwara courtiers to positions of leadership within the court. A prime, and fatal, example of this was Sugawara no Michizane (843–903), a statesman, poet, scholar and calligrapher. Although admired for his poetry and statesmanship, and patronized by Emperors Uda and Daigo, Michizane was no match politically for the Fujiwara. He was outmaneuvered by Fujiwara Tokihira (871–909) and forced into exile in Dazaifu, Kyushu, where sickness and grief soon brought his death. His revengeful ghost was believed to have afflicted the capital with fire, storm and plague. To appease the angry spirit he was returned to favor, promoted posthumously, apotheosized into the patron *kami* of letters, and had a shrine erected in his honor at Kitano in Kyoto.

The Fujiwara reestablished regency control in 967 and held on to it. The period until 1068 is known as the period of regency (*sesshō* and *kampaku*) politics, emphasizing Fujiwara control. The emperors of this period were all born of Fujiwara mothers and controlled by their uncles, fathers-in-law or grandfathers in whose households they were raised. The Fujiwara reached the apogee of glory with Fujiwara no Michinaga (966–1028). More glorious and powerful than the emperors, Michinaga dominated the imperial court for more than 30 years. He acquired great landholdings, and built fine palaces for himself and his family. He was father of four empresses, uncle of two emperors and grandfather of three more. In 1016 he became *sesshō* for his nephew Go-Ichijō. Although he never formally assumed the post of *kampaku*, Michinaga exercised all its powers and maintained tight control over the throne and the court. In 1017 he was appointed Grand Minister of State and showered largesse on allies and rivals. Having set up his sons as regents and ministers of state, he retired from active political life in 1019, took the tonsure and established the Buddhist monastery of Hōjōji. He came to be known as the Midō Kampaku because he had in effect exercised the powers of *kampaku*. To secure military backing he allied himself with the Seiwa Genji clan of provincial warriors. In retirement he exercised power through his son Yorimichi (990–1074), whom he installed as regent. Like most Heian officials Michinaga was expert in music, poetry, Buddhist studies, Chinese literature and history. His diary, the *Midō kampaku-ki,* is a valuable source of information about court life. He inspired the *Eiga monogatari* (*Tales of Glory*) and is said to have been a model for Prince Genji, the hero of the *Tale of Genji*. It is this phase in which Michinaga was at his zenith around the year 1000 that is frequently thought of as the epitome of Heian court life and culture.

After Michinaga, Fujiwara influence at court and in the provinces declined. He was succeeded by his sons, Yorimichi, who was both *sesshō* and *kampaku*, and Norimichi (997–1075), who became *kampaku*. But neither was as splendid or forceful as Michinaga. In the provinces Fujiwara power was undercut by warrior bands, to whose leaders provincial families commended lands that they would formerly have commended to the Fujiwara. In the capital there was a more serious reaction against Fujiwara dominance. Several emperors who did not have Fujiwara mothers found a device for countering Fujiwara control: they abdicated, but continued to exercise power by controlling their young sons whom they installed on the throne. This was a policy of paternal politics in contrast to the politics of maternal relatives employed by the Fujiwara. This system of rule has come to be called *insei*, or cloister government. Cloistered Emperors Shirakawa (1053–1129), Toba (1103–56) and Go-Shirakawa (1127–92) were all long-lived, active rulers who challenged the Fujiwara for control of the court. Under their leadership the imperial house became a contender for political and economic power alongside other competing power groups. Cloistered emperors tried to build up a household goverment on the model of the Fujiwara chancellery or *mandokoro*. Like the Fujiwara they solicited commendation of landholdings. By these means they were partially successful in reviving the influence of the imperial house, if not of the *tennō* office itself. However, *insei* was considered by later emperors and historians as much of an aberration or reversion to indirect rule as Fujiwara dominance had been. In the mid-12th century the political competition within the court was further intensified by the intrusion of the Taira warrior family, led by Taira no Kiyomori. This intrusion, which will be considered in more detail below (see p. 98), was the first significant step in the eclipse of the imperial court and the emergence of warrior rule in Japan.

Privatization of land: the proliferation of private estates

Fujiwara power represented a privatization within the official *ritsuryō* bureaucratic system established in the Nara period. Economically the power of the Fujiwara rested increasingly upon another form of privatization that was taking place within the

Distribution of private estates
The medieval land system is commonly described as a system of private estates (*shōen*) and public domain (*kokugaryō*). Public domain had existed from the Nara period when all lands throughout the provinces were subject to the fiscal and administrative authority of the imperial court. During the Heian period absentee proprietors – including nobles like the Fujiwara, temples and shrines like Tōdaiji, Enryakuji or Kasuga, and members of the imperial family – acquired collections of private rights (*shiki*) in reclaimed or commended holdings scattered throughout the provinces. These holdings, known as *shōen*, were gradually sealed off from the taxing power and administrative supervision of state officials. Thus by the 12th century most provinces in Japan had complex patterns of landholding in which public and private holdings were intermingled.

The map shows a small fraction of the 4000 or so *shōen* that came into existence between the 9th and 12th centuries. During the 13th century warriors began to compete for *shōen* titles and to intrude into *shōen*, leading to their eventual erosion.

In an agrarian premarket economy *shōen* provided their absentee proprietors with the basic commodities of daily life. The researches of Professor Amino Yoshihiko and other medievalists have shown that annual taxes (*nengu*) from *shōen* were not paid exclusively in rice. Although precise figures are unobtainable, many of the *shōen* in the northeastern provinces may at times have paid the bulk of their annual tax in silk, iron or other commodities.

ritsuryō system, namely the privatization of rights to land. Although the ideal of a "public" land system persisted throughout Heian, privatization quickly set in. From their inception the public land and tax systems had not functioned well because it had been necessary to compromise with the interests of powerful *uji* in order to gain their acceptance of the new land and tax systems. Even before the close of the Nara period privatized holdings, known as *shōen*, were beginning to develop in the provinces. Gradually Japanese practice began to drift away from Chinese ideals.

The land allotment system adopted from China in the Nara period was complex and burdensome. In order to allow reallotment of fields, they had to be reshaped into a regular grid pattern. This involved heavy labor and the transformation of the countryside in many parts of central Japan. Under the new land system fields and peasant cultivators were no longer to be considered as privately owned. They were to belong in principle to the central government. Farming land and the cultivators who worked it were treated as imperial (public) property. This bureaucratic Chinese ideal ran counter to deeply embedded clan interests and hereditary practices in Japan. Families viewed themselves as a continuum and sought to provide themselves with hereditary plots. The new system, with its periodic land surveys, censuses and reallotment of land to peasant families in accordance with the number of mouths in the family, stood in the way of plots being treated as family property. The full extent of the application of the "equal-field" (*jōri*) and allotment systems is open to question, but excavation has revealed fairly extensive remnants of equal-sized fields from Kyushu to the Kanto Plain. However, by the time the new land system was being applied in southern Kyushu in the late 8th century, it was already breaking down in other regions and *shōen* holdings were beginning to appear.

The origins of *shōen* can be traced from the very inception of the centralized state in the Nara period. Although the Japanese adopted a version of the "equal-field system," under which taxable rice paddy land was distributed to peasant cultivators and redistributed at death, certain lands were exempt. These included lands held by the imperial family and fields granted to court nobles in recognition of high rank or office or meritorious service to the state. Fields granted to the great Buddhist monasteries and Shinto shrines and agricultural lands "reclaimed" from the wild were also commonly exempted. Land assignments tended to become hereditary, especially those granted for meritorious service, high rank or religious purposes.

The practice of reclaiming land—that is converting it to irrigated rice fields—underlay the beginnings of privatized control over land. The pressure of population and the need to provide land for redistribution made it necessary constantly to

major *shōen* (private estate) 9th–12th centuries

◆ imperial family

◆ Fujiwara family

◆ Tōdaiji monastery

◆ other

‐ ‐ ‐ province boundary

commodity used for annual tax payment

▢ rice

▢ silk thread

▢ silk flax

▢ silk cloth

▢ iron

▢ other

bring more land into cultivation. The government seldom had funds for reclamation and government projects suffered from abuses, inefficiency and high costs. Only the prospect of unhampered ownership could persuade people to undertake costly reclamation projects. Land-hungry nobles and temples had the capital and labor to open new lands and their political influence allowed the activity to proceed despite its illegality. Land reclaimed by the government remained in the public domain, but from the early Nara period land reclaimed by private hands became the property of the reclaimer for set periods. In 724 reclaimed marshland was declared to be the property of the reclaimers for three generations; land reclaimed from unirrigated fields to paddy for one generation. An edict of 743 allowed privately reclaimed land to become the reclaimer's permanent property, not subject to reallotment. Rural population was frequently lured away from public lands. Competition to reclaim land ensued, and this increased the percentage of private lands and peasants who preferred to be tenants on private estates, which vied for their labor in reduced tax burdens, rather than to remain on public lands. The cumbersome reallotment system, starved for new land, fell into abeyance. The last recorded redistribtuion was in 844.

Shōen created by reclamation were soon surpassed in numbers by commended *shōen*. To secure protection and tax immunities, small landholders commended their lands to an absentee proprietor, a noble or temple in the capital. In return for paying annual tax the cultivator kept the right to cultivate his fields while assigning title to the noble or temple. If the new proprietor did not feel capable of fully protecting the land, he in turn might commend it to a high-ranking Fujiwara family member or imperial consort who would have a voice in court. To secure their good offices, he would in turn cede a right (*shiki*) in the land. These shared and divided *shiki* were essentially rights to a percentage of the income from land. *Shiki* were divisible, salable and heritable. An institution or individual, man or woman, might hold different kinds of *shiki* in the same estate, or a variety of *shiki* in many different estates, without ever visiting any of the estates in question. This system has been described as a "hierarchy of tenures." To protect their interests, monasteries and nobles sent out their own land stewards to establish an office on the estate, to map it and to collect taxes in rice, silk or some other commodity. These overseers also took a cut from the tax income.

In that *shōen* were privatized landholdings they had something in common with European manors. They differed, however, in that they were widely scattered and involved not full possession of the land but a proprietory interest in it. *Shōen* were very different from manor houses surrounded by their demesne. Structurally *shōen* involved four or five levels of cultivators of various kinds: local proprietors (*shōmin*), who had controlled the land prior to commendation, and estate officials (*shōkan*), who managed the estate for its absentee proprietor; the central proprietors (*ryōshu*) and the principal patrons (*honke*) above them lived in Nara or the capital.

The mere documentary recognition of a *shōen*

did not automatically remove it from tax-paying obligations to, or the supervision of, the public authorities. Proprietors, however, naturally wished to secure full immunity. The development of private landholdings alongside public lands within the provinces during the mid- and late Heian periods was accompanied by the acceptance of tax exemptions (*fuyu*) granted to influential aristocrats and temples. In time, their *shōen* were also granted immunity from entry or inspection by civilian officials (*funyū*) and thus were effectively sealed off from central government control.

Shōen proliferated in spite of occasional efforts to halt the process. Several emperors and cloistered emperors in the Heian period issued edicts stating that no new *shōen* titles should be recognized. These efforts were half-hearted and never consistently enforced. Those who issued decrees curtailing the diffusion of private holdings, especially the Fujiwara and cloistered emperors, were themselves competing for, and profiting from, the growth of *shōen*. The pace of *shōen* creation was moderate until the 11th century but quickened significantly in the 12th. John W. Hall has estimated that as late as 1086 rice lands in Bizen consisted of roughly 75 percent public domain and 25 percent private proprietorships. During the 12th century, however, the rate of *shōen* entitlement increased as cloistered emperors actively sought commendations. According to land registers (*Ōtabumi*) of the 13th century, the bulk of the land in many provinces was privatized in the form of *shōen*. With public office becoming hereditary, what had hitherto been public domain was also being treated very much like "public *shōen*."

Shōen represented a move in the direction of a closed or self-sufficient economic and cultural world. Instead of relying exclusively on the state treasury or on the public markets for commodities, nobles and temples relied heavily on their estates to provide them with the luxuries as well as the necessities of life. *Shōen* supplied temples and nobles with rice and silk, lumber and building materials, swords and horses, lacquer and wax, ink and brushes, fish and fowl, laborers and warriors. The elegant and leisured cultural life of the Heian nobility rested on a solid foundation of generous income from both public and private treasuries.

Heian period culture

The brilliant culture of the Heian period is generally viewed as the exclusive product of the imperial court. Certainly many of the most enduring products of Japanese culture were created during this period within the chambers and courts of the imperial palace or the residences of the Fujiwara. Moreover, such literary works as the *Tale of Genji* and the *Pillow Book* provide us with a clearer picture of court life and cultural activities than is available for any other period in early Japanese history. These literary riches tend to focus attention on the court. Revealing as this picture is, however, we should bear in mind that life went on beyond the confines of the capital. The mid- and late Heian periods saw the emergence of warriors. The shaping of early warrior culture can also be seen as a facet of the cultural life of this period. So too can the culture of Buddhist monasteries and cloisters. Unfortunately, the documentary record is

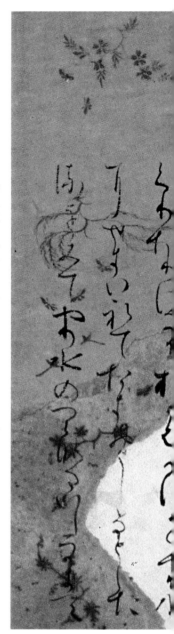

This page of calligraphy dating from the early 12th century contains poems by the poetess Ise (?877–?940) who was known for her passionate and witty verse and was counted among the 36 illustrious poets designated by Fujiwara Kintō. The Heian period saw the development of *kana* syllabaries and *kana* calligraphy. It also saw the refinement of superb papermaking techniques in which subtly colored papers were superimposed in daring collages and decorated with brushwork, powdered silver, mica or gold flakes. Here the vertical lines of the cursive calligraphy blend with the abstract pattern of the paper and with the decorative printed and painted embellishments in powdered metal.

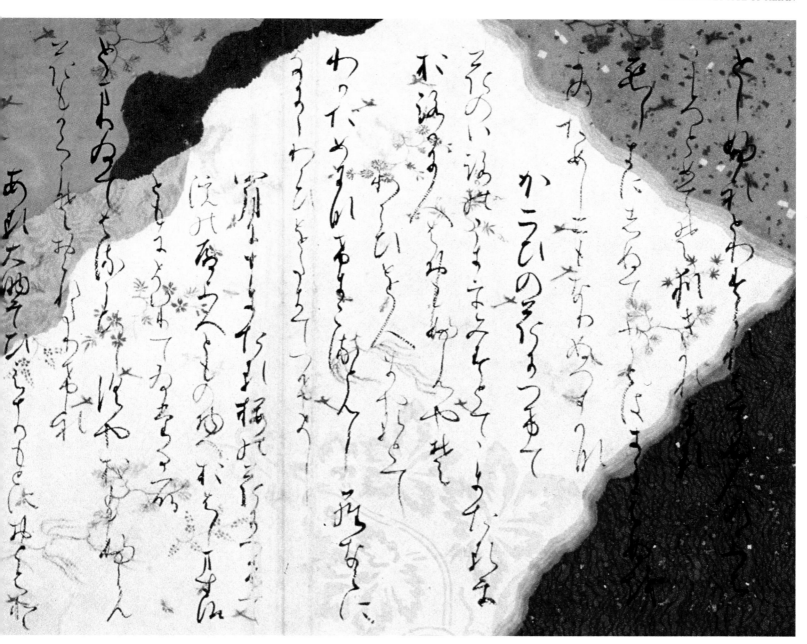

The *Lotus Sūtra* is one of the most enduring and eloquent statements of the Mahayana message of universal salvation. It has been venerated in Japan since the 6th century. Devotion to the Lotus teaching reached a peak in the late Heian and Kamakura periods. In this late 12th-century fan the text of part of the *Lotus Sūtra* is written over a scene from ordinary life in which court servants clean the veranda of a residence or temple. The combination of colored fan painting, decorative paper and the radiating calligraphy of the text creates an elegant blending of religious and secular themes.

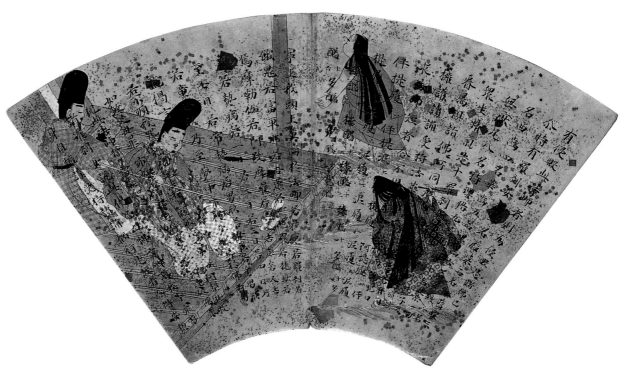

小大君

三源院東宮時芬蔵人左とき や

翩天皇孫三品敦明親王丗母貞得

古女一条院御文人

いそしくのあらさもも絶めつ

すること知られてこくこる秤

too fragmentary to allow us to say very much about the cultural lives or spiritual experiences of the commoners who cultivated the soil and made up the bulk of the population.

Aristocratic life and culture

The highest cultural standards were set by the small group of aristocrats who made up the courtly society of the palace enclosure and nearby aristocratic residences of Heian-kyō. This group of several hundred nobles, palace ladies and members of the imperial family comprised a highly refined, leisured, intensely literate and literary-minded elite. From the copious literary records that survive it is clear that it was a society in which niceties of birth, rank and breeding counted for everything. Within the hierarchical world of the court mastery of protocol and etiquette, of calligraphy and music, of dress and deportment became more important than skill with a blade or a horse. At its best this cultivation of an aesthetic of refinement (*miyabi*) brought a fusion of life and art. The expression of art in life, life in art, was characteristic of almost every facet of Heian aristocratic culture. The care lavished by Heian noblewomen on the choice of colors in their 12-layered silken robes, or on their long black tresses, whitened faces and blackened teeth was part of a constant cultivation of an aesthetic of refinement in a daily life which was a living expression of artistic sensibility. It was a society in which suggestion and indirect expres-

sion of the emotions were cultivated. Noblewomen lived behind screens and curtains. Relationships might start not by direct conversation but by the sight of a woman's long black hair, a hint of her fragrance, a glimpse of her elegant silken sleeve or, most revealing of all, the quality of her calligraphy, the fullest measure of a person. For men, too, cultivation of dress, physical appearance, calligraphy and literary skills was essential for success in the intrigues of courtly politics and love.

Among the fullest records for understanding Heian aristocratic society are poetry, tales and diaries. Through these records it is hard to escape the impression that the art of love was the most demanding activity in court society. Sensitivity was the rule for men and women. Constancy was less rigorous. Heian aristocratic society was polygamous. Marriages were arranged by and for family interests and the production of heirs. Wives and their offspring commonly lived with their families, where their husbands visited them. When a Heian nobleman had conducted the proprieties toward his principal wife, a woman of birth comparable to his own, and she had conceived an heir, there was nothing to prevent him establishing liaisons, more and less permanent, with other secondary wives or more casual partners. Women, for their part, were free to engage in liaisons with men other than their spouses. Some court ladies like Izumi Shikibu aquired reputations for their amorous conquests. Others, less attractive, like the

In the early 11th century the poet and critic Fujiwara Kintō compiled a list of 36 illustrious poets from the age of the *Manyōshū* to his own day. The list included such luminaries as Kakinomoto Hitomaro, Ono no Komachi and Ise as well as such lesser-known poets as the court lady Kodai no Kimi shown here. The listing preserved interest in the poets and their work.
By the late 12th century portraits of individual poets, with brief biographies and sample poems, were being produced, bringing together the arts of poetry, painting and calligraphy. The painting, in strong colors and *Yamato-e* technique, is less a portrait than an idealized abstraction of a court beauty with long black hair flowing over her twelve-fold robes.
The poem, from the Heian period anthology *Shūi-shū*, reads as follows:
Though pledges of love made in the night should be eternal, dawn brings only loneliness like that felt by the *kami* of Katsuragi.

author of the *Kagerō nikki* (*The Gossamer Years*), found themselves abandoned by their husbands and left prey to gnawing jealousy.

At its worst, Heian courtly culture could be petty, overrefined and sterile. It was also a rather closed and inward-looking society. In 894 the court ceased sending large-scale official missions to China. Some contact continued through the coming and going of monks and private traders but Japan's horizons had narrowed. During the 9th and 10th centuries too the central government of the imperial court began to lose some of its effective control over the provinces. Courtiers did not travel far afield and when they did move outside the confines of the palace enclosure, some were inclined to shudder at unwonted contact with any commoners they met: "They looked like so many basket-worms as they crowded together in their hideous clothes, leaving hardly an inch of space between themselves and me" (*The Pillow Book of Sei Shōnagon*).

This very introspection and self-absorption may well have contributed to the very high level of cultural activity in courtly circles. The culture of the Heian era is frequently described as the first truly Japanese culture. Actually much Chinese influence remained, but it was transmuted in distinctively Japanese ways.

During the early part of the Heian period the cultural influence of China was still strong and periodic large-scale embassies brought back to Japan new texts and ideas from China. The Chinese language was the principal vehicle for literary expression in poetry and prose. It is conceivable that Chinese might have remained the only literary vehicle but for the fact that it did not cater adequately to the need for emotional expression by the Japanese, and especially women, who were not expected to master it. Nor, therefore, did it meet the needs of poetic expression in courtship which was frequently conducted in verse and called for nuanced expression in Japanese if women were to reciprocate and express their deepest feelings. To meet the needs of simpler vernacular expression Japanese syllabaries (*kana*) were developed by simplyfing and standardizing elements from basic Chinese characters. Tradition ascribes their development to Kūkai but this is uncertain. *Kana* replaced complex and cumbersome methods of writing Japanese employed in the *Kojiki* and *Manyōshu* with simple and accurate phonetic transcription of Japanese sounds.

Kana opened up doors to literary expression for men, but especially for women. Among the first great literary products in *kana* text were the poems included in the *Kokin wakashū* (*Anthology of Poems Old and New*, 905) a collection of more than 1000 poems in Japanese (*waka*). In his preface to the *Kokin wakashū* the editor, Ki no Tsurayuki (859?–945), expressed one enduring ideal of Japanese literature, the primacy of emotion over intellect:

> The poetry of Japan has its roots in the human heart and flourishes in the countless leaves of words. Because human beings possess interests of so many kinds, it is in poetry that they give expression to the meditations of their hearts in terms of sights appearing before their eyes and sounds coming through their ears. Hearing the warbler sing among the blossoms and the frog in his fresh waters—is there any living being not given to song? It is poetry which, without exertion moves heaven and earth, stirs the feelings of gods and spirits invisible to the eye, softens the relations between men and women, calms the hearts of fierce warriors.

The *Kokin wakashū* established a poetic diction observed by most *tanka* poets over the next 1000 years. It also established the literary canon of poetic themes, moods and seasonal concerns. Its 20 books were dominated by seasonal and love poetry. The seasonal poetry dwelt on cherry blossoms and reddening maple leaves and set a stereotype that in later, less capable, hands proved stultifying. But love that "softens the relations between men and women" was the central theme. This concentration on love took Japanese verse away from Chinese. But love was treated less in terms of describing passion, or intimacy, or depth of relationship and more in terms of subtlety and delicacy, beginnings and ends: the uncertainty of a relationship beginning, the sadness at its ending. This was in keeping with the delicate mood and brevity of the *tanka* form.

Kokinshū poets have been criticized for superb technique but little individuality or emotional intensity. Some, however, like the poets Ariwara no Narihira (823–80) and Ki no Tsurayuki or the poetesses Ono no Komachi (fl.850) and the Lady Ise, consort of Emperor Uda, show greater depth and emotional intensity. Take, for instance, these poems by Ono no Komachi:

Hito ni awamu	This night of no moon
Tsuki no naki yo wa	There is no way to meet him.
Omoiokite	I rise in longing—
Mune hashiri hi ni	My breast pounds, a leaping flame,
Kokoro yakeori	My heart is consumed by fire.

and:

Wabinureba	So lonely am I
Mi wo ukigusa no	My body is a floating weed
Ne wo taete	Severed at the roots.
Sasou mizu areba	Were there water to entice me,
Inamu to zo omou	I would follow it, I think.

Or this by Ise:

Yume ni da mo	Not even in dreams
Miyu to wa mieji	Can I meet him any more—
Asa na asa na	My glass each morning
Wa ga omokage ni	Reveals a face so wasted
Hazuru me nareba	I turn away in shame.

Ki no Tsurayuki, the compiler of the *Kokin wakashū*, also wrote the *Tosa Nikki* (*Tosa Diary*, 935), an account in Japanese of a homeward journey from Tosa in Shikoku to the capital. It was written in the form of a travel diary, but like most Japanese literary diaries and much classical fiction it blended poetry and prose. The work is suffused with sadness because his young daughter had died in Tosa. Because he wished to use Japanese instead of Chinese, the normal language for male diaries, Tsurayuki pretended that the author was a woman servant of his.

This was the first in an important genre in Japanese literature, the diary (*nikki*). Fine examples of this genre from the Heian period were written by several court ladies. Among them the *Kagerō nikki* (*The Gossamer Years*) is a largely fictionalized diary covering the years 954–74 by an embittered court lady, abandoned by her husband the Fujiwara nobleman Kaniie. He has had a child by another and rarely comes to visit her. She still waits, obsessed with grief and jealousy:

Summer came, and a child was born to his paramour. Loading the lady into his carriage and raising a commotion that could be heard through the whole city, he came hurrying past my gate—in the worst of taste, I thought. And why, my women loudly asked one another, had he so pointedly passed our gate when he had all the streets in the city to choose from? I myself was quite speechless, and thought only that I would like to die on the spot. I knew that I would be capable of nothing as drastic as suicide, but I resolved not to see him again.

Three or four days later I had a most astonishing letter: "I have not been able to see you because we have been having rather a bad time of it here. Yesterday the child was born, however, and everything seems to have gone off well. I know that you will not want to see me until the defilement has worn off."

I dismissed the messenger without a reply. The child, I heard, was a boy, and that of course made things worse. He came calling three or four days later, quite as though nothing unusual had happened. I did my best to make him uncomfortable and shortly he left. . . .

It began to appear that the lady in the alley had fallen from favor since the birth of her child. I had prayed, at the height of my unhappiness, that she would live to know what I had been suffering, and it seemed that my prayers were being answered. She was alone, and now her child was dead, the child that has been the cause of that unseemly racket. The lady was of frightfully bad birth—the unrecognized child of a rather odd prince, it was said. For a moment she was able to use a noble gentleman who was unaware of her shortcomings, and now she was abandoned. The pain must be even sharper than mine. I was satisfied. . . .

Another, related, genre of fiction that was developing through *kana* in the mid-Heian period was the fictional tale, or *monogatari*. *Monogatari* were narrative works which included prose as well as verse. Among the finest of these is the *Ise monogatari* (*Tales of Ise*), a collection of 125 brief incidents involving the partly fictionalized Ariwara no Narihira, each involving one or two *tanka*, many attributed to Narihira. The *Ise monogatari* opens by introducing the young protagonist with characteristic elegance:

In former times there lived a young nobleman named Narihira. Upon receiving the ceremony of initiation into manhood, he set forth upon a ceremonial falconry excursion, to review his estates at the village of Kasuga, near the former capital of Nara.

In that village there dwelt alone two young sisters possessed of a disturbing beauty. The young nobleman gazed at the two secretly from the shade of the enclosure around their house. It filled his heart with longing that in this rustic village he should have found so unexpectedly such lovely maidens. Removing the wide sleeve from the silk cloak he was wearing, Narihira inscribed a verse upon it and sent it to the girls. The cloak he was wearing bore a bold pattern of passion-flowers.

Kasugano no	Young maiden-flowers
Waka-murasaki no	Of Kasuga, you dye my cloak;
Surigoromo	And wildly like them grows
Shinobu no midare	This passion in my heart,
Kagiri shirarezu	Abundantly, without end.

The maidens must have thought this eminently suited to the occasion, for it was composed in the same mood as the well-known

Michinoku no	For whom has my heart
Shinobumojizuri	Like the passionflower patterns
Tare yue ni	Of Michinoku
Midaresomeneshi	Been thrown into disarray
Ware naranaku ni	All on account of you.

The literary world of the *Tale of Genji*

While most Heian *monogatari* confined their attention to the world of the court, a few reveal a broader interest. The *Taketori monogatari* (*The Tale of the Bamboo Cutter*) is a fairy tale of a moon maiden found by a childless bamboo cutter inside the stalk of a bamboo. The *Taketori monogatari*, in its encounter between the human and the divine, has much in common with fairy tales of other countries. In its fantastic elements it can be compared with the earlier *Nihon ryōiki* (*Miraculous Stories of Karmic Retribution of Good and Evil in Japan*), an early Heian collection of Buddhist miracle stories stressing the workings of *karma* and the immediate effects of good and evil actions. *Konjaku monogatari* (*Tales of Times Now Past*) is a varied collection of didactic tales from India, China and Japan dealing with peasants, princes, monks and nuns, warriors and many other human types.

But the finest of the *monogatari,* and by common consent the supreme masterpiece of Japanese literature, is the *Genji monogatari* (*Tale of Genji*) by Murasaki Shikibu who died around 1014. The author is a shadowy figure. Even her name is uncertain. The name Shikibu derives from the fact that she was the daughter of a lower-ranking courtier, from a minor branch of the Fujiwara, in the Board of Rites (*Shikibu*). The name Murasaki, meaning "purple," came from one of the principal characters in the *Tale of Genji*, Murasaki (no Ue). Shikibu married Fujiwara no Nobutaka in 999. She gave birth to a daughter but Nobutaka died two years later. In 1006 or 1007 she went into the

Hand-written copies of Murasaki Shikibu's *Genji monogatari* were probably passed avidly around the imperial court or read aloud. By the 12th century scenes from the tale were being illustrated in handscrolls that, when unrolled, allowed the viewer to savor highlights of the story. In this scene, from the "Azumaya 1" chapter of the tale, Naka no Kimi, the consort of Prince Niou, has just rescued the young Ukifune from an unwanted seduction by Niou. To comfort Ukifune she invites her to her room where a maid is drying her damp hair. Naka no Kimi tries to take Ukifune's mind off her recent ordeal by showing her an illustrated tale and having one of her maids read aloud from the accompanying text. The depersonalized "line eyes and hook noses," the "blown-away roofs" and the obliquely angled interiors are all characteristic features distinguishing the developing *Yamato-e* tradition from its Chinese (*Kara-e*) counterpart.

service of Shōshi, one of the consorts of Emperor Ichijō. In Shōshi's quarters in the palace Shikibu became the center of a brilliant group of literary women. Her fellow attendants included the poetesses Izumi Shikibu and Akazome Emon. In the quarters of Teishi, another of Ichijō's consorts, was the talented and witty Sei Shōnagon. It was a stellar group and literary rivalry probably brought out the best in each of them. It is not known when Murasaki retired from the court or died.

The *Tale of Genji* was probably completed in very much like its present form in the first decade of the 11th century. It is in 54 chapters. The work is episodic and complex with many characters appearing, but the *Genji* has a discernible structure, unfolding somewhat like a narrative scroll painting in which each scene can be savored separately while still being clearly a part of a larger whole. The first two-thirds describe the youth and maturity of Genji, the "shining prince" of the Heian court. The remainder is devoted to the world after his death. Genji frequently voices a Buddhist sense of transience of the world. That feeling becomes stronger after his brilliant presence vanishes from the story.

Genji is the ideal Heian courtier—the son of an emperor, an accomplished musician, poet, painter, dancer, kickball player; but his greatest accomplishment is the art of love, the art most prized and most carefully cultivated in Heian courtly society. *Genji monogatari* is thus a record of many love affairs. Some are fleeting and shallow, some endur-

ing and deeply, painfully felt. Some are conducted with the highest-ranking court ladies, some with unknown beauties found in the back streets of the capital. In each of these affairs Genji shows a tact and consideration that makes him more than a mere philanderer. But the spotlight is not entirely on Genji or the male characters. Murasaki presents a series of brilliant portraits of sensitive women, vulnerable in their dependence upon men. Murasaki was interested in the thoughts and feeling of her characters. She does more than concern herself with the surface forms of court life and the mere chronicling of liaisons. Her characters can be introspective and psychologically complex.

It is hardly possible to do justice to the richness of *Genji monogatari* in a single brief quotation, but the following will give at least a hint of the author's understanding of her characters. Genji's most enduring relationship is with Murasaki. Although she is the daughter of a prince, she ranks beneath Genji and cannot hope to become his principal wife. She is therefore deeply distressed when Genji agrees to take into his chambers, and eventually marry, his niece the Third Princess, daughter of Emperor Suzaku:

The Third Princess was, as her father had said, a mere child. She was tiny and immature physically, and she gave a general impression of still greater, indeed quite extraordinary, immaturity. He thought of Murasaki when he had first taken her in. She had even then been interesting. She had a character of her own. The Third Princess was like a baby. Well, thought Genji, the situation had something to recommend it: she was not likely to intrude and make Murasaki unhappy with fits of jealousy. Yet he did think he might have hoped for someone a *little* more interesting. For the first three nights he was faithful in attendance upon her. Murasaki was unhappy but said nothing. She gave herself up to her thoughts and to such duties, now performed with unusual care, as scenting his robes. He thought her splendid. Why, he asked himself, whatever the pressures and the complications, had he taken another wife? He had been weak and he had given an impression of inconstancy, and brought it all upon himself. . . . She withdrew to her boudoir and they helped her into bed. She was lonely and the presence of all these women did little to disguise the fact. She thought of the years of his exile. She had feared that they would not meet again, but the agony of waiting for word that he was still alive was in itself a sort of distraction from the sorrow and longing. She sought to comfort herself now with the thought that those confused days could so easily have meant the end of everything.

The wind was cold. Not wanting her women to know that she could not sleep, she lay motionless until she ached from the effort. Still deep in the cold night, the call of the first cock seemed to emphasize the loneliness and sorrow.

She may not have been in an agony of longing, but she was deeply troubled, and perhaps for that reason she came to Genji in his dreams. His heart was racing. Might something have happened to her? He lay waiting for the cock as if for permission to leave, and at its first call rushed out as if unaware that it would not yet be daylight for some time. Still a child, the princess kept her women close beside her. One of them saw him out through a corner door. The snow caught the first traces of dawn, though the garden was still dark. "In vain the spring night's darkness," whispered her nurse, catching the scent he had left behind.

The patches of snow were almost indistinguishable from the white garden sands. "There is yet snow by the castle wall," he whispered to himself as he came to Murasaki's wing of the house and tapped on a shutter. No longer in the habit of accommodating themselves to nocturnal wanderings, the women let him wait for a time.

The 18th-century classical scholar Motoori Norinaga (1730–1801) praised *Genji monogatari* for its representation of *mono no aware*, a difficult term to translate, implying a sensitivity to things, an awareness of the qualities of joy or sadness in things which move the heart. The tale is suffused with the tragic implications of a single moment or gesture and of the sense of ephemerality of beauty and love and life itself. It is not hard to see in this resonances with the fundamental Buddhist teaching that life is an illusion, insubstantial and fleeting

as a dream. Also expressive of Heian cultural values as exemplified by the hero of the *Tale of Genji* was the word *miyabi* suggesting elegance, refinement and courtliness; the polishing of manners, speech and feelings to remove all roughness or crudity. Together *aware* and *miyabi* expressed an aesthetic ideal of art and life.

Murasaki Shikibu has also composed a brief diary or journal, the *Murasaki Shikibu nikki*, covering some 15 months of service as an attendant to Empress Shōshi. The diary reveals something of Murasaki's own feelings and provides us with some fascinating insights into the day-to-day life of the court. Murasaki had been trained from childhood in the Chinese classics but like many women then, and since, she had to conceal her intellectual accomplishments from her peers:

There is a woman called Saemon no Naishi, who, for some strange reason, took a dislike to me, I cannot think why. I heard all sorts of malicious rumors about myself.

His Majesty was listening to someone reading the *Tale of Genji* aloud. "She must have read the Chronicles of Japan!" he said. "She seems very learned." Saemon no Naishi heard this and apparently jumped to conclusions, spreading it abroad among the senior courtiers that I was flaunting my learning. She gave me the nickname Our Lady of the Chronicles. How utterly ridiculous! Would I, who hesitate to reveal my learning in front of my women at home, ever think of doing so in court?

When my brother, Secretary at the Ministry of ceremonial, was a young boy learning the Chinese classics, I was in the habit of listening to him and I became unusually proficient in understanding those passages which he found too difficult to grasp. Father, a most learned man, was always regretting the fact: "Just my luck!" he would say. "What a pity she was not born a man!" But then gradually I realized that people were saying, "It's bad enough when a man flaunts his learning; she will come to no good," and ever since then I have avoided writing even the simplest character. My handwriting is appalling. And as for those classics, or whatever they are called, that I used to read, I gave them up entirely. Still I kept on hearing these malicious remarks. Worried what people would think if they heard such rumors, I pretended to be unable to read even the inscriptions on the screens. Then Her Majesty asked me to read to her here and there from the collected works of Po chū-i, and, because she evinced a desire to know more about such things, we carefully chose a time when other women would not be present and, amateur that I was, I read with her the two books of Po-chū-i's New Ballads in secret; we started the summer before last. I hid this fact from the others, as did Her Majesty, but somehow His Excellency and the Emperor got wind of it and they had some beautiful copies made of the various Chinese books, which his excellency then presented to Her Majesty. That gossip Saemon no Naishi could never have

The literary influence of China was powerfully felt in Heian Japan, and continued even after the ending of official embassies in 894. Japanese emperors, nobles and monks and nuns all admired Chinese poetry and calligraphic styles and sought to master them. This calligraphy, ascribed to Emperor Saga, is his copy of a poem by the Tang poet Li Zhiao in the calligraphic style of the Chinese master Ouyang Xiu, whose calligraphy was particularly appreciated in early Heian.

found out that Her Majesty had actually asked me to study with her, for, if she had, I would never have heard the last of it. Ah what a prattling, tiresome world it is!

The diary also tells us that she admired Izumi Shikibu as brilliant but erratic and somewhat loose in her behavior, and that she regarded Sei Shōnagon as conceited and pedantic:

Now someone who did carry on a fascinating correspondence was Izumi Shikibu. She does have a rather unsavory side to her character but has a genius for tossing off letters with ease and can make the most banal statement sound special. Her poems are quite delightful. Although her knowledge of the canon and her judgments leave something to be desired, she can produce poems at will and always manages to include some clever phrase or other that catches the eye, and yet when it comes to criticizing or judging the work of others, well she never really comes up to scratch; the sort of person who relies on a talent for extemporization, I feel. I cannot think of her a poet of the highest quality. . . . Sei shōnagon, for instance, was dreadfully conceited. She thought herself so clever, and littered her writings with Chinese characters, but if you examined them closely they left a great deal to be desired.

Sei Shōnagon may indeed have been conceited and perhaps a little shallow, but she was also a witty, astringent observer of the men and women who made up the narrow world of the court. In *Makura no sōshi* (*The Pillow Book*) she shows a fine talent for pointing out the incongruous and disjointed and for seeing the comic overtones (*okashi*) in serious moments, as in this description of a woman's irritation in observing a lover's fumbling departure from a tryst at dawn:

If someone with whom one is having an affair keeps on mentioning some woman whom he knew in the past, however long ago it is since they separated, one is always irritated.

It is very tiresome when a lover who is leaving one at dawn says that he must look for a fan or a pocket-book that he has left somewhere about the room last night. As it is still too dark to see anything, he goes fumbling about all over the place, knocking into everything and muttering to himself, "How very odd!" When at last he finds the pocket-book he crams it into his dress with a great rustling of the pages; or if it is a fan he has lost, he swishes it open and begins flapping it about, so that when he finally takes his departure, instead of experiencing the feelings of regret proper to such an occasion, one merely feels irritated at his clumsiness.

It is important that a lover should know how to make his departure. To begin with, he ought not to be too ready to get up, but should require a little coaxing: "Come, it is past daybreak. You don't want to be found here . . ." and so on. One likes him, too, to behave in such a way that one is sure he is

unhappy at going and would stay longer if he possibly could. He should not pull on his trousers the moment he is up, but should first of all come close to one's ear and in a whisper finish off whatever was left half-said in the course of the night. But though he may in reality at these moments be doing nothing at all, it will not be remiss that he should appear to be buckling his belt. Then he should raise the shutters, and both lovers should go out together at the double doors, while he tells her how much he dreads the day that is before him and longs for the approach of night. Then, after he has slipped away, she can stand gazing after him, with charming recollections of those last moments. Indeed, the success of a lover depends greatly on his method of departure. If he springs to his feet with a jerk and at once begins fussing round, tightening in the waistband of his breeches, or adjusting the sleeves of his court robe, hunting jacket, or what not, collecting a thousand odds and ends, and thrusting them into the folds of his dress or pulling in his over-belt—one begins to hate him.

Here we see very clearly the merging of art and love and life in a single aesthetic. It is this aesthetic that has come to be seen as the epitome of the aristocratic Heian cultural ideal.

Religion in the Heian period

Religion and the supernatural pervaded Heian society. For the Heian aristocrat, hardly a day went by without the performance of some rite that had religious or supernatural implications. For the warrior, devotion to Hachiman, the god of war, or some other local *kami* or Buddha offered a source of spiritual comfort. Buddhism was an increasingly powerful force. To the six schools of Nara Buddhism were added the two newly introduced schools of Tendai and Shingon in the early Heian period. Late in the period devotion to the Buddha Amida began to gain ground in Tendai circles, hastened by a sense of urgency and pessimism brought about by belief that the Latter Age of the Buddha's teaching was at hand.

But Buddhism was not the only influence on Heian spiritual life. The eclectic current of thought known as *honji suijaku*, which blended devotion to the Buddhas with worship of the native *kami*, also became more prevalent during the period, especially under the influence of esoteric Buddhism. Mountain devotion flourished. Taoist notions, ideas of Yin and Yang and the Five Elements, and ritual taboos were also part of the fabric of Heian spirituality. Buddhism began to move out of monastic cloisters and into the residences of the aristocracy, where it showed a variety of manifestations: in textual study, in esoteric ritual, in artistic expression, and in pious works intended to accumulate merit such as copying *sūtras,* building statues and commissioning private temples.

Although the subtleties of Buddhist teaching were not yet well understood by provincial warriors or cultivators, generalized notions of *karma* and of the Buddhas as protective and healing deities became widespread as an increasingly Budd-

The two most powerful religious movements of the early Heian period were those of Tendai and Shingon Buddhism. This idealized portrait of Saichō (767–822), the founder of Japanese Tendai, produced long after his death, shows the scholar-monk seated in meditation on a carved abbot's chair. The meditative posture, gently withdrawn expression and prelate's robes give an iconic character to the painting. It is one of a set showing Prince Shōtoku and the 10 Chinese and Japanese patriarchs of the Tendai school.

Left The Taira were generous patrons of the Itsukushima shrine: Taira Kiyomori and his family dedicated 33 illuminated scrolls of the *Lotus Sūtra* to it. In keeping with the aestheticism in art and religious expression that the Taira had learned from Heian courtiers, the scrolls were gorgeously decorated and illustrated. The rollers of the scrolls were embellished with filigree bronze, gilt and crystal knobs. Each scroll opens with a vivid illustration in the *Yamato-e* or mixed Yamato and *Kara-e* traditions depicting the ineffable merits and promise of spiritual salvation offered by the *Lotus Sūtra*. This title-page from Chapter 21 shows a hermit ecstatically chanting the *sūtra* from his hut on a crag overlooking a lotus pond.

hist world view took hold. In the early Heian period, although the Mahayana message of salvation for all was embedded in the *Lotus Sūtra,* one of the most fundamental texts of Japanese Buddhism, in practice the path to salvation was still restricted to monks and nuns who had the literacy, training and time to devote themselves fully to the religious life. Toward the end of the period, in the late 12th century, however, Hōnen and other priests began to preach a message of salvation accessible to ordinary men and women.

Compared with his predecessor Shōmu or his successor Saga, Emperor Kammu was not an enthusiastic sponsor of Buddhism. His interest was rather in Confucianism as a basis for imperial rule. Buddhism was not entirely excluded from the new capital, however. Kammu patronized two young monks Saichō (767–822), known posthumously as Dengyō Daishi, and Kūkai (774–835), known posthumously as Kōbō Daishi. They turned again to China as the source of a revitalization of Japanese Buddhism. These two able young monks became the founders of the most powerful, prolific and enduring currents of Japanese Buddhism: the Tendai and Shingon traditions.

Saichō and the Tendai tradition

Both Saichō and Kūkai journeyed to China with the embassy of 804. Kūkai traveled on the first vessel, which was blown to the south and eventually reached land in Fujian Province. Saichō, on the second vessel, made a more direct crossing and soon found his way to Mount Tiantai, Heavenly Terrace, in Zhejiang Province. There he was impressed by the vigor and comprehensiveness of the syncretic Tiantai interpretation of the *Lotus Sūtra* elaborated by Zhiyi (538–97).

In Tiantai (Japanese: Tendai) thought the *Lotus Sūtra* is the supreme crystallization of the Buddha's teaching and contains all that is necessary for salvation. Whereas the teachings of other schools are provisional or incomplete, only those based on the *Lotus* are complete. Thus, the *Lotus* is viewed as the perfect teaching, reconciling the various imperfections of the other schools in a comprehensive, all-inclusive synthesis. At the core of this synthesis are the great messages of the *Lotus Sūtra,* that all sentient beings share Buddha nature, that is to say they are innately enlightened, and can be brought to salvation, and that the Buddhas and Bodhisattvas are eternally at work helping to realize that salvation. Zhiyi stressed that contemplative and intellectual approaches to religion were like the two wings of a bird; thus Tendai Buddhism was characterized by a strong philosophical inclination combined with a vigorous emphasis on meditation. The practices emphasized in Tendai included strict monastic discipline, prayer and textual study, esoteric rituals, and intensive meditation (*shikan*) through which the individual can grasp the interpenetration of the 3000 realms of existence, or aspects of reality, in a single thought and attain the realization that nirvana is immanent in *samsara* (the world of transmigration).

Saichō expressed man's innate potentiality for enlightenment in the image of the lotus emerging from mud and water: "In the lotus-flower is implicit its emergence from the water. If it does not emerge, its blossom will not open; in the emergence

is implicit the blossoming. If the water is three feet deep, the stalk of the flower will be four or five feet; if the water is seven or eight feet deep, the stalk will be over ten feet tall. That is what is implied by the emergence from the water. The greater the amount of the water, the taller the stalk will grow; the potential is limitless. Now all human beings have the lotus of Buddhahood within them. It will rise above the mire and the foul water of the Hīnayana and the Quasi-Mahāyāna, and then through the stage of the bodhisattvas to open leaves and blossoms together, in full glory."

Returning to Japan in 805, Saichō established the monastery of Enryakuji on Mount Hiei, to the northeast of the capital. Small at first, Enryakuji was rapidly to grow into the greatest monastic center in Japan. Because of its proximity to the capital Enryakuji enjoyed the patronage of the imperial court and the nobility. It was not long before younger sons of the nobility and the imperial family were enrolling as monks. To win acceptance for the new Buddhist teachings Saichō stressed the role of Buddhism as the protector of the state. He dreamed of making Buddhism the pillar of the nation and the spiritual support of the revived government in the new capital below the monastery. His ideal was to produce spiritual leaders, "Treasures of the Nation," who would combine the spiritual dedication and compassion of the Bodhisattva with the Confucian virtues of service to the state and society: "What is the treasure of the nation? The religious nature is a treasure, and he who possesses this nature is the treasure of the nation. That is why it was said of old that ten pearls big as pigeons' eggs do not constitute the treasure of the nation, but only when a person casts his light over a part of the country can one speak of a treasure of the nation."

To this end, he established a rigorous 12-year program of religious discipline for Tendai monks. Those few who completed the program with the highest distinction would be kept on Mount Hiei to train others. Less qualified monks would be sent to the provinces to serve as teachers or functionaries there. Saichō planned to use monks in an active life of social service very different from the traditional Theravadan ideal of the mendicant seeker:

Students of both disciplines shall be appointed to positions in keeping with their achievements after twelve years' training and study. Those who are capable in both action and speech shall remain permanently on the mountain as leaders of the order: these are the treasures of the nation. Those who are capable in speech but not in action shall be teachers of the nation. Those who are capable in action but not in speech shall be functionaries of the nation.

Teachers and functionaries of the nation shall be appointed with official licences as Transmitters of Doctrine and National Lecturers. The national lecturers shall be paid during their tenure of office the expenses of the annual summer retreat and provided with their robes. Funds for these expenses shall be deposited in the provincial offices, where they will be supervised jointly by provincial and district governors.

They shall also serve in such undertakings which benefit the nation and the people as the repair of ponds and canals, the reclamation of uncultivated land, the reparation of landslides, the construction of bridges and ships, the planting of trees and ramie bushes, the sowing of hemp and grasses, and the digging of wells and irrigation ditches. They shall also study the sūtras and cultivate their minds, but shall not engage in private agriculture or trading.

If these provisions are followed, men possessing the religious nature will spring up one after another throughout the country, and the way of the superior man will never die.

Responding to the religious environment in Japan, Saichō transformed Tendai in several ways. He was at pains to distinguish the Tendai universalism of the Great Vehicle from what he called derisively the Hinayana (Lesser Vehicle) and Quasi-Mahayana Buddhism of the old Nara monasteries. Rejecting the Hinayana ordination precepts used in the Nara monasteries, he adopted the so-called Bodhisattva precepts as the proper vows in ordaining Tendai monks. To free Tendai monks from control by Tōdaiji, where ordinations were customarily performed, he also appealed to the court to allow Enryakuji to conduct its own ordinations. This appeal was only acceded to after his death, but his insistence upon Tendai ordination and the use of the Mahayana Bodhisattva precepts represented a major breach with Nara Buddhism. Nara clerics, for their part, resented Saichō's assertiveness and ready access to imperial patronage and opposed him at every step.

Saichō also transformed Japanese Tendai in a very different way. He was powerfully drawn to esoteric Buddhist teachings (*mikkyō*). He had come across these ritual practices while in China and incorporated some in his own brand of Tendai. But he also sought to acquire more knowledge of esoteric teachings from his contemporary Kūkai. He had himself initiated into Shingon traditions by Kūkai, sent students to study with him, and borrowed works on Shingon ritual from him. The relations between them were embittered, however, when Kūkai refused to lend Saichō books and insisted that if he wished to study Shingon he should become a regular student. Kūkai's point was that esoteric truth was not revealed in texts, only in mind-to-mind transmission which only Kūkai could impart. This personal alienation did not prevent the continued permeation of Tendai by Shingon esoteric thought and practice. Shingon added a powerful ritual and aesthetic aspect to Tendai Buddhism, making it even more appealing to the court aristocracy in the capital.

Nor were Saichō and Enryakuji immune from the inclination to seek association between the Buddhism and the cults of the native *kami*. Saichō himself expressed a particular reverence for the ancient tutelary deity of Mount Hiei known as Oyamagui no Mikoto, or Mountain King, Sannō. The Hie shrine, dedicated to Sannō, was established on the eastern slopes of Mount Hiei overlooking Lake Biwa. Enryakuji monks always looked to Sannō as their protective deity and performed rituals in its honor. Through this associ-

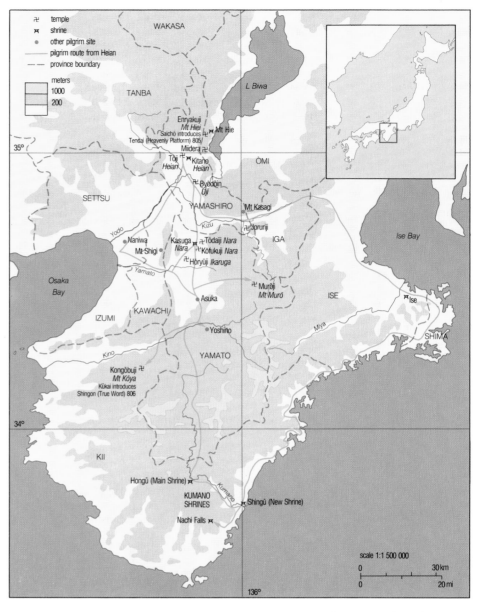

ation with Enryakuji and Tendai Buddhism what had been a minor local cult was drawn into the mainstream of the religious life of the capital. The deliberate association between the Buddhist temple and this deity is indicative of the efforts made by Japanese Buddhist leaders to overcome lingering local hostility to the "foreign" religion by incorporating within their respective spheres of influence the Shinto gods of those regions where they sought to establish their temples.

Enryakuji continued to grow after Saichō's death under the leadership of Ennin (794–864) and Enchin (814–91). Using esoteric teachings imported from China as well as those adopted from Japanese Shingon Buddhism, they elaborated a Tendai form of esoteric Buddhism known as Taimitsu in contrast to the Tōmitsu of the Japanese Shingon school. By the 10th century Enryakuji had become an extensive religious complex. In its halls were trained many of the most creative figures in Japanese Buddhism including Genshin, Ryōgen, Hōnen, Eisai, Dōgen, Shinran and Nichiren. During the 10th century there was a rift between monastic factions within Enryakuji and one group left to establish the rival monastic center of Onjōji (Miidera) at the foot of the mountain.

Like the great Nara monasteries, Enryakuji was

Pilgrimage in the Heian period
In general Heian nobles did not move far beyond the walls of the Heian palace. Emperors, nobles and commoners, however, did make arduous pilgrimages. The seven great temples of Nara could be visited in a week's journey. To maintain their influence they encouraged pilgrims. From Nara pilgrims could proceed to the mountain centers of Mount Kōya, Murōji (one of few mountains open to women) or the stone Buddhas at Mount Kasagi. The mecca for all devout Buddhists, however, was the very much more arduous pilgrimage to the Kumano shrines. Retired Emperor Uda was the first member of the imperial family to undertake it in 907. The 320-kilometer round trip, made on foot or by palanquin over rough mountain tracks, took nearly a month. Later pilgrims preferred to take the coastal route to Kumano, which allowed them to visit the Ise shrines as well.

awarded tax-free landholdings under the provisions of the *ritsuryō* system, and like them it used its resources and influence to create provincial branch temples and privatized holdings (*shōen*) either by reclamation or by seeking commendations. By the 12th century Enryakuji and its many branch temples had hundreds of *shōen* holdings scattered throughout the provinces immediately below the mountain and further afield. Again, like the powerful Nara monasteries, as well as Mount Kōya and Negoro, Enryakuji built up a powerful private army of monk-soldiers (*sōhei*) to protect its interests and its landholdings. Whenever the monastery felt its interests to be in jeopardy its monk-soldiers carried the sacred symbol of the Sannō cult down into the capital and used it as a spiritual sanction to try to force the court to accede to the monastery's demands. Rivalry between monastic armies from the Nara monasteries and Enryakuji, and between Enryakuji and warrior bands protecting the court and the Fujiwara, contributed to the growing political turmoil in late Heian Japan. Unruly monastic armies went virtually unchecked until the 16th century when Oda Nobunaga and Toyotomi Hideyoshi acquired the military power to take the necessary drastic measures to bring them to heel.

Kūkai and the doctrine of Shingon
The brilliant young monk Kūkai traveled to China on the same embassy, though not on the same ship, as Saichō in 804. Like Saichō, Kūkai was seeking a universal and unifying Buddhist teaching more appropriate to his needs and those of his countrymen than the abstract doctrines of the Nara schools. In China, Kūkai went with the embassy to the capital at Chang'an where he studied Buddhism with the famous master Huiguo (746–805). Kūkai was a learned young man, already well versed in Chinese. According to Kūkai, the 60-year-old Chinese master greeted him warmly as if he had been waiting for his arrival and soon made him his chosen disciple, initiating him into the secrets of esoteric Mantrayana Buddhism.

Kūkai's description of his encounter with his master is worth quoting at length because it also introduces basic features of Shingon teaching, ritual and iconography:

The founder of Japanese Shingon Buddhism, Kūkai (774–835) is shown holding the magical implements of Shingon Buddhism, a bronze thunderbolt and prayer beads. After Kūkai's death Shingon teachings and rituals permeated Tendai Buddhism and mingled with mountain asceticism to produce Shugendō. With Shingon running as a powerful current throughout the medieval period, Kūkai remained a venerated figure. He was believed not to have died, but to have entered a state of deep meditation (*samādhi*) to await the coming of the future Buddha Maitreya. Thus pilgrims could believe that Kūkai appeared to them in remote parts of Japan.

During the sixth moon of 804, I, Kūkai, sailed for China aboard the Number One Ship, in the party of Lord Fujiwara, ambassador to the T'ang court. We reached the coast of Fukien by the eighth moon, and four months later arrived at Chang'an, the capital, where we were lodged at the official guest residence. The ambassadorial delegation started home for Japan on 11 March 805, but in obedience to an imperial edict, I alone remained behind in the Hsi-ming Temple where the abbot Eichū had formerly resided.

One day, in the course of my calls on eminent Buddhist teachers of the capital, I happened by chance to meet the abbot of the East Pagoda Hall of the Green Dragon Temple. This great priest, whose Buddhist name was Hui-kuo, was the chosen disciple of the master Amoghavajra. His virtue aroused the reverence of his age; his teachings were lofty enough to guide emperors. Three sovereigns revered him as their master and were ordained by him. The four classes of believers looked up to him for instruction in the esoteric teachings.

I called on the abbot in the company of five or six monks from the Hsi-ming Temple. As soon as he saw me he smiled with pleasure, and he joyfully said, "I knew that you would come! I have been waiting for such a long time. What pleasure it gives me to look on you today at last! My life is drawing to an end, and until you came there was no one to whom I could transmit the teachings. Go without delay to the ordination altar with incense and a flower." I returned to the temple where I had been staying and got the things which were necessary for the ceremony. It was early in the sixth moon, then, that I entered the ordination chamber. I stood in front of the Womb Mandala and cast my flower in the prescribed manner. By chance it fell on the body of the Buddha Vairochana in the center. The master exclaimed in delight, "How amazing! How perfectly amazing!" He repeated this three or four times in joy and wonder. I was then given the fivefold baptism and received the instruction in the Three Mysteries that bring divine intercession. Next I was taught the Sanskrit formulas for the Womb Mandala, and learned the yoga contemplation on all the Honored Ones.

Early in the seventh moon I entered the ordination chamber of the Diamond Mandala for a second baptism. When I cast my flower it fell on Vairochana again, and the abbot marveled as he had before. I also received ordination as an āchārya early in the following month. . . .

I later studied the Diamond Crown Yoga and the five divisions of the True Words teachings, and spent some time learning Sanskrit and Sanskrit hymns. The abbot informed me that the Esoteric scriptures are so abstruse that their meaning cannot be conveyed except through art. For this reason he ordered the court artist Li Chen and about a dozen other painters to execute ten scrolls of the Womb and Diamond Mandalas and assembled more than twenty scribes to make copies of the Diamond and other important esoteric scriptures. He also ordered the bronzesmith to cast fifteen ritual implements. . . .

One day the abbot told me, "Long ago, when I was still young, I met the great master Amoghavajra. From the first moment he saw me he treated me like a son, and on his visit to the court and his return to the temple I was as inseparable from him as his shadow. He confided to me, 'You will be the receptacle of the esoteric teachings. Do your best! Do your best!' I was then initiated into the teachings of both the Womb and Diamond, and into the secret mudrās as well. The rest of his disciples, monks and laity alike, studied just one of the Mandalas or one Honored One or one ritual, but not all of them as I did. How deeply I am indebted to him I shall never be able to express.

"Now my existence on earth approaches its term, and I cannot long remain. I urge you, therefore, to take the two Mandalas and the hundred volumes of the Esoteric teachings, together with the ritual implements and these gifts which were left to me by my master. Return to your country and propagate the teachings there.

"When you first arrived I feared I did not have time enough left to teach you everything, but now my teaching is completed, and the work of copying the sūtras and making the images is also finished. Hasten back to your country, offer these things to the court, and spread the teachings throughout your country to increase the happiness of the people. Then the land will know peace and everyone will be content. In that way you will return thanks to Buddha and to your teacher. That is also the way to show devotion to your country and to your family. My disciple I-ming will carry on the teachings here. Your task is to transmit them to the Eastern Land. Do your best! Do your best!" These were his final instructions to me, kindly and patient as always. On the night of the last full moon of the year he purified himself with a ritual bath and, lying on his right side and making the mudrā of Vairochana, he breathed his last.

That night, while I sat in meditation in the Hall, the abbot appeared to me in his usual form and said, "You and I have long been pledged to propagate the esoteric teachings. If I am reborn in Japan, this time I will be your disciple."

I have not gone into the details of all he said, but the general import of the Master's instruction I have given. [Dated 5 December 806]

The quotation provides us with a very good sense of the teachings, ritual practices and implements that Kūkai took back to Japan with him. At the core of Shingon teaching is the belief that there is a transcendent and all-embracing Buddha, Vairocana, or Dainichi in Japanese. This Buddha is at the heart of the cosmos and in the center of the two great mandalas, Womb (or Matrix) and Diamond World, used to represent the cosmos in Shingon art. The myriad other Buddhas and Bodhisattvas are merely manifestations of Dainichi, and all realities—sentient beings and natural objects—are emanations from him. Hence it is possible for a person to "attain Buddhahood in this very body" when they recognize the immanence of Dainichi.

To assist in the attainment of this realization Shingon advocated three principal forms of religious practice. These three ritual practices represented respectively the thoughts, words and actions of Dainichi embodied through the believer. One practice involved meditation on the two mandalas of the Diamond World (Kongōkai) and the Womb World (Taizōkai). These were graphic representations of Dainichi's immanence throughout the universe and his transformation into the myriad forms and beings. A second form of religious practice in Shingon was the repeated

Mandalas and Shingon Art

The esoteric teachings (*mikkyō*) introduced to Japan by Kūkai in the early 9th century rooted quickly and flowed through Heian Buddhism in several powerful currents. One of these currents was Kūkai's own Shingon (True Word) school, based at Kongōbuji (Kōyasan) and Kyōōgokokuji (Tōji) in Kyoto. The other esoteric current flowed within Japanese Tendai Buddhism. Esoteric teachings promised that enlightenment was possible in this life without long years of waiting for birth in a distant paradise. The way of doing so lay not in study of the *sūtras*, but rather through the understanding of teachings transmitted secretly by the Buddha, containing the inner secrets of enlightenment. Through initiation in cosmic diagrams (mandalas), secret gestures (mudras) and mystical symbols (mantras) the adept could find access to these inner secrets. The two great esoteric mandalas are the Womb World (Taizōkai) and Diamond World (Kongōkai) mandalas, both illuminating aspects of the wisdom and compassion of Mahāvairocana (Dainichi), the primordial Buddha and source of all other Buddhas and beings.

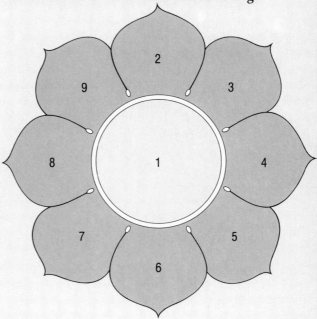

Above This diagram illustrates the central court of the Womb World Mandala. At the center sits Mahāvairocana. On alternate petals sit four Buddhas and four Bodhisattvas.
1. Dainichi Nyorai (Mahāvairocana)
2. Hōdō Nyorai (Ratnaketu)
3. Fugen Bosatsu (Samantabhadra)
4. Kaifukeō Nyorai (Samkusumitarāja)
5. Monju Bosatsu (Manjushrī)
6. Muryōju Nyorai (Amitāyus)
7. Kannon Bosatsu (Avalokiteshvara)
8. Tenkuraion Nyorai (Divyadundubhimeghanirghosa)
9. Miroku Bosatsu (Maitreya)

Right The Womb World (Taizōkai) Mandala represents the cosmos of Mahāvairocana's eternal and all-encompassing enlightenment. The idea of "womb" implies that this universal enlightenment is the all-embracing principle underlying and nurturing all phenomena. The mandala, in the shape of a long rectangle, consists of 12 sections or courts filled with 414 Buddhas and Bodhisattvas, around a central court (*above*) in which Mahāvairocana sits on a lotus throne. Above the lotus is a triangle, representing absolute wisdom. Beneath the lotus are the five great kings of wisdom.

Below Esoteric Buddhism makes great use of rituals from simple hand movements to complex ceremonies. Among them, the ceremony of ritual initiation (*abhiseka*), as performed by Kūkai in China, is described on page 90. Another important ritual was the *goma* fire ceremony, a burning of wooden stakes inscribed with prayers. Other elaborate ceremonies were performed to commemorate various phases in the careers of the Buddhas or the Shingon patriarchs, or to mark stages of initiation in the religious lives of monks and laypeople. These ceremonies were performed with elaborate bronze implements and accompanied by the ringing of bells and chimes. Esoteric art and ritual had a potent influence in shaping the aesthetic sensibilities of the Heian nobility. The illustration, from a medieval scroll painting, depicts an esoteric ritual at the Shingon'in within the imperial palace.

Left The Indian *vajra* (Japanese *kongō*) is one of the most characteristic ritual implements of esoteric (Shingon) Buddhism. Said to be endowed with "the hardness of diamond and the energy of a thunderbolt," it symbolizes the indestructible character of ultimate truth.

Above Here Mahāvairocana (Dainichi: the great sun), the primordial Buddha, source of all matter, energy and consciousness, of all other Buddhas and Bodhisattvas and of wisdom and compassion, is shown seated on a lotus throne at the center of the Diamond World (Kongōkai) Mandala. He appears among the myriad Buddhas and Bodhisattvas of this mandala in his aspect of diamond-like immutable universal wisdom that destroys delusion.

Above Within the vast esoteric pantheon were many ferocious deities who served the Buddhas by protecting the faithful. Among them were the Myōō (Skt. Vidyārāja), kings of knowledge and attendants of Mahāvairocana. Fudō Myōō (Skt. Acala), "the Immovable One," shown here, symbolizes the psychospiritual state of steadfastness in the face of passion, folly, egoism and temptation.

utterance of secret incantations, "true words," known as mantras and *dharani* (*shingon*). The third practice was that of ritual hand gestures or mudras (*ingei*).

As is clear from Kūkai's own experience with his master, the truths of Shingon were not accessible simply by textual study. They were secret, or esoteric, teachings imparted by a master to a ritually initiated disciple. The ceremony of *abhiṣeka* (*kanjō* in Japanese), a ritual sprinkling with water, was one of the principal initiation rituals in Shingon. These esoteric teachings (*mikkyō*), the sublime truths of the Buddha's teaching, were believed to be superior to openly propounded teachings (*kengyō*).

Shingon rituals and practices were expressed in elaborate ritual forms. In addition to mandalas, mudras and mantras, Shingon ceremonies involved the use of a variety of ritual intruments known as *vajra*, pronged instruments derived from Indian weapons, used to shatter the illusions that obscure true insight. The complexity, color and artistic sophistication of Shingon ritual gave the teaching a particular appeal to Heian courtiers and the monks of other Japanese Buddhist schools. Shingon quickly gained acceptance in the great Nara temples, as well as in Saichō's monastery of Enryakuji.

Emperor Kammu had died before Kūkai returned to Japan in 806. However the young monk, who was already renowned as a fine poet and calligrapher as well as a master of esoteric Buddhism, was patronized by Kammu's successors, especially Emperor Saga. In 809 he was installed by the court in the Takaosanji (later Jingoji) on the outskirts of Kyoto where he began to establish himself as a religious and cultural leader in Heian society. Here he conducted *abhiṣeka* initiations and built up a small community. In 810 he was honored with appointment as administrative head of the Tōdaiji. This provided the opportunity for him to introduce Shingon into the teachings and rituals of this great center for monastic ordinations.

In 816 Emperor Saga acceded to Kūkai's request that he be granted Mount Kōya, a mountain wilderness in Kii Province, as a site for a contemplative community. There Kūkai established a great monastic center that was to rival Enryakuji in religious, political and economic influence. The monastery was in itself conceived of as a mandala expressing the truths of Shingon Buddhism and the interpenetrating non-duality of the Womb and Diamond realms. Kūkai viewed Mount Kōya as the matrix realm symbolized by the lotus flower. The eight peaks surrounding the central plateau were the petals of the lotus. He named the monastic complex at the center of consecrated ground within the Womb realm Kongōbuji, Vajra or Diamond Peak Temple, representing the Diamond realm of eternity and of infinite activity and wisdom. Seated in the great central pagoda of the Diamond realm was the ultimate universal reality, Vairochana of the Diamond realm, surrounded north, east, south and west by the four Buddhas of the Womb realm.

Kūkai and a small group of followers spent several years establishing a community on Mount Kōya. On the mountain he devoted himself to meditation, prayer and writing. But he also needed

economic support for his building efforts and had to maintain his ties with the capital. In 823 he was entrusted by Saga with the monastery of Tōji, the Eastern Temple, in the capital. Kūkai had to complete its construction but it gave esoteric Buddhism a strong foothold within the capital. Again, the temple and its images were built to conform to Kūkai's spiritual vision of the Buddha realm of Vairochana. Kūkai was permitted to train 50 Shingon monks in Tōji. He was also granted the special privilege that it should remain exclusively Shingon. Sensing perhaps that his death was approaching, Kūkai returned to Mount Kōya in 831. He passed away in the third month of 834, although to his followers he had not died but entered a state of profound meditation (*samādhi*) in which he would await the coming of Maitreya, the future Buddha.

The cult of Amida

From the mid-Heian period a new devotional orientation began to develop within Japanese Tendai monasteries alongside meditation, study of the *Lotus Sūtra* and esoteric ritual. At first this new interest remained a contemplative monastic phenomenon. By the 12th century, however, this new devotionalism was spreading into lay society and offering renewed hope of salvation in a darkening world. The new religious movement advocated trust in the Buddha Amida (Amitābha) and held out the promise of salvation in the Pure Land of the Western Paradise. The emphasis in Pure Land Buddhism is less on the attainment of salvation or enlightenment by one's own efforts (*jiriki* in Japanese) than salvation through the saving power of another (*tariki*), in this case Amitābha.

Devotion to the Buddha Amida (Sanskrit Amitābha, Chinese Amituofo) and belief that through Amida's compassion the deceased can be reborn in his Western Paradise, or Pure Land, have been powerful currents in Mahayana Buddhism throughout Asia. In Japan, in particular, of all the Buddhas in the Mahayana pantheon, Amida has attracted the deepest devotion. The power of Amidism has lain in the promise it offers to ordinary men and women, as well as monks and nuns, that access to the Pure Land is open to them too and that it is not difficult to attain. All that is required is faith in Amida expressed in the invocation of the Buddha's name, known as the *nembutsu*: "Praise to the Buddha Amida," Namu Amida Butsu. Amidism also gave rise to a rich devotional literature and art depicting the delights to be found by the faithful in Amida's Paradise and the pains of the hells to which sinners could expect to be consigned.

The title Amida derives from the Sanskrit words *Amitābha*, meaning "Infinite Light," and *Amitāyus*, meaning "Eternal Life." The principal teachings relating to Amida and his Pure Land are found in the *Pure Land Sūtra*, or *Sukhāvati vyūha*. *Sukhāvati* means "Pure and Happy Land." The longer, and older, version of the *sūtra*, incorporating Theravadan notions of *karma* and individual striving for salvation, stresses the attainment of rebirth in the Pure Land through the performance of meritorious deeds and faith in Amitābha. The shorter version, which was more widely used in

When Kūkai returned from China in 806, he was appointed to the headship of Tōji (Kyōōgokokuji) in Kyoto which he turned into a great center of Shingon teaching. In 816 he was permitted by the court to build an ascetic training monastery, the Kongōbuji, in the wilds of Mount Kōya, south of the capital. Kūkai's tomb at the Oku-no-in remains a center of popular veneration. During the

Heian period Kōyasan grew into one of the most powerful monastic complexes in Japan, with extensive landholdings around the mountain and its own monastic army.

China and Japan, teaches that the only requirement for salvation is faith in Amida.

The origins of the cult of Amida are obscure. Amitābha is hardly mentioned in the earliest Buddhist scriptures. When he does appear, he is a very minor figure. He only begins to emerge as one of the Buddhas of the Mahayana pantheon around the 1st century AD when he is identified as a Buddha of longevity and infinite light presiding over a Western Paradise. The early cult may have blended Indian and western Asian notions. Ahura Mazda, a divinity of light in the Iranian Avesta, is also enthroned in a Western Paradise. The idea of Amida as a compassionate saving divinity who is frequently depicted as the central figure of a trinity may also have owed something to Greek or early Christian influences.

The cult of Amida was further developed in China. During the 3rd and early 4th centuries monks like Que Gongze (who died around 274),

Wei Shidu and Zhidun all expressed devotion to Amituofo, vowed to be reborn in his Paradise and sought to integrate Amidst ideas with indigenous Taoist notions of longevity and a Western Paradise presided over by a Queen Mother of the West.

Hui Yuan (334–417), disciple of Daoan and head of the monastic community at Lushan, is credited with the founding of the Pure Land School, as it later came to be called. Like Daoan, Hui Yuan was a master of the Prajnāpāramitā *sūtras* and of meditation. He taught that access to the glories of Amituofo's Paradise could be attained through meditation. Hui Yuan is sometimes said to have founded a group composed of monks and laypeople devoted to Amitābha and known as the White Lotus Society. Whether Hui Yuan actually founded such a group and whether this group of scholars and recluses actively spread Pure Land teaching are open questions. There is no doubt, however, that he and his followers meditated on Amituofo and made vows to be reborn in the Western Paradise. He thus served as an inspiration and a model and came to be regarded as the first Pure Land patriarch in China. Tan Luan (476–542), Dao Zhuo

(562–645) and Shan Dao (613–81) were also active in spreading Amidist devotion. In his *Essays on the Western Paradise,* for instance, Dao Zhuo argued that in an age of decline of the Buddha's teaching invocation (*nien-fo*) of the Buddha Amitābha's name was the surest way to assure rebirth in the Pure Land. As a result of the activities of these influential monks and their followers, Amidist devotion took root in China both as a school of Buddhism and as a current of popular devotionalism that persisted through the purges of Buddhism in the Tang dynasty.

Amidism came to Japan early. There is record that the *Sukhāvati vyūha* was recited publicly in 640. A Pure Land school was slower to develop. For several centuries Amidism was known mostly to monks and nuns within the scholarly framework of Nara Buddhism and then within Tendai and Shingon Buddhism as part of an esoteric practice of contemplation on the virtues of the various Buddhas. The practices of praying for the dead, invoking Amida through the *nembutsu* and circumambulating while concentrating on Amida (*jōgyō zanmai*) were also common.

The Byōdōin at Uji

The Byōdōin at Uji is a fine example of a Heian period palace converted into a temple and garden representing the Pure Land of Amida in terrestrial form. Originally a villa belonging to Fujiwara no Michinaga, the Byōdōin was converted into a temple by his son Fujiwara no Yorimichi in 1053. The core of the Byōdōin is the Phoenix Hall, or Hōōdō, so named for the bronze birds on its roof. It contains a wooden statue of Amida by the sculptor Jōchō, looking east over a lotus pond. Built like a great bird, the hall's wings extend as galleries, while the tail reaches across the pond. The interior presents a scene of Amida descending to welcome souls into his Pure Land.

Below left The facade of the Phoenix Hall, 48·7 meters long. This view, from the northwest, shows the central section of the hall with its two-story towered wings extending north and south. Recreating Amida's paradise in earthly form, the Phoenix Hall was built on an islet in a lake. The design derives from the towered corridor surrounding the great audience hall of the Heian palace and the winged mansions of the nobility.

Below The Phoenix Hall takes its name from its layout and from the two vigorous gilt-bronze birds that grace its roof and symbolize rebirth in the Pure Land paradise of Amida. It is possible that the phoenixes were designed by the sculptor Jōchō who made the central image in the Amida hall.

From the mid-Heian period Amidist devotion began to attract members of the court nobility. The vivid descriptions of Amida's Western Paradise and of the Buddhist hells provided by Genshin (942–1017) in his *Ōjō yōshū* (*The Essentials of Salvation*) helped to spread Pure Land devotion among monks and laypeople and inspired in their minds visions of bliss and terror. Genshin argued that mere repetition of the *nembutsu* was sufficient for rebirth (*ōjō*). Nobles copied *sūtras*, commissioned statues and built special halls and temples, such as the Byōdōin at Uji, in which to enshrine Amida. Fujiwara no Michinaga founded the Hōjōji as a lavish attempt to recreate the Pure Land on earth. He is reported to have died before the image of Amida at Hōjōji, clinging to ribbons attached to the image and chanting the *nembutsu* in the hope that Amida and his entourage of Bodhisattvas would come and welcome him into the Pure Land of bliss. Moreover, the strong belief that in the year 1052 Japan would enter the third and final age of devolution of the Buddha's teaching (*mappō*) strengthened the tendency to stress dependence on the "other power" or saving compassion (*tariki*) of Amida. The teachings of Ryōnin (1072–1132), Yōkan (1032–1111) and Chingai (1091–1152) further spread Pure Land devotion among the Heian aristocracy, while the wandering mendicant Kūya (903–72) began to carry the promise of rebirth to the common people.

However, it was only from the late 12th century with Hōnen (1133–1212), the founder of the Pure Land school (Jōdoshū), his disciple Shinran (1173–1262), founder of the True Pure Land school (Jōdo Shinshū), Rennyo (1415–99), eighth-generation patriarch of Jōdo Shinshū, and the medicant Ippen (1239–89), founder of the Timely school (Ji), that Amidism established its independence of the older schools. Only then did it begin to spread widely among ordinary people as a belief in which sincere faith in Amida, expressed through the *nembutsu*, held out the promise of easy salvation for all. The various Amidist schools established by these medieval pioneers came to comprise the most vigorous and popular current in Japanese Buddhism. There are today in Japan more than 13 million Jōdo Shinshū followers, some 3 million Jōdoshū devotees and 40 thousand Jishū followers.

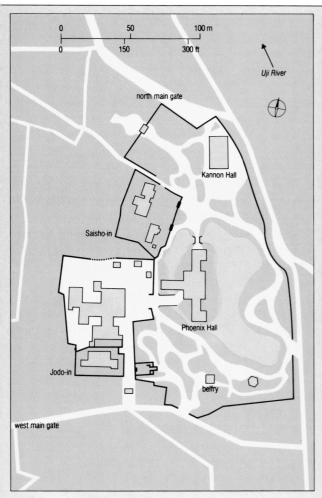

Above The plan shows the Byōdōin complex with the Phoenix Hall, containing its Amida statue, looking east and reflected in the lotus pond. The galleries forming the wings of the building run north and south. Until a fire in 1235 they extended much further into the pond. The building and its garden are a fine example of the unity of composition that was so characteristic of Heian architecture.

Right The central gilt wooden Amida figure is the work of Jōchō, the leading sculptor of the Heian age. It is built in the joined-block technique developed by Jōchō which allowed greater freedom of artistic expression than the early Heian method of carving from a single block. The volatile halo, showing Bodhisattvas floating in clouds or flames, contrasts with the tranquillity of the meditating figure on its lotus throne.

Paradise and Hell in Buddhist Theology

From the late 10th century devotion to the Buddha Amida (Amitābha) and belief in the accessibility of salvation (ōjō) in his Pure Land of the Western Paradise (jōdo) spread rapidly, first in aristocratic society and then among the common people. Devotion to Amida and the Pure Land was one of the most powerful currents of medieval Japanese Buddhism, and one that provided the basis for much of subsequent Buddhist practice in Japan.

Amidist devotionalism was part of a widespread religious reform movement that sprang out of the dislocations of an age in transition from the stability of aristocratic rule to one tormented by the instability of provincial warfare, struggles between rival warrior bands, monastic corruption, maurauding monastic armies and the growing conviction that Japan was entering the Later Age of the Buddhist Law (mappō). In the Later Age of the Law, believed to begin in Japan in the year 1052, salvation by the traditional means of accumulation of merit by one's own efforts (jiriki) was thought to be impossible. On the other hand it was believed that faith in the "other power" (tariki) of a compassionate Buddha such as Amida or Maitreya, the Future Buddha, would guarantee salvation. Early Pure Land advocates such as Genshin and Kūya argued that salvation in the Pure Land could be attained by a simple expression of faith in Amida's vow to save all sentient beings by repetition of the formula of the nembutsu, or sacred title of Amida (Namu Amida Butsu). Pure Land teaching spread first among the aristocracy, many of whom built Pure Land halls such as the Byōdōin or the Chūsonji or commissioned Pure Land paintings and sculpture. The teachings were carried to the people by dedicated preachers and itinerants.

Above Buddhist hells were depicted in *sūtras*, painting and sculpture as the punitive counterpart to the bliss of paradise. The hells were believed to be supervised by 10 judges or kings, headed by Emma, who were also depicted in painting and sculpture as in this wooden statue from the Muromachi period, late 15th century.

Below Most of the important paintings in the Pure Land tradition center on the figure of Amida, who is shown either seated in the midst of his paradise or in an attitude of welcoming descent (raigō), appearing before the devotee at the moment of death to conduct him to the Western Paradise. Here Amida is seen surrounded by a heavenly host of Bodhisattvas descending on purple clouds of evening to welcome men and women to paradise.

Left The path to salvation in Amida's Pure Land was commonly depicted in paintings on the theme of the white path between turbulent rivers of fire and water. These were based on a parable by Shan Dao (613–81 AD). In this painting we see the Pure Land seeker several times.

He is first being chased by thieves and beasts; then he is walking along the narrow white path toward the western shore between the rivers of fire and water containing vignettes of anger and greed; finally he is seen being reborn on a lotus throne in Amida's Pure Land.

Right The mendicant Tendai priest Kūya Shōnin (903–72), known as the "saint of the streets," wandered the length and breadth of Japan bringing the teaching of the Pure Land to all people, reciting the invocation to Amida (*nembutsu*), preaching, working miracles and

leading ecstatic dancing. This realistic statue by Kōshō (13th century) shows the itinerant priest beating a gong and chanting the *nembutsu* with tiny figures of Amida entering his mouth.

Above This Edo period printed edition of Genshin's *Ōjō yōshū* illustrates the terrors of the Buddhist hells as lictors repeatedly punish sinners in the hell of fiery vats.

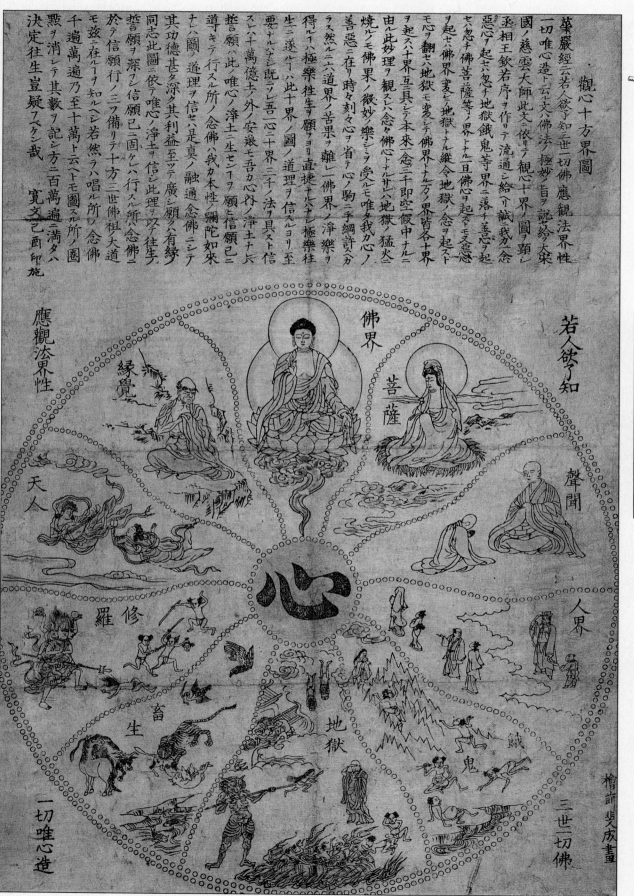

Left Devotion to Amida and the Pure Land blended with other currents of Buddhist thought. This woodblock print from the 17th century explains the 10 worlds of the *Avatamsaka (Kegon) Sūtra* for the layman and reconciles them with devotion to the Pure Land. The top four segments depict the worlds of private Buddhas, Bodhisattvas, Buddhas and Arhats. The lower six segments depict the six realms of transmigration: heavenly beings, humans, bellicose demons, hungry ghosts, beasts and hells. The character for heart at the center points the way to the Pure Land. According to the text, if the believer inks in one of the small circles each time he has invoked the *sūtra* 10000 times, he will reach the Pure Land when all are completed.

The rise of the warrior

Between the 9th and 11th centuries, while the Heian court was enjoying a period of relative tranquillity and cultural splendor, the provinces were slowly slipping into lawlessness and rebellion. The Fujiwara, although adept in court politics and intrigue, had little taste for the cut and thrust of battle or the rigors of military campaigns. Moreover, many were disinclined to leave the capital for administrative posts in the provinces and relied on agents and deputies to manage their public responsibilities and private landholdings. They turned increasingly to provincial warriors (*bushi*) for military support.

The privatization of landholdings that led to the proliferation of *shōen* was only part of a wider erosion of the public ideals of the Chinese-inspired *ritsuryō* system. By the 11th century the system of centrally appointed provincial governors was breaking down. Many nobles who did not wish to leave the comfortable and cultured environment of the capital for a post in some remote provincial office sold their appointment to a deputy. Such deputy governors were willing to stay in the provinces but were also naturally eager to recoup their outlay and take advantage of any local possibilities for their own enrichment. The most readily available sources of personal income were diversions of public taxes or contributions for the tacit acceptance of *shōen* creation within their assigned provinces. Some provincial governors and deputies found that life in the provinces had its own compensations. Whereas the *ritsuryō* codes officially required them to return to the capital after four years and give an account of their stewardship, they sought and secured reappointment and settled down in the provinces. The public treasury naturally tended to suffer when local administrators became entrenched in their assigned posts and ceased to account carefully for their activities. To entrench themselves and extend their interests they frequently made alliances with local warrior families.

Privatization and a return to what John W. Hall has called "familial authority" were also evident in the breakdown of the centralized military system and the emergence of warrior bands based on extended family or regional loyalties. As public land dwindled, the central government had fewer resources to support conscript armies. In 792 the peasant conscription system, which had not proved very effective in extending rule over Ezo tribes in the northeast, was abolished. Military responsibilities passed into private hands. Emperors, nobles, Buddhist temples and great families in the provinces raised militia units for public and private peacekeeping or warfare. There was a steady growth of provincial lawlessness, with the formation of robber and pirate bands, and the organizing of military forces by temples and shrines, by local public officials and managers of *shōen*.

The breakdown of any pretense at a centralized military system capable of ensuring the peace, combined with the growing need to protect private *shōen* and local public interests, hastened the development of provincial warrior bands (*bushidan*). These were not an entirely new phenomenon. There had always been armed families in the pro-

vinces. Prior to the reform effort of the Nara period the *uji* clans had maintained bands of trained warriors drawn from among their kin. Many of these clans had maintained their local influence within the *ritsuryō* system. When that system was eroded in the Heian period, they simply grew in local prominence. Fighting called for costly equipment: swords and armor, bows and arrows, horses and grooms, stables and fodder. It remained a function of the rural elite. These centuries saw the honing of professional military skills and the making of new alliances by these rural elites.

Leaders of the proliferating warrior bands included not only long-resident local chieftains and their kin but officials who had settled down in the provinces, the managers of private estates, and in some cases scions of the imperial or other noble families who had been been cut loose from the court, given a family name and set up in the provinces. Those warriors who had, or could claim, noble ancestry became the nuclei around which several of the largest regional warrior leagues, including the Taira and Minamoto, clustered.

The development of hardened warrior bands was especially evident in the rough frontier region of the northern Kantō where there was sporadic fighting against the Ezo tribes. Here warrior leagues flourished and clashed among themselves. It was these eastern warriors, frequently under the leadership of chieftains claiming noble lineage (*kishu*), who refined the techniques of mounted warfare and elaborated the "way of the bow and horse," the warrior tradition that was eventually to develop into the fully fledged notion of *bushidō*, or the "Way of the Warrior," under Confucian influence in the 17th century.

Unlike the nobles (*kuge*) who spent their lives within the confined and ceremonious world of the court, and unlike the warriors of the later Tokugawa period (1600–1867) who were deliberately separated from the peasantry and obliged to live in garrison towns, warriors (*bushi*) of the Heian and Kamakura periods lived in the countryside. When they were not engaged in warfare or guard duties they managed their holdings. They were repeatedly encouraged by their chieftains to maintain their martial heritage, to cultivate military skills, to practice hunting and hawking, to live frugal, arduous, outdoor lives, and to prize valor, loyalty and family honor.

The vital personal bond between lord and retainer was expressed in the contemporary terms of *hōkō*, or service, and *goon*, favor. In return for their lord's favor expressed most tangibly in spoils in battle or the confirmation of landholdings, the retainer was expected to provide military service in war, ceremonial attendance on guard duty, or economic support in the form of gifts, corvée or tax levies. Prior to the 17th century, however, exhortations to loyalty were frequently more ideal than actual. In an age of frequent instability and warfare many warriors followed their instincts for personal or family aggrandizement, or for sheer survival. The turncoat was probably as common as the selfless vassal.

We find a growing vocabulary of expressions describing the life-style of the warrior in the medieval period. Many of these terms distinguished the customs of warriors from those of

This is one of the set of 33 *sūtra* scrolls commissioned by Taira no Kiyomori and his family for the Itsukushima shrine. Each scroll is mounted on a wooden rod with metal mountings, silk bindings and knobs of crystal and gilded metal. Reflecting the ideals of universal salvation and the compassionate intervention of Bodhisattvas inherent in the *Lotus Sūtra*, this scroll contains an illustration and text describing the compassion of Kannon. The scrolls reveal the high level of craftsmanship in the late Heian period, the religious piety of the Taira, the fusion of Buddhism and Shinto – in that Buddhist texts are presented to a Shinto shrine – and the powerful influence of courtly culture on the warrior Taira family.

courtiers or contrasted the harsher customs of eastern *bushi* from their counterparts in the western provinces. Expressions like *yumiya toru mi no narai,* the customs of those who draw the bow and arrow, *kyūba no michi,* the way of the bow and horse, *mononofu no michi,* the way of the soldier, were all in common use in the late Heian and Kamakura periods to describe the *bushi's* profession of arms and to set it apart from the sequestered life-style of the court nobility. *Bandō musha no narai,* the customs of the Kantō warriors, expressed the strong sense of martial identity of the *bushi* of the eastern provinces. This developing vocabulary and image of the warrior ideal is enshrined in the chronicles and war tales (*gunkimono*) that were compiled in the late Heian and Kamakura periods. Early military tales like the *Mutsuwaki* (*A Tale of Mutsu*) or some of the stories in the *Konjaku monogatari* (*Tales of Times Now Past*) vividly portray the bloodshed and valor of the warrior's way of life: "I stand ready to give my life in your service, pledged Takenori. I look on it as nothing more than a feather. Though I may die facing the rebels, never shall I turn my back on an enemy in order to live" (*A Tale of Mutsu*). Some of these tales began as oral records and were compiled by courtiers or wandering balladeers. Many were no doubt savored as much by courtiers as they were by warriors.

While warrior leagues were small and merely clashed among themselves in the provinces, they did not represent a severe threat to the central authority of the court. By the mid-10th century, however, it was becoming evident that extensive bands of warriors with charismatic leadership were capable of exerting control over whole regions of Japan and that the court could only put down such challenges to its authority with great difficulty and by turning to some rival warrior league for support. Among the larger warrior leagues were those bearing the names Fujiwara, Taira and Minamoto. The leaders of the Taira (also known as the Heike) claimed descent from Emperor Kammu. The Minamoto (or Genji) claimed Emperor Seiwa as their founding ancestor.

Between 935 and 940 there were major challenges to the authority of the central government in eastern and western Japan. In the Kantō in the 10th century branches of the Taira clan were numerous. Taira no Masakado, who died in 940, an eastern warrior who claimed direct descent from Emperor Kammu, led a revolt against civilian authority in 935 and took over most of the eight Kantō provinces. The revolt began as a power struggle between several rival Taira bands from which Masakado emerged victorious. He then expelled court-appointed district governors from Musashi and Hitachi provinces. By 939 Masakado, calling himself the ruler of the Kantō, was in open revolt against the central government. At the same time Fujiwara no Sumitomo, who died in 941, had been sent by the court to put down piracy in the Inland Sea and turned rebel himself. The court thus faced revolt on two fronts. Armies led by imperial princes and the Minamoto chieftain Tsunemoto, who died in 961, were dispatched to deal with the uprisings. The revolts were quelled with difficulty. The court seemed to have reasserted its authority, but it had only done so with

great difficulty and by relying heavily on Minamoto warriors who were thus able to strengthen the Minamoto presence in eastern and western Japan. Some Minamoto established close ties with the Fujiwara at court and became the "claws and teeth" of the Fujiwara. The weakness of the court was now exposed, the power of provincial warrior bands shown all too clearly.

Powerful warrior bands continued to build up their power in eastern and western Japan during the 11th century. In the northeast the Minamoto (Genji), under the leadership of Minamoto no Yoriyoshi (988–1075) and his son Yoshiie (1039–1106), grew in strength through the Former Nine Years' and Later Three Years' Wars (1051–62). Yoriyoshi and Yoshiie were appointed by the court to quell a revolt by the Abe family in Mutsu. They did so after bitter fighting. In the process the Minamoto warriors became hardened campaigners and strengthened their grip on the Kantō. Their leaders began to receive commendations of land by local proprietors eager to secure their protection.

The exploits of Yoriyoshi and Yoshiie are the subject of the *Mutsuwaki* mentioned above. The *Mutsuwaki* was written by a courtier in the 11th century and chronicles the victories of Minamoto Yoriyoshi and his son Yoshiie in the wars of pacification of the northern provinces. The long campaigns in the north provided many opportunities for the display of warrior courage. Yoriyoshi's victories established his reputation as a great chieftain and, through the granting of spoils, allowed him to forge strong vassal bonds with the eastern *bushi* who joined his armies. The *Mutsuwaki* already contains many of the facets of the warrior ideal more fully developed in later war tales.

Yoriyoshi is presented as the seasoned leader and master of the way of the bow and horse:

At that juncture the court nobles met in council determined to appoint a general to punish [Abe] Yoriyoshi, and settled unanimously upon Minamoto-no-ason Yoriyoshi, a son of Yorinobu-no-ason, the governor of Kawachi province. Yoriyoshi was a cool, resourceful man, well suited to command. Numbers of eastern warriors had long ago joined their fortunes to his, won by his courage and enterprise as a soldier under his father during the Chōgen era [1028–37], when Yorinobu-no-ason went on behalf of the court to subdue Taira Tadatsune and his sons— rebels who were perpetrating shocking outrages in eastern Japan. For a time Yoriyoshi had served as a third-ranking official in Kōichijōin's household. Kōichijōin was a prince who delighted in the hunt. Whenever one of his parties came upon a deer, fox, or hare in the field, it was invariably Yoriyoshi who took the game, for although he carried a weak bow by preference, his aim was so deadly that every arrow buried itself to the feathers in his prey, and even the fiercest animal perished before his bowstring.

But Yoriyoshi is also the ideal type of warrior chieftain who wins the loyalty of his followers by his generous concern for them as well as by sheer force of arms: "Yoriyoshi provided a filling meal for his men, saw that their weapons were put to rights, and personally visited the injured to care for their wounds. The warriors were deeply touched. 'Our bodies shall repay our debts; our lives shall count as nothing where honor is at stake. We are ready to die for our general now.' "

Minamoto no Yoshiie, who like Yoriyoshi played an important role in the consolidation of Minamoto power in the eastern provinces, is presented as being cut from the same heroic mold as his father:

Nevertheless, the great hero of the battle was Yoriyoshi's eldest son, Yoshiie. He shot arrows from horseback like a god; undeterred by gleaming blades, he lunged through the rebels' encirclements to emerge on their left and right. With his great arrow heads he transfixed one enemy chieftain after another, never shooting at random but always inflicting a mortal wound. He galloped like the wind and fought with a skill that was more than human. The barbarians fled rather than face him, calling him the firstborn son of Hachiman, the god of war.

One of the warrior bands which assisted Yoshiie in the final conquest of the Abe was a branch of the Fujiwara family. These Northern Fujiwara, as they were known, established their castle at Hiraizumi and remained a military and cultural force in the northeast until their destruction by Minamoto no Yoritomo in the late 12th century. The golden hall of the Buddhist temple they built, the Chūsonji, is one of the most splendid examples of late Heian provincial architecture.

Closer to the capital, in the Ise region, a branch of the Taira family was also building up its power during the 11th and 12th centuries. Under the astute leadership of Taira no Kiyomori (1118–81) this lineage was called upon by cloistered emperors to intervene in court politics. Here the Taira came into direct conflict with the Fujiwara and the Minamoto warriors who were used by the Fujiwara. Once powerful warrior clans became involved in political disputes in the capital, they could not easily be dislodged. The cloistered emperors and courtiers therefore adopted, whenever possible, a policy of neutralizing warrior influence by playing one warrior faction off against another. As long as no single warrior clan achieved hegemony, the court could hope to maintain its own preeminence. From the mid-12th century, however, first the Taira, then the Minamoto achieved a preponderance of power over the court, giving warriors the chance to seize political leadership.

When a succession dispute broke out in 1156 between a cloistered emperor and a reigning emperor, the court took sides. There were Fujiwara family members on both sides of the dispute. The rival military clans Taira and Minamoto were also involved. By skillfully eliminating all his rivals in the Hōgen and Heiji disturbances of 1156 and 1159, Kiyomori killed off most of the Minamoto leadership and established for himself and the Taira a commanding position within the court. Characteristically, the emperors, the cloistered emperors and the Fujiwara clan were not swept away. Chagrined, they continued to play a largely ceremonial role,

waiting for an opportunity to oust the Taira. They were overruled at will by Kiyomori and the Taira leaders who took court ranks and offices and assigned themselves provincial titles and landholdings. Like the Fujiwara before them they used marriage politics in an attempt to coopt the imperial office. Kiyomori married his daughter into the imperial line in the hope of producing a Taira emperor. The infant emperor Antoku seemed to be a realization of the dream.

By settling in Heian-kyō (Kyoto) and becoming in effect a new group of courtiers, the Taira clan under Kiyomori cut itself off from its provincial military base and its martial tradition. At court they were regarded as arrogant upstarts by Fujiwara nobles and cloistered emperors who waited only for a countervailing military power to topple the Taira. Meanwhile the remnants of the Minamoto were mustering their strength in the eastern provinces around the young Yoritomo who had been spared by Kiyomori and sent into exile. From 1180 Yoritomo felt strong enough to challenge the Taira hegemony. His cousin Minamoto no Yoshinaka and half-brother Yoshitsune conducted the devastating military campaigns which drove the Taira from the capital to their destruction in the sea battle at Dannoura in 1185 in which the child emperor Antoku met his death in the waters of the inland sea. The Taira leaders were either killed or committed suicide to avoid capture and the clan was put to the sword.

The pathos of the sudden rise and disastrous fall of the Taira provides the central unifying theme in the *Heike monogatari* (*Tale of the Heike*). Recited by ballad singers, these tales of heroism and sadness, with their Buddhist overtones of dissolution, emptiness and change, were assembled in something like their present form in the mid-13th century. The distinctive martial values of the *bushi*, so clearly perceived by the anonymous courtier who compiled the *Mutsuwaki,* were vaunted and embellished in the war tales of succeeding centuries culminating in the splendid declamatory prose of the *Heike monogatari*. Strength, courage, cunning, loyalty to one's lord, generosity in victory, bravery in defeat, hunger for personal and family honor were all prized; cowardice, meanness and treachery castigated. The *Heike monogatari* frequently draws a contrast, exaggerated but striking, between the hardened Minamoto warriors of the eastern provinces and their courtierized Taira counterparts from the west:

. . . Commander-in-chief Koremori summoned Sanemori of the Saitō clan. He was from the village of Nagai and knew the east well. Koremori asked him: "Sanemori, in the eight eastern provinces are there many men who are as mighty archers as you are?"

"Do you then consider me a mighty archer?" asked Sanemori with a scornful smile. "I can only draw an arrow thirteen hand-breadths long. In the eastern provinces there are any number of warriors who can do so. There is one famed archer who never draws a shaft less than fifteen hand-breadths long. So mighty is his bow that four or five ordinary men must pull together to bend it. When he shoots, his arrow can easily pierce

The emergence of warrior bands
With the loosening of the central authority of the imperial court and the breakdown of the conscript military system local warrior bands (*bushidan*) proliferated in the provinces from the 10th century. The map shows some of the major warrior bands and the campaigns important in charting the rise of the *bushi*. In order to guard the capital, assert control over the north, protect *shōen* and villages, and put down regional revolts such as those led by Taira Masakado (940), Fujiwara Sumitomo (941) and Taira Tadatsune (1028), emperors, cloistered emperors, nobles, temples and shrines were forced to make use of the chieftains of regional warrior bands like the Minamoto or Taira, giving them an opening to involve themselves in court politics. Great temples such as Enryakuji, Kōfukuji, Mount Kōya and Negoro had armies of monk soldiers several thousand strong. Shrines such as Kumano and Usa could also field substantial military forces.

The eastern provinces were home to some of the toughest and most independent warrior bands. Many eastern *bushi* followed Minamoto Yoriyoshi and Yoshiie in their wars against the Abe and Kiyomori during the earlier nine-year campaign (1051–62) and later three-year campaign (1083–87). Minamoto military successes gave them control of much of the east and swelled their vassal band.

Inset This scene, from one of three surviving medieval scrolls depicting the exploits of Minamoto Yoshiie in the three-year campaign (1083–87), shows the warrior hero, who was known as Hachiman Tarō, the firstborn of Hachiman, god of war, in action against his enemies. According to legend he determined their position by noting the flight of startled wild geese. The scroll painting is rather simple in execution but it does convey a sense of the medieval warrior as mounted bowman who engaged in personal combat or sporadic sorties rather than pitched battles.

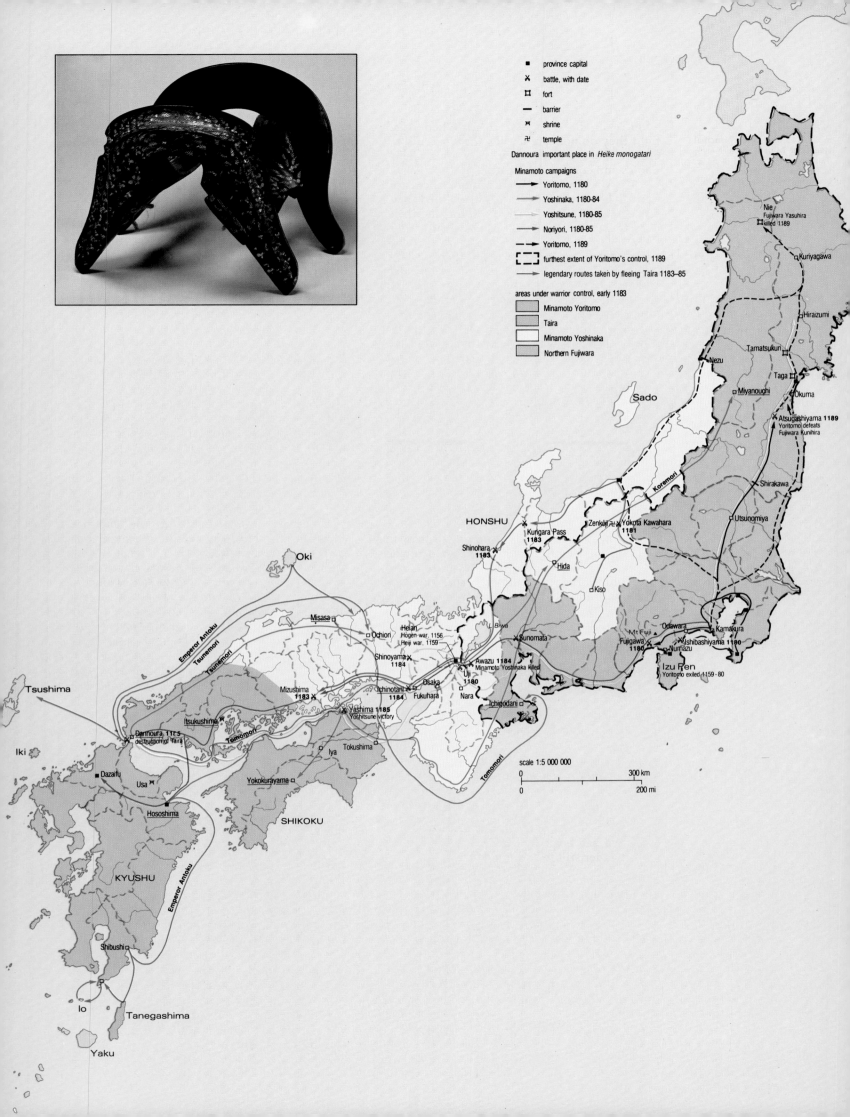

province capital
battle, with date
fort
barrier
shrine
temple

Dannoura important place in *Heike monogatari*

Minamoto campaigns

Yoritomo, 1180
Yoshinaka, 1180-84
Yoshitsune, 1180-85
Noriyori, 1180-85
Yoritomo, 1189
furthest extent of Yoritomo's control, 1189
legendary routes taken by fleeing Taira 1183-85

areas under warrior control, early 1183

Minamoto Yoritomo
Taira
Minamoto Yoshinaka
Northern Fujiwara

Nie
Fujiwara Yasuhira
killed 1189

Kuriyagawa

Hiraizumi

Tamatsukuri

Miyanoughi

Taga

Okuma

Atsugashiyama **1189**
Yoritomo defeats
Fujiwara Kunihira

Shirakawa

Nezu

Koremori

Sado

Utsunomiya

HONSHU

Kurigara Pass
1183

Zenkōji Yokota Kawahara
1181

Shinohara
1183

Hida

Kiso

Oki

Misasa

Ochiori

Heian
Hogen war. 1156
Heiji war. 1159

L. Biwa

Sunomata

Mt Fuji

Odawara

Kamakura

Fujigawa
1180

Numazu

Ishibashiyama **1180**

Emperor Antoku

Tsunemori

Tsunemori

Shinoyama
1184

Awazu **1184**
Minamoto Yoshinaka killed

Uji
1180

Izu Pen
Yoritomo exiled 1159 - 80

Tsushima

Mizushima
1183

Ichinotani
1184

Osaka
Fukuhara

Nara

Ichigodani

Itsukushima

Yashima **1185**
Yoshitsune victory

Tomomori

Iya

Tokushima

Iki

Dannoura **1185**
destruction of Taira

Tomomori

Yokokurayama

scale 1:5 000 000

0 _____ 300 km
0 _____ 200 mi

Dazaifu

Usa

Hososhima

SHIKOKU

KYUSHU

Emperor Antoku

Shibushi

Io

Tanegashima

Yaku

Gempei wars and the destruction of the Taira
With their sweeping victories in the Hōgen and Heiji uprisings (1156 and 1159) Taira Kiyomori and the Ise Taira were able to dominate the court, seize titles to land and destroy their principal rivals, the Minamoto chieftains. Taira arrogance turned courtiers and the retired Emperor Go-Shirakawa against them. In 1180 Prince Mochihito led an abortive coup against the Taira but was killed at the battle of Uji. In the east Minamoto Yoritomo also led a revolt but was defeated at Ishibashiyama (1180). At the battle of Fujigawa in the same year he was more successful. From 1180 Yoritomo consolidated his power in the east, adding to his vassals (*gokenin*) and beginning to build offices of warrior government.

In 1183 Yoritomo's cousin Yoshinaka, moving from Shinano, routed Taira troops and marched on the capital. When Yoshinaka burst into the capital, the Taira fled westward, taking the child emperor Antoku. Mutual suspicion between Yoshinaka and Yoritomo led Yoritomo to send his brothers Noriyori and Yoshitsune to deal with Yoshinaka and complete the rout of the Taira. Yoshitsune, a brilliant tactician, drove the Taira from Yashima in March 1185 and crushed them in a sea battle at Dannoura in April. The major Taira leaders were killed or took their own lives. The Taira child emperor Antoku is believed to have drowned with the imperial regalia.

Following the Minamoto victory, Yoritomo concentrated on the elimination of Yoshitsune, whom he branded a rebel, the consolidation of his military power in the east by crushing the Northern Fujiwara who had given Yoshitsune refuge, and formal recognition by the court of his de facto warrior government in Kamakura with the grant of the title of shogun and the consolidation of his Bakufu.

Although all the Taira leaders were killed at Dannoura, they lived on in legend and literature. There are many folk legends of "fallen people" or divine visitors, including disgraced nobles or defeated warriors who fled to remote areas. As many as 100 places are said to have given refuge or been founded by fugitive Taira who somehow escaped the destruction at Dannoura. The tragic story of the Taira, as told in the *Heike monogatari* and spread by blind lute players, had a powerful emotive appeal to villagers in remote areas.

Inset This saddle of wood and mother-of-pearl inlay, decorated with cobwebs and fronds of bush clover, aptly symbolizes the two aspects of the medieval martial tradition, the arts of war (*bu*) and those of peace (*bun*). The way of the medieval warrior was known as the "way of the bow and horse." But accoutrements of war were decorated with motifs suggestive of poetry and religion.

two or three suits of armor at once. Even a warrior from a small estate has at least five hundred soldiers. They are bold horsemen who never fall, nor do they let their horses stumble on the roughest road. When they fight they do not care if even their parents or children are killed; they ride over their bodies and continue the battle.

"The warriors of the western provinces are quite different. If their parents are killed they retire from the battle and perform Buddhist rites to console the souls of the dead. Only after the mourning is over will they fight again. If their children are slain, their grief is so deep that they cease fighting altogether. When their rations have given out, they plant rice in the fields and go out to fight only after reaping it. They dislike the heat of summer. They grumble at the severe cold of winter. This is not the way of the soldiers of the eastern provinces."

By the time of the compilation of the *Heike monogatari* the ultimate test of idealized warrior heroism was the willingness to die for one's lord, and to disembowel oneself if necessary to avoid the ignominy of capture and disgrace. At the same time this grisly ritual is sometimes modulated in the tale by the emphasis on a code of chivalry and an admiration of the courtly arts even for warriors. In the *Heike monogatari* the ideal warrior was not merely a master of the military arts, he was also sensitive to human emotion and skilled in the composition of poetry. Minamoto no Yorimasa may be said to have represented that ideal. Yorimasa had called for Prince Mochihito to raise a revolt against the Taira in 1180. When that revolt was crushed, he took his own life with all the ferocious bravery expected of a warrior after composing a verse that would have done credit to a courtier:

Yorimasa summoned Watanabe Chōjitsu Tonau and ordered: "Strike off my head." Tonau could not bring himself to do this while his master was still alive. He wept bitterly. "How can I do that, my lord?" he replied. "I can do so only after you have committed suicide." "I understand," said Yorimasa. He turned to the west, joined his palms and chanted "Hail Amida Buddha" ten times in a loud voice. Then he composed this poem:

> Like a fossil tree
> Which has borne not one blossom
> Sad had been my life
> Sadder still to end my days
> Leaving no fruit behind me.

Having spoken these lines, he thrust the point of his sword into his belly, bowed his face to the ground as the blade pierced him through, and died. No ordinary man could compose a poem at such a moment. For Yorimasa, however, the writing of poems had been a constant pleasure since his youth. And so, even at the moment of death, he did not forget. Tonau took up his master's head and, weeping, fastened it to a stone. Then, evading the enemy, he made his way to the river and sank it in a deep place.

The glory of the Taira was finally extinguished at the great sea battle of Dannoura in 1185. Again, in describing defeat, the storytellers transmute a disastrous naval encounter into a moving statement about the illusory nature of glory and the heroism that can arise from devotion and find expression even in defeat. As the Taira fleet is broken by the Minamoto, one court lady determines to die with the child emperor Antoku on whom so many Taira hopes had been fastened:

Then the Lady Nii, who had already resolved what she would do, donned a double outer dress of dark gray mourning and tucking up her long skirts put the Sacred Jewel under her arm and the Sacred Sword in her sash. She took the Emperor in her arms and said, "Though I am but a woman, I will not fall into the hands of enemy. I will accompany our Sovereign Lord. Let those of you who will, follow me." She moved softly to the gunwale of the vessel.

The Emperor was seven years old that year but looked much older than his age. He was so lovely that he seemed to shed a brilliant radiance about him, and his long black hair hung loose far down his back. With a look of surprise and anxiety on his face he asked the Lady Nii, "Where are you taking me?"

She turned to the youthful sovereign, with tears streaming down her cheeks, and answered, "Perhaps Your Majesty does not know that he was reborn to the Imperial throne in this world as a result of the merit of the Ten Virtues practiced in former lives. Now, however, some evil karma claims you. Turn to the east and bid farewell to the deity of the Great Shrine of Ise and then to the west and say the *nembutsu*, that Amida Buddha and the Holy Ones may come to welcome you to the Pure Western Land. Japan is as small as a grain of millet, but now it is a vale of misery. There is a pure land of happiness beneath the waves, another capital where no sorrow is. It is there that I am taking my Sovereign."

She comforted him, and bound up his long hair in his dove-colored robe. Blinded with tears the child sovereign put his beautiful little hands together. He turned first to the east to say farewell to the deity of Ise and then to the west to repeat the *nembutsu*. The Lady Nii took him tightly in her arms and with the words, "In the depths of the ocean is our capital," sank with him at last beneath the waves.

Even before the destruction of the Taira, Minamoto no Yoritomo was building up institutions of warrior rule in Kamakura, in eastern Japan. The establishment of Yoritomo's warrior government in Kamakura marked not only the end of the Heian period, but also a severe shift in the balance between courtly and warrior power, and the opening of a new cultural era. The age of courtly domination of Japanese culture was coming to an end. Learning from courtiers, but also drawing on their own customs and looking to Zen Buddhist monks and visitors from China, medieval warriors were forging a distinctive cultural style for themselves.

Samurai Society in the Medieval Age

The warrior elite who dominated Japanese society from the 12th to the 19th century were commonly known as *bushi* or samurai. *Bushi* means "fighting men" and is generally used for the warriors of the medieval period, most of whom lived in villages and managed their lands while training in military arts and keeping themselves ready for service to their chieftains on the battlefield. Some of these provincial warriors were retainers (*gokenin*, literally "housemen") of the shoguns. From an early period the word "samurai" had the association of armed service by a retainer. After the 16th century it is commonly used to describe warriors who were removed from the countryside to live as stipendiary retainers in castle towns. From the medieval period warriors developed their own martial, spartan, outdoor life-style. Through cultivation of the Way of the Warrior (*bushidō*) chieftains sought to inculcate the virtues of loyal service and family honor. In extreme cases loyalty might be expressed in willingness to immolate oneself for one's lord in the grisly ritual of *seppuku*. In the peaceful Edo period loyal service increasingly meant administrative or ceremonial duties.

Right In this scene from one of the Mongol Invasion scrolls the mounted warrior Takezaki Suenaga, by whom the scrolls were commissioned, is shown leading a sortie against Mongol archers who have established a beachhead on Japanese soil. His badly wounded horse is clearly startled by the strange fireball unleashed by the Mongols. The longbow and curved sword (*tachi*) used by the Japanese warrior are contrasted with the short bows and straight swords of the Mongol archers. Suenaga had the scrolls painted and presented to a Shinto shrine so that his exploits would be remembered when spoils and honors were distributed. Lest his heroic role should be mistaken, he is named in most of the scenes in which he appears.

Above This strikingly stylized portrait shows Minamoto Yoritomo (1147–99), the founder of the Kamakura shogunate, not as an armored warrior, but as ruler and administrator, dressed in court robes and holding a baton of office. This is fitting because Yoritomo is remembered less as a brilliant general than as an administrator and institution builder who planned and oversaw the rout of the Taira while building the basis of warrior government in Kamakura.

Right In the early medieval period warriors viewed themselves as mounted bowmen. Before long, however, blades, beaten, folded and tempered in solemn ritual forging by master swordsmiths in eastern Japan, came to be prized as the "soul of the samurai." This is a fine *tachi*, a sword intended to be slung at the waist by cords, made in the late 14th century. Swords of this quality were prized as objects of great beauty and spiritual force.

Left This fiery scene is from the scrolls illustrating the Heiji insurrection of 1159 by which the Taira came to power. Minamoto warriors are rampaging through the Sanjō palace in Kyoto as they seek to abduct the cloistered Emperor Go-Shirakawa who has sided with the Taira. As flames roar through the buildings, the maurauding *bushi* plunder the palace and massacre Go-Shirakawa's retainers. The painting is a vivid portrayal of the violence attending the intrusion of warriors into court politics.

Right Early manuals on the cultivation of martial arts showed warriors a variety of vital skills, including that of donning armor in emergency without a page to help.

CULTURE AND SOCIETY IN THE MEDIEVAL AGE

The long span of Japanese history between the 12th and 16th centuries—embracing the late Heian, Kamakura and Muromachi periods—is generally referred to as Japan's "medieval age" (*chūsei*). Some scholars might extend or narrow the temporal boundaries of the age, and others would perhaps prefer to describe it as the early feudal age in Japan, but most would accept this periodization without serious modification. It has been characterized as an age of war and warriors. Certainly it was an age of increasing instability and spreading warfare, but it was also an age of institutional growth and change, commerical activity, religious vitality and cultural creativity. Warriors achieved much greater social and political prominence during these centuries, but it would be misleading to see only their imprint on the politics and culture of the age. Courtiers maintained powerful cultural influence, Buddhist monks were active, and for the first time in Japanese history we can begin to discern popular elements in the cultural texture of the age.

Beneath the instability we can distinguish broad, long-term currents of change in politics, society, religion and the arts. A few of these developments might be described as distinctively medieval. Most, however, had their antecedents well before the 12th century or continued to be felt long after the 16th. Because the intermingling of these various currents shaped the larger features of traditional Japanese society and culture and because, in many cases, their impact can still be detected today, it is no exaggeration to suggest that the medieval heritage is as important for Japan as the medieval heritage has been to the history of any European society. In order to understand the significance of the cultural developments in this period it is essential to have some understanding of the political and social changes that were steadily transforming medieval society.

Currents of change in politics

Politically, we can distinguish three long-term currents, or phases, in the medieval age: the slow but relentless transfer of political leadership to a new elite; the erosion of stable central authority into decentralization and civil war; and then, when political fragmentation seemed to have reached an extreme, a fierce drive back through warfare to reunification. The first of these phases involved a shift in political power from the imperial court to warrior chieftains from the late 12th century, with the establishment of warrior governments (Bakufu or shogunates) on the one hand and the erosion of imperial authority and the political and economic power of the court nobility on the other. Whereas the early phases of warrior government, the Kamakura and early Muromachi Bakufu, were relatively strong and stable, the late 15th and early 16th centuries saw a loss of central control by the Muromachi Bakufu accompanied by provincial

unrest, endemic warfare and local initiative. This process has been referred to as the "lower toppling the upper" (*gekokujō*) in an age of provincial wars. Eventually, from the melee of warring lords (*sengoku daimyō*), emerged warriors such as Oda Nobunaga, Toyotomi Hideyoshi and Tokugawa Ieyasu who were impelled by larger visions of national unification and gifted with the tactical military genius to reunify the country and finally give it an enduring peace.

In the 10th and 11th centuries the imperial court in Heian still maintained its political authority. While emperors (*tennō*), who were frequently children, reigned, members of the Fujiwara family ruled by monopolizing the highest court offices and exerting influence as regents and maternal grandparents of the *tennō*. Those few *tennō* who challenged Fujiwara power did so by abdicating and setting themselves up as cloistered emperors (*in*) with their own offices of government. Already by the 10th century the administration, land-allocation, military and tax systems established in the Nara period were crumbling. Nobles, temples and shrines, and even members of the imperial family competed to carve privatized holdings (*shōen*) out of the public domain and began to provide themselves with the military means to protect them. With the collapse of any pretense of a centralized military system, provincial families armed themselves and formed regional warrior bands. The eastern warrior bands, in particular, forged strong vassal loyalties in skirmishes in the north. The officials, whose job it was to manage the scattered private estates of the nobility and temples, also called upon local warrior families for protection. The great monasteries built up their own armies of soldier-monks (*sōhei*) who were willing to use religious sanctions or military force to protect or extend monastic interests. There was periodic unrest in the provinces and disorder in the capital. The uprising by Taira no Masakado in the eastern provinces between 935 and 940 and the simultaneous rebellion by Fujiwara no Sumitomo in the west were severe challenges to central authority, but the court, by calling on provincial warrior bands for assistance, was able to suppress these early rebellions and cling to its authority and political preeminence until the 12th century.

This preeminence was seriously threatened, however, when provincial warriors (*bushi*) became embroiled in Kyoto politics and began to arrogate to themselves political power. The court sought to preempt this by playing off one warrior clan against another, especially the powerful Taira and Minamoto. This policy worked reasonably well until the mid-12th century when the Taira warrior family under Taira no Kiyomori wiped out their major rivals and established a virtual hegemony over the court. Much as the Fujiwara had done, Kiyomori and the Taira tried to monopolize court offices and to rule through the existing administra-

Mongol invasions of 1274 and 1281

In 1268, with Korea ravaged and most of Song China conquered, Khubilai Khan (1215–94) the Mongol chieftain sent envoys to Japan calling for the "king of Japan" to submit. The court in Kyoto and the warrior government in Kamakura ignored his demands and braced themselves for invasion. Samurai vassals of the Kamakura Bakufu were put on alert. Temples and shrines offered prayers for the protection of the nation. Finally in November 1274 a fleet of 900 vessels carrying more than 44000 troops and seamen (including Mongols, Tatars, Chinese and Koreans) set out from southern Korea. After devastating Tsushima it landed troops on the shore of Hakata Bay on 19 November. After forcing Japanese warriors to retreat the Mongols returned to their ships. At night they were hit by a fierce gale which sank many ships and scattered the fleet.

In 1275 and 1279 Khubilai renewed his demands. The Hōjō regents beheaded his envoys. They ordered the building of coastal ramparts around Hakata Bay, the construction of boarding vessels to harass the Mongol ships and the mobilization of non-vassals as well as vassals. With the final collapse of the Song in 1279, Khubilai was free to devote himself to the conquest of Japan. In 1281 he ordered the assembly of a great armada composed of two fleets. In early June 4400 warships bearing 140000 men set out simultaneously from Korea and the Yangzi River. While the southern fleet was delayed by several weeks, the eastern fleet arrived at Hakata on 23 June and engaged in sea battles with Japanese boarding vessels. On 16 August the joint fleet was struck by a typhoon and half the ships and men were lost. The Japanese attributed their two near-miraculous escapes to "divine winds" (*kamikaze*). This contributed to the belief that Japan was a "divinely protected land" (*shinkoku*). With no spoils to show for their efforts many samurai were discontented. Khubilai planned a third invasion but it was never launched.

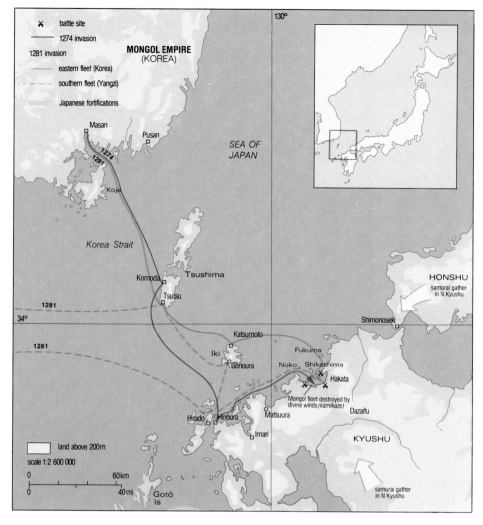

tive framework. In his efforts to dislodge the Taira, cloistered emperor Go-Shirakawa looked to the surviving Minamoto who were regrouping in eastern Japan under the young general Yoritomo and his half-brother Yoshitsune. While Yoritomo built up an institutional framework for Minamoto victory in eastern Japan, Minamoto Yoshinaka and Yoshitsune drove the Taira from Kyoto and pressed them westward to defeat and annihilation at the battle of Dannoura in 1185. The rise and fall of the Taira, or Heike as they were also known, is expressed with haunting poignancy in the *Heike monogatari,* the oral and literary narrative of their precipitous rise to power and calamitous fall.

The sweeping Minamoto victory over the Taira in the late 12th century replaced one military regime with another. It did not displace the imperial court, but neither did it restore power to the court. Yoritomo assumed the title of shogun, military agent of the *tennō,* and established his shogunate, or Bakufu, in Kamakura in eastern Japan. To reward his vassals, to handle spoils and disputed claims, to mete out justice and maintain order, Yoritomo set up a number of government offices headed by trusted vassals or by lower-ranking court nobles he brought from Kyoto. He thus established the model for subsequent warrior government in Japan. He also instituted two offices, those of provincial military protectors (*shugo*) and military estate stewards (*jitō*), that placed his vassals in positions of power in provinces and private estates (*shōen*) throughout the country. Thus Japan saw the creation of a dual structure of political

authority in which a military regime in Kamakura assumed many of the functions hitherto regarded as the preserve of the imperial court. At the same time the court was not displaced and continued to exercise some of its traditional functions. Yoritomo set a shogunal pattern of showing formal respect for the court while imposing his will on it and exercising surveillance over it.

As a warrior government, the Bakufu was primarily concerned with maintaining discipline in the warrior order headed by Yoritomo and his vassals. In time, however, under Yoritomo and his two short-lived sons and then the Hōjō warrior regents, who dominated it after the extinction of the Minamoto line of shoguns in the early 13th century, the Bakufu steadily assumed more and more legislative and judicial authority over landholding rights, tax payments and legal affairs affecting the whole of society. The Hōjō established a branch office of the Bakufu in Kyoto for oversight of western Japan. They intervened in the imperial succession. They assumed authority, too, in foreign affairs and it fell to Hōjō Tokimune to organize the defense of the country in the face of the Mongol invasions of 1274 and 1281. Suffering from reduced political and economic leverage and confronted with the institutional vitality of the Kamakura Bakufu, the court found its authority dwindling.

Unreconciled to its declining authority, the court made several attempts to recover political power. In 1221 the Jōkyū War, an ill-fated uprising led by cloistered emperor Go-Toba, was easily crushed by the Hōjō, giving them the power to exile emperors, confiscate more lands, install more military land stewards, punish courtiers and members of the imperial family and regulate the order of the imperial succession. In the 1320s resistance to the Hōjō family's control of the Kamakura Bakufu by disaffected warrior vassals clustered around Emperor Go-Daigo. With the support of the Ashikaga and several other powerful eastern warrior families, as well as that of armed bands of soldier-monks, Go-Daigo was able to overthrow the Bakufu in 1333 and reestablish what he called direct imperial rule. This imperial restoration of the Kemmu era lasted for only three years before the court-centered policies of Go-Daigo alienated his erstwhile warrior supporters. In 1336 Go-Daigo was forced to flee Kyoto, leaving Ashikaga Takauji to take the title of shogun and organize a new regime, the Muromachi Bakufu, under a rival emperor. For more than three decades the country was divided in a desultory civil war between supporters of Go-Daigo and his southern court and the northern court supported by the Ashikaga.

Thus the Muromachi Bakufu got off to an uncertain start. From the outset the Ashikaga shoguns, who had neither extensive lands nor military power of their own, had to rely on the cooperation of their leading vassals and provincial military protectors, the *shugo*. Strong shoguns, like the third shogun Yoshimitsu, who healed the breach between the northern and southern courts, or like the autocratic sixth shogun Yoshinori, were able to dominate and use the military power of this coalition to the advantage of the Bakufu and shogunal authority. The assassination of Yoshinori in 1441 by an aggrieved *shugo* exposed the Bakufu's intrinsic weakness. *Shugo,* and the local warriors beneath them, began to compete to enhance their local power while weak shoguns like Yoshimasa retreated from active political leadership into palace politics and cultural diversions. A dispute over Yoshimasa's shogunal title sparked the Onin War in 1467, a ten-year conflict between two rival leagues of *shugo* that laid waste much of Kyoto, scattered nobles and monks to the provinces and ushered in a century of sporadic provincial warfare known as the age of "warring provinces" (*sengoku jidai*).

In the disturbed conditions of the late 15th and early 16th centuries what counted was not an official title or the backing of an increasingly powerless shogunate but real power in terms of loyal vassals, tightly held lands, well-fortified castles, tactical ability and constant readiness for attack and defense. In these circumstances many of the *shugo,* whose administrative reach was overextended, were toppled by local warriors beneath them in a surge of *gekokujō* which produced the small, tightly knit domains of the warring states barons, the *sengoku daimyō*. By the early 16th century there were some 250 of these *sengoku* domains throughout Japan.

With the process of decentralization at its height, the political pendulum began to swing back in the direction of reunification. Oda Nobunaga, a tactical genius from a small domain in central Honshu, who claimed to be going to the aid of the shogunate, won a series of brilliant victories and marched into Kyoto in 1568. He soon ousted the shogun, isolated and crushed rival *daimyō,* armed religious groups in central Japan and made himself master of the realm. Nobunaga's conquests were ended by his assassination in 1582. His successor, Toyotomi Hideyoshi, pushed Nobunaga's conquests further west, set in motion a social transformation by the implementation of land surveys and the disarming of villagers and mounted bloody invasions of Korea. Hideyoshi, who, like Nobunaga, did not choose to take the discredited title of shogun, ruled as *kampaku* or regent, a title in the old court hierarchy. At Hideyoshi's death a council of warriors was established to serve as a regency for his son. Not surprisingly they vied among themselves for power. Tokugawa Ieyasu, in a great military victory at Sekigahara in 1600, destroyed his rivals and established a shogunate which endured until the 19th century.

The political legacy of the medieval age

These currents of political change in the medieval period left an important legacy. In many ways they established the discourse of ensuing centuries of political culture in Japan. On the one hand the idea of full-scale warrior government, headed by a shogun, detached from the imperial court, had been firmly established. There were occasional departures from this model, as in the case of Nobunaga and Hideyoshi, but on the whole it prevailed until the 19th century. Warrior rule was reinforced by warrior legal codes and by the notion of a shogun, or military regent, ruling under a reigning emperor. On the other hand, though weakened and financially hard-pressed, the imperial court survived. Once the idea of shogunal authority as the legitimate military expression of imperial rule was established, the need completely to eliminate court and *tennō* was removed. Although the imperial office was enfeebled and reduced to a ritual and legitimizing role, it was not stripped of sovereignty and its very weakness became something of a source of strength or, at least, of durability. At the same time the issue of the ultimate source of political authority remained latent and volatile. Courtiers and some warriors could always look back to a past when it could be claimed that emperors had ruled as well as reigned. This left open the possibility of using the court or the imperial office as a weapon against shogunal authority. Shoguns, and their enemies, could view the court and the

The rise and fall of the feudal barons
With the weakening of the central authority of the Ashikaga shoguns and the descent into civil war from the mid-15th century, the warring provincial lords (*daimyō*) became the leading political players. These three maps show some of the major *daimyō* houses involved in the political struggles of the late 15th through mid-16th centuries.

The top map shows the disposition of major *shugo daimyō* houses at the outbreak of the Ōnin War in 1467. While Shogun Ashikaga Yoshimasa watched helplessly, warriors of rival leagues led by the Hosokawa and Yamana ravaged Kyoto and carried war into the provinces. They thus set in motion the age of *gekokujō* in which many *shugo* were toppled by their underlings who emerged as the lords of more consolidated warring states (*sengoku daimyō*).

The lower maps show the disposition of major *daimyō* in 1560, the year in which Oda Nobunaga began his drive to conquer Japan, and 1572, when he had established himself in Kyoto. Defeating the Imagawa in 1560, Nobunaga made an alliance with Tokugawa Ieyasu (1562) and marched into Kyoto (1568). In rapid succession he razed Enryakuji (1571), crushed the Asai and Asakura (1573), drove Shogun Ashikaga Yoshiaki from Kyoto (1573), defeated the Takeda (1575), engaged in protracted warfare with Honganji followers and challenged the Mōri in the west.

Maps:

major shugo daimyō house c. 1467

Mogami
Date
Uesugi · Ashikaga
Hatakeyama
Kyōgoku
Satake
Shiba
Yamana · Toki
Akamatsu · Imagawa
Takeda · ? · Isshiki
Ōuchi · Hatakeyama
Shōni · Ōuchi · Hosokawa
Ōtomo
Shimazu

scale 1:15 000 000

major sengoku daimyō house c. 1560

Date
Suwa
Uesugi · Uesugi
Honganji · Satake
Hosokawa · Yamana · Asakura · Takeda · Hōjō
Kobayakawa · Amako · Asai · Oda · Imagawa
Urakami
Mōri · Hosakawa
Ryūzōji · Mōri · Chōsokabe · Hatakeyama
Ōtomo · Hosokawa
Shimazu

scale 1:15 000 000

major shokuhō daimyō house c. 1572

Date
Uesugi
Asakura
Asai · Takeda · Hōjō
Akita
Mōri · Oda · Tokugawa
Mōri
Ryūzōji · Chōsokabe
Ōtomo
Shimazu

scale 1:15 000 000

This detail from *The Mongol Invasions Picture Scroll* shows warriors from a small Japanese boarding vessel attacking a large Mongol ship during the second invasion. The two scrolls were painted around 1293 to record for posterity the exploits of the Japanese warrior Takezaki Suenaga who is shown here killing the Mongol leader.

imperial person as pawns while under control, but dangerous and volatile players if allowed to slip free of restraint.

Politically too the country had survived internal disintegration and external invasion. This left a legacy of unity and strengthened national identity. With the divine winds (*kamikaze*) that scattered the Mongol fleets came the belief that Japan was a divinely protected land (*shinkoku*). At the same time medieval men and women could see that their society was frequently torn by pestilence, natural disasters, instability and civil war. There was a hunger for new pathways to spiritual salvation and a powerful aspiration for peace and political stability. From the civil wars of the 14th and 15th centuries came the drive for reunification and a search for renewed political stability that found expression in the Tokugawa political balance in the early 17th century.

Currents of change in social and economic life

Warfare and political unrest brought changes beyond the political realm too. In the areas of social and economic life the medieval age saw the emergence of new classes, extension and erosion of the system of private estates (*shōen*), new patterns of landholding, growing agricultural production, increased market activity, more extensive commerce, greater use of coinage and substantial urban development, all of which contributed to, and benefited from, the release of new economic and commercial energies.

Prior to the 10th century it is difficult to portray Japan as anything other than an aristocratic society. Of course other social groups existed. Powerful rural families maintained and extended their local influence and armed themselves to pro-

tect their local interests. Poor farmers tilled the fields of public lands and private estates and bore the burden of taxation and labor service. Lower in the social scale there were landless peasants, slaves and outcasts whose presence we can only dimly discern through the sparse documentary record. These groups have left only faint traces in the historical records of the age. We know they were a vital part of the society but it is impossible to detail their role. It was the court nobles who dominated the society and the historical record. Public and private lands, and the peasants who farmed them, sustained the court nobility. They were the holders of political power whose function was to govern. Legal institutions catered to them. Apart from monks and nuns, many of whom came from noble families, it was the nobility that monopolized the intellectual and literary skills in the society. It seems fair, therefore, to describe the overall tone of Japanese society in these earlier centuries as aristocratic.

This aristocratic dominance was offset, however, by the emergence onto the center stage of Japanese history first of warriors, then of merchants and commoners. We have already seen how political power shifted during the medieval centuries from courtiers to warriors. As *bushi* gained political power, they began to set the tone for the society and culture. On the one hand, *bushi* were practitioners of the martial arts (*bu*) or "the way of the bow and arrow." On the other, they had to master skills of government and local administration which involved some measure of literacy and learning (*bun*). Moreover, they had their own spiritual and cultural aspirations that diverged from those of the Heian court nobility. By the end of the 13th century the ideal of the warrior as one who should have mastered literary and administrative skills (*bun*) as well as the arts of war (*bu*) was already established. By no means all warriors were literate. Throughout the medieval period, and especially in times of war, most rural *bushi* could not devote the time needed to meet the literary standards of this ideal, but the *bushi* elite certainly did. Learning from courtiers and monks, and consorting with them, the Hōjō regents, the Ashikaga shoguns and *sengoku* warrior leaders like the Ōuchi and Hosokawa became exponents and patrons of the arts of peace as well as students of the tactics of war.

Bushi were not the only newly emergent group to make their presence felt in medieval society. Merchants, artisans and small farmers also became a more visibly active presence. In the early 12th century what little local commerce there was was carried on by itinerant peddlers. There was little, if any, use of coinage, and hardly any market activity in Japan. Economic exchange was mostly in kind or in service, and the most pervasive economic activity was the payment of annual taxes (*nengu*) in rice or other products to *shōen* proprietors or to the local officials of the central government. *Shōen* economies were largely self-contained economic worlds. Nobles, temples and shrines, and members of the imperial family drew on their many scattered *shōen* holdings for their everyday needs and ceremonial activities. The bulk of farmers' output was absorbed in subsistence or tax payments. There was little surplus to sell in a market or to traveling merchants.

This rather static economic world began to change during the 13th century. One long-term economic and social transformation that was taking place during the medieval age was the steady dismemberment of *shōen*. The control formerly exerted over *shōen* by nobles or temples was undercut by warrior families living within, or on the fringes of, *shōen*. Erosion began in the Kamakura period. The land stewards (*jitō*) imposed by Yoritomo, and again by the Hōjō after the Jōkyū War, worked to entrench themselves and diverted more and more of the tax yield away from the proprietors. Nobles and temples were forced to make compromise settlements with *bushi* or physically to partition their estates. The warfare of the mid-14th and late 15th centuries brought further dismemberment to *shōen* as provincial protectors (*shugo*), local warriors and *sengoku daimyō* all sought to exert their control over lands in their locality held by absentee proprietors. The loosening grip of nobles and temples over *shōen* released more farmers' and artisans' labor for market-directed production. Although it is impossible to document, it is possible that Japan was producing an agricultural surplus during these centuries. There were also improvements in agricultural technology and farming practice. Greater use was made of draft animals and double cropping became more widespread. Markets within *shōen*, at crossroads and temple gates, became more widespread and more regular. Markets were held three times or six times monthly in many areas and permanent stores began to appear. These markets in remote areas were linked with the cities of Kamakura, Kyoto, Nara and Hakata by peddlers and merchants. Markets like the Horikawa lumber market in Kyoto or the

Yodo fish market drew produce from far afield and became wholesale markets. Forwarding merchants established themselves in port cities around the Inland Sea. Guilds of merchants trading in specialized commodities such as salt, oil, paper, silk or lumber under the protection of central *shōen* proprietors, temples and shrines, were active in the Kinai region and beyond.

This expanding economy was fostered by a growing availability of coinage. By the late 13th century copper cash were being imported from China and were coming into use in the Kinai and along the eastern seaboard. Until Hideyoshi began to mint gold coins, Japanese rulers preferred to import specie from China rather than minting it themselves. Although the supply of coins, especially good coins, was thereby restricted and subject to dislocation and hoarding, the use of money to conduct transactions became steadily more common. Taxes were increasingly commuted into cash, and moneylending by merchants, sake brewers and temples became a feature of daily life. Both the Kamakura and Muromachi Bakufu found themselves under pressure to issue debt moratoria edicts to assist warriors who had gone too deeply into debt to moneylenders. The activities of moneylenders added fuel to the uprisings (*ikki*) by *bushi* and farmers that became a feature of the 15th and 16th centuries.

Commercial and market activity continued to flourish during the Muromachi period. The location of the Bakufu and shogunal court alongside the imperial court in Kyoto spurred a recovery of vitality in the capital which became in the late 14th and early 15th centuries a national market and a major stimulus for trade. Unlike the Kamakura Bakufu, the Muromachi shogunate did not have a strong landed base. The more active of the Ashikaga shoguns turned to foreign trade and the promotion, and taxation, of domestic commerce to make up for this deficiency. Ashikaga Yoshimitsu sent official trading missions to China and fostered merchant groups in order to tax them. In the shadow of the official missions went so-called "Japanese pirates" (*wakō*), who were treated as marauders by the ruling authorities in Korea, China and Japan but who no doubt thought of themselves as freebooters and traders.

The warfare of the late 15th and 16th centuries was destructive, but not necessarily depressing to economic activity. Kyoto was badly damaged in the Ōnin War and much of its population of nobles and monks dispersed. Recovery came quickly, however, and the city was clearly flourishing again under Nobunaga and Hideyoshi. Both of these hegemons, particularly Hideyoshi, engaged in major building projects in the city. The Jesuit missionary João Rodrigues, who was in Kyoto in the late 16th and early 17th centuries, described the capital as "the noble and populous city of Miyako." Rodrigo de Vivero y Velasco gave its population as "over 800 000 people, while according to different estimates between 300 000 and 400 000 folk live in the vicinity." He also reported: "The viceroy told me that in the city of Miyako alone there were 5000 temples to their gods, as well as many hermitages. He also said there were some 50 000 registered public women, placed by the authorities in special districts."

Trade and piracy in the medieval age
The Chinese and Korean name for the freebooters who carried on illicit trade, ravaged coastal towns and shipping and carried off hostages was "Japanese pirates" (*wakō*). Neither Korea nor China recognized anything other than carefully regulated official trade. In the 15th and 16th centuries bands of fishermen and warriors from villages in Tsushima, Matsuura and the Inland Sea coasts marauded the Korean coasts in fleets ranging in size from two or three vessels to several hundred. While the official tally trade was in effect in the 15th century, their activities were somewhat restricted; but by the end of the century large fleets of *wakō* extended their activities along the Chinese coasts. These bands contained many Chinese and Portuguese rebels and freebooters. They were difficult to control because many Chinese merchants had their own vested interest in illicit trade. Little was done to stifle piracy effectively until Hideyoshi, who wanted regulated international trade, began to enforce anti-piracy edicts from the 1580s.

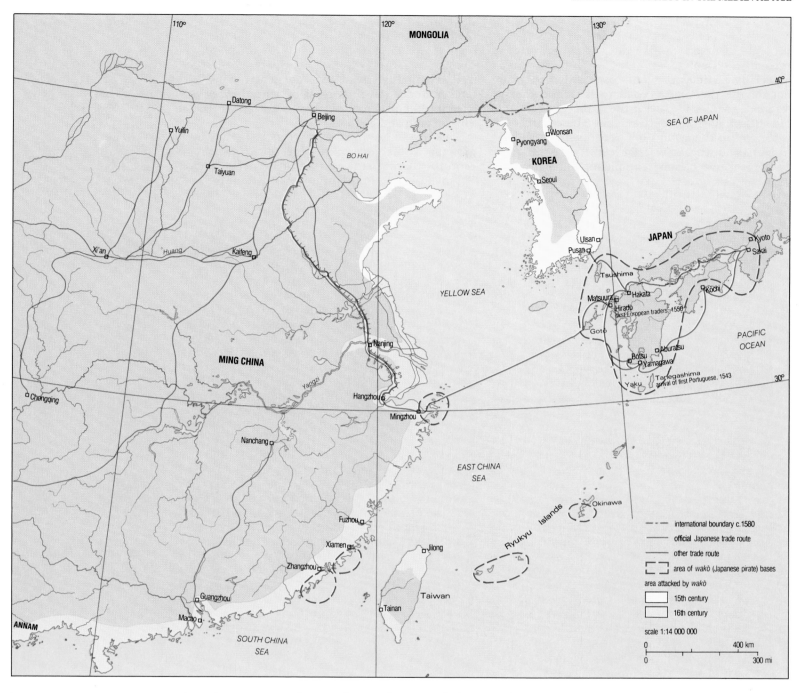

In other respects the warfare and many of the policies adopted by *sengoku daimyō* and the unifiers were a spur to commerce. Provision merchants were needed to supply arms, armor and horses for larger armies; food, drink and clothing for garrisons; building materials for fortifications and castles; timber for bridges and ships. Merchants from the port city of Sakai during the 16th century grew rich on the China trade and the provision of guns for Nobunaga and other warring *daimyō*. Early castle towns served as commercial centers for their domains as *daimyō* favored local merchants, whom they could more easily control, in the face of the older guilds. The Rokkaku family of Ōmi were among the first to try to break the old guild monopoly on markets and open them to new groups of local merchants. Oda Nobunaga followed suit in Azuchi. By these policies commerce was fully released from its earlier *shōen*-based restrictions.

The years between the mid-16th and mid-17th century are frequently referred to as the Christian century. Until Hideyoshi turned against the Christian mission effort in the 1580s, it looked as though millions of Japanese would be converted to Christianity and that the Catholic Church would establish a powerful presence in Japan. Trade accompanied the cross. Portuguese, Spanish, Dutch, English and Chinese merchants put Japan in contact with the commerce of Europe, the Indies and Asia. Japanese merchant houses, too, ventured further afield. Licensed Japanese trading vessels sailed for Luzon and south Asia where groups of Japanese merchants established themselves. The 16th century also saw an outpouring of gold and silver from newly opened mines in Japan. Hideyoshi, who was well aware of profits to be derived from trade and commerce, took first choice of imported items, imposed levies on traders, and directly controlled mines and set up gold and silver mints. As part of their drive for unification and legitimacy both Nobunaga and Hideyoshi destroyed barriers, worked for a uniform system of currency, reassessed and revalued land, encouraged Chinese and European merchants, shared in the proceeds of the overseas trade, and engaged in conspicuous consumption and castle building on the grand scale.

The social and economic changes witnessed by Japan in the medieval period were therefore substantial. Warriors set their imprint on society. But more than that, merchants and farmers also made their presence felt. Until the *sengoku daimyō*, especially Hideyoshi, began to separate samurai from their villages, Japanese medieval society was relatively fluid. Warriors lived in the villages and managed lands, if they did not actually farm them. Intermarriage among the various groups in Japanese society was relatively unrestricted. But the separation into status groups, which has been characterized as a mark of early modern society, was already underway in late medieval Japan. In an effort to rationalize the military and economic potential of their domains many *sengoku daimyō* had sought to draw their vassals more tightly around them. Hideyoshi was not the only *daimyō* to see the dangers of village-based armed uprisings like those engaged in by followers of the True Pure Land (Jōdo Shinshū) school of popular Buddhism and known as "uprisings of the single-minded."

In the Edo period the population of the country and the scale and complexity of economic life increased. In large part this was due to the unification of the country by Tokugawa Ieyasu, the solidity of the Tokugawa Bakufu and the effects of the *sankin kōtai* system of alternate attendance of *daimyō* in Edo. Medieval Japan did not yet have cities on the scale of Edo or Osaka: medieval castle towns were fewer and smaller. Nor did it have a rice market like the Osaka Dojima market, nor the commerce generated by the fully developed system of alternate attendance in Edo by *daimyō*. The merchant groups of the late Muromachi period in Kyoto, Sakai, Nara or Hakata were not as numerous, well organized or prosperous as their later Edo and Osaka counterparts. But, allowing for these differences of scale, it is also fair to suggest that most Edo period developments were already evident in the medieval period. It is hard to think of features of the Edo period economy, other than perhaps the ripple effects of the alternate year attendance system, that were not present in the late medieval economy.

Japan's international relations have been marked by periods of active contact with, and relative openness toward, the outside world and periods of relative withdrawal. In contrast with the preceding late Heian period, when official embassies to China were abandoned, and the succeeding Edo period, in which relations with the West were drastically curtailed, the medieval centuries were relatively open. The Taira reopened active commercial contacts with China and encouraged commerce in the Inland Sea. The Mongol invasions interrupted these relations but they were revived by the Ashikaga shoguns, and by trade-conscious *daimyō* like the Ōuchi and Hosokawa. Freebooters and marauders, many of them from Japanese ports, were active along the coasts of Korea and China. The 16th century, with the arrival of Western traders and a vigorous Asian trade in which Japan was an active participant, was perhaps the most "open" era in Japan's premodern history.

New paths to salvation

The medieval centuries also witnessed far-reaching changes in religious and cultural life, changes that were to lay the foundations of modern Japanese spirituality and aesthetic sensibility. From the late 12th century there was a surge of revival within Buddhism that was to carry hopes for salvation to the mass of the population. This surge was set in motion by a profound sense of social dislocation and the conviction of some young monks that all was not well with Buddhism, that it catered exclusively to the elite, that the rules of monastic life were not strictly observed and that the age was one of spiritual decline. It was widely believed that Japan, from the year 1052, had entered the "Later Age" of devolution in the Buddha's teaching (*mappō*) when it loses its force to assist men to salvation. In the age of *mappō* it was believed that old paths to salvation by self-effort through prayer and good works were impossible, even to the clergy and to sincere lay seekers.

In looking for new and easier paths to salvation, paths that would be available not only to themselves but to the newly emerging groups in society, these young reformers turned to teachings of Amitābha (Amida) and the Pure Land, the *Lotus Sūtra* and Zen. In doing so, they provoked a hostile reaction from the older schools of Buddhism, but also stimulated movements for reform within the older sects. Although there were many doctrinal differences among the newer branches of medieval Buddhism, we can detect some shared features in their attitude toward salvation. One pervasive current was that of reliance, in an age of despair, on the promise of compassion and salvation of some Buddha or Bodhisattva or *sūtra*. This path of faith is known as *tariki,* or "other power," and found expression in the Amidist and Lotus movements. A complementary current, reflected in the Zen schools, emphasized "one's own power" (*jiriki*), channeled through meditation, as the most direct means of breaking through the delusions of the senses which prevented men and women from recognizing their own Buddhahood. Another powerful current involved a rejection of the traditional monastic life in favor of a family-centered or lay community ideal. This was most evident in the Pure Land movement. On the other hand, Zen, which incorporated lay practice, tended to reaffirm the monastic community and rule. In reaction to the current rejecting monasticism in medieval society, there was a countercurrent stressing reinvigoration of the monastic rule.

The Amidist movement was the broadest and most powerful of these medieval religious currents. The teachings relating to Amitābha and the Pure Land were not new. They had been articulated in early Chinese Buddhism out of *sūtras* detailing the compassionate vows made by Amida to save all sentient beings who were trapped in the cycles of birth and rebirth, unable to help themselves, and bring them in bliss to his Western Paradise of the Pure Land where they could be sure of attaining nirvana. Pure Land texts were introduced to Japan in the Nara period and for centuries these texts were studied as subordinate teachings within Tendai monasteries. Monks, nuns and their aristocratic patrons practiced contemplation on the attributes and vows of Amida and the repeated sincere invo-

True Pure Land (Jōdo Shin) and the Timely (Ji) schools. Common to all of these reformers was the belief that devotion to Amida was the best possible route to salvation, that this route was open to all men and women, however poor, unlettered or sinful, and that the full force of Amida's vows could be triggered by the simplest of means, the sincere invocation of the *nembutsu*.

The differences among them, sharp enough to create schools and subschools, hinged on definitions of what constituted "faith" or "trust" in Amida, how that trust could be expressed through the *nembutsu* and how salvation (*ōjō*) could be assured. Hōnen, who taught that the *nembutsu* held exclusive efficacy in an age of *mappō*, believed that constant invocation was the sure means of salvation for all. Shinran, his disciple, argued that a single sincere invocation, triggered by Amida's compassion, and expressing complete surrender of self, was sufficient. More than the invocation itself, he emphasized the mind of faith which lay beneath any expression of the *nembutsu*.

Shinran's notion of faith called for the realization by individuals of their sinfulness, complete helplessness and inability to attain salvation by any self-effort, even the sincere invocation of the *nembutsu*. Faith, for Shinran, involved the spiritual recognition that salvation—and the *nembutsu* and faith which lead to it—is totally dependent on Amida's compassion and that people can attain that salvation only by abandoning any belief that they can contribute to their salvation and throwing themselves on the saving power of Amida. This need for recognition of one's own helplessness explains Shinran's famous assertion that it may be easier for a sinful person than a good person to attain salvation.

Ippen had a powerful belief in the efficacy of the *nembutsu* itself. He spent most of his life, accompanied by a ragged band of followers, wandering the roads and tracks of Japan. On his way he distributed printed amulets (*fuda*) bearing the *nembutsu* to everybody he met and encouraged them to invoke the name of Amida. The possession of one of these *fuda* was itself an invocation that would open the doors of the Western Paradise. Like Shinran, Ippen moved among the common people and helped to ensure that the message of the Pure Land was carried to the poorest and most desperate of people. His chanting of the *nembutsu* at the homes of the faithful developed into ecstatic dancing (*odori nembutsu*) as a spiritual practice which blended with folk culture. The itinerant life of Ippen, including many scenes of his followers dancing the *nembutsu,* is the subject of one of the finest medieval scroll paintings, the *Life of Ippen the Holy Wanderer* (*Ippen hijiri-e*). The scroll gives an unusually vivid insight into popular religious practice and fervor in the medieval period.

At the close of the 13th century these Pure Land schools were still small. But they were growing and finding followers in all sectors of society. By the 16th century they were firmly and fully established as the major schools of Japanese Buddhism. In particular, the Jōdo Shin, or True Pure Land, school founded by Shinran was revived and reorganized by Rennyo (1415–99). He brought many disparate groups of followers (*monto*) under the leadership of the Honganji temple complexes.

Although Buddhism had taken root in Japan in the 6th century, it was only after the 10th century that the promise and means of salvation were offered to the humble and unlettered. The guarantee of salvation in the Pure Land of Amida to anyone who would express their trust in Amida by intoning his sacred title "Namu Amida Butsu" was made by Kūya, Hōnen and Ippen (1239–89). These priests wandered the country with ragged bands of followers and spurred devotion to Amida by distributing talismans (*fuda*) bearing his name and by organizing ecstatic dances during which the *nembutsu* (title of Amida) was chanted. This scene shows Ippen (the tallest figure) and his followers dancing the *nembutsu* in Kyoto before a throng of nobles and commoners.

cation of Amida's sacred name, the *nembutsu*: "Namu Amida Butsu" ("I take refuge in the Buddha Amida"). From the 10th century, however, monks like Genshin (942–1017) and Kūya (903–72) began to emphasize faith in Amida as the most effective teaching in an age of *mappō*. While Kūya took his message to the people with dances and simple verses, Genshin wrote graphically in his *Ōjō yōshū* of the glories of Amida's Western Paradise and the terrors of the Buddhist hells and the six realms of birth and rebirth. These teachings struck a responsive chord with the Heian nobility. Pure Land halls and gardens, like the Byōdō'in or the Chūsonji, were built as earthly representations of the Western Paradise, and statues and paintings were commissioned depicting Amida coming to greet the faithful and lead them into the Pure Land or showing the Ten Kings of Hell and sinners suffering in the various hells. Many people on their deathbeds grasped ribbons tied to a statue of Amida as cords to draw them surely into the Pure Land. Others believed they had seen Amida as an exhalation in the form of a purple cloud.

In the late Heian and Kamakura periods Hōnen (1133–1212), Shinran (1173–1262) and Ippen (1239–89) further broadened the spiritual promise of the Pure Land practice. They took Pure Land teachings out of their monastic context, broke with the Tendai school and established separate schools of Pure Land devotionalism: the Pure Land (Jōdo),

Kamakura

Bottom This cave at Tōshōji in Kamakura commemorates the destruction of the Kamakura Bakufu in 1333. From 1331 many warriors rose in support of Emperor Go-Daigo against the Bakufu. When the forces of Nitta Yoshisada took Kamakura in 1333, Hōjō Takatoki, his family and 800 retainers committed *seppuku*.

Only 45 kilometers southwest of Tokyo, Kamakura is now a busy residential city and resort. Visitors come to enjoy its beaches in summer or to view temples and walk in the hills surrounding the town. Until the late 12th century it was a fishing village with a small shrine sacred to the Minamoto warrior clan. Yoritomo chose Kamakura as the seat of his Bakufu because of these spiritual associations, but also because the town was easily defensible. Under the Kamakura Bakufu Kamakura became a major garrison town, with warrior residences, Shinto shrines and Buddhist temples.

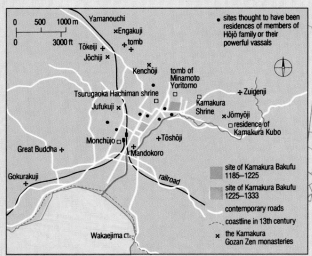

SONG CHINA

Yangzi

Hangzhou

Chuang

Mingzhou — Mt Ayuwang
Mt Taiping

Mt Tiantai
Eisai–1168 toured Tendai
monasteries for 4 months
1187–91 studied at Mt Tiantai
Dōgen–1223–25 pilgrimage to Tendai
1225–27 studied at Mt Tiantai

EAST CHINA SEA

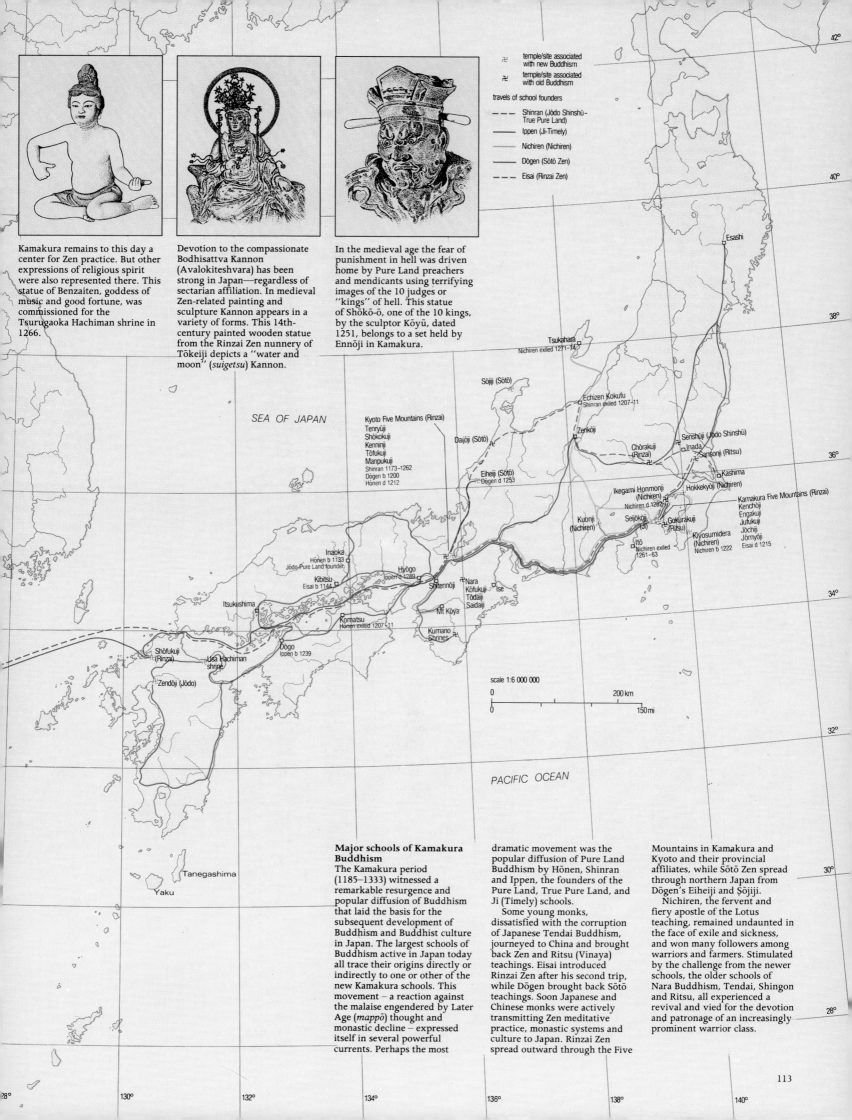

Kamakura remains to this day a center for Zen practice. But other expressions of religious spirit were also represented there. This statue of Benzaiten, goddess of music and good fortune, was commissioned for the Tsurugaoka Hachiman shrine in 1266.

Devotion to the compassionate Bodhisattva Kannon (Avalokiteshvara) has been strong in Japan—regardless of sectarian affiliation. In medieval Zen-related painting and sculpture Kannon appears in a variety of forms. This 14th-century painted wooden statue from the Rinzai Zen nunnery of Tōkeiji depicts a "water and moon" (*suigetsu*) Kannon.

In the medieval age the fear of punishment in hell was driven home by Pure Land preachers and mendicants using terrifying images of the 10 judges or "kings" of hell. This statue of Shōkō-ō, one of the 10 kings, by the sculptor Kōyū, dated 1251, belongs to a set held by Ennōji in Kamakura.

卍 temple/site associated with new Buddhism
卍 temple/site associated with old Buddhism

travels of school founders
- - - Shinran (Jōdo Shinshū–True Pure Land)
—— Ippen (Ji-Timely)
—— Nichiren (Nichiren)
—— Dōgen (Sōtō Zen)
- - - Eisai (Rinzai Zen)

SEA OF JAPAN

PACIFIC OCEAN

Esashi

Tsukahara
Nichiren exiled 1271–74

Sōjiji (Sōtō)

Echizen Kokufu
Shinran exiled 1207–11

Daijōji (Sōtō)

Zenkōji

Chōrakuji (Rinzai)

Senshūji (Jōdo Shinshū)
Inada
Sansonji (Ritsu)

Kashima

Eiheiji (Sōtō)
Dōgen d 1253

Ikegami Honmonji (Nichiren)
Nichiren d 1282

Hokkekyōji (Nichiren)

Kamakura Five Mountains (Rinzai)
Kenchōji
Engakuji
Jufukuji
Jōchiji
Jōmyōji
Eisai d 1215

Kuonji (Nichiren)

Seijōkōji (Ji)

Gokurakuji (Ritsu)

Kiyosumidera (Nichiren)
Nichiren b 1222

Kyoto Five Mountains (Rinzai)
Tenryūji
Shōkokuji
Kenninji
Tōfukuji
Manpukuji
Shinran 1173–1262
Dōgen b 1200
Hōnen d 1212

Itō
Nichiren exiled 1261–63

Inaoka
Hōnen b 1133
Jōdo-Pure Land founder

Kibitsu
Eisai b 1144

Hyōgo
Ippen d 1289

Shitennōji

Nara
Kōfukuji
Tōdaiji
Saidaiji

Ise

Mt Kōya

Itsukushima

Komatsu
Hōnen exiled 1207–11

Kumano Shrines

Shōfukuji (Rinzai)

Usa Hachiman shrine

Dōgo
Ippen b 1239

Zendōji (Jōdo)

Tanegashima
Yaku

scale 1:6 000 000
0   200 km
0   150 mi

Major schools of Kamakura Buddhism

The Kamakura period (1185–1333) witnessed a remarkable resurgence and popular diffusion of Buddhism that laid the basis for the subsequent development of Buddhism and Buddhist culture in Japan. The largest schools of Buddhism active in Japan today all trace their origins directly or indirectly to one or other of the new Kamakura schools. This movement – a reaction against the malaise engendered by Later Age (*mappō*) thought and monastic decline – expressed itself in several powerful currents. Perhaps the most dramatic movement was the popular diffusion of Pure Land Buddhism by Hōnen, Shinran and Ippen, the founders of the Pure Land, True Pure Land, and Ji (Timely) schools.

Some young monks, dissatisfied with the corruption of Japanese Tendai Buddhism, journeyed to China and brought back Zen and Ritsu (Vinaya) teachings. Eisai introduced Rinzai Zen after his second trip, while Dōgen brought back Sōtō teachings. Soon Japanese and Chinese monks were actively transmitting Zen meditative practice, monastic systems and culture to Japan. Rinzai Zen spread outward through the Five Mountains in Kamakura and Kyoto and their provincial affiliates, while Sōtō Zen spread through northern Japan from Dōgen's Eiheiji and Sōjiji.

Nichiren, the fervent and fiery apostle of the Lotus teaching, remained undaunted in the face of exile and sickness, and won many followers among warriors and farmers. Stimulated by the challenge from the newer schools, the older schools of Nara Buddhism, Tendai, Shingon and Ritsu, all experienced a revival and vied for the devotion and patronage of an increasingly prominent warrior class.

113

The *Lotus Sūtra*

For centuries the *Lotus Sūtra* has been revered in Japan as the fullest expression of the ideal of the compassionate Bodhisattvas and of the promise of the accessibility of the Great Vehicle of Mahayana Buddhism on which all beings can ride to salvation. The teachings of the *Lotus* were probably brought to Japan shortly after the introduction of Buddhism in the 6th century. They gained a devoted following among the leading families of the period. Prince Shōtoku is believed to have written a commentary on the *Lotus Sūtra*, and Saichō incorporated the *Lotus* teaching as the basis of Tendai Buddhism. Devotion to the *Lotus Sūtra* continued into the medieval period. Nichiren (1222–82), who had been trained in Tendai Buddhism, became an aggressive apostle of the exclusive merits of the *Lotus*.

Where Amidists believed that faith in Amida, expressed through the *nembutsu,* was sufficient for salvation, Nichiren argued that the power of the *Lotus Sūtra*, released by the invocation of its sacred title *Namu Myōhō Renge Kyō* ("I Take Refuge in the Lotus of the Mysterious Law"), was the only effective practice. Where Amidists looked to salvation in the Pure Land, Nichiren offered a millennial vision of a terrestrial paradise where the faithful will enjoy peace and prosperity. He castigated other Buddhist teachings, except Tendai, as heretical sources of national disaster and called for their abolition. Nichiren's uncompromising attacks on rival schools, and on the political authorities for sustaining them, brought him punishment and exile. Unchastened and fearless, he used the periods of exile to write and to build up a devoted following among samurai and farmers in northern and central Japan. Some of his disciples were active in Kyoto and, with his message of promised rewards for the faithful through Buddhahood in this life, he won a large following among townsfolk there. Nichiren's followers shared his uncompromising stance. Rivalry between Nichiren school devotees and the older Buddhist schools was reflected in *Lotus* uprisings (*hokke ikki*) in the capital in the mid-16th century; and one group of Nichiren devotees, the Fuju Fuse branch, whose members refused to "accept offerings from, or to make them to" the political authorities, was subjected to severe political repression. In spite of repeated repression, Nichiren's energy and charismatic appeal, combined with the simple message of trust in the efficacy of the *Lotus Sūtra*, gave vitality and longevity to his teachings. Branches of Nichiren Buddhism, including Sōka Gakkai, are active in Japan today and have established branches in other countries.

Zen

Zen, the practice of seeking personal enlightenment through meditation, was also introduced to Japan prior to the medieval period. Intensive meditation was an intrinsic part of the religious practice of most traditions of Buddhism. However, Zen as an independent school, in which seated meditation (*zazen*) was stressed as the supreme practice, only began to take root when introduced from Song China in the late 12th and 13th centuries. The early Japanese advocates of Zen were in many cases monks trained in Tendai Buddhism who sought to use Chinese Zen as a means of reviving traditional Japanese Buddhism. When they met resistance and hostility from the leaders of the old Buddhist establishment, they were forced to seek new patrons and to try to give Zen an independent footing. It was perhaps fortuitous that the surge of introduction of Zen from the late 12th and 13th centuries coincided with the coming to power of warriors with a taste, and need, for appropriate spiritual practices. Much has been made of the association between Zen and the emerging Japanese warrior ethic. While it is true that many warriors were impressed by the directness of Zen training and insights and that most patrons of Zen were warriors, it would be mistaken to assume that all warriors were deeply influenced by Zen. Many of those that practiced Zen also showed devotion to Amida, the *Lotus Sūtra* or esoteric Buddhism. Not all warriors were patrons of Zen, but many were; and most patrons of Zen were warriors, who were attracted by its directness, the possibility of personal enlightenment, the rigor of meditation and the cut and thrust of direct confrontation with Zen monks.

In contrast to the stress on reliance on "other power," whether of Amidism or the *Lotus* teaching, Zen practitioners believed that enlightenment could be attained here and now by their own efforts, that indeed they were originally enlightened, imbued with Buddhahood, and that all that was called for was to recognize the intrinsic emptiness of self, to "look within and recognize the Buddha" (*kenshō jōbutsu* or *satori*). This recognition of Buddhahood was not helped by rational means, by study or by reading of the *sūtras*. These traditional methods were more likely to obscure the truth and divert the seeker. The best path to enlightenment, the early Chinese Zen patriarchs had taught, was that taken by the supreme exemplar for Zen practitioners, the Buddha himself, the middle path of meditation. Through intensive meditation one could hope to break through the delusions of the senses and the rational mind to grasp one's Buddhahood directly and spontaneously. Moreover Zen was straightforward and pragmatic. Enlightenment could be found not only in seated meditation in a monastic meditation hall but through a concentrated meditative self-awareness while engaged in the most mundane of everyday activities—whether working, eating or resting. Zen teachings and practices had developed over centuries in China. When Japanese monks went to China in the 12th century looking for the spiritual means to revitalize Japanese Buddhism, they were impressed by the vigor of Zen (Chan). Chinese Zen had developed in a rigorous monastic setting, which stressed intensive communal meditation as the core of monastic life and which employed such aids as the *kōan* or the use of slaps and shouts to awaken people to enlightenment.

Rinzai Zen, introduced by Eisai (1141–1215), Enni and other Chinese and Japanese masters, found eager patrons among warriors and nobles in Kamakura, Kyoto and the provinces. Emphasizing the teaching of "sudden enlightenment," Rinzai Zen stressed rigorous meditation and relied heavily on Chinese *kōan* collections and monastic regulations. Under the patronage of shoguns, emperors, Bakufu warriors and provincial warrior lords, Rin-

Right This remarkable portrait of the monk Myōe (1173–1232), showing him seated in austere meditation in nature, belongs to the mountain temple of Kōzanji in Kyoto where Myōe spent most of his life. Myōe entered the Tōdaiji in Nara at the age of 16 where he began to study the teachings of the Kegon and Vinaya traditions. In 1206 he was granted land at Toganoo near Kyoto by retired Emperor Go-Toba. There he devoted his life to reviving Kegon teachings and enforcing orthodox Vinaya rules. He resisted the spread of Pure Land teachings, advocating instead an amalgam of Buddhist esoteric rituals, textual teachings, meditation and Shinto beliefs. Myōe is said to have planted at Toganoo the tea which the Zen monk Eisai (1141–1215) brought from China.

zai monasteries were built in Kamakura, Kyoto and the provinces. A system of officially sponsored monasteries known as the *gozan,* or Five Mountains, system came to include several hundred well-endowed monasteries under Bakufu patronage. Rinzai monasteries, in particular, were centers for the cultivation of such Zen-related arts as landscape gardening, calligraphy, ink painting and the tea ceremony. Laypeople who patronized Rinzai monks such as Musō Soseki (1275–1351) of Tenryūji or Ikkyū Sōjun (1384–1481) of Daitokuji were deeply attracted by the arts and aesthetic, as well as the practice, of Zen and carried these arts into secular society.

Sōtō Zen teachings, introduced from China by Dōgen (1222–82), spread widely among farmers and local samurai in northern Japan. This was partly because Dōgen, who had met opposition from the established schools while trying to establish his community near the capital, eventually eschewed government patronage of the kind that bound Rinzai Zen to the ruling elite. Dōgen was a profound and subtle exponent of Zen. His collected writings cover all aspects of Zen, but at their core, and that of his religious practice, can be said to be an emphasis on ''just sitting,'' expressing Dōgen's conviction that meditation in itself held the secret of enlightenment. After Dōgen's death Sōtō Zen incorporated elements from esoteric Buddhism, folk beliefs and prayers for material benefits. This gave it a more popular appeal than Rinzai Zen, but at some cost to the rigor of its Zen practice and training.

The traditional schools of Buddhism
The medieval centuries were the great age of Buddhism in Japan. This period has been called a ''Buddhist episteme,'' an age in which Buddhism was the dominant mode of thinking for all members of the society and a vital source of cultural expression. This is a fair characterization. In discussing the religious life of these centuries, however, it is particularly tempting to focus on the powerful influence of Zen Buddhism or on the working out of the popular Buddhist upsurge of the Kamakura period, which was to lay the foundations for most subsequent popular Buddhist practice in Japan up until modern times and which can fairly be described as a revolutionary development. Both the development of Zen and the diffusion of popular Kamakura period Buddhism were vital manifestations of medieval Japanese spirituality and had profound long-term implications. However, in looking at medieval Japanese culture we should take an even broader perspective. At the popular level there were powerful devotional cults to Maitreya, the Future Buddha, to the compassionate Kannon and Jizō and the warlike Fudō Myōō. The faithful buried copies of the *Lotus Sūtra* in anticipation of their rebirth. They held ceremonies to exorcise or appease tormented spirits. They erected stone statues at roadsides to protect travelers. They listened to preachers expound texts and pictures describing the world of hell and hungry ghosts.

There were other important religious developments within the older-established Buddhist world. The older branches of Japanese monastic Buddhism were not suddenly pushed aside with the emergence of Zen and the popular schools. In

Kumano Shrines

The Kumano Shrines

The three shrines of Kumano at the southern tip of the rugged Kii Peninsula comprise a natural mandala blending elements of ancient folk religion, mountain asceticism, Shinto and Buddhism in a numinous natural environment. The three shrines are the Hongū Shrine, deep among mountains and gorges, venerating Susano-ō no Mikoto, the storm god, the Shingū Shrine on the coast, sacred to Kumano Hatayama no Kami, and the Nachi Shrine at the Nachi waterfall, dedicated to Kumano Fusumi no Kami. From ancient times, mountain sites such as Kumano were regarded as the dwelling places of gods and Buddhas.

With the spread of the Pure Land Buddhist movement from the late Heian period, and the vogue for Shinto-Buddhist syncretism, the deities of Kumano were associated with Amida and other Buddhas. The *kami*, or Gongen, of Kumano were regarded as local manifestations of the Buddhas.

reaction to the surge of popular Buddhist revivalism they too experienced reform and revival. Monks such as Myōe (1173–1232) of Kōzanji, Eison Shien (1201–90) of Saidaiji and Shunjō (1166–1227) of Sennyūji were all highly respected advocates of reform within the older schools—reform which emphasized renewed observance of the precepts of the monastic life. Tendai and Shingon Buddhism continued to provide the source from which much of medieval Buddhist thought and syncretic folk belief emerged. Shugendō, the practices of mountain ascetics (*yamabushi*), which was systematized and spread widely during this period, owed its spiritual content to esoteric practices derived from Tendai and Shingon Buddhism as well as from the deeply embedded native cult of mountain devotion. The mountain centers of Kumano and Ōmine in Kii, the Three Mountains of Dewa, Mount Fuji, Hakusan in northern Japan, and mountain complexes in Shikoku and Kyushu were all centers of ascetic practice. The Shōgo'in of the Onjōji branch of Tendai Buddhism and the Shingon monastery of Daigoji Sambō'in were esoteric monasteries having close connections with Shugendō in the medieval period.

The older schools of monastic Buddhism were influential in other ways. They were among the greatest landholders in medieval Japan. Although their scattered *shōen* holdings were being steadily eroded by warrior intrusion throughout the period, their landed base was still found to be substantial when subjected to land surveys by Hideyoshi in the late 16th century. Many of the older monastic centers, like Enryakuji, Kōyasan and Negoro, maintained armies of soldier-monks (*sōhei*) throughout the period. They were frequently at odds with warrior leaders and were thorns in the flesh of the unifiers of the 16th century. Oda Nobunaga wreaked a particularly savage vengeance on Enryakuji when he surrounded and burned the mountain complex and slaughtered several thousand soldier-monks,

monks and laymen and women. Hideyoshi and Tokugawa Ieyasu were less hostile to Buddhism but no less determined to bring the Buddhist religious establishment firmly under their control and absorb Buddhist landholdings into their own vast domains.

By the 16th century some of the spiritual vitality displayed by Buddhism in the 12th and 13th centuries was declining. Most schools showed signs of weakness and secularization. On the intellectual front, too, Buddhism faced new challenges in the 16th century. The temporary success of Christianity was a setback for Buddhism on the one hand, while Chinese neo-Confucian thought was beginning to break out of its medieval Zen Buddhist cocoon to flourish under samurai patronage on the other. In spite of these challenges to the religious, social and intellectual supremacy of Buddhism it would be misleading to suggest that it had declined completely by the end of the 16th century or that its influence was nullified by the reforms imposed by Nobunaga and Hideyoshi. It continued to exert a powerful influence on the spiritual lives of the people, and the use by the Tokugawa authorities of Buddhist temples as registration centers in their effort to eradicate Christianity enhanced its social position.

Other systems of belief

Although Buddhism was pervasive in medieval Japan, it should be remembered that Shinto, Confucian and Taoist threads were also part of the intellectual fabric of the age. Apart from, or sometimes together with, their devotions to the Buddhas and Bodhisattvas, medieval men and women expressed devotion to the native gods, the *kami* of Shinto and to figures like Hachiman, a patron of warriors, who combined Buddhist and Shinto features. The behavior of many people in the society was also regulated by belief in divination or the operations of Yin, Yang and the five elements. In embarking on a journey, or erecting a building, or naming a child certain days, directions and characters were auspicious, while others were believed to contain risk. These notions blended in medieval Japanese minds to blur sharp or exclusive distinctions between available forms of belief. It was quite possible for an individual to express devotion to several Buddhas and Bodhisattvas, to practice Zen, to revere the *kami* and seek their protection, to observe a variety of taboos, such as that of *katatagae* or changing direction so that one broke a journey to avoid arriving from an inauspicious direction, and to be interested in Confucian moral or political concerns. With the exception of Nichiren, there were few advocates of spiritual exclusivity in medieval Japan.

Throughout Japanese history there has been considerable mutual interaction between what we call Buddhism and Shinto. From the Heian period syncretic tendencies within Shingon and Tendai Buddhism were producing a complex alignment of Buddhas and the native *kami*. This trend of thought was known as the notion of "essence and manifestation" (*honji suijaku*). By this notion the Buddhas and Bodhisattvas were treated as invisible "essences" (*honji*), operating for the salvation of sentient beings, while the native *kami* were their local and visible manifestations (*suijaku*). As this

contemporary poem suggests, "traces" of the Buddhas might occasionally be manifest in dreams:

> Buddha is always present
> wherever we are.
> Yet he is not real to our sight.
> A sad regret.
> When there are no sounds of men,
> in the light of dawn,
> Then faintly, in our dreams,
> He will appear.

This "appearance" might easily take the form of a *kami* in human, animal or other natural form. In texts, statues, paintings and the popular imagination individual Buddhas were paired off with their Shinto counterparts. Amaterasu, the Sun Goddess, for instance, was paired with the cosmic Buddha Dainichi; Hachiman with Amida. This medieval blend of Shinto and Buddhism was to provide one pervasive mode of Japanese religious belief until Shinto and Buddhism were wrenched apart by government decree in the early 1870s.

Typical of the eclectic tendency in Japanese religious practice, one influential current of medieval Shinto thought was known as "twofold Shinto" (*ryōbu Shintō*), using as it did Shingon Buddhist notions of the two great mandalas (or cosmic diagrams), the Kongōkai, or Diamond World Mandala, and Taizōkai, or Womb World Mandala, to identify and explain the native *kami*. The inner and outer shrines at Ise, for instance, were each identified with one of the mandalas and the various *kami* represented at Ise were ordered within the hierarchy of the mandala.

Shinto cults and shrines flourished in the medieval period and the rather unstructured teachings of Shinto were refined and systematized. Many shrines were becoming centers of pilgrimage. Among the many vigorous cults were those at the Kumano and Kasuga shrines, at the Kitano shrine in Kyoto and at the Ise shrines. Ise was an increasingly active center. The Watarai family of the outer shrine at Ise, for instance, asserted both the prominence of Ise Shinto as a whole, and the superiority of the outer over the inner shrine. In the Muromachi period, Yoshida Kanetomo (1435–1511) of the Yoshida shrine in Kyoto planned unification of Shinto under his leadership and challenged the prevailing notions of the *kami* as manifestations of Buddhas. He stressed instead the exclusive path of the *kami*. Thus there were within medieval Shinto powerful eclectic currents mingling with Buddhist elements. But there were also currents which sought to assert the primacy of the native *kami* over the Buddhas and to see the Buddhas not as *honji* but as *suijaku*.

The sharper definition of the *kami* in their association with the Buddhas or with particular shrines and cults contributed to the flowering in the medieval period of what has come to be known as Shinto art, that is painting and sculpture dealing with themes relating to particular personages, cults, shrines or sacred settings. Among these we can mention artistic expressions of devotion to such cultic centers as Kumano and the Nachi Falls, Kasuga, Kitano and Mount Fuji, to such apotheosized cultic figures as Hachiman, Tenjin (Sugawara Michizane) or youthful deities (*wakamiya*), and to such sacred animals as deer, foxes and crows.

Left The slender arc of the Nachi waterfall has been regarded as an abode of the *kami* since ancient times. For centuries mountain ascetics (*Yamabushi*) have climbed to its rim to practice their austerities or sit in ritual purification in the icy pool at its foot.

Far left The most powerful divinity at Hongū is Susa-no-ō, the wild brother of the Sun Goddess. There are several other bark-roofed shrines at Hongū, each with its own *kami*. By the 12th century emperors and courtiers were making the arduous pilgrimage from the capital by steep mountain trails to worship at the shrines. Pilgrims believed that they might encounter Amida as a Gongen in human form and secure a promise of admission to the Pure Land.

CULTURE AND SOCIETY IN THE MEDIEVAL AGE

New trends in medieval culture

In contrast to the ancient period, in which most discernible cultural activity was the province of the court nobility or Buddhist temples, medieval culture was very much the product of all social groups. We can distinguish a blending of the cultural interests of courtiers, warriors, monks, merchants and the common people. Japan's renewed contacts with the continent brought a powerful cultural influx from Song, Yuan and Ming dynasty China and from Korea. And the arrival of the Southern Barbarians and the Christian missionary effort in the 16th century put Japan for the first time into direct contact with the culture of Europe.

Although the court was being pushed aside politically and was suffering economically during the medieval age, its cultural preeminence survived. Emperors and courtiers remained the arbiters of taste in literary expression, especially in Japanese poetry. Emperors like Go-Toba, Hanazono and Go-Mizunoo acquired reputations as scholars, poets and patrons of the arts. Male courtiers were schooled from childhood in the Chinese classics and in Chinese and Japanese history. Their wives and daughters were adept in Japanese literary pursuits. Under court patronage the tradition of Japanese-style painting (*Yamato-e*) survived and exerted an influence on the emerging Kanō and Tosa medieval schools of painting. Courtiers were patrons of Buddhism and students of Confucianism; and they set the style in etiquette and polite behavior.

In the Heian period talented court ladies like Murasaki Shikibu and Sei Shōnagon had written brilliant narrative tales and diaries. This narrative courtly tradition did not survive their deaths. In the medieval period the courtly tradition in the literary arts was perhaps best represented by calligraphy and Japanese poetry, especially the short verses known as *tanka*. Imperial collections and poetry gatherings still set poetic tastes. The *Shin Kokinshū* (*New Collection of Poems Old and New,* 1205), one of the finest collections of Japanese verse, contained many poems on nature by master poets like Fujiwara Shunzei (1114–1204), his son Teika (1162–1241) and the priest Saigyō. Their nature poetry, however, conveyed not simply the vivid colors of nature but a muted, bleaker, monochromatic vision. They found beauty in the loneliness, sadness and coldness of nature, an aesthetic that developed through the medieval period, under the influence of Zen and Buddhist ideas of the emptiness of things and the dangers of attachment, into the idea of *wabi* (cultivated poverty) expressed perhaps most fully in Tea as refined by the Tea master Sen no Rikyū in the 16th century. The following poem by Teika perfectly expresses the beauty of a lonely, bleak and colorless landscape in late autumn:

Miwataseba	Looking about
Hana mo momiji mo	I see no cherry blossoms
Nakari keri	And no crimson leaves:
Ura no tomoya no	A straw thatched hut by a bay
Aki no yūgure	In the autumn dusk.

What was impressive about this developing medieval aesthetic was not so much that poets, monks and ordinary laypeople should find beauty in loneliness, imperfection or in the faded qualities of things but that they should elevate this beauty into an aesthetic principle transcending the vivid beauty of the colorful world of spring cherry blossoms or fall maple leaves. This was the vital medieval contribution to Japanese sensibility and aesthetic feeling.

Through their association with courtiers the upper echelon of warrior society was introduced to the whole range of courtly learning and culture, as well as to the arts of government. This association began even before the Taira imposed themselves upon the court in the 12th century. Yoritomo deliberately established his Bakufu outside the orbit of court politics. He and later warrior leaders warned of the debilitating dangers of too close an association with the court and he constantly asserted the duty of warriors to maintain their martial heritage, the arts of *bu*. At the same time Yoritomo and his warrior successors needed, and enjoyed, the literary and administrative skills (*bun*) of which courtiers were the masters. Thus, even after courtiers had lost much of their political authority, and declined into near penury at times, they maintained their social position and cultural influence as the mentors and associates of powerful warriors. Yoritomo, his son Sanetomo, members of the Hōjō family, Ashikaga shoguns and many provincial warriors studied calligraphy and etiquette and wrote poetry under the guidance of courtiers and priests.

Warrior patronage of the arts

In many ways, as we have seen, the medieval age was the age of the warrior. Warrior values came to the fore, and a martial life-style took shape. Fortified warrior residences and hilltop castles became architectural features of the age. Scroll paintings like the *Obusuma Saburō Scroll,* contrasting the lives of a martially minded eastern warrior and his aesthetically inclined elder brother, or the *Mongol Invasion Scrolls,* depicting the exploits of a Kyushu warrior against the Mongol fleets, illustrated the obsession of the elite society with details of warrior exploits, life-style and dress. The making of swords, armor, helmets and horse trappings reached the highest technical and artistic levels. A warrior ethic of heroism, loyalty and willingness to die for one's lord was fostered by warrior chieftains and lauded in war tales like the *Heike monogatari* or *Taiheiki.* At the same time warriors were mastering those civilian arts essential for government, for easier social intercourse with the nobility and for cultural enjoyment. Many warriors were literate. Some, including Minamoto Yoritomo and his son Sanetomo and several of the Hōjō regents, wrote poetry that was considered sufficiently accomplished to be included in major anthologies. Many other warriors participated in literary salons with nobles and monks and patronized painters, dramatists and craftsmen. Ashikaga shoguns like Yoshimitsu and Yoshimasa, provincial warrior families like the Hosokawa and Ōuchi, and the unifiers Nobunaga and Hideyoshi were all lavish patrons and practitioners of the arts.

It was under this kind of warrior patronage that the Noh theater and Tea (*chanoyu*) flourished. Palaces, castles and provincial warrior residences were decorated with screens and panel paintings by masters of the Kanō and Tosa schools of painting. Warriors became devotees and patrons of the new branches of Buddhism, especially Zen, and acquired from monks some understanding of the secular as well as the Buddhist culture of China. A vogue for "Chinese objects" (*karamono*) ran through the medieval period. Ink landscape paintings, portraits, books, silks, ceramics and tea utensils from China were all in great demand. Shoguns and *daimyō* called upon monks and secular experts for advice in connoisseurship. There were few warlords who did not, in one way or another, seek to enhance their political and military power with trappings of cultural legitimation. Hideyoshi, with his castle building and commissioning of massive painting projects, his patronage of Tea masters and Noh actors, his avid collecting of Chinese and European artwork and his capture of Korean potters, was merely a prime example of the warlord as patron of the arts.

The warrior's prominent role in medieval society is clearly reflected in a literary genre that is characteristic of the medieval period, the war tale, or *gunkimono*. The finest of these tales is *Heike monogatari* (*The Tale of the Heike*). Based on a chronicle of the rise and fall of the Taira family probably written by a courtier in the early 13th century, the tale was disseminated and elaborated by blind wandering minstrels who chanted favorite sections from the tale to the accompaniment of the *biwa*, a kind of lute. Like many of the war tales, the *Tale of the Heike* does not take pleasure in the deeds of war. It is rather suffused with a sense of transience and the Buddhist conviction that this world is illusory, glory ephemeral. This somber tone is set in the opening passage which states that "The sound of the bell of the Gion temple echoes the impermanence of all things." Memorable scenes from the *Heike* were reworked in the Noh,

Jōruri and Kabuki theatrical repertoires and continue to move audiences to this day.

Buddhist patronage of the arts

Buddhist monasteries, especially Rinzai Zen monasteries, were also major nodes in the medieval cultural fabric. Monks, nobles and warriors mingled on equal terms at literary salons. The abbots' buildings in monasteries were centers of learning and cultural exchange. Zen monks in China and Japan shaped a new aesthetic out of the conviction of the universality of Buddhahood and the insights of meditation. This aesthetic, refined within monastic walls, proved so attractive to lay artists,

Centers of late medieval culture
The map shows some features of the cultural landscape in the 15th and 16th centuries. The principal patrons of elite culture throughout the medieval period were members of the imperial court, shoguns and powerful warriors, and Buddhist temples and Shinto shrines. There was an increasingly active urban culture in cities such as Kyoto and Sakai. There was also a vigorous popular, frequently oral, transmission of culture to towns and villages by wandering balladeers, preachers, *sarugaku* dancers and picture explainers. In Kyoto in the late 14th and 15th centuries the Ashikaga shoguns, especially Yoshimitsu and Yoshimasa, set the cultural style. In the provinces, *daimyō* families with cultural interests, including the Ōuchi, Asakura and Kikuchi, patronized traveling monks, Noh troupes, tea masters, painters such as Sesshū Tōyō and poets such as Iio Sōgi. The Ashikaga school and the Kanazawa Library were both supported by provincial warrior families. Woodblock printed editions of Buddhist texts, Confucian classics and Chinese poetry were produced by Zen monasteries in Kyoto, by *daimyō* families such as the Ōuchi, Kikuchi and Shimazu, and by monks and merchants in Sakai.

patrons and men of culture that it quickly infused the cultural style of the medieval age. Zen monasteries incorporated in their layout and monastic buildings the styles of Song architecture. Their gardens introduced and refined the concept of "dry landscape" (*kare sansui*) in which raked gravel, sand, moss and stones replaced water, flowers or borrowed scenery. Zen monks brought to Japan mastery of the Song dynasty ink-painting (*suibokuga*) and broken-ink (*haboku*) techniques. Zen portraits and portrait sculpture sought to capture the spiritual energy of the Zen master they depicted. Religious paintings of Rakan, Zen patriarchs, Zen encounters or scenes from the life of the Buddha used in religious ceremonies or daily monastic life were also a stimulus for artists inside and outside the monasteries. Painters like Josetsu, Shūbun, Oguri Sōtan, Kanō Masanobu and Sesshū, all of whom had close ties with Zen monks and monasteries, mastered and transcended Chinese ink-painting techniques to establish a Japanese tradition of *suibokuga* that had a profound influence on medieval cultural style. The late medieval period saw a shift away from the monochromatic world of Zen ink landscape to the large gilded wall and screen paintings needed to decorate the panels of walls of the great castles like those at Azuchi, Momoyama and Osaka. Painters of the Kanō school flourished on these commissions. Zen monks were also scholars and poets. They transmitted to courtiers and warriors knowledge of Song Confucian thought and of Chinese poetry. They introduced ideas of the Unity of the Three Creeds, the fundamental compatibility of the teachings of the Buddha, Lao Tzu and Confucius and illustrated them in ink monochrome.

The practice of drinking tea also spread from Zen monasteries to secular society. *Daimyō* and merchants, especially those of Sakai, consorted with Zen monks in tea gatherings. Tea masters like Murata Jukō, Takeno Jōō and Sen no Rikyū secularized and refined the practice of tea drinking through the incorporation of a Zen aesthetic of simplicity and rusticity known as *wabi*. The passion for tea that infected late medieval society served as a spur to a range of related arts and crafts. In ceramics rough Japanese ware, especially Raku, gained pride of place alongside elegant Chinese celadons. Tea room architecture, interior and garden design, flower arrangement, lacquerware, metalwork and the use of bamboo were all powerfully influenced by the developing set of aesthetics generated within the tea rooms. At work here, as in other areas of medieval intellectual life, was a tension and interplay beween "Chinese" and "Japanese" elements, between the perfect unblemished regular beauty of *karamono* and the imperfect, impoverished beauty of a *wabi*-inspired, increasingly Japanese aesthetic, between the refined elite tradition of Chinese and Japanese culture and a carefully contrived rusticity.

Underlying the literature of the medieval age were aesthetic ideals, such as *wabi,* that either resonated with Zen or were directly inspired by Zen. Strands of eremitism, the ideal of the monk's rustic retreat, for instance, were heightened by the meditative life of the Zen monk seeking enlightenment. This found expression in poetry in Chinese and Japanese written by Zen monks. It also found

expression in *An Account of My Hut* (*Hōjōki*) by Kamō no Chōmei (1153–1216). Chōmei was not a Zen monk, but the experience of sickness and disaster led him to flee the capital and all worldly possessions for the simple beauty of life in a tiny hermitage. His enjoyment of his simple retreat is tempered, however, by his recognition that his love for his poor hut is also a form of attachment and a hindrance to his salvation. In his *Essays in Idleness* (*Tsurezuregusa*) Yoshida Kenkō (1258–1350) crystallized much of this medieval aesthetic of non-attachment, of pleasure in the irregular, the broken and the imperfect, of the importance of becoming (as opposed to simply being), of beginnings and ends (as opposed to climactic moments) and of declining (as opposed to burgeoning). This theme of non-attachment, which so much pervaded medieval Japanese literature, also underlay the Noh drama which flowered in the 14th and 15th centuries. Most Noh plays introduce tormented spirits reliving the passion or violence of their former lives. These restless spirits seek deliverance through prayer and erasure from the memory of their attachments in their former existence.

Popular culture

No comment on the medieval age and its culture would be complete without a reference to the growing cultural awareness of the common people. Evidence of popular culture wells out of the cracks in a war-torn society. Perhaps the very warfare and disintegration which shattered the stability and dominance of the old aristocratic cultural and social order gave new groups and individuals their chance. If warriors could rise to power by force of arms, so too could men of culture; and in the looser society of the 15th and 16th centuries all social groups could more easily contribute to cultural life.

Messages of Buddhist salvation and retribution and tales of military heroism were carried into the provinces by traveling priests and minstrels. The Noh theater and Kyōgen had their origins in popular rural and religious entertainments. Even after its elevation by Kan'ami, Zeami and their successors into a refined dramatic form, Noh continued to be performed at village shrines throughout Japan. Tea likewise was enjoyed in villages as well as in the castles of warriors or the tea houses of wealthy merchants. Wandering linked-verse (*renga*) poets like Sōgi (1421–1508) exchanged verses with their village hosts. On urban riverbanks, free from taxation, lived a restless urban proletariat known as the *kawaramono*. They included dropouts and outcasts who made a living slaughtering animals and tanning hides. Among them were poor artists, craftsmen and popular performers.

The vitality of popular life and culture in the *chūsei* period is evident from scenes in scroll paintings like the *Ippen hijiri-e* of the late Kamakura period, paintings of artisans and tradespeople, scenes of agriculture, shrines or medieval warfare, or the "Southern Barbarian" screens and genre paintings of the late 16th century. It is also evident in the origins of Kabuki entertainment in the late 16th and early 17th centuries. This vitality and popular exuberance carried over into the Tokugawa period and flourished even more vigorously in the urban centers of Osaka, Kyoto and Edo.

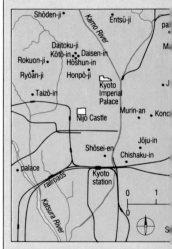

The Zen Gardens of Kyoto

Kyoto is famous for its temples and gardens. Some of these gardens reflect aristocratic or Pure Land influences. Many of Kyoto's finest gardens, however, are attached to Zen temples and were designed by Zen monks and their patrons in the medieval period. Zen meditation, the aesthetics of garden design, and landscape painting, which was also appreciated by Zen monks, were all closely interrelated. The garden designer could use trees, shrubs, moss, water, waterfalls and bridges. Or he could restrict himself to stone and gravel, much like the ink painter who rejected color. Such sand and stone gardens can be viewed as three-dimensional monochrome landscapes, with the gravel representing water and the rocks mountains or clouds, or enjoyed as abstract sculptures.

Below The garden of the Ryōanji Zen temple is widely recognized as one of the finest examples of the dry-stone landscape garden in Japan. Ryōanji was established by the warrior Hosokawa Katsumoto around 1450. The designer of the garden is unknown. The quietly dignified garden is simply an expanse of raked white gravel with 15 rocks, some of them edged in moss, set in three groups. The garden is framed by the monastery buildings and by a mellow earthen wall. The stones are sometimes said to represent a tigress shepherding her cubs across a stream or mountain peaks rising through clouds. It is probably wiser to accept no received explanation, but to find, as in Zen, one's own direct intuitive understanding in the garden.

Right and below Monks believed that enlightenment could be attained not only during meditation but in the mindful performance of such simple everyday tasks as cooking rice, swabbing the floor or working in the woodshed or garden. The creation and maintenance of gardens was thus a contemplative everyday activity as well as an aesthetic experience. There is a delightful story of a young novice, told to tidy a garden, who asked his master where he should throw the rubbish. "Where is the rubbish?" asked the master as he took broken twigs and leaves for kindling and carried small stones to catch rain drips from the eaves, leaving only a small pile of dust and gravel which he raked back into the garden. Seen here is one of the gardens within Daitokuji.

Japanese Gardens

Japanese gardens and garden design have intrigued and stimulated Western visitors since the Iberians first visited Japan in the 16th century. The Japanese art of garden design is ancient. Zen-inspired dry-landscape gardens are justly famous (see p.121), but they are not the only type of Japanese garden. A garden aesthetic was developing long before Zen was introduced. Zen simply added new aesthetic dimensions.

Gardens of the 7th and 8th centuries incorporated Chinese- and Korean-inspired ponds, bridges and lanterns or the Buddhist notion of Mount Sumeru as the center of the cosmos. Imperial palaces and the residences of the Heian nobility were built over ponds with fishing pavilions and "borrowed" mountain scenery. Emperors and courtiers enjoyed the recreation of floating poems or sake cups along a winding stream. By the Kamakura period provincial warriors, as well as nobles and monks, were beginning to develop an interest in garden construction. The earliest critical statement of Japanese garden design, the *Sakuteiki* ("Essay on Garden Making"), was written by Tachibana Toshitsuna in the early Kamakura period (1185–1333).

Above As a compositional feature water is incorporated into gardens in a variety of ways. In some cases a diverted stream may suggest a mountain ravine while an island of pines in a pond may evoke Matsushima or some other beauty spot. In Zen gardens white gravel and rocks may convey the impression of a fast-flowing river or ocean or, as here, water may provide a cooling soothing sound as it drips into and over an old stone basin.

Above left Nijo castle was built in 1626 as a Tokugawa strongpoint in Kyoto from which Bakufu officials could oversee the court and control western Japan. Its garden reflects the love of strikingly shaped rocks, no doubt received as gifts.

Left Among the most famous garden designers in Japanese history was the 14th-century Zen monk Musō Soseki (1275–1351). Until the age of 50 Musō lived as a wandering monk seeking enlightenment. On his wanderings he established many small mountain temples with gardens incorporating the natural scenery. In later life he was patronized by the Ashikaga shoguns and Emperor Go-Daigo and appointed abbot of the monasteries of Tenryūji and Rinsenji in Kyoto where he designed fine gardens. Toward the end of his life he withdrew to the small temple of Saihōji where he created a garden using moss as its principal compositional feature and incorporating the Chinese ideal of "ten splendid views."

Above Originally built in the late 14th century as part of the villa of the shogun Ashikaga Yoshimitsu, the Kinkakuji (Temple of the Golden Pavilion) survived until the 20th century, only to perish by fire in 1950. The present structure is a reconstruction completed in 1955 and regilded again in 1988. The garden incorporated elements from Zen garden design and Heian period water gardens. Shimmering in its own reflection, the pavilion seems to float on water. The garden is designed on a grand scale, using borrowed scenery and offering varied views of the pavilion.

Left This cluster of stone lanterns stands near the Tōshōgū shrine in Nikko where Tokugawa is enshrined. In some cases stone lanterns served a functional purpose. More often they are appreciated for the ancient, moss-covered stone itself or used as reminders of Buddhist themes of paradise or Mount Sumeru.

Noh Drama

Visitors to Japan today can take their choice of avant-garde or traditional theater. While modern experimental theater flourishes, the older forms of Noh, Kyōgen, Bunraku and Kabuki all have a following. Derived from a blending of earlier dance and dramatic forms and raised to a high dramatic intensity by Kan'ami and Zeami in the medieval period, Noh is a masked musical dance drama. Each of these four words says something important about Noh.

Most Noh plays revolve around a dramatic encounter between a troubled spirit (the *shite*) and a priest or bystander (the *waki*). Through this encounter the spirit may find some spiritual relief, though the audience is frequently left with the feeling that this haunting encounter can repeat itself. Noh is not acted but "danced," and the moments of greatest intensity in Noh are expressed in dance—slow and stately at first, gradually mounting to controlled intensity. The dance and drama are heightened by the music of flute and drums, and the accompanying chant. Actors (principally the *shite*) wear masks, as well as rich brocade robes. The masks denote characters or character types, or more often states of mind or spiritual conditions. They distort the voice, giving it an unearthly quality, and by movements of the actors they convey a variety of emotions.

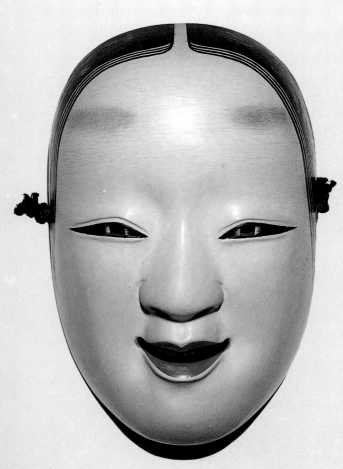

Above Originally Noh was performed outdoors or in shrines and temples. The modern Noh stage developed in the Edo period. The main stage (see plan, *top right*) projects into the audience. The action may occur here, or on the bridge. All plays are performed with only the simplest of properties, before the backdrop of an ancient pine. The flautist and drummers sit at the back of the stage. The chorus sits stage left of the actors. The main actor (usually masked) is known as the *shite*. The secondary actor (not masked) is known as the *waki*. The rule of the *waki* is to call the *shite* to the stage, to question him to expose the dramatic situation, and to provide incentive to dance.

Left The spiritual focus of a Noh performance is the mask, carved of cypress and painted, which the actor brings to life on stage. Most masks are variations on a type. This is the face of a beautiful young girl, Ko-Omote.

Right The puppets used in Bunraku are half-lifesize and worked by a principal operator and one or two black-robed assistants. Bunraku themes were derived from earlier Noh dramas, from history and legend. But the finest dramas were written specially for puppets by Chikamatsu Monzaemon.

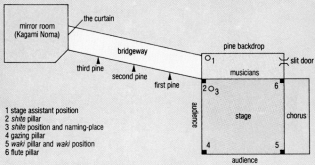

mirror room
(Kagami Noma)

the curtain

bridgeway

third pine

second pine

first pine

pine backdrop

1

musicians

slit door

2 ○ 3

6

audience

stage

chorus

4

5

audience

1 stage assistant position
2 *shite* pillar
3 *shite* position and naming-place
4 gazing pillar
5 *waki* pillar and *waki* position
6 flute pillar

Left Noh masks have always been regarded as having spiritual or mystic significance. The white-bearded mask of Okina, the holy sage, has been imbued with particular divinity. Some Okina masks, like this one, have pompom-like eyebrows. They are unique in being divided at the mouth line and joined with cord. All have expressions of happiness or merriment, with the mouth spread wide and the eyes narrowed to slits. The Okina mask is used only in the auspicious dance drama *Okina*, in which prayers for peace, longevity and fertility are offered in dance.

Center left Several masks are used in Noh plays to express the facial characteristics of young men. Some, such as the Semimaru and Atsumori masks, are used only to present the blind Prince Semimaru or the warrior Taira no Atsumori who died in battle at the age of 16. Others, like the Kassiki (acolyte) mask shown here, attributed to Echi, were more general.

Bottom left Many Noh plays revolve around the reincarnations of insane or jealous creatures, restless female spirits, vengeful ghosts and demonesses. Different demon masks express the various stages of transformation of women into demons. The Hashihime mask reflects a soul given to malice. The Hannya mask (shown here) reveals a character fighting an inner battle with rage. The most demonic mask is that of a woman transformed into a serpent.

Far left Traveling entertainers using small puppets probably presented simple stories in the ancient and medieval periods. The complex, half-lifesize puppets used in Bunraku were developed during the 17th and 18th centuries, as dramas by Chikamatsu, performed by master puppeteers and accompanied by the throb of *shamisens*, attracted large audiences of townspeople in Edo, Osaka and Kyoto. Like a Noh mask, the head of a puppet expresses a character type, whether maiden or matron, warrior or buffoon.

Castles in War and Peace

Iberian missionaries and merchants who found their way to Japan in the 16th century were amazed at the scale and grandeur of the great castles they saw. The Portuguese Jesuit missionary and chronicler Luis Frois (1532–97), who spent more than 30 years in Japan, provided this contemporary description of the castle at Azuchi, on a promontory overlooking Lake Biwa, built by Oda Nobunaga in his conquest of central Japan.

"On top of the hill in the middle of the city Nobunaga built his palace and castle, which as regards architecture, strength, wealth and grandeur may well be compared with the greatest buildings of Europe. Its strong and well-constructed surrounding walls of stone are over 60 spans in height and even higher in many places; inside the walls there are many beautiful and exquisite houses, all of them decorated with gold and so neat and well fashioned that they seem to reach the acme of human elegance. And in the middle there is a sort of tower which they call *tenshu* and it indeed has a far more noble and splendid appearance than our towers. It consists of seven floors, all of which, both inside and out, have been fashioned to a wonderful architectural design; for both inside and out, I mean, inside, the walls are decorated with designs richly painted in gold and different colors, while the outside of each of these stories is painted in various colors . . . In a word the whole edifice is beautiful, excellent and brilliant. As the castle is situated on high ground and is itself very lofty, it looks as if it reaches the clouds and can be seen from afar for many leagues. The fact that the castle is constructed entirely of wood is not at all apparent either from within or from without, for it looks as if it is built of strong stone and mortar." Sadly the castle at Azuchi was destroyed in 1582.

The map shows important surviving and restored castles including some, such as those at Himeji, Kumamoto and Matsumoto, that are among the finest examples of castle architecture in Japan. During the medieval period rival warrior chieftains built hilltop castles (*yamajiro*) as strong points. In the civil wars of the 15th and 16th centuries large castles (*hirajiro*) were built on raised mounds in the open river valleys commanding and protecting the rice fields and irrigation systems upon which the feudal lord and his retainers depended for survival.

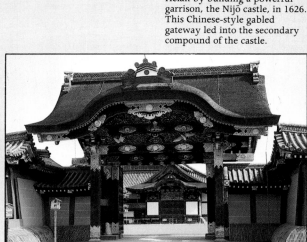

Below The Tokugawa shoguns asserted their power over the imperial court and the city of Heian by building a powerful garrison, the Nijō castle, in 1626. This Chinese-style gabled gateway led into the secondary compound of the castle.

Below As residences and centers of *daimyō* (warlord) culture, the great chambers of many castles were decorated with magnificent screen and door paintings by artists of the Kanō and other schools of Japanese painting. Here is the interior of an audience chamber designed originally for Hideyoshi's castle at Fushimi and later reinstalled in a temple in Kyoto.
Below right Matsumoto castle is a fine example of a *hirajiro*. Commanding a broad fertile valley among the mountains of Nagano Prefecture, the castle was built in 1594–97 by Toyotomi Hideyoshi.

Right Known as the White Heron (Shirasagi) castle, Himeji castle dominates the city of Himeji, Hyōgo Prefecture. First constructed by the Akamatsu warrior family in the 14th century, the castle was later controlled by Hideyoshi and the Ikeda family who greatly enlarged it. Set on a low hill, the castle comprises an intricate defensive system of moats, compounds and gates. The main donjon (see cross-section, *bottom right*) is five stories high on the outside, seven on the inside, and is connected with three minor donjons (see plan, *bottom left*). Castles served principally as garrisons and fortresses, but they were also the residences of shoguns and *daimyōs*, centers of national and regional government.

Below A *daimyō* procession is reenacted at Iwakuni in Yamaguchi Prefecture.

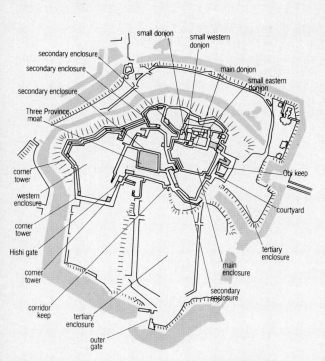

Overleaf Nijō castle and the bustling streets around it are shown in a contemporary screen painting.

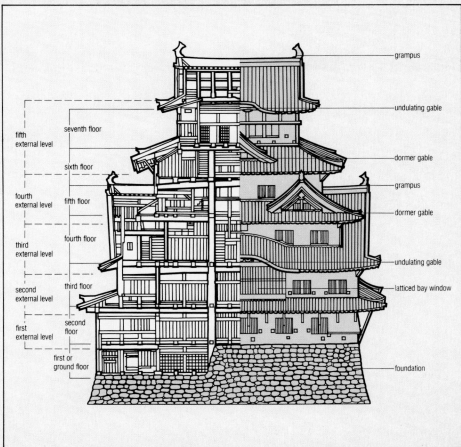

secondary enclosure
secondary enclosure
secondary enclosure
Three Province moat
small donjon
small western donjon
main donjon
small eastern donjon
Obi keep
courtyard
tertiary enclosure
corner tower
western enclosure
corner tower
Hishi gate
corner tower
main enclosure
secondary enclosure
corridor keep
tertiary enclosure
outer gate

grampus
undulating gable
dormer gable
grampus
dormer gable
undulating gable
latticed bay window
foundation

fifth external level
seventh floor
sixth floor
fourth external level
fifth floor
third external level
fourth floor
second external level
third floor
first external level
second floor
first or ground floor

127

Kabuki Theater

The two most popular dramatic entertainments for townspeople in Edo period Japan were Bunraku and Kabuki. There were decades in the late 17th and early 18th centuries when Bunraku eclipsed the Kabuki in popular appeal. By the mid-18th century, however, especially in Edo, it was the Kabuki theaters that were drawing the greatest crowds. Famous actors drew their own passionate followings, and in many cases the attentions of courtesans and ladies of the shogunal palace.

During the 17th century Kabuki actors had to survive by their wits when the Bakufu banned women's Kabuki (*Onna Kabuki*) in 1629. It was promptly replaced by boys' Kabuki (*Wakashū Kabuki*). When that was outlawed as socially disruptive in 1652, mature males assumed all the roles (*Yarō Kabuki*). Kabuki remained under Bakufu regulation as a necessary evil, a morally disruptive form of popular entertainment that simply could not be suppressed. In fact, this control probably helped in the maturation of Kabuki as theater. Mature male actors, deprived of the attractive forelocks and winsome appeal of women or boys, had to act and deepen the dramatic content of Kabuki to hold their audiences.

During the Genroku era, after 1680, Kabuki matured rapidly. Simple skits created by the actors gradually gave way to more complex plots crafted by playwrights. In the early decades of the 18th century the puppet theater surpassed Kabuki in popular esteem. Kabuki actors won their audiences back by absorbing the dramatic masterpieces and many of the theatrical techniques of the puppet theater.

Right This *ukiyo-e* by Okumura Masanobu (1686–1764) shows the interior of a Kabuki theater in Edo in the mid-18th century during a performance of the historical drama *The Revenge of the Soga Brothers*. By this time the wildly popular Kabuki theater had developed the runway through the audience (*hanamichi*) which could be used as a secondary stage, as well as a revolving main stage and draw curtain. The lanterns on the ceiling bear the emblems of the principal actors. Kabuki was a social occasion and an all-day entertainment, with eating and drinking, conversation and ogling of beauties in the galleries going on through the performance. Okumura Masanobu was a versatile print artist who painted parodies of classical themes, actors and beauties but also, as in this print, experimented with Western perspective.

Below This print by Utagawa Kunisada (1786–1864) shows a Kabuki actor in a typically masculine pose in a scene from the play *Yoshitsune Senbon Zakura* (''The Thousand Cherry Trees of Yoshitsune''). According to the legends, Yoshitsune, the hero of Dannoura, while fleeing from his brother Yoritomo, who has ordered his death, encounters an old enemy, Taira no Tomomori, the admiral of the Taira fleet destroyed by Yoshitsune. Killed at Dannoura, a reincarnation of Tomomori confronts the fleeing Yoshitsune but is defeated again. Tying a huge anchor to his waist, he leaps into the sea.

Below In Kabuki costumes, wigs and makeup are carefully integrated to maximize the role. In historical plays such as *Shibaruku* makeup is thick, elaborate, fantastic and mask-like (*kumadori*). In domestic dramas it is more restrained and realistic. The female impersonators (Onnagata), the cornerstone of Kabuki, wear striking makeup in the roles of young women and courtesans. As with Noh, Kabuki actors come mostly from theatrical families and begin their training at a very early age, mastering not only the roles but all aspects of Kabuki movement, costume and makeup.

Above This lively screen painting by Hishikawa Moronobu (died 1694) shows a scene backstage at the Nakamura-za Kabuki theater as actors robe and make up for the performance of a historical drama. Moronobu was the pioneer popularizer and preeminent artist of woodblock prints in his day. He was particularly skilled in depicting genre scenes and groups of colorful, vigorous figures with powerful brush strokes. His painting style and *ukiyo-e* inspired later print makers.

Right The Kabuki theater derives much of its popularity from lavish staging, larger-than-life action and colorful costumes. This scene was performed by the Ichikawa Ennosuke Troupe in 1987.

THE EDO PERIOD

Oda Nobunaga, "master of the realm"

Japan in the year 1500 was at an extreme of political decentralization. Neither the imperial court nor the Muromachi Bakufu commanded political authority or respect. The country was divided among more than 250 warring feudal lords (*daimyō*). Some of these *daimyō* hoped to use regional victories to catapult themselves into a drive for national hegemony. They watched for any chance to strike at the capital as a base from which to assert control over central Japan. The *daimyō* who achieved this first was Oda Nobunaga (1534–82), the young leader of the small domain of Owari on the Pacific coast. Nobunaga's achievement was to begin the reunification of the country. After his assassination the task of unification was carried on by his successors Toyotomi Hideyoshi (1536–98) and Tokugawa Ieyasu (1542–1616). In a series of brilliant tactical battles Nobunaga fought his way out of the ruck of warring *daimyō* to establish control over the capital region in 1568.

Nobunaga distinguished himself as a military genius at the age of 27 during the battle of Okehazama in 1566, when he not only defeated the very much larger army of the Imagawa clan, the greatest military force on the Pacific coast at that time, but also captured Imagawa Yoshimoto, the *daimyō* himself. In overpowering other *daimyō* Nobunaga dreamed of establishing a unified realm. In order to express this determination he used a seal bearing characters reading: *tenka fubu*, "the realm in military glory." The word *tenka*, "all under heaven," refers to the whole realm of Japan and implies control of the nation. Nobunaga viewed himelf as a *tenkajin*, or a person who rules the *tenka*. In entering Kyoto, he claimed that he was merely restoring the fifteenth Ashikaga shogun Yoshiaki (1537–97) to power. This was just a pretext. Yoshiaki was soon discarded and the Ashikaga shogunate terminated.

Nobunaga's road to mastery of the *tenka* was not an easy one: there were many hurdles. First, ambitious rival *daimyō* still held power in the provinces and were ready to crush him if they could. Secondly, he encountered fierce resistance from Buddhist monastic armies and militant lay believers. In disposing of rival *daimyō* Nobunaga displayed a rare tactical genius for isolating them and destroying them with superior strategy and technology. In the crucial battle of Nagashino in Mikawa (1575) Nobunaga allied with Tokugawa Ieyasu to defeat Takeda Katsuyori. The primary reason for Nobunaga's victory was his skillful use of muskets, a technology which had been introduced from Europe only 30 years earlier. Nobunaga organized a 3000-man musket brigade, rotated them in three ranks, and made it possible to fire a volley every 10 seconds. The Takeda forces, still relying on mounted swordsmen and pikemen, were powerless in the face of such fusilades.

Nobunaga's struggles with the military forces of militant Buddhist communities were equally fierce. The *Ikkōshū*, or devotees of the True Pure Land school, under the leadership of the monastic complex of Honganji, were a powerful spiritual and military force in the Kinai and surrounding provinces, as well as the Hokuriku and Tōkai districts. For almost a century the whole province of Echizen was effectively controlled not by a *daimyō* but by a council of *Ikkōshū* representatives led by local *bushi*. Echizen was even called "a nation ruled by the peasantry." The True Pure Land followers were so well armed and organized that they were a match in military power for any warring *daimyō*. Even a warrior as ruthless as Nobunaga had difficulty in bending them to his will. Over a 10-year campaign, the Ishiyama Honganji in Osaka refused to yield to Nobunaga's repeated onslaughts and returned his fire with several thousand guns. Reluctantly, Nobunaga was eventually forced to negotiate peace terms. However, the power of *Ikkōshū* followers in several of the central provinces was completely crushed by Nobunaga. In 1574 in Nagashima, Owari Province, Nobunaga surrounded 20000 *Ikkōshū* followers, men, women and children, and literally roasted them to death. It was the most brutal battle in an age of bloody battles—perhaps even the most brutal in the history of Japan.

From the callousness with which he crushed the *Ikkōshū* it is clear that Nobunaga had no respect for the authority of traditional religion. In 1571 he slaughtered some 3000 Tendai monks and laypeople and razed Enryakuji on Mount Hiei, a powerful political and religious authority from the early Heian period, because that monastery had challenged him militarily. Nobles and clergy, and even some warriors, were appalled at such sacrilegious acts. Nobunaga, however, was implacable toward any force that stood in his way. At the same time, it should be remembered that he did not deny imperial authority, nor did he deny the ancient authority of other temples and shrines as long as they did not challenge his hegemony. In dealing with the imperial court, Nobunaga tried to restore some of its domains, rebuild the imperial palace and refurbish some of its lost dignity.

Oda Nobunaga's attempt to unify the *tenka* was halted in the ascendant. In 1582, while he and his retainers were staying at the Honnōji in Kyoto, he was assassinated by Akechi Mitsuhide, one of his leading generals. Nobunaga's warriors withheld their allegiance from Mitsuhide and he was overthrown within a few days by another of Nobunaga's generals, Toyotomi Hideyoshi (1536–98), who succeeded as the new *tenkajin*.

Toyotomi Hideyoshi the unifier

Hideyoshi was the son of a peasant from Owari who served under Oda Nobunaga and won advan-

Top Nicknamed the "great idiot" for irreverent behavior at his father's funeral, Oda Nobunaga (1534–82) was the first of the three military unifiers of the 16th century. After putting down disorder in his own domain, Nobunaga conquered the realm (*tenka*) by crushing rival *daimyō* and religious institutions, securing control over Kyoto and ending the Ashikaga Bakufu. Ruthless and decisive, he began to institute some of the centralizing reforms later extended by Hideyoshi. Curious about Christianity, he allowed Iberian missionaries to spread Catholicism. Nobunaga's brilliant career was ended by assassination.

Above Toyotomi Hideyoshi (1536–98) was the son of a foot soldier who won the favor of Nobunaga. After Nobunaga's death he seized power, extended Nobunaga's conquests and ruled with the title of regent (*kampaku*). Hideyoshi's conquests, land surveys and sword hunts transformed Japan. Like Nobunaga he was a lavish castle builder and patron of the arts. He turned against Catholicism in 1587 and ended his life frustrated by his inability to conquer Korea.

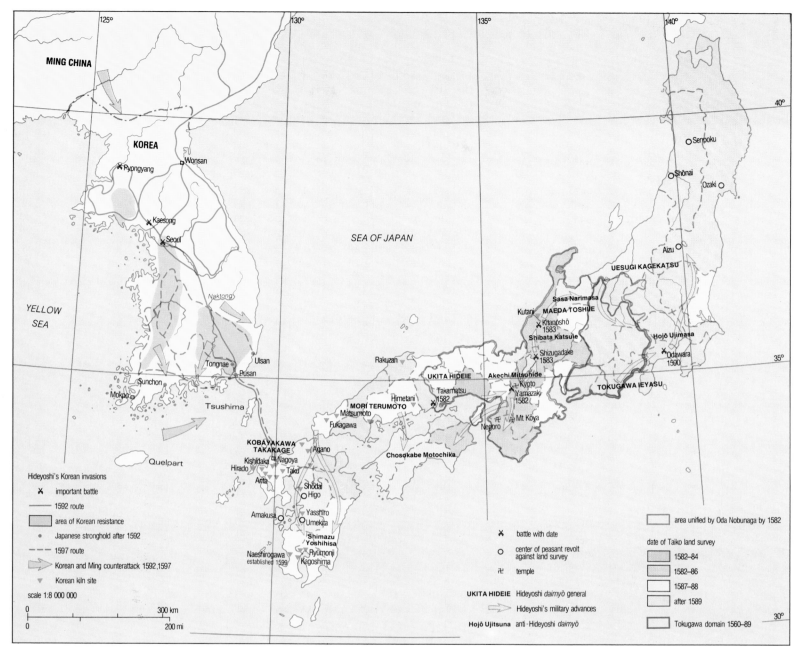

Hideyoshi's Korean invasions
- ✕ important battle
- —— 1592 route
- ▨ area of Korean resistance
- • Japanese stronghold after 1592
- --- 1597 route
- ⇨ Korean and Ming counterattack 1592,1597
- ▽ Korean kiln site

scale 1:8 000 000

0   300 km
0   200 mi

- ✕ battle with date
- ○ center of peasant revolt against land survey
- 卍 temple
- **UKITA HIDEIE** Hideyoshi *daimyō* general
- ⇨ Hideyoshi's military advances
- **Hōjō Ujitsuna** anti-Hideyoshi *daimyō*

- ☐ area unified by Oda Nobunaga by 1582

date of Taikō land survey
- 1582–84
- 1582–86
- 1587–88
- after 1589
- ☐ Tokugawa domain 1560–89

Campaigns of Hideyoshi
Hideyoshi made himself heir to Oda Nobunaga and his conquests by defeating Akechi Mitsuhide at Yamazaki in 1582. At Shizugadake in 1583 he gained control of Echizen, Kaga and Noto, distributing the provinces as rewards to loyal vassal *daimyō*. In 1584 and 1585 he subdued Wakayama and the Chosokabe domain in Shikoku. In 1587 he launched a major campaign against Shimazu Yoshihisa in Kyushu. As he pressed his conquests westward, Hideyoshi instituted detailed land surveys and, from 1588, his sword hunt. In 1590 he turned against the Hōjō in the Kantō and moved his rival Tokugawa Ieyasu out of central Japan, awarding him six Kantō provinces. Having made himself master of Japan, Hideyoshi launched two brutal and futile invasions of Korea – hoping to defeat Ming China and set up a pan-Asian empire. The only benefit to Japan came from enslaved Korean craftsmen who set up kilns in Kyushu and improved standards for pottery.

cement as a precocious strategist. At the time of his death Nobunaga controlled more than one third of the realm, including the cities of Kyoto, Osaka and Sakai. Hideyoshi pressed his conquests westward until by 1587 he had secured control of Kyushu. All that remained unbroken were the eastern provinces where productive power was relatively low. In 1587 Hideyoshi sent his armies eastward to force the Hōjō of Odawara into submission. In the same year he announced his grandiose design for invading Korea and establishing his supremacy over China. By 1590 he had secured eastern Japan and moved Tokugawa Ieyasu, his ally and most formidable rival, from Mikawa to Edo castle.

In 1591 Hideyoshi announced plans for attacking Ming positions in Korea. In the following year he conscripted over 150000 troops and launched an invasion. An army of 40000 warriors, led by *daimyō* from western Japan, marched on Seoul. Korean forces, however, counterattacked with the backing of Ming China and the Korean populace also conducted guerrilla operations against the invading Japanese armies. Gradually the signs of defeat became obvious. Hideyoshi was forced to

sue for peace and in 1588, nearing death, he ordered total withdrawal of the armies from Korea.

Hideyoshi enforced two important policies to solve other domestic structural contradictions. One was the policy of separation of samurai and peasants. The second was the enforcement of new land and tax systems. If we look first at the separation of *bushi* and peasants, the low-ranking samurai vassals of warring *daimyō* were part farmer and part soldier. They lived in rural villages which were consequently heavily armed. Samurai and peasants were closely linked in the rural community. In the confusion of the age of wars some powerful rural samurai, rejecting the authority of their nominal overlords, overthrew *daimyō* and themselves became *daimyō*. This process is known as *gekokujō* ("the lower toppling the upper"). In many ways Hideyoshi became a *tenkajin* by riding the tide of *gekokujō*. However, when he had seized power he realized that his position would always remain precarious if an untrammeled resort to *gekokujō* were allowed to continue. To try to stabilize society he determined to remove samurai from the villages, forcing them to live in castle towns under direct control of *daimyō* and to pledge loyalty to *daimyō*. Those who remained in the villages were disarmed and treated as farmers, working registered fields. Requisitioning of weapons, the so-called "sword hunt," was enforced throughout the country. Not all weapons were removed from villages, however, and the surrender of weapons was not the sole aim of the policy. The policy was accompanied by laws known as *sōbujirei* and *kenka teishrei* enforcing local peace by punishing private quarreling and resort to arms. Hideyoshi's aim was clearly to forbid private strife and show that only the government of the unifier and master of the realm (*tenkajin*) had the final discretionary power over disputes throughout the realm.

A new land and tax system emerged from Hideyoshi's extensive land surveys. Nobunaga had already started surveying fields with the aim of assessing the productive capacity supporting his newly won political power. Hideyoshi was more systematic. Land registers were drawn up containing the following information: size and location of fields; annual productive capacity in estimated yields of rice—*kokudaka* (even if the fields did not produce rice, he made villagers assess the land in terms of rice production); and the name of the cultivator of the fields. As a result, everybody from *daimyō* to the lowest-ranking *bushi* was clearly assessed by the same standard, namely how many *koku* of rice they were entitled to. Based on this standard, the unifier knew the productive and military power that he could mobilize and the labor force that could be taxed. A percentage of the yield of each village was assigned as its *nengu* (annual tax). Since the peasants whose names appeared in the land registers became the bearers of the tax, their cultivation rights were officially acknowledged. Land registration and the *kokudaka* system of assessment greatly simplified the complex medieval patterns of landholding and clarified relationships among those who lived in the villages. This rice-based yield system (*kokudaka-sei*) continued in force for 300 years until 1872 and can be said to have established the agrarian foundations of premodern Japan.

Establishment of the Tokugawa Bakufu

When Toyotomi Hideyoshi died in Osaka castle in 1598, his son Hideyori was still a child. Five powerful *daimyō* acted as a regency council and conducted the affairs of state. However, several of them had their own ambitions to seize the realm and the council quickly split into rival factions. Tokugawa Ieyasu (1542–1616), the most powerful of the five, broke the mutual understanding. He left Osaka, invited *daimyō* vassals and allies to his side and maneuvered for power. As he had anticipated, the anti-Ieyasu faction in Osaka, led by Ishida Mitsunari (1560–1600), raised an army and the struggle to control Japan began again. Two months later the issue was decided on the plain of Sekigahara (Mino) on 15 September 1600. In all, 160000 men took part and a fierce battle was fought from 8 o'clock in the morning. In the midst of the battle some of the *daimyō* in Ishida Mitsunari's western army secretly gave their allegiance to Ieyasu and by 2 o'clock in the afternoon the victory of the eastern army led by Ieyasu was certain.

Three years after the battle Ieyasu received imperial appointment as head of the feudal order (shogun) and formally established a new Bakufu. Unlike Oda Nobunaga and Toyotomi Hideyoshi who took official ranks in the court and used the highest rank of imperial regent as their source of political legitimation, Tokugawa Ieyasu assumed the highest rank in the warrior order and used the office of shogun with the intention of establishing a warrior government independent of the court. Ieyasu retired as shogun only two years later and turned the office over to his son, Hidetada. He thus established a dynastic precedent in which the shogunal office would be transmitted through Tokugawa descendants. For 264 years, until 1867, the Tokugawa shogunate survived for 15 generations. This long period of peace allowed for the ripening of a uniquely Japanese cultural style and spread higher levels of technology and education among the Japanese.

For most of its history the Tokugawa Bakufu state was an authoritarian centralized feudal state. Only during the latter part of the Tokugawa period did some decentralization of authority take place as the central power of the Bakufu weakened and some influential *daimyō* became more independent.

First, let us look at the centralization of the Bakufu from the viewpoint of the *daimyō* system. As mentioned above, Hideyoshi's land surveys set the pattern by which the assessment of the lands of the whole country was calculated in terms of rice productivity (*kokudaka*). *Kokudaka* became not only the basis for setting the land tax but also the standard of village size, and the basis for allotment of *daimyō* domains, samurai stipends and feudal obligations. Thus one characteristic of premodern Japan was that rice production became the standard for everything as indicated by the expression *komedate* (rice-based calculation).

The total production of the whole nation in the 17th century was estimated at 18 million *koku*. Approximately 7 million *koku* of that was from the lands held directly by the Bakufu and from the domains of shogunal vassals, called *hatamoto*. The other approximately 11 million *koku* were produced in the domains of some 260 *daimyō*. By definition *daimyō* in the Edo period were feudal lords who enjoyed incomes from their domains of 10000 *koku* or more. *Daimyō* had their own domains (*han*) and castles and were served by samurai vassals. Entrusted by the shoguns with the registers of lands and people in their domains, they enjoyed the right to govern the domain and collect annual land tax. In many respects the domains were like semi-independent states.

Independence was always tempered, however, by Bakufu power which controlled the *daimyō*. The Bakufu could and did relieve *daimyō* of office, move them at will to other domains, or confiscate all or part of their domains. In the 40 years after 1603, when the Bakufu was established, 71 *daimyō* households were subjected to attainder and the total *kokudaka* confiscated and reallocated reached 7200000 *koku*. Thus one third of the *daimyō* in the country were replaced. Their retainers suffered by losing not only their lords but their stipends and became *rōnin* (masterless samurai). The setting adrift of large numbers of masterless samurai in the

Tokugawa Ieyasu (1542–1616) was the third of the unifiers and founder of the powerful Tokugawa Bakufu. A patient and far-sighted tactician, Ieyasu used alliances with Nobunaga and Hideyoshi to build up his power in eastern Japan. He was appointed shogun three years after his victory at Sekigahara in 1600, and made Edo the center of a powerful system of political checks and balances that allowed him to control the more than 260 *daimyō*. The differences between the three unifiers are symbolized in this anecdote: confronted with a caged nightingale that would not sing, Nobunaga would kill the bird, Hideyoshi would force it to sing, and Ieyasu would wait for it to sing.

Edo

When Tokugawa Ieyasu first moved to Edo (now Tokyo) in 1590, it was a small castle town on Edo Bay. With the establishment of the Tokugawa Bakufu, the rebuilding of Edo castle and the enforcement of the alternate attendance system Edo grew rapidly into a teeming garrison, entrepôt and commercial city with a population, by the mid-18th century, of over a million.

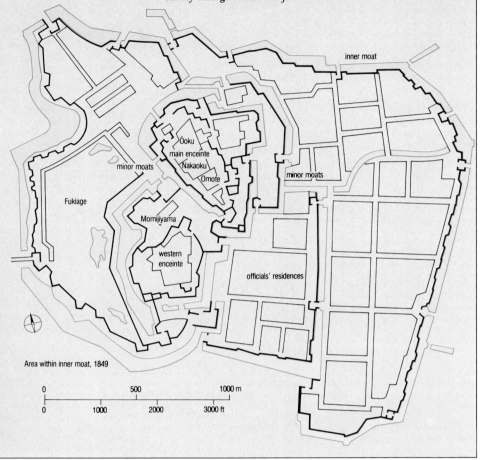

Below left Edo castle was a palace of the Tokugawa shoguns until 1868 when Edo was renamed Tokyo and, in the following year, became the new capital. The castle then became the residence of the Meiji emperor who moved with his entourage from Kyoto. Although it was hardly damaged in the Meiji restoration, the castle has suffered from fire and earthquakes in the intervening years and has now been substantially reduced and rebuilt. It is the residence of the present emperor and empress and used for such state occasions as banquets for visiting heads of state.

Area within inner moat, 1849

early 17th century created a serious problem of political order for the Bakufu.

Although there were a few *daimyō*, such as the Shimazu of Satsuma, who were so powerfully entrenched that even the Bakufu did not have the power to subject them to transfer or attainder, it is still true to say that *daimyō* were merely entrusted with the governance of the lands and people of their domains by the Bakufu. As seen in the records of the time, *tonosama* (lords) were temporary heads of the domains assigned at the will of the Bakufu while peasants remained permanently in their holdings. It was difficult to move the peasants who cultivated the land but one never knew when the *daimyō* might be transferred. Through this policy of attainder and transfer the Bakufu promoted long-standing loyal Tokugawa vassals to *daimyō* status. The Bakufu placed these hereditary *fudai daimyō* in Edo, where the Bakufu was located, and in surrounding areas, as well as those areas that were particularly crucial militarily and commercially. At the same time the Bakufu reduced the number of *tozama daimyō*, who had yielded to the Tokugawa at the battle of Sekigahara. They were moved to outlying districts, and separated from potential *tozama* allies by skillfully placing *fudai daimyō* in neighboring domains. As a result of these changes the Bakufu consolidated an extremely stable power structure, the so-called *baku-han* system, in which it and *han* shared power.

The Bakufu required two principal duties of the *daimyō*. One was regular, alternate-year attendance at the shogunal court of Edo known as *sankin kōtai*. The other was military service. *Sankin kōtai* derived from the hostage system of the age of wars. Tokugawa Ieyasu himself had been held hostage by his rival, the Imagawa, until the age of 14. He realized acutely the assertion of shogunal dignity and the limitations on *daimyō* power that could be enforced by the holding of hostages and the regular attendance of *daimyō* in Edo. The Bakufu ordered every *daimyō* to leave his wife and children in Edo and obliged *daimyō* to alternate their residence every other year between Edo and their home domains. As a result *daimyō* had to spend enormous sums on the *daimyō* processions during *sankin kōtai* and also on the double life of Edo and the domain, which involved maintaining several lavish residences in Edo as well as a castle in the domain. Consequently *daimyō* were drained financially. This was a deliberate design of the Bakufu.

Gun'eki (military service) included the military forces and various duties borne not only by *daimyō* but also by Bakufu retainers according to their *kokudaka*. For example, in time of war a 10000-*koku daimyō* had an obligation to contribute 20 guns, 50 spears, 10 bows and arrows and 14 horses as part of the overall Bakufu levy. The burdens were precisely stipulated per 100 *koku*, but in practice *gun'eki* had little relevance in peacetime.

Instead, the Bakufu commuted military levies into construction levies for such projects as the rebuilding of Edo castle or the Kyoto imperial palace, or the construction of harbors, roads or bridges.

Operation of the Bakufu system

Having looked at the *baku-han* system linking the Bakufu and *daimyō*, let us look briefly at the operation of the Bakufu itself. While some shoguns set policy, or at least set the tone, for Bakufu administration, the Bakufu was run on a day-to-day basis by those *daimyō* most trusted by the Tokugawa, that is to say the *fudai daimyō*, and by household retainers of the Tokugawa. Bakufu officials were selected according to their family status from among the *fudai* and *hatamoto* (samurai retainers with incomes of 10000 *koku* or less). The most powerful officials in the Bakufu were the *rōjū*, members of the shogun's senior council of elders appointed from among the senior *fudai*. Their role was to regulate the imperial court and the *daimyō* as well as to direct overall Bakufu administration. Occasionally a shogun might appoint a "great elder" (*tairō*). This post was established only in emergency situations and when there was an appropriate appointee available. Beneath the *rōjū* was a council of "junior elders" (*wakadoshiyori*), who assumed special responsibility for matters relating to the Tokugawa house. *Jisha bugyō* exercised special authority over temples and shrines, while *Kanjō bugyō* supervised Bakufu finances, and stewards (*daikan*) were sent out to oversee Bakufu domains (*tenryō*). These posts were usually staffed by several *fudai*, sharing responsibility. *Wakadoshiyori*, for instance, consisted of six or so *daimyō* officials who conferred together. During the early phase of Tokugawa Bakufu rule Ieyasu and his son, the second shogun Hidetada, had strong voices in the making of policy. This was a time of direct shogunal rule. Gradually, however, the operation of the Bakufu settled into that characteristically Japanese style of government where, instead of the highest authority demonstrating active leadership, a general consensus was worked out at lower levels and approved by the superior.

Among the most important pillars of Bakufu policy in the early modern period were policies adopted toward the imperial court and the religious orders. The imperial court consisted of the emperor, his consorts and the court nobles, some 140 families, clustered around a sacrosanct precinct in the Kyoto imperial palace. From ancient times this precinct enjoyed protection from intrusion by secular powers. From the Nanboku era (14th century) the emperor's effective political role was ended and, although he continued to be used as a legitimating symbol, the imperial will ceased to influence shogunal government. But no matter how little political power the emperor exercised, it was difficult to deny the emperor's role as a transcendent symbol of traditional authority and virtually unthinkable to regulate legally his conduct. The Tokugawa Bakufu, however, imposed severe legal regulations on the court and controlled it tightly. An Ordinance for the Court and Court Nobles in 17 articles (*Kinchū narabi ni kuge shohatto*) was issued in 1615. The first article stipulated the duties of the emperor and ordered him to devote himself to such non-political activi-ties as scholarship, especially Confucianism, and poetry.

Under the modern Japanese constitution the emperor is defined as the symbol of Japan. The Japanese people understand this to include the idea that the emperor is the symbol of traditional Japanese culture. The emperor (*tennō*) as a "cultural existence" was first defined legally in the *Kinchū narabi ni kuge shohatto*. On the one hand the Bakufu enriched the court economically by increasing its domains, but on the other restrained it by putting it under legal controls and placing senior Bakufu officials in Kyoto to supervise the court. The Bakufu also forbade the imperial granting of purple robes to important Buddhist prelates without permission. Emperor Go-Mizunoo (1596–1680), whose wife was the daughter of the second shogun Tokugawa Hidetada, suddenly resigned the imperial office in protest at Bakufu control over the court. It is commonly believed that the Tokugawa Bakufu's restoration of political authority to the emperor at the Meiji restoration in 1867 demonstrates that the relation between emperors and shoguns during the early modern era was one in which emperors merely entrusted shoguns with political power. However, the historical reality of the early Edo period was that the shogun was the ruler of the realm and the emperor a mere cultural authority.

The Tokugawa Bakufu also enforced tight control over the religious world and issued very concrete regulations (*Jiin hattō* or temple ordinances) for the temples of the various sects. These regulations established detailed rules for the promotion of monks and nuns and the ceremonies and customs to be observed within the temples. Based on these regulations, the Bakufu granted licenses (*shuinjo*) to approve temple and shrine land rights. Thus the temples and shrines received a guarantee of financial security in return for Bakufu control. Moreover, in the case of temples, the Bakufu established pyramidal hierarchies in which subordinate temples were put under the control of the head temple (*honzan*) of each sect.

Commoners were obliged to register at local temples. This policy was closely connected with the prohibition of Christianity. By registering at a Buddhist temple, people declared they were not Christian and were given supporting documentation to prove it. The Bakufu established a register of sponsors for each temple and controlled the masses through these registers. When a family moved to another area they needed a certificate to prove that they were registered with a temple which they had to submit to a temple in their new place of residence. Thus temples were not only religious organizations but also terminal organs in the Bakufu control system.

Although the Bakufu sought to regulate all religious groups, there were some groups of which the Bakufu did not approve and they, for their part, resisted Bakufu control. The most representative of these groups were the Kirishitan (Christians), especially Catholics, and a branch of the Nichiren school of Buddhism, the Fuju Fuse sect, which rejected compromise with political authorities.

The first ban on Catholicism was issued by Hideyoshi in 1587, but it was nominal and the

During the Edo period Japan remained a society ruled by a military elite, the samurai, who continued to emphasize their military traditions (*bu*) while espousing administrative and literary skills (*bun*). The mark of the samurai was his right to wear two swords (*daishō*). Commoners were forbidden to wear swords, though some favored merchants were permitted to wear one short sword, occasionally two. The cult of the warrior (*bushidō*) was fostered and controlled. In this warrior ethos samurai of all levels were eager to acquire fine arms and armor. At the same time, under the Tokugawa great peace, armor, helmets and swords were no longer needed for battle and tended to become decorative and luxurious ceremonial accoutrements and

The Bakufu began by proscribing Catholicism, then it limited foreign trade and prohibited Japanese overseas travel, and finally in 1639 it enforced virtual seclusion (*sakoku*) toward the West. The last stand by Japanese Catholics was made at an uprising in Shimabara, Kyushu, in 1637. Over 30 000 Christians, led by the 16-year-old Amakusa Shirō, took Hara castle and carried on a determined resistance to Bakufu forces for four months. After these Catholics were defeated and killed, only a few "covert Catholics" (*kakure kirishitan*) maintained their own form of Catholicism in secret in the islands off the coast of Nagasaki.

Crisis and reform in Bakufu politics

Although the Tokugawa Bakufu was a powerful institution, it was not immune to change. During the more than 200 years of Tokugawa rule, the shoguns and their senior Bakufu officials were obliged to respond to a variety of administrative problems created by changes in society and by problems within the Bakufu itself. Problems related to masterless samurai, dwindling Bakufu finances, peasant uprisings, *daimyō* succession, domain indebtedness and heterodox ideas all had to be dealt with. During the Tokugawa period there were several major Bakufu reform efforts, followed by reforms by *daimyō* attempting to restore the finances of their domains. The three great surges of Bakufu reform, the Kyōhō (1716–36), Kansei (1784–1801) and Tempō (1841) reforms, were named for the three eras in which they were carried out. Other Bakufu reform efforts were led by Arai Hakuseki early in the 18th century and Tanuma Okitsugu later in the century.

The first major problem to confront the Bakufu was a growing restlessness on the part of masterless samurai (*rōnin*) who were uprooted when their *daimyō* were subjected to attainder. As mentioned above, during the reigns of the first three shoguns the Bakufu replaced or demoted many of the older *daimyō* houses and promoted close Tokugawa vassals to the rank of *daimyō* or *hatamoto*. As a result the retainers of the attaindered *daimyō* lost their positions and became *rōnin*. During the first five decades of the Bakufu it is thought that more than 400 000 *rōnin* were created in this way. Assuming that half of them found service under some other *daimyō*, some 200 000 were still left without any regular income. Most were probably absorbed among the townsmen. Some became teachers, physicians and Confucian scholars.

It is not surprising that the anger of these impoverished samurai should be leveled against the Bakufu. In 1651, following the death of the third Tokugawa shogun Iemitsu, the Bakufu discovered a plot by Yui Shōsetsu (1605–51) and other frustrated *rōnin* to take advantage of the death of the shogun to lead uprisings in Edo, Osaka and Sumpu and to overthrow the Bakufu. Shōsetsu committed *seppuku* (suicide) and his fellow conspirators were captured. Put on notice by this incident, the Bakufu tried to respond more effectively to the problem of *rōnin* and a more flexible policy was adopted. The most common reason for attainder had been the lack of an heir and the consequent extinction of the *daimyō* line. The rules governing the adoption and succession of heirs were eased and prohibitions against posthumous adoption

heirlooms. The suit of red-laced armor with decorated mail sleeves (*right*) is of the *domaru* type that became very popular with *daimyō* in the Edo period. The helmet, with its symbolic horns, echoes earlier styles but with greater elaboration. The mounted sword from the mid-16th century (*left*) is a slung sword (*tachi*), decorated with a family crest and having the scabbard partially wrapped in silk cord to prevent damage by chafing. Sword guards (*tsuba*, *above*), originally simple pieces of iron or lacquer, tended to become finely wrought objects with designs in gold, silver and mother of pearl.

number of converts continued to increase. Catholic missions, closely tied in with trade, continued to flourish and as late as 1613 the *daimyō* Date Masamune could dispatch an embassy to Rome. However, in 1616 the Bakufu again prohibited Christianity, banned the activities of Spanish and Portuguese missionaries, and persecuted Catholics in Japan, creating many martyrs. There was a complex rationale for the prohibition of Christianity. It was suspected that Catholics did not accept the Bakufu as an absolute authority; there were fears that a common interest in Christianity might serve as a bond between potentially hostile western *daimyō*, and there was apprehension about possible economic intrusion by European powers. The issue was exacerbated by internal disputes between Spain and Portugal and among Jesuits, Franciscans and Dominicans.

following the sudden death of the *daimyō* were relaxed. The Bakufu also eased the policy whereby, as a way of controlling the *daimyō*, a *daimyō*'s relatives were obliged to serve in the Bakufu and live in specially designated dwellings. In this way some of the most oppressive aspects of the policy for controlling *daimyō* were eased and *daimyō* gained a somewhat greater degree of independence from the Bakufu. The Bakufu also prohibited the practice of ritual suicide (*junshi*) by samurai on the death of their lord. In strict feudal thinking warrior lords and their vassals were considered a single entity. When the lord died those samurai who had enjoyed their master's favor were expected to immolate themselves and follow him into the other world. In some cases retainers who had no desire for self-immolation were pressed into committing *seppuku* against their wills. In an effort to change the rough customs of the samurai of the age of wars and encourage a form of *bushidō* (Way of the Warrior) more suitable for peacetime, the Bakufu prohibited these meaningless *junshi*. The Bakufu also issued a prohibition against homosexuality, a common practice between *daimyō* and retainers which also contributed to *junshi*.

The new policies derived from the greater stability of the Bakufu but they were also influenced by a Confucian ideal of benevolence and the compassionate spirit of Buddhism. An extreme example was the *Seirui awaremu no rei* (Edicts Providing Compassion for Every Creature) issued by the fifth shogun Tsunayoshi (1646–1709). Tsunayoshi, who studied Confucianism and aspired to benevolent government, was an eccentric and loved dogs. He issued a protective law declaring that anyone who killed a dog should be executed. He created a huge 82 500-square-meter kennel in western Edo to feed and house stray dogs. The law was eventually extended to other creatures and the breeding or trading of fish, birds and turtles was forbidden. Angry commoners called Tsunayoshi the "Dog shogun." Upon Tsunayoshi's death this tyrannical rule was abolished but the *Seirui awaremu no rei* had other effects. In some mountain villages guns used mainly for hunting had survived, but due to the prohibition on killing birds and animals all guns, except for those owned by some hunters, were collected and the possession of guns by farmers was forbidden. At about this time townsmen were prohibited from wearing swords and the possession of weapons by anybody other than samurai was strictly controlled. This indicates that the social position of *shi-nō-kō-shō* (the status hierarchy of samurai, peasants, artisans and merchants) was now firmly established.

18th-century stability

The 18th century was a period of relative political stability in Japan. In the early years of the century the Bakufu was led by the samurai official and Confucian scholar Arai Hakuseki (1657–1725) who served Tokugawa Ienobu, the sixth shogun. Under the slogan of civilian reform Hakuseki sought to tidy up Bakufu administrative practice and strengthen a depleted treasury. He revised Bakufu legal codes and reformed Bakufu ceremonial practice and nomenclature. In diplomatic correspondence with Yi dynasty Korea, Hakuseki signed diplomatic documents with the seal of the Tokugawa shogun as "king of Japan" in an attempt to elevate the status of the shoguns. He tried to calculate the amounts of gold and silver which were draining out of the country to Holland and China via Nagasaki and, to prevent the worsening of the Bakufu economy, he ordered import restrictions on goods from overseas and the export of copper in place of gold and silver. Hakuseki was a rationally minded samurai official with a breadth of vision that went far beyond Japan. He looked critically at Japanese myths and tried to familiarize himself with conditions in the West by interviewing the imprisoned Italian missionary Giovanni Sidotti.

Although Arai Hakuseki withdrew from office after the death of his patron Ienobu, his political reform impulse carried on for some years. However, beneath the surface stability of the 18th century, changes were taking place that called for new efforts at reform. The eighth shogun, Yoshimune (1684–1751), one of the more politically active of the Tokugawa shoguns, set in motion the Kyōhō reform effort aimed at restoring Bakufu finances and reestablishing feudal control. During the first century of Tokugawa rule the shoguns had enjoyed not only their tax income from shogunal domains, but the residue of the vast wealth in gold and silver acquired by Ieyasu. The shogunal lifestyle, however, was lavish and resources, vast as they were, were eventually exhausted. At the same time, the rapid spread of a currency economy, combined with samurai indebtedness, weakened Bakufu and *han* finances, contributed to the extravagance as well as the destitution of samurai and domains, increased the growing influence of merchants, and created volatility in rural society, with some peasants gaining from access to a market network and others suffering from hardship and debt. In order to try to alleviate its financial decline the Bakufu reminted coins, reducing their gold and silver content. This, however, only brought inflation which hurt samurai who lived on fixed stipends.

Rejecting Arai Hakuseki's emphasis on civilian bureaucratic reforms, Yoshimune tried to restore things to the condition of Ieyasu's day, in the process reasserting direct shogunal rule. He stressed frugality, made taxes heavier and tried to enforce discipline on tax officials, imposed levies on the *daimyō*, encouraged reclamation of new land, tried to promote talented officials, revised the basic code of Bakufu laws, encouraged education and the building of domain schools, and relaxed bans on the study of Western learning, thus promoting Dutch studies in Nagasaki.

As a result of these policies Bakufu income in the mid-18th century, when the effects of the reforms began to show, reached a high point throughout the Tokugawa period, standing close to 1 million *ryō* in the black. Yoshimune was generally regarded as an able shogun. Other samurai officials also acquired reputations for distinguished service. Among them the *daikan* Ōoka Tadasuke (1677–1751), who became a hero of popular stories, earned a reputation as a wise and compassionate judge. Perhaps due to these reform efforts there was some mitigation of the rigors of the penal system.

The official who carried Bakufu policy furthest

in a mercantile direction was Tanuma Okitsugu (1719–88) who established close ties with merchant capital. Tanuma's father was a middle-level samurai (600 *koku*) serving the Kii Tokugawa family. When Tokugawa Yoshimune came into office as the eighth shogun, Tanuma's father accompanied the shogun from Kii to Edo. His son Okitsugu became a page to the ninth shogun and a favorite of the tenth shogun, Ieharu, and rose to become a *daimyō* of 57000 *koku*. Tanuma's policy stressed commercial development by using commercial capital on daring land reclamation of lakes and swamps and the development of Hokkaido. However, his close ties with merchants fostered corruption. Wealthy merchants scrambled to bribe Tanuma, who had dictatorial power, to grant them commercial privileges. Tanuma attempted to make Bakufu policy more responsive to the commercial realities of the age but in the process earned an unenviable reputation for graft.

The Kansei reforms

From 1781, after about 20 years of Tanuma rule, Japan was hit by a series of natural disasters. When, in 1783, Mount Asama (Nagano Prefecture) erupted, the death toll reached 20000. An area of several hundred square kilometers was smothered in volcanic ash. But the worst damage was famine caused by unusual weather conditions exacerbated by the volcanic eruptions. In the Tōhoku region, because of the cold weather, almost no crops were harvested. In Tsugaru *han* (Aomori) 80000 people, one third of the domain population, starved to death and 20000 *chō* of fields, one third of the total cultivated area of the domain, were abandoned. Throughout the Tōhoku the damage was more or less the same as in Tsugaru. Infanticide was practiced. Women and children were sold. Records of the time indicated that starving people even ate corpses. This famine continued to spread in the following years. The harvest of 1785 was one third that of an average year. Peasants left their empty fields and drifted into the cities in their thousands. But there too, because of the shortages, rice prices shot up and the masses suffered from dire poverty. Some of those in the depths of despair attacked the houses of wealthy merchants and the shops of rice

dealers and plundered the towns in urban rioting.

In 1784 in several castle towns, including Edo, Osaka and Kyoto, these riots flared up one after another. In villages peasants who could not bear the high rates of annual tax imposed by the Bakufu or *daimyō* joined in uprisings. Between 1782 and 1780 there were 230 riots throughout the country. The primary cause was a succession of natural disasters but such man-made suffering as the high tax rates prevailing since the Kyōhō reforms should not be overlooked. Peasants no longer had much in reserve and when poor harvests continued they suffered starvation and despair.

In these circumstances Tanuma Okitsugu fell from power. In his place the *daimyō* Matsudaira Sadanobu was appointed *rōjū* and introduced what have been called the Kansei reforms. Sadanobu set out to repair the misrule of the Tanuma years and to revert to frugal administration. One objective was to restore the villages desolated by famine and poverty. A second objective was to relieve samurai who were being impoverished by the reduction of tax incomes. A third objective was to organize the newly risen merchant class. To achieve the first objective peasants who had absconded to Edo were ordered to return to their villages and able deputies (*daikan*) were selected to manage the lands under the direct control of the shogun. To relieve the samurai, debts more than four years old were repealed. Those samurai who had borrowed money from merchants were naturally relieved, but the merchants who suffered financial loss simply refused to make more loans to samurai. So, in the end, lower-ranking samurai suffered even more poverty. Economically, the Bakufu made greater efforts to restore its finances by inviting powerful merchants to participate in policy discussions. Among Matsudaira Sadanobu's Kansei reforms there was an effort to control ideology. He prohibited heterodox studies and tried to promote the Neo-Confucian school of Chu Hsi studies. He exercised control over publications and suppressed subversive comment on Bakufu policy.

While the Bakufu was carrying out the Kansei reforms, many *daimyō* were trying to impose *han* reforms. Clearly, from the mid-18th century the income of the samurai class as a whole had declined. Virtually all the *daimyō* were heavily in debt to merchants. There were cases in which one or even two years' *nengu* was put up as security. When some *daimyō* came close to bankruptcy they entrusted to merchants everything from tax collection and the household economy of the *daimyō* himself to his retainer's stipends. Some *daimyō* who felt urgency about the problem applied emergency measures. In some cases they simply repudiated their debts or promoted *han*-sponsored monopolies in special products, such as the carrots for medicinal use and paper in Matsudaira *han* in Izumo. Those *daimyō*, like the Shimazu of Satsuma or the Mōri of Chōshū, who were successful in developing monopolies and reforming their finances, came to resemble small independent countries both economically and politically. In the 1860s, with the country in turmoil and the Bakufu struggling to cope with the threat from the Western powers, their solvency would stand them in good stead and allow them to purchase the guns to challenge and overthrow the Bakufu.

The Bakufu's Kansei reform was partially successful, and the prosperity of Edo revived. In the cities and villages commoners grew in influence and prosperity. On the other hand, the reforms aroused popular opposition and did little to stem the decline in the power of the Bakufu and the living conditions of samurai. The Bakufu no longer exerted such power over the *daimyō*. It was as much as Bakufu officials could do to maintain a crumbling Bakufu economy.

The final reform effort

In the early 1840s the Bakufu again tried to institute reforms, aimed at strengthening control over the Bakufu's Kantō base around Edo and making Edo independent of Osaka, the commercial center of the country. This final Bakufu reform effort of the Tempō era was led by the *rōjū* Mizuno Tadakuni (1794–1851). Tadakuni's reform effort was a reactionary reassertion of feudal controls, in the spirit of the Kyōhō and Kansei reforms. It included the old standbys of recoinage, dismissal of samurai officials to cut costs, forced loans on merchants, the breaking up of merchant monopolies, demands for frugality, the tighter regulation of morals and the strengthening of discrimination against lower social status groups. In an effort to raise production and tax yields edicts were again issued urging peasants to return to their plots. Tadakuni even came up with a proposal to have small *daimyō* and *hatamoto* moved from the environs of Edo and Osaka to give the Bakufu greater control over these cities.

Tadakuni's determination was spurred by worsening social unrest and the obvious erosion of feudal discipline. There seemed no end to the protests against the Bakufu's policies or the harsh economic conditions. Four hundred incidents of violent protest in villages and towns were recorded between 1813 and 1868. In Osaka in 1837 Ōshio Heihachirō (1793–1837), a low-ranking Bakufu official, led an uprising to secure relief for an impoverished urban population. The uprising was quickly suppressed but it gained nationwide sympathy. Tadakuni's reforms aroused hostility from *daimyō*, samurai, merchants and commoners. Several of his proposals were unworkable and most of them failed, bringing serious criticism against the Bakufu. Moreover, the foreign situation was as bleak as that at home. From abroad the Bakufu received disturbing news of the Opium War in China (1840–42) and of growing Western intrusion in East Asian waters. British and Russian vessels were probing the inadequate Japanese coastal defenses. With the arrival of Commodore Matthew Perry's squadron in 1853 the stage was set for the domestic and foreign crisis that was to end in the overthrow of the Bakufu, the restoration of imperial rule, the reopening of the country and the making of modern Japan.

Economy and society in the Momoyama era

During the late 16th century the Japanese economy was thriving. The old agrarian medieval economy, with its scattered private enclaves, its toll houses and other physical barriers to trade, and its restricted guilds, had been shattered by the rise of the warring *daimyō* and their struggles for regional and national hegemony. In its place during the late 16th century Japan was developing an outward-looking market-oriented economy fueled by war, bullion and international trade.

Domestically, the nationwide campaigns of unification and the invasion of Korea brought ceaseless military mobilization and created an insatiable demand for weapons, especially guns, provisions, pack animals, boats and building materials. The unifiers exploited the mines of Japan for gold and silver which flowed into the economy as never before. Nobunaga fostered trade by opening markets, breaking up old guild monopolies, patronizing newer merchant groups, destroying toll stations and encouraging road construction and shipbuilding. Hideyoshi continued these policies and began the minting and standardization of reliable gold coinage. His policies of land registration and confiscation and sword collection provided him with enormous resources in land and metals. He asserted direct control over the cities of Kyoto, Osaka, Sakai, Fushimi and Nagasaki. His great castle at Osaka became the nucleus of a busy port city that quickly eclipsed its neighbor Sakai.

Portuguese trading vessels had come to Japan in the 1540s bringing firearms, Chinese and Western goods, and missionaries. They were followed later in the century by Spanish, Dutch and English traders. Not only the major *daimyō*, but also Nobunaga and Hideyoshi, though wary with regard to Japan's national security, welcomed and profited from commercial contacts with the West and the rest of Asia. A vigorous interregional trade developed. Hideyoshi took an active interest in overseas trade, suppressed piracy and undertook other measures to encourage international commerce. Japanese trade and commerce with Southeast Asia flourished. Merchants, *daimyō* and temples joined to sponsor commercial trading ventures that were licensed under red seals by the political authorities. From 1604 to 1636 (after 1636 all vessels were forbidden to leave territorial waters) more than 300 red-seal vessels sailed to Asian ports. The main traders profiting from the red-seal vessels were *daimyō* such as the Shimazu and wealthy merchants such as Suminokura Ryōi (1554–1614). Chaya Shirojirō (1542–96) and Sueyoshi Magozaemon (1570–1617). Their trading vessels sailed to Luzon, Annam, Tonkin, Cambodia and Siam. Japanese trading quarters were founded in these countries. Silver, gold, copper and swords were exported. Guns, Chinese ceramics, books, raw silks and silk fabrics flowed into the country.

Economy and society in the Edo period

As Japan settled into a long period of peace under a new and powerful regime, economic attitudes changed in the decades after Sekigahara and the siege of Osaka castle. The Tokugawa emphasis on dynastic stability ran counter to freedom of commerce and overseas trade. Ieyasu still permitted active overseas trading under red-seal licenses. His successors, in the interests of stability and the eradication of Christianity, sought first to disentangle trade from Christianity and then steadily to restrict trade and contact with the West. By 1640 Japan was closing in upon itself commercially. Overseas ventures were forbidden. Portuguese and Spanish vessels were excluded. Only the English and Dutch were permitted to trade through Hirado

Peasant uprisings and Western intrusions
The map shows some of the domestic and international problems confronting the Tokugawa Bakufu in the late 18th and 19th centuries. Domestically, the *bakuhan* system remained strong until the 1860s. Its authority was tested internally, however, by a mounting wave of rural protest and urban riots and by its inability to deal decisively with the "barbarian" vessels probing Japanese ports. There were over 3000 recorded peasant protests during the Edo period, with their incidence increasing markedly in the late 18th century. Occurring nationwide in Bakufu and *han* territories, they were most numerous in the central and northeastern provinces which were particularly hard hit by famines.

The Gunnai uprising swept through Kai Province in 1836 as poor farmers protested the high cost of seed rice and demanded forced loans. The authorities had hardly contained this when they had to deal with the Ōshio Heihachirō uprising in Osaka and the ensuing Ikuta Yorozu protest in Echigo. Although these uprisings lacked a full-scale ideology of revolution, they embarrassed the Tokugawa Bakufu and *han* governments.

In 1792 Adam Laksman demanded trade with Russia in Nemuro. In 1804 Nicolai Rezanov sailed into Nagasaki harbor and demanded trade. In 1808 the English man-of-war *Phaeton* forced its way into Nagasaki harbor in search of Dutch vessels and demanded victuals before withdrawing. These incidents, together with the much more threatening news of the Opium War (1840–42), made it clear that the Western powers were advancing into east Asia. The arrival of Captain Matthew Perry's squadron in Uraga Bay in 1853 brought the Bakufu face to face with a problem that threatened its very foundations.

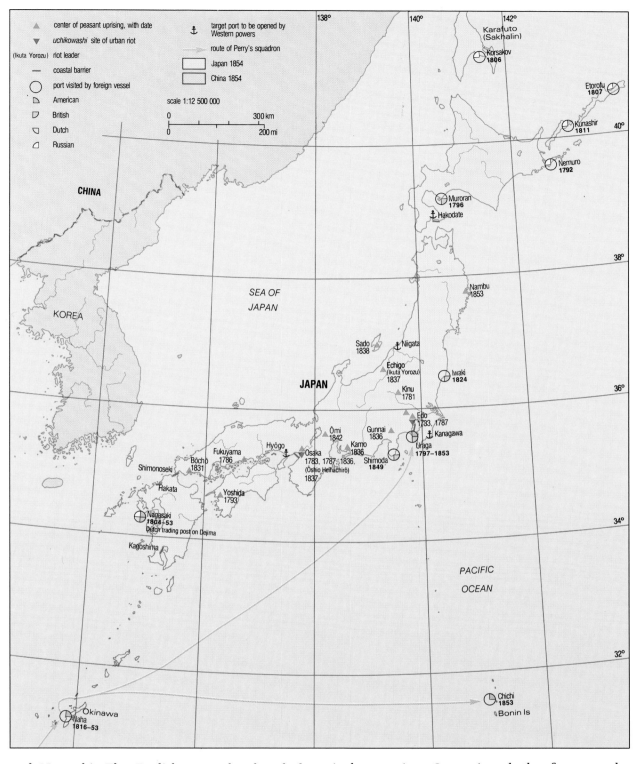

and Nagasaki. The English soon abandoned the effort and for the remainder of the Tokugawa period only the Dutch were left on a small island of Dejima in Nagasaki harbor as representatives of the European trading community. Japan still traded with China and Korea but this trade was restricted to Tsushima and Nagasaki when there was a thriving Chinese merchant community. Satsuma domain established control over the Ryukyus which it exploited as a source of sugar. Apart from these limited commercial contacts with the outside world, for the next 200 years what growth there was in the Tokugawa economy was to be domestically induced.

But domestically, too, the prospects of commercial development were not very bright in the early Edo period. The Tokugawa regime was instinc-

tively agrarian. Samurai and the farmers who supported them were important, not merchants. The Tokugawa shoguns, following the lead of Hideyoshi, sought to compartmentalize Japanese society into four hereditary status groups: samurai (*shi*), farmers (*nō*), artisans (*kō*), and merchants (*shō*), with *eta* (outcasts) and *hinin* (non-people) below them. Intermarriage between status groups was frowned upon. Inevitably there was some interaction which grew as time progressed. Some samurai gave daughters as brides to merchant families. Struggling farmers quit the soil and moved into the cities. Impoverished *rōnin* slipped into anonymity in the cities or set themselves up as village schoolteachers. Wealthy merchants or rural entrepreneurs bought permission to wear swords. On the whole, however, we can think of Edo society

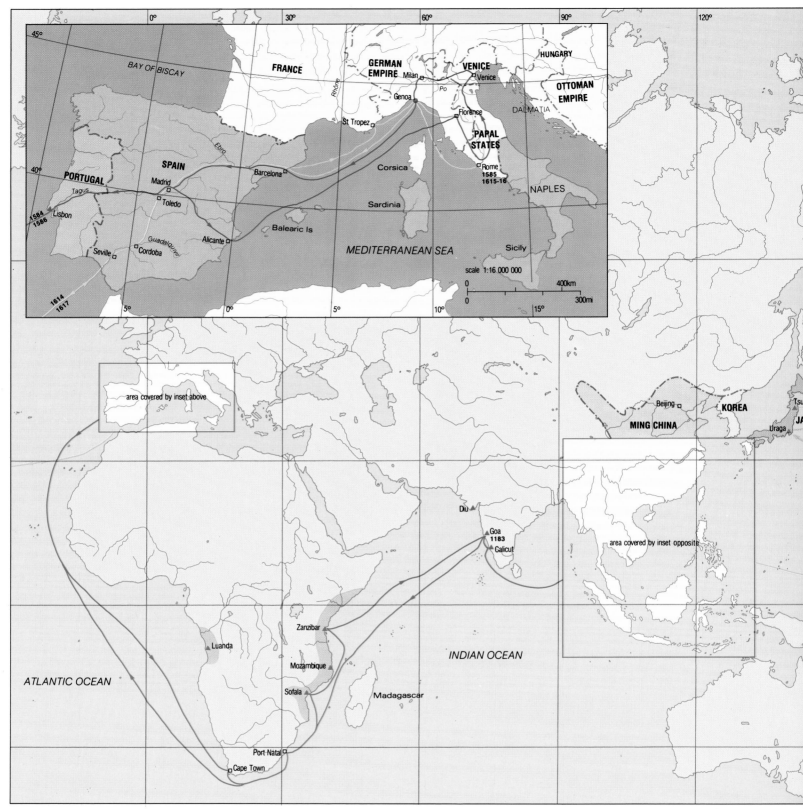

as deliberately, and very effectively, compartmentalized. The creation of such an inflexible status hierarchy was not conducive to mobility, freedom of trade or market activity. Samurai were detached from agricultural and commercial activities. Farmers were forbidden to engage in trade and were exhorted to live frugally on what they themselves could produce. The Bakufu and domain governments issued a stream of sumptuary injunctions to all classes urging frugality and actively discouraging consumption. There was no encouragement of saving for productive investment, however, and the growing of extra crops for market was discour-

aged. Merchants were forbidden to buy or reclaim land on their own initiative, closing major investment opportunities to them. Roads were poor, carts were excluded from major routes, and direct communication and trade among the domains was actively discouraged.

In spite of the throttling of foreign trade and the rather unpromising domestic environment, there was still a remarkable growth in the urban and rural economy during the Edo period. This growth was spurred by peace, increasing agricultural productivity, soaring urban demand, improvements in technology, the demands of alternate attendance

Trade in the 16th and 17th centuries
Prior to the restrictions imposed on trade and travel by the Tokugawa shogunate from the early 17th century, while Portuguese, Spanish, Dutch, English and Chinese merchants visited Japanese ports, Japanese traders sailed the seas of east Asia and the world.
Several *daimyō* were active in promoting Asian trade and cultural or religious contacts with the West. In 1582 three Kyushu *daimyō* sent an embassy of five Christian children to visit Pope Gregory XIII in Rome and

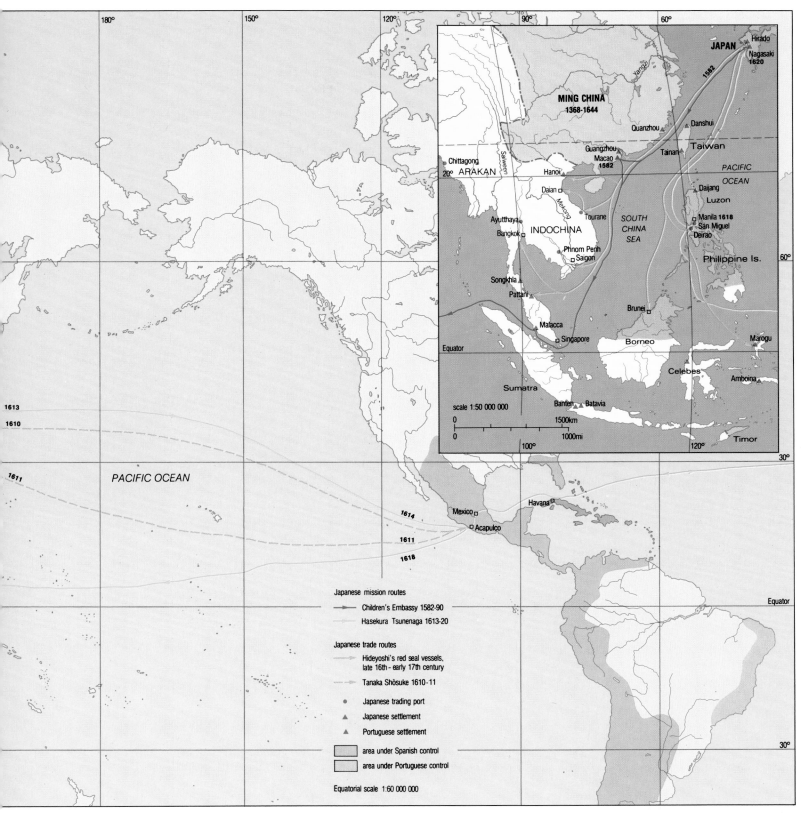

Japanese mission routes

→ Children's Embassy 1582-90

→ Hasekura Tsunenaga 1613-20

Japanese trade routes

→ Hideyoshi's red seal vessels, late 16th - early 17th century

→ Tanaka Shōsuke 1610-11

● Japanese trading port

▲ Japanese settlement

▲ Portuguese settlement

■ area under Spanish control

■ area under Portuguese control

Equatorial scale 1:60 000 000

Philip of Spain. They were greeted warmly in Europe and the prospects for contact with Europe seemed good; but by the time they returned in 1590, Hideyoshi had already turned against the Catholic missionary effort. In 1610 Tanaka Shōsuke, a Kyoto merchant, sailed to Mexico hoping for trade but returned to Japan frustrated the following year. In 1613 Hasekura Tsunenaga, a retainer of Date Masamune of Sendai, led an embassy to Mexico, Madrid and Rome. He returned to Japan in 1620 to find that Catholicism was now proscribed in Date domains.

by *daimyō* and a rising population. Although precise population figures are uncertain, the population probably rose from about 18 million at the beginning of the Tokugawa period to over 30 million by the end of the period. Population increase was steepest in the 17th and early 18th centuries. From then until the end of the period there was a more moderate growth rate, which may have been reduced somewhat by three major famines in 1732–33, 1783–87 and 1833–36.

Social and economic changes in the countryside

Over 80 percent of the population of Tokugawa Japan lived on the land. In the four-part Tokugawa status hierarchy farmers ranked immediately after the samurai rulers in importance. Their valued function in Confucian economic theory was to sustain society through their labor. Although Confucian theory urged benevolent treatment of peasants, *daimyō* and Bakufu officials naturally wanted to squeeze as much tax from them as possible. One contemporary adage stated that "peasants are like rape seed: the more you squeeze them the more oil you get out of them." The ideal of local administration was to squeeze as much tax as possible from villagers without driving them

143

from the land. Some *daimyō* and Bakufu officials squeezed too hard and drove their peasants to protest or abscond.

With the samurai removed from the land, villages were treated as autonomous units of adminstration and tax collection. Villagers were held mutually responsible for the direct payment of annual tax to samurai officials of the Bakufu or the local domain. In theory the ideal distribution of tax yield was six parts for the lord, four for the farmer. In practice the authorities probably had to be satisfied with much less. Peasants and villages pleaded poverty or natural disaster. Fields and yields were hidden and underreported. Reclaimed land was not reported. The Bakufu and most domain governments did not take the trouble to make the periodic surveys and reassessments that would have been necessary to keep tax incomes proportionate to increased yields.

The Tokugawa no doubt conceived of their agrarian settlement as perfected in the early 17th century. Within the villages, and among villages, considerable variations in wealth and influence opened up over time. Those families, newer as well as older, who were able to open up new land, increase their yields by better farming methods, produce extra crops for markets, or venture into soya sauce production, tea growing, silk making or sake brewing, were able to increase their incomes and build up capital with which to extend their commercial ventures or buy more land from their less successful neighbors. Those villages that were close to urban markets, were blessed with good soil, and spared natural disasters and harsh officials had greater opportunity to prosper than their poorer neighbors.

In spite of harsh officials and such natural calamities as famines, typhoons and locusts which brought periodic and widespread devastation and forced people to resort to infanticide or the selling of children to urban geisha houses, agricultural productivity increased markedly over the course of the Edo period. Cultivated acreage probably doubled. The increased output owed much to improvements in technology, the practice of multiple cropping, better seed strains and improved fertilizers. Good farming practice was disseminated by agricultural manuals such as the 10-volume *Nōgyō zensho* (Cyclopedia of Agriculture, 1696), compiled by the agriculturalist Miyazaki Yasusada (1623–97). Rice continued to be the basic crop throughout the country, but the spread of regional and nationwide market networks and the reach of maritime routes around the whole of Honshu were accompanied by local specialization in such crops as cotton, mulberry trees for the rearing of silk worms, indigo, tobacco, sugar cane and tea. Many coastal villages found a market for maritime products.

The growth of urban demand and local markets, and the diffusion of cash throughout the countryside, frequently undermined the traditional village social order. The village elders, the older extended families and the entrenched main houses were not always the most successful in seizing new opportunities offered by an increasingly commercial economy. Successful villagers did not always look to extended-family connections for help but turned more and more to hired labor or tenant farmers to work their land. They also put their money to

work in rural commerce and industry, and engaged in moneylending, the processing of vegetable oils, the production of soya sauce and sake brewing. Since these wealthy families did not always belong to the older main house, or necessarily see eye to eye with it, there were considerable tensions within villages. These tensions were accentuated by widening economic disparities. While some farmers were benefiting from commercialization and technological improvements in agriculture and elbowing their way up in the villages, others, less successful, pledged or sold their land and became tenants for their richer neighbors. In times of famine, flood or crop failure they were the most vulnerable.

As pointed out in the discussion of Bakufu reform efforts, peasant unrest was endemic in Tokugawa Japan. It was worse in some areas and times than others, but tended to increase over the period. Averaging less than six outbreaks a year over the 17th century, its incidence increased to 10 a year in the 18th century and reached a crescendo in the late 18th and early 19th centuries. During the great famines rural protests averaged more than 25 outbreaks a year. Peasant unrest was most prevalent in the harsh conditions of northeastern Japan, but no part of the country was exempt from such disturbances. In the early Edo period peasant uprisings were often led by village elders and directed against the exactions of domain officials or the Bakufu's *daikan*. Later uprisings were often directed as much against the local and commercial interests of the more prosperous villagers and rural merchants as they were against the exactions of *daimyō* or Bakufu officials.

Since the peasants were unarmed, their uprisings were generally crushed quickly. Some of their demands might be met, but the leaders were executed. Peasant uprisings, however violent, were protest movements directed at economic amelioration, not revolution. They did not reject the Tokugawa social order but appealed for the correction of its worst abuses. Even the mass millenarian protest movements of the 1850s and 1860s that burst out under the shoguns of *yonaoshi* ("world-correcting") or *ee ja nai kai* (ain't it grand?) lacked a concrete agenda for social revolution or the destruction of the Tokugawa power structure.

The impact of economic change on samurai society

Samurai, the *shi*, who made up between 7 and 10 percent of the population, enjoyed a privileged place at the top of Tokugawa society. As rulers and administrators they lived by the labor of others. As symbols of their authority they alone had the right to wear swords and to "cut commoners down." Commoners feared samurai. Even a poor samurai would show disdain for a wealthy merchant or substantial farmer. When *daimyō* processions passed along the roads to and from Edo, commoners had to step aside and kneel in the dust.

The category of *shi* also included nobles, some 140 families at the imperial court in Kyoto, and priests of the Buddhist monasteries and great Shinto shrines. In total this elite group, with their family members, amounted to less than 10 percent of the total population. As we have seen, the Bakufu treated the court and Buddhist orders with

Morikage was a Kanō school painter from Kaga in northern Japan. A fine ink painter, he specialized in agricultural and village scenes. His work shows greater sympathy and affection than that of any other Tokugawa period artist for the lives of ordinary people in the countryside. Morikage was a Confucian scholar as well as a painter. From the look of the costumes, the village scene here is set in China rather than Japan. Japanese villages in the Edo period experienced famines, floods, poverty, harsh taxation and occasional resort to desperate violence. They also saw technological improvements, double and triple cropping, commercial agriculture, greater prosperity, village schooling and active communal life.

the whole, however, temples proliferated and the Buddhist clergy lived a comfortable existence within the Bakufu power structure. With the challenge from Christianity removed, there was little pressure for internal reform or revitalization. The Buddhist clergy suffered most from the shift in intellectual interest toward Confucianism, Shinto and National Learning and from the criticisms that Buddhism was alien, otherworldly, superstitious and exploitative. Although Tokguawa Buddhism showed less creative vitality than in the medieval period, it was still a vigorous presence in the society at all levels. Zen was active and there were many popular expressions of devotion in the form of pilgrimages to Zenkōji or to the various Kannon pilgrimage circuits.

Although they were lords of society, economically the position of the samurai was less enviable. Separated from the land, living as stipendiary retainers in garrison towns, they were cut off from their original village roots and had lost the opportunity to farm or increase their incomes by acquiring land or selling produce. On the other hand, they were forbidden by edict and Confucian prejudice from engaging in trade. Trade was seen as subversive of the proper warrior life-style and of stable social hierarchy since some would prosper and others fail. They were expected to live on their stipends, not to need money but rather to despise it. Anything that samurai households needed other than rice was to be produced themselves or acquired by exchanging rice for it. Thus they lived on fixed inelastic incomes through two centuries when prices of all commodities tended to rise as fast as or faster than the price of rice. Many were left behind by economic development and found it difficult to scrape along.

The ruling samurai class in Tokugawa Japan was unskilled in dealing with a spreading money economy. The Bakufu tried to live off the taxes from its own direct domains (*tenryō*). As we have seen, it failed and was forced to resort to periodic attempts at retrenchment and reform. By 1700 its budget was beginning to show a deficit. For the next century or so in its various reform efforts it tried to deal with its chronic fiscal crisis by forced loans and devaluation of the currency, but without much success. Except in the Tanuma era, it never came close to channeling the tremendous wealth of merchants to its own fiscal needs, or to wresting control of the economy from the moneylenders and merchant houses of Osaka and Edo. Even the Tokugawa shogunate came to depend heavily on merchants for financial services, loans and provisions.

Daimyō were expected to live within their assigned *kokudaka*, provide for their samurai and pay all the costs of running the domain and maintaining several residences in Edo. The Tokugawa did not encourage interdomain trade and the domains tended to remain small-scale, localized and fragmented economies. Surplus produce in rice and other commodities found its way into the national produce market centering on Osaka. All *daimyō* tried to bring new land into cultivation and before long the actual rice yields of most *han* were greater than their nominal *kokudaka*. These increases, however, were rarely sufficient to keep abreast of expenses. The *daimyō* of the most power-

respect, guaranteed their incomes and gave them a place in the power structure but supervised and regulated them. Emperors and courtiers lived secluded lives in the imperial palace, devoting themselves to poetry studies and an annual round of court ceremonies. In particular the Bakufu tried to prevent *daimyō* or samurai making direct ties with the court that might undercut Tokugawa supremacy. This fear was realized in the 1860s when, in the face of Bakufu indecision in dealing with the demands of the Western powers, disaffected samurai turned to the court for leadership.

Although the political and military power of the Buddhist religious orders had been broken by Nobunaga and Hideyoshi and temples deprived of most of their lands, Buddhist clergy and temples continued to play an important role in Tokugawa society. The clergy retained considerable local influence because Buddhist temples were made responsible for the detection of Christians and the registration of the local population. Villagers had to become sponsors (*danka*) of some temple. Temples held considerable power over them. Unless villagers gave regular contributions they risked being designated covert Christians. Many villagers were also forced to borrow seed or money to tide themselves through hard times. Temples were active moneylenders and drove hard bargains. At the same time, some priests opened local schools and taught village children to read and write. In a few domains, such as Okayama and Mito, the *daimyō* ordered a drastic reduction in the number of Buddhist temples and the laicization of the clergy. On

ful domains, like the Maeda of Kaga, lived like petty shoguns. With incomes of from 500000 to more than 1 million *koku* from their domains they and their families and leading retainers were insulated from economic hardship. Most *daimyō* and their domains, however, were hard pressed.

The various Bakufu and *han* reforms were principally directed at alleviating the plight of impoverished samurai but few got to the heart of the problem. Toward the end of the period a few domains, notably Satsuma and Chōshū, managed to break out of the cycle of domain indebtedness by developing special products, reneging on their debts or reorganizing domain finances. Their relative solvency put them in a stronger position to challenge the Bakufu in the 1860s.

Several important changes took place in the cultural character of the samurai over the long Edo period. In the early 17th century samurai were still warriors who had had, or fully expected to have, experience on the battlefield. Throughout the Edo period they were encouraged to preserve this martial tradition by frugal living, practice of the military arts and the maintenance of their minds and weapons in a state of constant readiness for warfare. The confucianized cult of *Bushidō*, the Way of the Warrior, urged them to give single-minded loyalty to their lords, even at the sacrifice of their own lives.

On the other hand, after the siege of Osaka castle and the Shimabara uprising, few samurai saw any military action other than perhaps the quelling of occasional peasant uprisings. The Bakufu and domain governments worked to rein in the most exuberant expressions of samurai behavior by curtailing acts of *junshi* and vendetta. The samurai steadily became administrators and functionaries, who dedicated more of their time to the literary

arts (*bun*) than they did to the arts of war. It was the samurai who became the leading intellectuals of the age, the students of Confucianism, Dutch studies, and later of national defense and Western studies. For the performance of their official administrative duties literacy and basic numeracy became essential for all samurai. By the late 18th century most domains had opened schools where they employed Confucian scholars and experts in martial arts or Western studies to educate young samurai. A few domains also supported schools for the children of farmers and merchants. Thus the Edo period saw the transformation of samurai from warriors into administrators.

But it should be remembered that these were administrators with a practical bent, accustomed to leadership, who still carried two swords which they were trained to use. In the crisis of the 1860s, when the Bakufu fumbled, young samurai were again to take up their swords, this time in the service of the emperor and the nation, to forge a new beginning for Japan. Decisive, courageous, willing to act, accustomed to discipline, willing to bear hardship, literate and aware of the realities of power, the samurai provided strong leadership for a small country facing threats from abroad and instability at home.

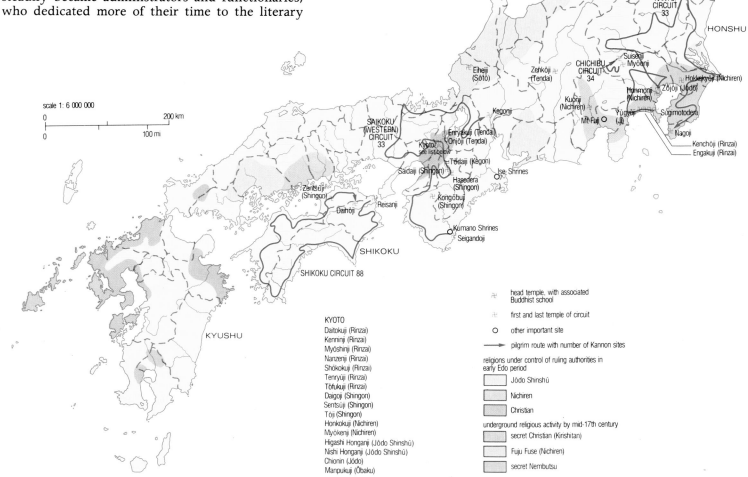

Economic changes in urban society

Against expectations, merchants, artisans and townspeople flourished in Tokugawa Japan. Politically powerless and acquiescent, they built up considerable wealth and long before the end of the period were living easier lives than many samurai. The artisans and merchants, who had enjoyed commercial opportunity and social acceptance in the Muromachi and Momoyama periods, were placed in the bottom ranks of the Tokugawa status hierarchy. As we have seen, Tokugawa feudal thinking favored an agrarian economy in which samurai would govern and farmers produce food and other vital commodities. These were both socially desirable activities. Merchants were unwanted parasites, relegated to the lowest category of society. Little effort was made by the authorities to understand their activities or the effect they might have on the economic life of the country.

Tokugawa economic principles stressing self-sufficiency for the various groups were in many ways naive. Farmers could live off the land, and perhaps be self-sufficient, but daimyō and samurai, separated from the soil, certainly could not. Stipends in rice had to be converted into cash to exchange for other commodities such as swords, armor, horses, clothing, furniture, saddles, robes, paper, writing brushes, ink and sake. Merchants were needed to conduct these market functions. When domain merchants in the castle town could not cope with the scale of the exchanges involved, merchants from Osaka, Kyoto and Edo were resorted to.

The authorities found it easy to control merchants and keep them in their place socially, but they needed their services too badly to be able to restrict fully their opportunities for commercial success. Population growth, urbanization and the sankin kōtai system all added to the need for the services of merchants. The swelling population and building and rebuilding booms in the cities, especially the shogunal capital of Edo and its great satellites Osaka and Kyoto, provided a rising demand for provisions, building materials and services of all kinds. Another factor contributing to mercantile and economic growth was the whole sankin kōtai apparatus. Intended to drain daimyō coffers, it created a need for daimyō loans and swelled merchant coffers and financial services in the domains and in Edo.

In Edo, the shogunal capital and a vast garrison town, more than half the population were townspeople (chōnin). Osaka, which developed as a prosperous commercial and shipping center, was almost entirely inhabited by merchants and townspeople. Kyoto, the site of the old imperial court and the Bakufu's strongpoint Nijō castle, was a thriving city of skilled artisans, monks and townspeople. The castle towns of the 250 or so domains, which like Edo castle had originally been founded as military strongpoints and centers of local rule, also became the nodes of local market networks and centers of trade in local products. Privileged merchants, usually operating under license from the shogunate or daimyō, served as the links between cities, castle towns and their rural hinterlands. Well-developed coastal navigation networks funneled rice and other commodities from the

domains to the Osaka market. Freight vessels plied regularly between Osaka and Edo.

Merchants did a lucrative business in brokerage, forwarding, money changing and moneylending. They ran the warehouses for rice and other commodities from the domains and were licensed to operate han monopolies. Brokers converted rice into cash or credit for individual samurai as well as the domains. The larger merchants acted as financial and forwarding agents for daimyō, handling shipments to Osaka for exchange or to Edo for the daimyō's consumption. They supplied banking services, exchanged the welter of han currencies, transferred funds and issued loans to the Bakufu, daimyō and hard-pressed samurai. Loans to daimyō were a profitable but risky business. More than one merchant house collapsed when daimyō unilaterally cancelled the debt. But these failures as well as Bakufu efforts to force merchant creditors to reduce or cancel bad debts did not stifle merchant activity or profits. They simply had the effect of raising the cost of credit, since neither Bakufu nor the domains were able to establish lasting solvency or reduce their dependence on the merchant sector.

With the Bakufu, daimyō and samurai all depending on merchants as financial agents and sources of provisions, merchant houses prospered and branched out into other businesses. By the second half of the 18th century there were more than 200 merchant establishments valued at over 200000 gold ryō (about one koku). Some of the great modern Japanese commercial enterprises trace their origins to Tokugawa period merchant houses. Mitsui began in the early 17th century as an Osaka trading house making high-interest loans. In 1673 Mitsui Takatoshi (1622–44) established a chain of dry-goods stores in Edo known as Echigoya. Under the slogan "cash down and no markups" he sold a wide range of goods at fair prices. The Echigoya flourished and is said to have taken in as much as 1000 ryō per day. It became the predecessor of the modern Mitsukoshi department store.

As in the villages, there were great differences in status and wealth among the town dwellers. For every great merchant house there were hundreds of shopkeepers, innkeepers, artisans, bathhouse owners, booksellers, art dealers, brothel keepers and clerks struggling to make their living and offering the myriad services called for in urban life. As with peasants and samurai, the Bakufu bombarded townspeople with sumptuary regulations urging them to live frugally. Most merchants and artisans heeded these regulations and established their own house codes which inculcated the principles of thrift, hard work, loyalty to the institution, service to clients and provision for the future that laid the basis for enduring family businesses. Some, however, flaunted their wealth in lavish costumes, entertainment or cultivation of the social graces.

Momoyama culture

The cultural style in the late 16th century was set by the unifiers, or tenkajin, Oda Nobunaga and Toyotomi Hideyoshi who had gained control over the country by conquest. They naturally looked for grandiose cultural expression to flaunt their new power. The primary cultural symbol of this age, reflecting their conquest and power, was the great

Religion in the Edo period
The map shows some important features of the religious life of the Edo period. Following the curbing of militant Buddhism by Nobunaga and Hideyoshi, the early Tokugawa shoguns reformed and reorganized Buddhism by issuing edicts for temples and shrines, clarifying sectarian lineages and supporting the authority of the head temples of the various Buddhist schools. Buddhist temples were used as registration centers in the eradication of Catholicism. By 1650 only a small number of covert Kirishitan clung to their faith in Kyushu. The Fuju Fuse and Nembutsu branches of Buddhism were also suppressed by the shogunate or daimyō such as the Shimazu.

Pilgrimage to Ise, to sacred mountains such as Fuji and to many other shrines and temples proliferated during the Edo period. Ise alone attracted thousands of pilgrims in regular years and millions in particularly auspicious years of "pilgrimages of thanks." Other famous pilgrimage centers included the Shikoku circuit venerating Kūkai (Kōbō Daishi), and the Saikoku (Western), Chichibu and Mogami circuits, all expressing the remarkable efflorescence of devotion to Kannon in the Edo period.

castle with its deep moats, huge walls, intricate courtyards and soaring keeps. Two castles (Nobunaga's Azuchi castle and Hideyoshi's Momoyama castle at Fushimi) have given the name to the age: the Azuchi-Momoyama (or simply Momoyama) epoch. Whereas early castles were usually mountain forts (*yamajiro*), built defensively on crags and protected by mountains and rivers, during the 16th century huge castles were built on the plains to command river valleys, communications nodes and rice fields. There was space around them for garrison towns to grow, to which samurai, artisans and merchants were drawn. With their layers of moats, towering, finely cut stone walls, soaring white wooden superstructures, and brilliantly colored roof tiles these great castles must have been awesome and forbidding sights in the late 16th and early 17th centuries, dominating the surrounding countryside, the symbols of power and personality of a new breed of powerful *daimyō* and unifiers.

These great castles were not simply fortresses. They were also centers of administration and living quarters for the hegemons and *daimyō*. To relieve

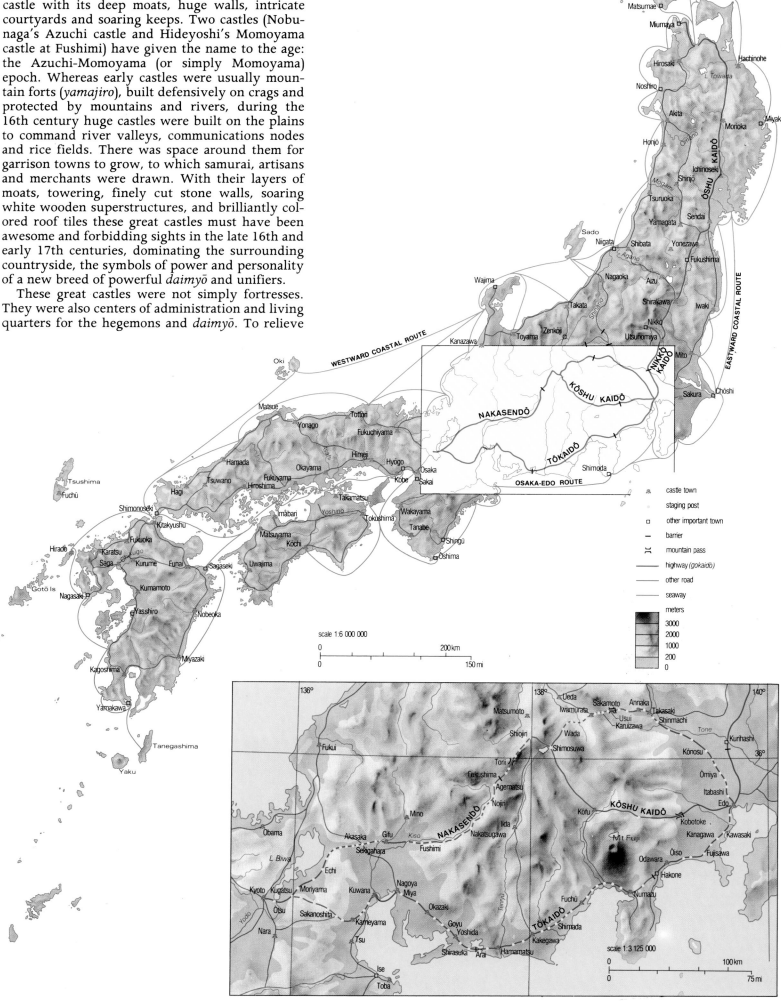

castle town

staging post

other important town

barrier

mountain pass

highway (*gokaidō*)

other road

seaway

Sen no Rikyū (1522–91) became the leading arbiter of taste during an age of cultural and artistic experience in Japan. The son of a fish merchant in Sakai, Rikyū studied tea (*chanoyu*) with several masters before becoming tea master for Nobunaga and Hideyoshi. Rikyū's love of the simple, natural and restrained (*wabi*) set a curb on the aesthetic excesses of the age. He reduced the size of the tearoom (*chashitsu*) from four tatami mats to two and introduced flower holders made of bamboo, rough irregular Japanese tea bowls and simple iron kettles. He also refined and simplified the meal (*kaiseki*) served with tea. He based his aesthetic of *wabi* in Zen Buddhist thought and practice. For reasons that are still debated, Rikyū aroused the anger of Hideyoshi and was obliged to commit suicide. Rikyū triumphed over Hideyoshi in that his aesthetic ideals, diffused by his successors, have continued to inspire Japanese culture.

Transportation in the Edo period
The Edo period saw the completion of a well-developed, carefully regulated system of road and maritime transportation. The road network centered on the five centrally administered highways traversing Japan and converging at Nihonbashi in Edo (now Tokyo). These five highways were the Tōkaidō, Nakasendō, Kōshu Kaidō, Nikkō Kaidō and Ōshu Kaidō. *Daimyō* fulfilling their alternate attendance (*sankin kōtai*) obligations rested at the staging posts along these highways or had their travel documents checked at the barriers (*sekisho*). At Hakone barrier guards were on the lookout for guns entering Edo and women leaving. The highway system symbolized the supremacy of the Tokugawa Bakufu in regulating communications, controlling military alliances and regulating movement of the population, especially of the *daimyō* and their retinues. Because transportation by road was slow and expensive, rice and other commodities were shipped by sea. Large freighters regularly plied the coast between Osaka and Edo, while the products of the most remote domains could be shipped to Osaka via a coastal shipping network that embraced the whole of Japan.

the dark and spartan interiors, their walls and screens were gorgeously decorated. These palatial residences spurred the development of wall painting, screens and panels employing expanses of gold leaf and vivid colors that are among the finest expressions of Momoyama art. The unifiers lavishly patronized the painters and craftsmen who decorated these castles. For Azuchi castle, for instance, Nobunaga employed Kanō Eitoku as his master artist. It was an immense project. With several square kilometers of space to transform, Eitoku organized teams of painters to create the outlines for his designs. Each story of the keep was decorated with a different theme. In the topmost rooms in the castle, for instance, and obviously symbolizing Nobunaga's aspirations to rule all Japan, the sliding screens were covered with gold-leaf paintings showing ancient Chinese rulers and culture heroes. On lower stories the rooms were decorated with Buddhist themes, the four accomplishments of the gentleman, horses, falcons, birds and flowers, and landscapes. The castle contained a Buddhist chapel and a Noh stage. The magnificence of Azuchi and the entertainments given there by Nobunaga dazzled Luis Frois and other observers. Splendid as it was, however, it did not outlast its builder and was burned to the ground in 1582.

Kanō Eitoku (1543–90) was the most influential of Momoyama era painters. The fourth-generation head of the Kanō school, which blended Chinese styles with Japanese Yamato-e techniques and themes, Eitoku responded creatively to the opportunities presented by the age for powerful and flamboyant works of art. He enjoyed the patronage of Hideyoshi as well as Nobunaga. In addition to the project at Azuchi he was also the master designer of Hideyoshi's three fortress-palaces: Osaka castle, the Jurakutei and Fushimi castle. Eitoku was already making his mark as a painter at the age of 24 when he painted a series of flowers and birds of the four seasons on sliding screens in the Jukōin subtemple of Daitokuji in Kyoto. In this painting he helped to establish the Momoyama style. On one set of four panel screens (1·7 meters high, 5·4 meters wide) he painted a gigantic gnarled plum tree, its branches spread, with a river flowing beneath it and water birds swimming. While retaining some of the characteristics of medieval monochrome ink painting, there is greater use of color and the branches and water are dramatically vibrant. With brilliant colors becoming more assertive, and the subjects more dramatic, the Momoyama style was complete. Befitting their imposing scale, Eitoku's images are rendered in simple dramatic forms, bold, coarse brush strokes, and strong opaque colors. Other fine paintings attributed to Eitoku include a very powerful gold painting of fantastic Chinese lions and a giant cypress. Painted when he was 48 and now mounted as an eightfold screen, a monumental aged cypress tree spreads its great branches against a background of gold-leaf clouds and blue water. He created an extremely dynamic composition in an unusual space restricted in height but relatively free in width.

After Eitoku, the Kanō school continued to produce fine painters under the protection of the powerful rulers of the time and gradually developed a decorative, elegant, sensitive style, transforming

Chinese styles and themes to Japanese taste. Kanō Sanraku (1559–1635), Eitoku's adopted son, who helped decorate Osaka castle, produced strong decorative bird and flower paintings and the Kanō tradition continued as a powerful artistic force through the Tokugawa period.

The Kanō school did not have the field of decorative art to itself. Independent painters like Hasegawa Tōhaku (1539–1610), Kaihō Yūshō (1533–1615) and Unkoku Tōgan (1547–1618) all competed with Kanō painters for the commissions of the warriors, courtiers, temples and townspeople. Hasegawa Tōhaku, who claimed Sesshū as his exemplar, was a brilliant and versatile artist who painted equally well in ink monochrome and in gold and vivid colors. Some of the paintings attributed to him express a lyricism that seems almost modern in mood. His ink wash of scattered pine trees emerging from morning mist mounted on a pair of sixfold screens has an ageless quality that has made it a stimulus for modern Japanese painting. In a completely different vein his vividly colored painting of an aged maple tree in full blossom in the Chisakuin in Kyoto displays an easy mastery of the decorative presentation of natural beauty on the grand scale.

If the power of the warlords is reflected in the great panel paintings of the age, the bustle of the growing urban population is captured in the screen paintings showing scenes of popular entertainments and public pleasures in and around the capital (*rakuchū rakugai-zu*). These paintings, looking not to a classical past but to the Momoyama world as it was, were decorative guide maps to the sights of the capital and its streets filled with merchants, townspeople, samurai and "southern barbarians."

Tea and the aesthetics of cultivated poverty
The late 16th century saw the perfection of what we refer to in English as the "Tea Ceremony." This is a rather imperfect translation of the Japanese term *chanoyu* which simply means "hot water for tea." To many observers and participants it may seem at times like a very stiff and formal "ceremony," but in fact it is more of a performing art, in which a host invites guests to share the enjoyment of tea and appreciate prized utensils in a carefully cultivated atmosphere. The word "ceremony" conveys more formality and distance than may be intended. It is not simply the host who performs a ritual of dispensing tea. Host and guests together share in the enjoyment of a ritualized aesthetic and emotional experience. With this proviso in mind we can use the term "ceremony."

During the late 16th century *chanoyu*, as we now know it, was perfected by the articulation of an aesthetic that came to inspire much of Japanese art and taste, the ideal of *wabi* (literally "lonely" or "impoverished"). Raised to an aesthetic principle, we can think of it as an ideal of cultivated poverty which contains within itself intimations of great richness. The style of tea ceremony developed during the 16th century that contained the perfected ideal of *wabi* has come to be known as "*wabi*-tea" (*wabicha*). This ideal was perfected by three tea masters—Murata Jukō (1422–1502), Takeno Jōō (1502–55) and Sen no Rikyū (1522–91)—all from the merchant community and all steeped in Zen Buddhism.

The Tea Ceremony

The following illustrations show some features of a tea gathering (*chaji*) as it might be conducted at the Mushanokōji Senke Tea School in Kyoto. The Mushanokōji Senke school, together with the larger Ura Senke and Ōmote Senke schools, traces direct descent from Sen no Rikyū through 16 generations. A *chaji*, at which food as well as tea will be served, is a formal social event and guests, as well as host, prepare themselves for the occasion. *Chanoyu* seeks to create the illusion of separation from the everyday humdrum world. Here the guests make their way quietly from the outer gate via the small rustic tea garden (*roji*) to a middle gate. At the Mushanokōji Senke this gate is called the Amigasa-Mon (woven umbrella gate).

Chanoyu (the "Tea Ceremony," literally "hot water for tea") has been one of the vital nodes in traditional Japanese culture. Here many cultural threads came together and were reshaped. Through *chanoyu* the ideal of *wabi*, cultivated poverty, was refined. This in turn allowed the Japanese to find as great a value in rough, simple, irregular Japanese and Korean pottery as in perfect, regular Chinese ware (*karamono*). This opened the way to a new aesthetic. The small, rustic tearoom became a separate world in which social barriers were temporarily reduced. Here merchants and townsmen could mingle with powerful warriors or nobles, all sharing a passion for simplicity on the one hand and for prized utensils on the other. There are many schools of tea in Japan today. Most trace their lineages back directly or indirectly to Sen no Rikyū in the 16th century. Some catered to shoguns, *daimyō* or courtiers, others to ordinary samurai or commoners. All shared the same ritual discipline, etiquette, aesthetic and interest in Zen. The three schools active today are the Ura Senke, Ōmote Senke and Mushanokōji Senke in Kyoto.

Passing through the Amigasa-Mon, they leave the outer world still further behind them as they admire the garden and move closer to the tearoom. They are now in the inner garden (*uchi roji*) of the tea house. The inner garden contains an arrangement of stones, in the center of which is a carved stone basin containing water. The guests crouch here to rinse their hands and mouths from a wooden dipper. Rikyū, drawing on Zen, stressed mindfulness in the performance of even the simplest tasks. The discipline of *chanoyu* also stresses economy and gracefulness of movement. There is a way to handle even something so mundane as a water dipper.

Entry to the tea house itself is frequently via a tiny entrance (*nijiriguchi*), 70 centimeters wide by 80 centimeters high, so that all guests have to crouch and crawl through. This further emphasizes the sense of having entered another world, remote from everyday anxieties. The *nijiriguchi* served an equalizing function in feudal times in that samurai had perforce to remove their swords before entering. The last guest to enter closes and locks the sliding entrance door.

Having entered the *nijiriguchi*, the guest finds himself facing the alcove, or *tokonoma*. By the end of the medieval period *tokonoma* were being incorporated into tea houses and domestic architecture as spaces in which to display prized scrolls, ceramics or bamboo flower vases. At the opening of a *chaji* a single scroll will be displayed in the *tokonoma*. Very often this is a single line of calligraphy by a Zen priest. In this case the calligraphy reads "Honrai mu ichibutsu" ("Originally there is nothing"), a famous phrase from *The Platform Sūtra of the Sixth Patriarch*, often used as a *kōan* to encourage the search for enlightenment. Calligraphy by the eccentric Zen monk Ikkyū of Daitokūji is particularly prized in tea circles. The guests acknowledge the scroll, aware that it has been chosen carefully by the host to reflect the season or the mood of the *chaji*.

After examining the scroll, the guests seat themselves around the small square hearth let into the center of the floor. The hearth, echoing a country farmhouse, is another feature perfected by Rikyū. At this point the host enters. The principal guest thanks the host for the invitation and the thoughtfulness of the preparations and inquires about the calligraphy scroll and other objects. At every stage in the *chaji* gestures, movements and speech are carefully modulated. Conversation is brief and limited to what is going on in the tearoom. Yet within this restricted environment the emphasis is on naturalness and spontaneity.

The host now serves a light meal (*kaiseki*) which has been prepared in a pantry (*mizuya*) beside the tearoom.

Right Styles of tea houses vary considerably. Sen no Rikyū favored very small tea houses, large enough for only one or two tatami mats. A two-mat room measures less than 2 meters square. This was the extreme pole of the ideal of rustic simplicity and cultivated poverty (*wabi*). Hideyoshi, Rikyū's patron, no doubt used two-mat tearooms, but he also built himself a golden tea house as an assertion of his power. Tea houses used by nobles and *daimyō* were often elegant pavilions of eight mats or more. Most tea houses are raised off the ground on posts. Exterior and interior walls are roughly finished in mortar, wood or bamboo. Roofs are thatched with reed or bark or shingled. This tea house stands in the Gosho Imperial Palace grounds in Kyoto.

The rise and fall of a tea master

Sen no Rikyū was a disciple of Jōō. He was born at Imaichi in Sakai. During his teens he studied the arts of tea with Jōō and by his twenties was already renowned as a tea master. Rikyū's family were fish wholesalers, probably quite wealthy but not ranked among the great merchant houses of Sakai. Rikyū soon came to the attention of Oda Nobunaga. Nobunaga also used Imai Sōkyū (1520–93) and Tsūda Sōgyu (died 1591) as his tea masters. While these two men served as both Sakai merchants and tea masters, Rikyō was employed purely as a specialist in the way of tea.

Hideyoshi's passion for tea was both Rikyū's fortune and misfortune. At first things went well between them. Under Hideyoshi's sponsorship *chanoyu* became the rage. The tea ceremony offered refinement for the samurai, a symbol of wealth to the merchant and cultural legitimacy to the ruler. Rikyū existed at the pinnacle of the world of tea. In 1587 Hideyoshi ordered that a great tea party be held in the grounds of the Kitano Shrine in Kyoto. Hearing that prized pieces (*meibutsu*) were going to be used at the party, as many as 800 tea masters were said to have gathered from all over Kyoto and neighboring provinces. But anyone who enjoyed tea was invited. Irrespective of wealth or social status, the townspeople could watch Hideyoshi and other tea masters conduct tea ceremonies and display famous utensils. In this popular festival of tea there was a breath of *gekokujō*, a dissolution or reversal of social hierarchy before the hardening of status distinctions. Rikyū was still in favor at this time and he and Hideyoshi shared in the planning for the occasion.

After this event, however, relations between Hideyoshi and Rikyū became strained. Many reasons have been advanced to explain the estrangement. Looking at it in cultural or aesthetic terms, we can suggest that the growing aesthetic severity of Rikyū's *wabicha* made an autocratic ruler like Hideyoshi uncomfortable. Rikyū's aesthetic ignored the whims of Hideyoshi and his desire for entertainment and made Rikyū the supreme arbiter in the world of tea. From the ruler's point of view Rikyū had become a cultural rival and heretic. Moreover, Rikyū's assertion of his aesthetic leadership may be seen as an expression of a spirit of *gekokujō* that challenged the rigid social hierarchy being imposed by Hideyoshi. According to the *Yamanoue Sōjiki*: "Since Rikyū is the master, it is tasteful if he freely breaks the way of tea, making mountains into valleys, west into east." This claim that Rikyū could freely overturn traditional values in the world of tea may well have been unacceptable to Hideyoshi, who claimed that authority as his own.

Rikyu's fate may also have been affected by the politics of the age and the eclipse of Sakai. In 1587, the year when the great Kitano tea party was held, Hideyoshi had virtually succeeded in unifying the nation, except the Hōjō family in eastern Japan. Hideyoshi's next target was Korea. As a base from which to launch an invasion, the merchant port of Hakata in Kyushu rose in importance. The sudden rise of Hakata meant eclipse for Sakai, and perhaps a consequent weakening of Rikyū's position within the factions around Hideyoshi. The merchants and tea masters Kamiya Sōtan and Shimai Sōshitsu of

Above According to Rikyū, the *kaiseki* should be light and delicately cooked and should appeal to the eye as well as the palate. The word *kaiseki* was taken, like many other facets of *chanoyu*, from Zen Buddhism. Buddhist monks were forbidden by the Vinaya to take food after noon. Chinese and Japanese Zen monks did physical work and many Zen masters permitted their monks to take an evening snack. Instead of calling it "food," however, they referred to it as a warm stone placed in their robe—*kaiseki*.

Above To each guest the host serves a tray bearing covered lacquered bowls of rice, soup, fish and vegetables with new cedar chopsticks and invites them to eat. Sake, served from a simple iron kettle, is drunk from shallow bowls. After being served a simple sweet of fruit or other seasonal dessert, the guests leave the tearoom for a brief recess. While the guests are relaxing, the host prepares the tearoom for the serving of thick tea.

Below left When the guests return to the tearoom, they find that the calligraphy has been replaced by a single flower in a vase in the *tokonama*.

Above center The host heats water in an iron kettle, rinses and wipes the tea bowl and utensils, places powdered green tea in the bowl with a bamboo spoon, adds hot water with the bamboo dipper, whips the tea with a bamboo whisk until the surface is slightly frothy, and serves it to his guests. Tea is made in two consistencies. Thick tea (*koicha*), the more formal, is creamy in consistency, though bitter in taste. It is drunk in small quantities by all the guests from the same bowl. The less formal thin tea (*usucha*) is served later in the ceremony in individual bowls.

Above Tea bowls vary according to the taste of the person making the tea and the season or occasion. "Summer" bowls tend to be shallower and broader to disperse the heat and give an impression of coolness. "Winter" bowls, like that shown here, are taller to contain the heat.

Hakata, for instance, were taken into Hideyoshi's confidence. Rikyū seems to have been involved in confrontation with the powerful *daimyō* Ishida Mitsunari and Maeda Gen'i who were strong supporters of dispatching troops to Korea. After the destruction of the Hōjō family in 1590 Tokugawa Ieyasu, who sympathized with Rikyū, was sent to the Kantō and the isolation of Rikyū within the factions around Hideyoshi worsened. The death in 1591 of Hidenaga, Hideyoshi's brother and Rikyū's last protector, opened the way for the tragedy. On the pretext that it was an expression of lese majesty to install a wooden statue of Rikyū wearing leather-soled sandals above the Daitokuji gate, through which Hideyoshi might pass, Rikyū was obliged to commit *seppuku*.

Rikyū's insistence on the ideals of *wabi* and simple natural beauty lived on. The *wabi* ideal of unpretentious rustic beauty that Rikyū had perfected within *chanoyu*, the beauty of a simple thatched roof, bare wood, unpainted walls, simple earthern vessels, a single flower, a small fire, continued to inspire the various schools of tea that claimed descent from him. Moreover, the ideal of *wabi* made its influence felt through Japanese aesthetics, well beyond the tea house. It is found in architecture, gardens, flower arrangement, pottery, painting, calligraphy, poetry and cooking. *Chanoyu* can therefore be seen as one of the central nodes in Japanese culture, bringing together, transforming and redistributing the various elements that went to make up the distinctively Japanese aesthetic ideal of *wabi*.

"Southern Barbarians" and Momoyama culture

During the late 16th century, the great age of navigation, Japan was open to cultural influences from east Asia and the Western world. Knowledge of Japan and its customs was carried to Asia and Europe by merchants and missionaries. The Japanese, for their part, were curious about the outside world and eager to experiment with new ideas, technologies and fashions. Among the many disparate cultural influences that poured into Japan in the late 16th century we have already mentioned the role of firearms and their impact on war and unification. In the cultural arena Christianity was a temporary but powerful source of stimulus.

Introduced into Kyushu in the 1540s, Christianity spread rapidly. St Francis Xavier (1506–52) viewed Japan as a promising mission field, one in which the Catholic Church would find new souls for Christ to offset its losses in Reformation Europe. Within 20 years of Xavier's departure there were more than 25000 Christians and 35 years later some 150000. Although Xavier enjoyed the patronage of the Portuguese king and certainly recognized that expansion and commerce were beneficial to Portugal, he had little personal interest in colonization or trade. His single-minded concern was in spreading Catholicism and providing relief activity. Although Christianity and commerce went hand in hand, commerce, for the most part, was left to merchants. The Jesuit missionaries did their best to win souls, from the *daimyō* down.

To help them make converts, the Jesuit missionaries enthusiastically studied Japanese customs and language. Their cultural interest is reflected in detailed letters and reports describing contemporary society and customs in Japan and in the famous Japanese-Portuguese Dictionary (*Nippo jisho*). This is a unique research tool because it records the Japanese language of the day, not transformed into Chinese characters, but written down exactly as the Jesuits heard it. Colleges and seminaries for training Japanese preachers were built. Missionary activity also brought the introduction of such European technology as printing; and new medical, astronomical and architectural knowledge was also introduced. The cultural influence of Catholicism was, however, short-lived. The threat implicit in Hideyoshi's prohibition against Catholic missionaries in 1587 was enforced more aggressively in the early Edo period when the Bakufu proscribed Christianity, first in Bakufu domains, then throughout the country. Under bitter persecution over the next few decades much Christian culture was rooted out.

But foreign cultural influences in the late 16th century were not limited to Christianity. Many entertainments, pastimes and foodstuffs newly introduced from Asia or the West found widespread acceptance among the common people. Here we have space to look briefly at only three or four of these popular fashions: the *shamisen*, playing cards, tobacco and foreign foods.

The three-stringed instrument known as the *shamisen* was imported during this period from the Ryukyu Islands, a point of cultural contact between Japan and China. Achieving rapid popularity, the *shamisen* was heard in geisha houses, Kabuki theaters and private homes. According to one account in a work called *Pine Leaves*: "Around the mid-17th century an instrument made of snakeskin with two strings was introduced to Nakakoji, a lute-playing minstrel who lived at Izumi in Sakai. As a result of a prophetic vision vouchsafed by the Hase Kannon, one more string was added. Thus it was commonly called the *shamisen* (three-stringed instrument).

It was also during the 1570s and 1580s that playing cards (*carta* in Portuguese) were introduced to Japan. One of the prohibitions in the Tosa *daimyō* Chōsokabe warrior code of 1597 forbade "gambling, cards and other games of chance." This seems to have been the first use of the word "karuta" in Japanese documents. But it is likely that card games were known in Kyoto and the Kinai region some time before they became the rage in Tosa. The card game introduced to Japan in the 16th century was the Portuguese version of the game played with 48 cards marked with four different symbols: swords, sticks, wine cups and coins. The *Ukiyo monogatari* (Tales of the Floating World) states that: "A game called *karuta* was introduced from the Southern Barbarian lands. The game was decided by dividing the cards into four suits of 12 cards." Later Portuguese versions of the game had five suits of 15 cards each.

Many colorful pastimes are shown in the fine genre screen paintings which allow us to enter the pleasure world of the early 17th century. In one screen painting a blind *shamisen* player seems to be teaching several young women how to use the instrument. In another painting a *shamisen* player is entertaining a circle of dancing figures. Upstairs

The Christian century
The Iberian Catholic (Kirishitan) missionary effort in Japan began with the arrival of the Jesuit St Francis Xavier at Kagoshima in 1549. In two years and three months in Japan Xavier preached in Hirado, Hakata, Yamaguchi, Kyoto, Shimabara and Omura and won the respect of such *daimyō* as Ōuchi Yoshitaka and Ōtomo Sōrin. He was followed by many more dedicated padres, Jesuits at first, followed by Franciscans and Dominicans, who strove to convert *daimyō* and commoners. Driven by a genuine interest in Catholicism as well as the attraction of trade and cultural contact with the West, more than a dozen *daimyō* were baptized after 1563, led by Ōmura Sumitada, Naitō Nyoan and Takayama Ukon. With the sympathy of Nobunaga and many *daimyō*, churches and seminaries were built in Azuchi and many other parts of Japan. By 1580 the Jesuits could claim 200000 converts and were training Japanese missionaries. Even after Hideyoshi's edict ordering the expulsion of missionaries in 1587 the number of converts continued to grow, reaching a peak in the first decade of the 17th century. Rivalries among the various Catholic missionary orders, criticism by Dutch and English Protestants, and increasingly relentless persecution after 1612 by the early Tokugawa shoguns, who were determined to eradicate Catholicism, weakened and eventually crushed the Catholic missionary effort. After the defeat of the Shimabara uprising in 1638 the few Kirishitan who clung to their faith did so secretly in the islands off the coast of Kyushu.

Inset This portable Christian shrine, or retable, reminds us that the first European art introduced to Japan was religious in inspiration. With the surge of conversions in the late 16th century it was impossible to meet the demand for religious art with imports from Europe and talented Japanese novices in the Jesuit seminaries began to produce very proficient versions of European themes. This shrine, richly decorated in gold lacquer and shell inlay with a design of flying birds and mandarin orange trees, has the emblem of the Society of Jesus on its pediment. The head of Christ, crowned with thorns, was probably painted by an unknown European hand. European art and Japanese craftsmanship combined to produce a moving expression of 16th-century Japanese Catholicism.

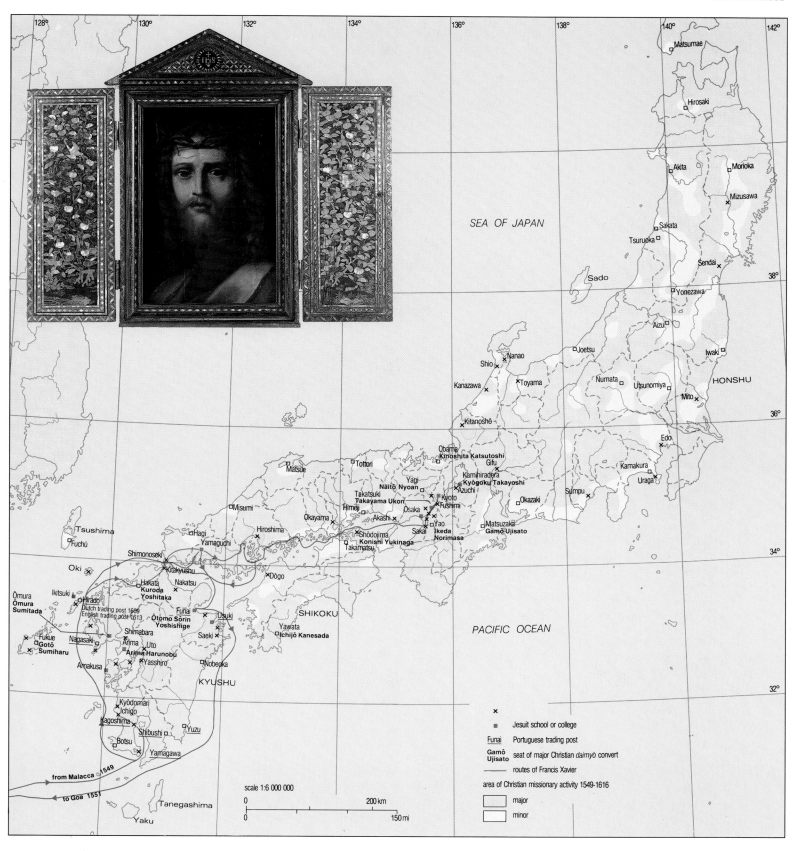

scale 1:6 000 000

0   200 km

0   150 mi

×   Jesuit school or college

Funai   Portuguese trading post

Gamō Ujisato   seat of major Christian *daimyō* convert

——   routes of Francis Xavier

area of Christian missionary activity 1549–1616

major

minor

four men and women are playing cards and back-gammon. Downstairs people are enjoying tea and playing with small arrows, while two men are smoking. It was almost a rule that paintings of contemporary amusements included scenes of men and women playing cards, strumming the *shamisen* or smoking tobacco. These were clearly the popular cultural vogue of the early 17th century.

The pungent tobacco leaves that the inhabitants of the New World smoked spread throughout Europe and at the end of the 16th century the custom was brought to India from Portugal. Tobacco smoking was introduced to Japan sometime after that, but no definite date is known. A work called the *Enroku*, written by Ōtsuki Bansui, states that tobacco plants were being grown in Nagasaki in 1606. Other views suggest that it was introduced in the 1560s or 1570s. It is fairly clear that by about 1590 tobacco was well known in Japan, if not as a plant, at least as a product. We know that by this time even Zen monks were using tobacco as a gift. An entry in the *Rokuon nichiroku* (a diary of the Zen abbot of the Rokuonji in Kyoto) for 1593 says: "Went to Shūyo's cloister in the evening; brought tobacco with me."

The Japanese in this period were introduced to other new tastes in food and styles in dress. Some of these took root, others were more ephemeral. The Portuguese and Spanish brought pepper and other new spices. They introduced bread, cakes and the fried dishes that became the basis of the deep-fried vegetable dish known as *tempura*. Japanese were also fascinated by Iberian dress. Even non-Christian *daimyō* affected rosaries and earrings bearing likenesses of Christ or the Virgin Mary. Hideyoshi on occasion amused himelf by dressing in Western fashion, and the pantaloons known as *calção* were adapted to use by commoners under the name *karusan*. Many new words were added to the language and are still in use today. The Portuguese *pao* (Spanish *pan*) gave the Japanese word for bread: *pan*. *Carta* gave *karuta*. The Japanese word *tempura* was derived from *temporas* (meatless Friday), while *konpeitō*, sugar confectionery, came from *confeitos*.

Early Edo culture: *kabukimono* and the Kabuki theater

The Kabuki theater, perhaps the most vigorous and compelling expression of the vitality of popular culture in the Edo period and a source of enjoyment for Japanese and non-Japanese today, had its origins in the precincts of temples and shrines and streets of Kyoto in the late 16th and early 17th centuries. The three Chinese characters used to write *Ka-bu-ki* today mean song, dance and skill. They describe the principal components that contribute to the spectacle and energy of Kabuki as we know it. The word *kabuki* may well have had other roots, however. There is more than an echo in it of the word *kabuku*, literally meaning to lean, or be eccentric, rakish, deviant, extraordinary, outlandish or erotic. Certainly, in the early days of Kabuki, it was a blend of seemingly strange and erotic combinations of song, dance and drama. The earliest manifestations of Kabuki may have been popular dances held in shrines and temples. By around 1600 dance troupes made up of lissome young women were drawing enthusiastic crowds in Kyoto. Young women, dressed in men's robes with their hair cut short, mimicked men's roles, while singing and dancing. These activities were traditionally identified with a single actress, Izumo Okuni, who danced with her troupe before admiring crowds beside the Kamo River in 1603. The entertainment spread rapidly around the country to Edo, Osaka and other cities and began to take on clearer theatrical form as actors adapted dramas from the repertory of the Noh and puppet theaters.

In the early decades of the 17th century the development of Kabuki as a theatrical form went hand in hand with the phenomenon of the bands of wild young blades known as *kabukimono* who roamed the streets in outlandish dress. They wore long sidelocks; their clothes were dyed with a patchwork of colorful crests; and they wore extravagantly long swords. Tokugawa Ieyasu and his shogunal successors, who were intent on imposing order on the country, did not look favorably on either the *kabukimono* or the Kabuki dancers.

How do we account for the outburst of *kabuki-mono* in early 17th-century culture? The age of *gekokujō*, or social disorder, was passing. The Tokugawa were tightening their control over society, but there were still fissures through which this kind of youthful energy could escape. In a sense the volatility of their outburst of self-expression may have owed something to the pressures for regularity and comformity that were being imposed on the society. These *kabukimono* expressed a common sense of anger at being born too late for the freewheeling, topsy-turvy world of *gekokujō*. Young as they were, they felt they had lived too long and were at odds with the strictures of the Tokugawa order. The sword belonging to Oshima Ippei, ringleader of the *kabukimono*, had a joke carved on it: "Haven't I lived too long at 25, Ippei?" In any age of drastic change heterodoxy may overcome orthodoxy and burst out in intense spurts of energy. In many ways the *kabukimono* were a menace. They teased merchants' wives and challenged others to fight with swords over trivial matters. They were known as *ibara* (thorns). However, the swaggering young blade was also the favorite spoiled child of the time. In the face of a powerful Bakufu trying to contain the energy of *gekokujō*, masterless samurai with their shaky samurai status, poor samurai children with their restricted futures, eccentric merchants and court nobles found a new ideal in the swaggering self-expression of the *kabukimono*.

It was in 1603 that the sensuous Kabuki dancing of Izumo Okuni swept Kyoto. Not surprisingly the youthful *kabukimono* found their way on to the Kabuki stage. Kabuki dances in which *kabukimono* consorted with courtesans were all the rage. Forgetting their stations in life, people in the audience were intoxicated at the sight of *kabukimono* appearing on stage singing: "Now let's be rakish . . . Come on, be rakish!" The *kabukimono* who appeared like bubbles in the stream of history clearly left their mark on Kabuki dance which achieved dramatic development in the Kabuki theater.

The Bakufu also frowned on Kabuki and fought a constant, but largely unsuccessful, battle to suppress the enormously popular actors and their colorful plays. In 1629 the Bakufu forbade women's Kabuki on the grounds that competitions for the favors of the actresses led to bloodletting and violence. Women actors were immediately replaced by elegant young men. These youths, dressed as women with hair flowing, created as much, or even more scandal. They were banned for loose morals in 1652. The enterprising actors then had adult men play all the parts, women as well as men.

The Bakufu eventually recognized that Kabuki could not be suppressed. The authorities had to be satisfied with regulating it by licenses and allowing it to persist as a form of plebeian amusement. Samurai were officially discouraged from wasting time or money on such frivolous pleasures but they, no less than other sections of the population, were drawn to the theaters. In 1714 there was a major scandal in Tokyo when a passionate liaison between one of the shogun's consorts Ejima and a famous actor was exposed. The Bakufu ordered a purge of the women's quarters in Edo castle, Ejima was exiled and some 1500 others were implicated and punished.

Artists and their patrons in the Momoyama era were fascinated by the novel and exotic, by everyday activities, and by leisure and entertainment. This screen shows a variety of activities that were fashionable in the contemporary pleasure quarters and society at large. The *shamisen*, introduced in the late 16th century, became the popular musical instrument of the Edo period. Played at first by blind lute players, it was picked up by courtesans, entertainers and ordinary townspeople. Tobacco became an addiction at about the same time. Board games such as backgammon had been known for centuries, but remained extremely popular and fed a passion for games of chance.

Thus, by the early 18th century, the Genroku period, the theaters had become wildly popular. Kabuki had moved far from the simple dances of Okuni. It offered full-blooded action and melodrama, music and dance, bravura poses, brilliant makeup and gorgeous costumes, and lavish scenery on large stages. It was very much an actors' theater, dominated by families of famous actors who specialized in particular roles and who took considerable liberties with their texts, making individual plays into vehicles for their own artistic personalities. Kabuki actors rivaled the courtesans of the Yoshiwara pleasure quarters and the famous sumo wrestlers in the fascination they aroused in men and women of all classes. As leading denizens of the floating world (ukiyo) they quickly became a favorite subject for the ukiyoe woodblock print artists. Many of their exaggerated poses and virtuoso performances, which must have been greeted with shouts of approval from their audiences, have been immortalized by the prints of Sharaku and other artists. The female impersonators were particularly famous. Conveying an idealized but sensual femininity, they set styles in dress and movement for the fashionable women of Edo and Osaka.

If Kabuki took Edo by storm, Bunraku, the puppet theater, flourished in Osaka. Bunraku is the modern name for a kind of recitative narrative known as Jōruri, used to carry the dramatic action of puppet dramas. The name comes from the Bunrakuza, or Bunraku theater, established in Osaka. The puppets were half-lifesize figures manipulated by two or three handlers who acted out a story told by a group of chanters accompanied by shamisens. Much of the success of the puppet theater was due to the fact that Chikamatsu provided splendid dramatic material for the puppeteers. Chikamatsu stated explicitly that he preferred puppets to the live actors who mauled his dramas to suit their own preferences. Moreover, inanimate puppets like the masks in Noh allowed the dramatist and the puppeteers to create a stylized and symbolic drama that moved into realms of beauty beyond the commonplace dimension of everyday life.

Chikamatsu came from a samurai background and many of his Jōruri were stirring military tales of fantastic heroism like *The Battle of Coxinga* (*Kokusenya kassen*) or *The Soga Successors* (*Yotsugi Soga*), but his most popular dramas dealt with topical themes. Several of his most famous dramas, including *The Love Suicides at Sonezaki* and *The Love Suicides at Amijima*, deal with desperate love affairs between poor shopkeepers and beautiful geisha from the licensed quarters. The weak men have deserted their families out of infatuation but are unable to buy their lover's freedom from her geisha house. Torn between duty and love, the lovers find release only in flight and suicide together. These dramas were so compelling that they set a vogue for real-life double suicides until the Bakufu stepped in to ban any play with the words "love suicide" in the title.

Protection and regulation

In destroying or pushing aside their rivals and superiors, the unifiers took advantage of the tide of gekokujō to rise to power; but having seized control of the realm, they sought to close the path by which they had climbed, to suppress volatile social mobility and replace it with a new and tighter social order. This pressure was also felt in the cultural arena. The enforced self-immolation of Sen no Rikyū and Furuta Oribe on the orders of Hideyoshi and Ieyasu can be viewed as cultural expressions of a freezing of gekokujū.

Furuta Oribe (1543–1615) was daimyō with a fief of 35 000 koku. He was the closest disciple of Rikyū. After Rikyū's death Oribe served the second shogun Tokugawa Hidetada as tea master of the realm. However, in 1615, following the summer campaign at Osaka castle, Oribe and his kin were accused of treachery as secret supporters of the Toyotomi and ordered to commit seppuku.

Okochi Kinbei, a Bakufu official, predicted Oribe's violent death. He criticized Oribe for "ruining treasures." He objected to the fact that Oribe found special beauty in once faultless tea bowls and caddies he had deliberately broken and repaired. This suggests that Oribe rejected the existing aesthetic value hierarchy of named pieces (meibutsu). Instead he asserted his own aesthetic consciousness by breaking, or deforming, the perfect meibutsu. His attitude had something in common with the wild young kabukimono who rejected the existing order and persisted in an eccentric self-expression which, in the end, ruined them. Oribe's death was thus not merely the death of one cultured daimyō. It was a symbolic event of cultural destruction.

From their appearance in the early 17th century kabukimono were banned many times. On the other hand the existence of thousands of unemployed masterless samurai (rōnin) constantly created more kabukimono. The Bakufu tried to enforce a twofold cultural policy, on the one hand to deal with rōnin, on the other to encourage and protect culture in such a way that kabukimono could not come about. Rōnin who could not find service with some daimyō forfeited samurai status. From their ranks came the leaders of a new cultural wave.

The Genroku age: the culture of the floating world

The late 17th and early 18th centuries witnessed a vigorous cultural efflorescence centering on the merchant city of Osaka. This is commonly known as the culture of the Genroku era (1688–1703). Among its principal representatives were the dramatist Chikamatsu Monzaemon, the popular writer Ihara Saikaku and the poet Matsuo Bashō. These and other artists and writers represented a new cultural leadership responding to the tastes of a growing urban population and more affluent rural merchant class. Growing prosperity and the improvement of roads were making travel easier. Bashō, for instance, was welcomed by literary disciples everywhere. He typifies a diffusion of culture in which merchant and samurai amateurs paid specialists to guide them in the arts.

It is from about this era that we see the development of a very characteristic feature of Japanese culture, the iemoto system. Iemoto, or "house heads," were the hereditary masters of lineages or schools of tea, flowers, poetry, kickball, archery, swordsmanship, calligraphy and other arts who

This smoking box in inlaid lacquer in the shape of a sixfold folding screen exemplifies not only the growing fashion of pipe smoking but also the playfulness and highly decorative quality of Edo period crafts. The wild young blades known as kabukimono led the craze for smoking tobacco in the early Edo period, but it was quickly adopted by residents of the pleasure quarters and ordinary citizens. Repeated Bakufu bans against tobacco as an illicit cash crop and fire hazard did little to curtail the enthusiasm for smoking.

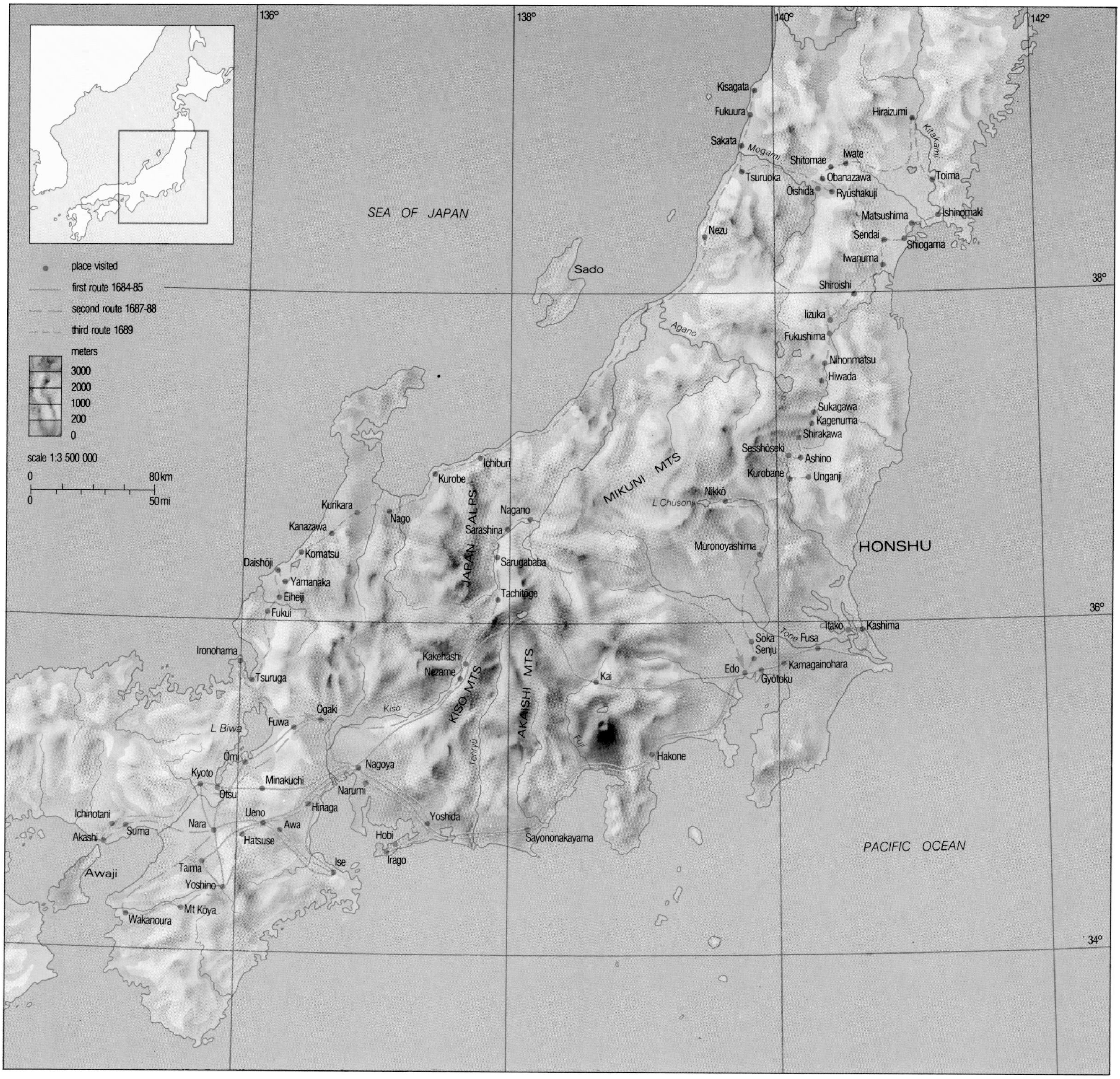
136°
138°
140°
142°
38°
36°
34°
SEA OF JAPAN
PACIFIC OCEAN
HONSHU
Sado
Awaji
place visited
first route 1684-85
second route 1687-88
third route 1689
meters
3000
2000
1000
200
0
scale 1:3 500 000
0
80km
0
50mi
Kisagata
Fukuura
Hiraizumi
Kitakami
Sakata
Mogami
Shitomae
Iwate
Tsuruoka
Obanazawa
Toima
Ōishida
Ryūshakuji
Matsushima
Ishinomaki
Nezu
Sendai
Shiogama
Iwanuma
Shiroishi
Iizuka
Agano
Fukushima
Nihonmatsu
Hiwada
Sukagawa
Kagenuma
Shirakawa
Sesshōseki
Ashino
Kurobane
Unganji
MIKUNI MTS
Nikkō
L Chusonji
Muronoyashima
Ichiburi
Kurobe
JAPAN ALPS
Nagano
Sarashina
Kurikara
Nago
Kanazawa
Komatsu
Daishōji
Sarugababa
Yamanaka
Eiheiji
Tachitoge
Fukui
Itako
Kashima
Tone
Fusa
Sōka
Senju
Kamagainohara
Ironohama
Kakehashi
Nezame
Edo
Gyōtoku
Tsuruga
Kai
KISO MTS
AKAISHI MTS
Ōgaki
Kiso
Fuwa
L Biwa
Tenryū
Fuji
Hakone
Ōmi
Kyoto
Minakuchi
Nagoya
Ōtsu
Narumi
Hinaga
Ichinotani
Ueno
Nara
Awa
Yoshida
Akashi
Suma
Hatsuse
Hobi
Sayononakayama
Irago
Ise
Taima
Yoshino
Mt Kōya
Wakanoura

dispersed their skills to followers for fees. These "schools" allowed widespread cultural participation and a graded progression in various arts while reserving ultimate cultural primacy for the *iemoto*.

In art Genroku saw the activity of decorative artists like Ogata Kōrin (1658–1716) and the early development of woodblock prints, the pictures of the floating world (*ukiyoe*). Kōrin, who came from a Kyoto merchant family, was influenced by the Kyoto *yamato*-style painters Hon'ami Kōetsu (1558–1637) and Tawaraya Sōtatsu (died 1643). His brilliant decorative paintings laid the basis for what is known as the Rimpa school of painting in which nature was portrayed in soft curves and brilliant colors. Kōrin painted vivid kimonos and helped to encourage the development of the *furisode*, or long flowing sleeved kimono, that became the fashion from Genroku on.

During the Genroku era many books containing woodblock printed illustrations were produced to satisfy the demands of an increasingly literate urban population. These early prints included many black and white illustrations of city life. With Suzuki Harunobu (1725–70), who specialized in prints of beautiful women, the possibilities of color were first fully exploited. Of the many *ukiyoe* artists active in Edo in the later 18th century the most creative were undoubtedly Kitagawa Utamaro (1753–1806) and Tōshūsai Sharaku (fl. 1794–95). Utamaro showed a particular genius for capturing not just the features or flesh of women but their changing moods. Sharaku, a fleeting and myster-

Right This print was intended to promote the philosophy of "self-help" and the encouragement of industry (*shokusan kōgyō*) in mid-19th-century Japan. The caption describes how Josiah Wedgwood (the one-legged figure) overcame childhood infirmities and physical handicaps to build up a successful pottery industry that trained craftsmen and contributed to the great wealth and strength of England.

Travels of the poet Bashō
The poet Matsuo Bashō (1644–94) used travel as a means of enlarging the scope of his life and poetry and deepening his vision of reality. He made three major poetic journeys from his native Edo. In 1684–85 he traveled westward to Nagoya, Nara and Kyoto. This journey is described in the travel journal *Nozarashi Kikō* (*The Records of a Weather-Exposed Skeleton*, 1685). After visiting Kyoto Bashō made a trip to Kashima, a scenic town northeast of Edo, to see the harvest moon. He later produced the travel sketch *Kashima Kikō* (*A Visit To Kashima Shrine*, 1687). In 1687 he again set out on a long trip to the west, this time visiting Suma and Akashi on the Inland Sea and returning to Edo via the mountain route passing through Sarashina in the Japan Alps. These journeys are recorded in two poetic diaries, *Oi no Kobumi* (*The Records of a Travel-Worn Satchel*, 1688) and *Sarashina Kikō* (*A Visit to Sarashina Village*, 1688). In the late spring of 1689 Bashō set out on what was to be his longest and most creative poetic journey. His travels took him to some of the loneliest, most underdeveloped parts of northern Japan. He covered 2500 kilometers in 156 days. The journey produced some of his finest *haiku* included in *Oku No Hosomichi* (*The Narrow Road to the Deep North*, 1694).

During the Edo period the kimono saw remarkable development in style and design. The short-sleeved *kosode*, originally an undergarment, was adopted as the dress of townspeople. Sleeves grew wider and longer, giving rise to the long, swinging sleeve (*furisode*), shown here.

ious artist, concentrated on prints of actors and scenes from the Kabuki. Blurring backgrounds, he dramatized and deformed his subjects to create exaggerated facial expressions in striking abstract designs. In the early 19th century *ukiyoe* masters like Katsushika Hokusai (1760–1849) and Andō Hiroshige (1797–1858) turned increasingly to landscapes, cityscapes or scenes of travel. The freshness, vitality and abstract qualities of *ukiyoe* prints captivated European and American impressionist artists when Japanese prints were exhibited in Paris, London and Philadelphia in the second half of the 19th century and set in motion a wave of Japonisme.

Intellectual life and popular culture in the late 18th and early 19th centuries

Until the Genroku era the Osaka-Kyoto area was the cultural pace setter. By the mid-18th century, however, the teeming garrison city of Edo was assuming the intellectual and cultural primacy. The presence of the shogunal court and *daimyō* residences, temples, shrines and a large population created a huge demand not only for commodities and services, but also for learning and entertainment. Moreover, Tanuma's unalloyed commercial interests gave Edo merchants the wealth and confidence to patronize culture.

Edo quickly became a center of samurai scholarship, orthodox and unorthodox. In an age when Japanese could not visit China, Chinese Confucian thought—especially the neo-Confucian synthesis derived from Chu Hsi—flourished as never before. The Bakufu favored the orthodox neo-Confucian teachings espoused by Hayashi Razan (1583–1657) and his successors. But the rival Wang Yang-ming and ancient learning traditions of Confucian scholarship were favored by many samurai scholars and the *daimyō* who employed them. Ogyū Sorai (1666–1728), who challenged neo-Confucianism from the standpoint of a return to the ancient learning of the sages, argued that the Way was not an immutable moral system laid down by Heaven but a flexible political artifice. This has been seen as a critical breakthrough toward a modern political consciousness. Sorai was known as a great Sinophile and the vogue for Chinese studies, Chinese poetry, Chinese books and Chinese themes in prints and paintings was a powerful intellectual current throughout the period.

But by the late 18th century the intellectual primacy of China was being undercut from two directions, by looking inward to Japan's own native traditions and outward to the West. Kamo no Mabuchi (1697–1769) and Motoori Norinaga (1730–1801) initiated a renewal of interest in the Japanese classics that led to a surge of awareness of Japanese cultural tradition. This broadened into a powerful movement of national learning (*Kokugaku*) in which Buddhism and Confucianism were ultimately rejected as alien to Japanese sensibilities. Norinaga emphasized a Japanese culture that was to be found in the simple, the fleeting and the emotional. Later thinkers pushed *Kokugaku* in a more nationalist and zenophobic direction, calling for the expulsion of the foreign threat that seemed to be pressing in upon Japan in the 19th century.

From the late 18th century there was also a perceptible upsurge of interest in Dutch studies

and Western learning by samurai eager to acquire pragmatic knowledge. Hiraga Gennai, for instance, a brilliant but eccentric young samurai from Shikoku, quit his domain to study Chinese and Western science in Nagasaki. Moving to Edo, he experimented with thermometers, static electricity machines and Western-style painting techniques. Sugita Genpaku (1733–1817) and Maeno Ryōtaku (1723–1803) overcame formidable linguistic obstacles to translate the medical book *Tafel Anatomia* from Dutch into Japanese. This growing interest in Dutch and Western learning may not have undermined the Tokugawa feudal system, but it did represent a clear shift away from the prevailing Chinese intellectual hegemony.

The late 18th and early 19th centuries saw the achievement in Japan of a mass popular culture. This vibrant culture was evident by day in city and village schools, street entertainments, festivals, sightseeing and pilgrimages and by night in the pleasure quarters and entertainment districts. Nighttime entertainments (*yomise*), catering to urban populations of avid pleasure seekers, proliferated. The officially approved pleasure quarters of the Yoshiwara in Edo, Shinmachi in Osaka and Shimabara in Kyoto all throve on evening patrons. Moreover, because the Yoshiwara was a whole day's outing from Edo, and therefore an expensive proposition, some of the courtesans from the Yoshiwara brought their trade to their patrons in Edo where an assignation could be had for the equivalent of 20 or 30 dollars. Day and night the streets of Edo and other cities and towns offered cheap and popular entertainments.

By the early 19th century people were traveling more. Travel for pilgrimage and pleasure was all the rage. Pilgrims headed for sacred mountains like Fuji or Ontake; they visited the 88 temples of the Shikoku circuit or headed for Ise in their thousands and, in some years, millions. In an 1830 pilgrimage of thanks (*okage mairi*) 5 million pilgrims visited the Ise shrines within a few months. In the 1850s and 1860s the roads and city streets saw other expressions of mass elation and millennialism in the form of *ee ja nai kai* (ain't it grand?) and *yonaoshi* (world-restoring) movements. Many of the pilgrimages ended at local bars or brothels which sprang up at shrine and temple gates to beguile travelers. Those travelers who did not visit shrines or temples set out to view maples, cherry blossoms, famous sights or firework displays and other entertainments. To cater to this taste for travel, guidebooks to temples, shrines, pilgrimage routes and famous places were printed.

By the early 19th century Japan was becoming a more literate, mobile, affluent, entertainment-oriented society. In addition to the *han* schools, which brought education to the young samurai in most domains, private academies and one-room schools (*terakoya*) provided literacy and basic education for commoners in villages and towns. There were 800 teachers of calligraphy in Edo alone. Ronald Dore in his study of Tokugawa education has estimated that 43 percent of males and 10 percent of females had some schooling by the end of the Edo period. Whatever the precise percentage, it is clear that the basis for mass literacy, education and modern popular culture was solidly laid by the late Edo period.

Everyday Life in the Edo Period

Dramatists and storytellers, poets, printmakers and painters were all inspired by the vitality of the personalities and scenes of daily life they saw around them in urban society of the Edo period. The "Floating World" of the pleasure quarters, Kabuki theaters, downtown streets and riverbanks held a particularly powerful appeal. But artists were also stimulated by scenes along the highways or in the villages, and a small number of artists and printmakers reflected the constant hardships and occasional pleasures of the peasants who worked the fields and made up the bulk of the population. Edo society was increasingly literate and open to the diffusion of books and woodblock prints. The vigorous artistic and literary output of the period gives a far clearer view of everyday life and popular culture than we can gain for any preceding period.

Below Torii Kiyohira (fl. 1751–63), a member of the Torii school of printmakers, specialized in prints of Kabuki actors, erotic pictures (*shunga*) and scenes of everyday life. This fresh and youthful print captures what must have been a common child's pastime in gentle and universal terms.

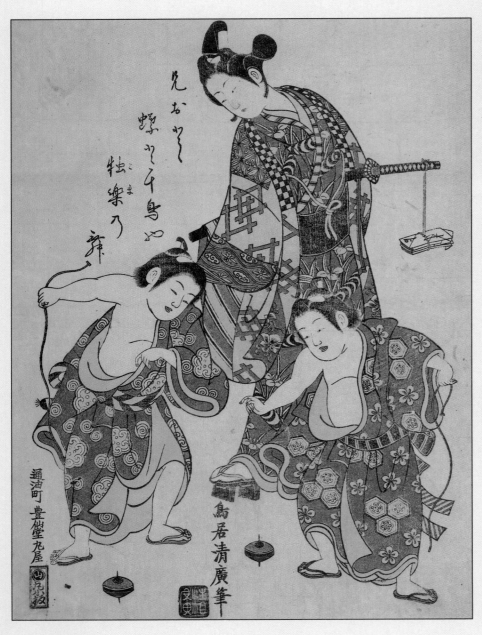

Above The Sumida River running through Edo was a place for entertainment. Along its banks were tea shops, drinking shops and houses of pleasure. On summer nights its waters reflected fireworks and festival lanterns. This print by Torii Kiyonaga (1752–1815) shows a typical pleasure boat carrying geisha and serving food and drink.

Left This unsigned print from a picture calendar for 1790 (year of the dog) shows an obviously impoverished doll maker in a crumbling workroom. He caters to the most popular local taste in making Daruma dolls and animals of the zodiac. Many masterless samurai (*rōnin*), with little or no stipend to depend on, were forced to take up simple crafts of this kind to eke out a living.

Right Shrines and temples throughout Japan held regular local festivals in which all the parishioners participated. This is one of "Five Scenes of the Spring Crossing Festival on the First Night of the Rat at Futaura Shrine in Shimotsuke Province," (c. 1815). "Shrine crossing" refers to the transporting at night of the gods of the shrine from one side of the precinct to the other as a protection against fire. The festival was held in the first and last months of the year.

Above Master of the scenes and moods of nature and of ordinary people engaged in everyday activities, Katsushika Hokusai (1760–1849) made many prints of travelers and pilgrims on the roads and mountain passes of Japan. His great work was the series "36 views of Fuji." This print, from an untitled series of stages of the Tōkaidō dated 1804, is entitled "Mitsuke: four *ri* and eight *chō* to Hamamatsu." The two travelers at the Mitsuke stage are eating millet noodles (*soba*), costing, according to the shop sign, 16 *mon* per bowl.

Japanese Ceramics

Far left From the mid-17th century the Dutch in Nagasaki began to buy Japanese porcelain to export to Southeast Asia and Europe. In particular they bought from potters in Arita (Kyushu) who had mastered Korean and Chinese techniques of making cobalt blue and white porcelain and overglaze enamel pigments. These wares were called Ko-Imari (old Imari) and Kakiemon. Kakiemon was admired for its whiteness, clear persimmon red and translucent glazes.

Japanese ceramics have an unbroken 10 000-year tradition behind them. Young potters are aware that they are heirs to this rich tradition as they reach for personal contemporary forms of artistic expression.

After the flamboyant vigor of Jōmon earthenware (p. 35) and the more symmetrical sophistication of Yayoi ware (p. 38), Japanese pottery tended to remain under the influence of Chinese and Korean potters for most stylistic and technical changes. By the mid-5th century Korean techniques for making high-fired ceramics were being incorporated. The Nara period saw the introduction and imitation of Tang dynasty lead-glazed three-color ware. While traditional earthenware continued to be produced in many medieval kilns, the vogue from the 13th century was for Song dynasty porcelains (*karamono*), introduced by Zen monks and traders. The late 16th and 17th centuries brought a great enrichment. The capture of Korean potters, who were to lay the basis of Edo period ceramics, the aesthetics of *wabi* and the popularity of the tea ceremony, the demands of *daimyō* and merchants and a growing urban population all contributed to an efflorescence of Japanese ceramics.

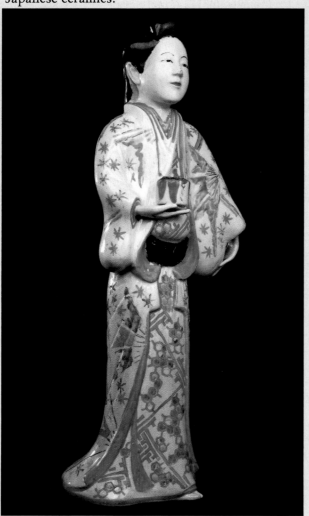

Left Kutani ware was produced principally in Kaga (Ishikawa Prefecture) from the mid-17th century under the patronage of the Maeda *daimyō* family. Kutani porcelains, usually decorated with overglaze, are of two major types—green Kutani and painted Kutani. This Kutani dish shows a design of Hotei, a Bodhisattva seen in human form as a rotund, smiling eccentric carrying a sack full of treasures.

Right The first orders by the Dutch for Arita porcelain were shipped to Europe in 1658. Japanese potters produced large quantities of blue and white ware, like this early 18th-century dish, in the Chinese Wanli style.

Below This incense burner, in the shape of a brilliantly plumaged pheasant overglazed with enamels, was created by Nonomura Ninsei, a Kyoto potter active in the mid-17th century. In his kiln at Ninnaji, a Kyoto temple, Ninsei produced a variety of ware ranging in style from single glaze pieces to highly decorated multi-colored enameled ware. Most of his pieces were made for the tea ceremony or tea-related meals.

Below right The innovative "informal" *wabi*-inspired tea style of Sen no Rikyū with its insistence on simplicity and naturalness called for ceramics that were quiet, unobtrusive and unsophisticated. This black tea bowl with a design of plum blossoms is attributed to an early 19th-century Raku master.

Below center Another type of ware much used in the tea ceremony is that produced in the Shino kilns of Mino Province from the 16th century. In this water jar of the Momoyama period decorated with a design of reeds touched by wind a triangular patch has been left unglazed.

Bottom Ceramics are highly appreciated and fine pieces fetch high prices in contemporary Japan. In this piece by Seto Hiroshi gold stripes undulate on a pale purple surface. Vases and other objects with crystal-glazed gold and silver stripes combine modern forms with traditional coloring and design motifs.

Netsuke

Western visitors to Japan in the 19th century were intrigued by the whimsical miniature, intricately carved, wood and ivory toggles (*netsuke*) and the elegantly decorated little medicine boxes (*inrō*) to which they were frequently attached. The Japanese kimono, held with a sash at the waist, was not provided with pockets. There were few places in which to keep such small personal belongings as tobacco pipes and pouches, seal boxes or medicine holders. These *inrō* were frequently slipped into the waist sash (*obi*) where they tended to slip unless anchored by a toggle.

By the late 17th century *netsuke*—still flat, simple toggles—were being carved and decorated. During the 18th century townsmen in Edo, Osaka and other cities looked for more elaborately carved *netsuke*. They were one means of flouting Bakufu sumptuary regulations against ostentation in dress. The *Sōken Kishō* (1781), by Inaba Tsūryū, an Osaka sword merchant, mentions 57 amateur and professional *netsuke* carvers, mainly in Osaka,

Kyoto, Edo and Nagoya. By the early 19th century, the great age of *netsuke* carving, many *netsuke* were being signed, as materials and themes became richer and more varied. While most *netsuke* were carved from ivory or wood, both of which developed a sheen in use, bone, lacquer and metal were also used.

Netsuke themes are limitless: a few are illustrated here. They include subjects from nature, Chinese legend, Japanese mythology, history and literature, Buddhism (including Zen), Shinto, and Noh and Kabuki.

Netsuke tended to become more humorous and expressive as ingenuity and novelty were emphasized. They were easily appreciated, amusing, relatively inexpensive and easy to transport. Large numbers were exported to private collections and museums in the West. The Meiji restoration, however, dealt a blow to traditional crafts and cultural interests, and changes in dress made *netsuke* and *inrō* increasingly redundant.

Center left The elegant ivory figure signed by Yoshimasa (c. 1800) depicts the legendary Chinese *kirin*, an auspicious creature and symbol of good fortune.

Center right This wooden carving on a Chinese theme depicts the dragon king of the sea as an old man bearing the tide jewel.

Center bottom This ivory Chinese lion (*karashishi*), clasping a jewel of omnipotence, is signed by Eijusai Masayoshi.

Bottom This 19th-century wooden *netsuke* by Masakatsu depicts a Chinese theme. The deity of scholastic attainment (Jurojin in Japanese) dozes comfortably in the company of his stag.

Below Bishamon Ten, guardian of the north, is one of the Buddhist heavenly kings guarding the four quarters of the universe. This piece, made of boxwood, is signed by Masanao.

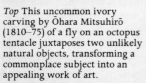

Top This uncommon ivory carving by Ōhara Mitsuhirō (1810–75) of a fly on an octopus tentacle juxtaposes two unlikely natural objects, transforming a commonplace subject into an appealing work of art.

Above The seated wild boar is carved in wood, with tusks inlaid in ivory. It is signed by Sakai Masakiyo. The coiled snake is signed by Shunchosai.

Right This carving by Tametaka of Owari (Nagoya) depicts an old drum that might once have summoned warriors to battle, monks to prayer or actors to their roles, now abandoned and used as a roosting place.

Left In this intricately carved ivory piece by Masahiro the popular seven gods of good fortune are depicted sailing in their dragon-headed treasure ship loaded with lucky charms.

Above The martial art (now the sport) of Kendō, the way of the sword, developed during the Edo period as a way of keeping samurai in training. This 19th-century fencer's mask, signed by Nagayasu, is unusual in being made of metal.

Above left This smiling attendant, signed by Yasumasa, is made of ivory and stained and inlaid.

Left In one famous incident Bodhidharma sat in meditation facing a wall for nine years until his legs atrophied and fell off. This gave rise to the roly-poly Daruma doll that springs back when pushed over.

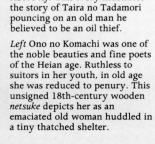

Above This ivory figure, signed by Mitsuhirō, depicts the magical monkey described in Wu Ch'eng-en's story *Monkey* who performs miracles to help his Buddhist priest friend.

Above left This ivory illustrates the story of Taira no Tadamori pouncing on an old man he believed to be an oil thief.

Left Ono no Komachi was one of the noble beauties and fine poets of the Heian age. Ruthless to suitors in her youth, in old age she was reduced to penury. This unsigned 18th-century wooden *netsuke* depicts her as an emaciated old woman huddled in a tiny thatched shelter.

Above Masks were a popular theme. This wooden Bugaku dance mask represents a gluttonous barbarian.

Above right Bodhidharma (Daruma) was the legendary Indian monk who brought Ch'an (Zen) to China. In one incident he is said to have crossed the Yangtze River on a reed. Here he is seen floating on a lotus leaf.

Right Nakasaina Sonja was one of the 16 ascetic disciples of the Buddha known as *rakan* in Japanese and usually depicted as eccentrics. This 20th-century wooden *netsuke* shows him holding a mysterious bowl from which water constantly flows.

The Floating World

Many of the world's great cities have pleasure districts, sections of town devoted to entertainment, gambling and prostitution. In some cities these are bleak, vicious and dangerous. In others they are harmless places of entertainment. The great cities of Tokugawa Japan all had their licensed quarters, frowned upon but tolerated by the authorities. Together with Kabuki theaters, street entertainments and sumo performances, these constituted the floating world of Tokugawa Japan.

In the floating world the normal order of society was rejected or turned upside down. Here the samurai's status gave precedence to the merchant's wealth; here the outcast Kabuki actors, rakes and courtesans were the arbiters of style and mores; and Confucian moral exhortations to frugality, order and rectitude were scorned. *Ninjō*, not *giri*, was the driving impulse, and Bakufu sumptuary regulations were flouted. The chroniclers of this world were the writers, painters, printmakers and authors of popular and risqué novelettes who fed, and whetted, an almost insatiable popular interest in the floating world.

Below This Genroku era print (c. 1730) by Mitsunobu shows a courtesan accosting a possible client in the geisha quarter. The spider's web motif on her kimono is no doubt a reference to her profession. Like many visitors to the pleasure quarter, the young man seems to be hiding his face under a hat.

Right The vortex of the floating world was the licensed quarter of Edo known as the Yoshiwara, originally established near Nihonbashi in the center of the city in 1618. It was razed in the great fire of 1657, rebuilt in an area to the north of Asakusa and renamed "New Yoshiwara" (Shin Yoshiwara). This print by Torii Kiyotada (fl. 1720–50) plays with perspective in showing courtesans and their patrons in the Daimojiya, one of the larger geisha houses. While a young courtesan relaxes with a pipe, two others play backgammon (*sugoroku*). Further in, other geisha are entertaining customers.

Far left Once an ancient ritual performed to please the gods, by mid-Edo sumo wrestling had become a professional sport and mass entertainment. Several tournaments were held each year in temporary stadiums erected in the Edo'in temple and other sites. The best of the wrestlers were as famous as great Kabuki actors or celebrated geisha and drew a passionate following. Utagawa Kunimasa (1723–1810) concentrated on portraits of actors, beautiful women and wrestlers.

Left These two courtesans are the work of Kitagawa Utamarō (1754–1806), perhaps the most celebrated print artist of the demimonde.

Above This portrait by Haga Isshō shows the writer and poet Ihara Saikaku in his later years. A witty chronicler, and shaper, of the floating world and its aesthetic, Saikaku recorded astringently the twin passions—of love and money—that drove the Genroku urbanite. Like Chikamatsu, he explored the tensions between duty (*giri*) and human feeling (*ninjō*) and showed the darker as well as the lighter side of urban society.

Above left Many printmakers produced stylized, brilliantly colored prints of individual actors in roles and poses for which they were famous. In this print by Utagawa Kunimasa the actor Ichikawa Ebizō is shown in the Shibaraku role.

Pilgrimage and Travel

The map on page 86 looked at pilgrimage in the Heian period. Over the centuries more pilgrimage sites and circuits were added. Peace, prosperity, better communications, all contributed to an upsurge of travel and pilgrimage in the Edo period. Although the Tokugawa Bakufu restricted travel, pilgrimage was treated more leniently. Many townspeople and villagers therefore combined pilgrimage with pleasure. Having visited a sacred temple or shrine, they felt free to indulge in the pleasures of food, drink and sex liberally available near most famous shrines and temples. For many the spiritual exercise of pilgrimage was very much secondary to the companionship of the road and the more mundane pleasures found along the way.

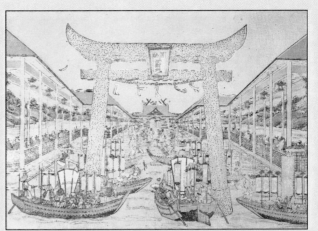

Left The island shrine of Itsukushima with its great red *torii* standing in the waters of the Inland Sea was one of the great sights of Japan. This print by Utagawa Toyoharu (1735–1814) shows pilgrims and pleasure seekers in boats thronging the shrine at the festival of Benten.

Below Ise, regarded as the most sacred shrine in Japan, easily became the greatest single pilgrimage site during the Edo period. This Ise mandala shows the inner and outer shrines with pilgrims purifying themselves and offering prayers at the shrines.

PART THREE
MODERN JAPAN

THE MEIJI RESTORATION AND ITS LEGACY

The restoration of imperial rule

The announcement of the "restoration" of imperial rule in January of 1868 brought to an end a decade of controversy over management of foreign relations. The first stage had seen a strong reassertion of shogunal prerogatives with the insistence of Ii Naosuke on ratification of the commercial treaty negotiated by Townsend Harris in 1858. Opponents of the Tokugawa policy had clustered around the imperial court and tried to use its authority to tie ratification of that treaty to the candidacy of Hitotsubashi Keiki in a succession dispute within the shogunate. Ii Naosuke's strong-arm methods in the purge that followed had led to his assassination in 1860. Thereafter, Tokugawa leaders had vacillated with attempts to work out a political consensus by conciliating and incorporating some of the great lords in advisory positions. That process opened the way for competition between those lords. The middle years of the 1860s saw Satsuma, Chōshū and Tosa put forward successive proposals for reconstruction, each more favorable to the cause of the imperial court—and to themselves. As shogunal officials countered with displays of loyalty to the imperial court, and then with punishment of Chōshū for its temerity in daring to try to seize the gates to the imperial palace in 1864, Tokugawa primacy began at last to be challenged. Tokugawa house vassals, bewildered by the shifting policies of their superiors, sought safety in inaction. Shogunal calls to restore the *sankin-kōtai* system of attendance, which had been relaxed in 1862, went unobserved a few years later, and cooperation against Chōshū, available in 1864–65, was lacking in 1866. The need to incorporate the imperial court in a larger role seemed clear, and when the shogun was advised to surrender his office in 1867, he agreed, expecting to retain his relative importance in a new and more collegial political structure. Events proved him wrong, as his rivals outmaneuvered him to obtain an "imperial" authorization to punish him as an "enemy" of the court. The Boshin Civil War, in which "imperial" armies of Satsuma, Chōshū and Tosa marched through Tokugawa domains, came to an end in late spring of 1869.

The stormy politics of that decade brought to an end the 268 years of Tokugawa dominance. But they had settled very little else. Japan was not in social tumult, for the warfare was carried out by samurai against samurai. The cities and countryside were quiet, and revenue continued to be extracted as before. Yet there was also economic disorder. The years 1866 and 1869 saw large-scale crop failures which resulted in conditions of desperate want in many areas. This was worsened by the demands of rapacious armies moving across the land. Combined with runaway inflation of the 1860s, this helped produce tremulous fears and hopes of betterment, shown in the eruption of a number of popular rumors of "world renewal."

The most remarkable of these was touched off by rumors of the mysterious appearance of magic portents, usually on the premises of propertied persons. The celebration of such happy portents led to expectations of shared good fortune and erupted in a carnival spirit of dancing, celebrating and drinking that distinguished the "*ee ja nai kai*" (ain't it grand?) movement from more angry and destructive expressions of unease.

In some areas representatives of the "imperial" armies that moved against the Tokugawa held out hopes of greatly diminished tax levies to the peasant leaders they encountered, and facts and rumors of such promises undoubtedly contributed to a flurry of hope and optimism. In the event, of course, such hopes were soon dashed, and popular teachers and preachers who predicted a bright new world were soon morose and disappointed. More serious was the fact that the violence of samurai warfare directly damaged the welfare of the commoners who did not participate. When Chōshū units failed in their effort to control the gates to the imperial precincts in Kyoto in 1864, their violence touched off fires that laid much of the ancient city

Although "civilization and enlightenment," Western dress, trains and other changes swept into downtown Tokyo and Yokohama in the wake of the Meiji restoration, the lives of ordinary Japanese in towns and villages were not transformed overnight and there was considerable rural hardship and protest.

Right Until the Meiji restoration Buddhism and Shinto were inextricably intertwined. Through the dual Shinto (Ryōbu Shinto) synthesis, Buddhist deities and Buddhist clergy dominated many shrines. Under pressure from Shinto advocates and looking for the basis for an emperor-centered national religion, the Meiji government ordered the separation of Shinto and Buddhism after 1868. Throughout the late 19th and early 20th centuries the Japanese government sought to realize the ancient ideal of *Saisei itchi* (unity of religious ritual and government administration) using Shinto to enhance belief in the divinity of the emperor and the uniqueness of Japan's "national polity" (*kokutai*). The formal structure of state Shinto was created in 1871 when the government decreed that: (1) shrines were places for the observance of "national rites"; (2) priests were to be government functionaries; (3) all citizens must register at local shrines. This photograph, taken around 1900, shows two Shinto priests, one of whom is carrying a portable shrine.

waste. It was so in each city visited by warfare in the years that followed. In Aizu Wakamatsu, a particular target of the restoration armies, the defenders first fired the entire city in order to free themselves from the inconvenience of the commoner presence. This continued to be true in cities visited by samurai disturbances into the 1870s, resulting in the verdict of the restoration leader Kido Takayoshi that townspeople in Hagi were so indignant with a samurai leader who had led an 1876 insurrection that if "Maebara is treated leniently, the people in Hagi castletown are saying that they want to behead him themselves." Everywhere, in the aftermath of the Boshin War, there was fear of more destructive violence to come. The Satsuma-Chōshū dominance had settled nothing, and there was fear of a falling out between Satsuma and Chōshū as well.

Such misgivings were well founded. The political coup that ousted the shogun from the power structure did nothing to provide an alternative structure. Satsuma and Chōshū leaders had been rivals far longer than they had been allies. As allies they were widely mistrusted in many parts of Japan; much of the resistance to the imperial armies in the Boshin War had been motivated by that distrust. In northeast Japan a coalition of *daimyō* led by Date of Sendai had in fact asserted their loyalty to the imperial house, while justifying their military resistance by suspicion of the southerners. Often, though, the announced intentions of the new regime to honor Japan's commitments to the foreign powers resulted in recriminations and threats of violence against the presumed leaders of the new regime. Several outstanding samurai statesmen of late Tokugawa days were assassi-

nated. Yokoi Shōnan, one of the most influential of the group, was accused by his murderer of pro-Western inclinations and killed in 1869. Hirosawa Saneomi, a leading Chōshū figure, met his end in 1871. For at least a decade no major restoration figure lived without the threat of assassination. Kido Takayoshi several times arrived at his appointed place to find his hosts had heard rumors that he had been killed on his way there.

The Charter Oath of April 1868

In the face of this uncertainty the leaders moved cautiously to utilize the numinous aura of the boy emperor Mutsuhito. On 6 April 1868 a five-point promise was issued in his name that became known as the Charter Oath. Phrased with generality and designed to minimize resistance among the *daimyō*, it promised fairness and change in the pursuit of national objectives:

(1) Deliberative assemblies shall be widely established and all matters decided by public discussion.

(2) All classes, high and low, shall unite in vigorously carrying out the administration of affairs of state.

(3) The common people, no less than the civil and military officials, shall each be allowed to pursue his own calling so that there may be no discontent.

(4) Evil customs of the past shall be broken off and everything based upon the just laws of nature.

(5) Knowledge shall be sought throughout the world so as to strengthen the foundations of imperial rule.

This remarkable document was worked out by a small group of restoration leaders in successive drafts. It was meant for the elite (at the same time edicts told ordinary commoners to continue to observe instructions on notice boards as before) and yet it had provision that would become meaningful for "the common people, no less than the civil and military officials." It promised change and improvement (who could not be against "evil customs of the past"?) but specified little, and reassured the feudality that "assemblies" in which matters would be "decided by public discussion" would find their opinions heard. The "search for knowledge . . . throughout the world" gave promise of a system that would "strengthen the foundations of imperial rule" and end the peculiarities of Japan's divided authority structure which pre-restoration petitions had repeatedly deplored as an embarrassment and reproach. Everything was promised, but nothing was specified.

Four years later Kido Takayoshi found himself in Washington, D.C., as a member of a commission "seeking knowledge throughout the world." When he found the mission's scribe struggling to translate the American Constitution, he remarked that Japan needed a document of that sort too. Kume, the scribe, reminded him of the Charter Oath, to which Kido had contributed; after reading it again, Kido was exhilarated to discover the broader relevance of what must have seemed, at the time it was issued, a temporary palliative for feudal alarm. In the decades after World War II the emperor Hirohito also drew attention to his grandfather's promises as justification for the democratization of Japan's political institutions. Clearly the generality of the phrasing helped give the docu-

Above Beset by the Western powers demanding to open the country and by pro-imperial voices to drive off the barbarians, the Tokugawa Bakufu reluctantly entered into a network of unfavorable treaty relations in 1858. From 1860 the Bakufu sent several embassies to the West to try to negotiate more favorable treaty terms or to obtain new technological knowledge. This photograph shows the first embassy to Paris in 1862-63; 38 samurai, led by Takeuchi Yasunori, were sent to ask for an extension of the opening of the ports of Edo, Osaka, Hyōgo and Niigata. These Bakufu embassies gave young scholars such as Fukuzawa Yukichi (1835–1901), who joined the first embassies to the United States and Paris, and Fukuchi Gen'ichirō (1841–1906, standing fourth from the right) their first introductions to Western culture.

scale 1:6 000 000

0	150km
0	100mi

Chōshū forces repel Bakufu sorties July – Dec 1864 Aug 1866 – Apr 1865

Ezo
Goryōkaku 27 June 1869
Hakodate
Takeaki resists imperial forces 20 Oct 1868 – 18 May 1869
Matsumae

Tsugaru
Hirosaki 15 July
Hachinohe

Nambu

Satake
Akita 4 July
Morioka 24 Sept

Sakata
Ichinoseki

Sakai
Mogami

Shōnai 27 Sept
Date

Sakai
Yamagata
Sendai 15 Sept

Murakami
Sōma 6 Aug

Uesugi
Yonezawa 29 July
Fukushima

Hoshina
Wakamatsu 6 Nov

Shirakawa

Iwaki 24 Jun

Nikkō
Utsunomiya

Tokugawa
Mito

Sado

Aikawa
Niigata

Kamo

Kanazawa
Toyama
Nagano
Ashikaga

Maeda
KAGA
Maebashi

Maeda
KAGA
Matsumoto
Ueda

Fukui
Matsudaira ECHIZEN

Tokugawa

Edo 11 Apr July 1868 renamed Tokyo
Kamakura

Ogaki
Tokugawa OWARI
Nagoya
Shizuoka

Oki

Ii
Hikone
Shimoda

Tottori
Matsue

Ikeda

Kyoto 3 Jan
Fushimi 27 Jan 1868
Hamamatsu

Sakakibara
Himeji
Osaka
Tsu
Matsuzaka

Ikeda
Okayama
Nara
Sakai

Asano AKI
Nichihara
Hiroshima
Iwakuni

Sō

Tsushima

Hagi
Mōri CHŌSHŪ
Shimonoseki
Kitakyushu

Tokushima
Hachisuka

Yamanouchi TOSA
Kōchi

Tōdō ANOTSU

Tokugawa

Wakayama

Iki

Kuroda
Fukuoka
Kurume
Hita

Hirado

Arima
Saga
Nabeshima HIZEN
Hosokawa

Gotō Is
Nagasaki
Kumamoto

Shimazu SATSUMA
Miyazaki

Kagoshima

Tanegashima

Yaku

—	route of imperial army
—	major domain boundary
Ikeda	important *daimyō* house
KAGA	domain name if different from castle town

domains

	Tokugawa - governed
	fudai (Tokugawa-related)
	tozama (outside *daimyō*)
	alliance against Bakufu

•	castle town
3 Jan	date of capture by imperial forces, 1868
✗	battle, with date
●	castle town sending troops to imperial army
●	castle town joining Bakufu league
Osaka	town with Bakufu officials

A giant of a man by Japanese standards, Saigō Takamori (1827–77) earned the respect of friends and foes alike by means of his role in the Meiji restoration and his concern for the plight of samurai. When his Korean proposals were rejected, he returned to Satsuma where he became the reluctant leader of the Satsuma rebellion (1877). In death he became a paragon of selfless devotion and national idealism.

Left: Overthrow of the Tokugawa shogunate
The series of battles in 1868–69 that brought about the military defeat of the Tokugawa shogunate and the restoration of imperial rule is generally known as the Boshin War (for the year Boshin in the sexagenary cycle). On 3 January 1868 a pro-imperial alliance led by Satsuma and Chōshū forces seized the imperial palace in Kyoto and proclaimed an imperial restoration. Bakufu troops, trying to dislodge them, were defeated at the battle of Fushimi on 27 January. They then fell back to defend Shogun Yoshinobu and Edo. Under an agreement worked out by Saigō Takamori of Satsuma and the Bakufu official Katsu Kaishū Edo surrendered peacefully. In northern Honshu an alliance of 31 pro-Bakufu domains resisted throughout the summer and fall of 1868. This resistance was crushed with the defeat of Aizu domain on 6 November at Wakamatsu. A pro-Bakufu fleet of eight warships commanded by Enomoto Takeaki continued resistance in Hokkaido (which Enomoto declared a "republic") until June 1869. With the conclusion of hostilities the whole country came under the control of the new imperial government. The problems of paying for the war and dealing with the feudal structure of *daimyō* domains remained to be dealt with.

ment enduring importance in Japanese political life and imagination.

The leaders used the emperor's person as well as his words. The young sovereign was carried about as a totem in grand imperial processions to acquaint his subjects with his person and to acquaint him with his people. As the modern state solidified, he was increasingly restricted to his palaces and grounds, "above the clouds," but in the formative years of the regime and particularly its first decade grand regional tours and frequent local excursions—a total of 693—made him a silent participant in the struggle to "strengthen the foundations of imperial rule." The emerging press lent its efforts to the task. As late as 1881 the *Yomiuri* had to lecture its readers that "Tomorrow, the third, is *Tenchō setsu. Tenchō setsu* is the birthday of Japan's emperor, his majesty Mutsuhito. Formerly the shogun ruled our country, but now it is different . . . everybody must be joyous, for it is a great holiday . . . There are a good many people who do not know the name of Tenchi Sama. But to be born in this country and not to know it is like not knowing your parents' age. This is unforgivable. It must be carefully remembered . . ."

The aura of the court was from the first a central factor in the young regime's ability to secure cooperation from the high feudality, and in time it became its greatest lever in securing the cooperation and obedience of Japan's commoners.

Political centralization

The most visible and enduring result of the Meiji restoration was administrative centralization. The samurai leaders who brought the restoration about did not have a fixed plan for centralization, and in the early stages of their work it would have been dangerous to reveal it even if they had had one. But they did have a sense of what Japan needed if it was to maintain its sovereignty in a world dominated by nation-states. The adoption of the era name "Meiji" (enlightened rule) and establishment of a national capital (Tokyo) at the shogun's castle city of Edo were early announcements of a plan to modernize political institutions.

The assertion of rule by the emperor was necessarily a significant step toward centralization, for it implied an end to the extremes of political parcelization of the Tokugawa Bakufu system. The saliency of the problem of foreign relations, dramatized by the presence of foreign garrisons in the treaty ports that had been established by the Harris and later treaties, also served to heighten the sense of a single "Japan" which had to confront *gaikoku*, "outside countries."

Victory in the Boshin War of 1868–69 did not of itself, however, lead to immediate centralization. That victory eliminated the main Tokugawa house from further political competition, but the new regime kept only the main Tokugawa *tenryō* as its own "territory." It even reestablished the Tokugawa house—under new leadership—as lord of a domain, albeit drastically reduced in territory. Tokugawa vassals scrambled to dissociate themselves from the former shogun's cause and condemnation, and vied with other *daimyō* in protestations of imperial loyalty. The overwhelming military predominance of Satsuma and Chōshū, the restoration fiefs of the southwest, raised suspicions that

they might have shogunal ambitions of their own. The restoration as such, in short, left the institutions of late Tokugawa feudalism intact.

Partly to allay suspicions of their motives, and partly to reduce the military responsibilities that were beginning to weigh heavily on their treasuries, the restoration domains of the southwest petitioned the court to accept the return of their feudal registers in 1869. Satsuma, Chōshū and Tosa leaders persuaded those of Hizen to join them and urged their *daimyō* to join their number and present the throne with a joint memorial. "The abode where we the undersigned dwell is the sovereign's land," they wrote. "The people over whom we rule are his people. Why should we privately own them? We pray that the imperial government, according to its judgment, give what should be given and take what should be taken away . . . and also that all the regulations, from the ordering of laws, institutions and military affairs . . . issue from the imperial government." That done, the empire would "stand beside the foreign powers." This still did not mean an end to domains; the document requested the court to reallocate where appropriate, and to unify administration, all for the sake of enabling Japan to conform with international practice. Other *daimyō* saw themselves outmaneuvered once again, and rushed to present their own petitions, many insisting that they had long been planning to do so. Kido Takayoshi, in a diary notation, asserted that this should now provide a sure foundation for the *daimyō* houses.

The court accepted these petitions in July 1869 and immediately reappointed the *daimyō* as governors of the areas they had ruled as feudal lords. The change in their status, however, provided the logic for directives to make administration more uniform. One tenth of domain revenue was set aside for the private needs of the *daimyō*-come-governors, and standardization of administration, which had begun with regulations issued in 1868, was now increased. These steps toward centralization justified a change in nomenclature: the new "governors" were joined with the old court nobility (*kuge*) in a new class to be designated *kazoku*. Additional instructions arranged domains in categories of income.

It would seem that the next step, to do away with domains altogether, was by now preordained, but distrust made it impolitic to advocate this openly. Leaders of the restoration domains returned to their home territory to carry out reforms on a local level; the sweeping nature of steps like those in Chōshū, where samurai stipends were lowered, subdivisions were abandoned and samurai were permitted to enter agriculture or commerce, gave some indication of what lay ahead. Similarly the central government moved faster in its limited territory, the core Tokugawa lands, than it did in national pronouncements. In addition 13 of the 260-odd domains also petitioned to be absorbed into the "imperial" domain, usually citing insoluble fiscal difficulties. "Public expenditures," one petition read, "have grown larger and larger; there is no conceivable way to meet the crisis, and the people's cries for relief fill the air; we humbly request the imperial government to extend its rule over us."

Born in 1852, Mutsuhito, the Meiji emperor, was still a very young man when he came to the throne in 1867 and was swept up in the Meiji restoration. With the overthrow of the Tokugawa Bakufu by the forces of Chōshū, Satsuma and Tosa, the young emperor and his court moved to Tokyo to become the numinous leader of the new regime. Although he did not exercise great personal power within the Meiji oligarchy, he was directly involved in many of the most significant political events of his reign including the promulgation of the Charter Oath, the rescripts for Education and Soldiers and Sailors, and the Imperial Constitution which elevated his authority while opening the door for representative government. His death in 1912 was seen as the close of an era, and prompted the suicides of General Nogi Maresuke and his wife.

In January 1871 the restoration fief military leaders merged their armed forces to form a 10 000-man imperial guard. Eight months later, in August, the domains were declared abolished, and new administrative units, in steadily declining numbers and increasing size, were pronounced "prefectures." *Haihan chiken*, abolition of domains and establishments of prefectures, was hailed by some of its proponents as "a second Meiji restoration." Preparation and lobbying for it had been led by second-level administrative and military leaders from the restoration centers, men who cautiously approached, persuaded and assisted the major restoration statesmen. Some leaders on the national central scene, notably Iwakura Tomomi, were not even aware of these plans until shortly before they matured. However logical and, in long-range terms, inevitable, the step was carried out cautiously and skillfully.

Each of these steps brought with it increased responsibility for the central government. Naming *daimyō* as governors brought them appointment and designation as *kazoku*, and responsibility for all domains brought the government responsibility for their samurai. Those worthies soon found themselves part of a new class designated as "gentry" (*shizoku*), and those of lower military rank as *sotsu*. Before long *sotsu* merged with *shizoku* and this large and expensive, non-productive military class became a major problem for the new regime.

Composition of the new government

As the central government grew in power and importance, its makeup changed as well. At first, when the need for cooperation was greatest, a generous infusion of high court nobles and mighty *daimyō* held leading posts. The samurai leaders of the restoration fiefs, their numbers augmented by particularly congenial or able men they coopted from other areas, contented themselves with secondary titles. Early documents like the Charter Oath made much of shared decision making and "general discussion," and domains were ordered to station representatives in Tokyo to represent their lords with suggestions and relay directives. As the government gained in territory and confidence, there was less need and room for symbolic figureheads and greater opportunity for the leaders of the southwestern domains. Formal abolition of their home domains made it possible for them to turn their attention more exclusively to problems at the center. Some of their erstwhile colleagues returned home in dissatisfaction, reproaching them with disloyalty to their lord and fief, and some of the lords who held office in early months withdrew voluntarily, realizing that the future lay with active participants and not titled aristocrats. The government gradually became less open, more assertive and authoritarian, quicker to override local demands and expectations. Upon the dissolution of domains the central government managed to avoid almost completely the appointment of samurai to high prefectural posts in their native areas. This was true even of Chōshū (though not of Satsuma), where the first appointive governor was a former Tokugawa retainer.

In addition to military and bureaucratic superiority the government mobilized tradition in the cause of modernization. With the return of the registers in August 1869 it established a state structure modeled on that of 8th-century Nara Japan. The *Dajōkan* (Council of State) established at that time remained in authority until the modern cabinet system was established in 1885. The Shinto claims surrounding the young emperor made it seem appropriate to sponsor a state religion. A Bureau of Shinto, established to confirm the link between the Sun Goddess and her imperial descendant, gave the regime and its pronouncements a theocratic cast; from 1869 to 1871 the Bureau was above even the Council of State. With the progress of administrative modernization, however, it could safely be downgraded, and it ended as a subdivision in the Ministry of Home Affairs in 1877—significantly, the last date the regime was seriously threatened by rebellion.

The Council of State was first headed by the court noble Sanjō Sanetomi, who later gave way in 1874 to Iwakura Tomomi, as Minister of the Right. Below them and four *dainagon* (imperial nobles) were the actual decision makers, samurai councillors from Satsuma (Ōkubo Toshimichi), Chōshū (Hirosawa, then Kido Takayoshi), Saga (Soejima Taneomi, then Ōkuma Shigenobu). The conscious use of nomenclature of the Nara court led the samurai officials to adopt for a time names redolent of an earlier age: Ōkubo Toshimichi, for instance, styled himself Fujiwara Ason ("imperial servant") Toshimichi. Court ranks of an earlier age were recreated to arrange those so honored in the nine ranks utilized in Tang China, designations that survived the creation of the new European-style nobility of 1885 and endured until the end of World War II.

The samurai at the center thus managed to raise their own influence and status steadily, utilizing antiquity and the sovereign, to carry out measures of centralization in a remarkably short time. Localism remained for a generation, of course. In some areas it exploded in violent resistance, while in others it could be extinguished by administrative amalgamation and threats of force. Nonetheless, with domains abolished and private *daimyō* armies disbanded it became possible to take further steps to enable Japan to "stand beside the foreign powers" as a modern nation-state.

The end of warrior rule

The Meiji restoration was brought about by a coalition of samurai leaders of southwestern domains who allied with court nobles to outmaneuver the Tokugawa Bakufu. Their victory was assured when their army units proved better prepared, motivated and led than those of the Tokugawa vassals. The new government, utilizing the aura of the emperor and harnessing the waning prestige of parts of the high feudality, was led by samurai administrators who had learned to govern in the restoration domains. For a generation *shizoku* dominated Meiji Japan. Yet during that same period the samurai, hereditary military who had held the reins of power since the 11th century, were systematically disestablished. Hereditary income was first reduced and then replaced by a one-time grant of interest-bearing bonds. Samurai swords, long a badge of honor and of class, were put away as heirlooms. The samurai monopoly of violence symbolized by those swords came to an end; security and military services were transferred to new conscript forces. Samurai perquisites of legal status, dress, surnames and forms of address disappeared in the new egalitarianism of a largely single-class society conveyed by the slogan "one ruler, 10 000 subjects."

That this was possible tells a great deal about the faltering prestige and real position of samurai in late Tokugawa society. Marooned with fixed incomes in a sea of rising fortunes and expectations, the relative well-being of the military had declined over time. Military skills, sharpened in the warfare that preceded Tokugawa rule, had dulled during the long inactivity of centuries of peace. Administration and cultural pursuits had motivated the best of the samurai, but the large majority had fallen on indolence and pointless punctilio in a setting of idleness. The irrationality of overstaffed administrations had created a setting in which few had more than a day of "duty" a week. Meanwhile peacetime commerce and productive agriculture had produced commoners whose leaders were as well educated as, and more independent and more enterprising than their military betters. Throughout Japan expectations of justice and fairness brought outbreaks of demonstrations and resistance when samurai administrators tried to solve their own problems at the expense of others through higher levies of tax and corvée. As Western weapons reappeared in the rearmament programs that followed the opening of

Japan, several of the domains had experimented with mixed commoner-samurai military units and found the commoners easier to train and drill than samurai. International example too showed the advantages of popular participation in military preparations. It seemed better to mobilize a "nation of samurai" than to trust things to samurai alone. Foreign example served to reinforce indigenous gropings, expressed in "practical learning" Confucianism and the personal morality of popular religion, toward separating the samurai ideal of service from the samurai in person.

The way this transition was brought about illustrates the caution and practicality of the new leaders. After the dissolution of the domains the government first assumed responsibility for all samurai stipends. It was soon clear that this burden set limits on its ability to sponsor reforms. The government tried a mix of steps, reducing pensions, then grouping them; it taxed larger incomes, offered optional commutation, and finally in 1876 ordered commutation into interest-bearing bonds in the hope that the former retainers would convert their hereditary privileges into constructive enterprises in the new society. In 1876, the year in which commutation was decreed, samurai were forbidden to wear their swords. What had been compulsory was now illegal. By the end of the

century popular moralists like Nitobe Inazō were praising the samurai code of Bushidō as a lofty set of standards for personal conduct comparable to Western chivalry, but in early Meiji years government leaders more often took a dim view of their erstwhile peers. Some, to be sure, thought the government was moving too fast and niggardly in its treatment of a class that had served so long, but most felt that their fellow samurai were being obstructive and troublesome.

One alternative to dismissing the samurai was, of course, to use them in warfare. Korea seemed to offer such an opportunity. The limits of "Japan" in Tokugawa times had not been clear-cut. Satsuma ruled Okinawa, but managed to have it continue its tributary relationship with China in order to carry on trade. A Tokugawa vassal named Matsumae was responsible for the northern island of Hokkaido, but quite incapable of preparing for a stronger Russian advance on Sakhalin and through the Kurils. The lord of Tsushima carried out trade with Korea, but accepted a patterned inequality for a trading station at Pusan.

The Korea case loomed largest. It had become an issue within the Tokugawa administration as early as the mid-1860s. If the foreign presence at all the edges of Japanese territory was to be offset, Japan would require clear-cut understandings with its

The Satsuma rebellion of 1877 was the last major armed uprising protesting the reforms of the new Meiji government, especially those reforms disestablishing the samurai class, ending their social privileges, reducing their income and curtailing their traditional way of life. Many Satsuma samurai left the government with Saigō in 1873, resentful over the rejection of Saigō's policy of invading Korea and angry at the process of reform that seemed to reject their interests. Rebellion erupted in January 1877 and lasted until Saigō's suicide in September. According to legends of the day, as visualised here, Kyushu women armed themselves with pikes to take on government forces.

neighbors. The new Meiji government thus sent a mission to Korea to inform it of the change of regime in Japan, cancel the arrangements that had existed between Korea and the Tokugawa vassal lord of Tsushima, and establish direct, state-to-state relations. The Koreans wanted none of this, but informed the Japanese that if they chose to behave like the West, with formal diplomatic treaties, then they would have to be grouped with barbarians and excluded. This response inflamed samurai leaders who, tired of their long subservience to the West, wanted to force the issue. Not the least attractive aspect of the opportunity was the possibility of using the restless and unproductive warriors. By 1873 it had been decided by the leaders in Tokyo to try to resolve the matter. Saigō Takamori, the greatest of the military leaders of the restoration, proposed that he be sent as emissary to Korea to settle things one way or another. Should he be slain or even insulted, Japan would have a clear cause for action.

Within months this decision was overturned by other leaders who were returning from a tour of the world to carry out the Charter Oath's promises to "seek wisdom throughout the world." Conscious of the gap in national strength between Japan and the powers, the returnees argued that an expedition to Korea was premature and could benefit only rapacious European powers who would deny Japan the fruits of any success and appropriate them for themselves. This argument carried the day, but important sectors of the samurai leadership retired in protest against what they saw as arbitrary and unresponsive government. They remained unmollified when the government carried out an expedition against Taiwan the following year (thereby establishing Japan's claim to Okinawa) to punish aborigines for the murder of Ryukyu fishermen.

The possibility of combining personal resentment and dissatisfaction with charges that national honor had been violated triggered some of the largest expressions of samurai discontent the new regime would know. Discontent flared most sharply in restoration domains, where samurai expectations of continued prominence had been highest. In the north the warfare of the restoration had served to reduce *shizoku* expectations. After the split in the government over Korean policy, however, several revolts were led by disgruntled members of the core leadership group. In 1874 Etō Shimpei led a rising by the "Punish Korea Party" in Saga; in 1876 similar risings were crushed in Chōshū (Hagi) and Kyushu (Akitsuki and Kumamoto), and in 1877 the restoration hero Saigō Takamori organized and led a large-scale *shizoku* rising in Satsuma that taxed the military capabilities of the young government to their very limits.

Saigō's failure marked the highwater mark of samurai opposition, and his inability to prevail meant that no other group or locality would try. The *shizoku* risings were rooted in feudal localism, and not at all coordinated. Resentful of lost class privileges, the samurai were incapable of recruiting no less resentful elements of the commoner population. In the extreme case of the Kumamoto "Divine Wind" rising, the rebels even refused to utilize guns in a futile effort to retain the mystique of the samurai sword. The Satsuma rising, by its size and

location, presented the government with its sternest challenge. No domain had a higher proportion of samurai, and no samurai population had more militaristic predispositions and higher morale. Consequently government units, fighting at great distance from their supply centers, found it necessary to supplement their numbers with those of the fledgling police units and even to recruit in other areas of Japan which had only recently felt the edge of Satsuma victory in restoration warfare. Fortunately for the government, it had superior communications and superior tactics. Saigō, who died by his own hand, would later be posthumously pardoned, restored to his honors and reemerge to stand as a hero of modern Japanese militarism and nationalism.

Legislation for conscription and education

If samurai were not to do Japan's fighting, others would. Conscription legislation was announced late in 1872 and implemented the following year. Participation of commoners—usually younger sons of village leaders—had been tried by a number of domains before the restoration, and at the very end the Bakufu itself was considering a tax on samurai stipends in order to defray the costs of commoner military formations. Western models of well-trained commoner units provided additional spur to such steps. The Franco-Prussian War of 1870–71 found several restoration leaders in Europe, and on their return they contrasted the high sense of participation shown by Parisian citizens in the defense of their city with the indifference most Japanese commoners had shown during the restoration warfare. Clearly, they argued, the path to national safety in the violent international environment Japan had entered lay in educating and training ordinary people so that Japan could become a "nation in arms" instead of relying on a class with arms. Tradition, too, could be cited, for ancient Japan had peasant conscripts when its institutions were modeled on those of China.

Japanese conscription legislation, like that of France on which it was based, exempted first sons (the Japanese added adopted sons as well) in order to avoid damage to the integrity of the family system. Exemptions could also be purchased. The need was not for a large force, however, and since volunteer recruits were also accepted, it was some time before conscription was really important. During the 1870s conscripts made up only about 3 percent of men in the appropriate age cohorts. After the suppression of the Satsuma Rebellion the government's needs were for the most part the suppression of farmer protests which flared in the confusion of the early land tax revision. As institutional changes began to bear fruit later, Japanese leaders could think about larger units and challenges. Not until the 1890s, with the completion of the constitutional order, was the government ready to deal with problems of Korea once more. From that point on military expenditures rose rapidly. In the meantime an officer corps, largely samurai-based, had been built and trained. The samurai tradition guaranteed that bearing arms in the emperor's service would continue to bulk large in Japanese consciousness.

Meanwhile national strength required the participation of an educated populace. In 1872 the

Fundamental Code of Education laid out a grid of eight university districts and 32 middle school districts, each with 210 primary schools. For many years it was the lower levels of this plan that mattered, but the ringing tones of the Code left no doubt of the importance attached to the measure. "Learning is the key to success in life," it announced, "and no man can afford to neglect it. It is ignorance that leads man astray, makes him destitute, disrupts his family and in the end destroys his life." In the past, it went on, learning had been too much the prerogative of the samurai, and even "the samurai and his superiors who did pursue learning were apt to claim it to be for the state, not knowing that it was the very foundation of success in life." This had been due to "our evil traditions." Hereafter "every man shall, of his own accord, subordinate all other matters to the education of his children."

Support for and content of that education continued to be debated for the better part of two decades. When local education taxes supplemented the land tax, farmers complained, and when textbooks seemed too liberal, conservatives complained that the aims of the state were being sacrificed. Ultimately the system received its formative guidance from Minister of Education Mori Arinori, a Satsuma samurai who held that post from 1885 until his assassination by a reactionary in 1889. Mori held out the prospect of a system that would produce a highly disciplined and motivated citizenry. Central to this was a teacher corps that would be educated in normal schools which were to stress a sense of discipline and commitment worthy of the military, who indeed played an important role in the normal schools. On the higher levels, however, university structures were to operate with the greatest possible degree of intellectual freedom in order to enable Japan to compete in the wider marketplace of science and ideas.

Japan was remarkably successful in combining these two seemingly antithetical structures. By the early 20th century all grade-age children were experiencing lower-school training. A system of uniform national textbooks incorporated "morals" training in patriotism and loyalty. At the Imperial University of Tokyo, established in 1877 and supplemented by that of Kyoto at the end of the Meiji period, inquiry was however remarkably free in all except sensitive areas associated with the origin and descent of the imperial house. Not until the perfervid ultranationalism of the 1930s was the value of a reasonably free atmosphere for higher education brought seriously into question.

Land tax reform

All of these reforms required a predictable income for government. Under late Tokugawa feudalism tax rates had varied by domain, and within domain sometimes by fief holder. The government's assumption of responsibility for the domains, and then its assumption of and discharge of samurai support, made a new and uniform system of land assignment and assessment possible and necessary. The year that saw the implementation of conscription and education, 1873, was also the year in which the land tax revision was addressed. After much discussion it was determined to work out an assessment of farm land on the basis of a capitaliza-

These two photographs present a striking contrast between the young samurai from Satsuma, Chōshū and Tosa (*above*) who overthrew the Tokugawa shogunate and the conscript army (*left*), trained and organized on Western models, which the samurai leadership of the Meiji restoration believed would be better suited as a modern national army than samurai bands with strong regional, domainal and elitist sympathies. The groundwork for the new national army was laid by Ōmura Masujirō and Yamagata Aritomo of Chōshū. From his experience in Chōshū, Ōmura had become convinced that peasants, if properly trained, could fight as well as samurai. Ōmura was an admirer of Napoleon and he organized the new Japanese military on the French model. Yamagata and other government leaders, impressed by Prussia's victory in 1871, later switched to the German general staff system. The conscription ordinance of 1873 was unpopular with the commoners who were the targets of the draft. It did, however, provide the troops to put down the Satsuma rising in 1877, the first real test for the new army.

tion of recent harvests. The tax set for the figure that resulted was initially to be 3 percent per annum paid in specie. In addition local taxes would add 1 percent, making a minimal tax of 4 percent.

The tax so devised was meant to be revenue-neutral. A government heavily in debt from its recent assumption of domain and samurai obligations, still paying off indemnities to foreign powers for the numerous untoward events of late Tokugawa times, and determined to remake its society, was not about to forgo possible revenue. On the other hand it was anxious to make good on its announced intention to even out taxes in the interests of equity. Problems lay ahead, of course, in the implementation of the plan, especially with establishing the evaluations on land. Surveys of arable land continued until 1876 and those of forest and watershed until 1881. In the case of Satsuma very little was done until after the rebellion. For the most part, farmers ended up paying approximately what they had before. The Tokugawa areas, most highly commercialized and most favored in the old system (partly because they were also least militarized), ended up paying rather more, while the restoration areas, harshly levied in the drive for remilitarization in late Tokugawa times, may have felt some slight relief.

Be that as it may, there is little doubt that farmers felt, correctly, that they were being called upon to pay for the costs of the new regime. It had no other dependable source. They also had to pay in specie, and in areas more distant from urban markets that often put them at some disadvantage. During the late 1870s numerous demonstrations and protests were mounted in the expectation that authorities would shrink from forceful suppression as had been the pattern in Tokugawa times. Instead the regime, with dependable units of the new conscript force at its disposal, did not hesitate to put them down harshly.

Japan's farmers thus experienced mixed results from the innovation made by the new regime. The decade of the 1870s tended to be one of steady inflation, as the regime could not afford to wait for sound financing in its hour of emergency. Consequently agricultural prices rose steadily and with them farmers' expectations. Farmers were also benefited by measures that freed them from the restrictions of Tokugawa status rules. They were permitted, and then told, to adopt surnames. They were free to grow what they wished instead of remaining subject to the mercantilist practices of the Tokugawa domains. Restrictions on permanent sale of land were abolished in 1872, and marriage across the old class and status lines was permitted. But farmers also became subject to the market in a way that had not been the case, and firm legal and police sanctions replaced the patterns of customary tenure and negotiated assessment that had prevailed. The result was certainly increased opportunity for the fortunately placed and able, and probably penalty for the remnant. In the 1880s, as inflation gave way to deflation, the proportions of these shifted sharply.

The institutional foundations for the formal end of warrior rule thus came with remarkable speed. Certainly most samurai had not bargained for anything like the capitalist society into which Japan was heading during the activity that led to the

Meiji restoration. They wanted a strong and effective government and polity, but they had never doubted that they and their fellows would head it. In the event, those that continued to head it were indeed former samurai, but many fewer than before, and the measures they adopted made it certain that the future would make better provision for the able, educated and prosperous than the past had. Yet that future society was also to be dedicated to national strength and militarist ideals, and its most basic civil legislation adopted the patriarchal samurai family as the norm just as lower educational institutions held up military virtues. On the other hand thousands of samurai were soon separated from their government-issued bonds, poorly equipped to compete in the new and more competitive society, and ended up living under conditions of usually genteel, but often shabby, poverty.

If one asks how reforms as sweeping as these, with all the consequences they had for future Japanese society, could be implemented as rapidly as they were, the answer probably has to be found in the distinctive nature of Tokugawa society. The *daimyō*, whatever they thought, did not really own their realms, but administered them in trust. Their vassals were allocated, but not really given, the lands from which they drew their income. The 1869 petition of the four restoration *daimyō* which argued that "the abode where we the undersigned dwell is the sovereign's land" spoke for the entire military class. Had there been a genuinely landed class like those in Europe, greater accommodation would have had to be made for the owners, and dislodging them might have required a revolution. Accordingly a process that required centuries in Prussia, for one contrast, was accomplished within a decade in Japan. There was revolutionary spirit and enthusiasm abroad in early Meiji Japan, but revolutionary action was not required.

Japan's encounter with the West

The 1870s were full of political problems and decisions for Meiji leaders, but it is important to remember that these came at a time when a cultural shift of the most profound sort was taking place. The most significant aspect of the early Meiji times was Japan's encounter with the Western world and its deliberate adoption of Western civilization and examples. For a millennium China had been a neighboring cultural colossus in terms of which Japan had formed and in a sense defined itself. Japanese culture and taste, blended with those of China, had come to be referred to as east Asian (Tōyō), and that remained permanently a part of Japanese consciousness. But the country of China was now no longer an object of esteem; instead it provided an object lesson of the dangers of stagnation and overconfidence. In the early 18th century the scholar Ogyū Sorai, in some ways a spokesman of his age, could refer to himself as an "eastern barbarian"; but by the 1880s Fukuzawa Yukichi, the leading figure in Japanese intellectual life at that time, warned his countrymen to avoid letting themselves be confused with China or Asia in Western eyes and argued that Japan should "get out" of Asia.

To be sure this shift was not a sudden one. Tokugawa intellectuals were inclined to distinguish

between Chinese civilization and the contemporary Manchu Qing state, and even Ogyū vaunted himself upon an ability in literary Sinology he felt was in no sense inferior to that of Chinese scholars. Nor was it universal and unanimous. Other Meiji figures argued the importance of affiliating with, and helping, Japan's continental neighbor, though they in turn ran the risk of condescension and arrogance in doing so. There had also been intellectual forerunners of the Meiji who turned to the West and found Western books, which they knew through the medium of Dutch contact at Nagasaki, more accurate and impressive than those of China. Even tradition could come into play: "Our ancestors traveled to China," wrote the vice minister of the first mission sent to the West in 1860; "but now we travel to the West." His mission of 1860 was followed by six others before the Tokugawa fall, and at the time of the restoration the shogun's younger brother was in Paris as a student, preparing himself for service in a modernized Bakufu.

Those preparations were nevertheless small in scale and restricted in personnel when compared to the sudden influx of ideas and the dramatic movement of Japanese to the West in the early Meiji years. Books and concepts entered Japan in considerable confusion and enormous numbers. Renaissance, enlightenment and Victorian ideas all came at once. In cultural terms, the Japanese historian Irokawa Daikichi writes, "the Meiji era was the most turbulent era in all of Japanese history . . . Compared with the confusion that developed in the Meiji period . . . earlier influence was restricted in scope, and its impact was weak. In Meiji times the impact was not something that affected just those in power; it roused violent emotions in the middle strata of society, and its influence extended down to the lower levels as well."

The context for the turn to the West on the part

of officialdom was encapsulated in the slogan *fukoku-kyōhei* ("rich country, strong army")—a search for ways to make the country strong. Late Tokugawa scholars like Sakuma Shōzan had argued the case in terms of combining "Western techniques" with "Eastern values" by applying what was clearly useful in order to bolster Japan's civilization. By the 1870s, however, it seemed clear to travelers and students that more was required; Western civilization posed a more compelling challenge. The slogan *bummei kaika* ("civilization and enlightenment") suggested the priorities of intellectuals who devoted themselves to the reform of their culture. Fukuzawa Yukichi's series of pamphlets entitled "The Encouragement of Learning" (*Gakumon no susume*) began with the assertion that "heaven does not create one man above or below another man. This means that when men are born they are by nature equal . . . The distinction between wise and stupid comes down to a matter of education." The object of education, he went on, should be "practical learning that is close to ordinary human needs . . . For the purpose of studying each of these areas, a person should investigate translations of Western books . . . A lad who is young and talented in letters should be taught to read Western languages." This work, written in simple language and addressed to ordinary people, circulated in hundreds of thousands of copies, and it is reasonable to suggest that a very high fraction of the literate had access to it.

In 1875, while the sections of *Gakumon no susume* were still appearing, Fukuzawa drew on Buckle to write a more complex work, *An Outline of a Theory of Civilization*. In it he argued that Japan had reached a crossroads and had to decide between the alternatives of advancing forward into modern civilization or falling back into barbarism. "Civilization," he felt, was the only choice, and

In 1858 a treaty was concluded between five foreign nations and Japan, opening several ports to foreign trade. One of the designated ports was the fishing village of Yokohama, south of Edo (Tokyo). As the first foreign merchants and their families arrived, the Japanese became fascinated by their strange manners, costumes and occupations. To satisfy the curiosity of Edo audiences, print makers produced prints of scenes in Yokohama. This one, by Utagawa Sadahide (1807–73), shows the first Western-style iron bridge in Japan, opened in Yokohama in 1870. In 1872 the first railroad in Japan was constructed between Yokohama and Shimbashi in Tokyo.

Of the men who carried out the Meiji restoration and shaped the government in its early years, Iwakura Tomomi was the only court noble, apart from the less forceful Sanjō Sanetomi. Shrewd, wily and skillful in political intrigue, he mediated between Chōshū and Satsuma factions and kept the interests of the imperial house in the forefront of the restoration. Iwakura believed firmly in a strong imperial institution and opposed the Freedom and People's Rights Movement. His journey to Europe, however, taught him the wisdom of adopting a constitutional system, if only to secure acceptance among Western nations. In 1881 he had Inoue Kowashi begin drafting a constitution.

since the modern West had evolved into a higher stage than Japan had yet reached, it was incumbent upon his country to catch up with the West by learning from it. For Fukuzawa "civilization" incorporated more than the material; it rested primarily upon internal spirit. He found the West's restless spirit and individual and national independence essential to the preservation of Japan's sovereignty and future dignity. Japanese progress had been stunted by governmental forms which prevented the development of an independent spirit among its people, and the country needed to cultivate the atmosphere of independence by promoting intercourse with the West. In these and other works Fukuzawa emphasized the importance of emulating the higher civilizations of the West in order to advance the civilization and independence of his country. As educator (and founder of Keiō, the oldest of Japan's private universities) and publisher (of the daily *Yūbin hōchi*) Fukuzawa was in many ways the spokesman of his age. His publications were so numerous that "Fukuzawa books" became a byword for progressive cultural discussion.

Translations of Western books came from Japan's presses in immense confusion, but none had a greater impact than the unlikely little work by Samuel Smiles, *Self-Help*. Tranlated by Nakamura Masanao, a Tokugawa-sponsored student who brought it back to Japan with him on his return, this little compendium of biographies of Western exemplars of ingenuity and enterprise became almost the textbook for an age, and its sentences appeared in national school readers into the 20th century. In 1871, the same year he published his translation of Smiles, Nakamura also translated John Stuart Mill's *On Liberty,* thereby providing the basic text for what would soon become an advocacy of representative institutions.

The Iwakura Mission

This enthusiasm for direct access to the Western experience was not limited to intellectuals and the growing number of students who went overseas. The early government, despite its financial and political problems, did everthing it could to encourage such interests, and the emperor himself issued a rescript exhorting the members of the old court aristocracy to do their share in furthering civilization and modern knowledge. Indeed, no sooner were the domains absorbed into a new system of prefectural government than the core of the Meiji government set out on a tour of the West to see for themselves.

The Iwakura Mission, as it became known for the chief ambassador, was abroad for a 21-month period from 1871 to 1873. Vice ambassadors included Ōkubo Toshimichi (Satsuma), Kido Takayoshi and Itō Hirobumi (Chōshū), the future architect of Meiji constitutional government. As each government department attached members, the mission grew until its total number neared 50. But even that number was almost doubled as recent feudal lords came and court nobles signed on, attended by their former retainers. Five young women were added as pioneers in Western education, and several dozen additional students were headed for Western schools. In a farewell ceremony the emperor charged the travelers to visit all countries with which Japan had formed contacts and observe and report on aspects of their institutions.

Few governments have the courage to send off their most powerful and influential members for so long a trip within a few years of their establishment. Affairs in Tokyo were left in the hands of a caretaker administration, of whose numbers the best-known was probably the Satsuma military figure Saigō Takamori. They were constrained by a

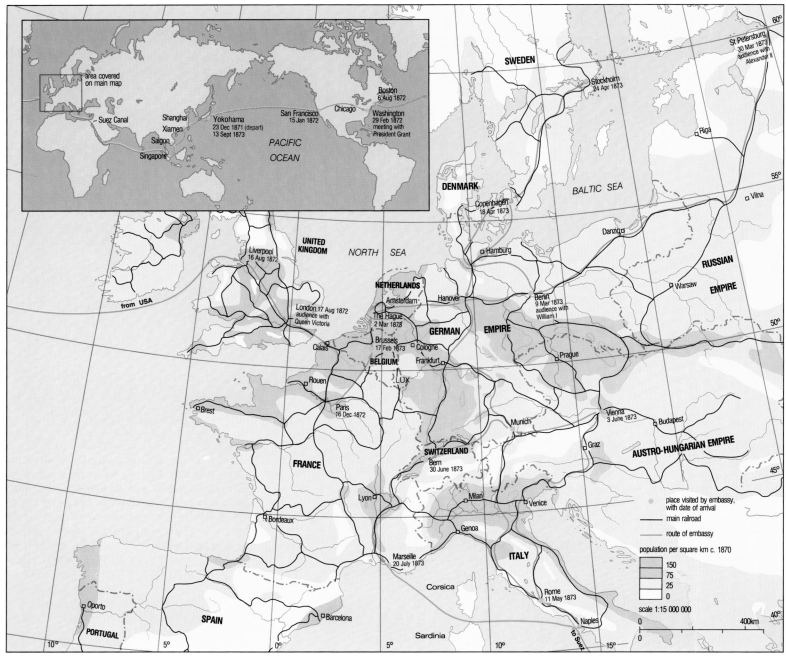

set of promises that specified that "since it is our intention to carry out major reforms in home affairs when the mission returns, the introduction of further reforms will in the meantime be avoided as far as possible." In fact the Tokyo remnant worked vigorously while the mission was abroad; the promulgation of the education and conscription ordinances and work toward the revision of the land tax all continued without letup. An additional reform, which alarmed some of the travelers when they learned of it, was the substitution of the Gregorian calendar for the lunar calendar. Most important, however, was the determination to force a decision on the Korean government, one which was reversed by the ambassadors upon their return.

The importance of the journey for some of the principal leaders of later Japanese policy can scarcely be exaggerated. The mission divided into teams that made particular studies of legal systems, education and industry. The importance of commerce and industry to the advanced nations of the West became clear to the ambassadors. As Ōkubo wrote to a colleague from London, "Factories have increased to an unheard-of extent, so that black smoke rises to the sky from every possible kind of plant . . . This is a sufficient explanation of England's wealth and strength." Kido Takayoshi, in the United States, was impressed by public education. As he wrote, "when it comes to things like schools and factories it is impossible to tell you everything, for it defies description. From now on, unless we pay a great deal of attention to the children, the preservation of order in our country in the future will be impossible . . . To prevent trouble ten years from now, there is only one thing to do and that is to establish schools worthy of the name." Kido was also impressed by parliaments. As a check upon arbitrary government, he wrote, "the people have parliamentary representatives whose duty it is to inspect everything that is done and to check arbitrary proceedings on the part of officials. Herein lies the best quality of these governments."

The ambassadors returned to Japan just in time to block the Korea moves; Japan's strength, they realized, was not sufficient for adventures abroad.

The Iwakura Mission 1871–73
The Iwakura Mission left Japan on the steamship *America* in late December 1871. One of its aims – that of securing revision of the unequal commercial treaties – was frustrated in Washington after conversations with President Grant in March 1872 led nowhere. From then on, the leaders of the mission confined themselves to goodwill visits and exchanges of views with an impressive roster of European rulers and statesmen, to observing every possible aspect that might help them to understand the individuality and sources of wealth and strength of Western nations, to placing Japanese students in the West, and to identifying foreign specialists who might be useful to Japan's own growth. Iwakura and the main body of the mission returned in September 1873. Kido and Ōkubo hurried back earlier in the year on learning that a full-scale political crisis was brewing over proposals to chastise Korea.

Basic institutional reforms would have to come first. But they were more encouraged than discouraged by what they had learned. For one thing, Japan's independence did not seem immediately threatened. More important, the strength of Europe was of recent date; as Ōkubo wrote, "this great growth of trade and industry in the cities has all happened in the last 50 years." The embassy's official chronicler confirmed this by pointing out that "if one compares the Europe of today with the Europe of 40 years ago, it can be imagined how great the changes are; on land there were no trains, on sea no steamers, there were no telegraphic communications, small boats were pulled along canals, sails were hoisted at sea, horse-drawn carts moved along the roads . . ." In other words, Japan was not really out of the race, but it could still catch up. As Kido wrote, "Our people are no different from the Americans or Europeans of today; it is all a matter of education or lack of education." Further, Europe was not a unit, and its countries were different in their culture and relative strong points.

From this time the Meiji policy of selective borrowing became clear. The political institutions of Central Europe, and especially Prussia and Austria-Hungary, seemed attractive; also the centralized education system of France, and the industrial might of Britain. Americans' skill in developing virgin land led the ambassadors to hire away the Grant administration's Commissioner of Agriculture, Horace Capron, to help plan the development of Hokkaido. When the ambassadors returned home, the implementation of the land tax revision, agrarian unrest and *shizoku* rebellions lay ahead, but a view of what needed to be done was clear in their minds.

Toward constitutional government

Meiji Japan was the first non-Western state to adopt a constitutional form of government. There were ups and downs in the working of that document, but it endured until 1945 without alteration. The document and the system it formalized proved remarkably resilient. Consideration of its origins and development tells a good deal about the stability and strength of Japanese society.

Four elements came together in the making of representative government in 19th-century Japan: cultural assumptions about responsibility and reciprocity, the example of the West, interaction within the leadership group, and the response of Japan's rural commoner elite. Each of these deserves brief comment and discussion.

Cultural assumptions might seem an unlikely support for constitutionalism in a society that had experienced military and autocratic rule. By mid-Tokugawa times, however, the diffusion and interpretation of Confucianism throughout Japanese society had created a setting quite different from that of earlier days. The fact of patriarchal and autocratic domination by an elite that did not brook interference remains unquestioned. Yet prolonged exposure to terms like "universal reason" (*dōri*) and "justice" (*seigi*) had built up a network of reciprocal expectations that modified the capricious treatment of late medieval times. Lords, quick to demand sweeping increases in burdens, could expect to find themselves taken to task by the local elite in petitions and criticized by

the shogunal overlord if order became threatened. Lords, like shogun and emperor, increasingly became symbols of authority rather than wielders of it, and their principal retainers expected to be consulted on matters of moment. So too with the shogun himself: Perry's letter from President Fillmore was distributed to feudal lords with requests for comment in 1853; one respondent requested that his response be kept confidential because he had not had opportunity to consult his own retainers. Efforts to build a consensus in the last years of Tokugawa rule included councils of great lords, and the conciliar expectations of those years had encouraged the last shogun to lay down his powers on the assumption that he would be part of a new order. In a time of rapid change any Japanese government forced to make unpopular agreements with the Western powers needed to build a political consensus for its acts; this lay behind the language of the April 1868 Charter Oath with its talk of "deliberative assemblies" and "public discussion."

The example of the West served to stimulate some of the Meiji leaders and to warn others. Kido Takayoshi, as mentioned earlier, returned from his trip with the Iwakura Mission with an optimistic and rather idealistic view of the way parliaments served to unite Western populations and to prevent arbitrary governmental action. Others, notably Ōkubo and Itō, were more impressed by the way royal power in Britain had been eroded by the growth of parliamentary responsibility. No matter: there were other models of parliamentary participation to be found in Central Europe. In any case all were agreed of the need to bring Japan's institutions into some kind of parallel with those of the advanced Western states as prerequisite for gaining Western respect and equality of treatment.

Interactions within the leadership group were more complex and more interesting. Resolution of the 1873 debate over action to be taken on the Korean problem had cost the government the support of its principal members from Tosa and Saga as well as the services of Saigō Takamori. In 1877 Kido Takayoshi died of natural causes, and the following year Ōkubo Toshimichi was assassi-

Itō Hirobumi (1841–1909, *above*) and Itagaki Taisuke (1837–1919, *right*) were among the leading statesmen of the Meiji period. Although they had much in common and sometimes collaborated, they also represented two contrasting attitudes to political reform. Itō was the quintessential insider. Leader of the restoration, senior councillor and Home Minister, he drafted a conservative, Prussian-style constitution that reserved power for the emperor and granted only limited popular constitutional privileges. Itagaki, who was several times drawn into government by Itō, generally preferred to remain on the outside as a leader of the Freedom and People's Rights Movement and as an organizer of popular political parties, especially the *Jiyūtō* (Liberal Party), Japan's first major political party. Itagaki's famous cry when attacked by a would-be assassin—"Itagaki may die, but liberty never!"—was an inspiration to the Popular Rights Movement.

nated by a disgruntled former samurai. The "big three" of the first decade of Meiji politics thus disappeared within a year of each other. The next echelon of leaders—men like Itō Hirobumi of Chōshū and Matsukata Masayoshi of Satsuma— were able and experienced, but more likely to be seen as representatives of a "Satsuma-Chōshū" interest; for the rest of the Meiji period, "Sat-Chō" was a term of abuse for the government.

Itagaki Taisuke and Soejima Taneomi, the Tosa and Saga leaders who left the government after the Korean dispute, did not resort to arms the way Etō Shimpei (Saga) and Saigō Takamori (Satsuma) did, but instead joined with other discontented leaders in calling for a constitution. The crisis of 1873, they pointed out, had threatened the very foundations of the government. It had acted precipitously in reversing decisions that had been made in proper order, and it was losing the confidence of the country. "How is the government to be made strong?" their petition asked, and went on to reply, "The establishment of a council chamber chosen by the people will create a community of feeling between the government and the people, and they will mutually unite into one body." The document went on to point out that Japan could advance the timetable for such institutions over that followed in the West, which had had no examples with which to work; Western institutions "had to be discovered by actual experience . . . If we can select examples from them and adopt their contrivances, why should we not be successful in working them out?" Like technical and mechanical innovations, political institutions could be imported; it was not necessary to invent the wheel a second time.

Itagaki, who had been high in the government, was aware that discussions about a constitution were going on within the regime as well, and he hoped to anticipate them with his proposal. To a large degree he succeeded, for his name is permanently linked with the organization of what is know as the Freedom and People's Rights Movement (*Jiyū minken undō*). It began as a largely regional, and largely *shizoku* movement in Tosa, but it did not remain that for long. The *Risshisha* (Self-Help Society, named for Smiles's book), which Itagaki set up in Tosa, issued a statement that "We, the 30 million people in Japan, are all equally endowed with certain definite rights, among which are those of enjoying and defending life and liberty, acquiring and possessing property, and obtaining a livelihood and pursuing happiness. These rights are by nature bestowed upon all men, and cannot therefore be taken away by the power of any man." Thus the *shizoku* found themselves quoting John Locke and the Declaration of Independence. Within a few years a movement that began with disgruntled Tosa ex-samurai had moved beyond that social class to speak for rural leaders. By 1881, when the Liberal Party (*Jiyūtō*) was organized in Osaka, it had become a national organization and its support went well beyond the ex-samurai who started it. That same year the government, trying to divert attention from scandals that had been exposed in the sale of government industrial assets and trying to anticipate further growth in the popularity of the movement for Freedom and People's Rights, announced its

intention of establishing a constitutional order by the end of the decade. This announcement of intent to broaden the base of government was nevertheless accompanied by an actual narrowing, as it was accompanied by the expulsion of the popular Saga figure, Ōkuma Shigenobu. Ōkuma promptly organized his own political party, the Progressive Party (*Kaishintō*), the following year.

Recent scholarship has made it clear that the true significance of all this activity was the response of Japan's rural commoner elite. Throughout the country a constituency of village leaders—landowners, local entrepreneurs, timber and upland operators—were to be found in discussion groups, frequently organized around local intellectuals and schoolteachers, in passionate discussion of national issues. In a remote mountain village on the edge of the Tokyo Plain, for instance, a political discussion society met regularly to discuss translations of books on diplomatic treaties, foreign policy and constitutional systems. Its members discussed articles of a sample constitutional draft, listened to talks by reporters for central newspapers, signed petitions for the early implementation of constitutional government and endorsed requests for national leaders like Fukuzawa to draft their proposals. This went on without government encouragement and in fact in the face of active police efforts to discourage popular participation.

The movement toward constitutional government was thus by no means limited to the workings of a generous national elite encouraging ordinary Japanese to take an interest in the affairs of their country. It began with disagreements among the elite, but it swiftly moved into the mainstream of popular life and discourse. Japanese society was by no means inert and unresponsive. Strong-minded local leaders had developed the habit of articulation during Tokugawa times. Literacy had made it possible for them to acquaint themselves with the problems of their times, and the loose administration of late feudal times had encouraged their inclination to participate. The upheavals of late Tokugawa and Meiji times had also created a class of educated wanderers whose chances of prominence or service had been blighted by the defeat or dissolution of their domains in the maelstrom of reorganization and reconstruction. Catching on as teachers or tutors with relatively affluent and independent sectors of the village elite, such individuals were able to help generate and crystallize the discontent and ambition of the local gentry. It was an unusual moment in Japanese social history, and one the government, with its bureaucratic preference for order and hierarchy, did its best to extinguish.

Efforts to coopt some of this energy came with prefectural assemblies, which began in the 1870s and provided organizational preparation—though scarcely policy participation—for an electorate based upon the property tax. The assemblies were usually limited to discussing measures the (appointive) governors proposed, and they were often at loggerheads with those governors. Nevertheless they gave the local elite the experience of elective activity. When constitutional government was implemented in the 1890s, many candidates for office were drawn from those who had first gained familiarity with the prefectural assemblies.

The constitution of the empire of Japan was promulgated on 11 February 1889. On that occasion, visualized in this contemporary woodblock print, it was stressed that the constitution was a gift from the Meiji emperor, who, in his wisdom, had limited his powers and bestowed upon the people rights and liberties and a share in the administration of national affairs. Itō Hirobumi and those who had drafted the constitution sought to embody in it the principle of imperial sovereignty without excluding the possibility of limited constitutional government. The document was certainly not democratic but in its ambiguity it left the door open for parliamentary party government, as well as for absolutist, militaristic tendencies under the cover of imperial sovereignty. The Meiji constitution was replaced by the present constitution of Japan on 3 May 1947.

Drafting the Meiji constitution

Amid all this ferment the central government did its best to keep the initiative for what became the Meiji constitution in its own hands. In 1875 the government managed to persuade Itagaki Taisuke and Kido Takayoshi to return briefly to its ranks. It was soon clear that understandings that had been made for a kind of "senate," the Genrōin, would not be kept, but even so that body, organized that same year, prepared and submitted constitutional drafts to the Council of State. When these proved unsatisfactory to a government nervous about having its prerogatives impaired, leading members of the government were next asked to submit their personal ideas about a constitution. When Ōkuma Shigenobu, who had waited the longest, submitted his directly to the emperor in 1881, his angry colleagues ejected him from the administration and secured the emperor's promise of a constitution by the end of the decade.

Matters now proceeded at the center without further input from anyone outside the leadership group. Itō Hirobumi was made head of a commission for constitutional preparation and dispatched to Europe on a study tour. His group listened with approval to the advice of legal theorists in Berlin and Vienna, and hired a German constitutional theorist to return to Japan with them and begin work on a Japanese document. An early draft was written in German, in curious anticipation of the draft of the 1947 constitution prepared in English. In 1885 a cabinet system was announced to replace the Council of State, and Itō became the first prime minister. A new European-style peerage, made up of former court nobles and former daimyō, was established to provide a conservative bloc against rapid change in a House of Peers. By the end of the decade Itō and his colleagues were reviewing the document they had prepared in the presence of the emperor, in the format of a Privy Council which Itō also headed. The Meiji constitution was formally promulgated in 1889 as had been promised.

Cut off from participation in this, the political parties were left without a role and fell to squabbling among themselves. Agricultural discontent rose as new treasury officials headed by Matsukata Masayoshi came into office in 1881, determined to end inflation and restore balance in government finances. Agricultural income fell more rapidly than land taxes, and the distress that resulted drove many at the lower end of the rural production chain—small farmers and landless laborers—to violence. Some 60 riots stemming from agricultural indebtedness took place in all parts of Japan in 1884, and in Chichibu, on the northern edge of the Tokyo Plain, an army of several thousand peasants organized in two battalions fought for a self-proclaimed "Rule of Benevolence." They dated their decrees "year one of freedom and self-government," sent squads of guerrillas to attack usurers, and battled with police and army forces sent to crush them. This ferment was related to the jacquerie of Tokugawa Japan, but its slogans were expressed in the language and terms of the new Movement for Freedom and People's Rights. It alarmed the leaders of the political parties, and certainly the central government. The parties hastily dissolved themselves, to reform toward the end of the decade. A movement that had begun as a fundamental challenge to the legitimacy of the governing oligarchy had been tamed and brought into the political system.

When the Meiji constitution came into effect in 1890, it proved that its framers, despite their caution, had conceded significant elements of power which could, in time, create a new setting for Japanese politics. The document's caution was shown in its treatment of the throne. The emperor was granted full sovereignty. The document indeed was his free grant, and he graciously pledged himself to rule with the advice and consent of the Imperial Diet. Basic freedoms were laid down, but could be modified "according to law." A two-house legislature was established, that of peers elected by ranks within the peerage and augmented by imperial appointments and representatives of the highest taxpayers. The House of Representatives was elected by a limited franchise (initially slightly over half a million in number) based upon rather high property tax qualifications. Failure to approve a government budget meant that the previous year's budget would continue in force. The document was vague as to the locus of administrative power lest it seem to weaken the emperor's prerogatives. As things worked out, the prime minister was essentially a first among equals; his manner of selection was not specified, and in practice the leadership clique made its suggestions to the throne. At first the core leaders, later known as "senior statesmen" (genrō), alternated in office as prime minister, with weight shifting from Satsuma to Chōshū. Yet for all its deficiencies the document endured until Japan's defeat in World War II. Parliamentary weight shifted increasingly to the lower house, and entry into that house was consistently controlled by the ability of the rural elite to organize local election campaigns. The tax qualification for electoral participation was lightened in 1900 and 1920 and finally removed in 1925, but the ballot was not extended to women until after World War II.

Japan and the West

Japan in the mid-19th century had to deal with problems at home and face a growing threat from vigorous and expansive Western powers determined to prise China and Japan open for trade. Before 1853 there were many Western attempts to induce the Japanese to open ports for trade, but these efforts were sporadic and unsupported by substantial economic and political interests. In 1778 and 1792 the Russians requested trade relations in Hokkaido. In 1804 a similar request was made in Nagasaki. The Bakufu refused these and similar requests from British ships. In 1825 the Bakufu ordered that all foreign vessels be driven from Japanese waters. This order did nothing to relieve the pressure, which continued to mount.

Within Japan opinion was divided. Through the Dutch, Japanese were well aware of Western strength and Chinese weakness. The Bakufu and some domains sought to acquire Western technology. By the 1840s the domains of Mito, Hizen and Satsuma were casting guns using Western technology. In 1850 Hizen acquired the first reverberatory furnace capable of reaching the temperatures needed in the casting of iron canon. A few daring samurai students of Dutch and Western studies suggested abandoning the policy of expelling Western barbarians. Most members of the imperial court, however, called upon the Tokugawa Bakufu to perform its military function of protecting the country and the emperor from the growing threat to Japan's sovereignty by continuing the policy.

Above right When the forced treaties of commerce were ratified after 1858 foreign ships entered Yokohama and other open ports in ever increasing numbers and the foreign colony grew rapidly. Not surprisingly there were mixed reactions. While they resented the unequal treaties and the presence of foreigners on Japanese soil, they were curious about Western customs, civilization and power. This Nishiki-e print of 1861 by Ippōsai Hōtō (Yoshifuji) expresses the interplay of curiosity and resentment as a Japanese champion defeats a foreign seaman.

Right With the acquisition of California in 1848 the interest of the United States in Japan increased markedly. Nagasaki was a convenient fueling stop between San Francisco and Shanghai. President Fillmore sent Commodore Matthew Perry with 11 ships, three of them steam frigates. Perry and his squadron reached Uraga in July 1853, forced the shogunate to accept a letter to the emperor and announced he would return for an answer the following spring. This anonymous sketch dated 1854 shows some of his black ships in Uraga Bay.

Right Following the treaty of commerce negotiated by the American consul Townsend Harris in 1858, similar unequal treaties were demanded by the Dutch, Russians, British and French. Besides opening more ports, these treaties called for most-favored-nation privileges and extraterritoriality. Japan lost control over tariffs and could not impose high import duties. The new opportunities lured foreign merchants, adventurers and the curious to the new settlements. This foreign presence provoked samurai anger and there were assassinations in 1859, 1861 and 1862. They did little to stem the influx. Printmakers delighted in portraying such foreign customs as this "Parade of the People of the Five Western Nations," with their sedan chairs, coaches and musical accompaniment.

Below With the Meiji restoration came increased openness to the West. As the government imported technology and the foreign settlements expanded, in Tokyo and Yokohama there were signs of at least a superficial Westernization—foreign dress, watches, umbrellas, all came into vogue. It was not unusual to see Japanese dressed in Western shoes and traditional *hakama*. To most Japanese meat eating was vulgar and abhorrent and they took to the custom slowly. By 1860, however, a concoction of fried beef, bean curd and vegetables known as *sukiyaki* caught on in the treaty ports and some Japanese indulged. Beneath the surface of the vogue for civilization and enlightenment was an attempt to revive Shinto and find Japanese values for the restoration. In this Nishiki-e print of 1872 there is a playful blending of East and West as the seven lucky gods, bearers of gifts and good fortune, view the railroad and steamships.

Above No match militarily for Perry's fleet, the Tokugawa Bakufu had little alternative but to make some concessions and play for time. When Perry returned in 1854, an initial treaty was signed opening the small ports of Shimoda and Hakodate. News of the black ships spread like wildfire, helped by unknown artists who added their sometimes imaginary impressions of the red-faced, long-nosed barbarians. This painting of Perry, "age about 60, hair half-white," was done by an impromptu artist who signed himself Morihiro.

Japonisme

With the opening of Japanese ports from the 1850s and the growth of the foreign settlements, Americans and Europeans began to visit Japan and make first-hand contact with its art and culture. Reporters, essayists and photographers sent their impressions back to Europe. A culture that had been inaccessible, and largely ignored, for more than 250 years was suddenly very accessible and startlingly different.

The appreciation of Japanese art in Europe was whetted by an exhibition in London in 1862 displaying Sir Rutherford Alcock's collection of Japanese woodblock prints and books. This was followed in 1867 by the Paris Exposition Universelle which introduced Japanese arts and crafts and included 100 *ukiyo-e* by Hiroshige and others. It was the *ukiyo-e* that created particular excitement among artists and intellectuals.

Félix Bracquemond is said to have started a craze for Japanese art when he found a copy of Hokusai's sketches, *Manga*, in 1856 in a packing crate at the shop of the printer Delâtre and began to copy from these albums. Soon the Goncourt brothers, Zola, Degas, Manet, Whistler and many other luminaries were competing in the collection of Japanese art. This surge of enthusiasm for Japanese prints and culture in general was dubbed "Japonisme" by the French art critic Philippe Burty in 1872.

Above Kitagawa Utamarō (1753–1806) is famed for his compositionally masterful prints of beautiful women from the pleasure quarters of Edo such as the high-ranking courtesan or *oiran* known as Hinzauru shown here (c. 1796). Utamarō's concern was less to give precise portraits of individual women than to show different types of women in varying situations, moods and activities. His prints, intimate and narrowly focused, concentrate on the subjects in their most characteristic surroundings.

Below Mary Cassatt (1845–1926) was introduced to *ukiyo-e* by such enthusiasts as Degas and Pissarro and by visiting the exhibition of woodblock prints at the École des Beaux Arts in the spring of 1890 where 89 prints by Utamarō were shown. In this print from the series called "The Letter" the influence of Utamarō's *oiran* Hinzauru is evident. Cassat, however, has transformed the high-ranking courtesan into a comfortably placed bourgeois gentlewoman. The paper, with its connotations of the aftermath of lovemaking in Utamarō's print, reappears as perhaps a love letter.

Above Félix Bracquemond, an etcher and designer for the French ceramic industry, was among the first to feel the passion for Japanese design. In 1866–67 he used copies of Hokusai and Hiroshige's sketches in designing a porcelain faience service for the firm of Eugène Rousseau.

Left Monet is known to have had his own copy of this print by Hiroshige, "Wisteria Blooms over Water at Kameido," from *One Hundred Views of Edo*. Andō Hiroshige (1797–1858) was among the *ukiyo-e* artists who made the greatest impact on Western painters. Best known for his landscapes, he used light and atmosphere, moonlight, rain and snow with skillful shading and a rich range of color to impart new life to the woodblock print.

Above Claude Monet (1840–1926) first encountered *ukiyo-e* in the 1860s and began to collect seriously from 1871. He built up a collection of several hundred prints, especially those by Utamarō, Hokusai and Hiroshige, many of which hung on the walls of his home at Giverny. He was impressed by their mastery of atmosphere and light. The famous garden at Giverny with its water-lily pond, painted so frequently, was designed in the Japanese style.

Right Vincent van Gogh too was an enthusiastic admirer of Japanese *ukiyo-e* artists. He enthused about their command of line, color and perspective and their mastery of figure and landscape composition. This portrait of the art materials dealer Julien (Père) Tanguy, painted in 1887, shows the Parisian storekeeper against a background of Japanese prints. Van Gogh later picked up some of the motifs in the prints in his seasonal landscapes and costumed regional types.

Below James McNeill Whistler was among the first of the impressionists to respond to the craze for Oriental art. Like Manet, Degas and Dante Gabriel Rossetti he collected Oriental pottery, prints and screens and decorated his home in Chelsea with them. By 1864, four years before the Meiji restoration, Whistler was incorporating Oriental influences into his paintings—superficially at first, then more deeply. This painting, entitled "Caprice in Purple and Gold. No. 2: The Golden Screen," is signed and dated 1864. The model is Jo and the prints on the screen and floor are by Hiroshige. This and several other early paintings of 1864 have been described as Oriental "fancy dress" pictures. Whistler, however, went deeper, looking for an aesthetic of harmony in Japanese prints.

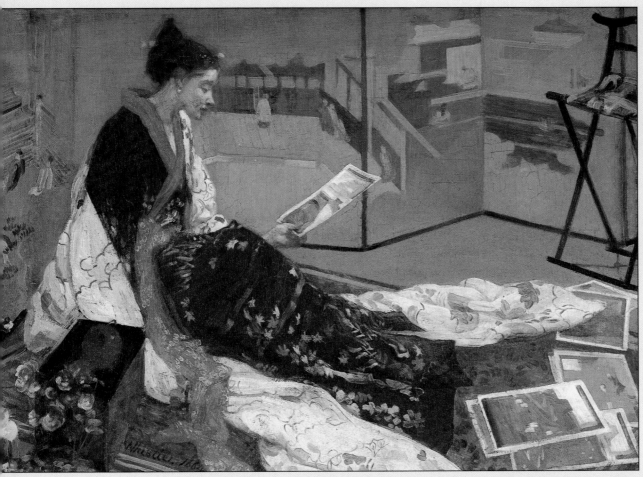

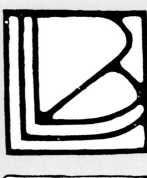

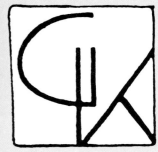

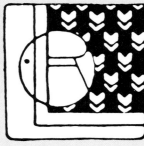

Above By the end of the century the vogue for Japanese art and influence was running its course. Its influence was still felt, however, in *fin-de-siècle* Vienna where Leopold Bauer, Gustav Klimt and other artists played with the notion of Oriental seals in designing monograms for themselves.

Left Among the impressionists, Toulouse Lautrec was one of those who captured the spirit of the floating world of the Japanese printmakers, the flatness of figure composition, the emphasis on the foreground, the angularity of perspective and transformed these into posters of the Parisian demimonde such as his "Divan japonais" of 1893.

IMPERIAL JAPAN

Japan's institutional structure

The institutional structure of the modern Japanese state was complete in 1890. Building and experimentation had resulted in a structure designed to give scope to individual energies and to channel the larger national ambition into paths productive of national strength. Once pulled together, those institutions produced a Japan able and anxious to demand equality with the treaty powers and join them in the late 19th-century imperialist competition. It will be useful to summarize that institutional structure.

The first decisions concerned local government. The builder of the modern Japanese army, Yamagata Aritomo of Chōshū, served as Minister of Home Affairs in the first cabinet and worked on steps to make sure that local government would not be affected by party rivalry and that agrarian disturbances would come to an end. In Yamagata's thought conscription and local self-government were closely related. By 1887 he was ready with plans for the election of lower-echelon officials to encourage the sense of self-government. All higher-level officials were to be appointed. The home minister was to be one of the most powerful officials in Japan. He appointed the governors, and they were able to block all local initiative. He could suspend the prefectural assembly. Towns and villages were given responsibility for their local budgets and assessments for local taxes; the chief significance of that was to relieve the national government from petty and inconsequential matters. The system met the objectives with which it had been conceived: after the 1880s Japan was free of agrarian insurrection, and local politics were separate from national politics for the better part of a generation.

A second area of institutional consolidation concerned the military. Disaffection within the armed forces in the early Meiji period had grown from their regional basis, and the exit and then defeat of the Satsuma leaders had produced justified concern about the army's dependability. Yamagata, again the central figure to deal with this, followed the advice of lieutenants he had dispatched to Germany to adopt the General Staff system. The army General Staff was established in 1878; and in 1883 the Army War College opened as an elite educational facility to train upper-level staff officers. The model, and two of its instructors, were German. The General Staff was directly responsible to the emperor. This guaranteed that in the future civilian politicians would have only limited ability to affect military budgets and policy. Ideology and spirit also drew Yamagata's attention. In 1882 the Imperial Rescript to Soldiers and Sailors exhorted them to avoid politics and pledged them to imperial loyalty. Emperor and male members of the imperial family moved into military uniform, and the later designation of the emperor as commander-in-chief in the Meiji constitution formalized a relationship

that had already been worked out. While military men were warned to avoid partisan politics, they were prominent in political office. The cabinets of the modern Japanese state had a heavy military cast; civilians did not form a majority of the cabinet until 1898, and during the Meiji period military officers held 45 percent of the civilian cabinet posts. The possibility of civilian control over military planning was even more firmly blocked by an imperial ordinance of 1900 that specified that the ministers of war and navy in the cabinet had to be drawn from generals and admirals on the active duty list. Thus either service could bring down a cabinet by withdrawing its service minister.

A third area of vital importance to all Japanese was the structuring of the modern police force. In the 1880s the government moved to centralize its police system through the creation in prefectural governments of a senior police official appointed directly by the home minister. In 1884 a police training school was established in each prefecture, and in 1886–87 work was begun on a network of one- and two-man posts dispersed throughout the countryside. This remarkable increase in the scope of police penetration of society made it possible to use the police as agents of the central government at the community level. Carefully selected, a police force with high morale became ubiquitous throughout Japanese society. It enforced public-health standards and conscription laws, supervised annual clean-up periods and enforced codes of appropriate behavior. In the cities police boxes at intersections occasionally became a focus of mob action during disturbances, but in the countryside these measures helped to enforce uniformity and discourage dissent.

The 1880s also saw the establishment of the infrastructure of the modern economy. Under the vigorous direction of Finance Minister Matsukata Masayoshi the government sold unprofitable investments and pilot plants to private purchasers, got the inflation of the 1870s under control and established the infrastructure of the modern economy through a national bank and postal savings system. Surveys without number tried to identify ways and places in which the modern economy might be advanced. Government influence worked to place the investments of banks that had been established with *daimyō* and samurai bonds where they would contribute to future growth; the railroad building program was a particular beneficiary of this. Matsukata's name is permanently associated with the agrarian distress of the decade that resulted from his deflationary policies, but when he left office almost a decade after assuming responsibility the Japanese economy had been made more stable and was ready for growth.

The 1880s were also a period of institution building in education. During the decade vigorous struggles were carried on about the nature and content of public education. Conservatives argued

Matsukata Masayoshi (1835–1924) came from a lower samurai family in Satsuma. Although younger than Saigō Takamori and Ōkubo Toshimichi, he knew them well and was used by them in the Meiji restoration. In April 1868 Matsukata was appointed a provincial governor in north Kyushu and assigned to raise funds from rich merchants for the support of the new government. In 1871 he moved to Tokyo to work with Itō Hirobumi on the land tax reform. In 1878 he visited Europe where he was impressed by French government finance policies. In 1881 Matsukata replaced Ōkuma Shigenobu as minister of finance. To deal with severe inflation caused by government overissues of banknotes in 1877 and 1878 and to pay for the cost of putting down the Satsuma rebellion, Matsukata enforced a strong deflationary policy by contracting the currency supply, increasing taxes and selling off government enterprises. His policies hit farmers hard. They laid the basis for sustained industrial growth and gave a start to many of the powerful entrepreneurs who established private financial empires known as *zaibatsu*.

The Mitsui family bank, shown here, provided the first modern commercial banking services in Tokyo. The family maintained close ties with the Tokugawa shogunate until the end of the Edo period. In the 1860s, however, Mitsui, seeing the wave of the future, also established relations with anti-shogunate leaders, making possible the company's continued enjoyment of government favor after the restoration. In 1871 Mitsui petitioned the government to be allowed to convert its moneylending and exchange business into a Western-type bank. Under the national bank ordinance (1872) it was permitted to open a private bank with 30 branches and a capitalization of 2 million yen. Mitsui dominated banking and enjoyed exclusive use of national tax revenues until the establishment of the Bank of Japan by Matsukata Masayoshi in 1882. Mitsui Bank became the cornerstone of the giant Mitsui financial, industrial and commercial combine (*zaibatsu*) that was eventually broken up during the allied occupation.

that the pro-Western slant of educators like Fukuzawa Yukichi risked deracinating future generations of Japanese and that the virtues of traditional Japanese society and thought should at all cost be retained. Closer central control of the lower schools, which had fared relatively poorly when dependent upon local taxes, also made it possible to take a firmer line with their content. Minister of Education Mori Arinori, mentioned earlier, was at odds with the emperor's Confucian tutor, Motoda Eifu, about the advisability of issuing a general proclamation about morality. Motoda won, although the final product was less prescriptive than he probably would have wished. The product, the Imperial Rescript on Education of 1890, was a document of great importance in the intellectual history of modern Japan. It was treated with religious veneration in the public schools and committed to memory by a large fraction of the school population. Its opening sentence suggests the whole: "Our imperial ancestors have founded our empire on a basis broad and everlasting, and have deeply and firmly implanted virtue; our subjects ever united in loyalty and filial piety have from generation to generation illustrated the beauty thereof. This is the glory of the fundamental character of our empire, and herein also lies the source of our education." There followed injunctions to observe the cardinal Confucian virtues of filiality and harmony; students (and subjects) were to "bear yourselves in modesty and moderation; extend your benevolence to all; pursue learning and cultivate arts, and thereby develop intellectual faculties and perfect moral powers; furthermore, advance moral good and promote common interest; always respect the constitution and observe the laws; should emergency arise, offer yourselves courageously to the state; and thus guard and maintain the prosperity of our imperial throne coeval with heaven and earth." Clearly the search for "wisdom throughout the earth" had led back to native founts of wisdom, and the search for foreign example had come to rest at native altars.

There were other indications of this. Restrictions on Christianity had been lifted in 1873 upon the advice of the Iwakura ambassadors. It grew enormously in number and strength during the 1880s. Missionary teachers and Japanese converts argued the necessity of replacing Japan's entire moral code with the new faith, on grounds that the nation needed and lacked an appropriate source of moral unity. In the course of preparing the constitution, however, Itō Hirobumi had decided that Japan did indeed have one. Writing to a friend from Germany, he argued that European constitutionalism had developed over time and that "religion has been the foundation of this form of government . . . The people thus have a fundamental consensus." In Japan, however, religion was formalistic and weak and could not play such a role. "Thus in our country the one institution which can become the cornerstone of our constitution is the imperial house."

Imperial loyalty, in other words, had to play the role that Christianity did in the West to bring about a consensus on morality and values. The Rescript on Education to some extent posited other value systems as a threat to the total unity that was supposed to bind Japanese together. An incident connected with its original proclamation seemed to bear this out. At the First Higher School of Tokyo, preparatory to the Imperial University, a Christian English teacher, Uchimura Kanzō, failed to follow the example of his colleagues in bowing to the document after it had been read. He was reviled as disloyal, and soon found it wise to resign his post. This inaugurated a vigorous debate about the possibility of combining patriotism and Christianity. The Education Ministry retained its doubts about the matter, since a few years later it eliminated religious (i.e. Christian) school students from exemptions for conscription. The openness of earlier Meiji days, when Japan was clearly in search of "wisdom" abroad, thus narrowed in the early months of the inauguration of the constitutional government.

Japan joins the Great Powers

With its institutional structure in place, Japan now found it was possible to turn to the problems of foreign policy which had had to wait. Meiji diplomats had succeeded in "opening" Korea to foreign relations in 1876 and they had worked out treaty relations with China, but a series of efforts to sponsor modernization in Korea in 1882 and 1884 had been clumsily handled and misfired. In 1885 Japan and China had agreed that both would stay their hand in Korea, but in the years that followed the Beijing government had been far more successful than Japan in advancing its interests and had installed a resident adviser in Seoul. Within Japan irritation with the continued indignity of the unequal treaties had built up steadily. During the 1880s the government had several times tried to get the approval of the Western powers for partial change in the treaty system, but each time these plans, when revealed, had stirred widespread indignation as being inadequate. Response ranged from public demonstrations to an assassination attempt on the Foreign Minister. Political party leaders had been quick to see that charges of weakness in foreign policy could be a highly effective

political device, and on the eve of constitutional government they had reformed and allied to fight for treaty revision.

When the constitution came into effect in 1890, the House of Representatives, dominated by members of the political parties, proved a refractory institution which the early cabinets found difficult to control. Efforts to manage it saw government leaders try to pressure party men through bribery, through dissolution of the house to force new elections, through strong-arm methods in elections and through imperial proclamations calling for harmony and progress; but the parties' tendency to think of the Satsuma-Chōshū government as their adversary proved tenacious.

Success in foreign policy brought a change in such attitudes. In 1894 a cabinet headed by Itō Hirobumi was able to achieve a successful solution to the problem of treaty reform. Full autonomy over tariffs was deferred until 1911, but the end of extraterritoriality finally secured full sovereignty for Japanese law. Henceforth Japanese would deal with foreigners as equals. While treaty reform was being negotiated, the outbreak of rebellion in Korea led to war with China; the ensuing Japanese victory brought membership in the circle of powers able to extract concessions from China.

At Korean request, China sent troops to help put down a rising there in 1894, and under the terms of the agreement worked out with China in 1885 Japan chose to send its own units also. Once they were there, the Japanese decided on a show of strength with demands that the Koreans make substantial reforms in administration with Japanese assistance. When the Chinese declined to cooperate in this the dispute led to war, and in the campaign that followed the modernized and well-led Japanese forces were everywhere successful. Within months Japanese armies had prevailed in Korea, occupied the Liaodong Peninsula in south Manchuria and sunk the northern fleet of the Chinese navy.

These diplomatic and military successes were greeted with jubilation by Japanese tired of second-class citizenship in the international order. "For the first time," wrote the liberal journalist Tokutomi, "I realized that the government I had been fighting was my government." The victories redounded especially to the benefit of the Japanese military, who were handsomely rewarded with peerage titles and budget allocations, and of the sovereign to whose paternal leadership the success was credited. The war was also profitable. The Treaty of Shimonoseki provided a large Chinese indemnity, the concession of Taiwan and the lease of the Liaodong Peninsula. At the last moment, however, Germany, France and Russia "advised" Japan to return Liaodong "for the peace of Asia" in what became known as the Triple Intervention. This provided a reminder that Japan had more work to do before it could consider itself fully the master of its fate. The treaty had additional important provisions. Japan received from China the privilege to establish manufacturing plants in China as well as additional treaty ports. Secondly, Korea was wrested from the Chinese tributary order and declared "independent," rendering it subject to a new competition between Russia and Japan.

The Sino-Japanese War of 1894–95 thus catapulted Japan from "semicolonial" status to imperialist. Occupation of Taiwan brought the first experience of imperial control and directed development. In 1898 Russian acquisition of a lease for the disputed Liaodong Peninsula revived Japanese resentment against a major European competitor. Russian influence in Korea soon began to outpace Japanese successes. Japan participated in the Great Powers' intervention against and suppression of the Boxer Rebellion in Beijing in 1900, and out of that came new respect and friendship with Great Britain which resulted in the Anglo-Japanese Alliance of 1902.

The Sino-Japanese War 1894–95

The Sino-Japanese War broke out in Korea. The catalyst was the Tonghak Revolt of 1894. The Tonghak ("eastern learning") movement had begun as a religious amalgam of Chinese, Buddhist and native Korean ideas. Outlawed by the Korean court, it took on nationalist overtones, protesting the corruption and poverty of Korean society and the presence of foreign powers (China and Japan). Both China and Japan responded to an appeal by the Korean court to help quell the revolt (June 1894) and then came to blows themselves in July 1894 when the Japanese kidnapped the Korean king and queen from the palace in Seoul. The Chinese were expected to win, but the Japanese, who were better led, equipped and trained, swept northward to Pyongyang and into the Liaodong Peninsula. The fighting was over by March 1895. At the Treaty of Shimonoseki in April harsh terms were imposed. The Qing court recognized the "independence" of Korea, leaving it vulnerable to Japanese intrusion. An indemnity of 200 million *taels* (310 million yen) was paid. The Liaodong Peninsula, Taiwan and the Pescadores were ceded to Japan, opening the door to imperial expansion, and the Chinese were forced to yield Japan commercial privileges in Chinese ports. Within months France, Germany and Russia had intervened to force Japan to return Liaodong to China, setting the stage for friction between Japan and Russia in Korea and Manchuria.

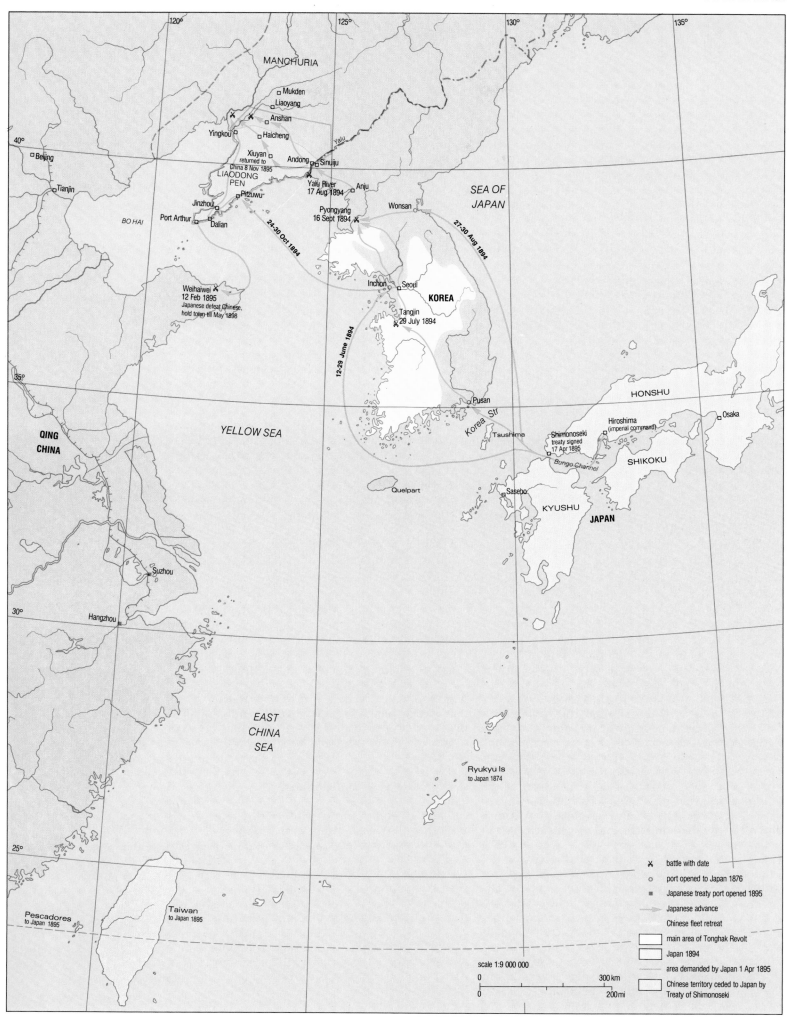

MANCHURIA

Mukden
Liaoyang
Anshan
Yingkou
Haicheng
Xiuyan
returned to
China 8 Nov 1895
LIAODONG
PEN
Andong
Sinuiju
Pitzuwu
Jinzhou
Port Arthur
Dalian

Beijing

Tianjin

BO HAI

Yalu River
17 Aug 1894

Anju

Pyongyang
16 Sept 1894

Wonsan

SEA OF
JAPAN

Yalu

24-30 Oct 1894

27-30 Aug 1894

Weihaiwei
12 Feb 1895
Japanese defeat Chinese,
hold town till May 1898

Inchon
Seoul

KOREA

Tangjin
29 July 1894

12-29 June 1894

HONSHU

Pusan

Korea Str

Tsushima

Hiroshima
(imperial command)

Osaka

QING
CHINA

YELLOW SEA

Shimonoseki
treaty signed
17 Apr 1895

SHIKOKU

Suzhou

Quelpart

Sasebo

Bungo Channel

KYUSHU

JAPAN

Hangzhou

EAST
CHINA
SEA

Ryukyu Is
to Japan 1874

Pescadores
to Japan 1895

Taiwan
to Japan 1895

battle with date

port opened to Japan 1876

Japanese treaty port opened 1895

Japanese advance

Chinese fleet retreat

main area of Tonghak Revolt

Japan 1894

area demanded by Japan 1 Apr 1895

Chinese territory ceded to Japan by
Treaty of Shimonoseki

scale 1:9 000 000

0   300 km

0   200 mi

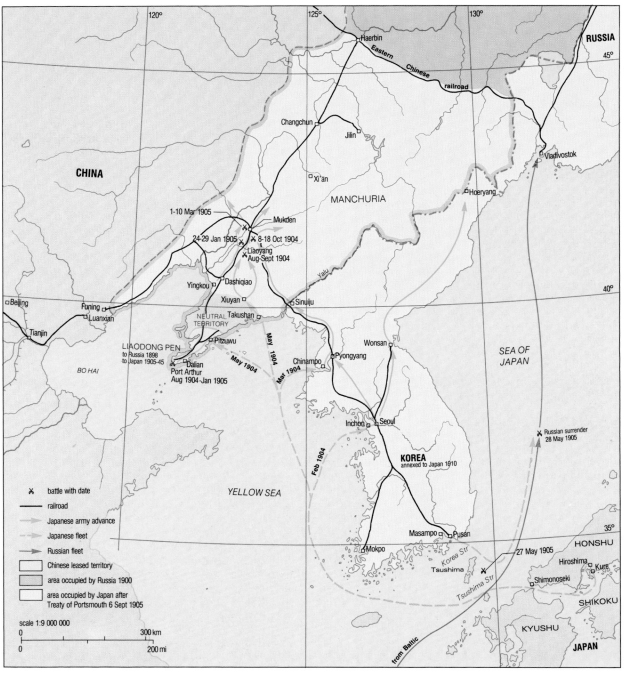

Left: the Russo-Japanese War 1904–05
Clashing imperial ambitions of Russia and Japan over Korea and the Liaodong Peninsula led to war in 1904. The Japanese struck first, blockading Port Arthur. In costly land action the poorly supplied Russian troops were driven back on Mukden, where 350000 Russian and 250000 Japanese troops fought a bloody but inconclusive battle. The Japanese high command recognized that their supply lines were stretched to the limit at Mukden. Meanwhile, the Russian Baltic fleet was sailing slowly halfway around the world. The Japanese fleet, waiting in the Tsushima Strait, destroyed the Baltic fleet in a decisive encounter in late May. Both combatants were exhausted and looking for mediation. They accepted an offer from President Theodore Roosevelt to make peace at Portsmouth, New Hampshire. Japan made striking territorial gains.

Right For most of the Meiji period small factories and shops—like this Tokyo metalworking shop—were characteristic of Japan's industrial production.

Below The first railroad in Japan, illustrated in this contemporary print, was built by the new Meiji government between Tokyo (Shimbashi) and Yokohama in 1872.

Fortified with a guarantee that the British navy would come to Japan's assistance if it should find itself at war with more than a single European power, Japan now prepared for a showdown with Russia. This came with Japan's naval attack on Port Arthur in 1904. As the Russian Far Eastern fleet was bottled up there, Japanese armies began the long and grinding effort to take that base, a drive that took the rest of 1904. Japanese armies then moved into Manchuria for the giant battle of Mukden. The Russian Baltic fleet, sent halfway around the world, was totally demolished by Admiral Tōgō Heihachirō at Tsushima Straits in the spring of 1905. President Theodore Roosevelt, partly at the behest of Baron Kaneko Kentarō, then helped bring the Russians to the conference table at Portsmouth, New Hampshire, for peace talks in the summer of 1905. By that treaty Japan regained Liaodong and secured the southern half of the island of Sakhalin. Russian influence was removed from Manchuria and, more important, Korea, to which Itō Hirobumi now moved as resident

general. Itō's efforts to stage-manage modernization in Korea were only partly successful, and after he was slain by a Korean nationalist in 1909 pressures for stronger steps led to the Japanese annexation of Korea in 1910.

The Russo-Japanese was the first of the 20th century's great wars. Enormously costly in lives, it forecast much of the futility of trench warfare on the Western front a decade later. Because the Japanese prevailed, however, foreign observers preferred to emphasize the positive aspects of that startling and unexpected success. Within Japan the prestige—and budgets—of the armed services rose ever higher, but this time there was no indemnity to defray the cost. Indeed, the failure to achieve more despite enormous expense made the Portsmouth Treaty intensely unpopular, and brought large-scale riots when the outcome was announced.

Nevertheless Meiji Japan's drive to great-power status had been successful. The emperor (he would die in 1912) had now neared the status of divinity,

and his photograph in uniform hung in the humblest home. With Chinese and Russian fleets at the bottom of the Pacific the navy had no enemies in sight so long as its alliance with Britain endured, as it did until the Washington Conference of 1922. Consequently it was General Yamagata's army that gained the most. His protegé, Katsura Tarō, was Prime Minister during the war. Fears of a Russian return and problems of disorder on the Chinese mainland after the Chinese Revolution of 1911 guaranteed that military considerations and needs would figure large in future political calculations. Soon the European powers were absorbed in the mutual destruction of World War I, enabling Japan to occupy German holdings in Shandong and attempt, in the 21 Demands of 1915, to work out a permanent position of leadership on the Asian continent. Imperial Japan had reached maturity just as imperialism was going out of fashion elsewhere in the world.

Industrialization and economic growth

From the time that late Tokugawa travelers to the West identified it as the source of Western strength, industrialization was the consistent goal of Japan's leaders. The journalist Tokutomi in one of his best-sellers in the 1880s predicted joyfully for his country that, "we will become like a great wharf in the Pacific, a great city of the Orient, a wholesaler of international commerce; the sun will be darkened by the smoke rising from thousands of smokestacks." Meiji wood-print artists took delight in showing steam locomotives puffing through the vernal settings that Hiroshige had depicted, and early textile plants at Tomioka threatened to replace Mount Fuji as subject for their talents.

The unequal treaties, however, limited Japan's freedom to raise its tariffs above 5 percent for most of the period, so that protection of infant industries was not possible. This may nevertheless have been a blessing in disguise, for it forced the Japanese to concentrate on areas of comparative advantage and discouraged massive investment in modern plants for which the economy was not prepared. In the 1870s the government had incurred heavy expenses with attempts to set up model plants, but in the retrenchment instituted after 1881 most of these were sold at a loss to private bidders. The purchasers, who shared the vision (and often the friendship) of the government leaders, were the founders of large conglomerates that would later be known by the pejorative term *zaibatsu* ("financial clique"). By the 1930s the term had overtones of the later Americanism, "malefactors of great wealth." But that eminence and opprobrium lay in the future and did not become widespread until after the Meiji period. Meiji Japan began with a single natural resource, that of coal, and much of it of low quality, and its exports to the West were limited to raw silk and tea.

Significant steps toward modern economic growth began with the incumbency of Matsukata Masayoshi as Minister of Finance in 1881. Matsukata was committed to financial orthodoxy. He carried out policies of public austerity and deflation, leading to the reintroduction of convertible currency. Public operation of expensive enterprises was discontinued, taxes on tobacco and sake

were raised and other indirect taxes introduced, and a redemption policy for the public debt was emphasized. The government succeeded in saving on average 28 percent of its current revenue, making possible steps toward capital formation. Deflation, in view of the fixed land tax, aided government and hurt farmers. The reduction in the quantity of money brought prices down by one quarter within three years. The Bank of Japan was established in 1885 and became the bank of issue. Rural distress, which was acute, was contained by police measures that have been described.

The mechanism of the economic growth that followed centered first of all on greater output from the traditional agricultural sector. Agriculture and crafts had the capacity for growth and provided the bulk of the capital until shortly after the turn of the century. The traditional economy proved capable of producing additional food and other goods for a growing population while at the same time labor was available for the gradual growth of industry. Thanks to Tokugawa patterns, relatively low levels of population growth and high death rates continued in the 19th century; modern medicine and death control would undoubtedly have slowed economic growth. Disorder on the Chinese continent and low standards of uniformity and quality control in China also gave Japan a regional advantage in its major exports of tea and raw silk. The authoritarian bent of Japan's leaders combined with their traditions of planning in a context of scarcity to make for strong government leadership. The mercantilist nature of domain planning in late Tokugawa times had developed in a context of competitive striving for resources in the programs of remilitarization. Chōshū, for instance, had produced surveys of domain capability commodity by commodity to ascertain its ability to provide the minimal sustenance essential to its population. Similar planning was carried out on a national scale in the 1880s, notably in a survey of industrialization that estimated the possibility for expanded production in each sector of the traditional economy. The Meiji state refrained from state management in all sectors but those of defense, but it was very active in other ways. Destructive competition between Japanese entrepreneurs that threatened the national interest in the face of foreign capital brought state guidance for mergers. In the case of coastal and China shipping the firm that emerged was then provided with government subsidies to enable it to prevail in the battle against the foreigners. For most of the period government was the largest and most important investor in the economy. Its share of capital formation, Henry Rosovsky writes, never averaged less then 40 percent, and it was only rarely that low. Out of this came a pattern which Chalmers Johnson has described as a "developmental" capitalist state in contrast to the "regulative" state. In the latter, private enterprise led and government stepped in to restrain monopolization. In modern Japan, however, the conviction of inherited disadvantage in international competition (through unequal treaties and through deficiency in natural resources) produced patterns of guidance and cooperation to compensate for those disadvantages.

The 1890s, which saw the institutional structure complete, also brought a change in economic balance. Government expenditures for armaments rose rapidly. The indemnity China paid as a result of the Treaty of Shimonoseki was used to establish the Yawata Iron and Steel Works, a decisive step toward heavy industry. Exports of textiles to China and Korea began to assume significant proportions. Natural increases within the modern manufacturing sectors of the economy were also beginning to make themselves felt. This was particularly noticeable around the time of the Russo-Japanese War. By 1905 exports of tea and raw silk were being replaced by the rapid rise of cotton fabrics, cotton yarn and silk fabric, and imports of consumer durables had fallen to about one quarter of domestic production. The internal market was also becoming incapable of satisfying the needs of producers of manufacturers' goods and exports were growing more important.

Despite all this it is important to note that in terms of scale Japan's modern economy was still at a very early stage. In 1900 the proportion of factory output was still well below 10 percent of the national product. It was something over 13 percent at the end of the Meiji period, and slightly over 25 percent in 1931. In 1909 barely 3 percent of the labor force worked in factories. By then cotton-goods production was the most developed modern industry, but more workers were employed by the silk industry in smaller units. In 1909 only 2·9 percent of factory workers were employed in enterprises employing 500 or more workers, 29·5 percent in units employing between 50 and 499, and a heavily preponderant 67·6 percent in enterprises employing fewer than 50 workers. In life-style and consumption patterns there was also remarkable stability over the half-century from late Tokugawa to the late Meiji period. The changes that did occur were partial and involved the substitution of Western for traditional paper umbrellas and of glass for paper in windows; they were only portents of the future. For most of the period traditional coexisted with modern. At court the royal family and officialdom moved into uniform and Western dress, and in the 1880s court ladies appeared in Victorian costume and even took part in dress balls in formal entertainment meant to demonstrate to foreigners the extent of Japan's transformation; but elsewhere throughout Japanese society the introduction of the new came in diminishing degree as the focus descended from elite to commoner and urban to rural. New foods such as bread and meat were luxuries and seldom an integral part of the diet. The continued demand for traditional goods helped to stabilize the economy and prolonged the utility of such goods and those who produced them as well as diminishing the demand for imports.

The impact of war on Japanese society
It was probably the military that had the strongest effect on diffusion of new life-styles and new goods, and the Sino-Japanese and Russo-Japanese Wars were major factors in transforming life in the late Meiji period, just as they transformed people's attitudes toward government, the throne and Japan's continental neighbors, Korea and China. It was not until the turn of the century that many Japanese began to make things Western a normal part of their daily lives.

World War I
By means of a very modest involvement in World War I Japan enhanced her international prestige and advanced her position in Asia and the Pacific. The involvement of the Western powers in the Great War in Europe provided Japan with the opportunity to seize former German colonial possessions in China and the Pacific and to put pressure on China to make other territorial concessions in Japan's favor. On 23 August 1914 Japan declared war on Germany. By November 1914 Japan had secured control of German possessions in Shandong and the German Pacific Islands. In the secret 21 Demands against China in 1915 the Japanese government pressed the Chinese to accede to Japanese control not only of Shandong but of other parts of China, Manchuria and Mongolia. When the demands were made public by the Chinese, they were greeted with condemnation in China and the West. They exposed Japanese imperial ambitions and set them athwart a rising tide of Chinese nationalism. In 1918, satisfying a long-standing ambition to be included among the great powers, Japan was invited to participate as one of the "big five" in the Versailles peace conference, where its control of Shandong and the former German Pacific Islands was recognized, and it was granted a seat on the council of the League of Nations.

The confusion attending the fall of the czar and the Bolshevik revolution in Russia aroused Japanese military ambitions to secure control of eastern Siberia. In July 1918 Japan sent 75000 troops, three times the number sent by her allies, as part of an allied expeditionary force to Siberia. Once in, the Japanese were reluctant to yield to international pressure to withdraw and maintained forces in Siberia until 1922.

100°　　　　　　　120°　　　　　　　140°　　　　　　　160°　　　　　　　180°

USSR

Kamchatka
(USSR)

SEA OF
OKHOTSK

Nikolayevsk
Magdagachi
Chita
Irkutsk
Blagoveshchensk
Amur
Sakhalin
Alexandrovsk-
Sakhalinskiy
Khabarovsk
Karafuto

MONGOLIA

EAST INNER
MONGOLIA

Haerbin

Kuril Is

Vladivostok

Mukden
Antung
KOREA
(CHŌSEN)
SEA OF
JAPAN
JAPAN
Beijing
Tianjin
Yantai
Dairen
Port Arthur
Weihaiwei
Pusan
Tokyo

CHINA

SHANTUNG
Qingdao
1914

PACIFIC

OCEAN

Huang

Nanjing
Hankow
Shanghai
Ningbo

Yangzi

EAST
CHINA
SEA
Okinawa

Bonin Is

Marcus

INDIA

FUKIEN
Fuzhou
Xiamen
Shantou

Iwo Jima

BURMA

Salween

Guangzhou
Hong Kong
(Br)

Taiwan

Hainan

Wake

SIAM
FRENCH
INDOCHINA

Mariana Is
Oct 1914

Mekong

Philippine Is

SOUTH
CHINA
SEA

Guam

INDIAN OCEAN

Eniwetok

Kwajalein

MANDATE, 1920

Truk

Marshall Is
Oct 1914

MALAYA

BRUNEI
N BORNEO
SARAWAK

Palau Is
Oct 1914

Caroline Is
Oct 1914

Borneo

Gilbert Is

DUTCH EAST INDIES

Sumatra

MANDATE, 1920
Nauru
1914

New Ireland

NEW GUINEA
Sept 1914

MANDATE, 1920

Java

PAPUA
(to Aust)

New Britain

Solomon Is
Sept 1914

Ellice Is

Timor

CORAL
SEA

MANDATE, 1920

possessions by Aug 1914

Japanese

British

German

French

Dutch

Portuguese

US

New Hebrides

Fiji Is

New Caledonia

AUSTRALIA

areas targeted by Japan in 21 Demands, 1915

Japanese Siberian expedition 1918–22

gains by 1919

Japanese

British

Australian

main treaty port

main railroad

1:48 000 000

0　　　　　　　　　　1500 km

0　　　　　　　1000 mi

NEW
ZEALAND

Tasmania

World War I brought even larger changes in economic and social life. Japan entered that conflict as an ally of England, but for the most part it limited its contribution to seizure of the German holdings in Shandong and the South Pacific. As the developed economies of the West became absorbed in the production of war materiel, Japan was able to produce for new markets in the West and particularly in Asia. It was now that the economic benefits of the victory over China became clear as Japanese capital was poured into the establishment of textile plants in Shanghai. Japanese shipyards also grew in scale and number. The imperial fleets that had fought the Chinese and Russians had been purchased abroad (as had those they sank), but from now on Japan emerged as a major shipbuilding power. The problem of foreign payments was suddenly solved as exports expanded more rapidly than import requirements. The windfall lasted for only five years, but the effects were felt much longer. Prices rose rapidly as did wages in the modern sector. For the first time, Japan experienced a labor shortage.

With the termination of the war exports fell rapidly and the inflation of the war years gave way to a new era of falling prices. In an effort to remain competitive in the modern sector firms increased investment and worked for higher productivity. From 1922 to 1933 product per worker in the modern sector rose by 60 percent. The same process, however, increased the differentiation in wages and well-being between workers in the modern sector and the traditional sectors. Along with this went a steady trend toward oligopoly in the modern sector, where the *zaibatsu* firms, structured around holding companies held in family hands by Mitsui, Iwasaki (Mitsubishi), Yasuda, Sumitomo, Ōkura and a few others came to assume giant proportions.

The division of the economy into a two-level structure had important consequences. In politics dissatisfied rural groups, thanks to the electoral system, had considerable political influence, an influence that served to further the political ambitions of the army which came to take the posture of spokesman and protector for rural recruits. In economic terms the differential structure perpetuated an unlimited supply of cheap labor because the modern economy, thanks to technical efficiency, required less additional labor. The domestic market also grew only slowly because much of the population was condemned to low productivity and low income.

The decade after World War I was thus full of problems for Japan, and it was a period that economic planners handled poorly. In part this was because the liberal trends of the Taishō period (1912–26) brought expectations of a worldwide shift away from governmental control. Within Japan expectations of governmental ability to manage had also been reduced by the government's disastrous failure to treat an inflation of rice prices that brought nationwide riots in 1918. The bureaucratic government that mishandled these, headed by an army protegé of General Yamagata, was replaced in 1918 by the first cabinet to be headed by a commoner who was also head of a political party. Bureaucratic control over business seemed to be on the wane. Japan seemed to be

following international trends. Until his assassination in 1921 Hara Kei (Takashi) showed considerable ability in maneuvering between entrenched bureaucratic and military interests to advance a more popular and representative interest.

The collapse of the wartime prosperity, however, brought large-scale strikes and worker protests. A 1921 strike of dock workers was particularly acrimonious and was followed by many others. In the countryside disputes between landlords and tenants also proliferated, and tenant unions were formed to try to ameliorate the conditions of tenancy. Importation of rice from Korea and Taiwan helped to depress prices and anger farmers. Many had been able to take full- or part-time work in industry during the war boom, and on their return to tenant farming they wanted more for their labor. Tenant agitation became significant with group petitions by tenants to landlords for rent reduction in 1921, and became a full-fledged movement by the time the left-wing Japan Farmers' Party was organized in 1926.

Above Financial panic swept Japan in the spring of 1927. It was rumored that banks in possession of so-called "earthquake bills" (discounted commercial paper) were in danger of collapsing before the government could redeem them. As many as 37 banks collapsed, among them the Bank of Taiwan. The crisis brought down the Wakatsuki Reijirō cabinet and provoked retrenchment in the banking industry.

Left Conditions in the Japanese countryside prior to the land reforms of 1946 were generally harsh. As a result of Matsukata Masayoshi's deflationary policies there was severe rural depression in the 1880s which cut raw silk prices and bankrupted 100000 farmers in 1885 alone. Many families were forced into tenancy. Some resorted to riots. After World War I cheap rice imports from Korea and Taiwan again drove down farm prices. Some farmers sought strength in unions. Disputes, evictions and rural poverty plagued the 1930s, barely alleviated by farmers' unions or attempts at political action. The photograph shows a Japan Farmers' Party political meeting in Nara Prefecture.

The 1920s marked a prolonged economic slump, one made worse by the enormous costs of the devastating earthquake that struck the heart of Japan on the Tokyo Plain in September 1923. The banking system was rendered unstable by the inability of many borrowers to repay notes, which had been guaranteed to banks by the Bank of Japan. These "earthquake bills," as they were known, helped to undermine bank portfolios because banks holding them were dependent on slow decisions by government bureaucrats. Still other banks were locked into patterns of loans to specific clients by costly commitments they had made to them previously. In 1927 the Bank of Taiwan precipitated a major banking crisis because of its symbiotic relationship with the Suzuki Trading Company, when it filed for bankruptcy. The aftermath of that crisis was so severe that Japan can be said to have entered the Great Depression two years in advance of other industrialized countries.

Out of all this came heightened industrial concentration around the major *zaibatsu* firms that survived. Their banks, the core of each network, were increasingly important to non-*zaibatsu* firms. At the end of the 1920s the Japanese economy was thus significantly different from the economy that had entered World War I. The seeds of later development were present in the Meiji origins of Japanese industrialization. The Taishō era brought vastly increased economic strength and diversity in electrical, chemical and machine industries, but that diversity was accompanied by an increased disparity in well-being between the two strata of the Japanese economy. Cartelization and oligopoly led to social and political unrest that was to figure in the politics and disorder of the 1930s.

Urban culture

By the time the Meiji government issued the Imperial Rescript on Education in 1890, many of its leaders wanted to slow or at least channel the flow of outside influence into Japanese culture and mentality. It could not be done; that influence continued without letup. It was easier to counter in lower schools than in literate society, and it was less welcome in the countryside than it was in the cities. In the 20th century Japan experienced more than a march toward industrialization, and its social history was much more complex than the tales of economic inequality would indicate. Nevertheless Japanese society was remarkable for the sustained growth of a lively urban culture which was the byproduct of the struggle and success of millions to improve themselves through modern education. There were dramatic increases in the number of higher schools and those attending them. By the end of the Meiji period virtually all Japanese were completing the minimal years of lower school, and basic literacy was universal.

The urban culture that developed had its roots in the commoner society of Tokugawa days, but it was enriched by a steadily increasing mix of cultural imports. Letters led in this new culture. Some Meiji authors experimented with adaptations of late Tokugawa fiction and others with translations and rewrites of English political novels, but they finally produced, by the last decade of the Meiji period, works which are regarded as classics

Right By 1890 Tokyo had its first skyscraper, the Ryōunkaku ("pavilion that rises to the clouds"). This 12-story building contained the first elevator in Japan (to the eighth floor). It was a pavilion of pleasure with shops, theaters, bars and restaurants on every floor. At the top were three observation towers and a cupola rising 68 meters above Asakusa. With the construction of the "12-story" (*Junikai*), as it was called, the Asakusa district (which had traditionally been one of the amusement districts) became the most important entertainment area in the city.

of modern Japanese literature. To cite only two: Mori Ōgai (1862–1922) and Natsume Sōseki (1867–1916) have earned a special place in national and, indeed, international literature. Mori, trained as a doctor, combined a career in the Japanese military with one in literature. In poetry and especially documentary fiction he explored the roots of Japanese sensibility with regard to feudal values and virtue to produce a body of work which is only now becoming known to Western readers. Natsume Sōseki, designated to become the successor of Lafcadio Hearn as specialist in English literature at the Tokyo Imperial University, studied in London for some unhappy years before concluding that his roots in Japanese and Chinese literary traditions were more secure. In 1907 he resigned his teaching post to begin editing the literary page of the great *Asahi* newspaper and there he began his novels in serial installments. By the time of his death he had produced a series of narratives which detail with immense skill the psychological and spiritual strains of a culture in rapid transition. He expressed particular horror at the ugliness of excessive egoism, and showed a deep skepticism about the civilization of his time. Many important writers emerged from the group of young disciples he gathered around himself.

Other areas of Meiji culture experienced comparable struggles to combine tradition with change. In art the Meiji leaders hired Italian painters to teach the principles of European representational art in a new Institute of Engineering, and out of that mélange of art and technology there began to emerge elements that would cohere in a new school of painting known as "Nihonga," Japanese painting. Music also found Western (in this case American) specialists imported to prepare song books suitable for the public schools. By the end of Meiji schoolchildren were singing an ode to fireflies drawn from a Stephen Foster melody ("My Old Kentucky Home") transformed into the Japanese harmonic mode.

In the years after World War I these beginnings seemed distant and old-fashioned. A new wave of cultural imports, spontaneous and not sponsored, brought far broader participation in international currents to Japan. Japan was one of the major allies and great powers and soon took a seat among its peers in the League of Nations. There was a much greater sense of belonging and of change among young people.

Not surprisingly this began with students. At Tokyo Imperial University a "New Man Society" (*Shinjinkai*), formed late in 1918, enrolled some of the most adventurous members of the intellectual elite. Its faculty sponsor was Professor Yoshino Sakuzō, an intellectual leader in the articulation of "Taishō Democracy" whose writings emphasized the democratic potential of the Meiji constitutional order. Ideals of internationalism, fired by the appointment of the educator Nitobe Inazō as assistant director general of the League of Nations, sparked many leaders of the new generation. The rebuilding of Tokyo after the great earthquake of 1923 eradicated many marks of the old city and of its culture and contributed to a sense of newness and of change. Popular culture eagerly embraced the superficial as well as the deeper aspects of a new Westernization. Motion-picture theaters and

cafés, dance halls and revues, appealed to the flapper and her counterpart. Student slang produced neologisms that stamp the generation; *modan* (modern), *moga* (for *modan gaaru*, or modern girl). The new world of entertainment had its economic consequence in the emergence of a large-scale beer industry as well as in ready-made clothing.

Throughout Japan the influence of the great metropolitan press grew steadily. The reading scene was further affected by a series of new periodicals of which the most popular was *Kaizō* or *Reconstruction*. As with the economic differentiation that has been discussed, the distance between this urban society and the poverty of backward sectors of rural Japan was particularly marked.

The new wave of influence included the writings of social reformers and radicals. The work of Karl Marx seemed to have new significance in a world in which it had found expression in the institutions of post-revolutionary Russia. Revolution and radicalism in China also reverberated in Japan to stimulate some and alarm others.

Bureaucrats in the Home Ministry had long been concerned about the possible spread of social radicalism to Japan. The Social Problems Division of the Home Ministry argued the need to anticipate such developments with social legislation like factory and labor laws, but interest groups of those affected argued that the "unique" paternalistic patterns of Japanese society rendered such innovations unnecessary. Factory legislation was slow in coming and slower in being enforced, but the tenant and labor ferment of the 1920s illustrated the need for a government response.

The government did respond with carrot and with stick. In 1925 universal manhood suffrage extended the ballot to males over 25. The electorate for the elections of 1928, the first carried out under its provisions, leaped to 12 million voters. With this was coupled the stick of police repression. The Peace Preservation Act also of 1925 established a Special Higher Police to deal with "dangerous thought" and instituted harsh penalties for forming or joining organizations which derogated private property or the "national polity." That vague term (*kokutai*) became increasingly important to conservatives; ultimately it involved the imperial system and symbol. In 1928 the Peace Preservation Act was strengthened to add provisions for capital punishment for crimes against the "polity." That same year a sweeping round-up of Communists and suspected Communists struck the left a body blow from which it did not fully recover before World War II.

The year 1928 also marked the enthronement ceremonies for the young emperor Hirohito, whose reign was to bear the era name Shōwa, Enlightenment and Harmony. The young sovereign was in some ways an exemplar of trends that have been discussed. Conservatives had opposed his consort on grounds of color blindness in her family, and though a son was long in coming he firmly refused to take a concubine as his forebears had done. In 1921 he was able to make a trip to England, a break in the decorum and ritual of the court he would long remember with nostalgia. Hirohito had succeeded his father as regent in 1922 for reasons of ill health. On the occasion of his enthronement in

Prominent among the writers who did most to establish modern psychological fiction in Japan were Mori Ōgai (1862–1922), *top*, and Natsume Sōseki (1867–1916), *above*. In their different ways they brought Japanese literature face to face with the ambiguities of modernity and the maintenance of cultural traditions. Ōgai, a German-trained physician, had cultivated an interest in Chinese, Japanese and Western literature. His stories dealt sensitively with sexuality in modern Japan and with historical and biographical themes. Sōseki, more than any other writer, probed the loneliness and guilt of the modern Japanese intellectual.

For Japan the 1920s and early 1930s were a period of growing democratic impulses, domestic urban prosperity and international stability. The young ladies peering into the telescope watching stars (*top right*) probably do not notice storm clouds already gathered over Manchuria or the political crises in Tokyo. They reflect an affluent urban life-style that offered new opportunities for leisure and popular culture. The Takarazuka and Shōchiku dance and entertainment troupes (*far right*) attracted crowds of middle-class young women to their performances of "strictly wholesome entertainment suitable for women and children from good families."

1928 the young emperor's rescript promised to nurture his people and to bring them up in harmony, to speed the nation's well-being and to work for peace throughout the world. A nervous police seized over 7000 of those same people, sometimes for nothing more than carrying a copy of the journal *Reconstruction*, and held them for questioning without charges for as long as a month until the celebration was accomplished. Small wonder perhaps, that Hirohito's reign would come to be divided into an era of war and one of peace.

The attack on Manchuria

The interwar period in Japan contained much evidence that trends of liberalism were in the ascendancy. After the death of Hara, the first prime minister chosen from the ranks of party leaders, cabinets fell under bureaucratic direction until 1924, when a united "Defend the Constitution" movement produced a coalition cabinet under the leadership of Katō Takaaki. Katō's Foreign Minister, Shidehara Kijūrō, followed a strongly internationalistic policy in line with Japan's commitment to the set of Pacific treaties that had been worked out at the Washington Conference in 1922. Shidehara refrained from interference during the stormy years in China that accompanied the rise of Jiang Jieshi's Guomindang, and he tried to follow this course again during his second term in office under the cabinet of Hamaguchi Osachi (1928–31). With the decline of the original *genrō* (only Saionji Kimmochi, who died in 1940, remained of the original group) Japan's leadership was less monolithic and cohesive, and representatives of the armed services, business, bureaucracy and agrarian interest groups competed for

Above The young Emperor Hirohito, who ascended the throne on 25 December 1926, adopted the era name Shōwa ("enlightenment and harmony") for his reign. Isolated from political conflict, he generally only approved decisions made by his advisers and officials. On one or two rare occasions he did assert his moderate views forcefully. His strong stand against the young military officers in the attempted coup of 26 February 1936 was largely responsible for its rapid suppression. He also broke the deadlock in deciding to accept the surrender terms of the Potsdam Declaration in 1945.

influence. Party cabinets seemed to be becoming the norm. Katō and his group made efforts to lessen the obstructive powers of the House of Peers, introduce social legislation and reduce the size and power of the armed services. They also extended the franchise, while implementing new police legislation. The Hara government carried through naval limitations worked out at Washington in 1922, and Hamaguchi did the same after the London Naval Conference in 1930. Such measures were denounced by ultranationalists. Both Hara and Hamaguchi were assassinated, and the era of party cabinets came to an end with the murder of Prime Minister Inukai in 1932. There were genuine currents making for internationalsim, but trends toward militarism proved stronger.

Countercurrents to internationalism were to be found at many points in Japanese society. At the very top, Meiji generation leaders who had spent a lifetime working for their country to reach the level of full participant in great-power imperialism were dismayed to find imperialism suddenly out of favor after World War I. The sudden end of empire for Germany, Russia, Austria-Hungary and Manchu China seemed to offer compelling opportunities for a rising power, but the Anglo-Saxon victors, while retaining their own colonies, were taking a strongly anti-colonial line. A young Prince Konoe Fumimaro, on his way to the Versailles Conference in 1918, came to notice with a strong indictment of such double standards. Then again, the Washington Conference system, for which Japan had to sacrifice its 20-year alliance with Great Britain, seemed a mixed blessing. While it promised co-operative action and respect for "China," it seemed to Japanese that the other signatories were over-eager to reach accommodation with Chinese nationalism and glad to have a newly imperialist Japan singled out for criticism. Advocates of living space for Japan argued that the northeastern provinces of Manchuria, at any rate, should receive special treatment. They had been paid for in the blood of the Russo-Japanese War, and they provided a burgeoning Japanese population with its only hope of expansion and growth. Even internationalists like Shidehara did not oppose such assertions for Manchuria; differences lay in opinions about the way Japan could proceed to lay claim to its legacy.

At lower levels of Japanese society, particularly within the military, there was impatience with what seemed the stultification of a defense establishment which had not known the sanction of real war and emergency since 1905. Young officers felt suffocated by the political caution and favoritism of a high command that had only begun to emerge from the Satsuma-Chōshū dominance of Meiji times. They were full of suspicion and contempt for what they considered the self-serving practices of politicians within the military. Periodic evidence of corruption in high places fueled additional discontent. Poorly prepared in history or in policy but convinced of their own patriotism, they were convinced that great opportunities lay at hand on the north Asian mainland and determined that the timidity and indecisiveness of civilian politicians and their military and bureaucratic allies should not be allowed to let them slip from Japan's hands. Just as there were "civilian" moderates within the military, there were "militar-ist" enthusiasts within the party-political and business worlds. The hardships which the Great Depression visited on the Japanese countryside, where the market for silk all but disappeared with startling suddenness, provided additional social pressures. The young officers charged that civilian politicians were indifferent to such suffering, and that they in fact helped cause it with policies geared to their business supporters.

It was natural that the northeast provinces of Manchuria should become the focus of some of the agitation as nationalist armies battled in China. In 1927 *Seiyūkai* politicians, tired of being out of power, entrusted their party to General Tanaka Giichi and charged Shidehara with pursuing a weak China policy. Shortly after Tanaka took office in 1927 he intervened twice in Shandong to block Jiang Jieshi's northern expedition. A year later, adventurers on the staff of the Guandong Army arranged the murder of the Manchurian war lord Zhang Zuolin. It was their hope that this would lead to a takeover of all of Manchuria, but instead it produced the fall of Tanaka, who was unable to satisfy his young emperor that the army had not been involved. Conspirators did not stop there, however; soon staff officers of the Guandong Army were at work again on more ambitious plans for a takeover of Manchuria and the construction of an ostensibly autonomous state that would ally with Japan.

In 1930 and 1931 economic conditions in Japan seemed to reach a nadir. The Hamaguchi cabinet had restored the gold standard at the worst possible time, producing a deflation that coincided with the world depression. Hamaguchi was at loggerheads with the Navy General Staff about acceptance of the London Naval Conference agreements, and young officers in the Army General Staff were organizing by graduation class to further their political agenda. In March 1931 a proposed coup d'etat in Tokyo narrowly misfired when a senior general decided not to cooperate with it. That September Guandong Army plotters struck, seizing the arsenal and command posts of the war lord, and began their systematic sweep of Manchuria.

Because of the institutional strength of the military and the strategic position of the Guandong Army within the military it would have required firm decisions by the Tokyo military leadership to reverse these actions. In fact there was strong support at lower levels in headquarters for what had been done, and hesitation at higher levels. Foreign Minister Shidehara, uninformed and anxious to put an end to the "Incident," made promises that he was unable to keep, and before the year was out the Guandong Army had seized all of Manchuria. The cabinet fell and Shidehara was soon out of the Foreign Office. Inukai, the new Prime Minister, groped for ways to restrain the military, but before he could make headway in this he was slain by young naval officers who had returned from a Shanghai Incident in 1932. It was their hope to seat a military government, but that was not to come for almost another decade. Conservative elder statesmen and court advisers instead experimented with a series of what they hoped would be national unity cabinets under respected naval figures of the recent past.

Japanese imperialism to 1941
From the mid-19th century, while much of Asia was being subjected to Western imperialism, Japan broke out of a net of unequal treaties, acquired great-power status as an ally of Great Britain and pursued imperial ambitions of its own. Japanese expansion was impelled by the example and rivalries of the Western powers, by the opportunity provided by the exposed weaknesses of Korea, China and Russia and by growing strategic conviction that Japan's security depended upon control first of Korea, and then of Manchuria, as "a line of advantage." It was also driven by the growing Japanese economic and military power and by eagerness for economic exploitation of the mineral wealth of Manchuria (Manchukuo). In 1874 Japan secured control of the Ryukyu Islands from China. In 1894 it went to war with China over Korea. Japan won a quick victory and under the Treaty of Shimonoseki (1895) acquired the Pescadores, Taiwan and the Liaodong Peninsula. Tripartite intervention by Russia, Germany and France forced the reversion of Liaodong. Victory over China put Japan squarely on the road to expansion and empire. It also marked a dramatic shift in the east Asian balance of power from China to Japan.

As a result of its spectacular victory over Russia in 1904–05 Japan secured undisputed control over Korea, Russian interests in southern Manchuria including the railroad and the Liaodong Peninsula, and the southern part of Sakhalin (Karafuto). In 1910 Korea was annexed outright and Japan proceeded to exploit Korea and Manchuria economically. By declaring war on Germany in World War I Japan acquired former German colonial possessions in China and the Pacific. Between 1918 and 1922 the Japanese sent a large expeditionary force into Manchuria and southern Siberia. From 1931 Japan extended control over Manchuria, created the puppet state of Manchukuo and pressed into China. In 1941, taking advantage of war in Europe and the German invasion of Russia, it advanced on Indochina. The Japanese challenge to the Western powers stimulated independence movements in several Asian countries, including Thailand and the Philippines. In December 1941 Japanese planes attacked Pearl Harbor and Japanese forces advanced through Asia and the Pacific, trying to fulfill the dream of a new Japanese imperial order in Asia.

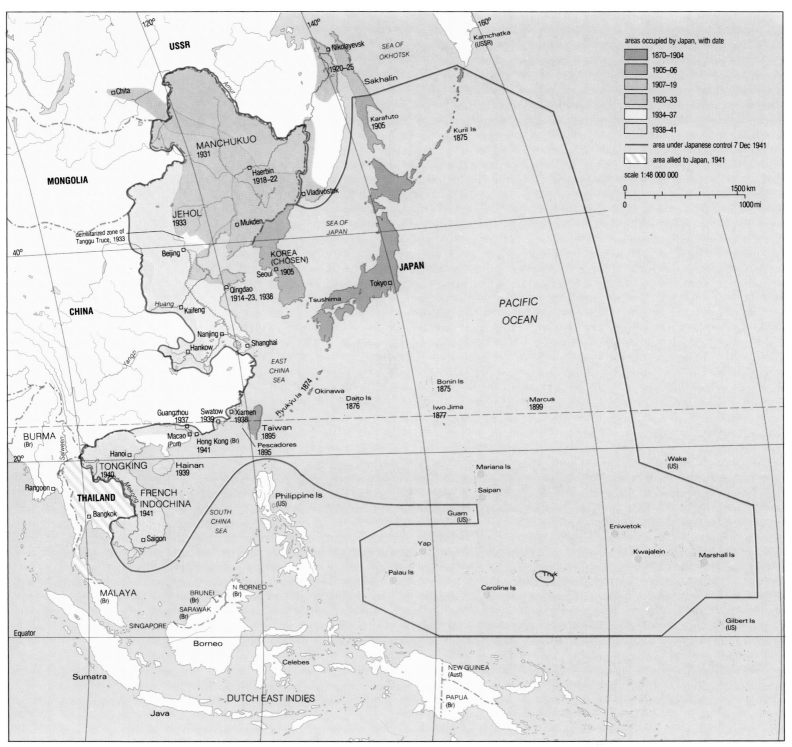

Militarism in the 1930s

The 1930s saw Japanese advance slowly south from Manchuria despite the lack of a clear policy. In 1933 Japan withdrew from the League of Nations to show its discontent with the conclusions of the League's Lytton Commission. That same year Japan recognized "Manchukuo" as an independent state. The first puppet state of the 1930s, the state was headed by "Henry" Pu Yi, the last Manchu ruler, and the commanding general of the Guandong Army doubled as Ambassador. Top posts were held by Manchus and Chinese, usually elderly gentlemen who had studied in Meiji Japan, but effective control lay with Japanese bureaucrats who were assigned to ministries on a fixed numerical scale. Japan poured substantial amounts of money into the development of its puppet state, and substantial beginnings were made in heavy

industry, but the Japanese defeat came before returns had been realized on these investments.

The arbitrary military steps that had been taken in the effort to achieve regional hegemony isolated Japan in international opinion. Tokyo governments, realizing the strong swing of popular favor for decisive acts in Manchuria and north China, waited for a more favorable time before trying to reverse such trends. Insubordination and plotting continued in the army, where talk of a "Shōwa Restoration" spread as hot-headed young officers compared themselves with the activists who had brought about the Meiji restoration. Army personnel shifts became explosive. In 1935 a lieutenant colonel murdered one of the army's foremost planners in his office, and the following year, on 26 February, an entire division about to be shifted to Manchuria obeyed the commands of its officers to rebel in the expectation of precipitating a crisis so severe that a military government would have to be formed. The rebels succeeded in surrounding the palace and murdering a number of senior government officials, but they failed in their purpose, in good measure because the emperor demanded that they be treated as rebels rather than patriots. The 26 February 1936 incident marked the high-water point of factional activity by the so-called "Imperial Way" (Kōdō) faction, and leadership now passed to a "Control" (Tōsei) group which pointed energy abroad.

Court conservatives, searching for an effective counterweight to the military, turned to the young Prince Konoe Fumimaro, who headed the first of his three cabinets in 1937. Almost immediately violence broke out at the Marco Polo Bridge in Beijing between units of a Japanese and Chinese garrison. For a period agreement against expansion of the fighting seemed to have been reached, but an unexpected firmness in the Chinese military response, together with strong-arm tactics on the part of Japanese military commanders, led to a war that was not over until 1945.

Japanese aggression in China and reports of Japanese atrocities, particularly at Nanjing, turned English and American opinion decisively against Japan. Germany, however, was less dismayed, and amateur diplomats among Japan's military-turned-ambassadors conceived the idea of restraining British and especially American action by uniting with Germany and Italy in an Anti-Comintern Pact which was signed in 1936. In 1938 Germany announced its recognition of Manchukuo, and in 1940 Foreign Minister Matsuoka Yōsuke negotiated a ten-year Triple Alliance with Germany and Italy. The pact contained promises of help in case any of the partners became involved with a country not yet at war, i.e. the United States. Matsuoka mistakenly thought that he had lessened the likelihood of war with America, but in fact his clumsy work had convinced United States Secretary of State Cordell Hull and many others that Japan was firmly committed to a course of fascism. Nevertheless that was not really the case.

Many Japanese, to be sure, became convinced during the decade that liberal democracy in the West was failing and speculated that some stronger form of government control which could retain elements of national individuality, and concentrate on the kokutai, should be substituted for the ineffective and contentious structure of party-political cabinets. By the late 1930s the popular and enigmatic Konoe Fumimaro seemed a possible symbol and leader for such a structure, and when he came to office a second time in 1940 there seemed considerable support for an "Imperial Rule Assistance Association" (Taisei yokusankai) that was to replace the political parties. Konoe himself worked with a brain trust of bright young academics, ultimately incorporated as the Shōwa Kenkyū Kai (Shōwa Research Association) which explored many such areas. Many "new bureaucrats" were also attracted to a system in which their ability to affect and control developments would be greater. Konoe's political association did come into being, and the political parties dissolved voluntarily to enter it, but it did not portend a basic change and never became an effective organization or movement.

Japan had no real mass party and never developed a Führer or Duce who was allowed to overshadow the imperial aura.

The outbreak of war in Europe in 1939 was followed by the Nazi victories in the west in 1940 and the attack on the Soviet Union in 1941. Matsuoka had followed Hitler's lead in developing a Neutrality Treaty with Russia in the belief that he was forming a great German, Japanese, Italian and Soviet coalition of revisionist powers against the Anglo-American nations that refused to cooperate with Japan in China. When that plan collapsed with the German attacks, Konoe parted company with Matsuoka, who wanted to join the Germans with an attack to the north. Japan's urgent needs for raw materials could now be satisfied only through further steps in Southeast Asia or by making concessions to the United States by relaxing its hold on China. Konoe argued for an attempt to work toward closer relations with the United States, in effect reversing the pattern of Axis-directed Matsuoka policy. At the last he tried to arrange a personal meeting with President Franklin D. Roosevelt in the hope that some arrangement could be worked out. When that failed, he resigned in despair and was replaced by General Tōjō Hideki.

Pearl Harbor and its consequences

Two factors prevented the meeting from taking place. One was the United States' insistence on some sort of agreement about China before a summit meeting took place. American leaders doubted that Konoe could sway the military, and they were afraid that apparent encouragement for Japan would lead Jiang Jieshi to accept Japanese blandishments on his own. The other was the insistence of the Japanese military on situating whatever discussions took place in the context of an "outline of fundamental national policy" that was adopted on 2 July 1941 in the presence of the emperor. By its terms Japan would try for a settlement of the China war, prepare for southern expansion and try to solve its northern problem in the course of "constructing a Greater East Asian

Above Prince Konoe Fumimaro (1891–1945) headed three prewar cabinets. In the early 1930s Japan's growing international isolation, rightist political assassinations at home and military interventions in China and Manchuria combined to undermine the authority of the parties and reassert the power of the military. The last prewar party prime minister, Inukai Tsuyoshi, was assassinated in 1932. In Konoe's cabinets most positions were occupied by military men. His first cabinet of 1937 saw the outbreak of war with China; his second and third brought Japan to the brink of war with the United States and strengthened militarist and authoritarian tendencies in Japanese domestic and foreign policy.

Right This captured Japanese photograph shows Pearl Harbor as it appeared to the Japanese pilots who swept in for a surprise attack on the morning of 7 December (8 December Japanese time) 1941. Four battleships and two other vessels were sunk, four battleships and 12 other ships were disabled and 3700 men were killed or wounded. The Japanese lost 64 men, 29 aircraft and five special submarines. The attack failed in its larger strategic aims of totally destroying the US Pacific fleet and shattering the American will to fight.

Co-Prosperity Sphere regardless of changes in the world situation." The empire would, in short, prepare for action at all points and be guided by circumstances in acting on those preparations. The army supreme command, sobered by recent defeats at the hands of Russian forces in undeclared warfare that had raged at Nomonhan in 1939, and aware that Russian defenses against a thrust from Manchuria remained strong, chose to occupy Indochina immediately to strengthen its strategic position in Southeast Asia. This destroyed any likelihood of effective negotiations with Washington and brought swift retaliation in the form of a freeze on Japanese assets and a cut-off of oil. Faced now with dwindling supplies and a deadline for possible success in initial strikes, the military were unenthusiastic about any Konoe-Roosevelt talks that would extend their timetable. When Admiral Nomura, Japanese ambassador in Washington, was unable to secure even moderate and provisional agreements from Cordell Hull in November, a decision for war brought the attack on Pearl Harbor in December 1941.

Japan's initial successes were tactically brilliant and strategically disastrous. The military, and particularly the navy, had not wanted war with the United States, realizing they could not prevail in a long struggle, but felt themselves constrained by shrinking capabilities in materiel to act while there was still the possibility of early victories. Those might change the setting for negotiation and heighten the probability of success. The reverse was the case; the resources of Southeast Asia were only briefly available and inadequately managed, while the initial humiliation of defeat produced an

American and Allied determination to accept nothing short of unconditional surrender.

The turning point in the Pacific War came early, at the battle of Midway in late May and early June of 1942. The shattering loss in aircraft carriers and trained pilots that Japan sustained there tilted the balance of forces. Grinding and expensive conquest of the Pacific islands lay ahead and thousands of lives would be lost; but for Japanese aware of what had taken place the war had been irretrievably lost. Political responses were coordinated with military defeats. The fall of Saipan brought down the Tōjō cabinet in 1944 and replaced it with one under General Koiso Kuniaki. In 1944 MacArthur's forces retook the Philippines, and in the spring of 1945 the invasion of Okinawa began a fierce battle that was resolved with the surrender of the surviving Japanese forces in June. Retired Admiral Suzuki Kantarō now became Prime Minister.

Frantic efforts had begun to find a way of extricating Japan from the war. B-29 raids based on Saipan and Tinian which began in March 1945 had laid waste all of Japan's principal cities except Kyoto with incendiary bombs. All over the Pacific, Japanese garrisons, cut off and bypassed, were unable to resupply themselves. Naval authorities had resorted to suicide flights of "divine wind" (*kamikaze*) units of inexperienced pilots as a way of offsetting diminished supplies of fuel and quality of aircraft. Japan itself was cut off from food supplies from its empire, without an adequate agricultural labor force, and reduced to uprooting ancient pines to extract oil from their roots. As early as February 1945 Konoe Fumimaro had

Above Shidehara Kijūrō was twice foreign minister (1924–27, 1929–31) and once prime minister (1945–46). As a prewar foreign minister he is remembered for "Shidehara diplomacy" which stressed internationalism and good relations with Britain and the USA. His internationalist, pro-Western views made his loyalty seem questionable to the nationalists in the 1930s. From 1931 to 1945 he remained in semiretirement as a member of the House of Peers. In 1945 he was elected to serve as prime minister. In his few months in office he worked to preserve the emperor system. His Progressive Party was defeated in the first postwar general election of 1946.

addressed a memorandum to the emperor arguing the need to end the war. Extension of the struggle, he warned, could lead only to a leftist revolution and permanent threat to the *kokutai*; indeed, as he now looked back on the 1930s, the self-styled patriots among the military had actually been Janus-faced agents of revolution and subversion.

On the American side Under Secretary of State Joseph Grew, the prewar ambassador in Tokyo, had been working on a modification of "unconditional surrender" to reassure the Japanese elite that *kokutai* and the imperial system could survive surrender. He was blocked in this, but at the Potsdam Conference in late July President Truman issued for the allies an assurance that the "Japanese should not be enslaved as a race or destroyed as a nation; . . . Japan shall be permitted to maintain such industries as will sustain her economy; . . .

eventual Japanese participation in world trade relations shall be permitted"; and "The occupying forces of the Allies shall be withdrawn from Japan as soon as these objectives [punishment of war criminals, the military disarmed and democratic reforms instituted] have been accomplished and there has been established in accordance with the freely expressed will of the Japanese people a peacefully inclined and responsible government."

The Suzuki cabinet was unable to respond to this, and used the term *mokusatsu*—literally "ignore," or "no comment"—to the public. Taking this as rejection, as it was, American leaders went ahead with their decision to utilize the first atom bombs. At Hiroshima, on 6 August, and Nagasaki, on 9 August, atomic horror was first revealed to the world. On 8 August the Soviet Union entered Manchuria and Korea to claim its share of the

World War II
In the summer of 1941, taking advantage of the German onslaught against the USSR, the Japanese army moved against French Indochina. The allies imposed an embargo on Japan, cutting off oil supplies and raw materials. While negotiating for peace, the Japanese leadership planned for war. On the morning of 7 December 1941 Japanese dive bombers struck Pearl Harbor in a devastating surprise attack and destroyed most of the US Pacific fleet. The Japanese army simultaneously advanced on Hong Kong and Malaya. The speed and strength of the Japanese advances brought rapid early victories across Asia and the Pacific. After the battle of Midway in 1942, however, the tide began to turn and Japan's defeat became inevitable.

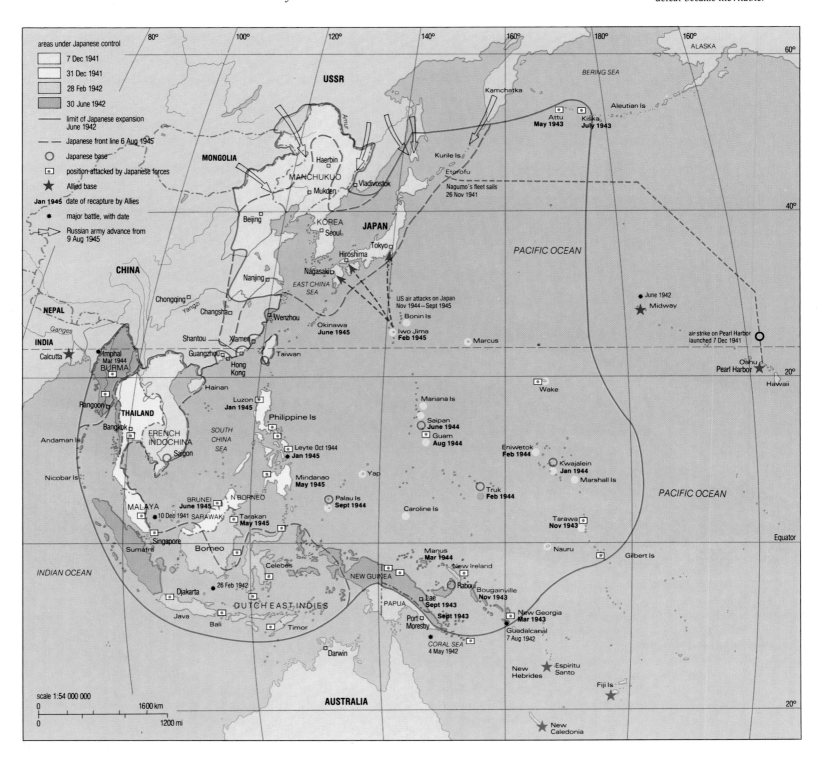

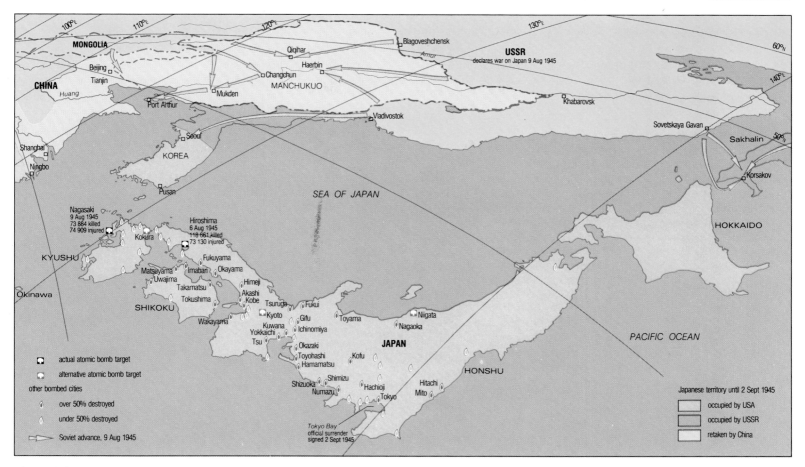

Above: defeat and occupation
By the spring of 1945, with Japanese cities being laid waste by bombing and fire, some Japanese civilian and military leaders recognized that the war was lost and that the time had come to extricate Japan. Others, especially in the army high command, either refused to admit defeat or argued that better terms would be gained by resisting to the end. When the Suzuki cabinet was unable to respond to the Potsdam Declaration of late July 1945 calling for a qualified unconditional surrender, the American leaders determined to unleash the atomic weapons developed by the Manhattan Project against Japanese cities. Among the targets discussed were Kyoto, Niigata, Kokura, Hiroshima and Nagasaki. As the former capital and cultural city Kyoto was spared. Hiroshima was bombed on 6 August and Nagasaki on 9 August. On 9 August Soviet forces advanced into Korea and Manchukuo. By 15 August the emperor had resolved the deadlock between the diehards and those willing to accept surrender. Japan surrendered and was open to occupation and reform. Scholarly opinion is divided on the ending of the war and its aftermath, but it is clear that the cataclysmic defeat and the subsequent reforms allowed the Japanese to rebuild a peaceful, prosperous, democratic society.

Right The first atomic bomb used against human targets was dropped at 8.15 am, 6 August 1945, on Hiroshima. On this watch found in the rubble the time of the blast has been etched into the face.

reward. In Tokyo the cabinet now wrestled with a decision. Army Minister Anami wanted to wait for the invasion, hoping that the enormous losses this would incur would force the Americans to provide a guarantee of the emperor system. A provisional response offered the United States this surrender with retention of the emperor, but Secretary of State Byrnes's masterfully ambiguous reply stated that the emperor would be subject to the occupying forces and that the ultimate form of government would be decided by the Japanese people.

Debate resumed in Tokyo; conservatives were dissatisfied, but optimists argued that a subject emperor was still an emperor and that they could count on their countrymen to make the right decision. Divided and deadlocked, the cabinet turned to the emperor himself for a decision. He resolved the issue in favor of acceptance of the Potsdam Declaration. A rescript announcing this was prepared, and the sovereign recorded it for broadcast at noon on 15 August, Tokyo time.

That night a final insurrection of guards officers killed their commander and invaded the palace to find and destroy the recording. It proved adequately hidden, and the next day the nation heard for the first time the voice of its ruler. The Surrender Rescript, when carefully read, is a powerful and fascinating document. The sovereign is endowed with a sacrificial and compassionate nature, and only his virtue can save humanity. "Should we continue to fight, not only would it result in an ultimate collapse and obliteration of the Japanese nation, but it would also lead to the total extinction of human civilization. Such being the case, how are We to save the millions of our subjects, and atone ourselves before the hallowed spirits of our imperial ancestors?'' The final message, reminiscent of a Boddhisattva, is expressed in the language of the *Sūtra in 42 Sections*: "We have resolved to pave the way for a grand peace for all generations to come by enduring what cannot be endured and suffering what cannot be suffered.''

In 1868, at the time of the Meiji restoration, an imperial prince led the triumphant armies north. Now several imperial princes traveled to distant battlefields to ensure the armies' surrender while another, Higashikuni, took the prime minister's chair.

REFORM AND RECONSTRUCTION

Postwar occupation and isolation

From September 1945 to the implementation of the San Francisco Treaty of Peace in the spring of 1952 Japan was under an Allied occupation commanded by General Douglas A. MacArthur. As Supreme Commander for the Allied Powers (SCAP) MacArthur received his orders from the War Department in Washington, and Japan's was essentially an American occupation. A Far Eastern Commission was set up in Washington to provide guidance and an Allied Council representing the British Commonwealth, Soviet Union, United States and China sat in Tokyo to oversee and report, but in practice the Commission was usually informed after the fact and the Council was ignored. MacArthur's headquarters worked under instructions provided shortly after the Japanese surrender by a joint State-War-Navy Department committee in Washington. But since American and European opinion, public and private, was concentrated on European problems, in practice MacArthur enjoyed wide latitude. Considerations of personnel, knowledge and language made it necessary to work through the Japanese government. SCAP directives were consequently filtered through the Japanese bureaucracy, and, as time went on, Japanese government agencies played increasingly important roles. Initially they professed astonishment at the range of SCAP expectations and responded only to directives.

Japanese were repatriated from abroad and Japan maintained no foreign relations or business establishments until the recovery of sovereignty in 1952. In a sense the Japanese were returned to an isolation comparable to that of Tokugawa days, except that outside information and influence now came from American rather than Dutch channels. When efforts to resume export trade began, they were carried on by officials of SCAP, while the personnel of Japan's great trading companies watched from the sidelines.

The MacArthur-sponsored changes can also be compared to those of the Meiji period. For a second time Japanese institutions were declared inadequate and outdated, "evil" customs of the past were to be discarded, and wisdom was to be sought abroad. Once again this was done from above, though this time not in the interests of making the empire strong but of making it peaceful and just. For a second time criticism was not brooked; censorship ruled out unfavorable comment by the Japanese media, and American or Western reporters who were thought negative found it difficult to renew the military permits that were required for entry into Japan. Yet despite all the ironies involved in the efforts to impose democratic reforms, SCAP's measures were in broad agreement with the sweep of modern Japanese history and beneficial for and pleasing to Japan's urban middle class. The nation was thoroughly disillusioned with its military masters, sobered to learn of the

actions of its troops in China and other occupied areas, and much too poorly fed, clothed and housed to retain the pride and arrogance of the early war years.

SCAP moved first to remove the military supports of the old state. Armed forces were disbanded, nationalist organizations banned, and several hundred thousand individuals, defined by categories or ranks, removed from positions of importance and purged. An International Tribunal for the Far East set to work trying to determine responsibility for the war decisions. Seven men, including former Prime Minister General Tōjō, were sentenced to death by hanging, and 16 sentenced to life imprisonment. Because there was no Nazi-style grand design to locate, however, the judgments of 1948 were gradually softened by history. Kishi Nobusuke, a member of the Tōjō cabinet, who was never brought to trial despite his early status as a grade A suspect, returned as prime minister in 1957, and postwar Prime Minister Yoshida Shigeru provided the calligraphy for a memorial inscription to "Seven Patriots" in 1959.

State Shinto was disestablished, and on New Year's Day in 1946 Emperor Hirohito renounced his claims to divinity in a proclamation explaining that the ties that bound him to his people did not rest on such fallacies. The Home Ministry, with its controls over police and local administration, was disestablished and its functions allotted to other agencies. *Zaibatsu* firms were ticketed for dissolution. In education the dominance of Tokyo Imperial University was challenged by a broadening of opportunities for higher education. All along the line deconcentration and liberalization replaced the rigid elitsm of the old society. Peace and democracy were the shibboleths of the day; Japan was not to be a "menace" to the world again, and its

After the dropping of the atomic bombs on Hiroshima on 6 August and Nagasaki on 9 August 1945 Japan accepted the terms of the Potsdam Declaration on 14 August and signed the Instrument of Surrender on 2 September aboard the USS *Missouri*. With the cessation of hostilities all administrative powers of the Japanese government were placed in the hands of the Supreme Commander for the Allied Powers (SCAP) General Douglas MacArthur. Under him were more than 150000 largely American troops and 5500 bureaucrats who made up the SCAP administration, working with Japanese statesmen and bureaucrats. Here American tanks parade past the SCAP headquarters in Tokyo overlooking the Imperial Palace.

Most of Japan's major cities and industrial facilities were burned out or reduced to rubble in the bombing of early 1945. The population suffered from unemployment, inflation and severe shortages of food, clothing and housing. Urban dwellers trekked into the countryside to barter family heirlooms for food. Black markets sprang up on street corners and people picked through urban rubble for things to sell or barter.

people were to have more to say in their government and a larger share of the fruits of their labor. A generation later much of the rhetoric that came out of SCAP seems naive and condescending, but in its context and time the occupation would probably compare favorably with other efforts to promote social change by outside forces.

The capstone of Japan's new institutional structure was a constitution proposed by the Government Section of SCAP and implemented in 1947. It begins with tones reminiscent of the Gettysburg Address. The emperor is defined as the "symbol" of the state who derives his position from the "will of the people with whom resides sovereign power." The document includes a 30-article Bill of Rights, which extend to "minimum standards of wholesome and cultured living," collective bargaining and academic freedom, and rules out discrimination on grounds of "race, creed, sex, social status or family origin." The peerage was dissolved, and a new Upper House of Councillors substituted; Privy Council and palace authority also disappeared.

The "Peace Constitution" derives its name from Article IX in which the language of the Pact of Paris is invoked to renounce war as a "sovereign right of the nation," followed by the pledge that "land, sea and air forces, as well as other war potential, will never be maintained." After the Korean War and the restoration of Japan's sovereignty a Self-Defense Agency was established with the rationale that Japan had an inherent right of self-defense, although such forces could not be used outside the boundaries of Japan, nor could their equipment be offensive in nature. These compromises have run the risk of casuistry, and no part of the postwar structure has generated more controversy. Suggestions for changing this language to conform with the reality of a defense structure have stirred fears of a reversal of other postwar institutional gains, and as a result the constitution, despite its manifest foreign origins and language, has gained in strength and support during its first four decades. The Meiji constitution, it will be remembered, endured 55 years.

Economic and social reforms

The most striking success in SCAP's program of economic reform converted tenant farmers into owners. The land reform was no less ambitious and portentous than the Meiji land tax revision, for it converted a struggling countryside into a dynamic society capable of providing more food and clamoring for the products of Japan's industries. The wartime government had anticipated this in some respects by interposing agricultural associations between tenants and landlords, and the relative well-being of villagers had improved as soldiers sent their wages home and the ravaged cities became desperate for agricultural produce. In 1946, by SCAP directive, land commissions with owner, landlord and tenant representation selected land eligible for purchase and resale to eligible tenant purchasers. The land was bought and sold at preinflation prices so favorable to purchasers that most had liquidated their debts within four years. At one stroke the land reform removed the injustice and hardship that had been the stock complaints of the 1930s. Conservative governments were initially uneasy about expropriating their rural supporters, but soon found themselves the beneficiaries of a satisfied, thriving and over-represented countryside. Advances in agronomy and protectionist policies against imports made for a level of rural prosperity that had never been known before.

Industrial deconcentration began with ambitious plans to break up some 1200 companies; these were carried out for only 28. The major *zaibatsu* concerns were restructured into their constituent units and separated from the families that had been at their center. For a time the very names were taboo as Mitsui Insurance, to name one example, became Central Insurance. With a relaxation of controls the firms gradually reverted to their former names. Instead of family-controlled networks the new formations, which could be traced to the old, were products of executive cooperation, and became clusters of enterprises grouped around the bank that formed their center. These industrial lineages, or *keiretsu*, remained immensely important and became more so as Japan's economy grew. As of 1985, for instance, nine large trading firms in Japan handled approximately 46 percent of Japan's exports and 78 percent of its imports. For the giant Mitsubishi Corporation, the percentages were 6 and 16. The program of industrial deconcentration thus changed the ownership and exclusiveness of *zaibatsu* conglomerates, but left them very powerful. On the other hand the interlude of uncertainty during which most high executives were "purged" did provide a period for new talent and new imagination. Individual entrepreneurs, like the founders of SONY and Matsushita, in all probability would have had a much harder time of it in the prewar economy with its patterns of oligopoly.

Another important shift in the economic picture involved labor. Prewar efforts to organize labor unions fared poorly, though during the long years of war "Patriotic Associations" had been encouraged in the interests of labor stability. Early occupation measures encouraged union formation, and the demoralization of management and hardships of life all helped to produce a burgeoning labor movement. Leftist organizers, who were no longer subject to police controls, worked hard to turn the union movement in radical directions and with considerable success. A general strike designed to cow both management and government was announced for February 1947. SCAP ruled this out on grounds of security and possible disorder, and from this time on it became clear that occupation aims, whatever their rhetoric, were not as revolutionary as many had thought. Conservatives in government and business took heart. During the next decade a new pattern of labor organization slowly developed in a process punctuated by major strikes like one that shook Nissan Automobile Company in 1953. Thereafter labor organizations, while affiliated with national organizations, were formed along enterprise rather than craft lines. Negotiations for working conditions and pay were conducted within the enterprise format, while the national organizations carried on propaganda for political and ideological issues. As Japan experienced several decades of almost uninterrupted growth and prosperity, worker loyalties to their enterprises became strong. Negotiations centered on the "spring struggle" about the size of the semiannual bonus rather than on confrontation. The enterprise format usually resulted in close cooperation between unions and management.

After several years of talk of reform and democratization in Japan SCAP rhetoric began to shift, and SCAP seemed more accessible to conservative than to socialist politicians. There were clear reasons for this. One was that many SCAP officials felt that their aims had been achieved and institutional changes completed. There was a gradual exit of the first generation of New Deal-style reformers who were replaced by less adventurous bureaucrats. The most basic, however, related to changes in the international climate. As it became clear that Guomindang rule in China was going to be succeeded by Communist, Japan's importance to the United States' strategic interest rose. Left-wing political activity in a free Japan began to be viewed with suspicion by SCAP officials who found themselves and their programs derogated. The banning of the general strike thus began a process that reached its apogee after the Korean War broke out in 1950. "Purge" decrees, earlier directed against right-wing conservatives, were now directed against Communists, and unions that had been the object of careful encouragement began to seem dangerous. School officials became objects of a "red purge" encouraged by the SCAP education authorities, and firms ticketed for dissolution were so no longer. It began to seem more important to rebuild the Japanese economy than to break it into smaller units.

By the end of occupation in 1952 there were numerous and unexpected ironies of recent history. Japanese leftists, often anti-American, championed the "Peace Constitution" and fought to protect it, while United States officials encouraged Japan to undertake programs of rearmament. Japanese bureaucrats who inherited the sweeping central powers that had been instituted by SCAP used them to protect Japan's struggling industries from American imports. Japanese leftists who had rashly assumed the early reforms were designed to promote revolution in Japan now worried about a United States tie that threatened to cut them off from their continental neighbors in China.

There can be no gainsaying that the sweeping changes the occupation instituted changed Japan into a middle-class, capitalist society. In some cases it would take time to "grow into" the institutions that had been laid down (as with those calling for female equality), but the contrast with wartime institutions that had stifled growth and change, and the popularity of most of the reforms among all sectors of Japanese society, spoke for the success of the experiment.

From September 1945 to April 1952 the Japanese government was officially responsible to an American-dominated occupation. In its earlier years the occupation insisted upon the demilitarization of Japan, war crimes trials, the purge of individuals held responsible for Japan's allegedly aggressive war, a new constitution, an American-style school system, and reforms in Japan's labor unions and the *zaibatsu*. Here Lt.-Col. D.R. Nugent, head of the education section of SCAP, discusses the newly reorganized school curriculum with members of the Japanese Ministry of Education. The prewar education system was believed to have been a source of elitism, nationalism and militarism. Educational reform was a key element in the effort to "democratize" Japan.

In the economic and industrial chaos following the war, SCAP initially encouraged the organization of labor unions as a means of democratization. Company- or government agency-based unions grew rapidly. By 1949 unionization reached a peak of almost 7 million members (more than 50 percent of wage and salary earners) in about 35000 basic plant- or enterprise-level unions throughout the private and public sectors of the economy. Already by 1947, however, SCAP was wary of strikes and calls for wage increases. It prohibited a proposed general strike on 1 February 1947, curbed union political activities and turned to policies of rebuilding the Japanese economy. Here representatives of a labor union picket the Diet Building in Tokyo in August 1949.

Recovery and prosperity

The memoirs of a recent Japanese foreign minister tell about a talk he had with a friend in April 1945, four months before the Japanese surrender. The two agreed that the war was lost, and that Japan had failed because it had overextended itself. Japan would surely be forced to disarm, but that would probably be a blessing in disguise. After all, they agreed, "an army in uniform is not the only sort of army. Scientific technology and fighting spirit under a business suit will be our underground army. This Japanese-American war can be taken as the khaki losing to the business suits."

Forty years later those reflections seem prophetic. With free access to the raw materials and markets of the world and no longer hemmed in by the colonial powers, Japan can be said to have achieved its aims without having to support a massive military machine. It has emerged as the chief beneficiary of the postwar trading system, and is the world's largest producer in commodity after commodity, from automobiles to consumer electronics to integrated circuits, each the bellwether of a stage of industrial and economic development.

In 1954 Japan's Gross National Product was slightly over $US21 billion. By 1967 it was three and a half times that figure, and it was to double again between 1966 and 1970, when it stood at $US200 billion. In 1980 it stood at one trillion. Japan had the world's third most productive economy after the United States and the Soviet Union, contributing 10 percent of the world's total goods and services.

The ingredients of this success have provided subject matter for economic and political debate. Chalmers Johnson, in a study of the Ministry of International Trade and Industry, stressed the role of government as partner with enterprise in an industrial policy that arranged the parts of capitalistic systems in a new way. The government's ability to coordinate and encourage planning through the allocation of foreign currency when it was scarce gave it great power, and its use of subsidies to help obsolescent industries phase out production, he suggested, reversed Western practice; it used its bureaucratic influence to protect healthy and growing, rather than failing, industries. Others argued that the powers of government in Japan were less sweeping than they seemed, and that it had failed in some of its efforts to rationalize and

organize industries, just as it was now failing in its efforts to diminish dependency on exports. Still others pointed to the dynamism of South Korea, Taiwan and Singapore as "new Japans" that were utilizing the Japanese experience. No one disputed the fact that the international economy had undergone permanent change and that the rise of Japan had been a primary factor in that change.

To describe this process is not to explain it, but a number of factors contribute toward both objectives. One of these would be that of political stability. With the exception of 1947–48, Japan's conservative politicians won every election, formed every cabinet and named every prime minister. They were operating under a system that favored the countryside by overrepresenting it; in an increasingly urban society 62 percent of Diet seats were allotted to rural and suburban districts. The healthy state of the economy, however, and the increasing affluence of all sectors of society had the effect of raising conservative majorities in urban elections in the 1980s at a time when commentators were predicting an end to conservative power. Modest shifts to even out representation from urban areas failed to shake the conservative edge in the 1980s. The conservative party, however, was far from monolithic. Leadership lay with factions that dated from the days of Yoshida Shigeru (1878–1967), who had set Japan's course during occupation and post-occupation days. After Yoshida's retirement the Ministry of Finance provided the principal career path for political leadership. Political leaders, who had had the conditioning of service as Minister of Finance, taxed moderately, pursued a consistent policy of trade expansion and protected the Japanese economy from foreign competitors. Long-range planning was a basic policy, and government-appointed commissions reported regularly on changes in the national and international prospects.

The Japanese economy profited from services the United States received during the Korean War. Wartime and postwar inflation had been brought to a halt by a series of reforms begun in 1949 by a Detroit banker, whose name became associated with the "Dodge line." Japan started from that point with a relatively balanced budget, stable currency and favorable exchange rate, and its enterprises were in a position to react instantly to opportunities the war offered for foreign exchange earnings and growth. The war can probably be described as having offered the first step in a turn from dependent isolation to full independence.

Japan profited from the international situation in other respects. It had come out of World War II with its industrial plant substantially destroyed, but its workers' productive skill had probably been sharpened during the long struggle with the world's most advanced industrial powers. As plants were rebuilt, they were naturally constructed along lines more advanced and more efficient than those in the countries that had not been bombed.

The facts behind the economic miracle

Japan's leaders had little real choice in their decision to stake their country's political and economic future on the maintenance of close ties with the United States, but it proved a fortunate choice. The American commitment to undertake the defense of Japan permitted Japan to spend a low 1 percent of its GNP on its own defense. Given the growth of GNP, that fraction grew constantly in real terms to sixth or seventh in the world, but it remained well below the United States' 6–7 percent and the United Kingdom's 5–6 percent, to say nothing of an estimated 15 percent for the Soviet Union. Probably more important were the United States' sponsorship of Japan's return to the world trading order and the availability of technology from American manufacturers who were initially glad to retrieve part of their development costs. The American market came to assume immense importance for Japanese manufacturers. This had consequences no one foresaw. In the 1950s Secretary of State John Foster Dulles advised Japanese leaders that they should try to develop markets in Southeast Asia as their products had only limited interest for American consumers. Thirty years later the largest problem in American-Japanese relations was the United States' enormous imbalance of trade with Japan. In prewar years Japanese products had been associated with inexpensive and shoddy merchandise, but through technological gains they now stood for dependable and high-quality goods. By the 1980s Japan was the first or second largest trading partner with every major country in the non-Communist world.

Japanese population growth had also been kept in check. Initially the prospect of supporting a population of 70 million swollen by repatriates from Manchuria and other Asian countries seemed daunting, but growing standards of expectation and affluence combined with the legalization of abortion in the 1950s enabled Japan to maintain population growth rates typical of highly industrialized countries. By the 1980s the distribution of age groups within a population that now stood at 120 million resembled that in other modernized countries, and Japanese planners were increasingly preoccupied with problems of an aging society that would soon require more social overhead and government welfare. Japanese life expectancy was the highest in the world.

Structural changes within the Japanese economy also figured importantly. The first was a dramatic change in the relative proportion of industrial to agricultural workers. At the end of World War II Japan was still an agricultural economy; agriculture accounted for approximately 25 percent of the GNP and employed close to 50 percent of the labor force, and consumers were devoting more than half of their consumption expenditures to food. The proportion of the labor force employed in primary industry declined rapidly; it stood at 48·3 percent in 1950, 32·6 percent in 1960, 19·3 percent in 1970 and 8·8 percent in 1985. During that same period employment in secondary industry rose by one third, and tertiary industry doubled from 29·8 to 56·9 percent. Meanwhile improvements in agronomy increased rural output and tastes in food changed. By the 1980s Japan had a large surplus of rice, which it had formerly had to import, and it was the United States' largest overseas market for agricultural goods. Conservative governments, responsive to agricultural voters, reciprocated with subsidies that were reflected in the rice surplus

and in the price consumers paid for rice. In the mid-1950s Japanese agricultural prices were 130 percent of international levels; in the early 1970s they were 200 percent, and in the early 1980s 250 percent. Foreign importers and Japanese consumers were demanding changes in the system, but the Tokyo government, having persuaded farmers to shift to other products like beef and citrus, hesitated to renege on its promises to them.

As Japanese manufactures increased in quality, there was a sharp increase in the proportion of value added through labor and a corresponding decline in the import cost proportion. In textiles cotton gave way to synthetics. In raw materials Japan became a principal beneficiary of bulk transport. Japan's industrial plants, like its labor force, were along the littoral, and to its ports came giant ore carriers and supertankers, most of them fabricated in Japanese shipyards. The Kure Naval Shipyard, now in private hands, that produced the giant battleship *Yamato*, the largest used in World War II, produced the first supertanker with some of the same plans from the same ways. The unit costs of new materials fell to even out the cost discrepancy Japan had experienced with American and European competitors. Japan's import needs gradually made it the largest market for virtually every category of raw materials, including oil. some observers thought that the oil crises of the 1970s would signal an end to Japan's economic growth rate, but in the 1980s cheaper oil and a higher stage of industrialization—integrated circuits and electronics, in which the import quotient was markedly less—found Japan competing with ease and success.

Japan's greatest resource was its people. Postwar legislation brought improved working standards, and the enterprise union system combined with permanent employment for favored workers to make for enterprise loyalty. In the 1950s and 1960s workers' productivity grew more rapidly than wages, and this combined with a favorable exchange rate to make Japanese products highly competitive. Since public welfare measures lagged well behind the rise of prices and since job transfers in large firms were relatively rare, workers had every reason to feel loyalty to enterprises. That loyalty was symbolized and sometimes satirized by the company song, worker excursions and morning calisthenics.

The discipline of the labor force was a reflection of the discipline of the masses. Into the 1960s opportunities for consumer spending were still limited; housing was in short supply, and most workers lived inexpensively though poorly. Thereafter they lived expensively but still well below the standard of amenities of their counterparts in Western countries. The inadequacy of public welfare measures made personal planning and saving essential. Government tactics encouraged this by not taxing postal savings accounts and by not exempting mortgage and other interest costs from taxation. This premium on saving resulted in a savings rate of 20 percent of disposable income, money which was transformed into investment and reinvestment by banks to fuel the continuing cycle of productive expansion.

Higher technology also required higher education, and this combined with the respect for learn-

Above By the early 1950s the Japanese economy was beginning to recover from the ravages of war and postwar dislocation. Between 1951 and 1955 GNP growth averaged 8·6 percent annually; it grew to 9·1 percent between 1955 and 1960, 9·7 percent between 1960 and 1965, and over 13·1 percent between 1965 and 1970. Shipyards, such as these Mitsubishi yards in Nagasaki, that had built battleships in wartime, were now producing oil tankers. Here shipyard workers, many of them women, are shown returning to their jobs after a lunch break.

Right Japan's economic miracle was not entirely free from industrial friction. Here strikers at a Tokyo mining machine factory in 1959 try to ram factory gates with a bus. Non-strikers inside the factory turned hoses on the strikers. The dispute, over pay increase demands, lasted for five months, involved several pitched battles between strikers and non-strikers and brought police intervention.

remained, then, of the traditional culture and its values?

An answer to this question would probably begin with emphasis on the work ethic. Throughout Japan work remained a positive good and not something from which to shrink. There was pride in performance and seeming satisfaction in role, from the brief ritual of preparation and dedication that came before department store doors opened to the smart salutes with which the subway dispatchers saw the crowded trains leave. Thomas Rohlen's study of the indoctrination program conducted by a bank for new employees described a period during which they were sent into the community to ask for useful work at no remuneration; the surge of gratitude for work that ended the embarrassment of idleness was the point of the lesson. Japanese worked longer hours and took fewer vacations than other workers. Few other countries have needed official campaigns to encourage people to take time off and relax. Hayami Akira, an economic historian, suggested that such attitudes dated from Tokugawa times, as Confucian morality combined with material incentives to produce an "industrious revolution" that lay before the industrial developments to come.

A second emphasis would surely lie with education. Proper educational qualification remained prerequisite to rewards at work and in society. Despite the rise in institutions of higher education, or perhaps because of it, entrance into those that brought prestige and favored access for employment opportunities became progressively more difficult because of the size of the cohort of applicants. Increasing numbers of young Japanese were spending much of their time preparing for and taking examinations into preferred schools—the best private schools, middle schools, high schools, and college and university, followed by examinations given by employers. It was typical that one of the largest new religions, Sōka Gakkai, arranged and rewarded its teachers and evangelists with academic rank, and that *sensei*, the term of respect awarded teachers, was used widely for elderly superiors. The enthusiasm for education dates from Tokugawa times, and in particular from the reform period at the turn of the 18th century as educational qualification was added to rank and birth as a criterion for public service. Most Japanese were agreed on the need to lessen the rigors of a lifestyle that centered on preparation for examinations, but they were also quietly proud of the dedication and commitment it demanded of young people. Thomas Rohlen's study of Japanese high schools concluded that over a 12-year cycle of public schooling Japanese students received four more years of schooling than did Americans and that the average Japanese student at graduation from high school was likely to have the basic knowledge equivalent to that of the average American college graduate. On international tests of science and mathematics Japanese mean scores were higher those of any other country. As family pressures tapered off, Rohlen suggested, it was the examination system that provided the discipline that prepared Japanese for the labor force.

Once in the labor force, the company and the peer group of employees provided the context for more of an individual's life than was the case in

ing that had been traditional. The number of students in institutions of higher learning, and the number of such institutions, rose steadily. In Japan in 1985 93·8 percent of junior high-shool graduates continued on to senior high school and 38·2 percent of high-school graduates went on to higher education. Proportionally Japan was graduating twice as many engineers in relation to population as was the United States, and the skills of the labor force remained high.

Contemporary Japanese society
Japan in the late 1980s was overwhelmingly urban, middle-class and salaried. The carefully calibrated degrees of status and rank of earlier days had disappeared in the homogenization of business suits and mass transportation. The variety of regional dialects and the complexity of status speech forms had given way to the standard media of radio and television. It would be difficult to imagine a society more consumer-oriented, or shoppers more materially conscious. What

other industrialized societies. At the preferred ranks permanent employment helped, but at all ranks company socialization through dormitories, group outings and group exhortation played a striking role. Furthermore throughout Japanese society assumptions of responsibility and reciprocity in meeting obligations remained strong. Commercial or corporate setbacks could be expected to bring the resignations of those at the helm. Corporate managers were expected to think of their authority as a period of stewardship for a firm that would far outlive them. Takeovers, mergers and buyouts to maximize short-range profits had little chance in a society that worked for the long view and derogated talk of profits. These characteristics, too, owed something to the Japanese past.

In terms of nationality, Japanese in the 1980s had outlived the intense repugnance their parents had shown for the wartime experience and shame of defeat. They were intensely conscious of their national history, and multivolume series of well-written histories, historical fiction and biographies drew enthusiastic reader response. No television series were more popular than those with historical coverage of Japan's past. As Japan loomed larger in international affairs, concern with what was Japanese brought a flood of writings about nationality, identity and uniqueness. Essays about "Japaneseness" were thus one aspect and consequence of the rapid change Japan had experienced.

In international affairs postwar Japan had been content to play an observer role, at first sincerely, and then conveniently, explaining its powerlessness and inability to affect larger patterns. As Japanese leaders began to be included in meetings of world leaders, they were usually content to be on the edge of or in the background of the photograph, perhaps uncomfortable with foreign languages, perhaps products of the political system in which factional backing, rather than eloquence or individuality, determined success. Japan had profited from the international order of postwar days, but seemed slow to contribute to that order by word or deed. At the same time, however, "internationalization" became the slogan of the day as Japanese reminded themselves of the responsibilities that accompanied their new power. International criticism of Japan for reluctance to open its markets and for its single-minded pursuit of export profits was also beginning to produce a hurt and resentful response from many Japanese.

It was possible, some suggested, to discern three distinct generational responses. Older Japanese, remembering the pain and destruction of war and reconstruction, were determined that Japan should play a helpful role and convinced of the favor their country had received. A generation of business leaders in mid-career, not having experienced the discipline of their elders, was more likely to show arrogance and to vaunt the advantages of their society's structures and products. Finally there was a student generation that had come to maturity in a setting of economic growth and plenty which took these for granted and seemed relatively indifferent to both anger and arrogance. Styled by their puzzled seniors as "new human beings" (*shin-jinrui*), they were better traveled, better trained and better experienced than Japanese had ever been. The future lay with them.

JAPAN TODAY

Work

Below One and a half million commuters pass through Tokyo's Shinjuku Station every morning rush hour. The growing acceptance of staggered work schedules ("flexi-time") may make this sight more of a rarity.

Below These women, taking local produce to market, are resting on a sea wall in the inner Tango Peninsula on the Sea of Japan coast.

Bottom left Morning calisthenics at this camera factory are more than physical exercise. They are intended to promote group solidarity and increased output. Japanese corporations overseas have introduced these practices—with mixed reactions from their workers.

Bottom right Automobile manufacture and electronics have been two pillars of Japan's postwar industrial success. The Mazda Corporation like other Japanese motor manufacturers was quick to introduce robots to the assembly lines.

Bottom Nishijin in Kyoto has long been a center of fine-quality silk weaving. From the streets one can still hear the clack of looms. Although many looms are now mechanized, there is a dwindling demand for the kimono fabric produced here. Nishijin weavers have been facing hard times.

In postwar Japan, as younger men looked for higher-paying work in towns and factories, farmwork fell increasingly on the shoulders of women and the elderly. The government and local agricultural cooperatives encouraged technological improvement and intensive production through farm subsidies and education. Here a specialist is advising farm women in Iwate Prefecture. The results have been impressive and the country has for years produced more rice than it can consume.

From the late 1980s Japan was subjected to growing demands from the international community, led by the United States and Australia, to open its markets fully to imported meat, citrus fruit and rice. City dwellers have stood to benefit from cheaper produce. The Liberal Democratic Party, however, which relies heavily on the farm vote, have resisted fully open markets, claiming they would lead to the obliteration of Japanese agriculture.

Food

Elegantly sliced and presented *sushi* and *sashimi* (raw fish on vinegared rice balls or served alone) are now almost as popular in London, Düsseldorf or New York as in Tokyo or Osaka—and much less expensive. Many Japanese also enjoy the conviviality of local cooking in small restaurants with names like "Inakaya" ("Country Cooking") that offer local specialities from Niigata or other prefectures, eaten with plenty of beer, sake or *shōchū* (neat liquor).

Sport and Leisure

Below Japanese fencing (Kendō) is a vigorous traditional sport, one of several thriving martial arts. Here masked barefoot fencers at the Metropolitan Police Academy practice with their bamboo swords.

Below left Sumō is the most ancient sport in Japan. Performed as a religious ritual in ancient shrines, it developed into an enormously popular sport in the Edo period, and draws enthusiastic audiences to six annual televised tournaments today.

Bottom left Some of Japan's ski resorts, such as Shiga or Zao with its ice-encrusted pines, are among the best in the world. They are also among the most crowded. To escape the crowds, seasoned skiers head for the higher slopes.

Below For centuries Japanese have partied under cherry trees on balmy spring days and nights. This contemporary scene in Ueno Park, Tokyo, echoes similar scenes in Japanese painting of Heian nobles and Edo townspeople enjoying cherry blossoms.

Bottom center Pinball (Pachinko) parlors are ubiquitous in Japanese towns and villages and it is not unusual to see a neon-lit temple of Pachinko towering among rice fields in rural areas. For some people it is merely a way of passing time while waiting for a train; for adepts it is an addiction.

Bottom right The slick all-girl Takarazuka Review has been entertaining patrons and fans—many of whom are young women—in Osaka and Tokyo for more than 50 years.

Most Japanese children, when their school day is done, go to a cramming school (*juku*). There are *juku* for every conceivable subject from abacus to mathematics or foreign languages. Many *juku* cram students for entrance to middle school or high school; others, as here, enhance interests such as calligraphy that have been learned in home or school.

Mastery of written Japanese is not easy and training in writing and brushwork begins early. The more proficient students take part in calligraphy contests for children organized by major newspapers. Some parents worry that the growing availability of Japanese word processors will kill calligraphy. But there is still a lingering feeling that calligraphy does indeed reveal the individual.

Beliefs and Festivals

A visitor to a Shinto shrine on an ordinary weekday, or a Sunday when there is no scheduled observance, may find only a few young mothers exercising their small children. At New Year and on festival days, however, shrines come alive and are thronged with worshipers and the merely curious.

Below A crane dance—for good fortune and longevity—held at the Yasaka shrine in Kyoto.

Bottom left A young Shinto priest makes a regular offering of fruit and sake to the *kami* of a waterfall at the Hie shrine on Mount Hiei, northeast of Kyoto.

Bottom right Respect for deceased relatives and ancestors is expressed by visits to family grave sites, especially during the midsummer Bon memorial.

Previous page The Shisendō (Hall of Immortal Poets) in the eastern hills of Kyoto was built as a contemplative space, part of the retreat of Ishikawa Jōzan (1583–1672). Jōzan, a Confucian scholar and author of poetry in Chinese (*kanshi*), served Tokugawa Ieyasu and fought at the battle of Sekigahara. He later resigned from military service, studied Zen and took Buddhist orders. He went into seclusion, built the Shisendō as a hermitage and devoted himself to poetry. With its azaleas sloping away down a hillside, the Shisendō still provides a quiet, contemplative experience.

Below Mountain Buddhism, such as that practiced today at Enryakuji on Mount Hiei or Kongōbuji on Mount Kōya (shown here) involves prayer, textual study, esoteric ritual and ascetic practice. These monks at the Oku-no-in on Mount Kōya, where Kūkai is interred, are practicing winter austerities.

Below There are still in Japan a few—a very few—individuals who resist the blandishments of the economic miracle and opt instead for an austere, rigorous, contemplative life, like that of the meditating Zen monks shown here.

Below center Asakusa in Tokyo is a much-frequented downtown entertainment area. It is also the location of the Asakusa Kannon temple, a site of popular devotion since the Edo period. This woman dispenses good-luck charms to the crowds who flock here on holidays and festival days.

Bottom left Palm reading is as popular in Japan as in any other society and has a long history.

Bottom right Japan still has phallic and naked festivals (*hadaka matsuri*). This one is held at Inazawa. During the festival young men in loin cloths carry the local *kami* around the district in a portable shrine. These festivals are a celebration of youth and manliness. They are often held in freezing weather or in the heat of summer, and the whole community joins in by preparing and sharing festive food and drink.

Below At any shrine a person can offer a prayer to the *kami* and hope that it will be answered. Many shrines, for a few yen, sell slips of paper bearing fortunes. Tying them to a tree or trellis, the person trusts that the *kami* may respond.

Below and bottom One of the oldest and most impressive festivals in Japan is the Gion *matsuri*, held in Kyoto each July almost continuously since the 16th century. It is a townspeople's festival with groups of merchants and storekeepers vying with each other in decorating and pulling the tall, heavy, wheeled floats from the Yasaka shrine at Gion through the streets of Kyoto.

The Future

The Japanese are looking to the future. They believe that security and prosperity in that future will depend on international cooperation and on information technology and youth. To prepare for the 21st century, kindergarten children (*below*) are being introduced to computers. Recent technology fairs at Tsukuba (*bottom*) and Saitama have also broached the theme of society in the 21st century. Mixed with feelings of international vulnerability and the unpredictability of domestic politics is a confidence that younger generations are being given some help in facing the challenges of a new century.

BIBLIOGRAPHY

There is now an enormous literature on Japan and Japanese culture in Western languages. This bibliography provides suggestions for further reading, mainly in English language materials. Preference has been given to general rather than narrowly specialized works, and to recent books with helpful bibliographies. For access to more specialized monographs and journal articles—as well as to the vast body of literature in Japanese of which the Western language literature is probably less than 1 percent—interested readers may refer to the bibliographic guides mentioned below, especially J. Dower, *Japanese History and Culture from Ancient to Modern Times.*

Bibliographic Guides to Western Language Materials
Association for Asian Studies, *Cumulative Bibliography of Asian Studies,* 1941–65 (1969) and 1966–70 (1973); and *Bibliography of Asian Studies,* annually, 1970–; Ann Arbor, Michigan.
J. Dower, *Japanese History and Culture from Ancient to Modern Times,* New York, Markus Wiener, 1986.
P. Grilli, ed., *Japan in Film: A Comprehensive Catalogue of Documentary and Theatrical Films on Japan Available in the United States,* Japan Society, New York, 1984.
International House of Japan Library, *Modern Japanese Literature in Translation,* Tokyo, 1979.
Japan Society, *What Shall I Read on Japan?* New York, 1984.

Historical and Geographical Surveys
The Cambridge History of Japan, 6 vols., Cambridge, Cambridge U.P., in progress.
Encyclopedia of Asian History, 3 vols., New York, The Asia Society, 1987.
J. K. Fairbank, E. O. Reischauer and A. M. Craig, *East Asia Tradition and Transformation,* Boston, Houghton Mifflin, 1978.
N. Ginsburg, "Economic and Cultural Geography," in Arthur Tiedemann, ed., *An Introduction to Japanese Civilization,* Lexington, Mass., Heath, 1974.
J. W. Hall, *Japan from Prehistory to Modern Times,* New York, Delacorte, 1970.
—— *Government and Local Power in Japan 500–1700,* Princeton, Princeton U.P., 1966.
Kōdansha Encyclopedia of Japan, 9 vols., Tokyo and New York, Kōdansha International, 1983.
G. B. Sansom, *Japan: A Short Cultural History,* London, Cresset, 1952.
—— *A History of Japan,* 3 vols., Stanford, Stanford U.P., 1958–63.
A. E. Tiedemann, ed., *An Introduction to Japanese Civilization,* Lexington, Mass., Heath, 1974.
H. P. Varley, *Japanese Culture, a Short History,* Honolulu, University of Hawaii Press, 1984.

General Introductions to Major Aspects of Japanese Culture
Art and music
T. Akiyama, *Japanese Painting,* Geneva, Skira, 1961.
E. Harich-Schneider, *A History of Japanese Music,* Oxford, Oxford U.P., 1973.
Heibonsha, *Survey of Japanese Art,* Translation of *Nihon no bijutsu* series. Published jointly by Weatherhill and Heibonsha, 30 vols.
L. P. Roberts, *A Dictionary of Japanese Artists,* Tokyo and New York, Weatherhill, 1976.
J. Stanley-Baker, *Japanese Art,* London, Thames and Hudson, 1984.

Literature and language
Y. Habein, *The History of the Japanese Written Language,* New York, Columbia U.P., 1984.
D. Keene, ed., *An Anthology of Japanese Literature: From the Earliest Era to the Mid-Nineteenth Century,* New York, Grove, 1955.
D. Keene, *Japanese Literature: An Introduction for Western Readers,* New York, Grove, 1955.
J. Konishi, *A History of Japanese Literature: The Archaic and Ancient Ages,* Princeton U.P., 1984; *The Early Middle Ages,* Princeton U.P., 1986; 3 vols. to follow.
E. Miner, H. Odagiri and R. E. Morell, *The Princeton Companion to Classical Japanese Literature,* Princeton, Princeton U.P., 1985.

H. Sato and B. Watson, trans., *From the Country of Eight Islands: An Anthology of Japanese Poetry,* New York, Doubleday, 1981.

Culture and ideas
R. F. Benedict, *The Chrysanthemum and the Sword: Patterns of Japanese Culture,* Boston, Houghton Mifflin, 1946.
B. Earhart, *Japanese Religion: Unity and Diversity,* California, Dickenson, 1974.
D. Keene, *Landscapes and Portraits: Appreciations of Japanese Culture,* Tokyo, 1971.
J. M. Kitagawa, *Religion in Japanese History,* New York, Columbia U.P., 1966.
I. Morris, *The Nobility of Failure: Tragic Heroes in the History of Japan,* New York, Holt, Rinehart and Winston, 1976.
H. Nakamura, *Ways of Thinking of Eastern Peoples: India, China, Tibet, Japan,* Honolulu, University of Hawaii Press, 1964.
R. Tsunoda, W. T. de Bary and D. Keene, eds., *Sources of Japanese Tradition,* New York, Columbia U.P., 1958.

Archaeological and Linguistic Origins
W. G. Aston, trans., *Nihongi, Chronicles of Japan from the Earliest Times to A.D. 697,* London, Allen and Unwin, 1896; reprinted 1956.
J. E. Kidder, *Japan before Buddhism,* London, Thames and Hudson, 1959.
—— *The Birth of Japanese Art,* New York, Praeger, 1965.
—— *Prehistoric Japanese Arts: Jōmon Pottery,* Tokyo and New York, Kōdansha International, 1968.
—— *Ancient Japan,* Oxford, Phaidon, 1977.
—— *Early Japanese Art: The Great Tombs and Treasures,* London, Thames and Hudson, 1964.
—— *Early Buddhist Japan,* London, Thames and Hudson, 1972.
G. Ledyard, "Galloping along with the Horseriders: Looking for the Founders of Japan," *Journal of Japanese Studies,* Vol. 1, no. 2, 1975, pp. 217–54.
F. Miki, *Haniwa,* Tokyo, Weatherhill, 1974.
R. A. Miller, *Origins of the Japanese Language,* Seattle, University of Washington Press, 1980.
E. S. Morse, *The Shell Mounds of Ōmori,* Tokyo, 1879.
R. Pearson, G. Barnes and K. Hutterer, eds., *Windows on the Japanese Past, Studies in Japanese Archaeology and Prehistory,* Ann Arbor, University of Michigan Press, 1986.
D. L. Philipi, trans., *Kojiki,* Tokyo, University of Tokyo Press, 1968.
—— trans., *Songs of Gods, Songs of Humans: the Epic Tradition of the Ainu,* Princeton, Princeton U.P., 1979.
—— trans., *Norito, A New Translation of Ancient Japanese Ritual Prayers,* Tokyo, 1959.
R. Tsunoda and L. C. Goodrich, *Japan in the Chinese Dynastic Histories,* California, P. D. and Ione Perkins, 1951.

Ancient Religion
W. T. de Bary, ed., *The Buddhist Tradition in India, China and Japan,* New York, Columbia U.P., 1969.
Japan Society, *Hōryūji, Temple of the Exalted Law,* New York, Japan Society, 1981.
H. Kageyama, *The Arts of Shinto,* Tokyo, Weatherhill, 1973.
H. Kageyama and C. Guth Kanda, *Shinto Arts,* New York, Japan Society, 1976.
K. Tange, Y. Watanabe and N. Kawazoe, *Ise: Prototype of Japanese Architecture,* Cambridge, Mass., M.I.T. Press, 1965.

Politics and Culture in the Nara Period
W. W. Farris, *Population, Disease, and Land in Early Japan, 645–900,* Cambridge, Mass., Harvard U.P., 1985.
R. Hayashi, *The Silk Road and the Shōsōin,* Tokyo, Weatherhill, 1975.
I. Hori, *Folk Religion in Japan, Continuity and Change,* Chicago, University of Chicago Press, 1968.
L. Hurvitz, trans., *Scripture of the Lotus Blossom of the Fine Law,* New York, Columbia U.P., 1976.
I. H. Levy, *The Ten Thousand Leaves: A Translation of Manyōshū, Japan's Premier Anthology of Classical Poetry,* vol. 1 (of projected 4 vols.), Princeton, Princeton U.P., 1981.
—— *Hitomaro and the Birth of Japanese Lyricism,* Princeton, Princeton U.P., 1984.
A. Matsunaga, *The Buddhist Philosophy of Assimilation,* Tokyo, Sophia U.P., 1969.
Nippon Gakujutsu Shinkōkai, comp., *Manyōshū: One Thousand Poems,* New York, Columbia U.P., 1965.
M. Ōoka, *Temples of Nara and their Art,* Tokyo, Weatherhill, 1973.

The Courtly Age: Heian Politics, Society and Culture
R. Borgen, *Sugawara no Michizane and the Early Heian Court,* Cambridge, Mass., Harvard East Asian Monographs, 1986.

J. W. Hall and J. P. Mass, eds., *Medieval Japan, Essays in Institutional History,* New Haven, Yale U.P., 1974.
G. C. Hurst III, *Insei: Abdicated Sovereigns in the Politics of Late Heian Japan, 1086–1185,* New York, Columbia U.P., 1976.
I. Morris, *The World of the Shining Prince: Court Life in Ancient Japan,* Oxford, Oxford U.P., 1960.

Heian Literature
R. Bowring, *Murasaki Shikibu: Her Diary and Poetic Memoirs,* Princeton, Princeton U.P., 1982.
R. Brower and E. Miner, *Japanese Court Poetry,* Stanford, Stanford U.P., 1961.
N. Field, *The Splendor of Longing in the Tale of Genji,* Princeton, Princeton U.P., 1987.
P. T. Harries, trans., *The Poetic Memoirs of Lady Daibu,* Stanford, Stanford U.P., 1980.
E. G. Harris, trans., *The Tales of Ise,* Tokyo and Rutland, Vt., Tuttle, 1972.
H. C. McCullough, trans., *Brocade by Night: Kokin Wakashū and the Court Style in Japanese Classical Poetry,* Stanford, Stanford U.P., 1985.
—— trans., *Kokin Wakashū: The First Imperial Anthology of Japanese Poetry,* Stanford, Stanford U.P., 1985.
H. C. and W. H. McCullough, trans., *A Tale of Flowering Fortunes (Eiga monogatari),* 2 vols., Stanford, Stanford U.P., 1979.
E. Miner, *Japanese Poetic Diaries,* Berkeley, University of California Press, 1969.
I. Morris, *The Tale of Genji Scroll,* Tokyo and New York, Kōdansha International, 1971.
I. Morris, trans., *The Pillow Book of Sei Shōnagon,* New York, Columbia U.P., 1967.
E. G. Seidensticker, trans., *The Gossamer Years: the Diary of a Noblewoman of Heian Japan (Kagerō nikki),* Tokyo and Rutland, Vt., Tuttle, 1964.
—— trans., *The Tale of Genji (Genji monogatari),* New York, Knopf, 1976.
M. Ury, trans., *Tales of Times Now Past: Sixty-two Stories from a Medieval Japanese Collection,* Berkeley, University of California Press, 1979.

Heian Buddhism
A. A. Andrews, *The Teachings Essential for Rebirth,* Tokyo, Sophia U.P., 1973.
T. Fukuyama, *Heian Temples: Byōdōin and Chūsonji,* Tokyo, Weatherhill, 1976.
P. Groner, *Saichō: the Establishment of the Japanese Tendai School,* Berkeley, University of California Press, 1984.
Y. Hakeda, *Kūkai, Major Works,* New York, Columbia U.P., 1972.
D. Hirota, trans., *No Abode, The Record of Ippen,* Kyoto, Ryūkoku U.P., 1986.
Kyōkai, *Miraculous Stories from the Japanese Buddhist Tradition: the Nihon ryōiki of the Monk Kyōkai,* trans. K. Nakamura, Cambridge, Mass., Harvard U.P., 1973.
D. and A. Matsunaga, *Foundations of Japanese Buddhism,* 2 vols., Los Angeles and Tokyo, 1974–76.
T. Sawa, *Art in Japanese Esoteric Buddhism,* Tokyo, Weatherhill, 1976.

Culture and Society in the Medieval Age
P. Arnesen, *The Medieval Japanese Daimyō,* New Haven, Yale U.P., 1979.
D. Brown, *Money Economy in Medieval Japan,* New Haven, Yale U.P., 1951.
D. Brown and Ishida Ichirō, trans., *The Future and the Past, A Translation and Study of the Gukanshō,* Berkeley, University of California Press, 1979.
P. Duus, *Japanese Feudalism,* New York, Knopf, 1969.
L. Frederic, *Daily Life in Japan at the Time of the Mongol Invasions, 1185–1603,* New York, Praeger, 1972.
K. Grossberg, *Japan's Renaissance, the Politics of the Muromachi Bakufu,* Cambridge, Mass., Harvard East Asian Monographs, 1981.
J. W. Hall and J. P. Mass, *Medieval Japan: Essays in Institutional History,* New Haven, Yale U.P., 1974.
J. W. Hall and T. Toyoda, eds., *Japan in the Muromachi Age,* Berkeley, University of California Press, 1977.
J. P. Mass, ed., *Court and Bakufu in Japan: Essays in Kamakura History,* New Haven, Yale U.P., 1982.
—— ed., *The Development of Kamakura Rule 1180–1250,* Stanford, Stanford U.P., 1979.
—— ed., *Warrior Government in Early Medieval Japan—A Study of the Kamakura Bakufu Shugo and Jitō,* New Haven, Yale U.P., 1974.
H. C. McCullough, trans., "A Tale of Mutsu" (*Mutsuwaki*), *Harvard Journal of Asiatic Studies,* 25 (1964–66), 178–211.
B. W. Robinson, *The Arts of the Japanese Sword,* London, Faber and Faber, 1970.
M. Shinoda, *The Founding of the Kamakura Shogunate 1180–85,* New York, Columbia U.P., 1960.
C. Steenstrup, *Hōjō Shigetoki,* London and Malmo, 1979.

S. R. Turnbull, *The Samurai: A Military History*, New York and London, Macmillan, 1977.
H. P. Varley, *Imperial Restoration in Medieval Japan*, New York, Columbia U.P., 1971.
—— *Samurai*, New York, Delacorte, 1970.
—— *The Ōnin War*, New York, Columbia U.P., 1967.
—— trans., *A Chronicle of Gods and Sovereigns: Jinnō shōtōki of Kitabatake Chikafusa*, New York, Columbia U.P., 1980.

Medieval Literature
K. Brazell, trans., *The Confessions of Lady Nijō*, New York, Doubleday-Anchor, 1973.
T. B. Hare, *Zeami's Style: The Nō Plays of Zeami Motokiyo*, Stanford, Stanford U.P., 1986.
D. Keene, ed., *Twenty Plays of the Nō Theatre*, New York, Columbia U.P., 1970.
D. Keene and H. Kaneko, *Nō, the Classical Theatre of Japan*, Tokyo and New York, Kōdansha International, 1966.
D. Keene, trans., *Essays in Idleness, the Tzurezuregusa of Kenkō*, New York, Columbia U.P., 1967.
H. Kitagawa and B. Tsuchida, trans., *The Tale of the Heike (Heike monogatari)*, 2 vols., Tokyo, Tokyo U.P., 1975.
K. Komparu, *The Noh Theatre: Principles and Perspectives*, Tokyo, Weatherhill, 1983.
W. R. LaFleur, *The Karma of Words, Buddhism and the Literary Arts in Medieval Japan*, Berkeley, University of California Press, 1933.
H. C. McCullough, trans., *The Taiheiki: A Chronicle of Medieval Japan*, New York, Columbia U.P., 1959.
—— trans., *Yoshitsune—A Fifteenth Century Japanese Chronicle*, Stanford, Stanford U.P., 1971.
E. Miner, *Japanese Linked Poetry*, Princeton, Princeton U.P., 1978.
D. Pollack, *Fracture of Meaning: Japan's Synthesis of China from the Eighth through the Eighteenth Centuries*, Princeton, Princeton U.P., 1986.
E. Pound and E. Fenollosa, *The Classic Noh Theatre of Japan*, New York, New Directions, 1975.
J. Rimer and M. Yamazaki, trans., *On the Art of Nō Drama, the Major Treatises of Zeami*, Princeton, Princeton U.P., 1984.
B. Ruch, "Medieval Jongleurs and the Making of a National Literature," in Hall and Toyoda, eds., *Japan in the Muromachi Age*.
A. L. Sadler, trans. *The Ten Foot Square Hut*, Tokyo and Rutland, Vt., Tuttle, rpt. 1971.

Paths to Salvation in Medieval Japan
A. Andrews, *The Teachings Essential for Rebirth*, Tokyo, Sophia U.P., 1973.
A. Bloom, *Shinran's Gospel of Pure Grace*, Tucson, University of Arizona Press, 1965.
A. Grapard, "Shintō," *Kōdansha Encyclopedia of Japan*, vol. 7, pp.125–32.
T. Kuroda, "Shinto in the History of Japanese Religion," *Journal of Japanese Studies*, 7.1 (1981), 1–21.
N. MacMullin, *Buddhism and the State in Sixteenth Century Japan*, Princeton, Princeton U.P., 1985.
L. Rodd, *Nichiren, Selected Writings*, Honolulu, University of Hawaii Press, 1980.
S. Weinstein, "Rennyo and the Shinshū Revival," in Hall and Toyoda, eds., *Japan in the Muromachi Age*.

Zen and Zen-Related Culture
M. Collcutt, *Five Mountains, the Rinzai Zen Monastic Institution in Medieval Japan*, Cambridge, Mass., Harvard U.P., 1981.
H. Dumoulin, *A History of Zen Buddhism*, New York, Random House, 1963.
Dōgen, *Record of Things Heard,—A Translation of the Shōbōgenzō zuimonki*, trans. Thomas Cleary, Boulder, 1980.
J. Fontein and M. L. Hickman, *Zen Painting and Calligraphy*, Boston, Museum of Fine Arts, 1970.
E. Herrigel, *Zen in the Art of Archery*, London, 1953.
P. Kapleau, *The Three Pillars of Zen*, New York, Beacon, 1964.
H. Kim, *Dōgen Kigen Mystical Realist*, Tucson, University of Arizona Press, 1975.
D. Pollack, trans., *Zen Poems of the Five Mountains*, Decatur, Ga., Scholars Press, 1985.
J. H. Sanford, "Mandalas of the Heart: Two Prose Works by Ikkyū Sōjun," *Monumenta Nipponica*, 35.3 (1980), 273–98.
Y. Shimizu and C. Wheelwright, *Japanese Ink Paintings*, Princeton, Princeton U.P., 1976.
H. Shin'ichi, *Zen and the Fine Arts*, Tokyo and New York, Kōdansha International, 1971.
D. T. Suzuki, *Zen and Japanese Culture*, New York, Pantheon, 1959.
—— *Essays in Zen Buddhism*, new ed., Rider, London, 1970.

Medieval Art
K. Hirai, *Feudal Architecture of Japan*, Tokyo, Weatherhill, 1973.
T. Ito, *The Japanese Garden: An Approach to Nature*, New Haven, Yale U.P., 1972.
L. Kuck, *The World of the Japanese Garden*, Tokyo, Weatherhill, 1968.
T. Matsushita, *Ink Painting*, Tokyo, Weatherhill, 1974.
S. Noma, *The Arts of Japan*, vol. 1, Tokyo and New York, Kōdansha International, 1967.
J. Rosenfield and S. Shimada, eds., *Traditions of Japanese Art: Selections from the Kimiko and John Powers Collection*, Cambridge, Fogg Art Museum, Harvard, 1970.
I. Schaarschmidt-Richter and Osamu Mori, *Japanese Gardens*, New York, Morrow, 1979.

The Way of Tea
R. Castile, *The Way of Tea*, Tokyo, Weatherhill, 1971.
L. A. Cort, *Shigaraki: Potters Valley*, Tokyo and New York, Kōdansha International, 1980.
R. Fujioka *et al.*, *Tea Ceremony Utensils*, Tokyo, Weatherhill, 1973.
T. Hayashiya, M. Nakamura and S. Hayashiya, *Japanese Arts and the Tea Ceremony*, Tokyo, Weatherhill, 1974.
R. Koyama, *The Heritage of Japanese Ceramics*, Tokyo, Weatherhill, 1972.
K. Okakura, *The Book of Tea*, New York, Dover, 1964.
Ura Senke Tea School, *Chanoyu Quarterly*, Kyoto, 1970–.

Political Unification in the 16th Century
M. E. Berry, *Hideyoshi*, Cambridge, Mass., Harvard U.P., 1982.
D. M. Brown, "The Impact of Firearms on Japanese Warfare, 1543–98," *Far Eastern Quarterly*, 7.3 (1948).
G. Elison and B. L. Smith, eds., *Warlords, Artists and Commoners: Japan in the Sixteenth Century*, Honolulu, University of Hawaii Press, 1981.
J. W. Hall and M. B. Jansen, eds., *Studies in the Institutional History of Early Modern Japan*, Princeton, Princeton U.P., 1968.
J. W. Hall, K. Yamamura and K. Nagahara, eds., *Japan before Tokugawa: Political Consolidation and Economic Growth, 1500–1650*, Princeton, Princeton U.P., 1981.

Overseas Contacts in the 16th and 17th Centuries
W. Adams, *Memorials of the Empire of Japan in the XVI and XVII Centuries*, London, Hakluyt Society, 1850.
A. Boscaro, *Sixteenth Century European Printed Works on the First Japanese Mission to Europe: A Descriptive Bibliography*, Leiden, E. J. Brill, 1973.
C. R. Boxer, *The Christian Century in Japan, 1549–1650*, Berkeley, University of California Press, 1951.
R. Cocks, *The Diary of Richard Cocks, Cape-Merchant in the English Factory in Japan, 1615–1622*, 2 vols., Tokyo, Sankōsha, 1899.
M. Cooper, SJ, *This Island of Japon: João Rodrigues' Account of 16th-Century Japan*, Tokyo and New York, Kōdansha International, 1973.
—— trans., *They Came to Japan: An Anthology of European Reports from Japan, 1543–1640*, Berkeley, University of California Press, 1965.
G. Elison, *Deus Destroyed: the Image of Christianity in Early-Modern Japan*, Cambridge, Mass., Harvard U.P., 1973.
D. F. Lach, *Asia in the Making of Europe*, Chicago, Chicago U.P., 1965.
G. B. Sansom, *The Western World and Japan: A Study in the Interaction of European and Asiatic Cultures*, New York, Knopf, 1950.

Momoyama Art and Culture
T. Doi, *Momoyama Decorative Painting*, Tokyo, Weatherhill, 1977.
I. Kondo, *Japanese Genre Painting*, Tokyo and Rutland, Vt., Tuttle, 1961.
B. Leach, *Kenzan and his Tradition: the Lives of Kōetsu, Sōtatsu, Kōrin and Kenzan*, London, Faber and Faber, 1966.
W. Malm, *Japanese Music and Musical Instruments*, Tokyo and Rutland, Vt., Tuttle, 1959.
H. Mizuo, *Edo Painting: Sōtatsu and Kōrin*, Tokyo, Weatherhill, 1972.
S. Noma, *Japanese Costume and Textile Arts*, Tokyo, Weatherhill, 1974.
—— *The Arts of Japan*, vol. 2, Tokyo and New York, Kōdansha International, 1967.
Y. Okamoto, *The Namban Art of Japan*, Tokyo, Weatherhill, 1972.
N. Ōkawa, *Edo Architecture: Katsura and Nikkō*, Tokyo, Weatherhill, 1975.
J. M. and A. Pekarik, eds., *Momoyama: Japanese Art in an Age of Grandeur*, New York, Metropolitan Museum of Art, 1975.
T. Takeda, *Kanō Eitoku*, Tokyo and New York, Kōdansha International, 1977.
Y. Yamane, *Momoyama Genre Painting*, New York and Tokyo, 1973.

Tokugawa Politics and Society
H. Bolitho, *Treasures among Men: the Fudai Daimyō in Tokugawa Japan*, New Haven, Yale U.P., 1974.
C. J. Dunn, *Everyday Life in Traditional Japan*, London, Putnam, 1969.
J. W. Hall, *Tanuma Okitsugu, 1719–1788: Forerunner of Modern Japan*, Cambridge, Mass., Harvard U.P., 1955.
J. W. Hall and M. B. Jansen, eds., *Studies in the Institutional History of Early Modern Japan*, Princeton, Princeton U.P., 1968.
S. Hanley and K. Yamamura, *Economic and Demographic Change in Preindustrial Japan, 1600–1868*, Princeton, Princeton U.P., 1978.
W. B. Hauser, *Economic Institutional Change in Tokugawa Japan: Osaka and the Kinai Cotton Trade*, Cambridge, Cambridge U.P., 1974.
K. Nakai, *Shogunal Politics: Arai Hakuseki and the Premises of Tokugawa Rule*, Cambridge, Mass., Harvard U.P., 1988.
G. Rozman, *Urban Networks in Ch'ing China and Tokugawa Japan*, Princeton, Princeton U.P., 1974.
T. C. Smith, *The Agrarian Origins of Modern Japan*, Stanford, Stanford U.P., 1959.
R. Toby, *State and Diplomacy in Early Modern Japan: Asia in the Development of the Tokugawa Bakufu*, Princeton, Princeton U.P., 1984.
C. Totman, *Politics in the Tokugawa Bakufu, 1600–1843*, Cambridge, Mass., Harvard U.P., 1974.
T. Tsukahira, *Feudal Control in Tokugawa Japan: the Sankin Kōtai System*, Cambridge, Mass., Harvard U.P., 1966.
H. Webb, *The Japanese Imperial Institution in the Tokugawa Period*, New York, Columbia U.P., 1968.
K. Yamamura, *A Study of Samurai Income and Entrepreneurship*, Cambridge, Harvard U.P., 1974.

Tokugawa Intellectual Life
R. Bellah, *Tokugawa Religion: the Values of Pre-Industrial Japan*, New York, Free Press, 1957.
R. P. Dore, *Education in Tokugawa Japan*, Berkeley, University of California Press, 1965.
H. Harootunian, *Toward Restoration: the Growth of Political Consciousness in Tokugawa Japan*, Berkeley, University of California Press, 1970.
M. Maruyama, *Studies in the Intellectual History of Tokugawa Japan*, trans. M. Hane, Princeton, Princeton U.P., 1974.
T. Najita and I. Scheiner, eds., *Japanese Thought in the Tokugawa Period 1600–1868: Methods and Metaphors*, Chicago, Chicago U.P., 1978.
P. Nosco, ed., *Confucianism and Tokugawa Culture*, Princeton, Princeton U.P., 1984.
H. Ooms, *Tokugawa Ideology: Early Constructs, 1570–1680*, Chicago, Chicago U.P., 1985.
B. T. Wakabayashi, *Anti-Foreignism and Western Learning in Early Modern Japan: The New Theses of 1825*, Cambridge, Mass., Harvard U.P., 1986.

Kabuki and Bunraku
J. R. Brandon, W. P. Malm and D. H. Shively, *Studies in Kabuki: Its Acting, Music and Historical Context*, Honolulu, University of Hawaii Press, 1977.
C. J. Dunn, *The Early Japanese Puppet Drama*, London, Luzac, 1966.
E. Earle, *The Kabuki Theatre*, Oxford, Oxford U.P., 1956.
M. Gunji, *Kabuki*, Tokyo and New York, Kōdansha International, 1983.
D. Keene, *Bunraku: The Art of the Japanese Puppet Theatre*, Tokyo and New York, Kōdansha International, 1965.

Edo Period Literature
H. Hibbett, *The Floating World in Japanese Fiction*, New York, Grove, 1959.
Ihara Saikaku, *The Life of an Amorous Woman and Other Writings*, trans. Ivan Morris, New York, New Directions, 1963.
D. Keene, *World within Walls: Japanese Literature of the Pre-Modern Era 1600–1867*, New York, Holt, Rinehart and Winston, 1976.
—— trans., *Chūshingura*, New York, Columbia U.P., 1971.
—— trans., *Major Plays of Chikamatsu*, Tokyo and New York, Kōdansha International, 1961.
Matsuo Bashō, *The Narrow Road to the Deep North, and Other Travel Sketches*, trans. Nobuyuki Yuasa, London, Penguin, 1966.

Edo Period Art: The Floating World
J. Earle, *An Introduction to Netsuke*, London, 1980.
E. Grilli, *The Art of the Japanese Screen*, Tokyo and New York, 1970.
J. Hillier, *Hokusai*, New York, Dutton, 1975.
C. Ives, *The Great Wave: the Influence of Japanese Woodcuts on French Prints*, New York, Metropolitan Museum of Art, 1974.

R. Lane, *Images from the Floating World: The Japanese Print*, New York, Putnam, 1978.
H. D. Smith, *Hiroshige: One Hundred Famous Views of Edo*, New York, Braziller, Inc., 1986.
D. Waterhouse, *Harunobu and His Age*, London, British Museum, 1964.

The Rediscovery of the West in the 18th and 19th Centuries
C. R. Boxer, *Jan Compaigne in Japan, 1600–1850*, The Hague, Martinus Nijhoff, 1950.
C. L. French, *Shiba Kōkan, Artist, Innovator and Pioneer in the Westernization of Japan*, Tokyo, Weatherhill, 1974.
G. K. Goodman, *Japan: The Dutch Experience*, London, 1986.
M. B. Jansen, *Japan and its World: Two Centuries of Change*, Princeton, Princeton U.P., 1980.
D. Keene, *The Japanese Discovery of Europe, 1720–1830*, Stanford, Stanford U.P., 1969.

The Meiji Restoration and its Legacy
W. G. Beasley, *The Meiji Restoration*, Stanford, Stanford U.P., 1972.
A. M. Craig, *Chōshū in the Meiji Restoration 1853–1868*, Cambridge, Mass., Harvard U.P., 1961.
T. M. Huber, *The Revolutionary Origins of Modern Japan*, Stanford, Stanford U.P., 1981.
M. B. Jansen, *Sakamoto Ryōma and the Meiji Restoration*, Princeton, Princeton U.P., 1961.
M. B. Jansen and G. Rozman, eds., *Japan in Transition: From Tokugawa to Meiji*, Princeton, Princeton U.P., 1986.
O. Statler, *Shimoda Story*, New York, Random House, 1969.
C. Totman, *The Fall of the Tokugawa Bakufu 1862–1868*, Honolulu, University of Hawaii Press, 1980.

Modern Political Development
G. Akita, *Foundations of Constitutional Government in Modern Japan, 1868–1900*, Cambridge, Mass., Harvard U.P., 1967.
W. G. Beasley, *The Modern History of Japan*, 3rd ed., London, St Martin's, 1981.
J. W. Dower, *Empire and Aftermath, Yoshida Shigeru and the Japanese Experience, 1878–1954*, Cambridge, Mass., Harvard U.P., 1988.
P. Duus, *The Rise of Modern Japan*, New York, Houghton Mifflin, 1976.
M. Hane, *Peasants, Rebels, and Outcastes: the Underside of Modern Japan*, New York, Pantheon, 1982.
J. P. Lehmann, *The Roots of Modern Japan*, London, St. Martin's, 1982.
T. Najita, *Hara Kei in the Politics of Compromise, 1905–1915*, Cambridge, Mass., Harvard U.P., 1967.
—— *Japan: The Intellectual Foundations of Modern Japanese Politics*, Chicago, Chicago U.P., 1974.
T. Najita and J. V. Koschmann, eds., *Conflict in Modern Japanese History: The Neglected Tradition*, Princeton, Princeton U.P., 1982.
E. H. Norman, "Japan's Emergence as a Modern State" (1940), in J. W. Dower, ed., *Origins of the Modern Japanese State*, New York, Pantheon, 1975.
T. J. Pempel, *Policy and Politics in Japan: Creative Conservatism*, Philadelphia, Temple U.P., 1982.
K. Pyle, *The Making of Modern Japan*, Lexington, Mass., Heath, 1978.
B. Shillony, *Revolt in Japan: the Young Officers and the Feb. 26, 1936 Incident*, Princeton, Princeton U.P., 1973.
R. Storry, *A History of Modern Japan*, London, Penguin, 1965.
N. Thayer, *How the Conservatives Rule Japan*, Princeton, Princeton U.P., 1969.

Modern Economic and Industrial Development
J. Abegglen and G. Stalk, Jr., *Kaisha, The Japanese Corporation*, New York, Basic Books, 1985.
R. Dore, *Flexible Rigidities: Industrial Policy and Structural Adjustment in the Japanese Economy, 1970–1980*, Stanford, Stanford U.P., 1986.
—— *Land Reform in Japan*, Oxford, Oxford U.P., 1959.
—— *Shinohata, a Portrait of a Japanese Village*, New York, Pantheon, 1980.
S. Garon, *The State and Labor in Modern Japan*, Berkeley, University of California Press, 1988.
A. Gordon, *The Evolution of Labor Relations in Japan: Heavy Industry, 1853–1955*, Cambridge, Mass., Harvard U.P., 1987.
C. Johnson, *Miti and the Japanese Miracle, The Growth of Industrial Policy, 1925–1975*, Stanford, Stanford U.P., 1982.
D. Okimoto, ed., *Japan's Economy: Coping with Change in the International Environment*, Boulder, Westview Press, 1982.
H. Patrick, ed., *Japanese Industrialization and its Social Consequences*, Berkeley, University of California Press, 1976.
H. Patrick and H. Rosovksy, eds., *Asia's New Giant: How the Japanese Economy Works*, Washington, D.C., The Brookings Institution, 1976.
R. Smethurst, *Agricultural Development and Tenancy Disputes in Japan, 1870–1940*, Princeton, Princeton U.P., 1986.
R. J. Smith, *Kurusu: A Japanese Village, 1951–1975*, Stanford, Stanford U.P., 1978.
A. Waswo, *Japanese Landlords, The Decline of a Rural Elite*, Berkeley, University of California Press, 1977.
D. E. Westney, *Imitation and Innovation: The Transfer of Western Organizational Patterns to Japan*, Cambridge, Mass., Harvard U.P., 1987.
K. Yoshihara, *Sōgō Shōsha: the Vanguard of the Japanese Economy*, Oxford, Oxford U.P., 1983.

Foreign Relations, Overseas Expansion and War in the Modern Century
D. Borg and S. Okamoto, eds., *Pearl Harbor as History: Japanese American Relations, 1931–41*, New York, Columbia U.P., 1973.
K. E. Calder, *Crisis and Compensation: Political Stability and Public Policy in Japan, 1949–1986*, Princeton, Princeton U.P., 1988.
K. E. Calder and R. Hofheinz, Jr., *The East Asia Edge*, New York, Basic Books, 1982.
Committee for the Compilation of Materials on Damage Caused by the Atomic Bombs in Hiroshima and Nagasaki, *Hiroshima and Nagasaki: the Physical, Medical, and Social Effects of the Atomic Bombings*, trans. by Eisei Ishikawa and D. L. Swain, New York, Basic Books, 1981.
F. H. Conroy, *The Japanese Seizure of Korea, 1868–1910*, Philadelphia, University of Pennsylvania Press, 1960.
J. B. Crowley, *Japan's Quest for Autonomy: National Security and Foreign Policy, 1930–38*, Princeton U.P., 1966.
J. Dower, *War without Mercy: Race and Power in the Pacific War*, New York, Pantheon, 1986.
E. Frost, *For Richer for Poorer: The New U.S.-Japan Relationship*, New York, Council on Foreign Relations, 1987.
J. Hershey, *Hiroshima*, New York, Bantam, 1946.
M. Ibuse, *Black Rain*, trans. J. Bester, Tokyo and New York, Kōdansha International, 1981.
A. Iriye, *The Search for a New Order in the Far East, 1921–1931*, Cambridge, Mass., Harvard U.P., 1965.
R. J. Lifton, *Death in Life: Survivors of Hiroshima*, New York, Random House, 1967.
M. Mayo, ed., *The Emergence of Imperial Japan: Self Defence or Calculated Aggression*, Lexington, Mass., Heath, 1970.
I. H. Nish, *Japanese Foreign Policy, 1869–1942*, London, Routledge and Kegan Paul, 1977.

Modern Intellectual and Cultural Developments
C. Blacker, *The Japanese Enlightenment: A Study in the Writings of Fukuzawa Yukichi*, Cambridge, Cambridge U.P., 1964.
B. H. Chamberlain, *Things Japanese*, London, 1905.
A. M. Craig and D. H. Shively, eds., *Personality in Japanese History*, Berkeley, University of California Press, 1970.
Y. Fukuzawa, *An Encouragement of Learning*, trans. D. A. Dilworth, Tokyo, Sophia U.P., 1969.
—— *Autobiography*, trans. E. Kiyooka, New York, 1966.
C. Gluck, *Japan's Modern Myths: Ideology in the Late Meiji Period*, Princeton, Princeton U.P., 1985.
L. Hearn, *Japan: An Attempt at an Interpretation*, London, Macmillan, 1913.
D. Irokawa, *The Culture of the Meiji Period*, trans. and edited by M. B. Jansen, Princeton, Princeton U.P., 1985.
S. Okuma, *Fifty Years of the New Japan*, London, 1909.
H. Passin, *Society and Education in Japan*, New York, Columbia U.P., 1982.
S. Picken, *Death and the Japanese*, London, Athlone, 1985.
D. W. Plath, *Long Engagements: Maturity in Modern Japan*, Stanford, Stanford U.P., 1980.
K. Pyle, *The New Generation in Meiji Japan: Problems of Cultural Identity*, Stanford, Stanford U.P., 1969.
D. Roden, *Schooldays in Imperial Japan*, Berkeley, University of California Press, 1980.
I. Scheiner, *Christian Converts and Social Protest in Meiji Japan*, Berkeley, University of California Press, 1970.
D. H. Shively, ed., *Tradition and Modernization in Japanese Culture*, Princeton, Princeton U.P., 1971.

Art Trends in Modern Japan
M. Harada, *Meiji Western Painting*, Tokyo, Weatherhill, 1974.
M. Kawakita, *Modern Currents in Japanese Art*, Tokyo, Weatherhill, 1974.
T. Miyagawa, *Modern Japanese Painting*, Tokyo and New York, Kōdansha International, 1967.
J. T. Rimer, "Tokyo in Paris, Paris in Tokyo," in Japan Foundation, ed., *Paris in Japan: the Japanese Encounter with European Painting*, Tokyo and St Louis, 1987.

Contemporary Japanese Society and Culture
J. Anderson and D. Richie, *The Japanese Film: Art and Industry*, Princeton, Princeton U.P., 1984.
G. Bernstein, *Haruko's World: A Japanese Farm Woman and Her Community*, Stanford, Stanford U.P , 1983.
C. Blacker, *The Catalpa Bow: A Study of Shamanistic Practices in Japan*, London, Allen and Unwin, 1975.
A. Bock, *Japanese Film Directors*, Tokyo and New York, Kōdansha International, 1978.
I. Buruma, *Behind the Mask*, New York, Meridian, 1984.
L. Dalby, *Geisha*, New York, Vintage Books, 1983.
G. De Vos, *Japan's Minorities: Burakumin, Koreans, Ainu, and Okinawans*, Minority Rights Group, 1983.
T. Doi, *The Anatomy of Dependence*, Tokyo and New York, Kōdansha International, 1973.
B. Duke, *The Japanese School*, New York, Praeger, 1986.
F. Gibney, *Japan the Fragile Superpower*, rev. ed., New York, Meridian, 1980.
H. Hardacre, *Kurozumikyō and the New Religions of Japan*, Princeton, Princeton U.P., 1986.
T. S. Lebra, *Japanese Women, Constraint and Fulfilment*, Honolulu, University of Hawaii Press, 1984.
T. S. and W. P. Lebra, eds., *Japanese Culture and Behavior: Selected Readings*, Honolulu, University of Hawaii Press, 1974.
J. D. Morely, *Pictures from the Water Trade*, New York, Fontana, 1986.
C. Nakane, *Japanese Society*, Tokyo and Rutland, Vt., Tuttle, 1970.
E. O. Reischauer, *The Japanese Today*, Cambridge, Mass., Harvard U.P., 1988.
D. Richie, *The Films of Akira Kurosawa*, Berkeley, University of California Press, 1984.
—— *The Japanese Movie*, New York and Tokyo, Kōdansha International, 1982.
T. Rohlen, *Japan's High Schools*, Berkeley, University of California Press, 1983.
I. Scheiner, ed., *Modern Japan: an Interpretive Anthology*, New York, Macmillan, 1974.
R. J. Smith, *Japanese Society: Tradition, Self, and the Social Order*, Cambridge, Cambridge U.P., 1984.
E. Vogel, *Japan as Number 1: Lessons for America*, Cambridge, Mass., Harvard U.P., 1979.
M. White, *The Japanese Educational Challenge*, New York, Free Press, 1987.

Modern Literature: Criticism
R. Bowring, *Mori Ōgai and the Modernization of Japanese Culture*, Cambridge, Cambridge U.P., 1979.
M. Miyoshi, *Accomplices of Silence: the Modern Japanese Novel*, Berkeley, University of California Press, 1974.
J. T. Rimer, *Japanese Fiction and its Traditions*, Princeton, Princeton U.P., 1978.
—— *Mori Ōgai*, New York, Twayne, 1975.
M. Ueda, *Modern Japanese Writers and the Nature of Literature*, Stanford, Stanford U.P., 1976.
H. Yamanouchi, *The Search for Authenticity in Modern Japanese Literature*, Cambridge, Cambridge U.P., 1978.

A Sampling of Modern Literature in Translation
Akutagawa Ryūnosuke, *Japanese Short Stories*, trans. Takashi Kojima, New York, Liveright, 1961.
Kawabata Yasunari, *Snow Country*, trans. Edward Seidensticker, New York, Knopf, 1958.
—— *The Sound of the Mountain*, trans. Edward Seidensticker, New York, Knopf, 1970.
Mori Ōgai, *The Wild Geese*, trans. K. Ochiai and S. Goldstein, Tokyo and Rutland, Vt., Tuttle, 1959.
I. Morris, *Modern Japanese Stories—An Anthology*, Tokyo and Rutland, Vt., Tuttle, 1962.
Natsume Sōseki, *Botchan*, trans. A. Turney, London, Owen, 1973.
—— *Kokoro*, trans. E. MacClellan, London, Owen, 1967.
—— *Mon*, trans. F. Mathy, London, Owen, 1972.
E. Seidensticker, *Kafū the Scribbler, The Life and Writings of Nagai Kafū, 1879–1959*, Stanford, Stanford U.P., 1965.
E. Shiffert and Y. Sawa, eds., *Anthology of Modern Japanese Poetry*, Tokyo and Rutland, Vt., Tuttle, 1972.
Tanizaki Junichirō, *Diary of a Mad Old Man*, trans. H. Hibbett, New York, Knopf, 1965.
—— *Some Prefer Nettles*, trans. E. Seidensticker, New York, Knopf, 1955.
—— *The Makioka Sisters*, trans. E. Seidensticker, New York, Knopf, 1957.
Yukio Mishima, *The Temple of the Golden Pavilion*, trans. I. Morris, New York, 1956.
—— *Death in Midsummer and Other Stories*, trans. E. Seidensticker, New York, 1966.

THE RULERS OF JAPAN

Emperors and reigning empresses

Number in traditional count	Sovereign	Birth and death dates	Reign dates	Year of enthronement (if later)
1	Jimmu			
2	Suizei			
3	Annei			
4	Itoku			
5	Kōshō			
6	Kōan			
7	Kōrei	legendary		
8	Kōgen	emperors		
9	Kaika			
10	Sujin			
11	Suinin			
12	Keikō			
13	Seimu			
14	Chūai			
15	Ōjin	late 4th to early 5th century		
16	Nintoku			
17	Richū	first half of the 5th century		
18	Hanzei			
19	Ingyō	mid-5th century		
20	Ankō			
21	Yūryaku			
22	Seinei			
23	Kenzō	latter half of the 5th century		
24	Ninken			
25	Buretsu			
26	Keitai			
27	Ankan	first half of the 6th century		
28	Senka			
29	Kimmei	509-571	531 or 539-571	
30	Bidatsu	538-585	572-585	
31	Yōmei	?-587	585-587	
32	Sushun	?-592	587-592	
*33	Suiko	554-628	593-628	
34	Jomei	593-641	629-641	
*35	Kōgyoku	594-661	642-645	
36	Kōtoku	597-654	645-654	
*37	Saimei	594-661	655-661	
38	Tenji	626-672	661-672	(668)
39	Kōbun	648-672	672	
40	Temmu	?-686	672-686	(673)
*41	Jitō	645-703	686-697	(690)
42	Mommu	683-707	697-707	
*43	Gemmei	661-722	707-715	
*44	Genshō	680-748	715-724	
45	Shōmu	701-756	724-749	
*46	Kōken	718-770	749-758	
47	Junnin	733-765	758-764	
*48	Shōtoku	718-770	764-770	
49	Kōnin	709-782	770-781	
50	Kammu	737-806	781-806	
51	Heizei	774-824	806-809	
52	Saga	786-842	809-823	
53	Junna	786-840	823-833	
54	Nimmyō	810-850	833-850	
55	Montoku	827-858	850-858	
56	Seiwa	850-881	858-876	
57	Yōzei	869-949	876-884	
58	Kōkō	830-887	884-887	
59	Uda	867-931	887-897	
60	Daigo	885-930	897-930	
61	Suzaku	923-952	930-946	
62	Murakami	926-967	946-967	

Fujiwara regents

	Sesshō	Kampaku
Yoshifusa (804-872)	866-872	—
Mototsune (836-891)	873-880	887-891
Tadahira (880-949)	930-941	941-949
Saneyori (900-970)	969-970	967-969
Koretada (924-972)	970-972	—
Kanemichi (925-977)	—	973-977
Yoritada (924-989)	—	977-986
Kaneie (929-990)	986-990	990
Michitaka (953-995)	990-993	993-995
Michikane (961-995)	—	995
Michinaga (966-1028)	1016-1017	(996-1017)
Yorimichi (990-1074)	1017-1020	1020-1068
Norimichi (997-1075)	—	1068-1075
Morozane (1042-1101)	1087-1091	1075-1087
		1091-1094
Moromichi (1062-1099)	—	1094-1099
Tadazane (1078-1162)	1107-1114	1106-1107
		1114-1121
Tadamichi (1097-1164)	1123-1129	1121-1123
	1142-1151	1129-1142
		1151-1158
Motozane (1143-1166)	1165-1166	1158-1165
Motofusa (1144-1230)	1166-1173	1173-1179
Motomichi (1160-1233)	1180-1183	1179-1180
	1184-1186	
Moroie (1172-1238)	1184	—

Kamakura shoguns

1. Minamoto no Yoritomo (1147-1199) 1192-1199
2. Minamoto no Yoriie (1182-1204) 1202-1203
3. Minamoto no Sanetomo (1192-1219) 1203-1219
4. Kujō Yoritsune (1218-1256) 1226-1244
5. Kujō Yoritsugu (1239-1256) 1244-1252
6. Prince Munetaka (1242-1274) 1252-1266
7. Prince Koreyasu (1264-1326) 1266-1289
8. Prince Hisaaki (1276-1328) 1289-1308
9. Prince Morikuni (1301-1333) 1308-1333

Regents of the Kamakura shogunate

1. Hōjō Tokimasa (1138-1215) 1203-1205
2. Hōjō Yoshitoki (1163-1224) 1205-1224
3. Hōjō Yasutoki (1183-1242) 1224-1242
4. Hōjō Tsunetoki (1224-1246) 1242-1246
5. Hōjō Tokiyori (1227-1263) 1246-1256
6. Hōjō Nagatoki (1229-1264) 1256-1264
7. Hōjō Masamura (1205-1273) 1264-1268
8. Hōjō Tokimune (1251-1284) 1268-1284
9. Hōjō Sadatoki (1271-1311) 1284-1301
10. Hōjō Morotoki (1275-1311) 1301-1311
11. Hōjō Munenobu (1259-1312) 1311-1312
12. Hōjō Hirotoki (1279-1315) 1312-1315
13. Hōjō Mototoki (d 1333) 1315
14. Hōjō Takatoki (1303-1333) 1316-1326
15. Hōjō Sadaaki (1278-1333) 1326
16. Hōjō Moritoki (d 1333) 1327-1333

Ashikaga shoguns

1. Takauji (1305-1358) 1338-1358
2. Yoshiakira (1330-1368) 1359-1368
3. Yoshimitsu (1358-1408) 1368-1394
4. Yoshimochi (1386-1428) 1395-1423
5. Yoshikazu (1407-1425) 1423-1425
6. Yoshinori (1394-1441) 1429-1441
7. Yoshikatsu (1434-1443) 1442-1443
8. Yoshimasa (1436-1490) 1449-1473
9. Yoshihisa (1465-1489) 1474-1489
10. Yoshitane (1466-1523) 1490-1493
11. Yoshizumi (1480-1511) 1495-1508
    Yoshitane 1508-1521
12. Yoshiharu (1511-1550) 1522-1547
13. Yoshiteru (1536-1565) 1547-1565
14. Yoshihide (1540-1568) 1568
15. Yoshiaki (1537-1597) 1568-1573
    Oda Nobunaga (1534-1582) 1568-1582
    Toyotomi Hideyoshi (1536-1598) 1582-1598

Tokugawa shoguns

1. Ieyasu (1543-1616)	1603-1605	9. Ieshige (1711-1761)	1745-1760
2. Hidetada (1579-1632)	1605-1623	10. Ieharu (1737-1786)	1760-1786
3. Iemitsu (1604-1651)	1623-1651	11. Ienari (1773-1841)	1787-1837
4. Ietsuna (1641-1680)	1651-1680	12. Ieyoshi (1793-1853)	1837-1853
5. Tsunayoshi (1646-1709)	1680-1709	13. Iesada (1824-1858)	1853-1858
6. Ienobu (1662-1712)	1709-1712	14. Iemochi (1846-1866)	1858-1866
7. Ietsugu (1709-1716)	1713-1716	15. Yoshinobu (1837-1913)	1867
8. Yoshimune (1684-1751)	1716-1745		

Early Meiji leaders

Ōkubo Toshimichi 1830-1878	Itō Hirobumi 1841-1909	Saigo Tsugumichi 1843-1902
Kido Takayoshi 1833-1877	Kuroda Kiyotaka 1840-1900	Yamagata Aritomo 1838-1922
Saigo Takamori 1827-1877	Matsukata Masayoshi 1835-1924	Inoue Kaoru 1835-1915
Iwakura Tomomi 1825-1883	Ōyama Iwao 1842-1916	Saionji Kinmochi 1849-1940

Prime Ministers

Itō Hirobumi 1885-1888	Katō Tomosaburō 1922-1923	Tōjō Hideki 1941-1944	Ikedo Hayato 1963-1964
Kuroda Kiyotaka 1888-1889	Yamamoto Gonnohyōe 1923-1924	Koiso Kuniaki 1944-1945	Satō Eisaku 1964-1967
Yamagata Aritomo 1889-1891	Kiyoura Keigo 1924	Suzuki Kantarō 1945	Satō Eisaku 1967-1970
Matsukata Masayoshi 1891-1892	Katō Takaaki 1924-1925	Higashikuni Naruhiko 1945	Satō Eisaku 1970-1972
Itō Hirobumi 1892-1896	Katō Takaaki 1925-1926	Shidehara Kijūrō 1945-1946	Tanaka Kakuei 1972
Matsukata Masayoshi 1896-1898	Wakatsuki Reijirō 1926-1927	Yoshida Shigeru 1946-1947	Tanaka Kakuei 1972-1974
Itō Hirobumi 1898	Tanaka Giichi 1927-1929	Katayama Tetsu 1947-1948	Miki Takeo 1974-1976
Ōkuma Shigenobu 1898	Hamaguchi Osachi 1929-1931	Ashida Hitoshi 1948	Fukuda Takeo 1976-1978
Yamagata Aritomo 1898-1900	Wakatsuki Reijirō 1931	Yoshida Shigeru 1948-1949	Ōhira Masayoshi 1978-1979
Itō Hirobumi 1900-1901	Inukai Tsuyoshi 1931-1932	Yoshida Shigeru 1949-1952	Ōhira Masayoshi 1979-1980
Katsura Tarō 1901-1906	Saitō Makoto 1932-1934	Yoshida Shigeru 1952-1953	Suzuki Zenkō 1980-1982
Saionji Kimmochi 1906-1908	Okada Keisuke 1934-1936	Yoshida Shigeru 1953-1954	Nakasone Yasuhiro 1982-1987
Katsura Tarō 1908-1911	Hirota Kōki 1936-1937	Hatoyama Ichirō 1954-1955	Takeshita Noboru 1987-
Saionji Kimmochi 1911-1912	Hayashi Senjūrō 1937	Hatoyama Ichirō 1955	
Katsura Tarō 1912-1913	Konoe Fumimaro 1937-1939	Hatoyama Ichirō 1955-1956	
Yamamoto Gonnohyōe 1913-1914	Hiranuma Kiichirō 1939	Ishibashi Tanzan 1956-1957	
Ōkuma Shigenobu 1914-1916	Abe Nobuyuki 1939-1940	Kishi Nobusuke 1957-1958	
Terauchi Masatake 1916-1918	Yonai Mitsumasa 1940	Kishi Nobusuke 1958-1960	
Hara Takashi 1918-1921	Konoe Fumimaro 1940-1941	Ikedo Hayato 1960	
Takahashi Korekiyo 1921-1922	Konoe-Fumimaro 1941	Ikedo Hayato 1960-1963	

Emperors and reigning empresses

Number in traditional count	Sovereign	Birth and death dates	Reign dates	Year of enthronement (if later)
63	Reizei	950-1011	967-969	
64	En'yū	959-991	969-984	
65	Kazan	968-1008	984-986	
66	Ichijō	980-1011	986-1011	
67	Sanjō	976-1017	1011-1016	
68	Go-Ichijō	1008-1036	1016-1036	
69	Go-Suzaku	1009-1045	1036-1045	
70	Go-Reizei	1025-1068	1045-1068	
71	Go-Sanjō	1034-1073	1068-1073	
72	Shirakawa	1053-1129	1073-1087	
			1086-1129†	
73	Horikawa	1079-1107	1087-1107	
74	Toba	1103-1156	1107-1123	(1108)
			1129-1156†	
75	Sutoku	1119-1164	1123-1142	
76	Konoe	1139-1155	1142-1155	
77	Go-Shirakawa	1127-1192	1155-1158	
			1158-1192†	
78	Nijō	1143-1165	1158-1165	(1159)
79	Rokujō	1164-1176	1165-1168	
80	Takakura	1161-1181	1168-1180	
81	Antoku	1178-1185	1180-1185	
82	Go-Toba	1180-1239	1183-1198	(1184)
83	Tsuchimikado	1195-1231	1198-1210	
84	Juntoku	1197-1242	1210-1221	(1211)
85	Chūkyō	1218-1234	1221	
86	Go-Horikawa	1212-1234	1221-1232	(1222)
87	Shijō	1231-1242	1232-1242	(1233)
88	Go-Saga	1220-1272	1242-1246	
89	Go-Fukakusa	1243-1304	1246-1260	
90	Kameyama	1249-1305	1260-1274	
91	Go-Uda	1267-1324	1274-1287	
92	Fushimi	1265-1317	1287-1298	(1288)
93	Go-Fushimi	1288-1336	1298-1301	
94	Go-Nijō	1285-1308	1301-1308	
95	Hanazono	1297-1348	1308-1318	
96	Go-Daigo	1288-1339	1318-1339	
97	Go-Murakami	1328-1368	1339-1368	
98	Chōkei	1343-1394	1368-1383	
99	Go-Kameyama	?-1424	1383-1392	
N1	Kōgon	1313-1364	1331-1333	(1332)
N2	Kōmyō	1322-1380	1336-1348	(1338)
N3	Sukō	1334-1398	1348-1351	(1350)
N4	Go-Kōgon	1338-1374	1351-1371	(1354)
N5	Go-En'yū	1359-1393	1371-1382	(1375)
100	Go-Komatsu	1377-1433	1382-1412	(1392)
101	Shōkō	1401-1428	1412-1428	(1415)
102	Go-Hanazono	1419-1471	1428-1464	(1430)
103	Go-Tsuchimikado	1442-1500	1464-1500	(1466)
104	Go-Kashiwabara	1464-1526	1500-1526	(1521)
105	Go-Nara	1497-1557	1526-1557	(1536)
106	Ōgimachi	1517-1593	1557-1586	(1560)
107	Go-Yōzei	1572-1617	1586-1611	(1587)
108	Go-Mizunoo	1596-1680	1611-1629	
*109	Meishō	1624-1696	1629-1643	(1630)
110	Go-Kōmyō	1633-1654	1643-1654	
111	Gosai	1637-1685	1655-1663	(1656)
112	Reigen	1654-1732	1663-1687	
113	Higashiyama	1675-1709	1687-1709	
114	Nakamikado	1702-1737	1709-1735	(1710)
115	Sakuramachi	1720-1750	1735-1747	
116	Momozono	1741-1762	1747-1762	
*117	Go-Sakuramachi	1740-1813	1762-1771	(1763)
118	Go-Momozono	1758-1779	1771-1779	
119	Kōkaku	1771-1840	1780-1817	
120	Ninkō	1800-1846	1817-1846	
121	Kōmei	1831-1867	1846-1867	(1847)
122	Meiji	1852-1912	1867-1912	(1868)
123	Taishō	1879-1926	1912-1926	(1915)
124	Hirohito	1901-	1926-	(1928)

* Empresses.   † Cloistered rule.

GLOSSARY

A Note on Pronunciation

Consonants in Japanese are pronounced much as they are in English with the exceptions that the *g* is always hard and *r* is unrolled, sounding somewhere between the English *r* and *l*.

Vowels are pronounced approximately as in Italian, Spanish or German: *a* as in *a*rt; *e* as in sp*e*nd; *i* as in m*e*; *o* as in c*o*ld; *u* as in r*u*de.

Macrons over *ō* and *ū* indicate that the sound should be lengthened to twice its normal duration. Macrons have been omitted from common geographic names such as Tokyō or Hokkaidō and from words like shōgun that have been accepted in English.

Amida (Skt. Amitābha) "Infinite Light." The Buddha who presides over the Western Paradise where the faithful trust they will be reborn after death. Personification of boundless light and compassion. The most popularly revered of the transhistorical Buddhas. Devotion to Amida and the Pure Land, expressed through the repeated invocation of Amida's name, was introduced to Japan from China in the ancient period, developed within Tendai Buddhist monasteries, and spread widely among ordinary people from the late 12th century.

Bakufu The term used to describe the administration of a SHOGUN, or military ruler. Also referred to as shogunate. The word Bakufu originated in China where it referred to the headquarters of the Tang emperor's inner palace guards or the headquarters of a general on a military expedition. The oldest reference in Japan, from the 10th century, describes the residence of an imperial guards' captain. The term was applied to Yoritomo's residence in Kamakura in his roles as captain of the imperial guards and as shogun. Gradually it came to mean not only the residence of a shogun but the organs of warrior government headed by the shogun. As such, it came to be applied to the Kamakura, Muromachi and Edo shogunates.

be Occupational serflike groups of farmers, potters, metalworkers or scribes serving the aristocratic lineage groups known as *UJI* in Japanese society prior to the Nara period. *Be* provided fixed amounts of produce, labor or domestic service for the *uji* they served.

Bodhisattva (Skt. Japanese *bosatsu*) "Enlightened Being." An inherently enlightened being on the verge of Buddhahood who postpones his own complete emancipation from the world and entry to NIRVANA so that he can save other sentient beings. Includes such compassionate figures as Fugen, Kannon, Miroku, Hachiman and Jizō.

bu Martial arts. The martial tradition and arts of the warrior, as opposed to the literary and civilian arts of government and letters, *BUN*.

buke The military houses. The great warrior families, as distinguished from the nobility, *KUGE*, and powerful temples, *jimon*.

bun Literary study. Civilian arts. In China and Japan there was frequent emphasis on the notion that the combination of the highest ideals of *bun* and *BU* were essential to government, civilization and moral order.

Bunraku Puppet theater. The modern name for a kind of JŌRURI, named for the Bunrakuza theater established in Osaka in the 17th century. Bunraku is dramatic performance by one-third lifesize puppets, manipulated by several skilled handlers and accompanied by chanted narrative and musical instruments. The genre flowered in Osaka in the late 17th century and maintains a popular following today.

bushi Armed men. Samurai or warriors. Especially those of the medieval period who still lived in the countryside and farmed their lands while honing their martial skills with horse and bow.

bushidan Bands of *BUSHI*. Local and regional warrior bands emerging in the provinces from the 10th century. Early warrior bands were based on kin or fictive kin relationships. With time, however, the largest bands clustering around famous chieftains grew on a regional basis. The most extensive *bushidan* were those with Fujiwara, Taira (Heike) or Minamoto (Genji) affiliations.

bushidō The Way of the Warrior, *BUSHI*. A martial ethic developing among warriors from the medieval period which involved patronage by the lord, *goon*, in return for military service, *hōkō*, by the vassal. In the earlier phases the relationship was conditional in that service was granted while victories and spoils were provided. In the Edo period, in works like the *Hagakure*, *bushidō* tended to be converted into a unilateral and unconditional bond of loyalty to the lord. At the same time the Tokugawa shoguns were at pains to tame some of the more violent expressions of *bushidō* such as *junshi*, following one's lord in death, or vendettas of the kind carried out by the 47 masterless samurai to avenge their lord.

chanoyu Literally "hot water for tea." The Japanese term for the "Tea Ceremony." Tea had been introduced to Japan before the 10th century. The custom of drinking tea did not really take hold, however, until the diffusion of Zen in the 13th century. Tea was drunk in Zen monasteries as a stimulant to help monks endure long periods of meditation and to entertain guests. The custom spread from Zen monasteries to the Sakai and Kyoto merchants and the provincial warriors who patronized Zen. In the process a distinctive aesthetic of rustic simplicity, *WABI*, was cultivated during the 16th century by such famed tea masters as Takeno Jōō and Sen no Rikyū.

chōnin City dwellers, especially those of Edo, Osaka and Kyoto in the Edo period. Embraces the world and cultural interests of merchants, artisans and storekeepers. Distinguished from nobles (*kuge*), samurai (*shi*), peasants (*nō*), outcastes (*eta*) and non-people (*hinin*).

daimyō Provincial feudal lords. Literally "great name." Originally referring to private named landholdings, the term *daimyō* during the medieval centuries was used to describe the provincial power holders, especially local warrior chieftains. In the age of wars in the late 15th and 16th centuries some 250 *daimyō* contended for local power. From among these warring *daimyō* Oda Nobunaga began a reunification of the country that was carried through by Toyotomi Hideyoshi and Tokugawa Ieyasu. Under the Tokugawa shoguns a *daimyō* was defined as the lord of a domain with an income of at least 10 000 *koku* (1 *koku* = 5 bushels of rice).

dhāranī Mystic and magical syllables used in esoteric Buddhism epitomizing the essence of *sūtras* and prayers.

dharma (Skt. "Law") Usually the law or truth of the Buddha's teachings. See *MAPPŌ*.

dogū Earthenware figurines from the late JŌMON (11 000–300 BC) period. Many are in the form of pregnant women with masklike faces and protuberant goggle eyes. No doubt intended to facilitate childbirth or to avert disease.

dōtaku Ceremonial bronze bells. Elegant, flattened, thin-walled bronze bell-shaped objects of the YAYOI period (300 BC–300 AD). By the 2nd century AD metalworkers in Japan were crudely reproducing small Korean bells. As technique improved, finer large bells with decorated panels and flowing-water designs were made in considerable numbers. Some of these bells provide us with the first simple illustrations of scenes from daily life in prehistoric Japan.

gagaku "Elegant music." Ritualized music and dance introduced from China or Korea during the Nara period. Took root as the ceremonial music of the imperial court.

gigaku Oldest of the imported continental music and dance traditions. Performed in Nara temples in the 7th and 8th centuries.

han The feudal domains of the Edo period. There were some 250 *han* headed by feudal lords, *DAIMYŌ*, and their samurai administrations. The Tokugawa power structure which controlled Japan from 1600 to 1867 is commonly known as the *baku-han* system, pointing to a sharing of powers between the Tokugawa shogunate, or BAKUFU, and the 250 or so *han*. After the Meiji restoration *han* were abolished and replaced by prefectures in a process known as *haihan-chiken*.

haniwa Literally "rings of clay." The clay cylinders, inanimate objects, animals and human figures placed on the slopes of mounded tombs in the 5th and 6th centuries AD. First made in the Kansai in the 4th century, they became the major art form of the tomb (KOFUN) period.

honji suijaku. The syncretic association of Buddhism and Shinto, developing from the ancient period, in which the *KAMI* are viewed as traces or native incarnations, *suijaku*, of the Buddhist deities who are their original forms, *honji*.

ikki Leagues of samurai or peasants in the medieval and early modern periods, frequently organized in resistance to local or central authority. Some *ikki*, including the *ikkō ikki* of the True Pure Land school of Buddhism and the *hokke ikki* of the Nichiren Lotus school, had a powerful religious motivation.

Jōmon Literally "cord pattern." Used first to describe cord-marked designs on the oldest prehistoric earthenware. Now applied to the entire period in which that pottery was made from around 11 000 BC to 300 BC. Jōmon society was also characterized by a hunting-and-gathering life-style.

jōri A term used to describe the basic units of land as it was laid out in the 7th and 8th centuries. These land allotments came to be known as the *jōri* system. *Jō*, measuring 360 *bu*, about 720 paces, ran north–south, while *ri*, also measuring 360 *bu*, ran east–west. *Jōri* left their physical mark on many parts of the country and can still be detected today in the patterns of rice fields. The aim was to provide equitably distributed taxable land, but the system foundered as public land was increasingly privatized and the supply available for redistribution dwindled.

Jōruri Stories with musical or chanted accompaniment. In the mid-15th century there appeared the chanted version of the sad tale of young Minamoto Yoshitsune and his lover, Jōruri Gozen, whose name provides the origin of Jōruri. Jōruri was brought to a peak of perfection by the dramatist Chikamatsu Monzaemon (1653–1724) and Takemoto Gidayū (1615–1714), a master reciter. During the 17th century the *shamisen* became the principal accompanying instrument. Performances with puppets, which we now frequently refer to as BUNRAKU, were known as *ningyō jōruri*. Jōruri was also a vital component of the KABUKI theater. Performances on stage by actors were called *kabuki jōruri*. There were also performances on the streets, in halls or temples.

Kabuki Originally colorful, extravagant, strange or erotic dance drama and song. Said to have begun with women performers like Okuni who performed with a troupe along the Kamo River in Kyoto in 1603, it spread rapidly. The Tokugawa authorities sought to suppress Kabuki. In 1629 women's Kabuki was banned for licentiousness. It was immediately replaced by young men's Kabuki, which was similarly banned in 1652 and replaced with adult male actors playing all roles. During the late 17th and early 18th centuries Kabuki deepened its acting and dramatic quality as actors and dramatists drew on NOH and JŌRURI for their themes. Kabuki was most popular in Edo and Osaka and reflected the concerns and interests of the townspeople, *chōnin*, of these great cities.

kami A Shinto deity. Includes apotheosized human beings, heroes and ancestors, as well as objects possessed of numinous power and non-tangible natural forces. *Kami* have their own hierarchy, and shrines are dedicated to some, but many are nameless. Usually aloof from human affairs, they are enticed to shrines for harvest and other festivals by the performance of proper rituals and provision of offerings.

kamikaze Winds of the gods. Divine winds. Used of the storms that saved Japan by wrecking the Mongol invasion fleets in the late 13th century. Contributed to the belief that Japan was a land divinely protected by the *KAMI*. Kyushu samurai resisting the Meiji government in 1876 used the same word in calling themselves the Jinpūren, or League of the Divine Wind. The word *kamikaze* entered the English language during World War II with reference to the young fighter pilots who made suicidal dive-bombing attacks on American and Allied vessels in the name of their emperor. In contemporary Japan it is used to describe reckless taxi-drivers and skiers.

kampaku A title in the imperial court hierarchy held by regents to emperors. The position of *kampaku* was held by members of the Fujiwara family from 880 to extend their influence over reigning emperors, especially those with Fujiwara mothers. The title of *SESSHŌ* was given to regents for child emperors. This position was also monopolized by the Fujiwara from 858. With time, both offices came to be held by the same Fujiwara family member. This system of Fujiwara domination of the imperial house through these offices has been called *sekkan* politics.

karma Ancient Indian belief, incorporated into Buddhism, that all life is a continuing process of cause and effect in which thoughts and actions in the past or from some previous existence affect the present; and present deeds affect the future.

kofun Ancient tomb. Describes the mound tombs, or tumuli, built as burial mounds for chieftains and their family members from the 3rd through 7th centuries AD. Tumuli varied in shape, size and structure. The largest of them, built on the plains of the Kinai region and western Japan, were enormous keyhole-shaped tombs with interior stone chambers containing sarcophagi and grave ornaments, including mirrors, swords, jewelry and horse trappings. The name has come to be used to describe the whole archaeological phase in which these tumuli were built.

kokubunji A network of government-sponsored provincial monasteries established after 741 on the orders of Emperor Shōmu. A monastery, *kokubunji*, and nunnery, *kokubunniji*, was to be built in every province and the prayers of their monks and nuns directed toward the protection of the nation. The monastery of Tōdaiji in Nara was the apex of the *kokubunji* system.

kuge Court nobles. Originally used to describe the emperors and courtiers. From the Kamakura period (1285–1333) it was used in distinction to *buke*, warrior houses. There were precise gradations of rank within the *kuge* class. Those of the third rank and above, with the right of imperial audience, were known as *kugyō*.

Kyōgen "Mad words." A type of drama that developed together with NOH drama, with which it is frequently performed as interludes. Whereas Noh is concerned primarily with the spiritual world, Kyōgen is frequently this-wordly, down-to-earth and humorous or farcical. Kyōgen plays usually have two or three characters such as a *daimyō* and servant, or two priests. There is more action than in Noh, and Kyōgen performers do not wear masks.

Mahayana (Skt. Japanese Daijō) "Great vehicle." That current of northern Buddhism flowing through Central Asia, Tibet, China, Korea and Japan emphasizing the possibility of salvation for all sentient beings on the great vehicle of the Buddha's teaching. Mahayana Buddhism developed an elaborate pantheon of Buddhas and compassionate Bodhisattvas offering the promise of salvation to all beings. It is the northern counterpart of THERAVADA Buddhism, the "Teaching of the Elders," sometimes referred to as Hinayana, the small vehicle.

mandala (Skt. Japanese *mandara*) "Circle." Formal geometric representations, painted or sculptural, showing Buddhist or Shinto deities or the relationships between deities. May also depict the abodes of deities in Paradise and in sanctuaries on earth. Commonly used in esoteric Buddhism and to designate images showing the *HONJI-SUIJAKU* relationship of Buddhist deities and native Japanese *kami*.

mantra (Skt.) "True Word." Mystically charged syllables or phrases recited to achieve identification with the Buddha. One of the three mysteries of esoteric Buddhism much used in Japanese SHINGON Buddhism.

mappō The End of the Law. Also translated as the Later Age of the Law. The third and final stage in the progressive devolution of Buddhist teaching from the first phase during the lifetime of the Buddha in which the *dharma* was understood and practiced perfectly. A period of strife and degeneration believed to have begun in Japan in 1052.

mudra (Skt. Japanese *in*) Gesture or sign made with the hands signifying the vows or enlightenment or practice of a Buddha, Bodhisattva or other divinity.

nembutsu (Skt. Buddhānusmrti) Originally, meditative recollection of the Buddha. With the development of Chinese Pure Land Buddhism it also came to mean invoking the name of the Buddha. In Japan it is generally used to indicate the six-character prayer formula Name Amida Buddha (Homage to Amida Buddha). The basis of popular Pure Land practice. One expression is the dancing *nembutsu*, *odori nembutsu*, the *nembutsu* sung and danced to a simple melody by mendicants like Ippen and his followers in the medieval age.

nirvana (Japanese *nehan* or *satori*) The supreme spiritual state of enlightenment, liberation from earthly existence and the cycle of rebirth, attained by extinguishing all illusions and attachments.

Noh Masked dance theatrical form that developed under the influence of Zen during the Muromachi period. Dramatists like Zeami imbued older literary, mythological and folk themes with deeper metaphysical overtones to create intense masked dance-dramas.

renga Linked poetry. Developed after the 12th century from an amusement into a serious art in which participants took turns in adding verses of 5-7-5 or 7-7 syllables to create a linked chain of poetry. *Renga* quickly developed its own rules and poetic conventions.

ritsuryō Civil and penal codes providing the legal basis of the centralized Chinese-style administrative systems adopted in the late 7th and 8th centuries. The Ōmi *ritusuryō* was issued in the late 7th century when Emperor Tenji was residing in Ōmi. These were superseded by the Taihō codes (701) and the Yōrō codes (718).

samurai From the verb "*saburau*" meaning "to serve." In the Heian period they were warrior guards used by the imperial court, Fujiwara nobles or cloistered emperors. The term was gradually extended to provincial warriors, BUSHI, in general. In the Kamakura, Muromachi and Edo periods the term samurai was generally applied to those warriors having some rank or office in shogunal or *daimyō* service.

satori Enlightenment. The Zen counterpart of rebirth, *ōjō*, in Pure Land Buddhism. An intuitive awakening to the truth of the permeation of Buddha nature throughout all existence. Seeing into one's own nature to realize that it is one with that of the Buddha (*kenshō jōbutsu*). The immediate awareness of emptiness. In Zen *satori* (or *kenshō*) is seen as a sudden experience free of all discrimination. See NIRVANA.

sesshō Regent for a child emperor. An office monopolized by Fujiwara leaders in the 9th, 10th and 11th centuries as one means of exerting influence over emperors. See KAMPAKU.

shamanism Religious devotion expressed through a medium believed to have supernatural powers and able to communicate with the *kami* through spiritual ecstasy. A major component of popular Japanese religious practice. Many prominent women in early Japanese records were shamans and these shamanic traditions persist to the present day.

Shingon (Skt. *mantra*) "True Word." Principal sect of esoteric Buddhism introduced into Japan by Kūkai (774–835) after his return from China in 806. Stresses use of mandalas and secret magical phrases such as MANTRAS and DHARANI. It is a Tantric branch of Buddhism using several *sūtras*, one of which is the *Mahāvairocana Sūtra*, an exposition on the nature of Dainichi. Shingon stressed ritual, magical practices, verbal transmission of doctrines and the use of all the arts. Before his death Kūkai had firmly established Shingon teachings at the Kongōbuji monastery on Mount Kōya and at Tōji in Kyoto.

Shinkansen New Trunk Line. The so-called "Bullet Train." Introduced in the 1960s, the super-express trains reach speeds of 250 kilometers per hour The first Tokaidō–Sanyō Shinkansen linked Tokyo with Hakata (Fukuoka) in northern Kyushu. Since then the Tōhoku Shinkansen has been built between Ueno in Tokyo and Morioka and the Jōetsu Shinkansen between Ueno and Niigata.

shogun Great General. Contracted form of *seiitaishogun*, meaning Great General who Quells the Barbarians. Originally a temporary title given to imperial princes who led punitive military campaigns for the imperial court in the Heian period. The title of shogun was later awarded briefly to the warrior Minamoto Yoshinaka and then to Minamoto Yoritomo, founder of the Kamakura BAKUFU. After Yoritomo it became customary for those warrior chieftains, *tōryō*, of Minamoto lineage—the Ashikaga and Tokugawa—who established Bakufu to assume the title of shogun as an expression of their legitimate military authority to rule the country as the military arm of imperial sovereignty.

shōen Privatized landholdings acquired by the nobility, temples and shrines, and warriors during the Heian, Kamakura and Muromachi periods. Although all land under the *RITSURYŌ* administrative codes was nominally public land belonging to the imperial government, nobles and temples reclaimed land, or received commended land, for which they sought permanent proprietorship, exemption from state taxation and exemption from entry by provincial officials of the central government. When these privileges were secured, large pockets of land in all the provinces of Japan were sealed off as *shōen* under the control of central proprietors who built up parcels of rights, *shiki*, in many scattered *shōen* holdings.

shugo Military constables. Warriors appointed as provincial constables by Minamoto no Yoritomo. Their function was to keep the peace and arrest troublemakers in the various provinces. The Ashikaga shoguns also appointed *shugo* to head provinces. Some of these extended their control over five or six provinces and are described as *shugo-daimyō* by modern historians.

sūtra (Skt. Japanese *kyō*) Sacred Buddhist texts alleged to convey the actual words and teachings of the Buddha though they only began to be composed some time after

his death. The Japanese normally read Chinese translations of Indian *sūtras*.

tanka Short poem. With *chōka*, long poem, one of the two principal forms of Japanese poetic expression. A *tanka* consists of only five lines of 5-7-5-7-7 syllables. After the Manyōshū era (9th century), during which *chōka* was the dominant mode of Japanese poetry, the *tanka* came into its own as the favored form of verse.

Tendai Name of Buddhist teaching introduced by Saichō (767–822) after his return from China in 805. Flourished first in Saichō's monastery of Enryakuji on Mount Hiei. Tendai was founded in China by Chih-i in the 6th century. The chief scripture was the *Lotus Sūtra* (*Hoke-kyō*), but value was seen in other *sūtras* as offering pointers to the truth revealed most perfectly in the *Lotus*. Tendai incorporated mystical SHINGON teachings and rituals alongside the practices of study and meditation, *shikan*. Its eclecticism provided the source for the later Pure Land, Zen and Nichiren movements.

tennō Heavenly Sovereign. The title given to the reigning member of the imperial family in Japan. The title came into use in the 7th century as the Japanese counterpart to such Chinese imperial titles as emperor, *huang-ti*, or Son of Heaven.

Theravada "The Teaching of the Elders." Term used to describe the Buddhism of south and southeast Asia to distinguish it from the MAHAYANA tradition which spread through Central Asia, China and Korea to Tibet. Sometimes referred to as Hinayana, or the "lesser vehicle," in contrast to the great vehicle of Mahayana.

uji Complex, extended elite families or clans organized on the basis of consanguinity in the ancient period. Controlled the local practices of government, religion and warfare. Asserted control over the service groups known as BE, which were held together more by shared locale or occupation.

wabi Coming from the word *wabishi* meaning a sense of loss or loneliness, *wabi* developed during the medieval period into an aesthetic of cultivated poverty in which the incomplete, imperfect, simple, poor and irregular were prized over the perfect, unblemished and refined. In the *wabi* ideal the moon partially obscured by scudding clouds or mist is more beautiful than the perfectly visible full moon. Reflected in poetry, architecture and garden design, the *wabi* aesthetic probably found its highest expression in the rustic simplicity of the Tea Ceremony, *wabicha*, shaped by Sen no Rikyū and other tea masters of the 16th century.

waka Japanese poetry. Frequently used to distinguish Japanese poetry and poetic sensibility from Chinese poetry, *kanshi*. *Waka* includes long poems, *chōka*, and the short verses, TANKA, which by the Heian period were becoming the dominant form of Japanese poetic expression.

Yang A paired complementary opposite of YIN. In ancient Chinese thought it was believed that the interaction of these two dynamic polarities lay at the basis of all life and activity. Yang is associated with the masculine, the active, the strong, the positive, the bright and the hot. Yin is associated with the feminine, the passive, the negative, the weak, the cold.

Yayoi A district in Tokyo where pottery finds were made early in this century. The name Yayoi was applied to the period (300 BC – 300 AD) in which the pottery was produced and during which rice and metals were introduced to Japan. The accompanying agricultural practices, crafts and ceremonies set fundamental patterns for subsequent social life in Japan.

Yin See YANG. Ideas of Yin, Yang and the Five Elements were introduced into Japan before the Nara period and were influential in shaping Japanese ideas about nature and human life.

zazen Seated meditation. The basic spiritual and physical practice in the search for Zen enlightenment, SATORI. The seeker sits quietly like the Buddha in the lotus or half-lotus posture, controls his breathing, empties his mind and enters a deep spiritual state of *samadhi*. The aim of *zazen* is to look inward and grasp directly the Buddhahood of self and other.

Zen (Skt. *dhyana*, Chinese *Chan*) One of the major traditions of MAHAYANA Buddhism that arose in China and flourished in Japan from the 13th century. Stressed self-discipline through meditation, *zazen*, and appealed strongly to the emerging warrior class, the *bushi*. Zen eschewed textual study, the ritualism of Shingon and the salvationist devotionalism of the Pure Land schools. It recognized manual labor and secular literary and art forms, as well as meditation, as possible vehicles for spiritual enlightenment and thus gave a powerful stimulus to all the arts.

LIST OF ILLUSTRATIONS

Abbreviations: t = top, tl = top left, tr = top right, c = center, b = bottom etc.

All maps by Lovell Johns Ltd, Oxford, and Alan Mais, Hornchurch, Essex.

Endpapers: map of western Japan showing 33 places sacred to Kannon: British Library, Map Room 62987(1).

We should like to thank the following for their particular help and guidance with finding the illustrations: Fusa McLynn, Bodleian Library, Oxford; Izumi Tytler, Bodleian Library, Oxford; Philippa Martin, Oriental Institute, Oxford; Greg Irvine, British Museum.

GAZETTEER

Chūgūji, 34°36'N 135°44'E, 59
Chūruimura, 42°34'N 143°17'E, 33
Chūsenji, 35°35'N 133°12'E, 41
Cologne (W Germany), 50°56'N 6°57'E, 180
Copenhagen (Denmark), 55°43'N 12°34'E, 180
Cordoba (Spain), 37°53'N 4°46'W, 142
Corsica (isl), (France), 42°00'N 9°10'E, 142, 180

Daianji, 34°40'N 135°49'E, 59
Daifang (N Korea), 37°52'N 126°30'E, 46
Daigi Gakoi shell mound, 38°18'N 141°01'E, 35
Daigoji, 35°00'N 135°46'E, 146
Daihōji, 34°13'N 134°18'E, 46
Daijang (Philippines), 18°22'N 121°40'E, 143
Daijōji, 36°40'N 136°36'E, 113
Daikandaiji, 34°32'N 135°50'E, 59
Daimyōjin, 39°32'N 141°00'E, 35
Dairen (China), 38°53'N 121°37'E, 195
Daisen*, 59
Daisen-Oki National Park, 35°15'N 133°38'E, 22
Daisetsu Mts, 43°43'N 142°47'E, 13
Daisetsu Mts National Park, 43°30'N, 142°55'E, 22
Daishōji, 36°18'N 136°19'E, 156
Daito Is (Pacific Oc), 25°00'N 131°00'E, 201
Daitokuji, 35°02'N 135°44'E, 146
Dalian (China), 38°49'N 121°48'E, 191, 192
Dalmatia*, 142
Damyōjin, 37°10'N 139°48'E, 33
Dannoura, 34°00'N 131°00'E, 100
Danshui (Taiwan), 25°20'N 121°38'E, 143
Danzig (Poland), 54°22'N 18°38'E, 180
Darwin (Australia), 12°23'S 130°44'E, 204
Dashiqiao (China), 40°36'N 122°33'E, 192
Datong (China), 40°10'N 113°15'E, 109
Dazaifu, 33°31'N 130°32'E, 59, 69, 100, 105, 119
Deirao (Philippines), 14°56'N 120°38'E, 143
Dengzhou (China), 37°30'N 122°05'E, 46, 69
Dewa, 38°50'N 140°02'E, 59, 73
Dewa*, 21
Dewa Cave, 32°48'N 131°27'E, 33
Diu (India), 20°42'N 70°59'E, 142
Djakarta (Indonesia), 6°08'S 106°45'E, 204
Dōgo, 33°52'N 132°43'E, 113, 153
Doigahama, 34°13'N 130°58'E, 39
Donghai (China), 34°35'N 118°49'E, 39
Dunhuang (China), 40°28'N 94°47'E, 68

East Inner Mongolia*, 195
Echi, 35°09'N 136°11'E, 75, 148
Echigo, 37°11'N 139°16'E, 141
Echigo*, 21
Echigo Mts, 37°20'N 139°25'E, 13
Echizen*, 21, 170
Echizen Kokufu, 37°10'N 138°12'E, 113
Edo *see* Tokyo
Ehime*, 21
Eigenji, 35°08'N 136°19'E, 113, 119, 146, 156
Ellice Is (Pacific Oc), 8°00'S 178°00'E, 195
Engakuji, 35°31'N 139°42'E, 113, 146
Eniwetok (isl), (USA), 12°00'N 161°00'E, 195, 201, 205
Enryakuji, 35°07'N 135°42'E, 59, 86, 99, 146
Erimo, Cape, 41°55'N 143°13'E, 13
Esashi, 39°13'N 141°12'E, 113
Espiritu Santo (isl), (Vanuatu), 15°50'S 166°50'E, 204
Etchū*, 21
Etchūyama, 38°24'N 139°44'E, 33
Etorofu (isl), (USSR), 45°00'N 148°00'E, 141, 204
Ezo*, 170

Fengzhou (China), 40°34'N 107°15'E, 68
Fiji Is (Pacific Oc), 18°00'S 178°00'E, 195, 204
Florence (Italy), 43°47'N 11°15'E, 142
Formosa *see* Taiwan
Frankfurt (W Germany), 50°06'N 8°41'E, 180
Fuchū (Honshu), 34°57'N 138°24'E, 119, 148
Fuchū (Tsushima), 34°18'N 129°20'E, 148
Fuji, 35°10'N 138°37'E, 22
Fuji*, 59
Fuji, Mt, 35°23'N 138°42'E, 13, 14, 18, 100, 146
Fuji-Hakone-Izu National Park, 34°50'N 138°43'E, 22
Fujisawa, 35°22'N 139°29'E, 39, 148
Fujiwara, 34°30'N 135°49'E, 72
Fukagawa, 34°27'N 131°20'E, 133
Fukien*, 195
Fukuchiyama, 35°19'N 135°08'E, 148
Fukuda, 34°34'N 134°20'E, 39
Fukue, 32°41'N 128°52'E, 153
Fukue (isl), 32°40'N 128°45'E, 13
Fukuhara, 34°40'N 135°10'E, 75, 100
Fukui, 36°04'N 136°12'E, 21, 22, 75, 148, 156, 170, 205
Fukui*, 21
Fukui Cave, 33°21'N 129°42'E, 33
Fukuma (isl), 33°46'N 130°23'E, 105
Fukuoka, 33°39'N 130°21'E, 13, 20, 21, 22, 33, 75, 126, 148, 170
Fukuoka*, 21
Fukushima, 37°44'N 140°28'E, 21, 22, 148, 156, 170
Fukushima, 35°50'N 137°42'E, 148
Fukushima*, 21
Fukuura, 39°11'N 139°54'E, 156
Fukuyama, 34°29'N 133°21'E, 126, 141, 148, 205
Funai, 33°17'N 131°30'E, 119, 148, 153
Funamoto, 34°28'N 133°24'E, 35
Funao, 33°08'N 131°47'E, 33
Funatsubara shell mound, 34°33'N 133°38'E, 35
Funayama, 32°54'N 130°36'E, 41
Funing (China), 39°52'N 119°15'E, 192
Fusa, 35°51'N 140°08'E, 156
Fushimi, 34°57'N 135°46'E, 59, 148, 153, 170
Fuwa, 35°21'N 136°24'E, 156
Fuzhou (China), 26°09'N 119°21'E, 69, 109, 195

Gassan, 38°33'N 140°02'E, 59
Genoa (Italy), 44°24'N 8°56'E, 142, 180
Gifu, 35°27'N 136°46'E, 21, 22, 126, 148, 153, 205
Gifu*, 21
Gilbert Is (Pacific Oc), 1°00'N 175°00'E, 195, 201, 204
Goa (India), 15°31'N 73°56'E, 142
Gokurakuji, 35°19'N 139°34'E, 113
Gōnoura, 33°45'N 129°41'E, 105
Goryōkaku, 41°50'N 140°44'E, 170
Gotō Is, 33°00'N 129°00'E, 13, 22, 105, 109, 148, 170
Goyu, 34°50'N 137°18'E, 148
Graz (Austria), 47°05'N 15°22'E, 180
Guadalcanal (isl), (Solomon Is), 9°32'S 160°12'E, 204
Guam (isl), (USA), 13°30'N 144°40'E, 195, 201, 204
Guangzhou (China), 23°08'N 113°20'E, 68, 109, 143, 195, 201, 204
Gumma*, 21
Gunnai, 35°41'N 139°26'E, 141
Gyōtoku, 35°44'N 139°54'E, 156

Hachijō (isl), 33°05'N 139°51'E, 13
Hachinohe, 40°30'N 141°30'E, 22, 148, 170
Hachioji, 35°40'N 139°20'E, 205
Haerbin (China), 45°45'N 126°41'E, 192, 195, 201, 204, 205
Hagi, 34°25'N 131°22'E, 148, 153, 170
Hague, The (Netherlands), 52°05'N 4°16'E, 180
Haguro*, 59
Haicheng (China), 40°53'N 122°45'E, 191
Hainan (isl), (China), 19°00'N 109°30'E, 195, 201, 204
Hakata, 33°38'N 130°24'E, 20, 69, 75, 105, 109, 119, 141, 153
Hakodate, 41°46'N 140°44'E, 13, 22, 141, 148, 170
Hakone, 35°14'N 139°06'E, 148, 156
Haku*, 59
Haku, Mt, 36°10'N 136°46'E, 13, 14
Hakusan, 36°10'N 136°38'E, 99
Hakusan National Park, 36°10'N 136°54'E, 22
Hakusukinoe (S Korea), 35°57'N 126°42'E, 69
Hamada, 34°56'N 132°04'E, 148
Hamakita, 34°48'N 137°54'E, 33
Hamamatsu, 34°42'N 137°42'E, 20, 22, 126, 148, 170, 205
Hamburg (W Germany), 53°33'N 10°00'E, 180
Hanaizumi, 38°50'N 141°03'E, 33
Hanawadai, 35°55'N 140°05'E, 35
Hangzhou (China), 30°14'N 120°08'E, 46, 109, 112, 191
Hankow (China), 30°35'N 114°19'E, 195, 201
Hanoi (Vietnam), 21°01'N 105°53'E, 143, 201
Hanover (W Germany), 52°23'N 9°44'E, 180
Haranotsuji, 33°45'N 129°43'E, 39
Harima*, 21
Hasedera, 34°30'N 135°51'E, 146
Hatsuse, 34°42'N 136°02'E, 156
Havana (Cuba), 23°07'N 82°25'W, 143
Hawaii (isl), (USA), 19°30'N 155°30'W, 204
Hayakawa, 35°26'N 39°26'E, 75
Heian *see* Kyoto
Heijō *see* Nara
Hida, 36°18'N 137°23'E, 100
Hida*, 21
Hidaka Mts, 42°30'N 142°46'E, 13, 14
Hie, 35°05'N 135°50'E, 59, 86, 99
Hie*, 59
Hiei, Mt, 35°05'N 135°50'E, 86
Higashi, Mt, 37°55'N 140°16'E, 18
Higashi Honganji, 34°59'N 135°46'E, 146
Higashiyama, 37°30'N 139°45'E, 33
Higo, 32°49'N 130°38'E, 133
Higo*, 21
Hijiridake, 32°45'N 131°16'E, 33
Hiko*, 59
Hikone, 35°17'N 136°13'E, 126, 170
Hikozaki shell mound, 34°27'N 133°42'E, 35
Himeji, 34°50'N 134°40'E, 22, 126, 148, 153, 170, 205
Himetani, 34°38'N 134°12'E, 133
Hinaga, 34°56'N 136°31'N, 156
Hinoura, 33°22'N 129°34'E, 105
Hirado, 33°22'N 129°31'E, 105, 109, 126, 133, 143, 148, 153
Hirado (isl), 33°17'N 129°28'E, 13, 170
Hiraide, 36°15'N 137°54'E, 35
Hiraizumi, 39°00'N 141°05'E, 99, 100, 156
Hirakawa, 31°29'N 130°31'E, 35
Hiranotono, 34°29'N 135°42'E, 75
Hiraoka, 33°35'N 133°32'E, 119
Hirosaki, 40°34'N 140°28'E, 126, 148, 153, 170
Hiroshima, 34°23'N 132°27'E, 13, 20, 21, 22, 126, 148, 153, 170, 191, 192, 204, 205
Hiroshima*, 21
Hirota, 30°27'N 130°58'E, 39
Hita, 33°20'N 130°56'E, 170
Hitachi, 36°35'N 140°40'E, 22, 205
Hitachi*, 21
Hitoyoshi, 32°12'N 130°48'E, 75
Hitsume, 39°31'N 141°07'E, 99
Hiwada, 37°30'N 140°22'E, 156
Hizen*, 21, 170
Hobi, 34°39'N 137°10'E, 156
Hoeryang (N Korea), 42°27'N 129°44'E, 192
Hōki*, 21
Hokkaido*, 21, 22
Hokkekyōji, 34°47N, 140°00'E, 113, 146
Hokkiji, 34°38'N, 135°44'E, 59
Hōkōji, 31°51'N 130°12'E, 39
Hokurikudo*, 59
Hong Kong (UK), 22°15'N 114°15'E, 195, 201, 204
Hongo, 34°05'N 131°24'E, 33
Hongū, 33°49'N 135°47'E, 86
Honjō, 39°27'N 140°02'E, 148
Honkokuji, 35°00'N 135°46'E, 146
Honmonji, 35°35'N 139°42'E, 146
Honyakushiji, 34°31'N 135°47'E, 59
Hora, 34°55'N 135°54'E, 72
Horie, 36°44'N 137°25'E, 75
Horinouchi, 35°41'N 139°39'E, 35
Hōryūji, 34°36'N 135°44'E, 59, 86
Hoshino, 36°20'N 139°38'E, 33
Hososhima, 32°25'N 131°38'E, 100
Hotta, 39°27'N 140°28'E, 73
Hungnam (N Korea), 39°49'N 127°40'E, 69
Hyakketsu, 36°10'N 140°21'E, 41
Hyōgo, 34°44'N 135°16'E, 113, 141, 148
Hyōgo*, 21
Hyūga, 32°25'N 131°38'E, 41
Hyūga*, 21

Iba, 34°40'N 137°40'E, 39
Ibaraki*, 21
Ichiburi, 37°00'N 137°48'E, 156
Ichigo, 31°45'N 130°14'E, 153
Ichigodani, 34°28'N 136°43'E, 100
Ichijōdani, 35°58'N 136°17'E, 119
Ichikawa, 35°45'N 139°55'E, 22
Ichinomiya, 35°18'N 136°48'E, 205
Ichinoseki, 38°56'N 141°08'E, 22, 148, 170
Ichinotani, 34°40'N 135°06'E, 100, 156
Idate, 37°50'N 140°30'E, 75
Idojiri, 35°52'N 138°14'E, 35
Iga*, 21, 72, 86
Iida, 35°35'N 137°50'E, 148
Iizuka, 37°49'N 140°23'E, 156
Ijuin, 31°38'N 130°22'E, 75
Ikara, 35°25'N 137°50'E, 75
Ikaruga, 34°52'N 134°35'E, 75
Ikeda, 34°52'N 135°23'E, 75
Ikegami Honmonji, 35°33'N 139°42'E, 113
Iki*, 21
Iki (isl), 33°47'N 129°43'E, 13, 33, 35, 39, 46, 59, 100, 105, 170
Ikunoshima, 34°18'N 132°47'E, 39
Imabari, 34°04'N 132°59'E, 22, 39, 148, 205
Imari, 33°18'N 129°51'E, 105
Imashiro, 34°43'N 135°36'E, 33
Imphal (India), 24°47'N 93°55'E, 204
Inaba*, 21
Inabayama, 35°20'N 136°40'E, 119
Inada, 36°20'N, 140°04'E, 113
Inakadate, 40°50'N 140°44'E, 39
Inaoka, 35°00'N 134°00'E, 113
Inariyama, 36°19'N 139°08'E, 41
Inchon (S Korea), 37°30'N 126°38'E, 191, 192
Ineda, 34°25'N 135°53'E, 75
Inland Sea National Park, 34°22'N 133°30'E, 22
Inubō, Cape, 35°41'N 140°52'E, 13
Inuyama, 35°22'N 136°58'E, 126
Io (isl), 30°48'N 130°16'E, 100
Ipponmatsu, 40°42'N 139°57'E, 35
Irago, 34°37'N 137°06'E, 156
Iriomote (isl), 24°20'N 123°55'E, 13
Irita, 32°56'N 132°57'E, 39
Irkutsk (USSR), 52°15'N 104°17'E, 195
Ironohama, 35°45'N 136°00'E, 156
Isaku, 31°27'N 130°18'E, 75
Isawa, 39°08'N 141°05'E, 73, 119
Ise, 34°29'N 136°41'E, 59, 86, 113, 119, 146, 148, 156
Ise*, 21, 86
Ise-Shima National Park, 34°25'N 136°53'E, 22
Ishibashiyama, 35°11'N 139°07'E, 100
Ishibutai, 34°30'N 135°52'E, 41
Ishigaki (isl), 24°20'N 124°05'E, 13
Ishigami, 40°44'N 140°12'E, 35
Ishiguchi*, 59
Ishikari Plain, 43°27'N 141°30'E, 13
Ishikawa*, 21
Ishinomaki, 38°25'N 141°18'E, 22, 156
Ishitobi, 32°10'N 130°36'E, 33
Ishiyama, 34°33'N 136°23'E, 41
Ishiyama Honganji, 34°42'N, 135°30'E, 119
Isumi, 35°11'N 140°23'E, 75
Itabashi, 35°43'N 139°43'E, 148
Itako, 35°57'N 140°31'E, 156
Itazuke, 33°36'N 130°24'E, 39
Ito, 33°30'N 130°30'E, 46
Itō, 34°58'N 139°04'E, 113
Itōzu, 33°53'N 130°52'E, 75
Itsukushima, 34°18'N 132°18'E, 100, 113
Iwado, 32°55'N 131°30'E, 33
Iwafune, 38°08'N 139°30'E, 73
Iwajuku, 36°22'N 139°16'E, 33
Iwaki, 36°58'N 140°56'E, 22, 141, 148, 153, 170
Iwaki, Mt, 40°38'N 140°18'E, 13
Iwakuni, 34°10'N 132°09'E, 126, 170
Iwami*, 21
Iwamizawa, 43°12'N 141°47'E, 22
Iwamurata, 36°20'N 138°25'E, 148
Iwanogawa, 34°04'N 135°18'E, 35
Iwanuma, 38°06'N 140°51'E, 156
Iwasakiyama, 34°18'N 134°08'E, 41
Iwase, 34°14'N 135°11'E, 41
Iwashimizu Hachiman, 34°52'N 135°42'E, 59
Iwate, 38°46'N 140°35'E, 156
Iwate*, 21
Iwate, Mt, 39°53'N 140°59'E, 18
Iwatoyama, 33°22'N 130°44'E, 41
Iwo Jima (isl), 23°40'N 142°10'E, 195, 201, 204
Iya, 35°39'N 133°51'E, 100
Iyo*, 21
Iyobeyama, 34°30'N 133°23'E, 39
Izawa, 39°17'N 141°05'E, 99
Izu*, 21
Izu (pen). 34°50'N 138°55'E, 13, 100
Izu Is, 34°00'N 139°30'E, 13, 15
Izumi*, 21, 72, 86
Izumo, 35°21N 132°46'E, 39, 59, 99
Izumo*, 21, 41

Japan Alps, 37°00'N 137°38'E, 13, 14, 156
Java (isl), (Indonesia), 7°25'S 110°00'E, 195, 201, 204
Jehol*, 201
Jiangning (China), 31°58'N 118°50'E, 54
Jilin (China), 43°53'N 126°35'E, 192
Jilong (Taiwan), 25°09'N 121°45'E, 109
Jingūji, 34°46'N 134°10'E, 41
Jining (China), 35°22'N 116°45'E, 68
Jinzhou (China), 41°06'N 121°05'E, 191
Jizōzaka, 35°24'N 139°24'E, 33
Jō-Shin-Etsu National Park, 36°40'N 138°40'E, 22
Jōchiji, 35°19'N 139°32'E, 113
Joetsu, 37°08'N 138°14'E, 153
Jōmō*, 41
Jōmyōji, 35°19'N 139°33'E, 113
Joruriji, 34°43'N 136°01'E, 86
Jufukuji, 35°19'N 139°32'E, 113

Kabul (Afghanistan), 34°30'N 69°10'E, 54
Kaesong (S Korea), 37°59'N 126°30'E, 133
Kaga*, 21, 170
Kagawa*, 21
Kagenuma, 37°12'N 140°14'E, 156
Kagoshima, 31°37'N 130°32'E, 13, 20, 21, 22, 33, 119, 133, 141, 148, 153, 170
Kagoshima*, 21
Kai*, 21
Kaifeng (China), 34°47'N 114°20'E, 46, 109, 201
Kaimon*, 59
Kaji, 37°48'N 139°13'E, 75
Kakegawa, 34°47'N 138°02'E, 148
Kakehashi, 35°46'N 137°41'E, 156
Kakuniyama, 38°34'N 140°14'E, 33
Kamagainohara, 35°39'N 140°02'E, 156
Kamakura, 35°19'N 139°33'E, 22, 100, 113, 119, 153, 170
Kamatsu, 36°37'N 136°36'E, 75
Kamchatka (pen), (USSR), 56°00'N 160°00'E, 15, 195, 201, 204
Kameyama, 34°52'N 136°28'E, 39, 148
Kamigamō, 35°00'N 135°47'E, 35
Kamihiradera, 35°08'N 136°00'E, 153
Kamikuroiwa, 33°30'N 132°56'E, 33, 35
Kamino, 34°04'N 135°17'E, 75
Kamo, 35°26'N 138°36'E, 39, 141, 170
Kamo, Lower, 35°04'N 135°46'E, 59
Kamo, Upper, 35°05'N 135°45'E, 59
Kanagawa, 35°29'N 139°36'E, 141, 148
Kanagawa*, 21
Kanazawa, 36°35'N 136°38'E, 13, 21, 22, 33, 119, 126, 148, 153, 156, 170
Kanazawa, 38°51'N 141°10'E, 73, 99
Kanazawa, 35°28'N 139°38'E, 119
Kanbara, 35°06'N 138°36'E, 75
Kannonyama, 36°25'N 139°04'E, 41
Kano, 34°55'N 138°59'E, 75
Kanō, 35°19'N 136°47'E, 39
Kanokogi, 32°48'N 130°50'E, 75
Kantō*, 22
Kantō Plain, 36°00'N 138°30'E, 13
Kanzaki, 33°22'N 130°16'E, 75
Karafuto (isl) *see* Sakhalin (isl)
Karako, 34°26'N 135°55'E, 39
Karatsu, 33°28'N 129°58'E, 126, 148
Kareda, 34°18'N 135°32'E, 75
Karita, 33°48'N 130°59'E, 75
Karuizawa, 36°22'N 138°37'E, 148
Kasagi, Mt, 34°48'N 136°01'E, 86
Kashima, 35°58'N 140°42'E, 22, 113, 156
Kasori, 35°37'N 140°10'E, 35
Kasuga, 34°40'N 135°45'E, 59, 86
Kasugayama, 37°10'N 138°13'E, 119
Katsumoto, 33°52'N 129°42'E, 105
Katsusaka, 35°23'N 139°31'E, 35
Kawachi*, 21, 72, 86
Kawagoe, 35°55'N 139°30'E, 119
Kawaguchi, 36°13'N 136°07'E, 22, 75
Kawai, 34°22'N 136°42'E, 75
Kawairi, 34°36'N 133°46'E, 39
Kawasaki, 35°32'N, 139°42'E, 20, 22, 99, 148
Kaya (S Korea), 35°04'N 129°03'E, 39
Kaya*, 39
Kazusa*, 21
Kegonji, 35°27'N 136°44'E, 146
Kenchōji, 35°20'N 139°33'E, 113, 146
Kenninji, 35°03'N 135°44'E, 113, 146
Kera, 33°30'N 133°24'E, 75
Kerama (isl), 26°21'N 127°20'E, 13
Khabarovsk (USSR), 48°30'N 135°06'E, 195, 205
Kibi*, 41
Kibitsu, 34°43'N 133°44'E, 113
Kii*, 21, 86
Kii Mts, 34°00'N 135°42'E, 13, 14
Kikai (isl), 28°18'N 129°56'E, 13
Kikuta, 36°55'N 140°47'E, 75
Kinai*, 41, 59
Kinki*, 22
Kinowa, 38°55'N 139°48'E, 73
Kinu, 36°11'N 139°39'E, 141
Kira, 34°47'N 137°05'E, 75
Kirishima, Mt, 31°57'N 130°50'E, 18
Kirishima-Yaku National Park, 31°53'N 130°54'E, 22
Kisagata, 39°12'N 139°55'E, 156
Kiska (isl), (USA), 52°00'N 178°30'E, 204
Kiso, 35°51'N 137°43'E, 100
Kiso Mts, 35°30'N 137°48'E, 13, 156
Kitagawa, 33°22'N 133°04'E, 35
Kitakami, 39°18'N 141°05'E, 22
Kitakyushu, 33°53'N 130°50'E, 13, 15, 20, 22, 148, 153, 170
Kitano, 34°59'N 135°47'E, 59, 86
Kitanoshō, 36°00'N 136°19'E, 133, 153
Kitashirakawa, 35°02'N 135°48'E, 35
Kiyosumidera, 35°10'N 140°02'E, 113
Kō, 34°24'N 135°36'E, 33
Kobe, 34°40'N 135°12'E, 13, 20, 21, 22, 148, 205
Kobotoke, 35°39'N 139°18'E, 148
Kōchi, 34°30'N 132°51'E, 21, 22, 109, 126, 148, 170
Kōchi*, 21
Kodoma, 36°16'N 139°10'E, 75
Kōfu, 35°42'N 138°34'E, 21, 148, 205
Kōfukuji, 34°41'N 135°49'E, 86, 99, 113
Koguryo*, 39, 46
Kokubunji, 35°20'N 133°42'E, 41
Kokura, 33°54'N 130°52'E, 205
Komaga, Mt, 42°05'N 140°41'E, 18
Komatsu, 36°25'N 136°27'E, 113, 156
Komoda, 34°14'N 129°12'E, 105
Kōmorizuka, 34°34'N 133°45'E, 41
Kongōbuji, 34°13'N 135°36'E, 86, 146
Kōnosu, 36°02'N 139°32'E, 148
Korea*/Chōsen*, 105, 141, 195, 201, 204
Koreharu, 38°43'N 141°03'E, 73
Kōriyama, 37°23'N 140°22'E, 22
Korsakov (USSR), 46°36'N 142°50'E, 141, 205
Kōya*, 59
Kōya, Mt, 34°14'N 135°36'E, 86, 99, 113, 133, 156
Koyahan (S Korea), 35°05'N 129°02'E, 46
Kōzu (isl), 34°10'N 139°10'E, 13
Kōzuke*, 21
Kubuiru, 34°35'N 129°42'E, 39
Kugatsu, 35°05'N 136°00'E, 148
Kujū, Mt, 33°07'N 131°14'E, 13
Kulp'ori (N Korea), 42°20'N 116°52'E, 33
Kumamoto, 32°50'N 130°42'E, 20, 21, 22, 126, 148, 170
Kumamoto*, 21
Kumano, 33°54'N 136°06'E, 59, 86, 99, 113, 146
Kunasir (isl), (USSR), 44°15'N 146°00'E, 141
Kungnaesong (China), 42°38'N 127°12'E, 46
Kuni, 34°47'N 135°52'E, 72
Kunu*, 46
Kuonji, 35°25'N 138°25'E, 113,146
Kurashiki, 34°36'N 133°43'E, 22
Kuratsuki, 36°30'N 136°32'E, 75
Kure, 34°14'N 132°32'E, 192
Kuribayashi, 36°48'N 138°26'E, 39
Kurigara Pass, 36°40'N 136°49'E, 100
Kurihashi, 36°09'N 139°40'E, 148
Kurikara, 36°39'N 136°50'E, 156
Kuril Is (USSR), 47°00'N 152°00'E, 13, 15, 18, 195, 201, 204
Kuriyagawa, 39°45'N 141°04'E, 73, 99, 100

Kurobane, 36°51'N 140°07'E, 156
Kurobe, 36°55'N 137°24'E, 156
Kuroda, 34°34'N 135°48'E, 75
Kurume, 33°20'N 130°29'E, 22, 148, 170
Kusatsu, Mt, 36°37'N 138°36'E, 18
Kushida, 36°41'N 137°01'E, 35
Kushinagara (India), 24°58'N 84°54'E, 54
Kushiro, 42°58'N 144°24'E, 13, 23
Kutani, 36°23'N 136°37'E, 133
Kuwabara, 36°06'N 136°14'E, 75
Kuwana, 35°04'N 136°40'E, 148, 205
Kuzū, 36°20'N 139°40'E, 33
Kwajalein (isl), (USA), 10°00'N 163°20'E, 195, 201, 204
Kyōdomari, 31°52'N 130°12'E, 153
Kyongju (S Korea), 35°52'N 129°15'E, 54, 69
Kyoto/Heian, 35°00'N 135°45'E, 13, 20, 21, 22, 33, 59, 69, 72, 73, 86, 99, 100, 109, 113, 119, 133, 146,148, 153, 156, 170, 205
Kyoto*, 21
Kyushu*, 22
Kyushu, North*, 41
Kyushu Mts, 32°30'N 131°00'E, 13, 14

Lae (PNG), 6°45'S 147°00'E, 204
Lanzhou (China), 36°01'N 103°46'E, 68
Leyte (isl), (Philippines), 10°40'N 124°50'E, 204
Lhasa (China), 29°41'N 91°10'E, 54
Liangzhou (China), 37°43'N 101°58'E, 68
Liaodong Pen*, 191, 192
Liaoyang (China), 41°16'N 123°12'E, 191, 192
Lisbon (Portugal), 38°44'N 9°08'W, 142
Liverpool (UK), 53°25'N 2°55'W, 180
London (UK), 51°30'N 0°10'W, 180
Luanda (Angola), 8°50'S 13°15'E, 180
Luanxian (China), 39°45'N 118°44'E, 192
Luofou (China), 23°22'N 114°48'E, 54
Luolang (N Korea), 38°45'N 125°45'E, 39, 46
Luoyang (China), 34°47'N 112°26'E, 39, 46, 54, 68
Luxembourg*, 180
Luzon (isl), (Philippines), 17°50'N 121°00'E, 143, 204
Lyon (France), 45°46'N 4°50'E, 180

Macao (Portugal), 39°33'N 8°00'W, 109, 201
Madagascar (isl), (Indian Oc), 17°00'S 46°00'E, 142
Madrid (Spain), 40°25'N 3°43'W, 142
Maebashi, 36°24'N 139°04'E, 21 170
Maeda, 37°27'N 140°30'E, 35
Magdagachi (USSR), 53°27'N 125°44'E, 195
Mahan*, 46
Makuni, 34°10'N 135°23'E, 75
Malacca (Malaysia), 2°14'N 102°14'E, 143
Manchukuo* *see* Manchuria*
Manchuria*/Manchukuo*, 191, 192, 201, 204, 205
Manila (Philippines), 14°36'N 120°59'E, 143
Manpukuji, 35°03'N 135°44'E, 113, 146
Manus (isl), (PNG), 2°00'S 147°00'E, 204
Marcus (isl), 24°18'N 153°58'E, 15, 195, 201, 204
Mariana Is (USA), 15°00'N 145°00'E, 195, 201, 204
Marogu (Indonesia), 1°05'N 127°30'E, 143
Marseille (France), 43°18'N 5°22'E, 180
Marshall Is (USA), 10°00'N 172°00'E, 195, 201, 204
Masampo (S Korea), 35°12'N 128°36'E, 192
Masan (S Korea), 35°10'N 128°35'E, 105
Masuda, 43°30'N 143°47'E, 33, 119
Matsubara, 34°35'N 135°33'E, 69
Matsue, 35°29'N 133°04'E, 21, 22, 126, 148, 153, 170
Matsugata Gakoi, 38°19'N 141°02'E, 39
Matsumae, 41°28'N 140°06'E, 148, 153, 170
Matsumoto, 36°18'N 137°58'E, 22, 41, 126, 133, 148, 170
Matsuo, 35°02'N 135°42'E, 59
Matsushima, 38°22'N 141°02'E, 156
Matsuura (Honshu), 35°17'N 139°37'E, 75
Matsuura (Kyushu), 33°21'N 129°44'E, 46, 75, 105, 109
Matsuyama, 33°50'N 132°47'E, 21, 22, 126, 148, 205
Matsuzaka, 34°33'N 136°32'E, 153, 170
Meakan, Mt, 43°24'N 144°01'E, 18
Megumi, 35°28'N 133°23'E, 39
Mexico (Mexico), 19°25'N 99°10'W, 143
Midway (isl), (USA), 28°15'N 177°25'W, 204
Mie*, 21
Mihara, Mt, 34°43'N 139°23'E, 18
Miidera, 35°01'N 135°52'E, 86
Mikawa*, 21
Mike, 33°01'N 130°25'E, 75
Mikkabi, 34°41'N 137°48'E, 33
Mikoshiba, 35°52'N 137°58'E, 33
Mikumo, 33°28'N 129°59'E, 39
Mikuni Mts, 36°54'N 139°00'E, 13, 14, 156
Mikura (isl), 33°54'N 139°39'E, 13
Milan (Italy), 45°28'N 9°12'E, 142, 180
Mimana*, 69
Mimasaka*, 21
Minakuchi, 35°00'N 136°10'E, 156
Minamata, 32°13'N 130°23'E, 22
Minami Alps National Park, 35°30'N 138°14'E, 22
Minami Oyama, 37°30'N 139°58'E, 39
Minatogawa, 26°16'N 127°43'E, 33
Mindanao (isl), (Philippines), 7°30'N 125°00'E, 204
Minebata, 35°55'N 137°50'E, 35
Ming China*, 133, 143
Mingzhou *see* Ningbo
Mino, 35°34'N 136°56'E, 148
Mino*, 21
Miri, 34°30'N 132°32'E, 75
Misasa, 35°31'N 133°54'E, 100
Misumi, 34°49'N 131°59'E, 153
Mito, 36°22'N 140°29'E, 21, 148, 153, 170, 205
Mitsu, 33°13'N 130°16'E, 39
Miumaya, 41°10'N 140°25'E, 148
Miwa*, 59
Miya, 35°04'N 136°57'E, 148
Miyagi*, 21
Miyake (isl), 34°08'N 139°33'E, 13
Miyako, 39°38'N 141°59'E, 148
Miyako (isl), 24°46'N 125°16'E, 13
Miyanodai, 35°41'N 140°41'E, 39
Miyanouchi, 38°10'N 140°06'E, 100
Miyata, 33°43'N 130°41'E, 35
Miyatayama, 34°52'N 134°50'E, 33
Miyazaki, 31°56'N 131°27'E, 21, 148, 170
Miyazaki*, 21
Mizusawa, 39°10'N 141°07'E, 153
Mizushima, 34°32'N 133°44'E, 22, 100
Mogami, 38°46'N 140°31'E, 170
Mokoto shell mound, 43°59'N 144°16'E, 35
Mokpo (S Korea), 34°50'N 126°25'E, 133, 192
Monō, 38°31'N 141°18'E, 73
Morioka, 39°43'N 141°08'E, 21, 22, 148, 153, 170
Moriyama, 35°03'N 136°00'E, 39
Morizaki, 34°13'N 134°36'E, 35
Moro, 35°33'N 139°47'E, 33
Mozambique (Mozambique), 15°00'S 40°44'E, 142
Mukden (China), 41°45'N 123°29'E, 191, 192, 195, 201, 204, 205
Munakata, 33°49'N 130°35'E, 59, 75, 99
Munakata (inner shrine), 33°55'N 130°26'E, 59
Munich (W Germany), 48°08'N 11°35'E, 180
Murakami, 38°13'N 139°28'E, 170
Murō, Mt, 34°29'N 136°05'E, 86
Murōji, 34°31'N 136°04'E, 86
Muronoyashima, 36°24'N 139°52'E, 156
Muroran, 42°21'N 140°59'E, 22, 141
Muroto, Cape, 33°13'N 134°11'E, 13
Musashi*, 21
Mutsu*, 21
Myōkenji, 35°00'N 135°46'E, 146
Myōonji, 36°02'N 138°58'E, 146
Myōrenjiyama, 35°22'N 132°39'E, 41
Myōshinji, 35°01'N 135°43'E, 146

Na, 33°34'N 130°42'E, 46
Nachi*, 59
Nachi Falls, 33°40'N 135°54'E, 86
Naeshirogawa, 31°32'N 130°24'E, 133
Nagai, 38°06'N 140°02'E, 39
Nagano, 36°39'N 138°10'E, 21, 22, 156, 170
Nagano*, 21
Nagaoka, 37°27'N 138°50'E, 22, 148, 205
Nagaoka, 34°55'N 135°42'E, 35, 72
Nagasaki, 32°45'N 129°52'E, 13, 20, 21, 22, 33, 141, 143, 148, 153, 170, 204, 205
Nagasaki*, 21
Nagashima, 33°08'N 130°06'E, 75
Nagato*, 21
Nago, 36°40'N 136°50'E, 156
Nagoji, 35°00'N 139°54'E, 146
Nagoya, 35°08'N 136°53'E, 13, 20, 21, 22, 126, 133, 148, 156, 170
Naha, 26°14'N 127°40'E, 13, 21, 33, 141
Nakabayashi, 36°26'N 138°38'E, 33
Nakahara, 36°08'N 137°56'E, 35
Nakamura, 33°02'N 132°58'E, 119
Nakao, 31°53'N 130°46'E, 35
Nakatsu, 33°37'N 131°11'E, 153
Nakatsugawa, 35°32'N 137°30'E, 148
Nakayama, 38°35'N 141°10'E, 73
Nakayama, 34°24'N 132°30'E, 39
Nakoso, 36°54'N 140°46'E, 73
Nambu, 39°38'N 141°58'E, 141
Nanao, 37°03'N 136°58'E, 119, 153
Nanchang (China), 28°37'N 115°57'E, 109
Nanhai (China), 23°09'N 113°20'E, 39
Naniwa, 34°40'N 135°30'E, 69, 72, 86
Nanjing (China), 32°02'N 118°52'E, 109, 195, 201, 204
Nankaido*, 59
Nantai, Mt, 36°47'N 139°29'E, 18
Nanzenji, 35°01'N 135°48'E, 146
Naples (Italy), 40°50'N 14°15'E, 180
Naples*, 142
Nara/Heijō, 34°41'N 135°50'E, 20, 21, 22, 59, 69, 72, 86, 100, 112, 119, 148, 156, 170
Nara*, 21
Narita, 37°00'N 140°25'E, 33
Narumi, 35°02'N 136°58'E, 156
Nasu, 37°00'N 140°07'E, 75
Nasu, Mt, 37°08'N 139°58'E, 18
Nauru (isl), (Pacific Oc), 0°32'S 166°55'E, 195, 204
Nayashi, 34°57'N 135°44'E, 75
Negoro, 34°13'N 135°16'E, 99, 133
Nemuro, 43°20'N 145°33'E, 23, 141
New Britain (isl), (PNG), 6°00'S 150°00'E, 195
New Caledonia (isl), (France), 21°30'S 165°30'E, 195, 204
New Georgia (isl), (Solomon Is), 8°11'S 160°36'E, 204
New Guinea*, 195, 201, 204
New Hebrides (isls), (Pacific Oc), 16°00'S 162°00'E, 195, 204
New Ireland (isl), (PNG), 2°30'S 151°30'E, 195, 204
Nezame, 35°41'N 137°38'E, 156
Nezu, 38°34'N 139°34'E, 73, 100, 156
Nichihara, 34°36'N 131°50'E, 170
Nicobar Is (India), 8°00'N 93°30'E, 204
Nie, 40°15'N 140°31'E, 100
Niho, 38°05'N 138°22'E, 75
Nihonmatsu, 37°37'N 140°26'E, 156
Nii (isl), 34°27'N 139°18'E, 13
Niigata, 37°58'N 139°02'E, 13, 21, 22, 141, 148, 170, 205
Niigata*, 21
Niigata Plain, 37°42'N 138°56'E, 13
Niihama, 33°57'N 133°15'E, 22
Niimi, 35°00'N 133°27'E, 75
Niiyama, 34°34'N 135°45'E, 41
Nijō, 35°01'N 135°45'E, 126
Nikkō, 36°45'N 139°37'E, 119, 148, 156, 170
Nikkō National Park, 37°00'N 139°30'E, 22
Nikolayevsk (USSR), 53°20'N 140°44'E, 195, 201
Ninagawa, 37°33'N 140°00'E, 75
Ningbo/Mingzhou (China), 29°56'N 121°32'E, 69, 109, 112, 195, 205
Nintoku, 34°34'N 135°29'E, 41
Nishi (isl), 36°11'N 132°08'E, 13
Nishi Honganji, 34°59'N 135°45'E, 146
Nishida, 39°25'N 141°10'E, 35
Nishishiga, 35°02'N 136°54'E, 39
Nitta, 38°36'N 141°00'E, 73, 75
Nobeoka, 32°36'N 131°40'E, 22, 148, 153
Nobi Plain, 35°10'N 136°40'E, 13
Nōbi*, 41
Nogawa, 35°31'N 139°30'E, 33
Nojiri, 35°44'N 137°43'E, 148
Noko (isl), 33°42'N 130°14'E, 105
Noshiro, 40°13'N 140°00'E, 148
Nota, 34°20'N 132°55'E, 75
Noto, 37°00'N 136°48'E, 69
Noto*, 21
Noto (pen), 37°20'N 137°00'E, 13
Nozaka, 35°40'N 136°05'E, 75
Nozawa, 36°38'N 137°41'E, 33
Numa, 39°19'N 140°31'E, 99
Numata, 36°38'N 139°03'E, 153
Numazu, 35°08'N 138°50'E, 100, 148, 205
Numazu shell mound, 38°26'N 141°24'E, 35
Nushiro, 39°57'N 140°04'E, 73
Nutari, 37°57'N 139°05'E, 73

Oahu (isl), (USA), 21°30'N 158°00'W, 204
Obama, 35°32'N 135°45'E, 119, 148, 153
Obanazawa, 38°37'N 140°22'E, 156
Ochiori, 35°18'N 134°29'E, 100
Oda, 35°55'N 136°00'E, 75
Ōdaino, 39°14'N 140°50'E, 33
Odawara, 35°15'N 139°08'E, 100, 119, 126, 133, 148
Ogachi, 39°03'N 140°29'E, 73, 99
Ōgaki, 35°22'N 136°36'E, 156, 170
Ōi, 35°22'N 136°36'E, 75
Ōishida, 38°35'N 140°25'E, 156
Ōiso, 35°18'N 139°19'E, 148
Ōita, 33°13'N 131°37'E, 21, 22
Ōita*, 21
Ojika, 38°25'N 141°09'E, 73
Ōjin, 34°34'N 135°39'E, 41
Okaya, 36°03'N 138°00'E, 22
Okayama, 34°40'N 133°54'E, 13, 20, 21, 22, 33, 126, 148, 153, 170, 205
Okayama*, 21
Okazaki, 34°58'N 137°10'E, 148, 153, 205
Oketo, 43°42'N 143°35'E, 33
Oki*, 21
Oki (isl), 36°10'N 133°10'E, 13, 39, 59, 100, 148, 153, 170
Okinahara, 36°55'N 138°36'E, 35
Okinawa*, 21
Okinawa (isl), 27°00'N 128°30'E, 13, 15, 18, 33, 109, 141, 195, 201, 204, 205
Okinawa Is, 26°30'N 128°00'E, 13
Okino erabu (isl), 27°21'N 128°34'E, 13
Okinoshima, 34°13'N 129°46'E, 39
Ōkuma, 38°09'N 140°54'E, 100
Ōkuni, 34°28'N 136°44'E, 75
Okushiri (isl), 42°00'N 139°50'E, 13
Okuyama, 38°04'N 139°20'E, 75
Ōmi, 35°08'N 136°05'E, 141, 156
Ōmi*, 21, 72, 86
Ōmiya, 35°54'N 139°39'E, 22, 148
Ōmori shell mound, 35°35'N 139°44'E, 35
Ōmura, 32°56'N 129°58'E, 153
Ōmuta, 33°02'N 130°26'E, 22
Onikiribe, 38°51'N 140°36'E, 99
Onjōji, 35°01'N 135°51'E, 146
Ono, 33°10'N 131°30'E, 75
Onomichi, 34°25'N 133°11'E, 22
Oporto (Portugal), 41°09'N 8°37'W, 180
Osaka, 34°40'N 135°30'E, 13, 15, 20, 21, 22, 33, 41, 100, 126, 141, 148, 153, 170, 191
Osaka, 35°57'N 137°17'E, 39
Osaka*, 21
Osaka Plain, 34°40'N 135°35'E, 13
Oshamanbe, 42°31'N 140°22'E, 22
Ōshima, 33°27'N 135°52'E, 148
Ōshima*, 59
Ōshima (isl), 34°45'N 139°25'E, 13
Osore*, 59
Osore, Mt, 41°17'N 141°03'E, 18
Ōsumi* 21
Ōsumi Is, 30°32'N 130°40'E, 13
Ōta, 35°10'N 132°29'E, 75
Otamadai, 35°43'N 140°42'E, 35
Otaru, 43°12'N 141°00'E, 22
Ōtsu, 35°00'N 135°50'E, 21, 72, 148, 156
Ōtsuka, 35°31'N 139°38'E, 39
Owari*, 21, 170
Ōyama, 35°12'N 135°04'E, 75
Ōyu stone circles, 40°25'N 140°53'E, 35
Ōzaki, 38°37'N 141°12'E, 133
Ōzuka, 33°35'N 130°31'E, 41

Paekche*, 69
Pagan (Burma), 21°07'N 94°53'E, 54
Palau Is (USA), 3°36'N 134°12'E, 195, 201, 204
Palembang (Indonesia), 2°59'S 104°45'E, 54
Papal States*, 142
Papua*, 195, 201, 204
Paris (France), 48°52'N 2°20'E, 180
Pattani (Thailand), 6°51'N 101°16'E, 113
Pearl Harbor (USA), 21°22'N 158°00'W, 204
Pegu (Burma), 17°18'N 96°31'E, 54
Pescadores (isls), (Taiwan), 20°50'N 121°55'E, 191, 201
Philippine Is (Pacific Oc), 13°00'N 123°00'E, 143, 195, 201, 204
Phnom Penh (Cambodia), 11°35'N 104°55'E, 143
Pingzhou (China), 39°33'N 118°56'E, 69
Pitzuwu (China), 39°17'N 122°20'E, 191, 192
Port Arthur (China), 38°46'N 121°15'E, 191, 192, 195, 205
Port Moresby (PNG), 9°30'S 147°07'E, 204
Port Natal (RSA), 30°44'S 30°27'E, 142
Prague (Czechoslovakia), 50°05'N 14°25'E, 180
Pusan (S Korea), 35°05'N 129°02'E, 13, 105, 109, 133, 191, 192, 195, 205
Puyo (S Korea), 36°17'N 126°54'E, 54
Pyongyang (N Korea), 39°00'N 125°47'E, 15, 39, 109, 133, 191, 192
Pyonhan*, 46

Qing China*, 191
Qingdao (China), 36°02'N 120°25'E, 195, 201
Qingzhou (China), 36°40'N 119°10'E, 69
Qiqihar (China), 47°23'N 124°00'E, 205
Quanzhou (China), 24°57'N 118°36'E, 143
Quelpart (isl), 33°18'N 126°33'E, 69, 133, 191

Rabaul (Solomon Is), 4°24'S 152°18'E, 204
Rakuzan, 35°28'N 133°05'E, 133
Rangoon (Burma), 16°47'N 96°10'E, 201, 204
Rebun (isl), 45°23'N 141°00'E, 13
Reisanji, 34°13'N 134°33'E, 146
Rikuchū Coastline National Park, 39°50'N 40°00'E, 22
Rishiri (isl), 45°10'N 141°12'E, 13
Rishiri-Rebun-Sarobetsu National Park, 45°20'N 141°12'E, 22
Risshakuji, 38°20'N 140°30'E, 119
Rome (Italy), 41°53'N 12°30'E, 142, 180
Rouen (France), 49°26'N 1°05'E, 180
Ryūgadō, 33°36'N 133°46'E, 39
Ryukyu Is, 26°00'N 126°00'E, 13, 15, 18, 39, 109, 191, 201
Ryūmonji, 31°46'N 130°38'E, 133
Ryūshakuji, 38°37'N 140°26'E, 156

Sado*, 21
Sado (isl), 38°00'N 138°24'E, 13, 22, 39, 59, 73, 75, 99, 100, 141, 148, 153, 170
Saeki, 32°58'N 131°51'E, 153
Saga, 33°16'N 130°18'E, 21, 148, 170
Saga*, 21
Sagami*, 21
Sagaseki, 33°14'N 131°52'E, 148
Sahashi, 37°14'N 138°18'E, 75
Saibezawa, 41°51'N 140°42'E, 35
Saidaiji, 34°42'N 135°47'E, 59, 113, 146
Saigon (Vietnam), 10°46'N 106°43'E, 143, 180, 201, 204
Saikachido, 35°41'N 139°32'E, 39
Saikai National Park, 33°07'N 129°18'E, 22
Saikaido*, 59
St Petersburg (USSR), 59°55'N 30°25'E, 180
St Tropez (France), 43°16'N 6°39'E, 142
Saipan (isl), (USA), 14°48'N 145°36'E, 201, 204
Saitama*, 21
Saitobaru, 32°05'N 131°24'E, 41
Saitobaru*, 41
Saitoyama, 32°49'N 130°38'E, 39
Sakai, 34°35'N 135°28'E, 20, 22, 35, 109, 119, 148, 153, 170
Sakamoto, 36°20'N 138°43'E, 148
Sakanoshita, 34°50'N 136°21'E, 35, 148
Sakarubaba, 33°23'N 129°38'E, 39
Sakashima Is, 24°50'N 124°50'E, 13
Sakata, 38°55'N 139°51'E, 153, 156, 170
Sakhalin/Karafuto (isl), (USSR), 50°00'N 143°00'E, 13, 15, 18, 33, 141, 195, 201, 205
Sakura, 35°43'N 140°13'E, 148
Sakuragaoka, 34°42'N 135°10'E, 39
Sakurai, 34°56'N 132°22'E, 75
Sakurai, 37°49'N 140°55'E, 39
Sakurajima, Mt, 31°36'N 130°44'E, 18
Samita, 34°35'N 135°44'E, 41
San Francisco (USA), 37°45'N 122°27'W, 180
San Miguel (Philippines), 15°48'N 120°36'E, 143
San'in Kaigan National Park, 35°43'N 134°30'E, 22
Sanchi (India), 23°38'N 77°42'E, 54
Sanindo*, 59
Sanrizuka, 35°45'N 140°24'E, 33
Sansonji, 36°12'N 140°16'E, 113
Santōnoda, 35°30'N 139°41'E, 39
Sanuki*, 21
Sanyodo*, 59
Sapporo, 43°05'N 141°21'E, 13, 15, 20, 21, 22, 33
Sarashina, 36°34'N 137°59'E, 156
Sarawak*, 195, 201, 204
Sardinia (isl), (Italy), 40°00'N 9°00'E, 142, 180
Sarugababa, 36°23'N 137°54'E, 156
Sasebo, 33°10'N 129°42'E, 22, 191
Satake, 36°44'N 140°32'E, 75
Satogi shell mound, 34°33'N 133°34'E, 35
Satohama shell mound, 38°19'N 141°04'E, 35
Satsuma*, 21, 170
Sawada, 40°47'N 140°22'E, 35
Sayononakayama, 34°45'N 138°08'E, 156
Seigandoji, 33°34'N 135°58'E, 146
Sekigahara, 35°22'N 136°26'E, 148
Sekijinyama, 33°10'N 130°32'E, 41
Sendai, 38°16'N 140°52'E, 13, 20, 21, 22, 33, 148, 153, 156, 170
Senju, 35°47'N 139°49'E, 156
Senjuji, 34°55'N 136°38'E, 119
Senpoku, 39°29'N 140°24'E, 133
Senpukuji Cave, 33°07'N 129°48'E, 33
Senshūji, 36°30'N 139°02'E, 113
Sentsūji, 35°00'N 135°46'E, 146
Seoul (S Korea), 37°30'N 127°00'E, 15, 109, 133, 191, 192, 201, 204, 205
Sesshōseki, 37°00'N 140°05'E, 156
Settsu*, 21, 72, 86
Seville (Spain), 37°24'N 5°59'W, 142
Shandong*/Shantung*, 195
Shanggu (China), 40°00'N 116°25'E, 39
Shanghai (China), 31°13'N 121°25'E, 180, 195, 201, 205
Shantou (China), 23°22'N 116°39'E, 195, 204
Shantung* *see* Shandong*
Shaozhou (China), 24°53'N 113°31'E, 68
Shibata, 37°57'N 139°20'E, 148
Shibayama, 34°44'N 135°40'E, 41
Shibayama, 36°22'N 136°24'E, 39
Shibushi, 31°30'N 131°07'E, 100, 153
Shibuya, 35°39'N 39°42'E, 75
Shida, 36°03'N 140°18'E, 75
Shiga*, 21
Shigaraki, 34°53'N 136°02'E, 72
Shigi, Mt, 34°37'N 135°40'E, 86
Shikashima, 33°42'N 130°26'E, 46
Shikashima (isl), 33°41'N 130°14'E, 105
Shikima, 38°24'N 140°49'E, 73
Shikoku*, 22
Shikoku Mts, 33°48'N 133°30'E, 13, 14
Shikotsu-Tōya National Park, 42°37'N 141°03'E, 22
Shima*, 21, 86
Shimabara, 32°48'N 130°20'E, 126, 153
Shimada, 34°50'N 138°10'E, 148
Shimane*, 21
Shimazu, 31°48'N 131°06'E, 75
Shimizu, 35°01'N 138°29'E, 22, 205
Shimo (isl), 32°25'N 130°06'E, 13
Shimoda, 34°40'N 138°55'E, 141, 148, 170
Shimojō, 32°58'N 131°53'E, 39
Shimonoseki, 33°59'N 130°58'E, 22, 105, 141, 148, 153, 170, 191, 192
Shimosa*, 21
Shimotsuke*, 21
Shinano*, 21
Shingū, 33°42'N 136°00'E, 86, 148
Shinjō, 38°45'N 140°18'E, 148
Shinmachi, 36°17'N 139°01'E, 148
Shinobu, 37°47'N 140°26'E, 75
Shinohara, 36°21'N 136°23'E, 100
Shinoyama, 35°03'N 135°08'E, 100
Shio, 36°58'N 136°47'E, 153
Shio, Cape, 33°25'N 135°48'E, 13

Editor Graham Speake
Art Editor Andrew Lawson
Map Editor Olive Pearson
Picture Editor Linda Proud
Index Ann Barrett
Design Adrian Hodgkins
Production Clive Sparling

AN EQUINOX BOOK

Published by Phaidon Press Ltd,
Littlegate House, St Ebbe's
Street, Oxford OX1 1SQ, England

Planned and produced by
Equinox (Oxford) Ltd, Littlegate
House, St Ebbe's Street, Oxford
England, OX1 1SQ

Copyright © Equinox (Oxford)
Ltd 1988

British Library Cataloguing in
Publication Data
Collcutt, Martin, *1939–*
    Cultural atlas of Japan.
    1. Japanese civilization, to 1987
    I. Title   II. Jansen, Marius B.
    III. Kumakura, Isao 952

ISBN 0-7148-2526-3

Origination by Scantrans,
Singapore

Maps drawn and originated by
Lovell Johns Ltd, Oxford, and
Alan Mais, Hornchurch, Essex

Filmset by Hourds Typographica,
Stafford, England

Printed in Spain by Heraclio
Fournier SA, Vitoria

Frontispiece Illustrations of
proper dress for a samurai family
of the Edo period.

Cultural Atlas of
JAPAN